PURCHASING AND SUPPLY CHAIN MANAGEMENT

Second Edition

Robert Monczka
Arizona State University and
The Center for Advanced Purchasing Studies

Robert Trent
Lehigh University

Robert Handfield
North Carolina State University

SOUTH-WESTERN
TM
THOMSON LEARNING

Australia · Canada · Mexico · Singapore · Spain · United Kingdom · United States

Team Director: Melissa Acuna
Senior Acquisitions Editor: Charles McCormick Jr.
Developmental Editor: Taney H. Wilkins
Senior Marketing Manager: Joe Sabatino
Production Editor: Robert Dreas
Manufacturing Coordinator: Doug Wilke
Cover & Internal Design: Imbue Design/Kim Torbeck, Cincinnati, Ohio
Design Project Manager: Michelle Kunkler
Media Technology Editor: Diane Van Bakel
Media Development Editor: Christine Wittmer
Media Production Editor: Robin Browning
Production House: Pre-Press Company, Inc.
Printer: R.R. Donnelley & Sons Company, Crawfordsville Manufacturing Division

Printed in the United States of America
2 3 4 5   04 03 02 01

For more information contact South-Western, 5191 Natorp Blvd, Mason, OH,
45040 or find us on the Internet at http://www.swcollege.com

For permission to use material from this text or product, contact us by
- **telephone: 1-800-730-2214**
- **fax: 1-800-730-2215**
- **web: http://www.thomsonrights.com**

Library of Congress Cataloging-in-Publication Data

Monczka, Robert M.
    Purchasing and supply chain management / Robert Monczka, Robert Trent,
Robert Handfield.—2nd ed.
        p. cm.
    Includes bibliographical references and index.
    ISBN 0-324-02315-4
    1. Purchasing.   2. Industrial management.   I. Trent, Robert J.   II. Handfield,
Robert B.   III. Title.

HF5437 .M648 2001
658.7'2—dc21   2001031350

$\mathcal{A}$BOUT THE AUTHORS

Robert M. Monczka is a Distinguished Professor in the Department of Supply Chain Management at Arizona State University, Professor Emeritus at Michigan State University, and Director of Project 10X in the Center for Advanced Purchasing Studies (CAPS). Project 10X is designed to create a rolling five-to-ten-year vision of strategies and best practices, and is committed to increasing performance by a magnitude of *ten times*. Outside of the academic arena, his career consists of consulting and research with more than 150 international organizations.

Robert J. Trent is the Supply Chain Management Program Director and Eugene Mercy Associate Professor of Management at Lehigh University. He received a Ph.D. in purchasing from Michigan State University. His research involves team-based approaches to purchasing, strategic sourcing, and global sourcing. He has presented many seminars to purchasing and supply chain managers and has published articles on these subjects in a variety of professional and academic journals.

Robert B. Handfield is the Bank of America Distinguished University Professor of Supply Chain Management in the College of Management at North Carolina State University. He is also the Director of the Supply Chain Resource Consortium at NCSU. His research focuses on field research with firms deploying supply chain management strategies, supplier development, and B2B e-commerce. He is Editor of the *Journal of Operations Management* and Area Editor (Supply Chain Management) for *Decision Sciences*. Handfield has served in consulting and executive education roles for more than a dozen Fortune 500 companies.

$\mathcal{B}$RIEF CONTENTS

$\mathcal{C}$ONTENTS

9 *Supplier Quality Management* 266

10 *Supplier and Development: Creating a World-Class Supply Base* 297

13 Strategic Cost Management 407

16 Purchasing Law and Ethics 518

Section 5
SUPPLY CHAIN MANAGEMENT

17 Managing Supply Chain Inventory 558

20 *Performance Measurement and Evaluation* 659

Section 6
FUTURE DIRECTIONS

21 Purchasing and Supply Chain Changes and Trends 688

PERFORMANCE IMPROVEMENT REQUIREMENTS 690

PURCHASING AND SUPPLIER IMPORTANCE 692

ORGANIZATION AND HUMAN RESOURCES 693

INFORMATION SYSTEMS DEVELOPMENT 696

PERFORMANCE MEASUREMENT 699

SUPPLY-BASE MANAGEMENT 701

PURCHASING RESPONSIBILITIES AND ACTIVITIES 704

Appendixes 710

Cases 721

Index 756

$\mathcal{P}$REFACE

The second edition of *Purchasing and Supply Chain Management* is the culmination of discussions with purchasing and supply chain managers across many industries from around the world. In this edition, we have combined our experience and research to create a managerial perspective of the core tasks and challenges required to effectively manage the purchasing function within the context of an integrated supply chain. Although prior books have dealt with many components of obtaining goods and services, we have created an integrated text that helps managers develop purchasing and supply chain strategies that contribute to corporate and business objectives. This new edition includes a number of innovative subjects that have been developed as a result of recent research projects undertaken by the authors. Some of the subjects that are newly introduced or expanded upon in this edition include:

- Cross-functional teaming
- Outsourcing and total cost analysis
- Supplier integration into new product development
- Automating purchasing through procurement cards and electronic systems such as Ariba and Commerce One
- Supplier development
- Strategic cost management and total cost of ownership
- B2B electronic commerce
- Enterprise Resource Planning
- Third party logistics
- Price analysis tools and techniques
- Negotiation simulations
- Contracting and Internet law
- Creating the lead supply chain
- Expanded and comprehensive cases

We are proud of this new text, and believe that it reflects many new themes that are only beginning to emerge in the public domain.

Course Description

Purchasing and Supply Chain Management is intended for college and university courses that are variously entitled purchasing, materials management, supply chain management, sourcing management, and other similar titles. The text is also well suited for training seminars for buyers, and portions of it have been used in executive education forums. Chapters have been used in both undergraduate and M.B.A. classes in purchasing, e-commerce, operations management, and logistics. Some instructors may also elect to use sections of the book for a class in operations management or logistics. The text is appropriate for either an elective or a required course that fulfills the American Assembly of Collegiate Schools of Business (AACSB) requirements for coverage of materials management issues. Most of the cases included in the book are based on actual companies or examples and have all been used and modified through classroom use by the authors.

Course Objectives

Depending on the placement of a course in the curriculum or the individual instructor's philosophy, this book can be used to satisfy a variety of objectives:

1. Students should be made aware of the demands placed on purchasing and supply chain managers by business stakeholders.
2. As prospective managers, students need to understand the impact of purchasing and supply chain management on the competitive success and profitability of modern organizations.
3. Students should appreciate the ethical, contractual, and legal issues faced by purchasing and supply chain professionals.
4. Students must understand the increasingly strategic nature of purchasing, especially the fact that purchasing is much more than simply buying goods and services.
5. Students entering or currently in the workforce must understand the influence of purchasing on other major functional activities, including product design, information system design, e-commerce, manufacturing planning and control, inventory management, human resource development, financial planning, forecasting, sales, quality management, as well as many other areas.

Special to This Edition

Many of the insights and topics presented throughout this book are based on examples developed through discussions with top purchasing executives and from various research initiatives, including research published by the *Center for Advanced Purchasing* studies and a project on supplier integration funded by the National Science Foundation. In addition, the revised text adopts a new chapter format that includes an opening vignette, a set of sourcing snapshots, and a concluding good practice case example that illustrates and integrates each chapter's topics. These new case studies and examples provide up-to-date illustrations of the concepts presented throughout each chapter.

The concept of teaming is emphasized throughout this book. Many of the case exercises require a team effort on the part of students. We recommend that the instructor have students work in teams for such projects to prepare them for the team environment found in most organizations.

Structure of the Book

This book is subdivided into six sections and 21 chapters that provide a through coverage of purchasing and supply chain management.

Section 1: Introduction

Chapter 1 introduces the reader to purchasing and supply chain management. This chapter defines procurement and sourcing, introduces the notion of the supply chain, and summarizes the evolution of purchasing and supply chain management as an organizational activity.

Section 2: Operational Purchasing

The chapters in Section 2 provide an in-depth understanding of the fundamentals surrounding the operational activity called purchasing. These chapters focus primarily on the fundamentals of purchasing as a functional activity. Without a solid understanding of purchasing basics, appreciating the important role that purchasing can play becomes difficult.

Chapter 2 provides an overview of the purchasing process by presenting the objectives of world-class purchasing organizations, the responsibilities of professional purchasers, the purchasing cycle, and various types of purchasing documents and types of purchases. Chapter 3 examines the organization and administration of purchasing. This includes a discussion of purchasing in the organizational hierarchy, how the purchasing function is organized, and the placement of purchasing authority. The chapter also describes the team approach as part of the organizational structure. Chapter 4 describes various categories and types of purchasing policies and procedures. Most firms have a set of policies outlining the directives of executive management. These directives guide behavior and decision-making and place boundaries on the behavior of personnel. Chapter 5 examines purchasing as a boundary-spanning function. Much of what purchasing involves requires interacting and working with other functional areas and suppliers. This chapter examines the intra-firm linkages between purchasing and other groups, including suppliers.

Section 3: Strategic Sourcing

A major premise underlying this book is that purchasing is as important an activity as manufacturing, marketing, or engineering in the pursuit of a firm's strategic objectives. Progressive firms have little doubt about purchasing's impact on total quality, cost, delivery, technology, and responsiveness to the needs of external customers. Section 3 addresses what firms must do to achieve a competitive advantage from their procurement and sourcing processes. Realizing these advantages requires shifting our view of purchasing from a tactical or clerically-oriented activity to one focusing on strategic supply management. Strategic supply management involves developing the strategies, approaches, and methods for realizing a competitive advantage and improvement from the procurement and sourcing process, particularly through direct involvement and interaction with suppliers.

Chapter 6 develops an understanding of how firms set purchasing strategies. This process should include a vision and plan of what a firm must do in its purchasing/sourcing efforts to support achieving corporate goals and objectives. Clearly, the strategic planning process should be the starting point for any discussion of strategic supply management. Chapter 7 describes an increasingly important topic today, insourcing/outsourcing. The insourcing/outsourcing process defines what activities a firm will perform internally and what activities it will outsource to suppliers. Once a firm decides to outsource a service, component, subassembly, or product, it must then support the outsourcing through its procurement and sourcing activities.

Chapter 8 focuses on one of the most important processes performed by firms today—that is, supplier evaluation, selection, and measurement. Selecting the right suppliers helps ensure that buyers receive the right inputs to satisfy their quality, cost, delivery, and technology requirements. Selecting the right suppliers also creates the foundation for working closely with suppliers, when required, to further improve performance. Chapter 9 describes how progressive firms manage and improve supplier quality once it selects its suppliers. Improving supplier quality may also create advantages that are not available to competing firms. Chapter 10 describes what firms must do to manage and develop world-class supply-based performance. Finally, Chapter 11 focuses on worldwide sourcing, which is becoming an important part of strategic supply management as firms search worldwide for the best resources.

Section 4: Strategic Cost Management

Purchasing professionals rely on an assortment of tools, techniques, and approaches for managing the procurement and supply chain process. Chapter 12 presents various tools and techniques that purchasers use when problem solving and pursuing performance improvements. The use of these tools and techniques can help purchasers achieve specific outcomes such as reducing cost/price, improving quality, reducing time, or improving delivery performance from suppliers.

Chapter 13 focuses on cost/price analysis. Progressive firms focus on cost control and reduction with suppliers as a way to improve (i.e., reduce) purchase price over time. Understanding cost fundamentals and appreciating how and when to use advanced costing techniques is critical for purchasers. This chapter details various types of costs, presents cost analysis techniques, and discusses the factors that affect a supplier's price. The chapter also discusses total cost analysis, cost-based pricing, and other innovative techniques designed to provide accurate and timely cost data.

Chapter 14 deals with purchase negotiation. Effective purchasers know how to plan for and negotiate contracts that create value within a buyer-seller relationship. Increasingly, purchase contracts emphasize more than simply purchase price. Buyers and sellers may negotiate cost reductions, delivery requirements, quality levels, payment terms, or anything else important to the parties. Purchase negotiation will become increasingly important as firms focus on non-price issues and longer-term, complex purchase agreements.

Chapter 15 addresses the fundamentals of contracting. The formal contracting process creates the framework for conducting business between two or more firms. As such, an understanding of contracting is essential when attempting to manage costs within a buyer-seller relationship. Chapter 16 addresses the major legal considerations in purchasing, including the legal authority of the purchasing manager. The chapter also discusses sources of U.S. law, warranties, purchase order contracts, breaches of contract, and patent and intellectual property rights. Because contracting is a part of the legal process, this chapter naturally follows the contracting chapter.

Section 5: Supply Chain Management

Section Five describes the major activities that relate to or directly support supply chain management. Some of these activities involve specific disciplines, such as inventory management or transportation; other activities relate to the development of supply chain support systems. These systems include performance measurement systems and computerized information technology systems. The activities presented in this section may or may not be a formal part of the purchasing organization. These activities and systems, however, are key elements of purchasing and supply chain management. Without them, purchasing probably cannot effectively pursue its goals and objectives. Therefore, purchasing students must be familiar with a range of supply chain activities.

Chapter 17 focuses on a topic of increasing interest—the management of a firm's inventory investment. The money that a firm commits to inventory usually involves a significant commitment of financial resources. This chapter discusses the function of inventory within a firm, factors leading to inventory waste, creating a lean supply chain, approaches for managing a firm's inventory investment, and future trends related to managing inventory. At some firms, purchasing is responsible for the day-to-day management of inventory.

Another area of interest involves the purchase of transportation services. We have witnessed major changes in transportation over the last 15 years, many of which have affected purchasing. Since Congress deregulated the transportation industry in the early 1980s, the role of the buyer has changed dramatically. More than ever, purchasing is involving itself in the evaluation, selection, and management of transportation carriers. Even if a buyer does not get involved directly with transportation, having a working knowledge of this dynamic area is critical. Chapter 18 highlights purchasing's role in transportation buying, presents a decision-making framework for developing transportation strategy, discusses ways to control and influence inbound transportation, and evaluates trends affecting the purchase of transportation services.

Information technology systems are changing business. Purchasing, too, can benefit from the development of current information technology systems. Chapter 19 examines the role of supply chain information systems and electronic commerce. The chapter also addresses the electronic linkage between firms through Electronic Data Interchange (EDI). Finally, this chapter discusses some advanced and future purchasing systems' applications. The availability of information technology systems greatly enhances purchasing's ability to operate at the highest levels of efficiency and effectiveness.

Chapter 20 focuses on performance measurement and evaluation. Increasingly, firms must develop measurement systems that reveal how well a firm is performing, including the performance of its purchasing and supply chain management efforts. Measurement systems support procurement and sourcing decision-making by providing accurate and timely performance data. This chapter examines why firms measure performance, defines various purchasing performance measurement categories, and discusses how to develop a purchasing performance measurement system.

Section 6: Future Directions

Chapter 21 focuses on what purchasing and supply chain management will look like in the 21st century. These trends, which are adapted directly from recent surveys of key executive managers from a variety of global organizations, can help students identify how the field of purchasing and sourcing management is changing, and what skills they will need to develop in view of these changes.

Case Studies and Instructor's Resources

Purchasing and Supply Chain Management contains 40 new and revised cases featured within the book and found at the product website, http://monczka.swcollege.com. These cases have been classroom tested and used within the industry. An instructor's manual and test bank are available on CD-ROM (ISBN: 0-324-02316-2) to help instructors identify how to best use and interpret these cases. Of particular interest are the negotiation and supplier selection cases, which allow students to experience the purchasing decision-making process in real time.

INTRODUCTION TO PURCHASING 1

1

The Importance of Purchasing at AlliedSignal

When Larry Bossidy became the new CEO of AlliedSignal (now part of Honeywell) in 1991, the $11.8 billion a year maker of auto parts and aerospace electronics was in a financial crisis. Debt was 42% of capital and cash outflows were outpacing revenues, creating serious liquidity problems. One of Bossidy's major initiatives focused on improving materials management through purchasing excellence. As Bossidy explained it, "We wanted to send a clear message to our suppliers, as well as to our own people. From here on out, AlliedSignal is going to take materials management very seriously."*

Two efforts illustrate this seriousness. First, AlliedSignal made material costs an explicit part of its productivity measures. Rather than tallying output per man-hour, the company began tracking *total cost productivity*. Productivity is defined as sales, discounted for price increases that do not reflect an increase in value, divided by all costs (including plant and equipment, materials, and labor), adjusted for inflation. This definition of productivity helps managers look beyond layoffs for sources of productivity gains. The head of the engineered materials division explained, "If I had to get 6% productivity growth from labor alone, there'd be nobody left in about three years. The real opportunities are in raising the value of what you sell and cutting material costs."

The second major effort involved drastic reductions in the company's supply base of 9,500 suppliers. This effort was seen as vital to improving productivity, lowering purchasing costs, and improving the quality of incoming goods and materials. In 1992, 1,500 of AlliedSignal's top U.S. suppliers were summoned to mass meetings to learn what the company had in mind. At a meeting of aerospace suppliers, some in the audience gasped when they heard that AlliedSignal expected them to develop credible plans to reduce their prices 10% to 15% and lead times 30%, while meeting stiff quality targets.

But AlliedSignal did not expect suppliers to achieve these gains by themselves. To give suppliers a cost reduction boost, the company arranged to let them tie in to AlliedSignal's purchases of office supplies, tooling, and corporate travel. The volume discounts meant major savings to both small and large suppliers.

More important, AlliedSignal formed "commodity teams," cross-functional squads of manufacturing engineers, designers, and purchasing and finance experts in such areas as castings, electronic gears, machine parts, and raw materials. Each team was responsible for identifying the best suppliers in its area and developing supply contracts. Key suppliers were given long-term contracts, and they were offered early involvement in product development and assistance in introducing total quality management (TQM) practices at their own companies. Furthermore, AlliedSignal established electronic linkages with these suppliers to reduce paperwork. In sum, AlliedSignal worked to establish a mutually advantageous relationship with these key suppliers.

→ → → →

The results of these efforts at AlliedSignal have allowed the company to enjoy major market share and stock price growth. Even as revenues grew 6% in 1994, AlliedSignal's purchasing costs actually decreased. In 1994, the company enjoyed a 21% surge in profits. Even when material costs were rising, AlliedSignal worked with suppliers to counter these increases with improved productivity, larger volumes, and improved quality and delivery performance. Even today, significant improvements continue due to the realization of the importance of purchasing and materials management.

*Tim Minahan, "AlliedSignal Soars by Building Up Suppliers," *Purchasing*, September 18, 1997, 38–47.

In the last two decades, managers have witnessed a revolution in how business is conducted. A variety of shocks occurring throughout global markets has radically changed the way managers view their environments. The accelerated rate of change in markets, products, technology, and the level of global competition is requiring managers to make decisions on shorter notice, with less information, and with higher failure costs. At the same time, customers are demanding quicker delivery of products, as borne out by the growth of express mail competitors. These same customers demand products that utilize state-of-the-art technology incorporating the latest features. Products are becoming less standardized, with options tailored to the unique requirements of individual customers.

The way customers evaluate products is also undergoing dramatic change. Electronic devices are evaluated based on their speed and cost, automobiles on their safety and reliability, and long-distance telephone carriers on price competitiveness. Even power and natural gas providers are facing complete deregulation of their markets and increasing competition. In every industry, products and services are becoming more complex, have a greater variety of options, and must be tailored to shrinking market "niches." Many product life cycles, which in the past were fairly stable, now last one or two months. These developments have led one popular management guru to compare current global markets to the fashion industry, in which products go in and out of style with the season.[1]

Another important change has been the development of the World Wide Web, spawning a new generation of "electronic commerce" featuring a seamless flow of information between marketing, sales, purchasing, finance, manufacturing, distribution, and transportation internally, as well as inter-organizationally to customers, suppliers, carriers, and retailers across the supply chain. The availability of information is transforming relationships throughout industry.

Managers throughout the supply chain, including purchasing managers, are feeling the full effect of these shocks. They are expected to continuously reduce costs, improve product quality, and provide greater product availability with less available inventory. Because sales growth is slowing in many markets, mistakes leading to lost sales cannot easily be dismissed and written off. Customers and suppliers are better at measuring performance, so mistakes are more easily detected. Customers are demanding exact quantities at exact times, which requires supply chains that are quick and precise, and that provide top-quality products and services every time.

What Is a Supply Chain?

With the increasing number of world-class competitors domestically and abroad, organizations have had to rapidly improve their internal processes to stay competitive. Throughout the 1960s and 1970s, companies began to develop detailed market strategies that focused on creating and capturing customer loyalty. Before long, organizations also realized that this required a strong engineering, design, and manufacturing function to support these market requirements. Design engineers had to translate customer needs into product and service specifications, which then had to be produced at a high level of quality at a reasonable cost. As the demand for new products increased throughout the 1980s, organizations had to become increasingly flexible and responsive to modify existing products, services, and processes, or to develop new ones to meet ever-changing customer needs. As organizational capabilities improved in the 1990s, managers realized that material and service inputs from suppliers had a major impact on their ability to meet customer needs. This led to an increased focus on the supply base and the responsibilities of purchasing. Managers also realized that producing a quality product was not enough. Getting products and services to customers—when, where, how, in the quantity required and in a cost-effective manner—constituted an entirely new type of challenge. More recently, the era of the "Logistics Renaissance" was also born, spawning a whole set of time-reducing information technologies and logistics networks aimed at meeting these challenges.[2]

As a result of these changes, organizations now find they must be involved in the management of (or at least take a serious interest in) all upstream firms (suppliers) that provide direct and indirect inputs. They must also be concerned with the network of downstream firms responsible for delivery and after-market service of the product to the end customer. From this realization emerged the concept of the *supply chain* (see Exhibit 1.1). We define the terms *supply chain* and *supply chain management* as follows:[3]

*The **supply chain** encompasses all activities associated with the flow and transformation of goods from the raw materials stage (extraction), through to end users, as well as the associated information flows. Material and information flows both up and down the supply chain. The supply chain includes systems management, operations and assembly, purchasing, production scheduling, order processing, inventory management, transportation, warehousing, and customer service. Supply chains are essentially a series of linked suppliers and customers; every customer is in turn a supplier to the next downstream organization until a finished product reaches the ultimate end user.*

EXHIBIT 1.1   *The Integrated Supply Chain*

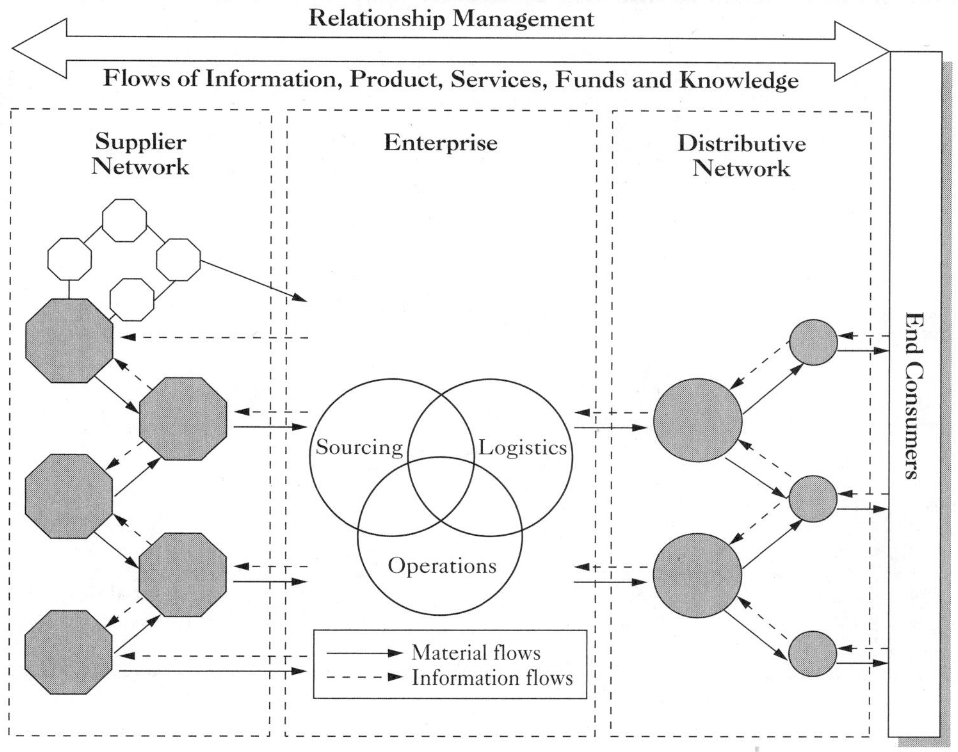

Relationship Management

Flows of Information, Product, Services, Funds and Knowledge

Supplier Network

Enterprise

Distributive Network

Sourcing   Logistics

Operations

———▶ Material flows
- - - -▶ Information flows

End Consumers

Resource Base (Capacity, Information, Core Competencies, Financial)

Supply chain management *is the integration of these activities through improved supply chain relationships to achieve a sustainable competitive advantage.*

If we consider a single firm within the context of this definition, we must include both its upstream supplier network and its downstream distributive network (see Exhibit 1.1). According to this definition, the supply chain includes the management of information systems, sourcing and procurement, production scheduling, order processing, inventory management, warehousing, customer service, and after-market disposition of packaging and materials. The supplier network consists of all organizations that provide inputs, either directly or indirectly, to the focal enterprise (i.e., the purchaser).

The increasing importance of supply chain management is forcing organizations to rethink their purchasing and sourcing strategies. As shown in Exhibit 1.1, supply chain management involves multiple organizations. Simple supply chains pull materials directly from their origin, process them, package them, and ship them to consumers. A

EXHIBIT 1.2   *A Cereal Manufacturer's Supply Chain*

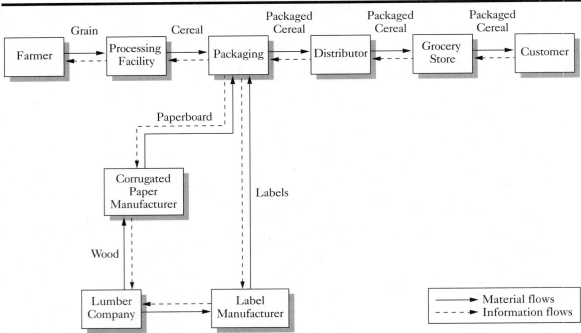

good example of a simple supply chain involves cereal producers (see Exhibit 1.2). A cereal company purchases the grain from a farmer and processes it into cereal. The cereal company also purchases the paperboard from a paper manufacturer, who purchased the wood to make the paper, and labels from a label manufacturer, who purchased semifinished label stock to make the labels. The cereal is then packaged and sent to a distributor, who in turn ships the material to a grocer, who then sells it to an end customer. Even for a simple product such as cereal, the number of transactions, material, and information flows are fairly complex.

For products such as automobiles, which have multiple products, technologies, and processes, the supply chain becomes more complicated. The material, planning, and logistics supply chain for an automotive company is shown in Exhibit 1.3, which illustrates the complexity of the chain, spanning from automotive dealers back through multiple suppliers. The automotive company's supplier network includes the thousands of firms that provide items ranging from raw materials, such as steel and plastics, to complex assemblies and subassemblies, such as transmissions and brakes. As also shown in the exhibit, the supplier network may include internal divisions within the company as well as external suppliers. A given material may pass through multiple processes within multiple suppliers and divisions before becoming assembled into a vehicle. A supplier for this company has its own set of suppliers that

EXHIBIT 1.3   *An Automotive Supply Chain: The Role of Material, Planning, and Logistics in the Production and Delivery System*

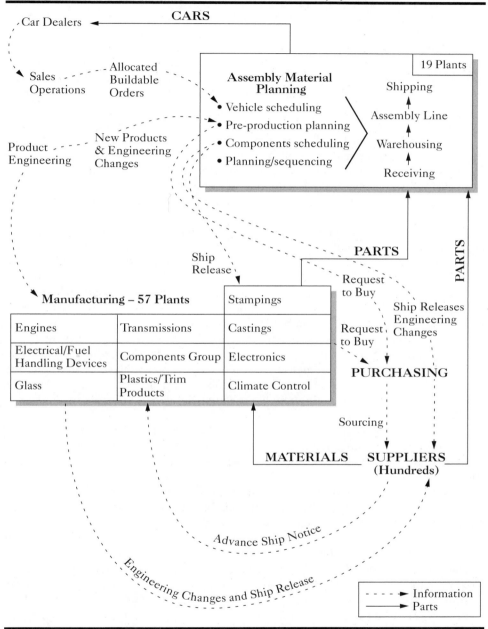

provide inputs (called second-tier suppliers) that are also part of this supply chain. The beginning of a supply chain inevitably can be traced back to "Mother Earth," which is the ultimate original source of all materials (e.g., iron ore, coal, petroleum, wood, etc.) that flow through the chain.

Several factors are driving the emphasis on supply chain management today. First, the cost and availability of information resources between entities in the supply chain allow easy linkages and eliminate time delays in the network. Second, the level of competition in both domestic and international markets demands that organizations be quick, agile, and flexible. Third, customer expectations and requirements are becoming much more important. As customers become increasingly demanding, organizations and their intermediaries must be flexible and quick, or face the prospect of losing market share. A strategic, proactive approach to managing the supply chain is critical for survival beyond the year 2000. To summarize one executive, "Competition today is not just between firms. It is between supply chains. In the future, the companies that put together the best integrated supply chains will be the winners!"[4]

From the focal firm's perspective (what we refer to as the purchaser), the supply chain includes (1) **internal functions,** (2) **upstream suppliers,** and (3) **downstream customers**. A firm's *internal functions* include the different processes used in transforming the inputs provided by the supplier network. This is usually referred to as *operations*. In the case of an automotive company, this includes its parts manufacturing (e.g., stamping, power train, and components), which are eventually assembled during final assembly into automobiles.

The coordination and scheduling of internal flows is challenging, particularly in a large organization. Some of the major functions include order processing, which is responsible for translating customer requirements into actual orders that are input into the system. Order processing may also involve extensive customer interaction, including quoting prices, possible delivery dates, delivery arrangements, and aftermarket service.

Another important internal function is production scheduling, which translates orders into actual plans and schedules. This may involve working with materials requirements planning and capacity-planning systems to schedule work centers, employees, and maintenance on machines.

The second major part of supply chain management involves **upstream suppliers**. In order to manage the flow of materials between all upstream organizations, firms employ an array of managers who ensure that the right materials arrive at the right time to the right internal users. Purchasing managers are responsible for ensuring that the right suppliers are selected, that they are meeting performance expectations, that appropriate contractual mechanisms are employed, and that a good relationship is maintained. They may also be responsible for driving supply-base improvement, and act as a liaison between suppliers and other internal supply chain members (engineering, accounting, etc.). Materials managers are responsible for planning, forecasting, and scheduling material flows from suppliers. They must work closely with production schedulers to ensure that suppliers are able to deliver material to the required locations, and that they have some advance warning as to future requirements so they can plan ahead.

Finally, a firm's **downstream customers** encompass downstream distribution channels, processes, and functions that the product passes through on its way to the end customer. In the case of an automotive company's suppliers, this includes finished goods and pipeline inventory, warehouses, dealer networks, and sales operations (see again Exhibit 1.3). This particular distribution channel is relatively short. Other types of supply chains may have relatively small internal supply chains but fairly long downstream distribution channels. For instance, Exhibit 1.2 shows the supply chain for a cereal manufacturer, and the extensive distribution network that is involved in getting the packaged cereal to the final customer. Within the downstream portion of the supply chain, logistics managers are responsible for the actual movement of materials between locations. One major part of logistics is transportation management, involving the selection and management of external carriers (trucking companies, airlines, railroads, shipping companies) or managing internal private fleets of carriers. Distribution management involves the management of packaging, storing, and handling of materials at receiving docks, warehouses, and retail outlets.

There are several major flows that take place in a supply chain (see again Exhibit 1.1). Obviously, materials and services flow down the chain (from suppliers to customers), and funds flow up the chain (from customers to suppliers), but there are other flows as well. Information and knowledge also flow up and down the chain. Participants in a supply chain are willing to share such information only when there is sufficient trust between members. Thus, the management of relationships with other parties in the chain becomes paramount. Organizations are effectively forming new types of relationships (sometimes called partnerships or alliances) that require a shared resource base. For instance, organizations may provide dedicated capacity, specific information, technological capabilities, or even direct financial support for other members of their supply chain so that the entire chain can benefit as a whole.

Why Purchasing Is Important

Despite the apparent complexity of managing supply chains, some organizations are thriving and exploiting their supply chains for competitive advantage. As companies strive to increase customer value by improving performance while simultaneously reducing costs, many companies are turning their attention to purchasing and to supply management—the part of supply chain management that focuses on the management of inbound goods and services into a firm. Organizations can realize major benefits from their focus on purchasing and supply management:

- Cost reduction or improvement
- Improved material delivery
- Shorter cycle time, including product development cycle times
- Access to product and process technology
- Quality improvement

Because manufacturers spend an average of 55 cents out of every dollar of revenues on goods and services, purchases are clearly a major area for potential cost savings. This fact was recognized first by many Japanese companies in the 1980s when superior management of relationships with suppliers gave Japanese automobile companies a $300 to $600 per-car cost advantage.[5]

Purchasing and supply management also has a major impact on quality. A supplier can make or break a company, in terms of providing products and services that either exceed their customers' expectations, or fail miserably to meet them. A poor-quality product can shut down a company's operations. In many cases, companies are seeking to increase the proportion of parts, components, and services they "outsource," in order to concentrate on their own areas of specialization and competence, and better meet their own customers' expectations. This further increases the importance of purchasing and external suppliers.

Finally, purchasing also can improve product and process designs and help introduce new technology faster into products and services. For example, when Chrysler introduced the new Neon automobile, the company realized that suppliers would furnish 70% of the value of the car. In order to bring the car out on schedule, the team invited 25 makers of key parts such as seats, tires, and suspension components to send engineers to Chrysler's engineering facility.[6] The result of this effort was that the car cost less to produce than previous models and included all of the proposed design features. Many managers agree that effective purchasing has become a critical way to gain competitive advantage. An executive vice president for telephone products at AT&T summarized this feeling very simply: "Purchasing is by far the largest single function at AT&T. Nothing we do is more important."[7]

The opening vignette illustrated how an emphasis on purchasing and supply management can result in dramatic payback. When AlliedSignal (now Honeywell) signs up a supplier, it requires a one-time reduction in price while demanding that the supplier commit to lowering total cost by 6%, adjusted for inflation every year. Typically, suppliers have been able to achieve this 6% target using a combination of price cuts and service improvements, such as increasing the frequency of deliveries to reduce the amount of inventory building up in the supply chain. Suppliers also pledge to eliminate defects. However, these agreements are not one-sided. AlliedSignal often enters into longer-term or partnership agreements with suppliers. The result is that everyone in this agreement emerges a winner.

TACTICAL PURCHASING VERSUS STRATEGIC SOURCING

This book focuses primarily on the processes and strategies used by companies to develop a sound purchasing organization that must operate in the context of supply chain management. There are two major forms of purchasing activities that take place in an organization: (1) **tactical purchasing** and (2) **strategic sourcing**. Each type of activity is important, but requires a different type of individual and skills to be successful. Let's examine each in more detail.

Tactical Purchasing

Tactical purchasing (or procurement) refers to a functional activity carried out in just about every organization. The term purchasing refers to the day-to-day management of material flows and information. (Note that the terms purchasing and procurement will be used interchangeably in this book.) These activities generally ensure that products or services are delivered to the right internal people at the right time but are often not carried out using a long-term horizon. The activities included in tactical purchasing may include (but are not limited to) the following:

- Commodity analysis—researching the requirements for purchased goods and services
- Market research—determining market characteristics for a commodity purchase
- Purchase order tracking and follow-up—managing the procurement process
- Determining the needs and requirements of internal customers—matching market and commodity information to customer needs
- Transmitting forecasts of future needs to suppliers—letting suppliers know what future requirements will be
- Transmitting actual orders for goods and services to suppliers
- Supplier performance measurement (ongoing)—tracking cost, quality, delivery, and service performance
- Management of supplier quality—ensuring that supplier products and services match the specified requirements
- Contract management and negotiation—developing appropriate contracts and terms
- Management of inbound/outbound transportation—ensuring that deliveries occur as scheduled and on time
- Price/cost analysis—carrying out ongoing analysis of price and cost trends

Strategic Sourcing Management

Strategic sourcing is related to purchasing activities but is somewhat broader in scope. Strategic sourcing is a cross-functional process that involves members of the firm other than those who work in the formal purchasing department. The strategic sourcing team may include members from engineering, quality, design, manufacturing, marketing, accounting, strategic planning, or other departments as needed. The focus of strategic sourcing management involves managing, developing, and integrating with supplier capabilities to achieve a competitive advantage. Advantages may be gained through cost reduction, technology development, quality improvement, cycle time reduction, and improved delivery capabilities to meet customer requirements. A variety of activities is associated with strategic sourcing management:

- Supplier identification—finding potential suppliers to meet existing or anticipated purchase needs
- Supplier evaluation and selection—determining if suppliers are capable of meeting needs
- Supplier management—ongoing management of the supply base
- Supplier development and improvement—taking actions to improve overall supply-base performance
- Supplier integration into ongoing processes—involving suppliers in new-product and -process development

As noted at the beginning of the chapter, it is no longer enough for purchasing managers to think simply in terms of internal efficiency as it relates to the processing of purchase orders. The purchasing process has changed dramatically over the years, and the rate of change in this functional area has increased most dramatically in the last five years. Moreover, the definition of purchasing is changing from a function emphasizing "clerical" activities to a strategic, proactive function that contributes effectively to a company's longer-term competitive advantage. Before discussing the specific concepts covered in this book, we will begin by reviewing some of the key historical events that have led to the current focus on purchasing.

THE EVOLUTION AND DEVELOPMENT OF PURCHASING

This section discusses the seven periods of purchasing development spanning the last 150 years.

Period One: The Early Years (1850–1900)

Some observers define the early years of purchasing history as beginning after 1850. Evidence exists, however, that the purchasing function received attention before this date. Charles Babbage's book on the economy of machinery and manufacturers, published in 1832, referred to the importance of the purchasing function. Babbage also alluded to a "materials man" responsible for several different functions. Babbage wrote that a key officer responsible for operating mines was "a materials man who selects, purchases, receives, and delivers all articles required."[8]

In the textile industry, purchasing was often handled jointly by the selling agent, who was also responsible for the output, quality, and style of the cloth. The selling agent was responsible for all purchasing decisions, since the grade of cotton purchased was a factor in determining the quality of cloth produced. These selling agents represented a simple and direct interface between market demand and production scheduling. Customer orders were directly transformed into purchase orders for cotton and subsequently into planned production.[9]

The greatest interest in and development of purchasing during the early years occurred after the 1850s—a period that witnessed the growth of the American railroad. The rail trade journals of this period often discussed purchasing issues. The predominance of the railroad in the American economy explains why the earliest writings about purchasing involved this industry.[10]

By 1866, the Pennsylvania Railroad had given the purchasing function departmental status, under the title of Supplying Department. A few years later, the top purchasing agent at the Pennsylvania Railroad reported directly to the president of the railroad. The purchasing function was such a major contributor to the performance of the organization that the chief purchasing manager had top managerial status.[11]

The Comptroller of the Chicago and Northwestern Railroad wrote the first book exclusively about the purchasing function, *The Handling of Railway Supplies—Their Purchase and Disposition*, in 1887. He discussed purchasing issues that are still critical today. For example, he discussed the need for technical expertise in purchasing agents, the need to centralize the purchasing department under one individual, and the lack of attention often given to the selection of personnel to fill the position of purchasing agent.

The growth of the railroad industry dominated the early years of purchasing development. Major contributions to purchasing history during this period consisted of early recognition of the purchasing process and its contribution to overall company profitability. The late 1800s signaled the beginning of organizing purchasing as a separate corporate function requiring specialized expertise. Before this period, this separation did not exist.

Period Two: Growth of Purchasing Fundamentals (1900–1939)

The second period of purchasing evolution began around the turn of the twentieth century and lasted until the beginning of World War II. Several features separate this period from the early years. First, articles specifically addressing the industrial purchasing function began appearing with increasing regularity outside the railroad trade journals. Engineering magazines in particular focused attention on the need for qualified purchasing personnel and the development of material specifications. Second, this era witnessed the development of basic purchasing procedures and ideas.

In 1905 the second book devoted to purchasing—and the first nonrailroad purchasing book—was published. *The Book on Buying* contained 18 chapters, each written by a different author. The editors devoted the first section of the book to the "principles" of buying. The second section (consisting of 11 chapters) described the forms and procedures used in various company purchasing systems.

Purchasing gained importance during World War I because of its role in obtaining vital war materials. This was due largely to purchasing's central focus of raw material procurement during this era (versus buying finished or semifinished goods). Ironically, no purchasing books of major consequence were published in the war years.

Harold T. Lewis, a respected purchasing professional during the 1930s through the 1950s, noted that there was considerable doubt about the existence of any general recognition of purchasing as being important to a company. Lewis noted that from World War I to 1945, at least a gradual if uneven recognition developed of the importance of sound procurement to company operation.

Period Three: The War Years (1940–1946)

World War II introduced a new period in purchasing history. The emphasis on obtaining required (and scarce) materials during the war influenced a growth in purchasing interest. In 1933, only nine colleges offered courses related to purchasing. By 1945, this number had increased to 49 colleges. The membership of the National Association of Purchasing Agents increased from 3,400 in 1934 to 5,500 in 1940 to 9,400 in the autumn of 1945. A study conducted during this period revealed that 76% of all purchase requisitions contained no specifications or stipulation of brand. This suggested that other departments within the firm recognized the role of the purchasing agent in determining sources of supply.[12]

Even before the end of the war, some observers questioned whether purchasing would continue to sustain its importance within the firm. Others raised the issue of whether or not the transition to a marketing culture would result in the redirection of a firm's primary emphasis.

Period Four: The Quiet Years (1947–Mid-1960s)

The heightened awareness of purchasing that existed during World War II did not carry over to the postwar years. After the war, purchasing managers struggled for recognition within the corporate hierarchy as the world witnessed the growth of marketing-driven U.S. multinationals. John A. Hill, a noted purchasing professional, commented about the state of purchasing during this period: "For many firms, purchases were simply an inescapable cost of doing business which no one could do much about. So far as the length and breadth of American industry is concerned, the purchasing function has not yet received in full measure the attention and emphasis it deserves."[13]

Another respected purchasing professional, Bruce D. Henderson, also commented about the state of affairs facing purchasing. He noted that purchasing was a neglected function in most organizations because it was not important to mainstream problems. He went on to say that some executives found it hard to visualize a company becoming more successful than its competitors because of its superior procurement. In his words, "Procurement is regarded as a negative function—it can handicap the company if not done well but can make little positive contribution."[14]

Articles began appearing during this period describing the practices of various companies using staff members to collect, analyze, and present data for purchasing decisions. Ford Motor Company was one of the first private organizations to establish a commodity research department to provide short- and long-term commodity information. Ford also created a purchase analysis department to give buyers assistance on product and price analysis.[15]

The postwar period saw the development of the value analysis technique, pioneered by General Electric in 1947. GE's approach concentrated on the evaluation of which materials or changes in specifications and design would reduce overall product costs.

Although important internal purchasing developments occurred during this era, there was no denying that other disciplines such as marketing and finance overshadowed purchasing. The emphasis during the postwar years and throughout the 1960s was on satisfying consumer demand and the needs of a growing industrial market. Furthermore, firms faced stable competition and had access to abundant material—conditions that historically have diminished overall purchasing importance. This period was one of long-term economic growth, normal (and minor) economic downturns, and material availability. The events that would normally cause an increase in purchasing importance were not present during the quiet years of purchasing history.[16]

Period Five: Materials Management Comes of Age (Mid-1960s–Late 1970s)

Beginning in the mid-1960s, firms initiated the dramatic growth of the materials management concept within American industry. Although interest in materials management grew during this period, the concept's historical origins date to the 1800s. Organizing under the materials management concept was common during the latter half of the nineteenth century in the U.S. railroads. They combined related functions such as purchasing, inventory control, receiving, and stores under the authority of one individual.[17]

External events directly affected the operation of the typical firm. The Vietnam War, for example, resulted in upward price and material availability pressures. During the 1970s, firms experienced widespread material problems related to oil "shortages" and embargoes. The logical response of industry was to become more efficient, particularly in the purchase and control of materials.

Widespread agreement existed about the primary objective of the materials concept and the functions that might fall under the materials umbrella. The overall objective of materials management was to solve materials problems from a total system viewpoint rather than the viewpoint of individual functions or activities. The various functions that might fall under the materials umbrella included material planning and control, inventory planning and control, materials and procurement research, purchasing, incoming traffic, receiving, incoming quality control, stores, materials movement, and scrap and surplus disposal.[18]

The role of purchasing throughout the age of materials management was notable. Purchasing managers emphasized multiple sourcing through competitive bid pricing and rarely viewed the supplier as a value-added partner. Buyers maintained arm's-length relationships with suppliers. Price competition was the major factor determining supply contracts. The purchasing strategies and behaviors that evolved over the last half-century were inadequate when the severe economic recession of the early 1980s and the emergence of foreign global competitors occurred.

Period Six: The Global Era (Late 1970s–1999)

The global era, and its effect on the importance, structure, and behavior of purchasing, has already proved different from other historical periods. These differences include the following:

- Never in our industrial history has competition become so intense so quickly. Global competitors from the Pacific Rim and Europe captured world markets from American firms. These firms emphasized quality at a lower cost in order to capture market share. Longer-term planning horizons became much shorter and uncertain.
- Global firms increasingly captured world market share and emphasized different strategies, organizational structures, and management techniques compared with their American counterparts. The individual-country-based organizational structure favored by most U.S. firms during the 1960s and 1970s became inadequate for competing in global markets.
- The rate of technology change during this period was unprecedented. The international product life cycle became shorter. Technological innovation spread rapidly around the world and product technologies changed over months instead of years.
- The ability to coordinate worldwide purchasing activity by using international data networks and the World Wide Web (via Intranets) emerged. This ability supported taking a global view of purchasing to achieve maximum performance benefit.

The swiftness of change and the importance of suppliers is reflected in the actual and anticipated purchasing practices of this period. In a study of U.S. and foreign firms, a new set of activities had already replaced those emphasized at the beginning of the global era (early 1980s).[19]

Period Seven: Integrated Supply Chain Management (2000 and Beyond)

Purchasing approaches beyond 2000 reflect a changing emphasis toward the importance of quality and the role of suppliers. Supplier relationships are shifting from an arm's-length adversarial approach to a more cooperative approach with suppliers. Purchasing strategy approaches with suppliers involve supplier development and improvement, early supplier design involvement, cross-functional teams for supplier evaluation, the use of full-service suppliers, total cost supplier selection, long-term supplier relationships, strategic cost management, and integrated Internet linkages and shared databases. Purchasing behavior is shifting dramatically to support the performance requirements of the new era.

It is possible to reach three conclusions about the new era. First, *the reshaping of purchasing's role in the modern economy is underway* in response to the challenges presented by worldwide competition and rapidly changing technology and customer expectations. Second, the *overall importance of the purchasing process is increasing*, particularly for firms competing in industries characterized by worldwide competition and rapid change. Third, *purchasing must continue to become more integrated with customer requirements, as well as with operations, logistics, human resources, finance, accounting, marketing, and information systems.* This is a natural evolution that may take some time to occur, but is inevitable in the long run.

This discussion provided a brief historical perspective about the evolution of purchasing within American industry. It is important to gain an appreciation of purchasing's roots in the mid-1800s and to grasp the importance of the function in today's global environment. Each historical period has contributed something unique to the development of purchasing, including the events that shaped purchasing history and the leaders who have contributed to the growth of the profession, particularly during the early periods.

LOOKING AHEAD

The remainder of this book discusses the major tasks and challenges facing the modern purchasing professional *operating within the context of a dynamic supply chain*. Section 2 provides a basic understanding of the activity called purchasing. Chapters 2 through 4 focus primarily on purchasing as a functional activity, often interacting with other functional groups. This discussion is largely restricted to the **tactical purchasing** processes discussed earlier in this chapter. Without a solid understanding of tactical purchasing processes, appreciating the strategic role that purchasing can play within a supply chain is difficult.

With this understanding, Section 3 considers how purchasing evaluates, selects, manages, and improves supplier performance. Chapters 5 through 11 relate to **strategic sourcing** activities. Realizing these advantages requires shifting our view of purchasing from a tactical or clerically oriented activity to one focusing on strategic supply management.

Every purchasing professional is expected to play a major role in reducing supply chain–related costs. Because strategic cost management is such an important factor in today's purchasing environment, purchasing professionals have developed an assortment of tools, techniques, and approaches for managing the procurement and sourcing process. The tools, techniques, and approaches presented in Section 4 illustrate how purchasing managers can contribute to meeting an organization's goals and objectives through **strategic cost management**. Chapters 12 through 15 address inventory and process management tools, cost and price analysis, negotiation, and contract management.

Section 5 deals extensively with the important role that purchasing plays within the integrated supply chain. The focus is on **supply chain management** and some of the important issues that must be considered as organizations form closer relationships with other supply chain partners and begin to link information systems. Some of these activities involve specific disciplines, such as legal or transportation support, while others relate to the development of purchasing information systems and business-to-business electronic commerce. Organizations must also have a rigorous and relevant performance measurement system to track its ongoing processes and make decisions regarding planned future changes. The activities presented in Chapters 16 through 20 may or may not be a formal part of the purchasing organization. They are, however, integral stepping-stones to effective supply chain management.

Section 6 (Chapter 21) deals with **future directions** identified during research and experience with a variety of global organizations. These trends can help us identify how the field of purchasing and supply chain management is changing, what is driving these changes, and how best to respond. As we move forward into the twenty-first century, this section will be updated on a continuous basis to reflect the ongoing changes occurring in the field of supply chain management.

DISCUSSION QUESTIONS

1.   What do you think was the critical element that led to the changes at AlliedSignal? Under what circumstances would the effort to move toward strategic sourcing have failed?
2.   Provide examples of "tactical" and "strategic" purchasing activities. What type of people should be assigned to each type of task?
3.   What are the historical origins of the "supply chain" concept? Who were the early pioneers in this area?
4.   Why do you think purchasing has taken so long to be recognized as a true management function? What led executives to realize the growing importance of purchasing?
5.   What do you think lies in store for purchasing in the future?

ADDITIONAL READINGS

Das, Ajay, and Robert Handfield. "A Meta-analysis of Doctoral Dissertations in Purchasing." *Journal of Operations Management* 15 (1997): 101–121.

Handfield, Robert, and Mitsumasa Onitsuka. "Process and Supply Chain Management Evolution in the American Cotton Textile Industry." *St. Andrew's University Economic and Business Review* (Kobe, Japan, December, 1995): 1–35.

Monczka, Robert, and Robert Trent. *Purchasing and Sourcing Strategy: Trends and Implications*. Tempe, AZ: Center for Advanced Purchasing Studies, 1995.

ENDNOTES

1.   Tom Peters, *Liberation Management* (New York: Knopf, 1992).
2.   *World Class Logistics: The Challenge of Managing Continuous Change*, Global Logistics Research Team, Michigan State University (Oak Brook, IL: Council of Logistics Management, 1995).
3.   R. Handfield and E. Nichols, *Introduction to Supply Chain Management*, (Upper Saddle River, NJ: Prentice Hall, 1998).
4.   Consortium Company Meeting, GEBN, Michigan State University, October 1996.
5.   Alex Taylor III, "The Auto Industry Meets the New Economy," *Fortune*, September 5, 1994, 52–59.
6.   David Woodruff, "Chrysler's Neon: Is This the Small Car Detroit Couldn't Build?" *Business Week*, May 3, 1993, 116–126.
7.   Shawn Tully, "Purchasing's New Muscle," *Fortune*, February 21, 1994, 56–57.
8.   Charles Babbage, *On the Economy of Machinery and Manufacturers*, 2nd ed. (London: Charles Knight Publishing 1832), 202, as reported by H. Fearon, "History of Purchasing," *Journal of Purchasing* (February 1968): 44.

9. Robert Handfield and Mitsumasa Onitsuka, "Process and Supply Chain
    Management Evolution in the American Cotton Textile Industry," *St. Andrew's
    University Economic and Business Review* (Kobe, Japan, December 1995): 1–35.
10. H. Fearon, "History of Purchasing," *Journal of Purchasing* (February 1968): 44–50.
11. Fearon, "History of Purchasing," 44–50.
12. Fearon, "History of Purchasing," 8.
13. John A. Hill, "The Purchasing Revolution," *Journal of Purchasing Management*
    (Summer 1975): 18–19. (*Note:* This is a reprint of a speech given by John Hill in
    1953.)
14. Bruce D. Henderson, "The Coming Revolution in Purchasing," *Journal of Purchasing
    and Materials Management* (Summer 1975): 44. (*Note:* This is a reprint of an article first
    appearing in 1964.)
15. Albert J. Browning, "Purchasing—A Challenge and an Opportunity," *Purchasing*
    (December 1947): 99–101.
16. The Korean War conflict did have some impact on material availability. The total
    impact was relatively minor compared to that of World War I and World War II.
17. Harold E. Fearon, "Materials Management: A Synthesis and Current View," *Journal
    of Purchasing* (February 1963): 34.
18. Fearon, "Materials Management," 37–39.
19. *Purchasing and Materials Management Seminar Research Survey* (East Lansing: Michigan
    State University, 1995).

2 THE PURCHASING PROCESS

Purchasing Objectives

Objective 1: Support Operational Requirements

Objective 2: Manage the Purchasing Process Efficiently and Effectively

Objective 3: Select, Develop, and Maintain Sources of Supply

Objective 4: Develop Strong Relationships with Other Functional Groups

Objective 5: Support Organizational Goals and Objectives

Objective 6: Develop Integrated Purchasing Strategies That Support Organizational Strategies

Purchasing's Span of Control

Evaluate and Select Suppliers

Review Specifications

Act as the Primary Contact with Suppliers

Determine the Method of Awarding Purchase Contracts

The Purchasing Cycle

Identify or Anticipate Material and Service Needs

Evaluate Suppliers

Select Suppliers

Release and Receive Purchase Requirements

Continuously Measure and Manage Supplier Performance

Purchasing Documents

Purchase Requisition

Request for Quotation

Purchase Order

Blanket Purchase Order

Purchase Release

Other Documents/Electronic Forms

Types of Purchases

Raw Materials

Semifinished Products and Components

Finished Products

Maintenance, Repair, and Operating Items

Production Support Items

Services

Capital Equipment

Transportation and Third-Party Purchasing

Improving the Purchasing Process

Good Practice Example: Lehigh University Makes the Purchasing Process Work

Conclusion

$\mathcal{P}$urchasing Helps Chrysler Make a Big Turnaround

It is hard to imagine that one day in 1979 Chrysler Corporation (now DaimlerChrysler) did not have enough cash to pay its employees, suppliers, and financial creditors, and almost had to declare bankruptcy. Keeping Chrysler in business required concessions from the United Auto Workers, a restructuring of bank debt involving hundreds of institutions, and more than a billion dollars of government-secured loans. While the recession that occurred in the late 1970s could be partly to blame for this, much of Chrysler's problems involved how it managed its operations. The company operated with strong functional silos—information flowed up and down the organization but rarely across functions or to other supply chain members. Management fought the union, purchasing fought with suppliers, and product developers, dominated by engineering, created products that customers did not want. It also didn't help that Chrysler was producing products with very poor quality.

Today, Chrysler is a far different enterprise than it was 20 years ago. How can this be explained? To better satisfy car buyers, the company adopted the "extended enterprise," a strategy that calls for greater integration of activities throughout all purchasing linkages—from raw materials through subassembly and component suppliers, through production, to dealers; and ultimately, to delivering the final product to the customer. By way of this tighter integration, Chrysler has become more responsive to the needs and desires of the marketplace. It has earned a reputation as being quite innovative in product design and development.

Purchasing has made a major difference in Chrysler's turnaround. The company is recognized as having some of the best supplier relationships in North America. Adversarial relationships have given way to more cooperative supply management approaches. Suppliers are early and active participants during new product development. In fact, major suppliers are now responsible for designing and building systems for virtually every car and truck developed by Chrysler. Purchasing has established an extremely successful supplier suggestion program called SCORE, which generates thousands of supplier suggestions each year. The savings realized from these suggestions are valued annually in the hundreds of millions of dollars.

These changes could not have happened without people who understand the purchasing process and know how to use that process to create value. Chrysler recognizes that purchasing is no longer a place for undertrained buyers to practice traditional, and usually adversarial, approaches to supply chain management. The company recruits highly educated individuals to be part of the purchasing team. These individuals must develop a thorough understanding of purchasing fundamentals as they progress along a career path that shifts from tactical buying to strategic sourcing. To aid in their development, Chrysler utilizes a training program that stresses purchasing fundamentals. Trainees rotate through

$\rightarrow\rightarrow\rightarrow$

different areas to gain well-rounded experience and knowledge. In short, management knows that future leaders in purchasing must be proficient in operational purchasing before they can assume responsibility for the development of purchasing strategies.

In the competitive environment at the start of the twenty-first century, executive management has been looking to purchasing to provide cost reductions, improve supply chain quality, gain access to new sources of technology, improve cycle time, involve suppliers in product and process development, and streamline processes. As the opening vignette highlighted, world-class organizations must have highly qualified staff members who are schooled in the fundamentals of purchasing. As one purchasing executive maintained, "You have to know how to block and tackle [know the basics] before you can be an effective purchaser."

Before we explore the more advanced purchasing topics presented in later chapters, we must first gain a thorough understanding of the purchasing process, just like the trainees at Chrysler. A world-class purchasing staff must continuously work to improve the efficiency and effectiveness of what we call the *purchasing process*. This chapter introduces the following topics and ideas associated with purchasing in almost all industries:

- Purchasing objectives
- Purchasing's span of control
- The purchasing cycle
- Documents that support the purchasing process
- Types of purchases
- Improving the purchasing process
- Good practice example from Lehigh University

$\mathcal{P}$URCHASING OBJECTIVES

The objectives of a world-class purchasing organization move far beyond the traditional belief that purchasing's primary role is to obtain goods and services in response to internal needs. To understand how this role is changing, we must understand what purchasing is all about, starting with the primary objectives of a world-class purchasing organization.

Objective 1: Support Operational Requirements

Purchasing must perform a number of activities to satisfy the operational requirements of internal customers, which is the traditional role of the purchasing function. More often than not, purchasing supports the needs of operations through the purchase of raw materials, components, subassemblies, repair and maintenance items, and services. Purchasing may also support the requirements of physical distribution centers responsible for storing and delivering replacement parts or finished products to end customers. Purchasing also supports engineering and technical groups, particularly during new product development.

In the past, many organizations used vertical integration as a means of managing sources of supply. Vertical integration means that an organization controls (i.e., owns) the inputs that support the supply chain. While vertically integrated enterprises have suppliers, they are internal rather than external suppliers. For example, with the development of mass production techniques, Henry Ford was faced with uncertainty regarding the flow of material inputs into his factories, and he relied on vertical integration to buffer demand and price uncertainty. Unfortunately, by extending control of the value chain over areas that were difficult to manage, such as mining, Ford's integration efforts were not successful in the long run. Henry Ford committed so many resources to vertical integration that he forgot to develop new car models.

Today, many industries are moving away from vertical integration and relying increasingly on external suppliers. Purchasing must support this movement by providing an uninterrupted flow of high-quality goods and services that internal customers require. Supporting this flow requires purchasing to

1. Buy items at the right price
2. From the right source
3. At the required specification
4. In the right quantity
5. For delivery at the right time
6. To the right internal customer

Purchasing must be *responsive* to the material and support needs of its internal operational customers. Failing to respond to the needs of internal customers will diminish the confidence these internal customers have in purchasing, and they may try to negotiate contracts themselves (a practice known as "backdoor buying").

Objective 2: Manage the Purchasing Process Efficiently and Effectively

Purchasing must manage its internal operations efficiently and effectively, including

- Determining staffing levels
- Developing and adhering to administrative budgets
- Providing professional training and growth opportunities for employees
- Introducing purchasing systems that lead to productivity improvements and better decision making

Purchasing management has limited resources available to manage the purchasing process, and must continuously work toward improved utilization of these resources. Limited resources include employees working within the department, budgeted funds, time, information, and knowledge. Organizations are therefore constantly looking for people who have developed the skills necessary to deal with the wide variety of tasks faced by purchasing.

Objective 3: Select, Develop, and Maintain Sources of Supply

One of the most important objectives of the purchasing function is the selection, development, and maintenance of supply. This is what strategic supply management is all about. Purchasing must select and manage a supply base capable of providing performance advantages in product cost, quality, technology, delivery, or new product development. Hewlett-Packard has improved on-time delivery and reduced cycle times by working closely with suppliers in sharing production schedules and forecasts, working with suppliers to reduce non–value-added time in their processes, and helping them to improve the scheduling of deliveries. Suppliers had to improve their scheduling processes, reduce setup times, reduce order-entry errors, change their facility layout, and do whatever was necessary to improve their delivery performance.

Supply-base management requires that purchasing pursue better relationships with external suppliers and develop reliable, high-quality sources of supply. This objective also requires that purchasing work directly with suppliers to improve existing capabilities or even develop new capabilities. Effectively maintaining and developing sources of supply often requires purchasing to first identify suppliers who have the potential for excellent performance, and then approach these suppliers with the objective of developing closer buyer-seller relationships. A good part of this text focuses on how purchasing can effectively meet this objective.

Objective 4: Develop Strong Relationships with Other Functional Groups

U.S. industry has traditionally maintained organizational structures that have resulted in limited cross-functional interaction and cross-boundary communication. During the 1990s, the need for closer relationships between functions became clear. Purchasing must communicate closely with other functional groups, who are purchasing's internal customers. If manufacturing personnel are complaining that parts received from a supplier are defective, than purchasing must work closely with the supplier to improve quality. In order to achieve this objective, purchasing must develop positive relationships and interact closely with other functional groups, including marketing, manufacturing, engineering, technology, and finance. In Chapter 5, we examine the importance of this cross-functional interaction in detail.

Objective 5: Support Organizational Goals and Objectives

Perhaps the single most important purchasing objective is to support organizational goals and objectives. While this sounds easy, it is not always the case that purchasing goals match organizational goals. This objective implies that purchasing can directly affect (positively or negatively) total performance and that purchasing must concern itself with organizational directives. For example, let's assume an organization has an objective of reducing the amount of inventory across its supply chain. Purchasing can work with suppliers to deliver smaller quantities more frequently, leading to inventory reductions. Such policies will show up as improved performance on the firm's balance sheet and income statements. However, the ability to support organizational goals requires a fundamental shift in the way that executive management views purchasing. Purchasing can no longer be a support function, but must be recognized as a strategic asset that provides a powerful competitive advantage in the marketplace. In order for this to happen, purchasing must help deliver timely results that contribute to organizational goals and objectives.

Objective 6: Develop Integrated Purchasing Strategies That Support Organizational Strategies

Far too often the purchasing function fails to develop strategies and plans that align with or support organizational strategies or the plans of other business functions. There are a number of reasons why purchasing may fail to integrate its plans with company plans. First, the training and selection of purchasing personnel has historically been for the performance of a demanding operational position. As a result, purchasing personnel have not participated at the highest levels of the corporate planning process. Second, executive management has often been slow to recognize the benefits that a progressive procurement function can provide. Accordingly, purchasing has had limited involvement or influence in the development of an organization's strategic plans. As these two reasons become less important, increased integration of purchasing within the strategic planning process will occur. A purchasing department actively involved within the corporate planning process can do the following:

- Monitor supply markets and trends (e.g., material price increases, shortages, changes in suppliers) and interpret the impact of these trends on company objectives.
- Identify the critical materials and services required to support company strategies in key performance areas, particularly during new product development.
- Develop supply options and contingency plans that support company plans.

PURCHASING'S SPAN OF CONTROL

Functional groups carry out certain duties on behalf of the organization. We refer to this as a function's *span of control*. Purchasing must have the legitimate authority to make decisions that rightfully belong to a purchasing group. While internal customers influence many important decisions, final authority for certain matters must ultimately be assigned to the purchasing department. This section details those decision areas that are rightfully part of purchasing's operating authority.

Evaluate and Select Suppliers

Perhaps the most important duty of purchasing is the right to evaluate and select suppliers—this is what purchasing personnel are trained to do. Presumably, the purchasing function has the expertise and specialization to carry out this responsibility. It is important to retain this right to avoid "backdoor" buying and selling—a situation that occurs when sellers contact and attempt to sell directly to end users (purchasing's internal customers). Of course, this right does not mean that purchasing should not request assistance when identifying or evaluating potential suppliers. Engineering, for example, can support supplier selection by evaluating supplier product and process performance capabilities. The right to evaluate and select suppliers also does not mean that sales representatives are not allowed to talk with nonpurchasing personnel. However, nonpurchasing personnel cannot make commitments to the seller or enter into contract agreements. A trend that is affecting purchasing's right to select suppliers is the use of teams to make buying decisions. Such teams still feature the involvement of personnel with purchasing expertise. The selection decision becomes more of a consensus process.

Purchasing's right to evaluate and select suppliers maintains the integrity of the purchasing process. Allowing nonpurchasing departments to select suppliers invites questionable behavior between buyers and sellers and risks the selection of less qualified suppliers. It can also result in poorly worded contracts, increased supply risk, redundant paperwork, and the lack of a unified buying policy. Organizations often issue a policy statement outlining the guidelines to follow in this area.

Review Specifications

The authority to review material specifications is also within purchasing's span of control, although engineering sometimes disputes this right. Purchasing personnel work hard to develop knowledge and expertise about a wide variety of materials but must also make this knowledge work to an organization's benefit. The right to question allows purchasing to review specifications where required. For example, purchasing may question whether a lower cost material can still meet an engineer's stress tolerances. The right to question material specifications also helps avoid developing material specifications that only a user's favorite supplier can satisfy. A review of different requisitions may also reveal that different users actually require the same material. By combining purchase requirements, purchasing can often achieve a lower total cost.

Act as the Primary Contact with Suppliers

Purchasing departments historically have maintained a policy that suppliers have contact only with purchasing personnel. While this makes sense from a control standpoint, some firms today are beginning to relax this policy. Today, we recognize that purchasing must act as the primary contact with suppliers, but that other functions should be able to interact directly with suppliers as needed. Xerox Corporation

EXHIBIT 2.1   *A Comparison of Two Communication Models*

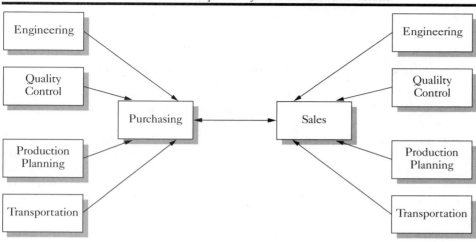

(a) Traditional Purchasing Communication Linkages

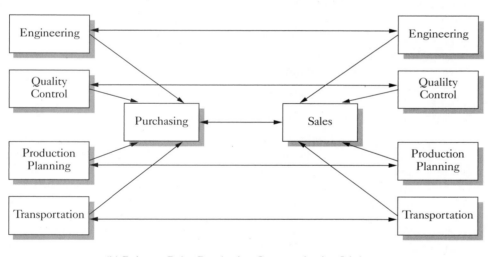

(b) Point-to-Point Purchasing Communication Linkages

allows its engineers to have direct contact with supplier engineers after the award-ing of a purchase contract, which allows the two technical groups to talk to each other and "speak their own language." It also makes the communication process between buyer and seller more efficient and accurate. Exhibit 2.1 compares two communication models. The first features all communication linkages moving through purchasing and sales, and the second model features expanded point-to-point communication linkages. While purchasing must retain the right to be the primary contact with suppliers, the right of exclusive contact encourages rigid departmentalization rather than the timely movement of personnel and information between organizations and functions.

Determine the Method of Awarding Purchase Contracts

According to this policy, purchasing is given the right to determine how to award purchase contracts. Will purchasing award a contract based on competitive bidding, negotiation, or a combination of the two approaches? If purchasing takes a competitive bidding approach, how many suppliers will it request to bid? Purchasing should also lead or coordinate negotiations with suppliers. Again, this does not mean that purchasing should not use personnel from other functions to support the negotiation process. It means that purchasing retains the right to control the overall process, act as an agent to commit an organization to a legal agreement, and negotiate a purchase price.

THE PURCHASING CYCLE

This section presents the purchasing process as a cycle consisting of five major stages:

1. Identify or anticipate material or service needs.
2. Evaluate potential supply sources.
3. Select suppliers.
4. Release and receive material requirements.
5. Continuously measure and manage supplier performance.

These stages may vary in different organizations, depending on whether purchasing is sourcing a new or repetitively purchased item. New items require that purchasing spend much more time up front evaluating potential sources. Repeat items usually have approved sources already available. The entire purchasing cycle, shown in Exhibit 2.2, applies only to new item requirements or changes to established sources of supply. For items that already have suppliers selected for them, the purchasing cycle consists of steps 1, 4, and 5. (In some instances, purchasing is not even involved in step 4.) Supplier evaluation and selection comes into play during the purchase of new items or services, or during a review of existing purchase contracts.

Identify or Anticipate Material and Service Needs

The purchasing cycle begins with identifying or anticipating a material or service need. Material requirements can be for equipment, components, raw materials, subassemblies, or even completely finished products. Examples of service requirements include a need for computer programmers, hazardous waste handlers, transportation carriers, or maintenance service providers. Users (also called internal customers) must identify their material and service requirements in order for purchasing to satisfy that need. Purchasing requirements are expressed in a variety of ways, including purchase

EXHIBIT 2.2   *The Purchasing Cycle*

1. Identify or anticipate material and service needs. . .

Purchase requisitions

Forecasts and customer orders

Reorder point systems

Stock checks

Cross-functional new product development teams

2. Evaluate suppliers. . .

Develop list of potential suppliers

Look at past performance

Determine important performance criteria

Visit supplier facilities as required

3. Select suppliers. . .

Evaluate past performance or site visit data

Analyze request for quotations or proposals

Negotiate with suppliers as required

Make selection decision and issue purchase order or finalize contract

5. Continuously measure and manage supplier performance. . .

Do not assume that purchasing cycle ends with receipt of material or service

Identify improvement opportunities or supplier nonperformance

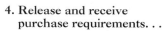

4. Release and receive purchase requirements. . .

Transmit purchase requirements electronically, by fax, or through the mail

Shorten order cycle time through electronic data interchange and bar-code technology

requisitions from internal users, forecasts and customer orders, routine reordering systems, stock checks, and material requirements identified during new product development. Let's take a closer look at these systems.

Purchase Requisitions Perhaps the most common way to inform purchasing of a requirement is through a purchase requisition—an internal document completed by a user that informs purchasing of a specific material need. A standard purchase requisition is used most often for routine, noncomplex items, which are increasingly being transmitted through online requisitioning systems linking users with purchasing. An online requisition system is an internal system designed primarily to save time through efficient communication and tracking of material requests. Users should use these systems only if they require purchasing involvement. It is possible that users have access to other systems that will allow them to purchase an item directly from a supplier, such as a corporate procurement card. In that case requisitions forwarded to purchasing are unnecessary.

Wide differences exist across organizations in the quality and use of electronic purchase requisition systems. A system that simply requires users to submit what they require for electronic transmission to purchasing is similar to electronic mail.

This type of system provides little added value except to speed the request to purchasing. Conversely, one system studied was so complex that users were afraid to use it. They bypassed online requisitioning and relied instead on the phone or intracompany mail.

Fidelty Investments, a leader in the mutual fund industry, has created a desktop online requisition system for its 23,000 users spread across diverse geographic locations. The Intranet system displays product information for 40 high-volume suppliers with point and click requisition capability. The system allows tracking of the request so users can determine the status of material requests. The average cost of a requisition has declined from $80 to $21. This represents major savings, especially since the company processes more than 60,000 requisitions anually. Also, the average processing time for requisition approval is two days versus six days with a paper-based system. Soon, users will have the ability to forward requests electronically to suppliers, bypassing purchasing entirely.[1]

Traveling Purchase Requisitions Material needs are also communicated through a traveling purchase requisition—a form consisting of a printed card filed for each item controlled in a manually operated system. This method is used primarily for very small companies that have not automated their purchasing or inventory management processes. Information on the card can include

- Description of item
- List of approved suppliers and addresses
- Last prices paid to suppliers
- Reorder point
- Record of usage

A traveling requisition can be helpful because it can conserve time when reordering routine materials and supplies. When stock levels reach a specified reorder point, an employee notifies purchasing by forwarding the traveling requisition maintained with the inventory. The employee notes the current stock level and desired delivery date. To eliminate the need to research information, the traveling requisition includes information required by a buyer to process an order. This system saves time because it provides information on the card for the item that otherwise requires research by a buyer. For example, the traveling requisition can include a list of approved suppliers, list prices, a history of usage and ordering, and lead-time information. Historical ordering information is noted directly on the record over a period of time. As inventory systems continue to become computerized (even at smaller companies), traveling requisitions are used less frequently. With an automated system, clerks simply enter the order requirement and the system generates a purchase requisition or automatically places an order.

Forecasts and Customer Orders Customer orders can trigger a need for material requirements, particularly when changes to existing products require new components. Customer orders can also signal the need to obtain existing materials. As companies increasingly customize products to meet the needs of individual customers, purchasing must be ready to support new material requirements. Market forecasts can also signal the need for material. An increasing product forecast, for example, may signal the need for additional or new material. If a supplier already is selected to provide that material, then an automated ordering system such as material requirements planning (MRP), may forward the material request to suppliers automatically.

Reorder Point System   A reorder point system is a widely used way to identify purchase needs. Such a system uses information regarding order quantity and demand forecasts that are unique to each item or part number maintained in inventory. Each item in a reorder point system, which is usually computerized, has a predetermined order point and order quantity. When inventory is depleted to a given level, the system notifies the material control department (or the buyer in some organizations) to issue a request to a supplier for inventory replenishment. This signal might be a blinking light on a screen, a message sent to the material control department's e-mail address, or a computer report. Most reorder point systems are automated using predetermined ordering parameters (such as an economic order quantity, which considers inventory holding and ordering costs). Computer-based systems can instantly calculate reorder point parameters. Most systems can also calculate the cost tradeoffs between inventory holding costs, ordering costs, and forecast demand requirements. Reorder point systems are used for production and nonproduction items.

An automated reorder point system efficiently identifies purchase requirements. This type of system can routinely provide visibility to current inventory levels and requirements of thousands of part numbers. The reorder point system is the most common method for transmitting routine material order requests today, particularly for companies that maintain spare part distribution centers. Students interested in learning more about reorder point systems should consult an inventory management textbook.

Stock Checks   Stock checks (or cycle counts) involve the physical checking of inventory to verify that system records (also called the record on hand) match actual on-hand inventory levels—also called the physical on hand (POH). If the physical inventory for an item is below the system amount, an adjustment to that part's record can trigger a reorder request for additional inventory. Why might physical inventory be less than what the computerized system indicates should be on hand? Placing material in an incorrect location, damage that is not properly recorded, theft, and short shipments from the supplier that receiving did not notice all can contribute to the POH being less than the record on hand (ROH).

Smaller firms that rely on standard, easy-to-obtain items often use stock checks to determine material ordering requirements. In this environment, the stock check consists of physically visiting a part location to determine if there is enough inventory to satisfy user requirements. No purchase reorder is necessary if there is enough to cover expected requirements.

Cross-Functional New Product Development Teams   When users contact purchasing with a specific need, we say that purchasing is operating in a *reactive* manner. When purchasing works directly with internal customers to anticipate future requirements, such as during new product development, purchasing is being *proactive*.

What does it mean to anticipate a requirement? If purchasing is part of new product development teams, then the opportunity exists to see product designs at early stages of the process. Purchasing can begin to identify potential suppliers for expected requirements rather than reacting to an engineering requirement at a later date. Anticipating requirements can contribute to faster product development cycle times and better supplier evaluation and selection. As firms continue to be forced to reduce the time required to develop new products, cross-functional interaction will increasingly be the means through which organizations identify, and hopefully anticipate, material requirements in the purchasing process cycle.

Evaluate Suppliers

Supplier evaluation is the second step in the purchasing cycle process. The potential evaluation of suppliers begins after determining that a purchase need exists (or is likely to exist) and the development of material specifications occurs. For routine or standard product requirements with established or selected suppliers, further supplier evaluation and selection is not necessary. However, potential sources for new items, especially those of a complex nature, require thorough investigation to be sure that purchasing evaluates only qualified suppliers.

The source evaluation process requires the development of a list of potential suppliers. This list may be generated from a variety of sources, including market representatives, experience with suppliers, information databases, and trade journals. For some items, companies may maintain a list of "preferred suppliers" who receive the first opportunity for new business. A preferred supplier has demonstrated capability through past performance. Relying on a list of preferred suppliers can reduce the time and resources required for evaluating and selecting suppliers.

Buyers use different performance criteria when evaluating potential suppliers. These criteria are likely to include a supplier's capabilities and past performance in product design, commitment to quality, management capability and commitment, technical ability, cost performance, delivery performance, and the ability to develop process and product technology. These factors are weighted in the supplier evaluation process. Specific examples of such weighting schemes appear in Chapter 8 on supplier evaluation. Final evaluation often requires visits to supplier plants and facilities. Because the resources to conduct such visits are limited, the purchaser must take great care in deciding which suppliers to visit.

Select Suppliers

Final supplier selection occurs once purchasing completes the activities required during the supplier evaluation process. Selecting suppliers is perhaps one of the most important activities performed by companies. Errors made during this part of the purchasing cycle can be damaging and long-lasting.

Identifying potential suppliers is different than reaching a contract or agreement with suppliers. Competitive bidding and negotiation are two methods commonly used when making a supplier selection decision. Competitive bidding in private industry involves a request for bids from suppliers with whom the buyer is willing to do business. This process is typically initiated when the purchasing manager sends a *request for quotation* form to the supplier. The objective is to award business to the most qualified bidder. Purchasers often evaluate the bids based on price. If the lowest bidder does not receive the purchase contract, the buyer has an obligation to inform that supplier why it did not receive the contract. Competitive bidding is effective under certain conditions:[2]

- Volume is high enough to justify this method of business.
- The specifications or requirements are clear to the seller. The seller must know or have the ability to estimate accurately the cost of producing the item.
- The marketplace is competitive, which means it has an adequate number of qualified sellers who want the business.
- Buyers ask for bids only from technically qualified suppliers who want the contract, which in turn means they will price competitively.
- Adequate time is available for suppliers to evaluate the requests for quotation.
- The buyer does not have a preferred supplier for that item. If a preferred supplier exists, the buyer may simply choose to negotiate the final details of the purchase contract with that supplier.

Buyers use competitive bidding when price is a dominant criteria and the required item (or service) has straightforward material specifications. In addition, competitive bidding is often used in the defense industry and for large projects (e.g., construction projects, information system development). If major nonprice variables exist, then the buyer and seller usually enter into direct negotiation. Competitive bidding can also be used to narrow the list of suppliers before entering contract negotiation.

Negotiation is logical when competitive bidding is not an appropriate method for supplier selection. Face-to-face negotiation is the best approach

- When any of the previously mentioned criteria for competitive bidding are missing. For example, the item may be a new and/or technically complex item with only vague specifications.
- When the purchase requires agreement about a wide range of performance factors, such as price, quality, delivery, risk sharing, and product support.
- When the buyer requires early supplier involvement.
- When the supplier cannot determine risks and costs.
- When the supplier requires a long period of time to develop and produce the items purchased. This often makes estimating purchase costs on the part of the supplier difficult.

As firms continue to develop closer relationships with selected suppliers, the negotiation process becomes one of reaching agreement on items in a cooperative mode. One thing is certain: the process that buyers use to select suppliers can vary widely depending on the required item and the relationship that a buyer has with its suppliers. For some items, a buyer may know which supplier to use before the development of final material specifications. For standard items, the competitive bid process will remain an efficient method to purchase relatively straightforward requirements. The bid process can also reduce the list of potential suppliers before a buyer begins time-consuming and costly negotiation. Chapter 14 discusses negotiation in detail.

Release and Receive Purchase Requirements

This phase of the purchasing cycle involves the physical transmittal of purchase requirements. This should be a fairly routine, although not necessarily the most efficient, part of the purchasing cycle. Some organizations transmit orders electronically, while others send material releases through the mail or by fax. Purchasing or materials planning must minimize the time required to release and receive material. Electronic data interchange (EDI), which involves the electronic transfer of purchase documents between the buyer and seller, can help shorten order cycle time. EDI transactions, particularly through the Internet, will increase over the next several years. Also, better relationships with suppliers can support a just-in-time ordering system. In some companies, once a contract is negotiated, internal end users may be directly responsible for "releasing" material orders covered under the terms of the contract, and purchasing is no longer involved until the contract is renewed.

Purchasing or a material control group must monitor the status of open purchase orders. There may be times when a purchaser has to expedite an order or work with a supplier to avoid a delayed shipment. A buyer can minimize order follow-up by selecting only the best suppliers and developing stable forecasting and efficient ordering systems. The receiving process should also be as efficient as possible by using bar-coding technology to receive and place supplier deliveries in inventory.

Continuously Measure and Manage Supplier Performance

One way to identify the best suppliers is to track performance after awarding a contract. Supplier measurement and management is a key part of the purchasing cycle. Buyers should not assume that the purchasing cycle ends with the receipt of an ordered item or the selection of a supplier. Continuous measurement is necessary to identify improvement opportunities or supplier nonperformance. A later chapter discusses purchasing measurement and evaluation tools. This section simply summarizes the key points about this phase of the purchasing cycle.

A desired outcome from performance measurement is improved supplier performance. If no formal evaluation takes place, a buyer has little insight into supplier performance over time, and tracking any performance improvement that results from supplier development efforts is not possible. Without a measurement and evaluation system, a buyer lacks the quantitative data necessary to support future purchase decisions.

A major issue when evaluating supplier performance is the frequency of evaluation and feedback. For example, should a buyer receive a supplier quality performance report on a daily, weekly, monthly, or quarterly basis? While most firms recognize the need to notify suppliers immediately when a problem arises, there is little consensus about the frequency for conducting routine or scheduled supplier evaluations. For many firms, this overall evaluation may occur only one or two times a year. Regardless of the reporting frequency, supplier performance measurement is an important part of the purchasing process cycle.

$\mathscr{P}$URCHASING DOCUMENTS

A document flow accompanies the movement of orders and material throughput the purchasing process. Historically, preparing and managing the proper purchasing documents has been a time-consuming process. Most firms have streamlined the document flow process to reduce the paperwork and handling required for each purchase. Companies are computerizing the flow of documents by (1) automating the document generation process and (2) electronically transmitting purchase documents to suppliers. The benefits of electronically generating and transmitting purchasing-related documents include

1. A virtual elimination of paperwork and paperwork handling
2. A reduction in the time between need recognition and the release and receipt of an order
3. Improved communication both within the company and with suppliers
4. A reduction in errors
5. Lower overhead costs in the purchasing area

A detailed discussion of the advantages of computerized purchasing systems occurs in Chapter 19 on purchasing information systems. This discussion focuses on the most common purchasing documents associated with the release of material requirements.

Purchase Requisition

The most common method of informing purchasing of material needs is through a *purchase requisition*. Exhibit 2.3 presents an example of one. Users may also transmit their needs by phone, word-of-mouth, or through a computer-generated method. Although a variety of purchase requisition formats exist, every requisition should contain

- Description of required material or service
- Quantity and date required
- Estimated unit cost
- Operating account to be charged
- Date of requisition (this starts the tracking cycle)
- Date required
- Authorized signature

This document moves manually or electronically from the individual or department requiring material to purchasing. While the user may suggest a supplier, purchasing has final selection authority. For routine, off-the-shelf items, the requisition

EXHIBIT 2.3   *Purchase Requisition*

AnyCompany

TO: PURCHASING DEPARTMENT, PLEASE FURNISH THE FOLLOWING

OUR P.O. NUMBER	**REQUISITION** No. **36010**

ACCOUNT CODE NO./A.F.E. NO./A.F.M. NO./W.O. NO./EQUIP. NO.	REQUESTED BY	VENDOR NO.
DATE	DATE DELIVERY REQ'D.	F.O.B.	DEPARTMENT OR LOCATION	TERMS
TO BE USED FOR			COST ESTIMATE	APPROVAL
			APPROVAL REQUIRED BY	

SUGGESTED SUPPLIER	SHIPPING INSTRUCTIONS
	☐ TAXABLE ☐ TAX EXEMPT

ITEM NO.	QUANTITY	PART NO.	DESCRIPTION	PRICE

DELIVER TO	INSPECTION REQUIRED

☐ CONFIRMING ORDER	TO	DATE	BY	METHOD

COPIES OF PURCHASE ORDER TO	☐ ACKNOWLEDGEMENT COPY	☐ PURCHASING APPROVAL OF INVOICE REQUIRED

REASON FOR AWARD

☐ Low Bid   ☐ Blanket Order   ☐ Priority Source
☐ Only Bid   ☐ Only Approved Source   ☐ Commitment made outside of Purchasing Department
☐ Only Available Source   ☐ Emergency   ☐ Low Bidder not acceptable (explanation attached)
☐ National Account/Contract Supplier   ☐ Small Purchase   ☐ Other – or additional comments

CORPORATE FORMS MANAGEMENT

may contain all the information that purchasing requires. However, for technically complex or nonstandard items, purchasing may require additional information or specifications with the requisition. Examples of such specifications include the grade of material, method of manufacture, and detailed measurements and tolerances. Purchasing may send an acknowledgment of the receipt of the purchase requisition to the requestor. This acknowledgment often takes the form of a confirming order requisition. The acknowledgment may be a separate form notifying the user that purchasing has received and is processing the requisition, or it may be a copy of the original requisition. The confirmation verifies the accuracy of the user's material request.

Request for Quotation

If the purchase requisition requests an item with no existing supplier, then purchasing may obtain quotes or bids from potential suppliers. Purchasing forwards a *request for quotation* (RFQ) to suppliers inviting them to submit a bid for a purchase contract. Exhibit 2.4 presents an example of a request for quotation form. The form provides space for the information that suppliers require to develop an accurate quotation, including the description of the item, quantity required, date needed, delivery location, and whether the buyer will consider substitute offers. Purchasing can also indicate the date by which it must receive the supplier's quotation. The supplier completes the form by providing name, contact person, unit cost, net amount, and any appropriate payment terms. The supplier then forwards the request for quotation to the buyer for comparison against other quotations. The normal practice is for a buyer to request at least three quotations. Purchasing evaluates the quotations and selects the supplier most qualified to provide the item.

If the requested item is complex or requires an untested or new production process, purchasing can include additional information or attachments to assist the supplier. This might include detailed blueprints, samples, or technical drawings. In addition, buyers can use requests for quotation as a preliminary approach to determine if a potential supplier even has the capability to produce a new or technically complex item. A buyer must identify suppliers with the required production capability before requesting detailed competitive bids. Further quotation and evaluation can then occur to identify the best supplier.

If the purchase contract requires negotiation between the buyer and seller (rather than competitive bidding), purchasing sends a *request for proposal* (RFP) to a supplier. In many firms, RFQ and RFP are synonymous. However, in the latter case, the item's complexity requires that a number of issues besides price need to be included in the supplier's response.

Purchase Order

The drafting of a *purchase order* (PO), sometimes called a *purchase agreement,* takes place after supplier selection is complete. Purchasing must take great care when wording a purchase agreement because it is a legally binding document. Almost all purchase orders include the standard legal conditions that the order (i.e., the contract)

EXHIBIT 2.4   *Request for Quotation*

USE ONLY 3 LINES FOR VENDORS 1 & 3
USE ONLY 4 LINES FOR VENDOR 2. NOTE
SMALL NUMBERS 1 2 & 3 FOR FOLDING
TO FIT STD. NO. 10 ENVELOPE

CORPORATE FORMS MANAGEMENT

SEPARATE BETWEEN PLIES 2 & 3 – RETAIN
1 & 2 INTACT WITH CARBON IN FOR LATER
ENTRIES. DISTRIBUTE 3 - 4 - 5 TO
VENDORS & PLY 6 TO REQUISITIONER.

AnyCompany

REQUEST FOR QUOTATION

THIS IS NOT A PURCHASE ORDER

DATE

SUMMARY OF QUOTATIONS   QUOTATION NO.

QUANTITY	NO. 1	NO. 2	NO. 3
DELIVERY DATE			
F.O.B.			
FREIGHT COST			
TERMS			

NO. 1 ▶

NO. 2 ▶

NO. 3
1 ▶

WE WILL [ ]   WE WILL NOT [ ]   CONSIDER SUBSTITUTE OFFERS.

2 **PLEASE QUOTE ON THE FOLLOWING ITEMS:**

3 FOR SHIPMENT TO

F.O.B.

DELIVERY REQUIRED BY

TERMS

REPLY MUST BE IN BY:

ADDRESS REPLY TO:

ITEM NO	QUANTITY	DESCRIPTION	UNIT COST	DISCOUNT	NET AMOUNT
1					
2					
3					

AnyCompany   PURCHASING DEPARTMENT   BY

IN COMPLIANCE WITH THE ABOVE AND SUBJECT TO ALL THE CONDITIONS STATED, THE UNDERSIGNED OFFERS AND AGREES, THAT IF HIS QUOTATION OR PART OF QUOTATION BE
ACCEPTED, THAT HE WILL FURNISH AND DELIVER THE ARTICLES OR SERVICES SO LISTED ABOVE, AT THE PRICES QUOTED, TO THE DESIGNATED POINT, AND WITHIN THE TIME SPECIFIED.

QUOTATION DATE _____   FIRM NAME _____   BY _____

QUOTATION MUST BE SUBMITTED ON THIS FORM   PURCHASING DEPT. COPY is subject to on the reverse side of the agreement. The purchase order details critical information about the purchase: quantity, material specification, quality requirements, price, delivery date, method of delivery, ship-to address, purchase order number, and order due date. This information, plus the name and address of the purchasing company, appear on the front side of the order. Exhibit 2.5 presents an example of a purchase order and Exhibit 2.6 illustrates a typical set of conditions and instructions.

In companies that have not switched to computerized systems, seven to nine copies typically accompany the purchase order. In computerized environments, a file containing a copy of the PO is sent to each department's computer mailbox. The supplier receives the original copy of the purchase order along with a file copy. The supplier signs the original and sends it back to the buyer. This acknowledges that the supplier has received the purchase order and agrees with its contents. In legal terms, the transmittal of the purchase order constitutes a contractual offer while the acknowledgment by the supplier constitutes a contractual acceptance. Offer and acceptance are two critical elements of a legally binding agreement.

Purchasing forwards a copy of the purchase order to accounting (i.e., accounts payable), the requesting department, receiving, and traffic (either electronically or manually). Purchasing usually keeps several copies for its records. There are good reasons for other departments to have visibility to purchase orders and incoming receipts:

- The accounting department gains visibility to future accounts payable obligations. It also has an order against which to match a receipt for payment when the material arrives.
- The purchase order provides the requesting department with an order number to include in its records.
- The requestor can refer to the purchase order number if he or she must inquire into the status of an order.
- Receiving has a record of the order to match against the receipt of the material. Receiving also can use outstanding purchase orders to help forecast its inbound workload.
- Traffic becomes aware of inbound delivery requirements and can make arrangements with carriers or use the company's own vehicles to schedule material delivery.
- Purchasing uses its copies of the purchase order for follow-up and monitoring open orders.
- Orders remain active in all departments until the buying company acknowledges receipt of the order and that it meets quantity and quality requirements.

Note that firms are increasingly using computerized databases to perform these processes, and are moving toward a "paperless" office. Paper transfer and handling in a manual purchase order system represents minimal, if any, value-adding activity.

Blanket Purchase Order

For an item or group of items ordered repetitively from a supplier, purchasing may issue a *blanket purchase order*—an open order, effective for a year, covering repeated

EXHIBIT 2.5   *Purchase Order*

CORPORATE FORMS MANAGEMENT		
ACCOUNT CODE NUMBER/A.F.E. NO./A/F/M/ NO.	REQUESTED BY	REQUISITION NO.	VENDOR NO.

AnyCompany

PURCHASE ORDER

No.

PURCHASE ORDER NUMBER MUST BE SHOWN ON ALL DOCUMENTS, ACKNOWLEDGEMENTS, SHIPPING PAPERS, PACKING SLIPS, PACKAGES, INVOICES AND CORRESPONDENCE.

**INVOICE IN TRIPLICATE
ATTN: ACCOUNTS PAYABLE**

DATE WRITTEN	DATE DELIVERY REQUIRED	F.O.B.	DEPARTMENT OR LOCATION	TERMS

TO

SHIPPING INSTRUCTIONS

THIS ORDER SUBJECT TO CONDITIONS ON REVERSE SIDE   ☐ TAXABLE   ☐ TAX EXEMPT

ITEM NO	QUANTITY	DESCRIPTION	PRICE

– IMPORTANT –
IF YOU CANNOT DELIVER THIS MATERIAL OR SERVICE
BEFORE DATE REQUIRED PLEASE NOTIFY US **IMMEDIATELY**

AnyCompany

_____
PURCHASING AGENT   ASST   BUYER

☐   ☐

NOTICE:
EQUIPMENT, MATERIALS AND/OR SERVICE UNDER THIS CONTRACT
MUST COMPLY WITH ALL APPLICABLE STATE AND FEDERAL SAFETY
CODES FOR PLACES OF EMPLOYMENT, INCLUDING OSHA.

AN EQUAL EMPLOYMENT OPPORTUNITY EMPLOYER

EXHIBIT 2.6   *A Typical Set of Conditions and Instructions for a Purchase Order*

1.   Any different or additional terms or conditions in Seller's (Contractor's) acknowledgment of this order are not binding unless accepted in writing by Buyer.

2.   Seller shall comply with all applicable state, federal and local laws, rules and regulations.

3.   Seller expressly covenants that all goods and services supplied will conform to Buyer's order, will be merchantable, fit and sufficient for the particular purpose intended and free from defects, liens and patent infringements. Seller agrees to protect and hold harmless Buyer from any loss or claim arising out of the failure of Seller to comply with the above, and Buyer may inspect and reject nonconforming goods and may, at Buyer's option, either return such rejected goods at Seller's expense, or hold them pending Seller's reasonable instructions.

4.   The obligation of Seller to meet the delivery dates, specifications and quantities, as set forth herein, is of the essence of this order, and Buyer may cancel this order and Seller shall be responsible for any loss to or claim against Buyer arising out of Seller's failure to meet the same.

5.   Buyer reserves the right to cancel all or any part of this order which has not actually been shipped by Seller, in the event Buyer's business is interrupted because of strikes, labor disturbances, lockout, riot, fire, act of God or the public enemy, or any other cause, whether like or unlike the foregoing, if beyond the reasonable efforts of the Buyer to control.

6.   The remedies herein reserved shall be cumulative, and additional to any other or further remedies provided in law or equity. No waiver of a breach of any provision of this contract shall constitute a waiver of any other breach, or of such provisions.

7.   The provisions of this purchase order shall be construed in accordance with the Uniform Commercial Code as enacted in the State of Georgia.

8.   Government Regulations:

(1)   Seller's and Buyer's obligations hereunder shall be subject to all applicable governmental laws, rules, regulations, executive orders, priorities, ordinances and restrictions now or hereafter in force, including but not limited to (a) the Fair Labor Standards Act of 1938, as amended; (b) Title VII of the Civil Rights Act of 1964, as amended; (c) the Age Discrimination in Employment Act of 1967; (d) Section 503 of the Rehabilitation Act of 1973; (e) Executive Order 11246; (f) the Vietnam Era Veteran's Readjustment Assistance Act of 1974; and the rules, regulations and orders pertaining to the above.

(2)   Seller agrees that (a) the Equal Opportunity Clause; (b) the Certification of Nonsegregated Facilities required by Paragraph (7) of Executive Order 11246; (c) the Utilization of Minority Business Enterprises and the Minority Business Enterprises Subcontracting Program Clauses; (d) the Affirmative Action for Handicapped Worker's Clause, and (e) the Affirmative Action for Disabled Veterans and Veterans of the Vietnam Era Clause are, by this reference, incorporated herein and made a part hereof.

(3)   Seller agrees (a) to file annually a complete, timely and accurate report on Standard Form 100 (EEO-1) and (b) to develop and maintain for each of its establishments a written affirmative action compliance program which fulfills the requirements of 41 C.F.R. 60-1.40 and Revised Order No. 4 (41 C.F.R. 60-2.1 et seq.).

purchases of an item or family of items. Exhibit 2.7 provides an example of a such a form. Blanket orders eliminate the need to issue a purchase order whenever there is a need for material. After a buyer establishes a blanket order with a supplier, the ordering of an item simply requires a routine order release. The buyer and seller have already negotiated or agreed upon the terms of the purchase contract. With a blanket purchase order, the release of material becomes a routine matter between the buyer and seller.

Almost all firms establish blanket purchase orders with their suppliers. In fact, blanket orders have historically been the preferred method for making the purchasing process more efficient and user friendly. Buyers usually use a purchase order for initial purchases or a one-time purchase, which purchasing professionals may also call a *spot buy*. Blanket purchase orders are common for production items ordered on a regular basis or for the routine supplies required to operate. A maintenance supplies distributor, for example, may have a purchase order covering hundreds of items. It is not unusual for the buyer or seller to modify a purchase order to reflect new prices, new quantity discount schedules, or the adding or deleting of items.

The blanket purchase order is similar to the purchase order in general content and is distributed to the same departments that receive a copy of a purchase order. The major difference between a purchase order and a blanket purchase order is the delivery date and the receiving department. This information on the blanket order remains open because it often differs from order to order.

When negotiating a blanket purchase order, the buyer and supplier evaluate the anticipated demand over time for an item or family of items. The two parties agree on the terms of an agreement, including quantity discounts, required quality levels, delivery lead times, and any other important terms or conditions. The blanket purchase order remains in effect during the time specified on the agreement. This time period is often, but not always, six months to a year. Longer-term agreements covering several years are becoming increasingly common with U.S. firms. Most buyers reserve the right to cancel the blanket order at any time, particularly in the event of poor supplier performance. This requires an "escape clause" that allows the buyer to terminate the contract in the event of persistently poor quality, delivery, and so on.

Purchase Release

Buyers use material purchase releases to order items covered by blanket purchase orders. Purchasing specifies the required part number(s), quantity, unit price, required receipt date, using department, the ship-to address, and the method of shipment and forwards this to the supplier. Purchasing forwards copies of this form to the supplier, accounting, receiving, and traffic. Purchasing retains several copies for its records. The copy to the supplier serves as a notification of a required item or items. Accounting receives a copy so it can match the quantity received against the quantity ordered for payment purposes. Receiving must have visibility on incoming orders so it can compare ordered quantities with received quantities. As with other forms, this part of the process is increasingly becoming electronic.

Different types of material releases exist. Organizations often use the material release as a means to provide visibility to the supplier about forecasted material

EXHIBIT 2.7 *Blanket Purchase Order*

CORPORATE FORMS MANAGEMENT

ACCOUNT CODE NUMBER/A.F.E. NO./A.F.M. NO. Refer to Blanket Order Release	REQUESTED BY J. M. Smith	REQUISITION NO. 20659	VENDOR NO. 02867

AnyCompany

Corporate Purchasing
Street Address
Any City, State 00000
Telephone

PURCHASE ORDER	
No.	**34833**

SEND INVOICE TO:
ATTN: ACCOUNTS PAYABLE

PURCHASE ORDER NUMBER MUST BE SHOWN ON ALL DOCUMENTS, ACKNOWLEDGEMENTS, SHIPPING PAPERS, PACKING SLIPS, PACKAGES, INVOICES AND CORRESPONDENCE.

DATE WRITTEN	DATE DELIVERY REQUIRED	F.O.B.	DEPARTMENT OR LOCATION	TERMS
1/3/01	As Requested	Our Plant	Various	2% 10, Net 30

TO

Miller Plumbing Supply Company
1616 S. E. 3rd Avenue
Anytown, Any State 90641

SHIPPING INSTRUCTIONS

☑ ATTN: SUPPLY ROOM

☐

☑ TAXABLE   ☐ TAX EXEMPT

ITEM NO.	QUANTITY	DESCRIPTION	PRICE
		BLANKET PURCHASE ORDER	

This Blanket Purchase Order is issued to cover our purchases of <u>valves, pipe and fittings</u> from you for the period 1/3/01 through 6/30/01. Prices are not to exceed your proposal dated 12/15/00 for the period of this order.

This order is not a commitment for any material until actual releases are made on our standard Blanket Order Release form #GP-3809 by an authorized AnyCompany employee whose name appears below.

All shipments, deliveries, and pick-ups will be accompanied by a delivery ticket or packing slip.

All packing slips, delivery tickets, invoices and any other documents relating to this order must reference this Blanket Purchase Order number and the applicable Blanket Order Release number.

AnyCompany reserves the right to cancel this order at any time without cost or obligation for any items not released against this order.

Personnel authorized to make releases against this Blanket Purchase Order:

THIS PURCHASE ORDER SUPERSEDES PURCHASE ORDER #40019, DATED JULY 1, 1998.

– IMPORTANT –
IF YOU CANNOT DELIVER THIS MATERIAL OR SERVICE BEFORE DATE REQUIRED PLEASE NOTIFY US **IMMEDIATELY.**

AnyCompany

John M. Doe

PURCHASING AGENT   ☐ ASST   ☐ BUYER

THIS ORDER SUBJECT TO CONDITIONS ON REVERSE SIDE

NOTICE: EQUIPMENT, MATERIALS AND/OR SERVICE UNDER THIS CONTRACT MUST COMPLY WITH ALL APPLICABLE STATE AND FEDERAL SAFETY CODES FOR PLACES OF EMPLOYMENT, INCLUDING OSHA.

AN EQUAL EMPLOYMENT OPPORTUNITY EMPLOYER

requirements as well as actual material requirements. One U.S. automobile producer provides suppliers with an 18-month forecast for replacement parts. The first three months of the release are actual orders. The remaining nine months represent forecasted requirements that help the supplier plan production.

Other Documents/Electronic Forms

The shipping and receiving processes require several other important documents (which also can be electronic), including the material packing slip, the bill of lading, and the receiving discrepancy report.

Material Packing Slip The *material packing slip*, which the supplier provides, details the contents of a shipment. It contains the description and quantity of the items in a shipment. It also references a specific purchase order and material release number for tracking and auditing purposes. A packing slip is a critical document when receiving material at a buyer's facility. The receiving clerk uses the packing slip to compare the supplier packing slip quantity against the actual physical receipt quantity. Furthermore, the packing slip quantity should match the material release quantity. The comparison between material release quantity and packing slip quantity is critical. It identifies if suppliers have over- or under-shipped.

Bill of Lading Transportation carriers use a *bill of lading* to record the quantity of goods delivered to a facility. For example, the bill of lading may state that ABC carrier delivered three boxes to a buyer on a certain date. This prevents the purchaser from stating a week later that it received only two boxes. The bill of lading details only the number of boxes or containers delivered. Detailing the actual contents of each container is the supplier's responsibility; that information appears on the packing slip.

The bill of lading helps protect the carrier against wrongful allegations that the carrier somehow damaged, lost, or otherwise tampered with a shipment. This document does not necessarily protect the carrier against charges of concealed damage, however. A user may discover concealed damages after opening a shipping container. Responsibility for concealed damage is often difficult to establish. The receiving company may blame the carrier. The carrier may blame the supplier or maintain that the damage occurred after delivery of the material. The supplier may maintain total innocence and implicate the carrier. While all this goes on, the buyer must reorder the material as a rush order. This can affect customer service or commitments.

Receiving Discrepancy Report A *receiving discrepancy report* details any shipping or receiving discrepancies noted by the receiving department. It is often the job of purchasing or material control to investigate and resolve material discrepancies. Material discrepancies usually result from incorrect quantity shipments. They can also result from receiving an incorrect part number or a part number incorrectly labeled.

Just-in-Time Purchasing Just-in-time (JIT) purchasing and manufacturing allows firms to eliminate most receiving forms. Honda of America, for example, assumes that if its production line does not shut down it must have received its scheduled shipments from its suppliers. The accounts payable department makes payment unless informed otherwise. Honda's JIT system eliminates the need for packing slips and inbound material inspection. The system also eliminates the need to examine, file, and forward multiple copies of each packing slip to various departments. If a receipt does not arrive on time or is not damage-free, Honda realizes this within minutes. With this system, no news means the shipment arrived and is production ready.

Black and Decker employs a similar system called *backflush accounting*. In this system, suppliers are paid only for the quantity of components that are used in each week's production runs. In the event that parts are tossed aside on the production line because of defects, Black and Decker does not pay for them.

Types of Purchases

Organizations buy many different goods and services. All purchases represent a trade-off between what an organization can make itself versus what it must buy externally. For many items, the make-or-buy decision is actually quite simple. Few firms could manufacture their own production equipment, computers, or pencils. However, all firms require these items to support continued operations. The challenge is deciding which suppliers offer the best opportunity for items an organization must purchase externally. The following sections outline the variety of goods and services a typical purchasing department is responsible for buying. Please note that for each category, organizations should establish measures that track the amount of goods in physical inventory.

Raw Materials

The raw materials purchase category includes items such as petroleum, coal, and lumber, and metals such as copper and zinc. It can also include agricultural raw materials such as soybeans and cotton. A key characteristic of a raw material is a lack of processing by the supplier into a newly formed product. Any processing that occurs makes the raw material saleable. For example, copper requires refining to remove impurities from the metal. Another key characteristic is that raw materials are not of equal quality. Different types of coal, for example, can differ by sulfur content. Raw materials often receive a grade indicating its quality level. This allows raw material purchases based on the required grade.

The quality of a raw material can affect an organization's production process. For example, DuPont's poly film plant in Whitby, Ontario, requires virgin and recycled resins as raw material inputs. The quality of the raw material is a primary influence on the effectiveness and efficiency of the production process, and therefore on the quality of the finished product. It is purchasing's responsibility to make sure the plant receives the required level of quality for its raw materials.

Uncontrollable forces or factors can influence raw material prices and availability. Events in the Middle East, which no buyer controls, affect the price and availability of petroleum. Civil unrest in central and southern Africa can impact the availability of strategic minerals. A drought in the Midwest or an early frost in Florida can affect agricultural raw material prices and availability. Experienced buyers must forecast the short- and long-term supply and demand trends affecting raw material price and availability. Buyers should also develop contingency plans in case of disruption to raw material markets. This involves identifying alternative supply sources and/or substitute materials. Even if an organization does not purchase raw materials directly, it must still concern itself with the condition of raw material markets. If a disruption affects a raw material market, the buyer will quickly feel the impact through disrupted shipments throughout the supply chain.

Semifinished Products and Components

Semifinished products and components include all the items purchased from suppliers required to support an organization's final production. This includes single part number components, subassemblies, assemblies, subsystems, and systems. Semifinished products and components purchased by an automobile producer include tires, seat assemblies, wheel bearings, and car frames.

Managing the purchase of semifinished components is a critical purchasing responsibility because components affect product quality and cost. Hewlett-Packard buys its laser jet printer engines, which is a critical part of the finished product, from Canon. HP must manage the purchase of these engines carefully and work closely with the supplier. Outsourcing product requirements increases the burden on purchasing to select qualified suppliers, not only for basic components, but also for complex assemblies and systems.

Finished Products

All organizations purchase finished items from external suppliers for internal use. This category also includes purchased items that require no major processing before resale to the end customers. An organization may market under its own brand name an item produced by another manufacturer. Why would a company purchase finished items for resale? Some companies have excellent design capability but lack production capability or capacity. The purchase of finished products also allows a company to offer a full range of products. Purchasing (or engineering) must work closely with the producer of a finished product to develop material specifications. Even though the buying company does not produce the final product, it must make sure the product meets the technical and quality specifications demanded by engineering and the end customer.

Black and Decker has developed a wide range of rechargeable handheld products. The company uses lower-cost producers to manufacture many of these items. This approach has allowed the company to bring many new products to market simultaneously. Xerox purchases small copiers from overseas producers for sale under the Xerox brand name. This allows Xerox to offer a full line of copiers to its customers. General Motors purchases small cars for sale under its Geo nameplate.

The decision to purchase a finished product is often part of a company's strategy. For example, many first-time car buyers will purchase a Geo from a Chevrolet dealer (the Geo marketing outlet). General Motors hopes these customers will trade up to other General Motors products during later years. GM also earns sales revenue that it otherwise would not earn if it did not purchase and market a smaller car line.

Maintenance, Repair, and Operating Items

Maintenance, repair, and operating (MRO) items include anything that does not go directly into an organization's product. However, these items are essential for running a business. This includes spare machine parts, office and computer supplies, and cleaning supplies. The way these items are typically dispersed throughout an organization makes monitoring MRO inventory difficult. The only way that most purchasing departments know when to order MRO inventory is when a user forwards a purchase requisition. Because all departments and locations use MRO items, a typical purchasing department can receive thousands of small volume purchase requisitions. Some purchasers refer to MRO items as nuisance items.

Historically, most organizations have paid minimal attention to MRO items. Consequently, (1) they have not tracked their MRO inventory investment with the same concern with which they track production buying, (2) they have too many MRO suppliers, and (3) they commit a disproportionate amount of time to small orders. With the development of computerized inventory systems and the realization that MRO purchase dollar volume is often quite high, firms have begun to take an active interest in controlling MRO inventory. An organization that once had 26,000 different MRO suppliers has aggressively attacked the "MRO monster." It now deals with only a handful of distributors. In exchange for a major contract, each selected supplier offered price reductions, 24-hour delivery on regular orders, two-hour delivery on emergency orders, and no paperwork (transactions are electronic), and it also agreed to expand the number of part numbers carried along with the amount of each part kept on hand. At FedEx, an agreement with Staples allows purchasing to be free of the burden of tracking office supply requests. Instead, Staples provides a Website listing all supplies with prices; users can point and click on the items they need, and the supplier will deliver to the user's location the next business day.

Production Support Items

Production support items include the materials required to pack and ship final products, such as pallets, boxes, master shipping containers, tape, bags, wrapping, inserts, and other packaging material. Production support items directly support an organization's production operation; this is a key distinction separating production support and MRO items.

A specialist is often responsible for the purchase of production support items. This specialist must identify the correct package that prevents damage at the lowest total cost. Packages may also require aesthetic appeal to customers. Although buying production support items may appear mundane compared to other types of purchased inventory, these items are a major source of inventory investment. Furthermore, an entire production line can shut down when production support items are unavailable. Thus, there is a tendency to maintain large inventories to prevent shortages, which increases inventory carrying costs.

Creative approaches are available to control even the most routine purchased materials. DaimlerChrysler's after-market division in Center Line, Michigan, is responsible for forecasting and packaging over 40,000 different parts and kits for its replacement market. Matching packaging requirements to individual part numbers and kits was a cumbersome, costly, and often inaccurate process. The company solved this problem by assigning a part number to each packaging container. The container's part number, which the production control system now recognizes as a valid component number, appears on each part's schedule of component requirements (also referred to as a *bill of material*). Chrysler's system aggregates each part number that requires a particular container into a single figure over specific time periods. For example, if ten part numbers scheduled for packaging during the third week of November require carton ABC, the volume requirement for carton ABC is the combined production quantity schedules for the ten part numbers. The company matches and times its container requirements to its production schedules. Purchasing can also forecast future container requirements based on forecasted packaging production runs. Another benefit resulting from this system is that Chrysler reduced the floor space required for storing production support items by 60%.

Services

All firms rely on external contractors for certain activities or services. An organization may hire a lawn care service to maintain the grounds around a facility or a heating and cooling specialist to handle repairs that the maintenance staff cannot perform. Other common services include machine repair, snow removal, data entry, consultants, and the management of cafeteria services. Like MRO items, the purchase of services occurs throughout an organization. Therefore, there has been a tendency to pay limited attention and to manage the service purchases at the facility or department level. A study by AT&T several years ago revealed that the company was spending over a *billion* dollars a year on consultants. As with any purchase category, careful and specialized attention can result in achieving the best service at the lowest total cost. More and more, companies are negotiating longer-term contracts with service providers just like they would with other high-dollar purchase categories.

Capital Equipment

Capital equipment purchasing involves buying assets intended for use over one year. There are several categories of capital equipment purchases. The first includes standard general equipment that requires no special design requirements. Examples include general purpose material handling equipment, computer systems, and furniture. A second category includes capital equipment designed specifically to meet the

SOURCING SNAPSHOT

Bank of Boston Streamlines the Purchasing Cycle for Nontraditional Service Purchases

Bank of Boston saved $50 million over two years by applying commodity management strategies to service purchases. The bank leveraged its purchasing power for services, introduced control to the purchasing process, and simplified acquisition by the end user. Purchasing teams, along with key functional business units, evaluated, selected, and negotiated contracts with service suppliers. Bank of Boston forecast its purchasing needs for nontraditional services by establishing a steering committee consisting of purchasing, human resources, operations, finance, advertising, marketing, and information technology personnel. The steering committee identified six large service areas for analysis of spending in those areas. Cross-functional teams, each with a representative from purchasing, reviewed invoices in the six spending areas and issued requests for information to qualified suppliers. Using information provided by suppliers, the teams developed detailed requests for proposals for use in the evaluation and negotiation of corporate agreements. Now, an automated system allows users to requisition certain materials from an electronic catalog. This approach creates efficiencies within the purchasing process and enables purchasers to focus on value-adding activities.

Source: Adapted from "Managing Costs Banks Savings," *Purchasing,* April 25, 1996, 73–77.

requirements of the purchaser. Examples include specialized production machinery, new manufacturing plants, specialized machine tools, and power generating equipment. The purchase of these latter items requires close technical involvement between the buyer and seller.

Several features separate capital equipment purchases from other purchases. First, capital equipment purchases do not occur with regular frequency. A production machine, for example, may remain in use for 10 to 20 years. A new plant or power substation may remain in operation over 30 years. Even office furniture may last over 10 years. A second feature is that capital equipment investment requires large sums of money. This can range from several thousand dollars to hundreds of millions of dollars. High-dollar contracts will require finance and executive approvals. For accounting purposes, most capital equipment is depreciable over the life of the item. Finally, capital equipment purchasing is highly sensitive to general economic conditions.

The selection of qualified capital equipment suppliers is critical. Buyers can rarely switch suppliers in the middle of a large-scale project or dispose of capital equipment after delivery because of dissatisfaction. Furthermore, the relationship between the buyer and supplier may last many years, so the buyer should also consider the supplier's ability to service the equipment. The consequences of selecting a poorly qualified supplier of capital equipment can last for many years. The reverse is also true. The benefit of selecting a highly qualified capital equipment provider can last many years. Up-front planning is critical when purchasing capital equipment.

Transportation and Third-Party Purchasing

Transportation is a specialized and important type of service buying. Few purchasing departments involved themselves with transportation issues before the early 1980s. However, legislation passed during the late 1970s and early 1980s deregulated the air, trucking, and railroad industries. This legislation allowed buyers to negotiate service agreements and rate discounts directly with individual transportation carriers. Previously, the U.S. government, through the Interstate Commerce Commission, established the rate (referred to as a tariff) that a transportation carrier charged. It was common for suppliers to arrange shipment to a purchaser and simply include the transportation cost as part of the purchase cost.

Purchasing has become involved with transportation buying and the management of inbound and outbound material flows. It is now common for purchasing to evaluate and select logistics providers the same way it evaluates and selects suppliers of production items. Buyers are also selecting suppliers who are capable of providing coordinated transportation and logistics services for an entire company, including warehousing, packaging, and even assembly. Because many carriers now provide service throughout the United States, a buyer can rely on fewer transportation carriers. The cost savings available from controlling and managing logistics are significant.

In some industries such as electronics and telecommunications, purchasing is responsible for contracting with third-party "contract manufacturers" such as Solectron or SCI. These organizations will design, source components, manufacture, and even distribute personal computers and other products that have a brand name such as IBM, Hewlett-Packard, or Sun on them. Purchasing managers must develop special capabilities in order to effectively manage the new realm of contract manufacturing.

Like service and capital equipment purchases, third-party purchasing is a specialized type of activity. It is also an area that provides tremendous cost reduction and service improvement opportunities. The chance to work directly with carriers, logistics providers, and contract manufacturers to coordinate the efforts of supply chain members makes this an exciting area. Chapter 18 discusses this subject in greater detail.

IMPROVING THE PURCHASING PROCESS

Most companies spend too much time and too many resources managing the ordering of goods and service, particularly lower-value items. Some purchasing departments spend 80% of their time managing 20% of their total purchase dollars. A. D. Little,

EXHIBIT 2.8   *Methods or Approaches Organizations Expect to Emphasize to Reduce the Effort or Transactions Required to Process Low-Value Purchases*

Method or Approach	Total Sample	Industrial	Nonindustrial
Online requisitioning systems from users to purchasing	66.3%*	64.9%	67.4%
Procurement cards issued to users	65.1	59.7	69.6
Electronic purchasing commerce through the Internet	60.9	68.8	54.3
Blanket purchase order agreements	57.4	63.7	52.2
Longer-term purchase agreements	54.4	58.4	51.1
Purchasing online ordering systems to suppliers	53.3	61.0	46.7
Purchasing process redesign	53.3	50.7	55.4
Electronic data interchange (EDI)	52.7	58.4	47.8
Online ordering through electronic catalogs	51.5	49.4	53.3
Allowing users to contact suppliers directly	49.7	54.5	45.7
User online ordering systems to suppliers	49.1	51.9	46.7
	N = 169	N = 77	N = 92

*Represents the percentage of total respondents expecting to emphasize a method or approach.

Source: Trent and Kolchin, "Reducing the Transactions Costs of Purchasing Low Value Goods and Services," Center for Advanced Purchasing Studies, Tempe, AZ, 1999.

for example, reported in a study of maintenance, repair, and operating (MRO) purchases that while the average MRO invoice was $50, the total cost of processing an MRO transaction was $150. In another example, a U.S. government agency reported that in a single year it processed 1.1 million transactions at an estimated cost of $300 per transaction! How can organizations create value through their purchasing process when they spend more time processing orders than what the orders are worth?

A recent study by Trent and Kolchin addressed how organizations are improving the purchasing process by reducing the time and effort associated with obtaining lower-value goods and services.[3] The study involved 169 randomly selected organizations, of which 77 are industrial companies and 92 are nonindustrial companies or organizations. Exhibit 2.8 identifies the methods or approaches that organizations expect to emphasize over the next several years to improve the low-value purchasing process. The following sections summarize the approaches and methods presented in the exhibit.

Online Requisitioning Systems from Users to Purchasing Online requisitioning systems are internal systems designed primarily to save time through efficient and rapid communication. Users should use these systems only if they require purchasing involvement to support a material or service need. If users do not require assistance, they should have access to other low-dollar systems that do not require purchasing involvement.

Advanced organizations are much more likely to say purchasing receives low-value purchase requests from users through internal electronic systems when the need requires purchasing involvement. Organizations that have made less progress

SOURCING SNAPSHOT

Disney Uses the Magic of Procurement Cards to Streamline the Purchasing Process

As Disney's kingdom grew dramatically throughout the 1990s, the company realized it needed to streamline its purchasing process. Rapid expansion was overwhelming purchasing's ability to support users. Furthermore, managers wanted to shift procurement emphasis from transaction processing to supplier management. To aid in this shift, the company decided to pursue procurement cards, which aligned well with Disney's "performance excellence," a program that emphasized increased efficiency across the company. When selecting the card provider, Disney relied on tax and internal audit groups to identify the provider that could best support Disney's reporting and tax information needs. Once Disney selected the card provider, purchasing performed a detailed analysis that identified high-volume users and suppliers for early inclusion. Purchasing assumed ownership for implementation and contacted suppliers directly to gain their support. Program benefits to date include major savings within the purchasing and accounts payable departments, as well as reduced cycle times for processing small dollar orders. Almost 70% of transactions now use procurement cards. The success of the program has made expanding the magic of procurement cards a top priority at Disney.

Source: Adapted from M. Cohen, "Making Procurement Cards Work for You," *Purchasing Today* (October 1998): 37–39.

managing low-value purchasing use company mail or the phone to receive user requests. Users should rely on efficient requisitioning systems for items that require purchasing involvement. A longer-term focus should be to create systems and processes that empower users to obtain low-value items directly from suppliers rather than involving purchasing.

Procurement Cards Issued to Users One tool or system that most organizations agree is central to improving the purchasing process is the use of the procurement card, which is essentially a credit card provided to internal users. When a user has a lower-value requirement, he or she simply contacts a supplier and uses the card to make the purchase. Cards work well for items that do not have established suppliers or are not covered by some other purchasing system. The users make the buying decisions (which come out of their department's budget) and bypass purchasing completely. The dollar value of the items covered by procurement cards is relatively low. The cost to involve purchasing or engage in a comprehensive supplier search would likely outweigh the cost of the item.

The study by Trent and Kolchin found that the average cost per transaction due to procurement card use decreased from over $80 to under $30. The primary benefits from using cards include faster response to user needs, reduced transaction costs, and reduced total transaction time. In most organizations, purchasing is responsible for introducing and maintaining the card program.

Electronic Purchasing Commerce Through the Internet   Electronic purchasing commerce through the Internet refers to a broad and diverse set of activities. Using the Internet to conduct purchasing business is not extensive today, although commercial Internet usage by purchasers should increase dramatically over the next several years. The highest expected growth areas in e-commerce purchasing include

- Transmitting purchase orders to suppliers
- Following up on the status of orders
- Submitting requests for quotes to suppliers
- Placing orders with suppliers
- Making electronic funds transfer payments
- Establishing electronic data interchange capability

Chapter 19 discusses electronic commerce through the Internet further.

Longer-Term Purchase Agreements   Longer-term purchase agreements usually cover a period of one to five years, with renewal based on a supplier's ability to satisfy performance expectations. These agreements can reduce the transactions costs associated with lower-value purchases by eliminating the need for time-consuming annual renewal. Furthermore, once a purchaser and a supplier reach agreement, material releasing responsibility should shift to user groups. Ideally, material releasing becomes electronic rather than manual, even for lower-value items.

Although the two approaches are conceptually similar, differences exist between a blanket purchase order, which purchasers routinely use, and longer-term purchase agreements. Both approaches rely on a contractual agreement to cover specific items or services; they may be for extended periods; they are legal agreements; and they are highly emphasized ways to manage lower-value purchases. However, blanket purchase orders are typically used more often for lower-value items compared with longer-term agreements. Longer-term agreements are usually more detailed in the contractual areas they address compared with blanket purchase orders.

Organizations often rely on longer-term agreements to provide the foundation for developing specific systems and approaches for managing low-dollar purchases. For example, a contract with a distributor that covers hundreds or even thousands of items, which we call a systems contract, usually involves a longer-term agreement that addresses issues that conventional or standard purchase orders do not address. These issues can include specified replenishment service levels, on-site supplier support personnel, inventory buy-back clauses covering obsolete inventory, continuous cost reduction requirements, and use of bar-code technology and electronic linkages that eliminate paperwork.

Online Ordering Systems to Suppliers   Online ordering systems involve direct electronic links from a purchaser's system to a supplier's system, often through a modem or other Web-enabled technologies. A major feature of online ordering systems is that suppliers often bear the responsibility for developing the software required to link with a customer's system. Online ordering is a logical approach once an organization has established a blanket purchase agreement or longer-term contract with a supplier. The strategic part of the sourcing process involves identifying, evaluating, and selecting suppliers. Online ordering systems allow purchasing or users to place orders directly into a supplier's order-entry system. Advantages of online ordering systems include

- Immediate visibility to backordered items
- Faster order input time, which contributes to reduced order cycle times
- Reduced ordering errors
- Order tracking capabilities
- Order acknowledgment from the supplier, often with shipping commitment dates
- Ability to batch multiple items from multiple users on a single online order
- Faster order cycle time from input to delivery

Suppliers establish online ordering systems so purchasers can have dedicated access to the supplier's order-entry system. The system creates a seamless tie-in or linkage between organizations. Third-party software providers such as Ariba provide turnkey solutions that will help to further this development in the future.

Purchasing Process Redesign Most organizations recognize that purchasing process redesign efforts often precede the development of low-dollar purchase systems, which are often the result of redesign efforts. Properly executed redesign efforts should lead to faster cycle times and simplified processes that result in reduced transactions costs.

The purchasing process is composed of many subprocesses, which means it can benefit from process mapping and redesign. The low-value purchase process affects hundreds or even thousands of individuals throughout a typical organization—users in every department, office, plant, and facility; accounts payable; receiving and handling; purchasing; systems; and of course, suppliers. Anyone with a need for low-value goods or services is part of the low-value purchase process.

Electronic Data Interchange Electronic data interchange (EDI) involves a communications standard that supports interorganizational electronic exchange of common business documents and information. It is a cooperative effort between a buyer and seller to become more efficient by streamlining communication processes. When used by buyers and suppliers, EDI can help eliminate some steps involved in traditional communication flows, which reduces time and cost.

While actual volumes through EDI have increased through the 1990s, actual EDI volume does not match the expected volume that was projected by companies. In 1993, for example, purchasing professionals estimated that 60 percent of the supply base, 70 percent of total purchase dollars, and 65 percent of total purchasing transactions would flow through EDI systems. Actual 1997 volume was 28 percent of suppliers, 38 percent of total purchase dollars, and 32 percent of total purchasing transactions flowing through EDI systems.[4] Part of this shortfall is due to the introduction of auto fax technology. For many organizations, especially smaller organizations, auto fax is a quicker and less expensive method of communicating with suppliers. Auto fax systems automatically fax requirements to suppliers once those requirements are known by the buyer. The Internet will also capture electronic volume that formerly would have passed through third-party EDI providers. Chapter 19 discusses this important topic in greater detail.

Online Ordering Through Electronic Catalogs Purchasers are increasingly using this approach in conjunction with other low-dollar purchase systems. For example, one organization allows its user to identify supply sources through the Internet and then use a procurement card to process the order. The key benefit of using electronic catalogs is their powerful low-cost search capability and, if users order directly instead of relying on purchasing, reduced total cycle time and ordering costs. Perhaps the greatest drawback to online ordering is the limited number of suppliers that offer electronic catalogs, along with security of electronic ordering and control issues.

Allowing Users to Contact Suppliers Directly This general method or approach involves different kinds of low-dollar systems. Procurement cards technically qualify as a system that allows users to contact suppliers directly. Online ordering systems also allow users to contact suppliers directly. Or, the system may involve nothing more than a multiple part form, such as a limited purchase order, that a user completes as he or she initiates an order. FedEx refers to its "pick up the phone" system, which allows users to contact suppliers directly, as its convenience ordering system.

Approaches that allow users to contact suppliers directly shift responsibility for the transaction from purchasing to the user. Even for items with no established supplier, purchasing still may have limited or no involvement unless the requirement reaches a predetermined dollar or activity level. If an item becomes a repetitive purchase, then purchasing may determine if the item warrants a blanket purchase order. Blanket purchase orders usually allow users to contact suppliers directly when a need arises for material. The following Good Practice Example describes a system that allows users to contact suppliers directly below some dollar threshold level.

GOOD PRACTICE EXAMPLE
Lehigh University Makes the Purchasing Process Work

■ ■ ■

Imagine a purchasing process where the need for standard or low-value items is the norm rather than the exception.[5] Developing the techniques, approaches, and systems to improve the purchasing process would be logical for any purchasing group operating within this environment. Lehigh University, confronted with pressure to reduce administrative costs over the previous ten years, was forced to redesign the purchasing process while reducing the full-time purchasing staff.

Purchasing determined that the way to make the purchasing process more effective was to (1) allow users greater flexibility in ordering by raising the dollar limit requiring purchasing support and approval and (2) provide the purchasing tools and systems to support users. The transition toward empowered user groups has helped redefine purchasing's role within the university. Now more than ever, purchasing professionals focus on creating value rather than managing material releases. An example of value-added activities is the development of negotiated longer-term contracts that provide favorable pricing.

A review of the various purchasing systems available to users occurred during 1996 at Lehigh. Administrators believed that too many systems were available and that these systems were not well controlled. The vice president of business services formed a continuous improvement team and charged it with reviewing ways to purchase goods and services, particularly the purchase of low-value goods and services. The team presented a set of recommendations designed to simplify the purchasing process. The following details the major initiatives taken by purchasing, accounts payable, and laboratory stores to improve the purchasing process.

Selected Use of Blanket Purchase Orders A blanket purchase order is an open order, effective for a year, that allows users to release against that order for repetitive, lower-value consumable items. At Lehigh, if the dollar value of an order is less than $2,000, purchasing conducts no formal bidding before establishing the blanket order. For orders with values between $2,000 and $5,000, purchasing secures three verbal quotations before establishing the blanket order. If the value is greater than $5,000, purchasing requests and reviews three written quotations before establishing the blanket order. An item must have at least six transactions per month to qualify for a blanket purchase order. This is one of the oldest purchasing systems within the university and, indeed, across most organizations. These orders or agreements, which purchasing usually does not negotiate, exclude rental, lease, and maintenance agreements. A recent review of the system revealed that 50% of existing blanket orders were no longer current and could be eliminated, further reducing transaction and maintenance costs. More efficient purchasing systems are available for items that no longer qualify for blanket orders.

Expanded Use of Systems Contracting Each department in the university uses office supplies, such as binders and accessories, clips, copier and computer supplies, envelopes, writing supplies, tape, and pads and paper. Purchasing has negotiated a single contract for all office supplies with a single supplier (Boise Cascade). Each department can order through the Internet all commonly purchased office items with their established discounts. The negotiated systems contract with guaranteed delivery allowed the university to close its central stores. The supplier guarantees next-day delivery to the requisitioner's office for orders received before 9 A.M. if the supplier has those items in inventory. Discussions with users reveal a high level of satisfaction with this system. The selected supplier is responsive, the contract covers most items required by departments, and the burden to order, file, and reconcile orders is not excessive. While purchasing does not calculate the hard savings from systems contracting, the consensus among departments is that this approach has greatly improved the ordering of office supplies.

Development of Limited Purchase Orders (LPOs) Perhaps the most significant change to Lehigh University's small procurement processes has been the introduction of the *limited purchase order* (LPO)—a purchase order initiated by user groups, such as departments, without direct purchasing involvement. The LPO can be used for items that do not have an established blanket purchase order and are less than $2,000. The system offers many advantages:

*   Ease of use by the user community
*   Ability of users to select their own supplier for small purchases
*   Ability of purchasing personnel to focus on more strategic activities, such as negotiating longer-term systems contracts
*   Faster ordering cycle times (the LPO is simple to complete and does not involve the cycle time associated with forwarding material requisitions to purchasing)
*   Clearly specified approval controls and limits
*   Higher user acceptance and satisfaction due to the flexibility and responsiveness of the system

Online User Requisitions The online user requisitioning system, part of the university's financial record system, allows users to transmit requisitions electronically to purchasing for items greater than $2,000. This system applies only to items that currently do not have an established blanket purchase order. If an item is less than $2,000 and does not have a blanket purchase order established, a limited purchase order or procurement card apply. Users can also submit requisitions to purchasing by mail or fax.

Direct Order-Entry Systems with Distributors Lehigh University has 15 departments and centers across the campus that use scientific supplies. The university has systems contracts with three large suppliers of scientific supplies: Fisher, VWR, and JWS Technologies. Two of these suppliers (Fisher and VWR) are distributors that have developed online ordering systems for lab store items. For comparison purposes, the lab store is conceptually similar to a tool or maintenance crib in a large manufacturing facility. Lab store items include glassware, lab ware, science items, and gasses. Purchasing requested bids for these contracts and negotiated with potential suppliers before reaching final agreement.

When users require material supplied by a contracted supplier, they submit a blanket purchase order release to the lab store clerk. Users transmit material requests to the lab store clerk in three ways: call or stop by the lab store and request items from the clerk, complete and forward a manual material request, or submit a request through the online requisitioning system. Once the lab clerk enters an online order, she receives a confirmation number. She processes all orders by 3 P.M. to take advantage of the supplier's same-day shipping service. Shipping costs are part of the contracted price for each item. The supplier delivers material directly to the requisitioner.

The clerk can monitor the status of all open orders by accessing supplier's system and requesting order status updates. The clerk verifies catalog numbers for errors before ordering and then maintains a hard copy of each order. Users must place a catalog number and description on all material requests. If an item is not in the catalog, then the online order system is not used. The distributors also make their most recent catalogs available online. Since several distributors have some overlap in their product lines, it is the user's responsibility to compare prices and determine the best distributor to use.

Introduction of Procurement Cards The team responsible for reviewing the university's purchase systems recommended procurement cards as a way to make the purchasing process even more efficient. Part of this group's effort included benchmarking existing card programs at other colleges and universities. The benchmarking group studied card limits, implementation, administration, and other issues critical to the introduction of procurement cards.

The university initiated a pilot program in February 1998 with nine departments participating. Currently, over a dozen departments are participating with 75 cards issued. Users of limited purchase orders are purchasing's target audience for procurement cards. The purchasing director expects the procurement card to eventually replace the LPO system. In conjunction with the introduction of procurement cards, purchasing increased the small-dollar threshold to $2,000 per transaction. This provides users with increased flexibility and purchasing power. At the same time, this will result in fewer transactions requiring purchasing support. Purchasing personnel expect to focus their time on larger-dollar purchases and contracts.

User Education Developing effective purchasing systems is not possible without the active support of internal customers—that is, the users of purchased goods and services. Purchasing has recognized the importance of educating users (mainly department personnel and some faculty) concerning appropriate purchasing practices. To meet this need, the department has published a condensed version of the

Lehigh University purchasing manual in pamphlet form and has also made this information available on the purchasing department's Website. This pamphlet

- Lists purchasing contacts throughout the university
- Provides a commodity index of purchases with contact names
- Details purchasing's mission statement, ordering and receiving procedures, and the order changes and cancellation process
- Identifies purchasing methods besides the standard requisition purchase order method, including limited purchase orders, procurement cards, and laboratory stores
- Provides a flowchart of requested goods and services from requisition to receipt and payment

The purchasing department also conducts seminars for internal customers and conducts an annual supplier exposition, a forum that introduces users to suppliers and allows purchasing to educate users about various forms and procedures.

Accounts Payable Initiatives Several years ago accounts payable analyzed Lehigh's purchase transaction volume and dollar values. As expected, the findings indicated that 80 percent of transactions and accounts payable time were spent managing 20 percent of total dollar items. Accounts payable processes more than 80,000 transactions a year, 60,000 of which are for purchases of less than $250.

Traditional invoice processing is a manually intensive procedure that not only involves processing of the invoice but also requires an inspection of the invoice for accuracy. When performed manually, each invoice requires several minutes to process and place in a batch with other invoices for payment. Time is also required to correct any errors detected (such as a wrong account number). Manual checks require verification that the supplier has a proper tax identification number and is established within the processing system.

One method used to reduce the effort required to process invoices involves data tapes provided by select suppliers. Instead of accounts payable processing these transactions manually, the department receives a data tape detailing the previous month's transactions. The tape feeds automatically into the accounts payable system and includes the supplier number, invoice number, and account number data, all of which are required for audit purposes. Without the tape provided by the suppliers, accounts payable would process receipts according to a set batch size. The tape feeds have reduced invoice processing time by 65% to 75%. While expanded data tape use would further reduce accounts payable transaction efforts, managers say that most suppliers are too small to justify automated invoice/accounts payable systems.

Has the Purchasing Process Improved? Lehigh University has not initiated the changes described throughout this case without resistance. A university community consists of many different departments and users, some with very traditional and inflexible views. Purchasing and accounts payable recognize the need to educate users and communicate changes at the department level, and have attempted to get users more involved in the change process. For example, the team responsible for developing the procurement card program included a "difficult" user as a member. The team's logic was to work early with groups and users who would present special challenges to the success of new systems.

A recent benchmarking study that focused on internal customer satisfaction with purchasing revealed that users at Lehigh are positive about purchasing's performance. Of 57 institutions participating in the benchmarking study, internal customers rated Lehigh's purchasing department as first or second across many performance areas:

- *Overall satisfaction with purchasing* (first),
- *On-time delivery*, which is the percentage of orders that arrive by the expected date (first),
- *Accuracy,* which represents the number of errors by purchasing in such areas as specifications, quantity, price, due date, and delivery location (second),
- *Quality of purchased items*, which represents how well delivered goods and services meet the internal customer's quality expectations (second),
- *Purchase order cycle time*, which is the average time from the generation of a requisition until the purchase order is sent to a supplier (first),
- *Professionalism*, which represents how well purchasing upholds standards of conduct, ethics, convention, and related areas (second),
- *Partnering*, which is how well purchasing develops team or partnership-type relations with internal customers (first), and
- *Responsiveness*, which includes indicators such as answering the phone, being available, answering questions, and providing assistance with specifications and problems (first).

This example illustrates that improving the purchasing process in terms of efficiency *and* effectiveness requires more than one single system or approach. Purchasing, accounts payable, user groups or departments, and those responsible for handling inventory and material can all benefit from a systematic approach to improving how goods and services flow into an organization. ■

CONCLUSION

This chapter provided an overview of purchasing and the purchasing process, including the objectives of a world-class purchasing function, purchasing's span of control, the purchasing cycle, and the documents used to manage the purchasing process.

These topics provide the foundation from which to introduce the tools, techniques, and strategies used by purchasing organizations in a competitive market.

This chapter also pointed out the many different categories of purchases. In addition to buying production material and items, purchasing can be responsible for buying transportation, services, packing supplies, MRO items, capital equipment, and even the corporate jet! There is no one system or approach that applies to all purchase situations. Purchases can vary according to type, importance, impact on quality, time frame for delivery, and dollar volume. We rarely find purchasing personnel who are experts in all the different types of purchases, which is why so many purchasing departments have specialized personnel. These personnel all have one thing in common, however—the opportunity to manage large amounts of resources through the purchasing process.

DISCUSSION QUESTIONS

1.   How can an effective purchasing department affect organizational performance?
2.   Discuss the concept of the internal customer. Who are purchasing's internal customers?
3.   Discuss the contributions a purchasing department can make to the corporate strategic planning process.
4.   List the areas typically considered within purchasing's span of control. Explain why it is important that purchasing have authority over each of these areas.
5.   Describe how purchasing becomes aware of purchase requirements.
6.   How is anticipating a material requirement or need through purchasing's involvement on a new product development team different from reacting to a purchase need?
7.   Why do some firms no longer rely only on competitive bidding when awarding purchase contracts?
8.   Discuss the advantages of electronically transmitting and receiving purchasing documents between a buyer and seller.
9.   Why is it important to measure and monitor supplier performance improvement over time?
10. How does a just-in-time purchasing and production system reduce the need for certain purchasing documents?
11. Discuss the advantages of point-to-point communication within a supply chain.
12. Why is purchasing becoming increasingly involved in the purchase of transportation services and other nontraditional purchasing areas?
13. Discuss how the purchase of capital equipment differs from the purchase of routine supplies.
14. Develop a list of topics that nonpurchasing personnel should be allowed to talk about with their counterparts at suppliers. Develop a list of topics that only purchasing should be allowed to talk about with suppliers.
15. What is the difference between a purchase order and a blanket purchase order? What are the advantages of using blanket purchase orders?
16. Assume you have been selected by management at your company to improve the purchasing process. Develop specific recommendations concerning how you would achieve a more efficient and effective process.

ADDITIONAL READINGS

Barry, J., J. L. Cavinato, A. Green, and R. R. Young. "A Development Model for Effective MRO Procurement." *International Journal of Purchasing and Materials Management* (Summer 1996): 35–44.

Harrington, James. *Business Process Redesign.* New York: McGraw-Hill, 1991.

Morgan, J. P. "Is Integrated Supply the Way of the Future?" *Purchasing* (May 1, 1997): 41–63.

Palmer, R. J., T. Schmidt, and J. Jordan-Wagner. "Corporate Procurement Cards: The Reengineered Future for Noninventory Purchasing and Payables." *Journal of Cost Management* (Fall 1996): 19–41.

"More Catalogs Go On-Line." *Purchasing* (September 21, 1995): 69–70.

Trent, Robert J., and Michael G. Kolchin. *Reducing the Transactions Costs of Purchasing Low Value Goods and Services.* Tempe, AZ: Center for Advanced Purchasing Studies, 1999.

ENDNOTES

1. From an industry presentation at the Executive Purchasing and Supply Chain Management Seminar, Michigan State University, 1997.
2. Donald Dobler, Lamar Lee, and David Burt, *Purchasing and Materials Management* (Homewood, IL: Irwin, 1990), 204.
3. Robert J. Trent and Michael G. Kolchin, "Reducing the Transactions Costs of Purchasing Low Value Goods and Services," Center for Advanced Purchasing Studies, Tempe, AZ, 1999.
4. From data collected annually at the Executive Purchasing and Supply Chain Management Seminar, Michigan State University, 1990–1999.
5. Adapted from Trent and Kolchin, 107–112.

PURCHASING AND SUPPLY CHAIN ORGANIZATION

3

Purchasing's Position Within the Organizational Structure

Factors Affecting Purchasing's Position

To Whom Does Purchasing Report?

Organizing the Purchasing Function

Specialization Within Purchasing

Purchasing Department Activities

Separating Strategic and Operational Purchasing

Placement of Purchasing Authority

Advantages of Centrally Controlled Purchasing

Advantages of Decentralized Purchasing Authority

A Hybrid Purchasing Structure

Organizing for Supply Chain Management

Supply Chain Activities and Functions

A Supply Chain Management Structure

The Team Approach as Part of the Organizational Structure

Creating the Organization of the Future: The Horizontal Organization

Good Practice Example: Making Centralized and Decentralized Purchasing Work at Black and Decker

Conclusion

American Airlines Organizes to Win the Gold

American Airlines has come a long way in purchasing over the last ten years. In fact, the airline has progressed so far that *Purchasing Magazine* recently awarded its coveted Medal of Excellence award to American. Achieving this level of excellence required a major transformation in how purchasing was organized and managed. "In the 1980s, we were not focused on developing relationships with suppliers that we could count on. We used to beat on maintenance for not having the part," said the chairman of AMR Corporation, the parent company of American Airlines. He also commented that developing supply chain relationships was not part of American's management process. "If there was a crisis at an airport that resulted in the cancellation of a flight because of parts availability," he said, "then there were no flights for American to sell. In addition, the reputation of the airline is damaged."

A review of the airline's supply management operation revealed the process was badly in need of an overhaul. Executive management turned to the manufacturing world and hired the former head of purchasing at Navistar as vice president of purchasing. The chairman of American then elevated this position, which is now only one level removed from the chairman. The newly hired vice president recruited and trained a staff that systematically applied supply management strategies to AMR's diverse purchases: fuel, aircraft maintenance, airport and customer service, and technology. Taking a team approach, purchasing slashed costs, consolidated the supply base, entered into a purchase consortium, and negotiated long-term agreements, saving over $250 million annually.

Today, the chief purchasing officer at the airline knows that success requires people with higher-level knowledge and skills. Less than ten years ago only 52% of the airline's purchasing managers had a college degree. Today, the number is 90%, with 21% having advanced degrees. The company actively recruits at universities with supply management programs. In addition, the vice president stepped up his recruiting efforts at other companies. He has recruited purchasing professionals who have worked at GE, Xerox, IBM, Motorola, AlliedSignal, and Honda. Each purchasing professional also receives 40 hours of training a year.

Purchasing has structured its operation so that managing directors of purchasing are responsible for sourcing all of the goods and services required to support each part of the business. Often, purchasing personnel are co-located next to internal customers. For example, buyers with responsibility for purchasing aircraft maintenance parts and supplies work at the company's maintenance center in Tulsa, Oklahoma. Buyers who purchase PCs and software work in the same location as AMR's technology unit. The purchasing vice president also created the position of strategic sourcing manager, who is responsible for putting together the strategy that is taking purchasing into the twenty-first century.

→ → →

A senior vice president commented that under the new leadership, purchasing has shifted from a reactive support organization to one that is strategically focused and tightly integrated with the airline's business units.

Perhaps the best validation of the changes that purchasing has made comes from the chairman of the company. "I can only underscore that MacLean (vice president of purchasing) and his team have certainly accomplished what we expected and, in fact, have exceeded our expectations in terms of taking manufacturing strategies and adapting them to the airline business with clearly a lot of innovation."

Source: Adapted from: Susan Avery, "AMR Lands the Medal!" *Purchasing* (September 15, 1998): 36–44.

In the emerging business model of supply chain management, organizational strategy and structure must go hand-in-hand. A proper organizational structure with the right people is essential to take advantage of and respond to supply chain and market opportunities. Conversely, the best-planned supply chain strategy will be useless if it is burdened within a bureaucratic organizational structure. Traditional organizational structures, including those that have historically characterized purchasing, must give way to the responsive organization. In the traditional bureaucratic organization, information is guarded, a large central staff usually dictates from the top, barriers separate a firm from its suppliers and customers, one-way communication and many management levels exist, and functional middle managers limit their thinking to their own areas of expertise. Organizational structures for the new century, on the other hand, must be responsive, which means they must be adaptive and innovative in their form, able to respond quickly to competitive and customer challenges, move people and information easily across boundaries, and pursue continuous improvement. Purchasing managers must emphasize cross-functional interaction with groups outside of purchasing, including suppliers. For some, managing in this environment does not come easily. Traditional practices are hard to change. In the new era of supply chain management, however, a familiar maxim that is often heard is that you had better lead, follow, or get out of the way!

A formal organizational structure serves several purposes. First, it shows an organization's division of labor—the way work is assigned along with the authority that accompanies those responsibilities. This division affects how organizations allocate resources. Second, a formal structure helps define how a firm communicates and integrates decision making across the groups comprising the organization (a process also referred to as coordination).[1] Leading-edge organizations have a dedicated stand-alone portion of their structure committed to the purchasing and sourcing process. In addition, such organizations have one or more managers responsible for the process who report to someone at a higher level, along with resources committed specifically to that process.

The effectiveness of the formal purchasing process and structure will affect the success of purchasing and inevitably the entire organization. This chapter explores purchasing within the context of formal organizations, which requires the presentation of certain topics:

- Purchasing's position within the organizational structure
- Organizing purchasing
- Placement of purchasing authority
- Organizing for supply chain management
- The team approach as part of the organizational structure
- Creating the horizontal organization

A discussion of organization structures for global sourcing occurs in Chapter 11.

PURCHASING'S POSITION WITHIN THE ORGANIZATIONAL STRUCTURE

Almost all organizations have a purchasing department or group separate from other functional groups.[2] Our concern here is with the *physical position* or *placement of purchasing* in the organizational hierarchy or reporting structure. Why is purchasing's position or placement in an organizational structure important? Basically, the physical placement and reporting relationship of a function usually indicate its organizational status and influence. A function whose highest responsible executive is a manager (or even several managers) lacks the organizational importance of a function whose highest responsible executive is a senior vice president. In some organizations, the highest purchasing professional's reporting status is on par with other major functions. In others, you have to search before finding an individual executive responsible for purchasing. With a totally decentralized purchasing function, a number of executives may be responsible for purchasing at different locations and at different reporting levels. This section presents some of the factors influencing purchasing's position or placement in the formal organizational structure.

Factors Affecting Purchasing's Position

History Perhaps the most important factor contributing to purchasing's position in the organizational hierarchy is history. For established organizations, early purchasing history emphasized the gradual development of the policies and procedures defining proper purchasing. A respected purchasing professional, Bruce D. Henderson, noted that purchasing had been a neglected function in most organizations because purchasing simply was not perceived to be important to mainstream problems. He emphasized that it was hard for some executives to visualize a company becoming more successful than its competitors because of its superior purchasing practices, even though organizations developed competitive edges from other functions such as research, marketing, finance, or operations.[3]

Older companies were primarily marketing oriented. As a result, the marketing side of the supply chain received corporate dollars and attention while purchasing suffered from benign neglect. For many years, an assignment in purchasing was viewed as a career with few prospects for promotion or increased decision making. In recent years, however, this trend has been reversing. Purchasing is slowly but surely becoming the focus of executive management's attention. Evidence of this change is borne out by recent reports in the business press of the impact that purchasing has on corporate profitability.

Type of Industry Purchasing's position in the reporting hierarchy varies significantly across industries. Some industries are not as driven by materials or external technological change as others. The need to constantly innovate and improve often places materials-related functions at a higher level compared with mature industries or those with a history of treating purchasing as a second-tier function. In rapidly changing industries or those where purchased goods and services comprise a larger portion of product or service costs, management usually recognizes the need to provide visibility to purchasing and materials. They achieve this visibility through a higher position in the organizational hierarchy.

Total Value of Goods and Services The amount spent on purchased goods and services strongly influences purchasing's organizational placement. Companies such as Deere, Honda, and DaimlerChrysler spend 60% to 70% of their sales dollars on purchased goods and services. In the computer and telecommunications industries, companies such as Nortel Networks, Compaq, Solectron, IBM, Cisco, Hewlett-Packard, and Sun rely on suppliers for parts as well as new technology—which means that purchasing plays a critical role within these corporate structures. A service organization spending 10% to 20% of its sales dollar for purchased goods and services will, on average, view purchasing differently than a firm spending over 60%.

Other Factors A variety of other factors can affect purchasing's organizational position. The philosophy of the founder (particularly when the founder still plays an active role) exerts a strong influence. This is especially true in high-technology organizations started during the last 25 years. The organizational structure often reflects the founder's background. If the founder is marketing oriented, the firm usually has a strong marketing perspective. If the founder is engineering oriented, the emphasis is usually on product and process development. For example, both Mr. Hewlett and Mr. Packard emphasized a strong engineering focus. Consequently, Hewlett-Packard's supply base also emphasizes technological proficiency. The founder of Herman Miller Inc, an industrial office furniture manufacturer, believed that organizations should be the "stewards" of the environment. Consequently, purchasing plays a strong role at that company in emphasizing environmental responsibility.[4]

The type of purchased materials influences purchasing's position. The purchase of routine, off-the-shelf items is quite different from the purchase of leading-edge high technology. Purchasing departments confronted with fast-paced change and uncertainty usually have closer contact with other key functions and a higher organizational reporting level.

The ability to influence the overall performance of a company is another factor affecting purchasing's position. When purchasing can strongly affect competitiveness, purchasing assumes a higher position in the organizational structure. The ability to influence performance is such a critical factor in some industries that it overrides any other factor that previously supported a lower purchasing profile.

To Whom Does Purchasing Report?

The reporting level to whom purchasing reports reveals a great deal about the importance of purchasing. When purchasing reports directly to the president or executive vice president, particularly in organizations with over $1 billion in annual sales, this indicates that it is considered a critical function by executives. Regardless of size, a clear trend during the last 25 years is that the level of executive to whom purchasing reports has increased. Bloom and Nardone reported that "during the 1950s and early 1960s, a high percentage of the purchasing departments reported in a second-level capacity to the functional managers, most commonly production and operations."[5] They also cited Heinritz and Farrell, who reported this:

> By the 1970s, the majority of centralized purchasing departments reported directly to the top executive officer responsible for profitable operation—president, executive vice president, or general manager. Whenever purchasing reported directly to top management, it was in the first tier of executives, on the same organizational plane with the production manager, sales manager, controller, manager of industrial relations, and the heads of other divisions.[6]

A study by the Center for Advanced Purchasing Studies (CAPS) provides further support for the continued elevation of purchasing within the organizational structure.[7] The study found that in almost 35% of the organizations surveyed, the highest purchasing executive reported to a senior or group vice president or higher. By 1995, 50% of the companies surveyed reported that the highest purchasing executive reported to a senior or group vice president or higher.[8]

Exhibit 3.1 illustrates three different purchasing reporting levels. In part (a) purchasing is an upper-level function reporting directly to the executive vice president. In part (b) purchasing is a midlevel function reporting to an executive one level below the executive vice president. In most companies today, purchasing is an upper- or second-tier function. Part (c) shows purchasing as a lower-level function at least two reporting levels from the executive vice president. These simplified diagrams show several possible placements of purchasing in the organizational hierarchy. Of course, actual organizational structures are much more complex and detailed. This exhibit simply shows that purchasing's placement in an actual organization occurs at different levels. In general, however, the higher that purchasing is in the corporate structure, the greater the role it plays in the corporate strategy debate. When a purchasing vice president can appeal to top executives in the company and make a case for additional resources (in the form of personnel training, hiring, and information system resources), there is a high likelihood that the organization's sourcing strategies will be successfully deployed.

EXHIBIT 3.1   *Purchasing at Different Organizational Levels*

(a) Purchasing as an upper-level function

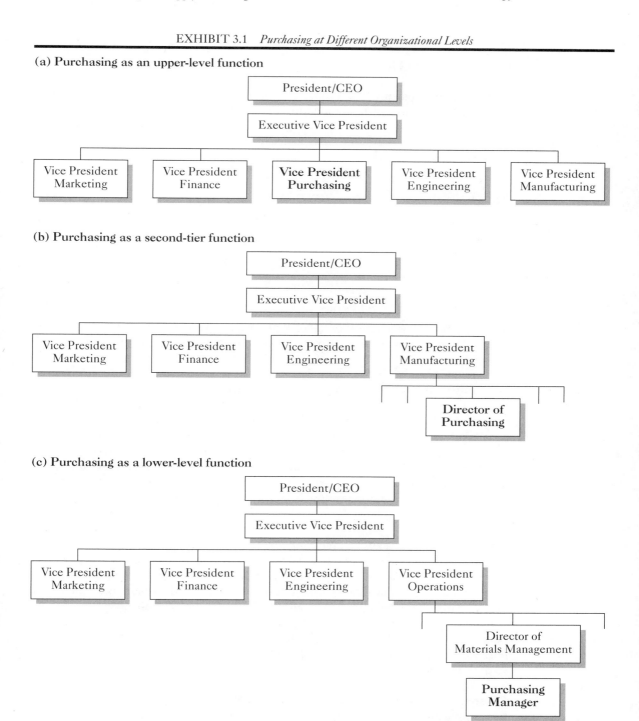

(b) Purchasing as a second-tier function

(c) Purchasing as a lower-level function

ORGANIZING THE PURCHASING FUNCTION

A purchasing department has clearly defined duties with specialized personnel. Specialization requires that an individual or subunit within a department have expertise in a particular area. This section discusses, among other things, the organization of the purchasing department into specialized subgroups and the different activities of today's purchasing function.

Specialization Within Purchasing

Purchasing departments in larger organizations usually structure themselves to support specialized purchasing activities, which are grouped into four major areas:

1. Sourcing and negotiating
2. Purchase research
3. Operational support and order follow-up
4. Administration and support

It is not efficient or practical to have all purchasing personnel responsible for every task within each group. Instead, most purchasing departments organize into specialized subgroups.

Sourcing and Negotiating   This group negotiates with suppliers and performs the buying of goods and services. Buyers are usually responsible for a specific range or type of item(s), which may be grouped into commodities or categories. For example, plastic injected parts are an example of a purchase commodity. Other buyers may specialize in raw materials, be responsible for packaging supplies, or specialize in negotiations with suppliers for higher-dollar items. Others may specialize in international sourcing. Very often, buyers will work in global commodity teams that have responsibility for negotiating contracts for the entire organization. This concept is discussed further in Chapter 6.

Purchasing Research   Purchasing research involves a range of activities. These include developing long-range material forecasts, conducting value analysis programs, assessing supplier capabilities, and analyzing the cost structure of suppliers. While some of these specialized tasks are the responsibility of individual buyers, more and more organizations recognize the benefit of developing specialized purchasing research personnel. The development of strategic product and material plans requires detailed and accurate research. Companies commit significant resources to the process of identifying sources that "push the envelope" in terms of cost, quality, service, technology, and cycle time.

Operational Support and Order Follow-up   This group includes the activities supporting the day-to-day operations of the purchasing or materials function. Order expediters and follow-up personnel fall into this group. The preparation and transfer of material releases to suppliers is also part of the operational support process. Many of the tasks that qualify as operational support are being streamlined or automated especially with the advent of business to business (B2B) e-commerce technologies (discussed in Chapter 19). As a result, the number of purchasing personnel committed to these types of tasks is declining. Because operational support activities represent a poor use of a buyer's time, organizations are increasingly separating buyers from operational support personnel. Support personnel may not even report to a purchasing manager.

Administration and Support   This group is responsible for a variety of tasks. Examples include developing the policies and procedures that purchasing personnel follow, determining required staffing levels, developing department plans, organizing training and seminars for buyers, and developing measurement systems to evaluate purchasing performance. Basically, this group concerns itself with making sure the purchasing department runs smoothly and meets its responsibilities.

Purchasing Department Activities

Today's purchasing department does much more than the traditional buying of materials, parts, and services. The role of purchasing is expanding to reflect the growing importance of purchasing and the performance contribution of suppliers. The following responsibilities are the most common tasks currently performed by a modern purchasing department. Not all departments perform every one of these tasks. The trend, however, is for more of these assignments to become purchasing's responsibility. Exhibit 3.2 presents the activities that have increasingly become purchasing's domain.

Buying   By definition, a primary responsibility of the purchasing function involves buying—a broad term describing the purchase of raw materials, components, finished goods, or services from suppliers, some of whom can be another operating unit within the organization. The purchase can be a one-time requirement or the release for material against an established purchase order. The buying process will require supplier evaluation, negotiation, and selection. Chapter 2 described the various types of purchase categories that require buying.

Expediting and Inventory Control   Expediting is the process of directly contacting suppliers to determine the status of past-due or near past-due shipments. In smaller organizations, expediting is often part of the purchasing function. In larger organizations, expediters often report to a separate material control department. The actual expediting process rarely provides new value within the purchasing process. Unfortunately, expediters are an accepted overhead cost at some organizations. Progressive organizations recognize that a need for expediters indicates that suppliers are not performing as required or that suppliers are not receiving realistic or stable material release schedules. It is also possible that the buying organization is making frequent and demanding schedule changes. To prevent this situation, more compa-

EXHIBIT 3.2   *Activities of the Purchasing Department*

Activity	Description
Buying	• Purchase of raw materials, components, finished goods, or services from an outside supplier • Specific processes involve supplier selection, evaluation, negotiation, contracting, and awarding the contract
Expediting and inventory control	• Contacting suppliers to determine the status of past-due shipments, and if necessary, increasing the priority of the order • Monitoring day-to-day management of purchased and in-process inventory at each using location
Transportation	• Purchasing inbound transportation services • Carrier selection • Transportation cost analysis
Managing countertrade arrangements	• Managing countertrade contracts, involving international or domestic trade where goods are exchanged for goods as payment for a firm's products
Insourcing/outsourcing analysis	• Analysis of whether a firm should make or purchase a proposed or existing item • Often involves strategic analysis of core competencies, total cost, and amount of vertical integration
Value analysis	• Organized study of an item's function as it relates to value and cost • Team study involves attempting to reduce cost without sacrificing quality, enhancing the function without increasing cost, or providing greater function above and beyond cost
Purchasing research/ material forecasting	• Anticipating short- and long-term changes in material and supply markets • Development of detailed strategic purchasing plans for critical commodities
Strategic supply management	• Progressive approach to managing the supply base • Development of a mission statement and a plan to increase cross-functional involvement, supplier quality assurance, supplier partnerships, and supplier development
Other Responsibilities	• May include: receiving and warehousing, travel arrangements, production planning and control, commodity futures trading, international materials management, economic forecasting, and subcontracting

nies are reducing their use of expediting by developing realistic material release schedules and doing business with suppliers capable of meeting material shipment schedules. For example, IBM-Rochester signed an agreement with suppliers called a "pull profile" that identifies the total to be purchased from the supplier in a given time period. On a total bill of materials of $50, there may be a $1 part that IBM agrees to buy a certain amount over the quarter. The supplier then commits to production of this quantity. If IBM does not pull to forecast, the supplier can bill IBM for the difference. That is, the supplier can request a reimbursement for production that IBM did not purchase, which is made up over the forecast of this item in the next time period.

Increasingly, purchasing is becoming less responsible for expediting and inventory control. With the deployment of sophisticated purchasing information systems and inventory control systems, many of the traditional expediting and inventory control decisions are being put into the hands of users. As businesses begin to track their costs more efficiently, functions are often able to better manage their inventory and material needs independently at a lower cost. Each function "owns" the inventory it purchases, and users are therefore much more careful in how much they order and how they use it. The sense of ownership often leads to a more "proactive" approach to expediting, wherein managers monitor deliveries and prevent delays rather than react to them.

The inventory control function routinely monitors the day-to-day management of purchased and in-process inventory at each using location. This activity usually relies on sophisticated equations or algorithms to determine the demand requirements for each operations location. In larger companies, the individual responsible for sourcing an item is usually not responsible for the maintenance or routine release of purchase requirements.

Transportation   The U.S. government deregulated transportation services in the early 1980s. Since that time purchasing has taken an active role in the evaluation, negotiation, and final selection of transportation services and carriers. Transportation is a highly specialized activity with its own set of requirements (discussed in Chapter 18).

Managing Countertrade Arrangements   Purchasing may have responsibility for managing countertrade—international or domestic trade where goods are exchanged for goods as payment—although at some companies it is a specialized activity separate from purchasing. This can involve a total exchange of goods or involve some partial payment in cash. Because countertrade involves the purchase of foreign goods, purchasing may be called upon to manage this specialized form of international trade. Chapter 11 discusses countertrade.

Insourcing / Outsourcing   Purchasing often analyzes whether a new or existing purchase requirement should be provided internally or sourced from external suppliers. Certain items or services, such as standardized or routine maintenance and supply items, do not require make-or-buy evaluations. For other items, however, the make-or-buy analysis takes on strategic importance involving more than simple cost comparisons. Make-or-buy decisions indicate where management is willing to commit the resources required to maintain production ability and also indicate the amount of vertical integration a firm is willing to pursue.

Purchasing's role in make-or-buy analyses is an important one. Regarding outsourcing, purchasing must identify whether qualified suppliers exist in the marketplace. Further requirements may include visiting potential suppliers, negotiating outsourcing contracts, and monitoring supplier performance. The process of conducting an insourcing/outsourcing analysis is discussed in Chapter 7.

Value Analysis   Value analysis, developed by Larry Miles at General Electric during the late 1940s, is the organized study of an item's function as it relates to value and cost. Value here is defined as the relationship between function and cost:

$$\text{Value} = \frac{\text{Function of an item}}{\text{Cost of the item}}$$

The objective of value analysis is to enhance the value of a good or service by one of three methods: (1) reducing the cost of an item without sacrificing quality, (2) enhancing the function of an item without increasing cost, or (3) providing greater function to the user above and beyond any increase in cost. Any one of these actions makes the numerator of the value analysis equation larger in relation to the denominator. Purchasing actively involves itself with value analysis through the study of materials, specifications, and suppliers. The role of purchasing in coordinating the interface between engineering and suppliers during value analysis is discussed in Chapter 12 on purchasing tools and techniques.

Purchasing Research / Material Forecasting   Purchasing should have responsibility for anticipating short- and long-term changes in material and supply markets. Research and forecasting are critical for any organization that sources raw materials or components. Detailed short- and long-term strategic purchasing plans are required for items subject to technological, economic, or political change. Developing these plans involves examining the factors that can impact purchasing's ability to obtain the right good or service at the right cost. Exhibit 3.3 highlights some of the topics that a purchasing research plan often covers. Chapter 6 discusses this topic further.

Strategic Supply Management   Supply management is a progressive approach to managing the supply base that differs from the traditional arm's-length or adversarial approach with sellers. It requires purchasing professionals to work directly with key suppliers who are capable of providing world-class performance. One expert defines strategic supply management as follows:[9]

- It involves purchasing, engineering, supplier quality assurance, and the supplier working together as one team, early on, to further mutual goals.
- It is long-term win-win relationship between a company and specially selected suppliers where a supplier is virtually an extension of the customer company (except for ownership).
- It is a process of concrete, on-site, and frequent help to suppliers in exchange for dramatic and continuous performance improvements, including steady price reductions.
- It is a new way of operating, involving internal operations, external suppliers (Tier 1), and a chain of subsuppliers (Tier 2) and sub-subsuppliers (Tier 3) to achieve advances in product development, shorter cycle times, and total quality control.

EXHIBIT 3.3   *Topics Covered in a Purchasing Research Plan**

A. CURRENT STATUS OF ITEM
  1. Description and use
  2. How the item is purchased
  3. Current price, terms, and annual expenditure
  4. Current contracts and expiration date
  5. Strategic importance of item

B. PURCHASE OBJECTIVES
  1. Short term
  2. Long term

C. REQUIREMENTS FORECAST
  1. Past and present usage
  2. Future requirements
  3. Source of forecast information
  4. Lead times

D. MARKET SITUATION
  1. Geographic considerations
  2. Analysis of market forces: political, technological, availability of substitutes, anticipated supply and demand
  3. Assessment of potential threats to supply

E. COST/PRICE EVALUATION
  1. Supplier production costs
  2. Cost/price history
  3. Material price forecast
  4. Price of substitute material

F. SUPPLIER EVALUATION
  1. Strengths and weaknesses of each producer
  2. Potential suppliers
  3. Buyer/seller relationships
  4. Make-or-buy analysis

G. PROCUREMENT STRATEGY
  1. Recommended short-term strategy
  2. Recommended long-term strategy
  3. Contingency procurement supply plans
  4. Value analysis opportunities

*For existing or proposed items or commodities.

Part of strategic supply management requires pursuing strategic responsibilities, which can be defined as activities that have a major impact on long-term performance. This definition excludes routine, simple, or day-to-day decisions that have a minor or shorter-term impact. The routine ordering and follow-up of basic operational supplies is not a strategic responsibility. The concept of strategic supply management, as broad as it appears, has become a purchasing responsibility. Examples of strategic responsibilities include developing material supply plans and commodity forecasts, negotiating longer-term contracts with suppliers of critical goods and services, developing supplier capabilities, and managing early supplier involvement during new-product development.

Other Responsibilities   Purchasing can also assume a variety of other responsibilities such as receiving and warehousing, managing company travel arrangements, production planning and control, commodity futures trading, international materials management, economic forecasting, and subcontracting. These topics are not covered in detail in this book because other textbooks specifically address each area.

Separating Strategic and Operational Purchasing

Managing day-to-day supply chain operations is quite different from managing longer-term strategic tasks. Can the personnel who are expected to manage the uninterrupted flow of materials also find time to practice strategic supplier management? Do these personnel even have the right skills to shift from operational to strategic purchasing? When pressed for time, strategic responsibilities take second place to the immediate needs presented by operational issues. Strategic responsibilities lack the immediacy of tactical duties and, as a result, are often ignored.

One way to ensure that both types of assignments receive adequate attention is to separate the staff according to tactical and strategic job assignments. Separation does not mean one group or area is more important than another. Both types of assignments are important and require specialized attention. Exhibit 3.4 highlights the characteristics of tactical and strategic buying at a division of a Fortune 500 electronics company. Both positions require buyers to work closely with internal groups while displaying the ability to think creatively. The skills required for a strategic focus will be different from the skills required for an operational focus.

This exhibit illustrates one possible arrangement for separating operational and strategic buyers. The operational buyer manages the efficient utilization of inventory resources and the day-to-day purchasing system. Closest internal contact occurs with the operations group (whom the operational buyer directly supports). The strategic buyer supports new-product development, identifies strategic suppliers through cross-functional commodity teams, and uses progressive procurement practices to support the longer-term needs of the organization. Closest internal contact occurs with research and development (R&D) and materials engineering. The separation of professional duties will become increasingly common as a means to satisfy operational and strategic performance objectives.

$\mathcal{P}$LACEMENT OF PURCHASING AUTHORITY

Placement of purchasing authority refers to how an organization structures its decision-making authority. Probably the best way to preface this discussion is to begin by evaluating where the authority for a decision exists within an organization

EXHIBIT 3.4   *Characteristics of Tactical and Strategic Buyers*

Tactical Buyer	Strategic Buyer
• Supports the needs of the strategic buyers (teamwork) • Implements plans for achieving performance goals regarding —Inventory —Supplier reviews —Systems data integrity —Latest system knowledge • Works effectively with the manufacturing departments • Monitors performance progress using charts and graphs • Achieves continuous cost reductions • Is a creative thinker	• Supports the needs of the technical groups (teamwork) • Works with R&D and materials engineering • Possesses strong interpersonal skills • Assumes commodity team leadership • Is knowledgeable regarding industry and technical trends • Understands latest trends and theories in procurement • Is an effective presenter

versus the physical location of personnel. If an executive at corporate headquarters must approve a decision, then a firm maintains a centralized authority structure for that decision, even if purchasing personnel are located throughout the organizational hierarchy. If purchasing authority for a decision exists at the divisional, business unit, or plant level, then a firm has various levels of decentralized decision-making authority.

We can envision the different types of purchasing organizations as existing on a continuum, with complete centralization at one end and complete decentralization at the other. Few organizations lie at these polar extremes; rather most organizations lie somewhere toward one end or the other of the spectrum. Certain decisions or tasks, such as the evaluation and selection of suppliers that will support an entire organization, may be centralized. The authority to generate purchase orders, however, rests with local buyers. A firm might centralize the authority for capital expenditure purchases over a specified dollar with lower-dollar decisions made at a facility level.

The 1970s version of centralized purchasing authority often resulted in complete purchasing control, along with a large staff, placed at the corporate level. If plant or divisional management required material sourcing or engineering changes, these changes had to be approved through the centralized office. Obviously, this additional layer of decision making quickly became unresponsive to the fast-paced needs of new-product development. Moreover, bloated organizational charts represented a major barrier toward a strategic approach to supply chain management. As foreign competition attacked U.S. markets during the early 1980s, organizations increasingly experienced lost market opportunities because of many levels of decision making. Today's version of centralized purchasing should emphasize support, integration, and coordination of different tasks at different levels to achieve maximum performance rather than strict control over the entire purchasing process. The challenge today is to know which activities, processes, and tasks to control or coordinate centrally and which to push down to the operating units.

Advantages of Centrally Controlled Purchasing

A centralized procurement group can provide some definite advantages, particularly when an organization has multiple buying centers. Centrally controlled purchasing does not necessarily mean that a central group actually does any buying. Instead, a central group may select suppliers and negotiate purchase contracts that others throughout the organization use. What are the potential benefits of centrally controlled purchasing?

Coordinate Purchase Volumes Historically, the primary advantage of centralized purchasing has been to realize a favorable price due to accumulated volumes. Unfortunately, when organizations pursued centralized purchasing, they not only centralized the sourcing of parts with suppliers but also the actual ordering process. This led to the widespread perception that centralized purchasing resulted in decreased responsiveness to the needs of internal customers. Many believed that centralization just added another time-consuming step in the decision-making process. Today, however, the systems technology exists for a firm to identify common purchased items between divisions or business units for centrally coordinated sourcing. To facilitate this process, local purchasing personnel can still retain the authority to generate purchase releases directly to a supplier. A firm can achieve material cost reductions by combining purchase volumes while still recognizing the operating requirements of division or plant buyers. In fact with electronic data interchange and electronic commerce, operating requirements are now often triggered by users and sent to suppliers, with little day-to-day involvement on the part of a corporate or higher-level purchasing department.

Organizations can also accumulate services to achieve a better purchase agreement. Almost all organizations rely on transportation services to support the inbound and outbound portions of their supply chain. Today, organizations often use centrally controlled transportation contracts not only to realize cost reductions but also to achieve uniform, consistent performance standards across all locations. General Electric established a central executive transportation committee comprised of divisional transportation managers. This committee acts as a central body to evaluate carriers for corporate transportation contracts, award corporate contracts to the best carriers, and establish uniform carrier performance standards for all divisions. Carrier selection is no longer a decision made at the divisional level. By combining transportation volumes, GE realizes cost and service improvements that benefit the entire corporation.

Reduced Duplication of Purchasing Effort Another reason for centrally controlling purchasing authority is to reduce duplication of effort. Consider an organization with ten locations and a completely decentralized purchasing structure. Should each location be responsible for developing its own purchasing policies, procedures, and systems? Think about some of the potential duplication among the locations:

- Ten sets of material release forms
- Ten supplier quality standards
- Ten approaches to supplier quality control
- Ten supplier performance evaluation systems
- Ten separate purchasing training manuals
- Ten approaches to strategy development
- Ten standards for electronic data interchange with suppliers

Duplication adds costs but very little in the way of unique value. It is costly and inefficient, and it creates a lack of consistency between operating units. Purchasing personnel should spend time on value-added tasks rather than developing redundant or separate policies between different operating units. The principle of standardization is being applied even across industries. For instance, the U.S. auto industry implemented the QS 9000 quality conformance standards to eliminate the need for suppliers to Ford, Chrysler, and GM to complete multiple sets of forms.

Ability to Develop and Coordinate Procurement Strategy It is a challenge to develop and coordinate a corporate procurement strategy without central coordination. One question is whether it is advantageous to develop a corporate purchasing strategy. Within most industries the answer is a definite yes. A strong corporate purchasing strategy provides operational direction before committing scarce resources. It also provides the proper match between opportunities and resources, operational guidance to managers, and flexibility as organizations adapt to a dynamic environment.

Several strategy development trends are occurring today. First, purchasing is becoming less of a tactical function and more of a strategic function. Second, organizations are linking corporate, operations, and purchasing strategy plans into an overall competitive strategic plan. These trends require a centrally controlled group responsible for developing purchasing strategy at the highest levels of an organization. Without this group, an organization cannot coordinate its purchasing strategy. Chapter 6 describes the strategy development process in greater detail.

Ability to Coordinate and Manage Companywide Purchasing Systems
The need for advanced purchasing systems is increasingly important. The design and coordination of sophisticated purchasing systems should not be the responsibility of individual units. If each division or unit is responsible for developing its own purchasing or part-numbering system, the end result will be a mixture of incompatible systems. A centrally coordinated approach to systems development supports a system design compatible with all locations.

Hewlett-Packard, historically a decentralized company, relies on its central procurement group to develop and manage company-wide databases. This results in visibility to common items between HP's dozens of divisions as well as the ability to evaluate supplier performance at the corporate level. The system also supports the development of company-wide material forecasts. Decentralized purchasing systems simply do not provide management with the capability to oversee the purchasing function at a higher level.

Development of Purchasing Expertise Purchasing personnel cannot become experts in all areas of purchasing, especially as the purchasing function becomes more complex and sophisticated. The ability to develop specialized purchasing knowledge and to support individual buying units is another advantage of a central purchasing group. The following list, while not exhaustive, presents some of the areas where a central group either develops specialized expertise, and/or provides training and support to divisional or business unit purchasing personnel:

- Purchase negotiations
- International purchasing
- Legal aspects of purchasing
- Training and development programs
- Supplier quality programs
- Budget and measurement systems
- Purchasing research, including macro economic trend analysis
- Value analysis techniques
- Corporate commodity management
- Total cost of ownership
- Team-building skills
- Total quality management
- Computer and information system skills

Additional information on training seminars and online learning can be obtained through the National Association of Purchasing Management at http://www.napm.org/.

Managing Change to Benefit the Entire Organization Recently, one of the authors of this book visited two companies that were putting in place a new process to manage purchases regionally (a region might be North America or Europe, for example), and globally if the opportunity existed. One company had a strong central focus to its major functional activities. The other had over 80 highly decentralized operating companies. As you might guess, the decentralized company struggled to initiate change because support or compliance with the corporate-wide global purchasing process was voluntary or not a priority. The centrally focused company indicated that it experienced very few problems getting participants around the world to support the suppliers selected through its global sourcing process. This example shows that managing the change process at one central point is often easier in a centrally controlled or coordinated purchasing environment.

Other Advantages Centralized authority can provide greater control over large capital expenditures. Inventory part number reduction, an objective of most organizations today, is also possible with a department that has the authority to oversee the activities of each operating unit. From its unique perspective at the top of the organization, a centralized group can focus on controlling the growth of total purchased part numbers.

A central group can develop a single approach to supplier development and support it by providing corporate resources or developing uniform guidelines. Such a group can also help to integrate first-, second-, and third-tier suppliers into a supply chain management program. Because significant resources and central coordination are needed for such an effort, centralized purchasing is a must to ensure the success of this strategy. Finally, a central purchasing group can effectively coordinate a supply-base reduction program. This approach ensures that the reduction process supports the goals of the entire organization, not just a particular purchasing department.

Advantages of Decentralized Purchasing Authority

With all the advantages that centrally coordinated purchasing appears to offer, why would any organization support a decentralized purchasing structure? While competitive pressures encourage a more centralized approach to certain tasks, these same pressures also support the decentralized placement of purchasing authority for other tasks. In other words, a firm can gain an advantage from placing purchasing personnel with sourcing authority directly "where the action is." So, what are the potential benefits of decentralizing purchasing authority?

Speed and Responsiveness It is frustrating to have critical decisions delayed in layer after layer of management decision makers. Organizations that respond quickly to market opportunities will have an advantage over those that delay their decision making. The ability to respond quickly to user and customer requirements has always been a major justification for decentralizing purchasing authority. Poor responsiveness often outweighed all the benefits of centralized purchasing during the 1970s. Purchasing, a critical *support* function, simply did not respond to the needs of its internal customers under centralized buying.

Organizations with a decentralized organizational structure usually have a decentralized purchasing function. Even today, organizations often resist a stronger centralized purchasing group simply because of previous experience with centralized management. Some organizations fear that any centralization of authority automatically results in slower response times. Whether this view is valid is not the issue—organizations must work within the context of their structures. Most purchasing professionals agree that a decentralized purchasing authority contributes to greater responsiveness and support throughout lower organizational levels.

Understanding Unique Operational Requirements Decentralized purchasing personnel should gain a greater understanding and appreciation of local operating requirements. These personnel become familiar with the products, processes, business practices, and the customers the division or plant serves. Increased familiarity allows a buyer to anticipate the needs of the departments it supports while developing solid relationships with local suppliers. This is especially important for global companies such as Colgate-Palmolive, which has plants located on every continent.[10]

Product Development Support   Because most new-product development occurs at the divisional or business unit level, a decentralized purchasing structure can support new-product development at the earliest stages. Purchasing can support new-product development by bringing key suppliers earlier into the product design process, evaluating longer-term material product requirements and developing strategic plans, determining if substitute materials are available, and anticipating product requirements and selecting the best suppliers available.

Ownership   Organizations often prefer decentralized purchasing authority because of an intangible reason called ownership. In essence, ownership refers to the assumption that local personnel understand and support the objectives of the business unit or division, and that centralized personnel are unable to comprehend these objectives. Local support personnel feel a personal commitment to a particular operation. Ownership means that everyone is on the same team, speaks the same language, works together toward common goals, and shares the responsibility for the group's problems.

A Hybrid Purchasing Structure

A number of research studies that focused on industrial companies have concluded that a majority of companies use a hybrid centralized-decentralized structure. Exhibit 3.5 presents the division across different structures from one sample of companies. Experience reveals that less than a third will be strictly centralized, and even less will be totally decentralized. Larger organizations tend to rely on a combination of centralization and decentralization, while smaller ones are more likely to be equally split between centralization and centralization-decentralization. Larger organizations usually have more operating units or divisions and are generally dispersed geographically. As a result, some purchasing authority must be decentralized. However, these organizations also maintain some centralized control over the purchasing process, particularly for high-value commodities purchased by multiple operations globally. Purely decentralized purchasing is the least preferred structure across all size organizations.

Most organizations should develop a structure that retains the benefits and expertise of a central purchasing group but also responds quickly to plant and divisional purchasing requirements. This is not as difficult as it sounds—if executive management is willing to make the necessary changes.

ORGANIZING FOR SUPPLY CHAIN MANAGEMENT

The need to coordinate and share information across organizations and functional groups has resulted in the development of higher level positions designed to oversee various supply chain activities. *Total supply chain management* is an organizational

EXHIBIT 3.5   *Decentralization Versus Centralization: Placement of Purchasing Authority*

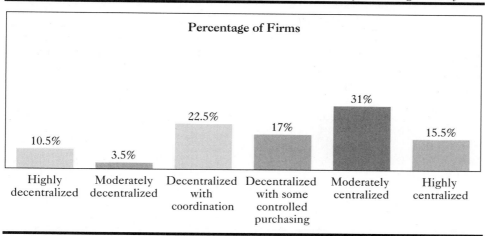

Source: From data collected from 69 firms at the Executive Purchasing and Supply Chain Management Seminar, Michigan State University, 1999.

concept whose primary objective is to proactively manage the two-way movement and coordination of goods, services, and information from raw material through end user. *Materials management* focuses on the coordination of goods, services, and information from suppliers through operations, and it is a subset of total supply chain management. *Physical distribution management* focuses on the coordination of goods, services, and information from operations through end user, and it is also a subset of total supply chain management. Conceptually, total supply chain management involves both materials management and physical distribution management. Exhibit 3.6 presents a widely held industry and academic view of the difference between the three terms.

A structure that coordinates the diverse activities within a supply chain contrasts greatly with one where separate supply chain groups or activities report to different executive managers. The latter model can result in each function or activity pursuing conflicting organizational goals and objectives. Organizing as an integrated supply chain structure requires traditionally separate activities to report to an executive responsible for coordinating the two-way flow of goods, services, and information from supplier through customer.

Most large organizations have a materials or supply chain executive responsible for coordinating separate supply chain activities. Earlier research revealed that 70% of U.S. operations organizations use the materials concept to some extent, a figure that is consistent across all sizes of organizations.[11] The materials management or supply chain executive may even report directly to the executive committee, which reflects the importance of this activity.

Historically, the greatest growth of the materials management concept occurred during the mid-1960s to late 1970s. This does not mean, however, that the materials concept began during this period. The origins of materials management date back to the 1800s. It was common during the latter half of the nineteenth century for U.S.

EXHIBIT 3.6   *Components of Total Supply Chain Management*

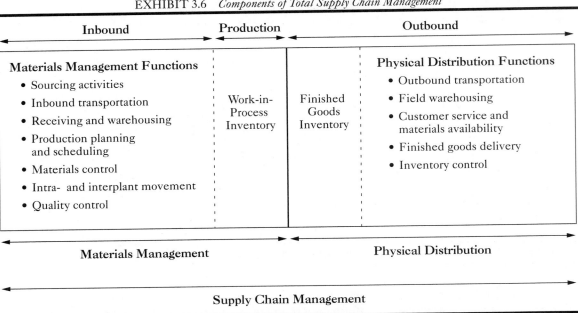

railroads to use a materials management structure. Related functions such as purchasing, inventory control, receiving, and stores reported to a single individual.

During the 1970s, most organizations experienced shortages of vital materials as well as rising materials prices. Organizations embraced the materials concept as a means to coordinate diverse material functions and to control materials-related costs, quality, and supply. Some purchasing professionals were concerned during this period that the creation of a materials management position would reduce purchasing's organizational importance. They argued that purchasing naturally assumes a lower position when management creates an executive materials position. Furthermore, if a nonpurchasing professional heads the materials position, this reduces purchasing's importance within the organizational structure even further.

To some degree, these fears were not unfounded. A survey conducted in 1968 during the initial growth phase of the materials concept found that 33% of materials management executives came from production control, 29% from purchasing, and 38% from departments outside the materials area.[12] Regardless of the background of the materials manager, most organizations today recognize purchasing's importance. Organizations that develop a coordinated approach to materials management show a greater interest in the control of materials costs. This can only increase the importance of purchasing within the organizational hierarchy because of purchasing's influence on cost and quality.

The materials manager must constantly balance trade-offs between the functions making up the materials organization. What does managing trade-offs mean? Consider, for example, two separate groups—a material control and inbound transportation group. Material control is responsible for maintaining raw material and work-in-process inventory levels as low as possible while still meeting production schedules, which allows a firm to minimize the capital it has committed to carrying inventory. Now consider a transportation department measured by its ability to reduce transportation costs. Conflicts exist because materials control managers seek to reduce average inventory levels (requiring frequent, fast, and often expensive transportation shipments of smaller quantities) while transportation seeks to minimize costs with full truckloads or slower (i.e., less expensive) methods of transportation such as rail carriers. Which viewpoint prevails? This situation creates conflict because each function pursues independent actions to satisfy its own (although conflicting) performance and cost objectives. A materials manager addresses these issues by developing the systems and performance measures that support cooperative action. This example illustrates the qualities required of a materials manager (and a supply chain manager as organizations begin to take a supply chain perspective): an unbiased total system perspective; the ability to direct diverse functions toward common organizational goals; the ability to manage trade-offs and conflict between groups; and recognition that the lowest cost for each separate activity or department does not necessarily mean the lowest total system cost.

It is easy to see why organizations have endorsed first the materials management concept and now an integrated supply chain concept. Both approaches can lead to some tangible benefits:

- Provide direct control over material and service costs.
- Develop awareness of managing the system trade-offs within a supply chain.
- Open channels of communication and stimulate the sharing of ideas across organizations and groups.
- Support the career paths of talented personnel by providing the means to develop well-rounded expertise.
- Develop greater operating efficiencies as supply chain activities work together to create material systems, coordinate procedures, and streamline the movement of material and data.
- Create a direct link from the customer back to external suppliers.

While the 1970s witnessed the growth of the materials management concept, we are now entering the era of total supply chain management. The sourcing snapshot about Eastman Chemical illustrates how a major company is practicing total supply chain management. While conceptually appealing, few organizations have created positions specifically responsible for managing the entire supply chain from supplier to end customer. This will change over the next several years.

In recent years, some organizations have evolved from the concept of materials management to the concept of integrated supply chain management. This latter concept, while still largely unrealized in 1997, refers to the integration of the materials function across multiple tiers of suppliers and through the end customer within the supply chain. An excellent example of integrated supply chain management in action is described by Ernest L. Nichols, Jr., who worked with four organizations seeking to supply one another in a supply chain: a computer retailer, a computer manufacturer, a component manufacturer, and a semiconductor manufacturer.[13] For the supply chain to function effectively, these four organizations had to work together to develop an integrated information system that allowed any party in the chain to have complete access and visibility to information on upcoming product demand forecasts, production requirements, and inventory levels at any stage backward or forward in the chain. By developing trust throughout the members in the chain, each party could better plan their own production and distribution requirements. The result? Lower inventories throughout the chain, shorter cycle times, improved planning, and lower costs. While supply chain management is often discussed in theory, few organizations have achieved this level of integration and success. One reason for this—the difficulty in developing the level of trust required to share information with so many parties—will remain a challenge in the future. Additional information on articles describing other supply chain partnering cases can be found in their journal entitled *Cycle Time Research* at http://www.people. memphis.edu/%7Ecctr/cycle.htm.

Supply Chain Activities and Functions

What are the activities that make up this concept called supply chain management? The following sections briefly describe some of them.

Purchasing   Most organizations include purchasing as a major supply chain activity. Since purchasing is the primary focus of this book, we do not need to elaborate. Purchasing's responsibilities in a supply chain are the same as those discussed earlier in this chapter in the section titled Organizing the Purchasing Function, except that it must create a dialogue and work with an expanded set of groups compared with a materials management focus.

Inbound Transportation   Larger organizations usually have a specialized traffic and transportation function to manage the physical and informational links between the supplier and the buyer. For some organizations, transportation is the single largest category of purchasing-related costs, especially for highly diversified organizations. While a firm may have minimal common purchase requirements between its operating units, opportunities usually exist to coordinate the purchase of transportation services.

Organizations that focus on supply chain management must pay close attention to transportation. They recognize the need to control inbound materials shipments as tightly as they control outbound shipments to customers. Allowing a supplier to arrange for inbound transportation may not provide the cost control or coordination required on the inbound side of the supply chain. Inbound transportation is often outsourced to a specialized transportation provider. Chapter 18 addresses transportation and logistics.

Inbound Quality Control Quality control has taken on increased importance during the last 15 years. Almost all organizations recognize the importance of the supplier quality and the need to prevent rather than simply detect quality problems. As a result, the quality emphasis has shifted from detecting defects at the time of receipt or use to prevention early in the materials-sourcing process. This requires a strong awareness concerning a supplier's role in the quality process. Progressive organizations work directly with suppliers to develop proper quality control procedures and processes. Chapter 9 discusses supplier quality management.

Receiving and Storage All inbound material must be physically received as it moves from a supplier to a purchaser. In a non–just-in-time environment, material must also be stored or staged. Receiving and storage is usually part of the materials management function because of the need to control the physical processing and handling of inventory.

Receiving and storage includes a variety of tasks. For example, a firm must process incoming receipt records, usually through a computer terminal, which updates the in-transit file, purchasing files, the accounts payable system, as well as any other systems requiring receipt information. Other tasks include the possible inspection of material and its storage awaiting final production. Material handling is also a critical part of the receiving and storage process, including movement within a facility along with any movement between facilities during the material transformation process. All material movement requires tight control.

Materials or Inventory Control *Materials control* and *inventory control* are sometimes interchangeable terms. Within some organizations, however, these terms have different meanings. The materials control group is often responsible for managing materials releases to suppliers. This includes generating the materials release, contacting a supplier directly concerning changes, and monitoring the status of inbound shipments. Materials control activities are sometimes the responsibility of the purchasing department, particularly in smaller organizations. In large organizations, however, purchasing and materials are often separate activities. Purchasing evaluates and selects sources of supply while materials control determines the actual order release quantities and shipment schedules. In this case, operational materials control and strategic purchasing duties are separate.

The inventory control group is often responsible for determining the inventory level of finished goods required to support customer requirements, which emphasizes the physical distribution (i.e., outbound) side of the supply chain. Integrated supply chain management requires that the materials and inventory control groups coordinate their efforts to ensure a smooth and uninterrupted flow to customers.

Order Processing Order processing is a vital link in ensuring that a customer receives material when and where it is needed. Order processing involves accepting a customer order and then sequencing that order internally for fulfillment. Historically, the problems with order processing involved (1) accepting and then scheduling customer orders before determining if adequate production capacity or machine time are available, (2) not coordinating order processing with order scheduling, and (3) using the producer's desired production date to drive the order schedule rather than trying to determine when the customer requires a good or service. Order processing is an important part of supply chain management—it represents a link between the producer's and customer's supply chains.

Production Planning and Scheduling This activity involves determining the aggregate levels of production for a family of items along with a time-phased, detailed schedule of production. While the production plan is not a sales forecast, it relies on forecasts from marketing to estimate the volume of materials that are required over the near term. Because operations is responsible for carrying out the production plan and meeting customer order due dates, order processing, production planning, and operations must work together closely.

Production planning and scheduling is a highly sophisticated process, which is not within the scope of this textbook. At many educational institutions, an entire course is devoted to this topic. Readers interested in production planning and scheduling should consult a production and operations textbook.

Warehousing Before a product heads to the customer, it may be stored for a period in a warehouse. This is particularly true for companies that produce according to a forecast in anticipation of future sales. Increasingly, as companies attempt to make a product only after receiving a customer order, this part of the supply chain may become less important. Chapter 18 addresses the changing role of warehousing in greater detail.

Shipping Shipping involves physically getting a product ready for distribution to the customer. This requires packing to prevent damage, completing any special labeling requirements, completing required shipping documents, or arranging transportation with an approved carrier. For obvious reasons shipping and outbound transportation must work together closely.

Outbound Transportation Fewer and fewer organizations "own" the transportation link to their customers. This is a part of the supply chain where full-service transportation providers, such as FedEx or other contract carriers, can design and manage entire distribution networks. Chapter 18 discusses this topic further.

Customer Service Customer service includes a wide set of activities that attempt to keep a customer satisfied with a product or service after the initial sale. Often, this means having dedicated customer account managers who help in managing customer promotions, inventory control, and delivery schedules. This may require providing customer training or having technical support personnel available to answer phone questions 24 hours a day. Customer service may also include a network of spare parts distribution centers that provide rapid replacement of parts and components.

Organizing for Supply Chain Management Helps Manage the Flow at Eastman Chemical

Just a decade ago, Eastman Chemical of Kingsport, Tennessee, kept on hand a three-month supply of wood pulp. Today the company gets by on a nine-day supply, which is not allowed to go up. Only after the company physically uses wood pulp is it allowed to replace what it used. Following the dictate of demand-pull management, the company tells suppliers to send just enough to replace what was used. The same is true for hundreds of other raw materials the company purchases.

How does Eastman manage the flow of material from supplier through customer? To make sure that as little inventory as possible sits idle, Eastman devised what it calls "stream inventory management." The vice president of materials management has designated that one person manage the inventory by looking at each raw material stream as a single company-wide number instead of tallying up the assorted amounts and reformulations as material progresses through the supply chain. This approach required a novel organizational structure that combines customer service and materials management. "Most companies would have established teams that bring together representatives from the usual functional areas," said Eastman's CEO. "We said, 'Let's define the process and put all of that in one organization.' The only thing we didn't put there is the actual manufacturing of the materials."

Stream inventory management has delivered a solid payoff. Because Eastman can monitor inventory while it is still at the supplier, and because it can also generate more accurate production forecasts due to working closely on the customer service end, it no longer needs a cushion of large stockpiles. Over the last ten years inventories have decreased from 11.5% of sales to 8% on average. The company expects even further gains as more raw materials are managed taking an integrated approach to supply chain management.

Source: Adapted from Eryn Brown, "The Push to Streamline Supply Chains," *Fortune,* March 3, 1997, 108C–108R.

A Supply Chain Management Structure

Exhibit 3.7 illustrates one possible way to structure around supply chain management. The actual groups under the supply chain umbrella can vary widely between organizations. Also, the reporting level of the supply chain executive can be higher or lower than shown here. In this exhibit, patterned after a high-tech company in Massachusetts, the vice president of supply chain management is responsible for material sourcing, production planning and scheduling, logistics, operations, and customer service. Materials quality reports directly to the director of material sourcing.

EXHIBIT 3.7   *Reporting Relationships in a Supply Chain Management Reporting Structure*

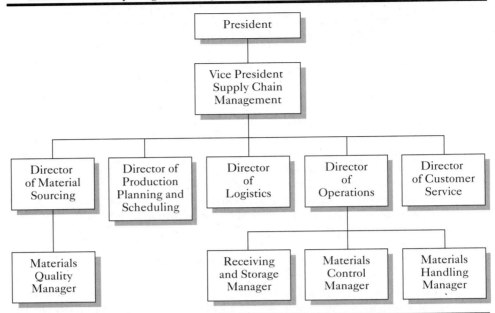

The director of operations is responsible for receiving and storage, materials control, and materials handling. This shows only one of many possible ways to emphasize supply chain management through the formal organizational structure.

THE TEAM APPROACH AS PART OF THE ORGANIZATIONAL STRUCTURE

Organizations are showing an increased willingness to use cross-functional teams to arrive at critical decisions or to implement major projects. Cross-functional teams consist of personnel from various functions brought together to achieve a specific task. Organizations that use cross-functional teams to manage some part of their supply chain typically have members that make a part-time commitment to the team. Team responsibilities are often in addition to regular job responsibilities. This can create a competition between the team and the functional group where the member normally resides. A team leader or executive sponsor may have to negotiate for a member's time.

When implemented properly, the team approach should result in improved performance and organizational decision making because it encourages group interaction across different functions. Problem solving is faster because the team assumes responsibility for problems and works together as an integrated unit. This approach supports the development of innovative methods to address traditional tasks and to "cut through the red tape."

The team approach can also break down restrictive communication barriers between functions. Cross-functional teams represent a new type of structure as organizations search for better ways to compete. Currently, a major use of cross-functional teams in purchasing is to evaluate and select suppliers for key items. A team will visit and rate potential suppliers against various performance areas. The team evaluates a supplier's quality, financial stability, product and process technology, delivery, and management strength. A team composed of functional experts should arrive at a better decision than an individual acting alone.

Another area supporting the use of teams is new-product development, which represents a radical departure from the traditional new-product development process. With the cross-functional approach, team members begin work simultaneously to reduce the total time it takes to move a product from the concept stage to the customer. This presents a clear contrast with the traditional or historical approach, where product development occurs within a series of sequential steps. Chapter 5 addresses this topic further.

CREATING THE ORGANIZATION OF THE FUTURE: THE HORIZONTAL ORGANIZATION

A major debate is currently underway concerning the best organizational structure, including how to organize for integrated supply chain management. The trend today is to move away from a vertical focus, where work and information are managed up and down through layers of the organization, toward a horizontal focus, where work and information are managed across groups and between organizations. The horizontal organization largely eliminates both hierarchy and functional or departmental boundaries. While there will always be a need for a group of key executives at the top of an organization, the remainder of the organization will work together "horizontally" in teams or groups to perform core processes.[14] Exhibit 3.8 compares the vertical and horizontal approaches to structuring organizations. It is easy to see how a horizontal focus applies to purchasing and supply chain management.

Vertical structures feature personnel that specialize within functional areas such as marketing, purchasing, engineering, and finance. Employees develop specialized knowledge, which will always be required to some degree. Information, however, does not flow freely between functional groups or across organizations. The greatest drawback to a strict functional or vertical structure is the inability to work with other groups and to see how "all the pieces fit" within an organization. This type of structure is not suited to managing trade-offs or conflict between groups because of the emphasis placed on functional, rather than organizational, goals and objectives. What is good for one group may not be best for another group or for the entire organization.

EXHIBIT 3.8   *Shifting from a Vertical to a Horizontal Organization*

The Vertical Organization

Organize in functional silos

Marketing   Finance   Purchasing   Engineering

The Horizontal Organization

Corporate infrastructure

Organize in full-time
cross-functional teams
around key processes

Supplier evaluation and selection

New-product development

Order generation, scheduling, and fulfillment

Integrated logistics

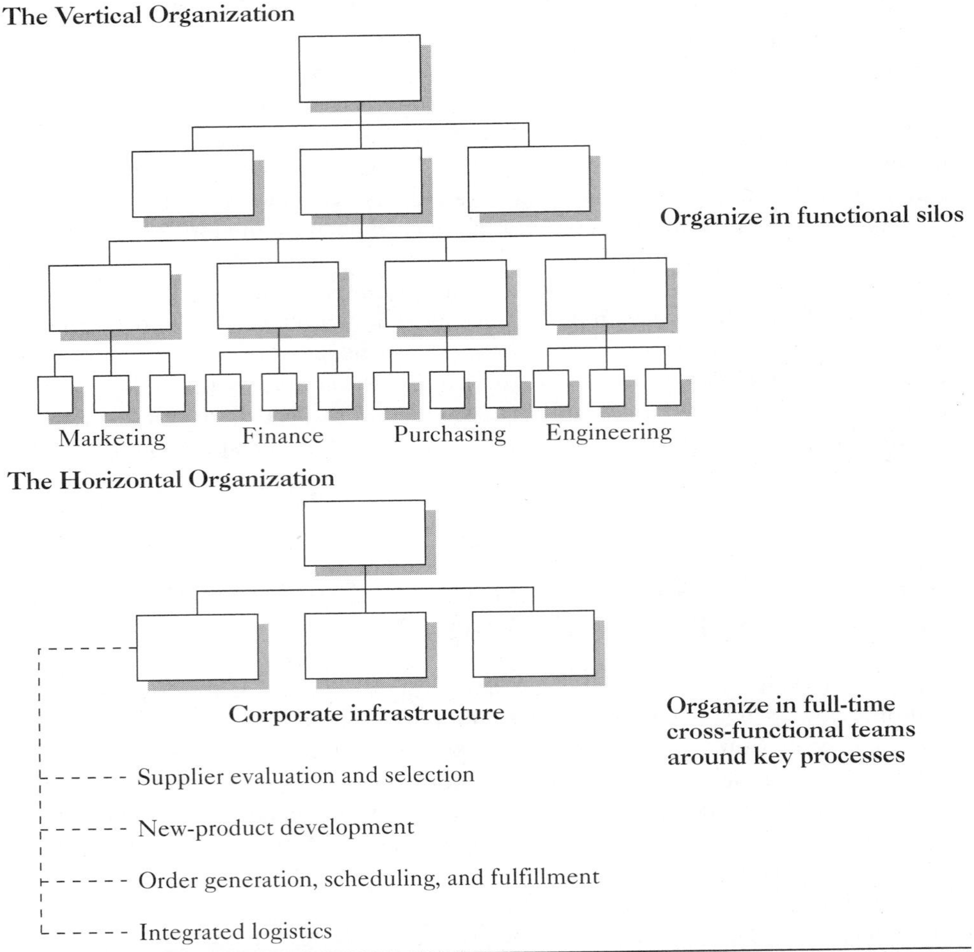

The horizontal structure is organized around processes rather than specialized work activities. General Electric's lighting business, for example, eliminated its vertical structure and instead adopted a horizontal design involving more than 100 processes. Motorola's Government Electronics unit redesigned its supply management organization as a process that directly involves external customers. Creating a team that focuses on new-product development, another important process, differs from assigning new-product development activities, such as product forecasting, to separate groups that do not coordinate their activities. In purchasing and supply chain management, different processes include supplier evaluation and selection, supplier management and development, customer order fulfillment, and logistics.

Instead of working on teams in addition to regular functional job responsibilities, which is usually the case for vertically aligned organizations that attempt to use teams, horizontal organizations often physically locate together those directly involved with managing a process. Instead of working in a functional area, individuals work on a full-time team basis with members from other areas. Because the work performed within a process naturally crosses functional boundaries, it makes sense to have those involved with the process working together closely.

Some evidence exists that purchasing is beginning to assume a horizontal rather than strictly vertical focus. Almost 80% of companies surveyed use cross-functional teams to manage some part of the sourcing process. Since 1990, we have also witnessed a shift from a commodity focus to one that is end-item or process focused. In 1990, purchasing organized around commodities in almost 80% of firms surveyed. Currently, purchasing is organized by commodity less than 65% of the time.[15] A shift has occurred toward organizing around end items (which supports new-product development efforts) and hybrid structures, such as organizing around processes. Of course, few organizations will choose to be purely vertical or purely horizontal in the future. Most will create structures that attempt to capture the best that vertical and horizontal alignments have to offer.

GOOD PRACTICE EXAMPLE
Making Centralized and Decentralized Purchasing Work at Black and Decker

■   ■   ■

Throughout the 1980s, Black and Decker (B&D) resembled a typical multinational U.S. firm.[16] Decentralized production and purchasing authority existed within each major country or market where the company operated. This multinational focus resulted in tremendous duplication of effort and inefficiency across B&D's product lines. For example, the lack of internal product control resulted in over 100 different motor sizes worldwide for its power tools. By the early 1990s, with the help of coordinated purchasing, the company reduced this figure to five different motor sizes.

Black and Decker's performance turnaround during the latter 1980s was due in part to the reorganization of purchasing. In fact, some executives maintain that purchasing helped lead the way during the company's global restructuring program. Instead of emphasizing a centralized or decentralized purchasing structure, B&D created a mixed centralized-decentralized authority structure, which still exists today. The new structure captured the benefits of centralized purchasing for some purchase decisions while still being responsive to the needs of each facility. The company achieved its competitive turnaround by emphasizing four primary cornerstones in its purchasing philosophy.

The first cornerstone—common to many major U.S. companies that are trying to improve purchasing and supply-base performance—is to *reduce the supply base* through a centrally controlled approach and then to identify one major supplier for each commodity. The major supplier receives 70% of the purchase volume while other suppliers receive the remaining 30%. The company believes this provides most of the benefits of single sourcing while still maintaining competition between suppliers. The company relies on a centrally controlled team approach to evaluate and select suppliers for key commodities that are common to different divisions or business units.

The second has been to *identify crucial commodities for centralized management*. Centrally managed commodities satisfy one or more criteria. The item or commodity is strategically important (e.g., motors), a few global suppliers produce the item (e.g., rechargeable batteries), the item is critical to product quality or is technically complex and/or important, or it is a high-dollar-volume item. Corporate purchasing is responsible for selecting corporate sources and for negotiating prices, contract length, and other contractual features for centrally managed purchases. Responsibility for day-to-day purchasing or material releasing remains the responsibility of divisional or business unit buyers.

A centralized commodity team evaluates and selects suppliers for items that meet the above criteria. Buyers at the plant level, however, are free to establish purchase orders directly with each selected supplier. They also have the authority to contact suppliers concerning delivery or quality problems, which helps alleviate the complaint that centralization is an inefficient process that is unresponsive to individual buying locations. This process allows local buyers to respond to operations's needs in a timely manner.

Local buyers also have the authority to source items that are not candidates for centralized commodity management. Items that have the volume for centralized sourcing but are competitively available from local or regional suppliers are purchased locally. For these items, management appoints a buyer at each location to become the resident buying expert as well as the commodity champion for that item.

The third cornerstone of Black and Decker's buying philosophy involves the *use of longer-term agreements*. Usually two to five years in length, these agreements have renewal options for suppliers who consistently meet performance expectations. They also include escape clauses when suppliers fail to perform as expected. The use of long-term agreements provides an incentive for a supplier to invest in productive equipment over the life of the contract. The contracts also provide some leverage for B&D with its suppliers.

The final cornerstone of the buying philosophy involves *organizational structure*. The company has created a structure designed to benefit from worldwide sourcing by maintaining foreign or international buying offices in key geographic

EXHIBIT 3.9   *Black and Decker Centralized-Decentralized Purchasing Organizational Structure*

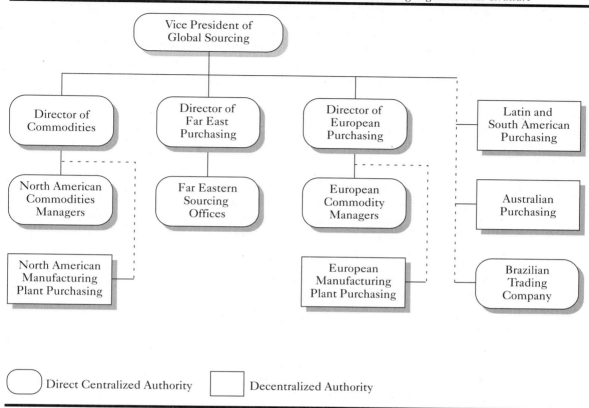

regions. Personnel at these offices search for the best suppliers to meet performance requirements. This structure allows purchasing to respond when economic and competitive factors make one region of the world more attractive compared to another region.

Black and Decker has an organizational structure that combines the best features of centralization and decentralization, and achieves purchasing economies of scale with world-class suppliers while still supporting the requirements of local facilities. Exhibit 3.9 is a partial representation of the company's organizational purchasing structure. Originally conceived during the late 1980s, this structure still serves the company today.

The structure presented in Exhibit 3.9 is a mix of a centralized and decentralized purchasing network. An executive at the highest level of the organization oversees the global purchasing process. Regional buyers, while granted autonomy to source noncommodity items and deal directly with corporate suppliers on non-price issues, maintain a dotted line reporting relationship with the central office. The foreign buying offices report directly to the vice president of global sourcing. For example, corporate purchasing controls the Far East buying office even though the director is physically located overseas. Finally, certain buying regions remain decentralized due to local government requirements or because the locations are too far removed geographically from mainstream operations. ▪

CONCLUSION

As customer requirements continue to become more demanding, organizations must become better at responding to change. New markets, rapid advances in communications, and shortages of skilled labor are forcing one of the most fundamental reorganizations since the multidivisional corporation became standard in the 1950s. Senior managers are struggling to adapt their organizations to the twenty-first–century business world that is rapidly taking shape. Thriving in the fast-paced environment requires a new kind of company and a new kind of leader. Organizations across many industries seem to be converging on a common management model to run their organizations, which relies on Western-style accounting and financial controls, yet stresses collaboration between groups and across organizations.

As it relates to purchasing and supply chain management, the organizational model for the twenty-first century has certain characteristics:

- Flattened hierarchies for faster decision making and freer flow of ideas
- Joint ventures and alliances with key suppliers and other supply chain members
- Cross-functional teams to pursue new opportunities and ensure cross-fertilization of ideas
- Global sourcing to capture the benefits from the world's best suppliers
- Greater decentralization of buying activity with centralized coordination of major spending categories
- Corporate cultures that nurture innovation, challenge assumptions, and seek new ideas
- Open information channels, with electronic mail, the Internet, Intranet, and information technology systems that make information widely available throughout the supply chain
- Diversified management, which rotates younger managers around the world for three-month to two-year assignments

As organizations continue to make changes, purchasing managers must learn to acquire new skills, become more flexible, and continually improve their capabilities. The twenty-first century will undoubtedly be full of uncertainty and risk. While rapid change frightens many purchasing managers, it is also exhilarating to be on the frontier of these changes. The next several decades will require the successful purchasing manager to be a supply chain risk and relationship manager rather than someone who reactively buys goods and services.

DISCUSSION QUESTIONS

1.   What are the advantages of organizing a purchasing department into specialized sub-units? What are the disadvantages? How can a firm overcome these disadvantages?

2.   What does it mean to say that an organization has organized to take a total supply chain management perspective?

3.   Discuss the major problem(s) with centralized purchasing during the 1970s. How did these problems affect a firm?

4.   Why is a function's placement in the organizational hierarchy important?

5.   What factors contribute to the increasing importance of purchasing within the organizational hierarchy?

6.   Why do some observers believe that the importance of purchasing diminishes when a firm organizes under the materials management umbrella?

7.   Discuss the two or three most important benefits to centralized purchasing authority. Justify your choices.

8.   Discuss the two most important benefits to decentralized purchasing authority. Justify your choices.

9.   What is the relationship between the total volume of purchased goods and the relative importance of purchasing in an organization? What are some of the organizational outcomes that are a result of this relationship?

10. Why was purchasing not perceived to be a higher-level function during the early industrial years in the United States?

11. What is the difference between strategic and operational purchasing? Provide some examples of strategic and operational tasks.

12. Discuss the advantages of a purchasing research staff. Are the advantages confined to purchasing? Why or why not?

13. Discuss the logic behind physically separating strategic and operational buyers.

14. You are the chief purchasing officer for a company with multiple production locations. Design a purchasing organizational structure that allows you to compete effectively. Describe the reporting structure, physical placement of personnel, and the placement of purchasing authority.

15. Discuss the advantages of using a cross-functional team to evaluate and select key suppliers.

16. Compare a vertical and horizontal organizational structure.

17. Identify five key processes that involve purchasing or supply chain management personnel.

18. What does it mean when a firm has centralized or decentralized its purchasing authority?

ADDITIONAL READINGS

Byrne, John A. "The Horizontal Corporation." *Business Week*, December 23, 1993, 76–81.

Jacob, Rahul. "The Struggle to Create an Organization for the 21st Century." *Fortune*, April 1995, 60–67.

Wellin, Richard S., William C. Byham, and George R. Dixon. *Inside Teams: How 20 World-Class Organizations Are Winning Though Teamwork*. San Francisco: Jossey-Bass, 1994.

ENDNOTES

1. Judith R. Gordon, *A Diagnostic Approach to Organizational Behavior* (Boston: Allyn and Bacon, 1987), 522–526.
2. While we may find a formal purchasing department, there is a trend to shift or distribute some of the activities historically performed by purchasing to users or internal customers. For example, the purchase of low-value items is increasingly becoming the responsibility of departments and users. This allows the formal purchasing organization to commit its limited resources to value-added activities rather than routine buying.
3. Bruce D. Henderson, "The Coming Revolution in Purchasing," *Journal of Purchasing and Materials Management* (Summer 1975): 44. (This article first appeared in the *Journal of Purchasing* in 1964.)
4. Based on discussion with managers at the Michigan State University Executive Purchasing Seminar, East Lansing, MI, 1996.
5. Harold Bloom and James Nardone, "Orgainzational Level of the Purchasing Function," *International Journal of Purchasing and Materials Management* 20, no. 2 (Summer 1984): 16.
6. Stuart Heinritz and Paul Farrell, *Purchasing Principles and Applications*, 5th ed. (Englewoods Cliffs, NJ: Prentice-Hall, 1971), 24.
7. Harold Fearon, "Organizational Relationships in Purchasing," *Journal of Purchasing and Materials Management* (Winter 1988): 7.
8. Michiel R. Leenders and Harold E. Fearon, *Purchasing and Supply Management* (Burr Ridge, IL: Irwin 1977).
9. Keki R. Bhote, *Strategic Supply Management: A Blueprint for Revitalizing the Manufacturing-Supplier Partnership* (New York: American Management Association, 1989), 13.
10. "Global Purchasing at Colgate," *Purchasing* (January 1997): 40–45.
11. Harold Fearon, "Organizational Relationships in Purchasing," *Journal of Purchasing and Materials Management* 24: no. 4 (1988): 2–12.
12. G. J. Zenz, "Materials Management, Threat to Purchasing?" *International Journal of Purchasing and Materials Management* 4 (May 1968): 44.
13. Ernst Nichols, "Supply Chain Management," *Cycle Time Journal* 1, no. 1 (1995): 3–10.
14. John A. Byrne, "The Horizontal Corporation," *Business Week* (December 20, 1993): 76–81.
15. From data collected at the 1999 Executive Purchasing and Supply Chain Management seminar, Michigan State University, East Lansing.
16. This section highlights Black and Decker's evolution over the last 12 years, including an original article that appeared in *Purchasing* magazine, September 29, 1988.

PURCHASING POLICY AND PROCEDURES 4

Can Not Understanding Policies Get Us in Trouble?

John Wilson, a recently hired buyer at an automotive company, was looking forward to a few days off to celebrate the December holidays with his family. While at work, he took a break and called his wife, Jill. During their conversation, Jill excitedly told him that an early gift had been delivered. It was a beautiful array of expensive gift-wrapping supplies. When John asked who sent the present, he was stunned to hear the gift came from a salesperson who was actively trying to win an upcoming contract with John's company. John felt uncomfortable about this and asked his wife to return the gift immediately. That might be hard to do, his wife explained, since this year's presents were already wrapped using the supplies "from that generous salesman!" As John thought about the gift, he realized he faced a dilemma. Should he accept the gift? Can he accept the gift? Should he try to return the gift, or should he simply report it to his manager? Does his new company even have a policy that covers this situation?

Later that day, John was having lunch with some of his colleagues. He mentioned the present the salesman had sent to his home and was surprised to learn that the other buyers received gifts on a regular basis. One had recently received 14 tickets to an NFL game from various suppliers. He did not go to the game himself but gave the tickets to employees in the plant. Another buyer had received two VIP passes to the U.S. Open Golf Tournament. The discussion really got animated when the table began to talk about an annual golf outing that was sponsored by a major supplier. Apparently, it was an event not to be missed, with free rounds of golf at the best course in the area.

When John asked if the company allowed buyers to accept these gifts and favors, the group admitted that no one really discussed the matter with them. One buyer then mentioned that his manager won a set of golf clubs at the golf outing! "The manager can't golf worth a darn," the buyer said, "but he sure has a nice set of clubs now."

It is clear that John Wilson and the other buyers in the opening vignette require some guidance concerning the acceptance of favors and gifts. Most organizations have a set of policies outlining or detailing the directives of executive management across a range of topics. These directives provide guidance while at the same time placing operating constraints on personal behavior. This chapter, divided into three major sections, discusses the role of purchasing policy and procedures in today's business environment. The first section provides a general overview and discussion of policy. This includes defining policy, the characteristics of an effective policy, the advantages and disadvantages of policy, and the policy hierarchy. The second section focuses on specific categories of purchasing policies, with examples provided for each category. The third section presents purchasing procedures, which are operating instructions detailing functional duties and tasks. The study of purchasing policies and procedures will help further our understanding of what purchasing is all about. Policies help clarify where purchasing lies within an organization, while procedures provide functional guidance for completing the mission of purchasing.

$\mathcal{P}$OLICY OVERVIEW

The term *policy* includes "all the directives, both explicit and implied, that designate the aims and ends of an organization and the appropriate means used in their accomplishment. Policy refers to the set of purposes, principles, and rules of action that guide an organization."[1] Rules of action refer to standard operating procedures along with any rules and regulations. While policies are usually documented in writing, unwritten or informal policies can also exist. Informal polices are understood over time and eventually become part of an organization's culture.

What Are the Advantages and Disadvantages of Policies?

Having written and implied policies offers a number of advantages. Perhaps their greatest advantage is that policies create an opportunity to define and clarify top management objectives. Policy statements are a means for executive management to communicate its leadership and views. Executive management should develop a series of high-level policy statements that provide guidance to employees at all levels.

Another advantage is that policies provide a framework for consistent decision making and action. In fact, one of the primary objectives of a policy is to ensure that personnel act in a manner consistent with executive or functional management's expectations. Finally, an effective policy provides an additional advantage by defining the rules and procedures that apply to all employees. This means each department within a division or business unit abides by the same standards and principles.

Potential disadvantages to policy development also exist. First, a policy is often difficult to communicate throughout large organizations. Simply because a policy exists does not mean that all personnel are aware of its intent and purpose. Accordingly, the greater the number of policies, the more difficult it becomes to create awareness. It may even be that some managers store the policy manual on a shelf. Second, a danger exists that employees view policies as a substitute for effective management. Policy statements are guidelines outlining management's belief or position on a topic. They are not a set of how-to instructions designed to provide specific answers for every business decision. A policy should provide guidance rather than answers. Third, policy development can also restrict innovation and flexibility. Too many policies accompanied by cumbersome procedures can become an organization's worst enemy. Too many rules can burden personnel with inefficient and counterproductive procedures for controlling each task. The product development manual at a major chemical company, for example, is over 200 pages in length. A detailed procedure addresses every step and conceivable situation encountered during development. Compare this to the product development procedures at a high-tech company. This company has a 20-page guideline outlining its new-product development process and milestones.

The guidelines support employee innovation and creativity—traits that are increasingly required in today's competitive environment.

What Makes an Effective Policy?

Unfortunately, simply having written or implied policies does not always lead to desired results. Certain features characterize an effective policy. To begin with, effective policies are *action-oriented* guidelines for providing guidance. They provide enough detail to direct behavior toward a specific goal or objective but are not so detailed that they discourage personnel from following the policy.

An effective policy is *relevant*—avoiding trivial or unimportant issues—and *concise*—stating a position with a minimum number of words. An effective policy is *unambiguous*, allowing personnel little doubt as to how to interpret the policy's intent and direction. Policies subject to different interpretations will, over a period of time, result in several possible outcomes. This can lead to inconsistent behavior, as people will simply ignore the policy because it is so difficult to interpret.

Another characteristic of effective policies is that they are *timely* and *current*, periodically reviewed for clarity and conformance. A policy is ineffective or counterproductive if it is confusing, ignored, or outdated. Policy formation and review should be a dynamic activity undertaken at least once every year or so. A review will indicate if employees understand and follow the policies. The review will also determine if a written policy is required where none currently exists. If a review indicates a policy is ineffective, management must identify the reasons why. A policy may be timely and correct but not properly enforced by management. In this case, it is management's responsibility to reeducate the workforce about the policy's intent. This sometimes occurs when an organization practices inappropriate or even illegal behavior and gets caught. Shortly after, executive management often publicizes an existing policy that addresses the issue or problem. The characteristics of effective policies can thus be summarized as follows:

- Action oriented
- Relevant
- Concise
- Unambiguous/well understood
- Timely and current
- Guides problem solving and behavior

The Policy Hierarchy—Moving from Executive Policies to Rules and Regulations

Policies exist within a hierarchy. Different levels of policy are present that, when taken together, guide the actions of people across an entire organization. Policies, procedures, rules, and regulations must be consistent and compatible throughout each organizational level. A hierarchy implies that upper-level directives flow downward to lower levels. Different departments or functions should not create policies and procedures that are inconsistent with higher-level policies. For example, a

EXHIBIT 4.1   *Major Levels of Organization Policy*

Executive Policies
- Outlines executive management's positions and directives
- Defines the purpose of the organization

Functional Policies
- Incorporates and aligns executive policies with functional policies
- Provides guidance for functional areas

Operating Procedures
- Describes functional duties and tasks in detail
- Describes steps required to complete specific tasks

Rules and Regulations
- Places constraints on individual behavior
- Describes organizational laws

purchasing policy cannot conflict with a policy directive sent down by executive management.

Policies range from the highest directives of executive management to the basic rules and regulations governing day-to-day operations. A major characteristic of policies is that they become more specific and rule oriented as they move toward lower organizational levels. Exhibit 4.1 presents policies and procedures as a pyramid. Fewer policy statements and directives occur at the highest executive levels compared with the functional level. After all, an organization has only a single executive level compared with many different functional and operating levels. Each function and level will have its own specific policies and procedures.

The top level of the policy hierarchy or pyramid includes major policies. A major policy is a "general statement of purpose that serves to guide the decisions of top management in particular, and all levels of management in general."[2] These include executive or corporate policies, which are fundamental statements concerned with an organization's purpose and constraints. The presence of an executive policy acts as a directive. Here is an example of a corporate or executive policy:

This company seeks to promote the well-being of our environment. To help accomplish this objective, business units will report twice a year, and an executive committee will evaluate, each business unit's compliance with corporate and government environmental regulations.

The second level of the policy hierarchy encompasses functional policies. Purchasing, finance, marketing, and engineering are examples of various functions. Not as broad in scope as the major executive policies, functional policies begin to translate and operationalize the executive policies as they relate to each function, provide guidance in areas where no executive policy exists, and relate to the areas where the function has responsibility. Functional policies eventually become the procedures and rules directing day-to-day behavior.

The third level includes operating procedures. A procedure is "a series of related steps or tasks expressed in chronological order and sequence to achieve a specific purpose. A standard operating procedure is a sequence of actions that become well established and accepted as a basic rule of conduct. Procedures are methods, techniques, and detailed ways through which an organization achieves or carries out its policies."[3] Procedures are more limiting than policies because they provide minimal operational discretion.

Procedures describe the process required to perform functional duties. For example, a functional purchasing procedure may specify details about what a buyer must go through to develop a purchase contract: the number of purchase agreement copies required, distribution and storage locations of the signed agreement, signature requirements, or a buyer's authority to enter into a purchase agreement without approval from higher management. Procedures help ensure that a function conducts business in a consistent manner by providing a level of detail greater than that provided by a policy. A later section discusses specific purchasing policies and procedures in detail.

The lowest level of the policy hierarchy includes the rules and regulations that constrain or direct behavior. While the operating procedures detail how to accomplish some business-related task, the rules and regulations, often called *organizational laws*, specify certain acceptable levels of individual behavior. Rules and regulations are specific and provide a minimum of interpretation and flexibility. For example, an organization may have a major policy prohibiting certain types of dangerous or inappropriate behavior—for example, horseplay, threatening other employees, running through a plant, gambling, or fighting. Contracts with employees often specify or clarify rules and regulations.

Although the primary discussion of this chapter concerns itself with purchasing policies and procedures, it is necessary to gain a general understanding of the role of policies. This helps us understand exactly where purchasing policies and procedures fit within the organizational framework and the general policy hierarchy.

PURCHASING POLICIES—PROVIDING GUIDANCE AND DIRECTION

Purchasing management develops policies to provide guidance and support to the professional purchasing and support staff. These policies are general outlines clarifying purchasing management's position on a subject. While many purchasing policies exist, most fall into one of five categories:

- Policies defining the role of purchasing
- Policies defining the conduct of purchasing personnel
- Policies defining social and minority business objectives
- Policies defining buyer-seller relationships
- Policies defining operational issues

The following discussion does not include all possible policies. Organizations will also develop policies to meet unique operational requirements.

Policies Defining the Role of Purchasing

This set of policies defines purchasing's authority. It usually addresses the objectives of the purchasing function and defines the responsibilities of the various buying levels. These policies often serve as a general or broad policy statement from which more detailed or specific policies evolve.

Origin and Scope of Purchasing Authority Personnel at all levels must be aware of purchasing's authority to conduct business and to represent organizational interests. An executive committee usually grants this authority and develops this policy. This policy may also detail the authority of purchasing to delegate certain tasks or assignments to other departments or functions.

An important section of this policy describes the areas where purchasing authority does or does not exist. The policy may exclude the purchasing function from any responsibility for purchasing real estate, medical insurance policies, or other areas where purchasing may not have direct expertise. However, purchasing is increasingly becoming involved in all types of purchases. This policy outlines the overall authority of purchasing as granted by the executive committee while describing the limits to that authority.

Objectives of the Purchasing Function A policy describing the general objectives or principles guiding the purchasing process often appears early in the policy manual. The following describes one company's purchasing objectives or principles:

- To select suppliers that meet purchase and performance requirements
- To purchase material and services that comply with engineering and quality standards
- To promote buyer-seller relations and to encourage supplier contribution
- To treat all suppliers fairly and ethically
- To work closely with other departments
- To conduct purchasing operations so they enhance community and employee relations
- To support all corporate objectives and policies
- To maintain a qualified purchasing staff and to develop the professional capabilities of that staff

While these objectives or principles appear broad, they are important because they set forth, in writing, management's commitment to a higher level of purchasing behavior. These principles are also important because they give rise to other policies that directly support purchasing activities.

Corporate Purchasing Office Responsibilities It is also useful to understand the duties and responsibilities of the central or corporate purchasing office (if a central office exists). This policy may also detail the relationship of the corporate office to purchasing centers located at the divisional, business unit, or plant level. The corporate purchasing office is usually a staff position directing, supporting, and/or co-ordinating the purchasing effort. This policy can provide guidance concerning the role of the corporate purchasing staff in these areas:

- Carry out executive policies.
- Develop and publish functional purchasing and material policies and procedures to support efficient and effective purchasing operations at all levels.
- Coordinate strategy development between purchasing departments or centers to maximize purchasing leverage of critical commodities.
- Evaluate the effectiveness of purchasing operations.
- Provide expert support to purchasing departments (i.e., international sourcing assistance, contract negotiations, systems development).
- Perform other tasks typically associated with a corporate support staff.

Exhibit 4.2 illustrates a policy detailing corporate purchasing office responsibilities.

Purchasing Policy on Cross-Functional Decisions Business decisions involving more than one function or department are becoming more commonplace today. The decision about whether to make or buy an item or service, for example, is receiving a great deal of attention. Purchasing plays a major role in the make-or-buy process and may have a policy detailing its responsibility in this area. This policy may also outline executive management's philosophy about the make-or-buy process. Management's goal may be to use its own manufacturing facilities if, over the long run, the company can produce the item at competitive quality and cost levels. Another policy may define purchasing's involvement in new-product development, or the role that suppliers play during that process. Policies that are structured strictly within functional areas may inadvertently encourage strict functional behavior.

Policies Defining the Conduct of Purchasing Personnel

These policies outline management's commitment to ethical and honest behavior while guiding personnel who are confronted with difficult situations. Some business practices are technically not illegal but are potentially unethical or questionable. Because of this, purchasing management must develop policies that provide guidance in these gray areas. Since purchasing personnel act as legal agents and representatives, they must uphold the highest standards as defined by executive policy and the law.

Ethics Policy Most organizations, particularly medium- and larger-sized ones, have a written policy describing management's commitment to ethical purchasing behavior. The opening vignette in this chapter highlighted what was clearly an ethical dilemma. Chapter 16 discusses purchasing ethics in considerable detail.

Reciprocity Policy A formal policy often exists detailing management's opposition to reciprocal purchase agreements. Reciprocity, discussed in the purchasing ethics section of Chapter 16, occurs when suppliers are pressured to purchase the buyer's products or services as a condition of securing a purchase contract. A reciprocity policy

EXHIBIT 4.2   *Example of a Functional Purchasing Policy*

ABC Technologies
Purchasing Policy

Policy Number: 2   Applies to: Corporate Staff
                                       Divisional Purchasing
                                       Plant Buyers
Date: 1-1-01

Subject: Corporate Purchasing Office Responsibilities

This policy outlines the responsibilities and authority of the Corporate Purchasing office and staff and its relationship to Division Purchasing and Buying Units.

Executive policy E-7, sets forth the principles supporting the organization and management of ABC Technologies and its operating Divisions:

ABC Technologies, by executive policy, is organized on a line and staff basis, with divisional operations largely decentralized. It is corporate policy to assign responsibility and delegate authority concerning operational matters to executive divisional management. All responsibilities not delegated to divisional management remain as official responsibilities of the corporate staff.

The Corporate Purchasing staff is one of the corporate staffs referred to in executive policy E-7. As such, it retains responsibility for the following functions, activities, and duties:

- Responsibility for carrying out and ensuring that each division and buying unit adheres to each corporate policy as stated by executive management.
- Responsibility for developing and publishing functional purchasing and material policies and procedures. The purpose of this is to support efficient and effective purchasing operations throughout the company.
- Coordinate strategy development between divisional purchasing and other buying units to support companywide efficiencies and reduced duplication of effort.
- Develop systems to evaluate companywide purchasing performance and operations.
- Provide expert support to purchasing departments and buying units throughout the company.
- Assume responsibility for (1) tasks typically associated with a corporate support staff and (2) tasks not directly assigned to divisional or plant purchasing.

This policy reaffirms the autonomy of the divisions and other buying centers to conduct operational purchasing duties and functions. It also reaffirms the company's commitment to efficient companywide purchasing operations through a strong corporate support staff.

---

usually describes management's opposition to the practice and lists the type of behavior to avoid. Personnel must *not* engage in behavior that suggests any of the following:

- A buyer gives preference to suppliers who purchase from the buyer's organization.
- A buyer expects suppliers to purchase the buying company's products as a condition for securing a purchase contract.
- A buyer looks favorably on competitive bids from suppliers who purchase the buyer's products.

This area requires an executive management policy because disagreement occurs regarding this topic. Reciprocity is relatively easy to control once management issues a policy on the subject.

Contacts and Visits to Suppliers An understanding must exist regarding direct visits or other communication contacts with suppliers or potential suppliers. This policy should address not only purchasing personnel but also other departments or functions that visit or contact suppliers. Purchasing wants to control unauthorized or excessive contacts or visits because these can impose an unnecessary burden on suppliers. Also, unauthorized supplier visits or contacts by nonpurchasing personnel undermine purchasing's legitimate authority as the principal commercial contact with suppliers. Purchasing wants to avoid situations where suppliers might interpret statements and opinions offered by nonpurchasing personnel as commitments.

Former Employees Representing Suppliers Occasionally, an employee may leave to work for a supplier. This is a concern because the former employee probably has knowledge about business plans or other confidential information, which may provide an unfair advantage over other suppliers. One way to address this issue is to establish a policy prohibiting business transactions with suppliers who employ former employees known to have inside or confidential information. This exclusion can range from a period of a few months to several years, depending on the employee and the situation. Another possibility involves including a clause in the employee's original employment contract prohibiting employment with a competitor or a supplier for a specified time. This can offset the advantage a former employee may have from his or her previous employment.

Reporting of Irregular Business Dealings with Suppliers This policy may establish a reporting mechanism for buyers or other employees to report irregular business dealings. Examples of irregular dealings include accepting bribes from suppliers, cronyism, accepting late bids, and other types of behavior that are not considered part of the normal course of business. The policy can specify the proper office to report the irregularity, the safeguards in place to protect the reporting party, and the need to report suspected irregularities as soon as possible. This policy sends the message that management will not tolerate irregular business transactions involving employees.

Policies Defining Social and Minority Business Objectives

In the long run it is likely in a purchaser's best interest to use its power to support social and minority business objectives. This may include supporting and developing local sources of supply or awarding business to qualified minority suppliers. Purchasing's actions help shape a perception of good corporate citizenship. Pursuing social objectives may require the development of policies specifically defining management's position.

Supporting Minority Business Suppliers Management's position concerning transactions with minority business suppliers provides guidance to buyers. A minority business supplier is a business that is run or partially owned by an individual classified as a minority by the U.S. government. Such policies typically state that these suppliers should receive a fair and equal opportunity to participate in the purchasing process. The policy may outline a number of steps to achieve the policy's objectives, including

- Setting forth management's commitment on this subject
- Evaluating the performance potential of small or disadvantaged suppliers to identify those qualifying for supplier assistance
- Inviting small and disadvantaged suppliers to bid on purchase contracts
- Establishing a minimum percentage of business to award to qualified small and disadvantaged suppliers
- Outlining a training program to educate buyers regarding the needs of the small and disadvantaged supplier

Policies supporting disadvantaged suppliers are common in contracts with the U.S. government, which encourages awarding subcontracts to small and disadvantaged suppliers. Other companies have formal procedures for including minority business suppliers. For instance, one large pharmaceutical company has developed a process for identifying minority suppliers, which includes the following questions:

- Is the supplier fully qualified?
- Does the supplier satisfy U.S. government criteria defining a minority business?
- Does the supplier meet our standard performance requirements?
- Is the supplier price competitive?
- How much business can we give the supplier given its capacity?

Links and information having to do with minority business development can be found at http://www.nmsdcfl.com/business.htm

Environmental Issues A set of policies outlining a position related to environmental issues is becoming increasingly important. Moreover, governments are now requiring such policies by law. These policies include the use of recycled material, strict compliance with local, state, and federal regulations, and proper disposal of waste material. The Clean Air Act of 1990 imposes large fines on producers of ozone-depleting substances and foul-smelling gases, and the Clinton administration introduced laws regarding recycling content in industrial materials. As a result, buyers must consider a supplier's ability to comply with environmental regulations as a condition for selection. This includes, but is not limited to, the proper disposal of hazardous waste.

A good example of environmental policy involves the chemical industry, which traditionally has been a major source of industrial pollution. This industry knows that if it does not adopt a set of environmental policies, then government regulators will initiate strict regulations. Dow Chemical, for example, considers environmental concerns a critical feature of its policies and procedures. As a member of the Chemical Manufacturers Association, Dow is a participant in Responsible Care, a program initiative that addresses a community's concerns regarding chemicals, including their manufacture, transportation, use and safe disposal, health and safety, prompt reporting of environmental accidents, and counseling of customers. These concerns were initially influenced and developed from the Valdez principles.[4] Supplier evaluation involves assessing the environmental policies of suppliers (primarily other major chemical companies). A key element of evaluation involves understanding and assessing the environmental risk associated with the particular chemical being purchased. Dow searches for suppliers who are "green" according to industry standards.

The Good Practice Example at the end of this chapter describes Home Depot's new policy regarding wood sourcing. Additional information on the responsible care program and Dow Chemical's commitment to the environment can be found at http://www.dow.com.

Policies Defining Buyer-Seller Relationships

The policies that are part of buyer-seller relationships cover a wide range of topics. Each topic, however, relates to some issue involving the supply base.

Supplier Relations The principles that guide relations with suppliers are often contained in a policy stating that buyer-seller relationships are essential for economic success. Furthermore, relationships based on mutual trust and respect must underlie the purchasing effort. This policy often describes a number of principles that support positive relationships, including

- Treating suppliers fairly and with integrity
- Supporting and developing those suppliers who work to improve quality, delivery, cost, or other performance criteria
- Providing prompt payment to suppliers
- Encouraging suppliers to submit innovative ideas with joint sharing of benefits
- Developing open communication channels
- Informing suppliers as to why they did not receive a purchase contract
- Establishing a fair process to award purchase contracts

Qualification and Supplier Selection Buyers may require guidance regarding the performance criteria used to evaluate potential sources of supply or to evaluate an existing supplier for an item not traditionally provided by suppliers. Management wants to make sure that supplier selection occurs only after purchasing thoroughly reviews all criteria. Supplier selection criteria include

- Price/cost competitiveness
- Product quality
- Delivery performance
- Financial condition

SOURCING SNAPSHOT

When Is a Minority Supplier Not a Minority Supplier?

Most large purchasers have policies promoting the use of minority and histori-cally disadvantaged suppliers. At a time when courts and voters have scaled back racial-preference programs, corporate America is headed along a different road. The National Minority Supplier Development Council, whose represen-tatives are drawn from the biggest U.S. corporations, certifies "minority owner-ship." Its 80-member board is likely to loosen its definition of minority-owned, which in government and corporate procurement has always required at least 51% minority ownership. Most board members expect the new requirement will be closer to 20%, along with proof of minority management.

Proposed changes in what defines minority ownership would allow minority firms to drastically diminish their minority ownership in order to go public. Not all the corporate representatives on the council, however, favor changing the definition of minority ownership. William Blue, who manages DuPont Company's efforts to increase minority contracting says, "If a company reaches the level where it needs to get institutional equity, great, go for it. But they aren't minority-owned anymore." According to Blue, if a firm wants to preserve its minority-owned status, it should sell equity to the growing numbers of pools of minority investors.

For smaller minority-owned firms unable to attract big infusions of capital, the idea that large, publicly held firms need a leg-up as a minority firm does not seem fair. Scott Flores, the Hispanic president of Die Cut Technologies, a Denver-based gasket-manufacturing firm with annual revenue of $4 million, says, "The rich will get richer" under the rule change, while "99% of the other minorities will get less business. And the Big Three (U.S. automakers) will say, 'Gee, we've reached our goals, we don't have to make an effort to mentor small business.'"

Source: Adapted from Paulette Thomas, "Number Crunching: What Does It Take to Deem a Business 'Minority-Owned'?" *Wall Street Journal*, July 26, 1999, A1.

- Engineering and manufacturing technical competence
- Management of its own suppliers
- Management capability
- Ability to work with the customer
- Potential for innovation

This policy may also outline management's position on single and multiple sourc-ing or the use of longer-term purchase agreements. It may also acknowledge purchas-ing's need to rely on nonpurchasing personnel to evaluate technical or financial crite-ria during the supplier selection process. For example, Nortel Networks has a policy that only those suppliers deemed acceptable and placed in a component database can be used. Nortel's site for supplier management (http://www.nortelnetworks.com/prd/suppliers/index.html) provides a self-assessment program that allows suppliers to assess their suitability as potential suppliers, as well as cost improvement suggestion information. Instead of just approving suppliers, the components provided by suppliers are approved as well. Each component in the database is assigned a classification code, based on the extent of risk associated with sourcing that component. Engineers consult this database whenever an engineering change or a new design is being considered to determine the impact of the change on current supply strategies. There are four possible categories in which a component can be classified: (1) preferred, (2) acceptable, (3) special purpose, and (4) not for new designs.

A *preferred* component is the optimum choice for use by product designers. Categorization of a component under this code indicates there are multiple sources available, that the sources are approved and preferred, and that the component meets all specifications implicit in the design. This category is most likely to be attained at the later growth and maturity portions of the component life cycle. In cases where a component meets most but not all of the criteria necessary for preferred status, it is considered *acceptable*. If only a single approved source exists, the component is classified as acceptable rather than preferred. *Special purpose* components are not intended for general use, but refer to those components that are used in specialized applications. Examples include new components requiring special treatment such as hazardous chemicals and gases, or high frequency or power applications. Components in the *not for new designs* category are least desirable, and fail to meet one or more of the evaluation criteria. As such, engineers should not use them in new designs or redesigns, and should instead identify substitutes in these cases.[5]

Principles and Guidelines for Awarding Purchase Contracts The process for selecting and awarding purchase contracts is central to effective purchasing. This policy covers a number of critical topics:

- Buyer's authority to award a contract within a certain dollar limit
- Conditions where the competitive bid process is and is not acceptable
- Conditions outlining the use of competitive bids
- Process of analyzing sealed competitive bids
- Conditions prompting the sourcing of an item to other than the lowest bid supplier
- Conditions prompting a rebid
- Operating guidelines that pertain to the negotiation of contracts with suppliers

Although there is a trend toward less reliance on competitive bids and more on negotiated longer-term agreements, many contracts are still awarded through the competitive bid process. Routine items available from many different sources are generally purchased through competitive bidding. It is important for purchasing to have a standard set of guidelines for awarding purchase contracts to suppliers. These guidelines provide assurances that purchasing awards contracts based on a fair set of principles.

Labor or Other Difficulties at Suppliers Management's position concerning supply or labor disruptions as well as possible courses of action provide guidelines during supplier strikes or other labor problems. One issue this policy can address is the legal removal of company-owned tooling from suppliers during a strike so that the buyer can establish an additional source during the interruption. The policy can provide details about this issue, which can be part of the contract with the supplier, to suspend temporarily any purchase contracts or outstanding orders with a striking supplier. An example of this occurred in 1997 when seat maker Johnson Controls experienced a strike. One of its major customers, Ford, began temporarily purchasing the seats from Johnson Controls's competition—Lear Corporation—to avoid a shutdown.

Other Policies Dealing with Buyer-Seller Relations Organizations must be cautious about liabilities associated with accepting and using ideas provided by suppliers interested in doing business with a purchaser. A policy may state the buyer accepts unsolicited proposals from interested suppliers only on a nonconfidential basis with no obligation or liability to the provider. Suppliers may even have to sign a waiver releasing the purchaser from liabilities in this area.

Another policy can clarify management's position on financial obligations to suppliers who provide early product design involvement. A buyer may request that suppliers submit cost-reduction ideas during the early phases of new-product design. This policy can provide guidance about the extent of financial obligation to suppliers, particularly to suppliers whose ideas were not accepted.

In cases where purchasing is attempting to integrate suppliers into the new-product development process, many companies have established a policy manual written by engineering, marketing, manufacturing, and purchasing. This manual specifies the steps when developing a new product and the triggers in the process that identify when and how suppliers should be part of the process. The policy may also specify the types of nondisclosure agreements used, the criteria for sharing patents, and other joint product development policies.

Policies Defining Operational Issues

The broadest of the five purchasing policy categories involves policies that provide guidance for operational issues that confront buyers during the normal performance of duties.

Hazardous Materials Purchasers must take an active role controlling hazardous waste. During the last ten years, new regulations and policies appeared, outlining the proper handling of toxic and hazardous material. In the period from 1899 to 1950, the U.S. government passed seven laws that involved environmental protection. From 1976 to 1978, nine laws passed Congress. More recent legislation has further emphasized the need for business to have a carefully considered response to environmental initiatives. Environmental policy is an issue that purchasers must take seriously or risk potentially large legal and financial liabilities.

The purchase of waste disposal services is often a purchasing responsibility. For companies that routinely use or produce hazardous materials, the law requires a policy that outlines in detail the legal requirements and conditions for the handling of toxic waste. Failure to have such a policy is considered a federal offense. This policy details the responsibility of purchasing to select only those contractors who conform to local, state, and federal laws. Before awarding a contract for the hauling and disposing of dangerous materials, some policies require that the contractor provide the following detailed information:

- Evidence of valid permits and licenses
- Specification of the types of disposal services the contractor is licensed to provide
- Evidence of safeguards to prevent accidents along with contingency plans and preparations if a hazardous spill occurs
- Detail of the specific process used to control hazardous material once it exits a buyer's facilities
- Evidence of adequate liability insurance on the part of the contractor
- Evidence that the waste transporter uses properly certified disposal sites

Selecting a qualified hazardous waste contractor is critical. On a larger scale, this requires an environmental policy that is clearly expressed. Increased government and public awareness of environmental issues is driving this issue.

Supplier Responsibility for Defective Material This policy outlines supplier responsibility for defective material shipments or other types of nonperformance. It usually details the various charge-back costs for which suppliers are liable in the event of nonperformance. These costs can include the cost of material rework, repackaging for return shipment, additional material handling costs, return shipping costs, or costs associated with lost or delayed production. Purchasers operating in a just-in-time environment are usually quite strict about the charges associated with supplier-caused material problems. A single defective shipment in a just-in-time production environment can shut down an entire production process.

Defective material policies may also outline purchasing's authority to negotiate and settle claims against suppliers. This requires purchasing to carefully review each nonperformance to determine a fair settlement. This policy provides protection for the purchaser due to supplier-caused problems.

Purchased Item Comparisons Another policy may outline management's position concerning the continued evaluation of purchased items. This evaluation may require buyers to periodically review purchased items or services to determine if existing suppliers still maintain market leadership. This evaluation can include cost, quality, delivery, and technological comparisons.

For items purchased through the competitive bid process, purchased item comparisons often mean requesting new bids for an item from qualified suppliers. This policy usually states how often management expects competitive comparisons and the general procedure for conducting a comparison. For items on longer-term purchase contracts, purchased item comparisons may involve benchmarking or comparing cost performance against leading competitors.

Other Operating Policies Many other operating policies guide purchasing. Additional examples include policies that outline

- Compliance with U.S. laws and regulations
- Restrictions on source selection outside of the purchasing function
- The proper disposal of material assets
- Purchasing's legal right to terminate a purchase contact or order
- Supplier responsibility for premium transportation costs
- Supplier-requested changes in contractual terms and conditions
- Supplier use of trademarks or logos

All the policies just discussed have something in common. They clarify management's position on a topic while providing guidance to the personnel responsible for carrying out the policy. The outcome of these policies should be consistent actions on the part of personnel at different locations or organizational levels. A basic set of policy statements outlining management's position on different topic areas should be readily available and distributed. All policies should be regularly reviewed and updated. Increasingly, progressive companies are posting their policies on their Intranet.

${\mathscr{P}}$URCHASING PROCEDURES

Procedures are the operating instructions detailing functional duties or tasks, and a procedure manual is really a "how-to" manual. A large purchasing department may have hundreds of procedures detailing the accepted practice for carrying out an activity. It is beyond the scope of this discussion to present but a brief overview of purchasing procedures, particularly since no uniform set of principles exist to guide the development of purchasing procedures. Every organization develops a unique set of operating instructions to meet its own specific requirements.

A procedure manual serves a number of important purposes. First, the manual is a reference guide for purchasing personnel and is especially valuable to new employees who require explanation about how to accomplish different activities or assignments. For experienced personnel, the manual provides clarification or simply reinforces knowledge about different topics. Second, the manual provides consistency and order by documenting the steps and activities required to perform a task. A well-documented procedure manual supports efficient operations and is usually more extensive and detailed than the policy manual. The procedure manual may also specify industry best practices to follow that are identified through benchmarking comparisons with leading firms.

Simplifying procedures should be a goal whenever possible. A primary emphasis should be on the development of a concise, accurate, and complete set of operating instructions. A word of caution is in order here. A procedure is ineffective if it specifies too many steps to carry out or presents unnecessary detail. Many companies have found that the traditional procedure for developing new products does not support cooperation between departments. Existing procedures are being replaced by streamlined procedures that encourage timeliness and responsiveness. As with a policy, management must review and evaluate its procedures to make sure that they are timely and accurate and that they contribute to rather than hinder performance.

Procedures often include information considered essential for successfully deploying purchasing strategies. While no standard or established format for purchasing procedures exists, many contain basically the same types of information. First, the purchasing department usually assigns a number, an effective date, and a subject heading to each procedure. The first section of the procedure is usually introductory in nature, setting forth the purpose of the procedure as it relates to the particular subject. Also, if the procedure is lengthy and includes many sections, it might require a table of contents or some other subject directory. It is also common to define key terms at this point. A second section often summarizes any functional or corporate policies relating to the procedure. Recall that a procedure resides below a policy in the hierarchy. Many procedures operationally define corporate or functional policies.

Another section specifies the position, department, or area responsible for the contents or directions of the procedure. For example, it may specify that a buyer is responsible for placing company-owned tooling with external suppliers. A final section often describes the actual procedure. This is usually the longest and most detailed part of the procedure—it is the nuts and bolts of the document. It describes the instructions, directives, and activities personnel must follow when completing a task.

Exhibit 4.3 shows a purchasing procedure for a major high-technology company.[6] This procedure, which details purchasing's authority to select sources of supply, includes the different sections just discussed. As with all procedures, this procedure will require future review to verify its timeliness and effectiveness. Increasingly, engineering and purchasing are locating closer together to reduce product development cycle times. When this occurs, the determination of source selection often occurs by a team rather than an individual. Existing procedures may no longer apply when well-established processes are changed.

Purchasing Procedural Areas

Procedures exist to cover just about any subject involving purchasing. Most purchasing procedures correspond to one of the following areas.

The Purchasing Cycle   Existing procedures usually document the proper steps to follow during each step of the purchasing cycle or process. The purchasing process, particularly for routinely purchased items, generally consists of the five steps detailed in Chapter 2: (1) identify or anticipate material and service needs, (2) evaluate suppliers, (3) select suppliers, (4) release and receive purchase requirements, and (5) continuously measure and manage supplier performance.

EXHIBIT 4.3   *Examples of a Functional Purchasing Procedure*

ABC Technologies
Purchasing Procedure

Procedure Number: 4.3   Date: 10/1/00

Subject: Sourcing Requests from Engineering

I.   INTRODUCTION

This procedure outlines the steps to follow when purchasing receives a material request from engineering with a Specified Source form attached (form SS-1). Processing a specified source request differs from processing a suggested supplier source listing. The purpose of this procedure is to evaluate engineering source requests in a fair, timely, and thorough manner.

II. RELATED POLICY

Executive policy grants purchasing the authority to obtain material, components, and other items that meet the delivery, quality, lowest total cost, and other competitive requirements of the company. Restriction of this authority can have a serious impact on purchasing's ability to perform its required duties and assignments. Certain conditions, however, may warrant the specification of sources by departments other than purchasing.

III. RESPONSIBILITY

It is the direct supervisor or manager's responsibility of the buyer that receives the Specified Source form to evaluate and determine the final disposition of the specified source request in accordance with the following procedure.

IV. PROCEDURE

A. Upon receipt of a SS-1 form submitted by engineering, purchasing departmental management verifies that each section of the form is properly completed.

B. Purchasing management must verify that the requested item is not currently an actively purchased item. If the item is currently purchased, purchasing must inform engineering of this.

C. For items not currently purchased, purchasing management must evaluate engineering's reasons for specifying a source for the required item. It is also within purchasing's authority to identify and evaluate equally qualified sources if the reasons for the specified source are found not to reflect acceptable purchasing or market principles.

D. If engineering's source request is accepted, purchasing management signs the Specified Source form and processes promptly the purchase order.

E. Rejected requests are sent back to engineering with reasons. In order to promote close working relations between purchasing and engineering, purchasing will respond to specified source requests within a reasonable amount of time. Furthermore, purchasing agrees to work with engineering to identify sources that satisfy engineering's technical requirements while meeting the commercial requirements of the company.

Proper Use of Purchasing Forms A typical purchasing function relies on many forms to conduct its business. Recall that Chapter 2 provided examples of commonly used purchasing documents and forms. The procedure manual is a valuable source for a description of the proper use of each form, the detailed meaning of each information field on the form, and a description of the proper handling and storage of each form. For the latter point, this usually includes information about where, and for how long, to store each copy of the form along with required signatures or approvals. Storage can be manual or electronic. The movement toward electronic storage of forms requires major revisions to procedures relating to this subject.

The Development of Legal Contracts The development of legal purchase contracts can require dozens of pages and address many topics. Most organizations have specific procedures for contracting with outside suppliers and individuals for goods and services. It is the purchasing employee's responsibility to become familiar with and follow the procedures covering legal contracts. Some of the topics discussed in legal contract procedures include:

- Basic features of the standard purchase contract
- Basic contract principles
- Execution and administration of agreements
- Essential elements of the contract
- Ensuring contract compliance and performance
- Formal competitive contracting procedures
- Contract development process
- Examples of sample agreements
- Legal definitions
- Use of formal contract clauses

The procedures covering the development, execution, and enforcement of legal purchase agreements and contracts are usually quite detailed (much like the contracts themselves!). A purchaser may rely on a specialized staff to provide assistance in this complex procedural area.

Operational Procedures Operational procedures provide instruction and detail across a broad range of topics. A procedure can be developed for any operational topic that benefits from following a specific set of steps, requires consistent action to promote efficiency and consistency, or carries out the directives of functional or executive policies. The following procedure topics appear in the material manual of a Fortune 500 company:

- Control of material furnished to suppliers
- Storage of purchasing documents
- Supplier qualification process
- Use of purchasing computerized systems
- Analysis of competitive quotations
- Use of single source selection
- Order pricing and analysis requirements

GM Limits Supplier-Provided Perks

General Motors has adopted a stringent new policy forbidding employees from accepting free meals, hockey tickets, golf outings and most other gifts and gratuities from suppliers. Some suppliers feel this will hurt their efforts to establish personal relationships with buyers. Already, supplier-sponsored business luncheons are getting smaller, and buyers are avoiding perks such as supplier hospitality tents at golf outings. Some anonymous suppliers said that the new rules would get bypassed because they are unrealistic. Reports from vendors suggest that GM employees are conscious of and abiding by the new rules by paying for their own lunches. Ford, Chrysler, and Honda's policies on entertainment are more lax, while Procter & Gamble does not allow employees to accept tickets to shows or sporting events.

Source: Adapted from David Sedgwick, "GM's New No-No Freebies Code Raises Anxiety Level for Staff and Suppliers," *Automotive News*, July 22, 1996, 1.

- Cost analysis procedures
- Acceptable cost reduction techniques and documentation
- Intracompany transactions
- Processing and handling of overshipments
- Supplier acknowledgment of purchase orders
- Disposition of nonconforming purchased material
- Removal of company-owned tooling from supplier

This is a small sample of the different operational topics that often require documented procedures. The topic of purchasing procedures is broad and sometimes mundane. However, an effective set of procedures can result in the efficient use of a purchasing professional's time. Procedures serve as a ready reference covering a host of questions. They also ensure that employees follow the same basic steps when performing similar tasks.

GOOD PRACTICE EXAMPLE
Home Depot Changes Purchasing Policy—Promises to Reduce Wood Sourced from Endangered Forests

■ ■ ■

The Home Depot, the world's largest home improvement retailer, took the occasion of its twentieth-anniversary celebration to announce a significant policy change regarding wood sourcing. President and CEO Arthur M. Blank used his keynote speech to Home Depot associates to highlight the next phase in the company's environmental commitment. Founded in 1978, the Home Depot today has 856 stores in the United States, Canada, Puerto Rico and Chile. Although the company sells less than 10% of the lumber in the world, it remains the largest single retailer of lumber.

"Our pledge to our customers, associates and stockholders is that Home Depot will stop selling wood products from environmentally sensitive areas. Home Depot embraces its responsibility as a global leader to help protect endangered forests," Blank said. By the end of 2002, the company plans to eliminate from its stores wood from endangered or old-growth areas with preference given to certified wood. Old-growth wood comes from forests that have never been logged commercially and are the most endangered forests on earth. They include lumber from ancient redwood and cedar forests in the Pacific Northwest, the temperate rain forests of British Columbia, old-growth stands from Southeast Asia, and big leaf mahogany from the Amazon. To carry the certified label, wood must be tracked from the forest, through manufacturing and distribution, to the customer, and must ensure a balance of social, economic, and environmental factors.

"This is indeed a bold step in advancing the cause of independent certification and responsible wood use throughout the industry," said David A. Ford, president of the Certified Forest Products Council, whose group connects buyers and sellers of products coming from certified well-managed forests. "We're pleased that Home Depot is taking decisive action to protect endangered forested ecosystems around the world."

Implementing this new policy is a huge challenge for Home Depot as well as its suppliers—made more complicated by the fact that the world supply of certified wood is extremely limited. So far, only about 1% of the world's wood is certified. "It's not impossible, but it's an immediate challenge," said Brian Shillington, a spokesperson with Canfor Corporation, the Home Depot's largest Canadian supplier of wood, which currently does not produce certified lumber. "We're in the process of getting areas certified, but we're struggling with the rules, how they'll be established and by whom."

The Home Depot has already begun favoring lumber suppliers offering certified wood that has been tracked from the forest where it was cut to the store to ensure that it did not come from environmentally sensitive forests. The company expects to get independent audits on where the wood is sourced. "It's a big challenge, but this is a responsibility, to give back to the community," said Annette Vershune, of Home Depot of Canada.

Environmental, economic, and social factors will be considered during the sourcing process, the company said. Home Depot officials said they have long planned to phase out the purchase of old-growth wood, which is used in a variety of products, including hammers, rakes, and doors. "We've been working on this for years and years and are now at a time when we feel we can make this work," said Jerry Shields, a senior public relations manager for Home Depot. "The forest industry is in a position where they can handle this."

Home Depot expects to use the power of its purchasing dollars to procure products that help preserve environmentally sensitive areas. The company is asking its vendors to help by dramatically increasing the supply of certified forest products. Home Depot is encouraging other home improvement retailers to follow its lead. The company expects its competitors to join the effort to save environmentally sensitive areas around the world and to promote alternative wood products. "We're also working to ensure that the transition is completely transparent to customers, and will not appreciably affect pricing or product availability. Our policy is rooted in environmental responsibility, and it makes good business sense because we believe people will see the value in what we're doing," CEO Blank said.

The company's change in policy may also be the result of public pressure. Conservation groups have accused the Home Depot of destroying irreplaceable woodlands in order to fill store shelves. Most recently, the environmental group Greenpeace focused its antilogging activities against the retailer, placing a giant Home Depot sign on a block of clear-cut land north of Vancouver, accusing the company of having a hand in the destruction of the world's remaining ancient forests. "It's about time Home Depot made this decision," said Darcy Riddell, a spokesperson with the Sierra Club of British Columbia, another environmental group that has also targeted the retailer for its use of environmentally sensitive wood. "Home Depot is a huge pin in the whole structure," she said.

The pledge was also hailed as a significant victory by the Rainforest Action Network (RAN), which for the last two years has led an international campaign against the retail giant's selling of wood from environmentally sensitive areas around the world. The group has picketed Home Depot stores in the United States and Canada and staged high-profile demonstrations at Home Depot's headquarters in Atlanta. RAN has urged the company to "go green" by phasing out sales of old-growth wood products. At a St. Patrick's Day demonstration at a Home Depot store in Canada, three protesters spent five hours chained by their necks to store shelves.

"Home Depot has taken a leadership role in the U.S. do-it-yourself industry. It is sending the message to lumber companies that it's barbaric to continue to cut down old-growth forests and is as outdated as slaughtering elephants for their ivory," said Michael Brune, old-growth campaign director for RAN, which is based in San Francisco. "Home Depot and other major retailers of old-growth wood no longer have a social license to convert 2,000-year-old trees into lawn furniture," Brune said. He said that Home Depot, as the world's largest retailer of old-growth wood, has now set an industry trend, which will compel other retailers who have not done so already to switch to certified wood products. "What Home Depot wants, the market will provide. This spells relief for endangered forests globally," said Brune. Fortune

EXHIBIT 4.4   *The Home Depot Environmental Responsibility Fact Sheet*

- The Home Depot offers many alternative products that provide environmental choices for consumers. Here are a few examples:
  - Finger-jointed moldings, casing trim, and door framing that use smaller wood pieces leading to increased wood efficiency
  - Paneling backed with chipboard, that uses waste and falloff from manufacturing processes
  - Royal Mahogany doors that come partially from an FSC certified forest
  - Plastic and composite decking materials
  - Insulation made from recycled glass or recycled newspapers
  - Garden hoses made from recycled tires
  - Flooring underlayment made from recycled newspapers
  - Garden planters made from recycled shrink-wrap
  - Energy efficient compact fluorescent bulbs
  - Biodegradable, enzyme-based drain cleaners

- The Home Depot will award more than $750,000 in grants to nearly 60 environmental non-profit organizations during 1999, to aid in the study of a variety of environmental issues. The company's focus areas include forestry and ecology, sustainable and green building practices, clean-up and recycling, lead poisoning prevention, and consumer education. Past grant recipients include the World Wildlife Fund, World Resources Institute, Keep America Beautiful, Conservation International, and Reforest the Tropics.

- The Home Depot has received numerous awards for environmental excellence, including the President's Council for Sustainable Development Award (1996), Vision for America award from Keep America Beautiful (1997), and an "A" rating for environmental programs for the Council on Economic Priorities' Corporate Report Card (1998).

- The Home Depot's environmental policies are formulated by the company's Environmental Council, consisting of senior-level managers representing every department in the company.

Source: The Home Depot public Website.

500 companies Nike, Kinko's, Johnson & Johnson, 3M, IBM, and Hewlett-Packard have all pledged to phase out the use of old-growth forest products.

This good practice example illustrates several points. First, policy changes often require changes to purchasing practices and operations. In this case, purchasing must now find reliable, certified suppliers that can provide cost-competitive products. Second, external parties can influence policies. In this case, environmental groups were relentless in their criticism of Home Depot's sourcing policies. Exhibit 4.4 highlights various steps that Home Depot has taken to demonstrate its support of environmental initiatives. Purchasing must play a major role in supporting the company's environmental policies and goals.

To find out what else Home Depot is doing to improve their commitment to the environment, go to http://www.homedepot.com/. The Website for the Forest Stewardship Council (FSC), an organization that provides certification in the environmentally and socially responsible management of the world's forests, is found at http://www.fscus.org The site provides principles and criteria for companies seeking certification, the benefits of certification, and more.

CONCLUSION

Understanding policies and procedures is essential for understanding how organizations operate and work. Policy is based on the idea that guidelines are documented and applicable to all the internal and external relations of an organization. A policy prescribes methods of accomplishment in terms broad enough for decision makers to exercise discretion while allowing employees to render judgment on an issue.[7] Well-formulated policies and procedures support efficient, effective, and consistent purchasing operations. On the other hand, policies and procedures that are out of date, require unnecessary actions, or do not address current issues or topics will not support effective purchasing operations

DISCUSSION QUESTIONS

1.   Why should an organization have a set of policies that outline the directives of executive and functional management?
2.   What are the advantages of policy development? What are some of the disadvantages and risks of policy development?
3.   Select a subject and write a brief policy statement that presents a position on that subject. What are the features or characteristics that your policy statement should have?
4.   How does an executive policy differ from a functional policy?
5.   How does a functional policy differ from a procedure?
6.   Why is it important to include a policy that outlines the origin and scope of purchasing authority? What might happen if such a policy did not exist?
7.   Why should management review its policies and procedures periodically? What are the potential consequences if management does not review policies and procedures?
8.   What are the benefits associated with a comprehensive policy and procedure manual?
9.   Discuss the concept of ethics. Why is the purchasing profession particularly sensitive to this topic?
10. What are the risks associated with backdoor buying and selling? Why is purchasing interested in controlling this business practice?
11. Do external groups affect purchasing policies? Provide examples of how groups can influence policy.
12. This chapter listed a number of different operational procedures. Describe and discuss three additional topic areas that might benefit from written procedures.

ADDITIONAL READINGS

Ethics Policy Statements for Purchasing, Supply, and Materials Management: Examples of Policies and Procedures. Tempe, AZ: National Association of Purchasing Management, a TECHnotes publication, 1995.

Procurement Policy Letters: A Compilation of Policies, 4th ed., Washington, DC: The Executive Office, 1992.

Purchasing Policies and Practices. Omaha: University of Nebraska, College of Continuing Studies, 1994.

U.S. Agency for International Development, *Statement of Procurement Policies.* Washington, DC: USAID, 1993.

ENDNOTES

1. W. H. Klein and D. C. Murphy, *Policy: Concepts in Organizational Guidance* (Boston: Little-Brown, 1973), 2.
2. E. F. Harrison, *Policy, Strategy, and Managerial Action* (Boston: Houghton Mifflin, 1986), 43.
3. G. A. Steiner, *Top Management Planning* (New York: Macmillan, 1969), 267, as quoted in Harrison, *Policy,* 44.
4. The Valdez principles are a set of guidelines established to help organizations develop environmentally sound decisions; they are named after the Exxon Valdez oil spill disaster in 1990.
5. Robert Handfield and Ronald Pannesi, "Managing Component Life Cycles in Dynamic Technological Environments," *International Journal of Purchasing and Materials Management* (Spring 1994): 20–27.
6. The name of this company is being withheld per the company's request.
7. Harrison, *Policy,* 3.

Purchasing as a Boundary-Spanning Function 5

NEC Integrates A Key Supplier in New-Product Development

Ryoji Furuya owns Sato Electronics, a supplier of metal machine parts. His largest client is the Nippon Electric Company (NEC). NEC makes many business machines, but its plant in Abiko, Japan, manufactures only fax and copy machines. During the 15 years that Sato and NEC have worked together, Sato has provided parts for many of NEC's fax machines. In fact, Sato Electronics supplies 90% of the metal press parts that make NEC's NEFAX 880e series fax. When planning the 880e and many of NEC's other fax machines, the two companies have worked together on design and development. Designers and engineers are an important part of this process, but so is NEC's purchasing department. Concurrent engineering with NEC suppliers began in the late 1990s in an effort to keep costs down, and ultimately design a higher quality fax machine.

Early in the development cycle for the NEFAX 880e, NEC purchasing managers visited the Sato facility. They wanted to determine whether Sato could make the parts NEC needed for the fax at a specified or target cost. A target cost for the entire product was developed based on marketing's input, and it was then broken down for different categories of parts based on historical costs. The target cost for the mechanical parts was further broken down into a target cost for each metal part needed to make the fax. When it was determined that Sato Electronics could supply almost all of the parts for the 880e at or below NEC's target cost, the two companies were able to move further, into the development and engineering phases.

At first, there was not a detailed design for the 880e. After general discussion, Ryoji Furuya submitted an initial design for the fax. As the development cycle evolved, the design became progressively tighter and more detailed. It started out with a basic frame and shape, and eventually was reduced to a set of detailed design specifications. At each stage of the design evolution, engineers from both companies worked together, with purchasing acting as a liaison. While engineering provided the technical information and specifications, purchasing personnel helped to coordinate meetings, and provided information on business volumes, pricing, cost management strategies, and contract specifics.

Many problems occurred in codesigning the product, including technical problems and difficulties in meeting the target cost. Furuya often traveled to NEC from his facility (more than three hours by train), but NEC engineers also visited Sato Electronics. There were meetings with mechanical engineers to discuss and resolve the problems. Purchasing also helped at this stage by facilitating brainstorming discussions and sharing their insights on further alternatives to reduce costs. In addition, a database maintained by purchasing that showed historical target costs for various plastic components was helpful in developing and refining target costs. All of this extra effort paid off for NEC by providing them with a highly successful product that was produced below the target cost.

→ → →

The joint venture has also paid off for Sato Electronics. In return for their cooperation and support, NEC mechanical design engineers have been using some of the same components for future generations of the product, and Sato will have the first opportunity at new business. Furuya has made several presentations to different NEC divisions to advertise the success of this project, which hopefully will generate additional business for his company. As he toured the NEC plant looking at the fax machines being assembled with his parts, he emphasized that "to succeed in concurrent engineering with NEC, we must open our know-how to meet their target cost. We know that we will benefit in the long run by sharing this information." Sato Electronics and NEC understand the interdependencies between them. They also understand the importance of relying on purchasing as a boundary-spanning function.

Different functions or groups within any organization must work together to achieve a wide range of common goals—from the reduction of product cost and improved product quality and delivery to the development of innovative new products. Purchasing plays an active role in supporting such performance objectives, interacting with and supporting the needs of groups within the organization and outside of it. It accomplishes this by professionally managing suppliers and developing close working relationships with different internal groups. The central theme of this chapter is that purchasing must be an integral member of teams that make decisions related to engineering, supply chain management, production, and new-product development. Companies that are able to capitalize on purchasing's knowledge and contribution should achieve a sustainable competitive advantage.

The first section of the chapter addresses purchasing's critical internal and external linkages with various groups, particularly the linkage between purchasing and engineering. The second section discusses the need to develop closer and more collaborative buyer-seller relationships. The third section discusses the cross-functional sourcing team—an increasingly important approach taken to achieve closer internal and external involvement in purchasing decisions. The final section focuses on purchasing's involvement in developing new products. Each section supports the central theme of this chapter: the need for purchasing to develop closer working relationships with other internal groups and suppliers.

PURCHASING LINKAGES

Purchasing must maintain a number of communication flows and linkages. Exhibit 5.1 illustrates the two-way linkages between purchasing and other key groups along with a sample of the information exchanged between these groups. The linkages between purchasing and other groups will become even stronger and more important as the role of purchasing continues to develop and evolve.

EXHIBIT 5.1   *Purchasing's Communications Flows and Linkages*

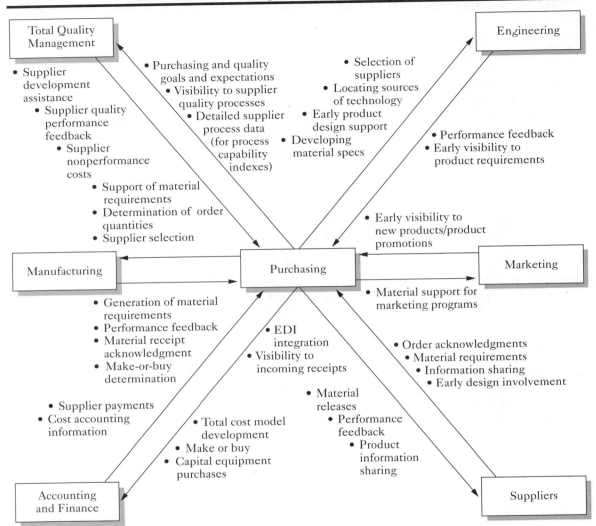

Purchasing's Internal Linkages

Purchasing's mission has been primarily as a support function to other groups and internal customers, particularly operations, in understanding their needs. Accordingly, other functions have had to recognize purchasing's need for information and the constraints under which purchasing operates. To facilitate information exchange, a number of critical communication linkages or interfaces have evolved between purchasing and other departments.

Operations Purchasing has always been a major supporter of the operations group. Because the links between operations and purchasing have been so close, it has not been unusual for purchasing to report directly to operations. Even today, purchasing still reports to operations in many firms, particularly smaller firms. This structure may also exist in firms where the cost of purchased materials is relatively low compared to other cost components.

A major link between operations and purchasing is through the development of operations strategy. Since purchasing directly supports manufacturing or operations effort, it must develop insights into its production strategies and plans. Purchasing's strategies and plans must be aligned with operation's plans. For example, purchasing must be aware of the components and services needed by operations as they plan to assemble a product or deliver a service. Because purchasing is responsible for sourcing the components to support operation's plans, purchasing managers must work with schedulers to coordinate the delivery of materials to the production site. Purchasing may also have to generate material releases and forecasts to suppliers to meet these schedules.

Purchasing and operations also maintain communication linkages through direct personnel contact. Some firms place purchasing departments or personnel directly at operating locations so purchasing can respond quickly to operation's needs. Even if purchasing does not report directly to operations, it can still support production needs directly.

Quality The purchasing-quality linkage has increased in importance during the last ten years. As firms externally source a larger percentage of finished product requirements, purchasing and total quality management must work together closely to ensure that suppliers perform as expected. Joint projects involving these two groups include supplier quality training, process capability studies, and corrective action planning. This linkage has become so important that some firms have placed the responsibility for supplier quality management directly with purchasing.

Engineering Perhaps the most important and challenging linkages exist between purchasing and engineering. The need to develop quality products in less time has drawn purchasing and engineering closer over time. There are still opportunities, however, to improve the level of interaction between these two groups.

Historically, engineering has been a very independent function. Some engineers do not accept that other functions should have direct input into product design. Engineers may not like "outsiders" affecting a product's design, its materials, or its component requirements. Some engineers also feel that buyers do not speak their "language" and therefore cannot contribute to the engineering design process in any meaningful way. This attitude is often prevalent in high-tech organizations that are primarily engineering-driven.

The need for greater teamwork has helped reduce the communication barriers between purchasing and engineering. The degree of cooperation between the two departments has increased over the last 15 years. Most professional engineers now recognize the contribution that a well-trained purchasing professional offers. Just as purchasing has historically supported the manufacturing group, it will also support the engineering group.

Firms can create stronger communication linkages and flows between purchasing and engineering in several ways. Engineers and buyers can develop open communication by working together on product development or supplier selection teams. Purchasing can also co-locate a buyer within the engineering group. The buyer can maintain direct contact with product and process engineers to respond quickly to their needs. A firm can also identify a liaison that coordinates interdepartmental communications and makes sure that each group is aware of the other group's activities. The two departments can hold regular meetings to report on items of mutual concern. Finally, many purchasing groups are recruiting commodity managers with very strong technical backgrounds, and who are able to "talk the talk and walk the walk" alongside their engineering counterparts. The key to a successful relationship between purchasing and engineering is open and direct communication, which in turn should lead to increased teamwork and trust.

Engineering looks to purchasing to perform certain tasks to support engineering's efforts. For example, engineering expects purchasing to identify the most technically and financially capable supplier for an item and to make sure each supplier meets engineering's quality and delivery targets. In addition, engineering expects purchasing to assess a supplier's production capabilities, actively involve suppliers early in the design process, and develop relationships that encourage a supplier to offer innovative ideas. Engineering also expects purchasing to identify sources of new technology that can be integrated into new products and services.

Accounting and Finance Purchasing also maintains linkages with the accounting and finance department. These linkages are not as strong, however, as the linkages with operations, engineering, and quality control. In fact, much of the communication linkage between purchasing and accounting today is electronic. For example, as purchasing transmits material releases to suppliers it also provides information of inbound material requirements to the accounting department. Upon receipt of the ordered material, the material control system updates the purchasing files from on-order or in-transit to a received status. The accounts payable system then receives the receipt information and compares the amount received to the amount ordered for payment.

Purchasing may require data from the cost accounting system. For example, purchasing must know handling and material rework costs for an item resulting from poor supplier performance. Purchasing usually does not maintain data about individual activity costs that can increase total cost. The purchasing performance measurement system relies on input from cost accountants to help calculate the total cost of an item, which is also important in make-or-buy decisions. Finally, purchasing must work closely with finance when making capital acquisition decisions.

Marketing/Sales Purchasing maintains indirect linkages with marketing. Many new-product ideas that purchasing must support start with marketing personnel who are the voice of a firm's end customers. Marketing also develops sales forecasts that convert into production plans. Purchasing must select suppliers and request material to support both marketing and production plans.

Legal Purchasing often confers with the legal department to seek counsel on specific elements of contracts. Issues that may arise include patent ownership terms in new-product development, intellectual property, product liability claims, antitrust, long-term contracts containing escape clauses, and other legal issues. Electronic commerce also raises many legal issues that require purchasing to consult with the legal department. Later chapters discuss legal issues in greater detail.

Environmental Management, Health, and Safety Purchasing may also confer with personnel from the environmental, health, and safety departments to ensure that suppliers are employing safe methods of transportation and are complying with Occupational Safety and Health Administration (OSHA) and safety regulations.

Purchasing's External Linkages

Purchasing also maintains extensive linkages with groups external to the firm—these linkages are in some respects more important than purchasing's internal linkages. Purchasing acts as a liaison with the external environment for multiple issues, including materials, new technology, information, and services. Purchasing, as well as marketing representatives on the outbound side, effectively create a firm's external reputation. The relationship between a buyer and a supplier will have a direct impact on how the supplier views the organization.

Suppliers Purchasing's primary external linkages are with its suppliers. It is purchasing's responsibility to maintain open communications with suppliers and select the suppliers with which to do business. Purchasing should be the primary communication linkage with suppliers, which does not exclude a non-purchasing department from contacting a supplier about a particular item or question. As discussed in Chapter 2, it is often better to bypass purchasing regarding certain communications between firms.

Purchasing has the responsibility to select suppliers and to remain the primary commercial linkage with the buying firm, including any matter involving the conditions of the purchase agreement or other issues of importance. Non-purchasing departments should not select, independently work with, or directly negotiate with potential suppliers for items for which the purchasing department is responsible.

Government Purchasing sometimes maintains communication linkages with governments at different levels and locations. For example, purchasing has an active role in international countertrade and often negotiates directly with foreign governments when establishing countertrade agreements. Purchasing may also need to consult with federal government agencies on various matters, including the Environmental Protection Agency, the Department of Defense, the Department of External Affairs, and other agencies that have authority over issues governed by public policy.

Local Communities Purchasing may have contact with local communities and leaders. Because purchasing controls a large budget, it has the potential to affect certain social goals. These goals include sourcing from local suppliers, awarding a certain percentage of business to qualified minority suppliers, and establishing ethical business practices in all dealings.

BUYER-SELLER RELATIONSHIPS

The traditional approach to buyer-seller relationships, which dates back to the 1920s for most industries, relies on using multiple suppliers for most purchased items. A purchaser might take three bids, then play one supplier against another to get the lowest price. This approach also features the use of short-term contracts where purchasers are unwilling to commit to a supplier over an extended period of time. This approach, while sometimes encouraging competition between suppliers, provides little incentive for a supplier to invest in longer-term productivity or quality improvements. Short-term contracts encourage profit maximizing as quickly as possible. Minimal commitment and trust exists between purchaser and seller, which further limits joint innovation and performance improvement. While this approach works for some items, it usually does not work well for high-value goods and service. It simply fails to tap into the value that closer relationships can create.

Advantages of Closer Buyer-Seller Relationships

A firm can gain many advantages by pursuing closer relationships with suppliers. The first is the development of *mutual trust,* which is the foundation of all strong relationships. While seemingly intangible, trust refers to the belief in the character, ability, strength, or truth of another party. Trust makes it possible, for example, for the seller to share cost data with a buyer, which can result in a joint effort to reduce a supplier's cost through a mutual sharing of ideas. Trust can also result in a supplier working with a purchaser early in the design of a new product.

Another advantage of closer buyer-seller relationships is the opportunity to evaluate which suppliers should receive longer-term contracts. Purchaser and seller both realize benefits from longer-term contracts. A long-term contract provides an incentive for a supplier to invest in new plants and equipment. This investment can make a supplier more efficient and result in lower costs to the purchaser. Longer-term contracts can also lead to the joint development of technology, risk sharing, and supplier capabilities.

Consider the following example provided by a purchasing manager from Honeywell Microswitch, who describes the advantages of working closely with suppliers:

Customers came to us with a product quality problem, and eventually we traced it back to the supplier. We had problems with the supplier's product, and we identified the problem as occurring because their process had shifted. Initially, we went to process quality assurance with the problem, and confronted them. At first, the supplier refused to believe that it was their fault, and claimed that we were not using the material correctly. Our group leader for the product

SOURCING SNAPSHOT

Relying on Buyer-Supplier Relationships for Supply Chain Improvement

Professional purchasers are starting to focus their cost-cutting and quality improvement goals with suppliers past their first tier. Reaching second- and third-tier suppliers is a challenging issue that requires a high level of trust with suppliers throughout a firm's supply chain. Increasingly, purchasers are looking to first-tier suppliers to exert leadership further down the supply chain. Often, manufacturers expect first-tier suppliers to provide highly engineered systems that interact with other systems in a final product. Faster product development time is a major goal as suppliers provide design engineering and prototypes earlier in the product development process. First-tier suppliers become more dependent on their supply base as they assume these new responsibilities. While training responsibility for lower-tier suppliers normally lies with first-tier suppliers, Honda of America provides training and support to important, value-adding second-tier suppliers if productivity improvements are feasible. General Motors Central Advanced Purchasing group evaluates cost and technology drivers of lower-tier suppliers to align them with tier-one suppliers. Training is an essential dimension in developing the supply chain. Original equipment manufacturers (OEMs) will show suppliers how to run workshops internally with expectations that this will spread throughout the supply base. Also, OEMs expect that cost, quality, and process control will improve. The recurring theme for success in such initiatives is complete trust between buyers and suppliers.

Source: Adapted from Kevin Fitzgerald, "Keys to Getting Past the First Tier," *Purchasing* (August 15, 1996): 64–65.

---

team found it difficult to coordinate with the supplier, and therefore requested an in-house person from their facility to work with us. The problem was resolved through many teleconferences, meetings at their facility, checking their processes, supplier teams coming to our plant, and many exchanges on specifications via e-mail, fax, etc. They identified the problem in their process, and since then they are performing very well. There was clearly a learning phase in transitioning from a traditional relationship, but resolving this problem clearly showed how to work together to strengthen our relationship.[1]

Clearly, quality problems such as this one cannot be resolved unless both firms are committed to the relationship.

Obstacles to Closer Buyer-Seller Relationships

A number of obstacles can prevent the development of closer relationships between a purchaser and a seller. A firm must evaluate whether these obstacles are present and identify ways to overcome them if the goal is to pursue closer interfirm cooperation.

Confidentiality The need for confidentiality regarding financial, product, and process information is the most frequently cited reason for not developing closer supplier relationships. Confidentiality is a concern for at least three reasons. Purchasing managers are sometimes reluctant to share critical information with suppliers who may also sell to competitors. There is also the possibility that a supplier is a direct competitor, or may become one in the future. For example, a major supplier to DaimlerChrysler is General Motor's Saginaw Steering Gear division. It is unlikely that DaimlerChrysler shares proprietary product plans with Saginaw Steering Gear. Finally, a purchaser and a seller may simply not trust one another. Each party may believe it has more to lose than to gain by providing or sharing information.

Limited Interest by Suppliers Closer relationships may not interest all suppliers. A supplier may have the leverage or power in some relationships, particularly when they are in a monopolistic or oligopolistic industry position. In such cases, the purchaser may be unable to pursue a closer relationship simply because of the relative size or power position of the two firms. Consider, for example, a small manufacturer of molded plastic injected parts who purchases specialty chemicals from Dow Chemical or DuPont. The purchaser is not the predominant party in this relationship, and the supplier may simply not see any advantages in a closer relationship. The type of relationship pursued can be a function of what the supplier wants it to be. The buyer may offer too few dollars to even be of interest to the supplier.

Legal Barriers In some industries, legal antitrust concerns may act as barriers or obstacles to closer buyer-seller relationships (covered in greater detail in Chapter 16 which discusses the legal aspects of purchasing).

Traditional Approach to Managing Suppliers Entire generations of purchasing professionals grew up using an arm's-length approach. A shift toward a more trusting approach is not easy. Resistance to change is a powerful force that takes time, patience, and training to overcome. One purchasing executive at a high-tech firm commented, "We can't simply wipe out an entire generation of buyers; they'll need to be retrained. If we have grown up maintaining an arm's-length relationship with suppliers, well, that time is gone; one could say that it [the arm's-length approach] didn't make much of a performance difference in the past."[2] Also, firms that practice traditional supply chain management may not have the skills or knowledge in their workforce to evolve toward closer supplier relationships.

Avoidance of Suppliers Who Are Not Technology or Product Leaders
A purchaser should avoid those suppliers who are not capable of providing technology or product leadership. It makes little sense to pursue longer-term involvement if a supplier is not capable (currently or in the near future) of meeting performance requirements, especially in high-tech industries where product life cycles are very short. The choice of a supplier who cannot follow through on technology promises can effectively cause a purchaser to be completely "locked out" of a potential market opportunity.

   The movement toward closer interfirm relationships has been gradual and difficult. Purchasing must develop new supplier management techniques and work with suppliers who are capable of world-class performance. Today, real performance improvement is more likely through a collaborative rather than a traditional, arm's-length approach to supplier management.

Collaborative Buyer-Seller Relationships

Most purchasers and sellers now recognize a need for joint cooperation to achieve cost, quality, delivery, and time improvements. During the 1980s, progressive purchasers eliminated poor or marginal suppliers from their supply base. They then developed collaborative relationships or alliances with many of the remaining suppliers. *Collaboration* is defined as the process by which two or more parties adopt a high level of purposeful cooperation to maintain a trading relationship over time. The relationship is bilateral; both parties have the power to shape its nature and future direction over time. Mutual commitment to the future and a balanced power relationship are essential to the process. While collaborative relationships are not devoid of conflict, they include mechanisms for managing conflict built into the relationship.[3]

The following characteristics define a collaborative buyer-seller relationship:

- *One or a limited number of suppliers for each purchased item or family of items:* Remaining suppliers often provide material under long-term contracts with agreed-upon performance improvement targets.
- *A win-win approach to reward sharing:* Chapter 14, which discusses negotiation, defines the win-win concept in detail.
- *Joint efforts to improve supplier performance across all critical performance areas.*
- *Joint efforts to resolve disputes.*
- *Open exchange of information:* This includes information about new products, supplier cost data, and production schedules and forecasts for purchased items.
- *A credible commitment to work together during difficult times:* In other words, a purchaser does not return to old practices at the first sign of trouble.
- *A commitment to quality, defect-free products having design specifications that are manufacturable and that the supplier's process is capable of producing.*

Exhibit 5.2 compares the characteristics of traditional and collaborative buyer-seller relationships. While not all relationships between purchasers and suppliers should be collaborative, the trend is toward greater use of the collaborative approach.

Evolving from Adversarial to Collaborative Relationships The movement toward collaborative relationships has been evolutionary for most companies. How do buyers and sellers move from an adversarial, arm's-length relationship to one of mutual trust and commitment?

- **Phase 1—Traditional school of supply management:** Each party views the other with minimal trust or respect. Relations are frequently confrontational—even hostile. Multiple sourcing, competitive bidding, and short-term contracts characterize purchasing strategy. Purchasers quickly replace suppliers who cannot provide price reductions. Relationships are described as *antagonistic.*

EXHIBIT 5.2   *Characteristics of Buyer/Seller Relationship*

	Traditional Approach		Collaborative Approach
Suppliers	Multiple sources played off against each other	→	One of a few preferred suppliers for each major item
Cost Sharing	Buyer takes all cost savings; Supplier hides cost savings	→	Win-win shared rewards
Joint Improvement Efforts	Little or none	→	Joint improvement driven by mutual interdependence
Dispute Resolution	Buyer unilaterally resolves disputes	→	Existence of conflict-resolution mechanisms
Communication	Minimal or no two-way exchange of information	→	Open and complete exchange of information
Marketplace Adjustments	Buyer determines response to changing conditions	→	Buyer and seller work together to adapt to a changing marketplace
Quality	Buyer inspects at receipt	→	Designed into the product

- **Phase 2—Mere suspicion rather than total distrust:** Multiple sourcing still provides a level of safety and control. Frequent sourcing changes still occur as purchasers search for the source capable of providing the greatest cost reductions. Although an arm's-length relationship exists, attitudes start to give way to the beginning of a working relationship. Relationships are described as *competitive* or *adversarial*.
- **Phase 3—Closer buyer and seller relations as a result of mutual goals:** Purchasers begin to recognize the advantages of maintaining a smaller supply base along with sophisticated measurement, design, and quality systems. A purchaser encourages suppliers to provide cost-reduction ideas. Strategies focusing on lead-time reduction become popular during this stage. For example, purchasers become aware of the benefits of supplier input during product design. Relationships are described as *cooperative*.
- **Phase 4—Total trust between purchaser and seller:** Both parties commit to working together and emphasize strategies supporting world-class performance levels. Purchasing is responsible for managing a supply base that best supports a firm's performance objectives. Trust and information sharing become common while both parties focus on the components of total cost to achieve joint cost reductions. The seller becomes an extension of the purchaser's organization. Relationships are described as *collaborative*.

Most firms have found it difficult to move from the first to the fourth phase. Others, like DaimlerChrysler, IBM, and American Airlines, have moved aggressively to reduce their supply base and develop closer relations with remaining suppliers. The majority of buying firms within the United States are generally moving toward Phase 3. A firm's industry also affects the phase that a firm is in. Globally intense

Long-Term Partnership and Teaming Between Chrysler and Rockwell

ChryslerDaimler and Rockwell have reached an agreement that allows Rockwell to work with Chrysler engineers during the design phase of a vehicle project. Rockwell makes computerized controls that run the machinery in assembly and component plants. If the controls are not mated properly with the vehicle design, it can affect quality and the time to bring vehicles to market. In the deal, Rockwell will be the exclusive supplier of controls for all of Chrysler's assembly, stamping, welding, and powertrain facilities through May 2001. This agreement may mark the first time an automaker has worked jointly with a control supplier during the vehicle design phase. If the control design and car design do not mesh, the quality and time to market can be adversely affected. By working closely with Chrysler design engineers, Rockwell will develop software that will allow the engineers to design the controls and vehicles simultaneously. Controls are one of the largest pieces of capital equipment in the plants and one of the most difficult to start up. Both parties expect smoother start-ups, cost savings, and quicker product launches. Reducing the current 26- to 28-month time-to-market is crucial to Chrysler in maintaining competitive advantage. Their targeted time-to-market is 24 months and their hope is that their new strategic alliance with Rockwell will help them achieve this goal.

Source: Adapted from Kathy Jackson, "Pact Links Controls to Car Designs," *Automotive News,* (July 1, 1996): 14.

---

industries, such as semiconductors, automotive, xerographic, and electronics, tend to be further along this model than less competitively-intense industries.

Strategic Alliances—A Special Type of Collaborative Relationship A purchaser does not require collaborative or strategic relationships with all suppliers. Some suppliers provide widely available standard items. For these items, the purchaser simply needs to maintain a solid business relationship with its suppliers. Other suppliers provide technical, complex, or high-value items or services.

In the early stages of developing collaborative relationships, organizations will often eliminate those suppliers that are clearly not suitable. The reasons will vary: they do not have the capabilities to serve the organization, are too distant, are not well aligned with the company, or are simply not interested in developing a relationship. After eliminating these firms from consideration, organizations may occasionally encounter a supplier that is willing to put forth the time and effort required to create a strong relationship. In such cases, firms may consider developing a very special type of supply chain relationship, in which confidential information is shared, assets are invested in joint projects, and significant joint improvements are pursued. These types of interorganizational relationships are sometimes called *strategic alliances:*

Strategic supplier alliances are long-term, cooperative relationships designed to leverage the strategic and operational capabilities of individual participating companies to achieve significant ongoing benefits to each party. These alliances continue as long as significant value accrues to both parties. Successful alliances require very high levels of coordination, trust, information sharing, creativity, and senior management support to fully exploit joint opportunities. Among the primary benefits of such relationships are alignment of goals, total cost reduction, improved quality and cycle time, and a strengthened overall competitive position, which exceeds the contributions possible from other traditional relationships.[4]

To be successful, both participants in an alliance must willingly modify basic business practices to reduce duplication and waste while facilitating improved performance.[5] Strategic alliances allow firms to improve efficiency and effectiveness by eliminating waste and duplication in the supply chain. The process of developing a strategic alliance takes a significant amount of time. One study found that there are four levels that managers must proceed through in assessing the strategic and operational issues involved in a strategic alliance:

- **Level 1—Alliance conceptualization:** A firm determines that a collaborative arrangement has appeal and provides a potential alternative to the current arrangement. This level involves significant joint planning to determine what the "ideal strategic alliance" would be in an ideal world and then to project what a more realistic type of alliance might be.
- **Level 2—Alliance pursuance:** The decision to form an alliance is finalized, and the firm establishes the strategic and operational considerations that will be used to select the alliance partner.
- **Level 3—Alliance confirmation:** The focus here is on partner selection and confirmation. Managers determine the strategic and operational expectations for the arrangement through joint meetings with the alliance partner, and the relationship is solidified.
- **Level 4—Alliance implementation/continuity:** A feedback mechanism is created to continually administer and assess performance to determine whether the alliance will be sustained, modified, or terminated. If a conflict occurs, the firm may need to explore different types of conflict resolution mechanisms.

Purchasing managers must ask a series of questions to determine the fit between the buying company and a potential longer-term strategic alliance supplier:[6]

- Has the supplier signaled a commitment to a relationship and a willingness to allocate resources such as time, people, and money?
- Does the supplier understand the level of commitment required to achieve long-term performance gains?
- Can the supplier's capabilities grow along with the buying company's capabilities?
- Does the supplier have up-to-date technical ability and innovative products and processes?
- Is senior management willing to commit to a longer-term relationship?
- Will the supplier share information about future product and technology plans?
- How much of the supplier's business will be committed to the purchaser's requirements?

- What is the financial condition of the supplier?
- Is the supplier honest and trustworthy?
- How well does the supplier know the purchaser's industry and requirements?

Purchasers should be warned that not all strategic alliances are successful. The challenges of creating and maintaining strategic alliance relationships are best recognized by the breakdown between Office Max and Ryder Integrated Logistics. In this case Office Max sued Ryder Integrated Logistics for $21.4 million, for breach of contract after 21 months of a seven-year contract. Ryder Integrated Logistics countersued Office Max for $75 million.

In one study, the following attributes of supplier alliances were found to be significantly related to successful outcomes: trust and coordination, interdependence, information quality and participation, information sharing, joint problem solving, avoiding the use of severe conflict resolution tactics, and the existence of a formal supplier/commodity alliance selection process.[7] One metaphor used to describe alliances is that of a marriage. Before entering into such a commitment, both parties want to make sure that they understand and know the other party relatively well. Each party also has a need to establish a set of expectations regarding future actions. These expectations are often expressed in the form of measurable performance objectives, which define what the buyer expects of the supplier, and vice versa.

IMPROVING PERFORMANCE AND RELATIONSHIPS THROUGH CROSS-FUNCTIONAL SOURCING TEAMS

The pressure to improve, already intense, is expected to increase even more in the years ahead. Many firms are responding to this pressure by creating organizational structures that promote cross-functional and cross-organizational communication, coordination, and collaboration. In support of this effort, cross-functional sourcing teams have become increasingly important as firms pursue leading-edge purchasing strategies and practices.

Cross-functional sourcing teams consist of personnel from different functions, and increasingly suppliers, brought together to achieve purchasing or supply chain–related tasks. This includes specific tasks such as product design or supplier selection, or broader tasks such as responsibility for reducing purchased item cost or improving quality. When executed properly, the cross-functional sourcing team approach can bring together the knowledge and resources required for responding to new sourcing demands, something that rigid organizational structures are often incapable of doing. However, in a classic work of 40 years ago, a researcher noted that groups and teams can accomplish much that is good, or they can do great harm. There is nothing implicitly good or bad, weak or strong, about teams, regardless of where an organization uses them.

Exhibit 5.3 segments cross-functional sourcing teams by the team's assignment (finite or continuous) and the member's personal commitment to the team (full- or part-time). While some progressive firms are creating full-time sourcing team assignments, in most cases sourcing team assignments are still part-time. The lower half of

EXHIBIT 5.3   *Purchasing at Different Organizational Levels*

	Time Frame	
	Finite	Continuous
Full-Time	Move from project to project	Assigned permanently to specific team with evolving or changing responsibilities
Personal Commitment		
Part-Time	Support a specific team assignment in addition to regular responsibilities Disband after completion	Ongoing support of team assignments in addition to regular responsibilities

this matrix (finite or continuous team assignments supported by part-time members) presents a special challenge. It is often a struggle to obtain the commitment of members who have other professional responsibilities. Experience reveals that cross-functional sourcing teams are usually part-time/continuous assignments, making the use of sourcing teams a challenging way to work.

The following discussion of sourcing teams examines the benefits and potential drawbacks to team interaction, identifies when to form a cross-functional team, and concludes with a set of questions and answers that will help us better understand how to make sourcing teams effective.

Information on the importance of cross-functional teams, as well as other areas of strategic planning and management can be found at http://www.hsmg.com/index. htm the Website for the Hamilton Group, a consulting company that tailors team approaches to different company cultures, visions, and strategies.

Benefits Sought from the Cross-Functional Team Approach

Firms commit the energy needed to form teams to realize specific performance benefits. When cross-functional teams meet their performance objectives, the benefits can far outweigh the cost of using teams. The following highlights some of the benefits that organizations hope to realize from cross-functional sourcing teams.

Reduced Time to Complete a Task Individuals working as a team can often reduce the time required to solve a problem or complete an assigned task. The traditional, rigid approach to organizational tasks often requires duplication of effort between groups, and the individual sign-off of different functional groups may take an extended amount of time. The team approach supports members reaching agreement together, which can result in reduced rework and the time required to execute a decision. For example, Honeywell's Building Controls Division abandoned the traditional approach to new-product development and replaced it with a cross-functional team approach. The company replaced a three-inch-thick volume documenting product development procedures with a 20-page guideline outlining the development process. This reduced the average product development cycle time from two to three years under the old method to 14 months with the team approach.[8]

Increased Innovation   Firms look to teams to develop innovative products and processes to maintain an advantage over competitors. Innovation is critical to long-term success. Research has revealed that lower levels of formal rules and procedures along with informal organizational structures support increased levels of innovation.[9] The team approach should require fewer formal rules and qualifies as a less formal organizational structure. Teams can be a means to encourage increased innovation among members.

Joint Ownership of Decisions   The team approach requires joint agreement and ownership of decisions among different members. Through team interaction, members begin to understand each other's requirements or limitations and develop solutions that different departments can support. Perhaps the greatest benefit of team interaction is that once a team makes a decision, implementing the decision often becomes easier due to group buy-in. The stakeholders involved in carrying out the decision are more likely to do so efficiently and effectively, since cross-functional agreement and ownership regarding a change or decision has been established.

Enhanced Communication Between Functions or Organizations
Those who have worked in an organization with rigidly separated departments know the inefficiency of interdepartmental communication. The problems are even worse as parties attempt to communicate across organizations. The cross-functional team approach can help reduce communication barriers because members are in direct contact with each other (either face to face or by electronic communication). For example, the team approach can help reduce design or material changes during product development because the team works together when developing product specifications. This cross-functional team approach, by design, encourages open and timely exchange of information between members.

Realizing Synergies by Combining Individuals and Functions   A primary objective of using teams is to bring together individuals with different perspectives and expertise to perform better on a task compared to individuals or departments acting alone. The synergistic effect of team interaction can help generate new and creative ways to look at a problem or approach a task. Ideally, a team works together to solve problems that individuals could not solve as well acting alone, to create new ways to perform routine (though time-consuming) tasks, and to develop ideas that only a diverse group could develop.

Better Identification and Resolution of Problems   Teams with diverse knowledge and skills have an opportunity to quickly identify causes of problems that may affect the team or the organization. Early problem identification and correction minimizes or even prevents a problem's total impact. Furthermore, a team should assume joint ownership of problems and accept the responsibility for problem correction, which helps prevent finger pointing for blame between departments.

Potential Drawbacks to the Cross-Functional Team Approach

The use of cross-functional sourcing teams does not guarantee a successful outcome to a project or assignment. The team approach requires careful management, open exchange of information between members, motivated team members, clearly understood team goals, effective team leaders, and adequate resources. Potential drawbacks to the team approach exist when conditions do not support an effective team effort. Purchasing managers must be willing to address these drawbacks if they begin to affect team performance.

Team Process Loss   Process loss occurs when a team does not solve its task in the best or most efficient manner or members are not motivated to employ their resources to create a successful outcome.[10] When process loss is present, the total group effort is less than the expected sum of the individual parts. A potential drawback exists if the benefits resulting from team interaction do not outweigh team process loss. For example, a supplier selection team with 12 members, five of whom are active on the team, would experience a loss and waste from a lack of team interaction and participation.

Negative Effects on Individual Members   Membership on a team can have negative effects on individuals. Teams can exert pressure to conform to a decision or position that the member does not support. An example might involve a materials engineer who is pressured by other team members to select the lowest price supplier, even though he or she knows that a higher-priced supplier will provide better quality. A team may also pressure an individual to support or conform to a lower productivity norm than the individual's personal norm. Also, some individuals may feel stifled in a team setting or may not interact well with other team members. When this occurs, individual performance suffers.

Poor Team Decisions   Although it seems counter to what we popularly believe, cross-functional teams can arrive at poor decisions. Groupthink—the tendency of a rational group or team to arrive at a bad decision when other information is available—may become a problem for individuals in a cohesive group. By striving for group uniformity and consensus, they may suppress their motivation to appraise alternative courses of action.[11] The team may arrive at a decision that careful evaluation of all available information or critical discussion normally would not support.

Purchasing and Suppliers Must Make Major Contributions to Future New-Product Development

Major automakers are planning cost reductions as large as 30% on their next generation of vehicles. Car companies are telling suppliers that they must do their part to achieve the targeted savings. The reasons for such stringent cost-reduction pressures: Automobile consumers are already unwilling to pay high prices, and federal regulations mandating safety equipment will "add another $400 between now and the end of the decade," said Tom Stallkamp, Chrysler's Vice President of Procurement. Auto companies announced the following goals during a purchasing seminar at the Automotive News World Congress: Chrysler will not permit any price hikes by suppliers and is seeking cuts. Honda will reduce costs for the next generation of the U.S.-produced Accord by 20%. Honda reported it has already signed contracts with suppliers that will enable it to meet its cost-reduction targets. BMW will seek 25% to 30% cost reductions for its next 3-series sedan. Ford wants to reduce component costs by an average of 20%. The challenge lies in determining what portion of the cost reduction suppliers must absorb, particularly at a time when automakers are expecting suppliers to commit major investment toward a global production capability.

Source: Adapted from David Sedgwick, "Makers Squeeze Parts Costs," *Automotive News* (January 15, 1996): 1.

When to Form a Cross-Functional Team

All organizations face resource constraints that affect the number of cross-functional teams, including sourcing teams, they can establish. Clearly, a firm cannot use the team approach for every business decision. Certain business decisions simply do not require a team approach. A team approach is useful when the task at hand satisfies certain characteristics.

A firm faced with a complex or large-scale business decision should consider the cross-functional team approach. Examples include new-product development, locating a new production facility, developing a commodity/purchase family strategy, or establishing a new business unit. These tasks are so large or complex that one person or function cannot effectively accomplish the assignment. A firm can also use the team approach when a team is likely to arrive at a better solution than a person or department acting individually. For example, purchasing may be able to handle the evaluation and selection of suppliers but may benefit from a team with diverse experience whose members are better equipped to evaluate suppliers from a number of perspectives. Engineering can provide technical specifications, marketing can provide details on the features required, accounting can provide material and labor cost data estimates, etc. In these situations, selecting a better supplier(s) for the situation at hand is more likely as better information becomes available and is analyzed by team members.

An assignment that directly affects a firm's competitive position, such as negotiation with a joint venture partner, might also benefit from the team approach. The cross-functional team approach is also useful when no single function has the resources to solve a problem that affects more than one department or function.

Improving Sourcing Team Effectiveness

The remainder of our team discussion presents a set of questions that require students and managers to think about various issues that affect the quality of sourcing team interaction and performance. Each question includes a brief discussion of major points and insights related to that question.

Question 1: Does Our Organization Consider Cross-Functional Team Planning Issues When Establishing Sourcing Teams? Successfully using teams requires extensive planning before a team should be allowed to pursue an assignment. Ignoring these issues or the needs of team members during team formation increases the risk of team failure. The following summarizes several sourcing team planning issues.

SELECTING A TASK Organizations should use teams selectively due to limited resource availability. Sourcing teams should work only on tasks that are important to an organization's success. One expert recommends selecting tasks that are "meaningful." A meaningful task is one that requires members to use a variety of higher-level skills, supports giving members regular feedback about performance, results in an outcome with a significant affect on the organization and others outside the team, and provides members autonomy for deciding how they will do the work. Once an organization understands the task it wants a sourcing team to pursue, then the functional groups and the size of the team required to support that task become clear. The team's broad performance objectives may also emerge as an organization selects appropriate tasks. For example, reducing purchase cost is an example of a broad performance objective.

SELECTING TEAM MEMBERS AND LEADERS Perhaps one of the most critical planning issues involves selecting the right members and leader. An effective team member is one that:

- Understands the team's task—the member has task-relevant knowledge
- Has the time to commit to the team
- Has the ability to work with others in a group
- Can assume an organizational rather than strict functional perspective

Team leadership is discussed shortly.

TRAINING REQUIREMENTS Interacting as a team requires a set of skills different from the skills required for traditional work. Organizations must consider carefully the training requirements of sourcing team members. Members may require training

---

EXHIBIT 5.4   *Organizational Resource Requirements*

---

1. **Supplier Participation**
   The degree to which suppliers directly support completion of this team's task assignments when supplier involvement is required
2. **Required Services and Help from Others**
   The services and help required from others external to the team to perform the team's assignment
3. **Time Availability**
   The amount of time that can be devoted by all team members to the team's assignment
4. **Budgetary Support**
   The financial resources needed to perform the team's assigned tasks
5. **Materials and Supplies**
   The routine items that are required to perform the team's assignment
6. **Team Member Task Preparation**
   The personal preparation and experience of team members, through previous education, formal company training, and relevant job experience, required to perform the team's assignment
7. **Work Environment**
   The physical aspects of the immediate work environment needed to perform the team's assignment—characteristics that facilitate rather than interfere with team performance
8. **Executive Management Commitment**
   The overall level of support that executive management exhibits toward the cross-functional team process
9. **Job-Related Information**
   The information, including data and reports, from multiple sources required to support team performance. Examples include data on costs, technical issues, suppliers, supply market, performance targets, and requirements.
10. **Tools and Equipment**
    The specific tools, equipment, and technology required to perform the team's assignment

---

Source: Adapted from L. H. Peters and J. O. O'Connor, "Situational Constraints and Work Outcomes: The Influences of a Frequently Overlooked Construct," *Academy of Management Review*, no. 3 (March 1980): 391–397.

in project management, conflict resolution, consensus decision making, group problem solving, goal setting, and effective communication and listening skills.

RESOURCE SUPPORT An earlier study of cross-functional sourcing teams by Monczka and Trent revealed that the types of resources that cross-functional sourcing teams had access to made a major difference in team performance. [12] Adapted from work by Peters and O'Connor, we can identify ten categories of team resources, as presented in Exhibit 5.4.[13] The resources that correlate the highest, on average, with effective sourcing teams (in order of importance) are supplier participation, required services and help from others, time availability, and budgetary support. Budget support is especially critical for teams whose members must travel from different geographical areas, or for teams that must visit suppliers during the course of their assignment.

Other planning issues not addressed here include determining the level of sourcing team authority, the types and frequency of team evaluations and rewards, and the physical location of team members. This list of planning issues reveals that organizations must give serious attention to some important considerations before allowing sourcing teams to begin work.

Question 2: Does Executive Management Practice Subtle Control over Sourcing Teams?

A major issue involves management's willingness to exert *subtle control* over cross-functional sourcing teams, a process that does not mean that management dictates or supervises team activities. Instead, subtle control involves activities undertaken by management to increase the probability of team success. There are several ways that management can practice subtle control over sourcing teams:

- Authorizing the creation of the sourcing team
- Selecting the team's task
- Establishing broad objectives (with the team later establishing specific performance targets or goals)
- Selecting the team leader and members
- Requiring performance updates at regular intervals or at key milestones (What team wants to report to executive management that they have made no progress?)
- Conducting performance reviews and holding teams accountable for performance outcomes

While management does not involve itself in a team's day-to-day activities, management must concern itself with moving the sourcing team process forward.

Question 3: Does Our Organization Recognize and Reward Team Member Participation and Team Performance?

A direct link exists between rewards and team member effort, and also between rewards and team performance. Unfortunately, many organizations still fail to recognize the time and effort members must commit to sourcing teams, particularly members of part-time teams. This lack of recognition often causes team members to commit their time to nonteam work activities.

How should organizations recognize and reward team member participation and team performance? While no single answer exists, there are some guidelines that will help in this area. First, team membership should be part of an individual's performance review. This sends a message that team participation is valued and recognized by the organization, just like an individual's other work responsibilities. Second, along with an evaluation of the entire team's performance, management should consider assessing each individual's contribution to the team. This helps ensure that nonparticipating members do not benefit unfairly from the efforts of other team members.

Rewards and recognition that organizations offer teams cluster into four broad categories:

1. Monetary bonuses and other one-time cash awards
2. Executive recognition, including plaques or mention in the company newsletter
3. Nonmonetary rewards, including dinners or sports and theater tickets
4. Merit raises awarded during the team member's annual performance review

Rewards offer an opportunity to reinforce desired activity and behavior. It is well understood that what gets rewarded gets done. If team members are positively reinforced for high performance, they will likely exert even greater effort. Furthermore, if members receive immediate reinforcement, they will exert greater effort than if the reinforcement is delayed. If positive work is never recognized or reinforced through rewards, the positive effort will likely be extinguished.

Question 4: Do We Have the Right Individuals Selected as Sourcing Team Leaders? The previously mentioned research by Monczka and Trent found that the effectiveness of the sourcing team leader is one of the strongest predictors of team success. An additional finding from that research was that most sourcing teams had formally designated leaders who usually were selected by management (see Question 3 on subtle control). Zenger and his colleagues, in extensive research with teams, found this to be true.[14]

- Most organizations report they should give more attention, training, and support to their team leaders.
- Within days of taking a leadership role, team leaders usually realize they need a new set of skills.
- Even when shared team leadership among members is the goal, the team as a whole still reports to someone who needs advanced team-leadership skills.
- Overly structured team leaders who see themselves as "top sergeants with a few extra duties" greatly increase the chance of team failure.

We may conclude that selecting and training an effective team leader is critical to team success. Being an effective team leader means satisfying a demanding set of essential operating responsibilities and requirements while still promoting the creativity, leadership ability, and cohesiveness of team members. Unfortunately, relatively few individuals have the qualifications, experience, or training to immediately assume such a demanding leadership position.

Appendix I, located on the Website, presents a measurement scale used by team members to assess the effectiveness of sourcing team leaders. Each item within this appendix identifies a requirement or responsibility that the sourcing team leader should assume. Using this scale allows organizations to (1) evaluate team leader strengths and weaknesses; (2) rank team leaders, which is valuable when considering future leadership responsibilities; (3) provide feedback regarding improvement opportunities, which can lead to training that is targeted to the specific needs of the leader; and (4) allow individual leaders, teams, and organizations to take corrective action as required. A failure to staff the position of team leader with qualified individuals greatly reduces the probability of sourcing team effectiveness.

Question 5: Do Our Sourcing Teams Effectively Establish Performance Goals? One of the most important activities relating to sourcing team interaction is the ability of teams to establish *quantified* goals that focus on end results (rather than desired activities). For example, a sourcing team that establishes a goal of 2% cost reduction for the first quarter of 2002 has likely established a more effective goal than one that establishes a goal of holding three team meetings in the first quarter.

Establishing sourcing team goals is important for several reasons. Teams with established goals often use those goals as a basis for evaluating how well the team is performing. The goals provide a benchmark for assessing progress, providing feedback, and allocating performance rewards for superior effort and results. Teams will also establish, on average, challenging rather than easy goals. Furthermore, external pressure on a team to set goals usually results in the setting of more challenging goals (recall our discussion of subtle control). We also know that teams with goals perform better, on average, than teams that are asked simply to perform their best without explicit end goals. Goal setting is a critical cross-functional team requirement.

Appendix J, on the Website, presents a three-part tool that sourcing teams can use to develop goals for which they will be held accountable. The first part of this tool requires a team to describe its task. For example, a team may be responsible for *managing suppliers that provide a certain commodity*. The second part of the tool requires the team to assess its ability to achieve certain outcomes on a scale ranging from 1 (no potential) to 7 (high potential). Finally, the team identifies those areas offering the highest performance potential (usually the items within the five to seven range) and develops quantified or specific objectives relating to that item. If the team believes it has the potential to improve material delivery, then it should develop an objective goal that relates to material delivery.

Question 6: Are Key Suppliers Part of the Sourcing Team Process?

The potential benefit of closer buyer-seller relationships is well understood by most organizations. Cross-functional sourcing teams are an ideal way to promote cross-organizational cooperation. Research reveals that relying on supplier involvement and input (when a team's assignment warrants involvement) demonstrates, on average, some positive characteristics compared with teams that do not involve suppliers.[15]

- They are rated as more effective than teams that do not involve suppliers.
- They are rated as putting forth greater effort on team assignments than teams that do not involve suppliers.
- They report greater satisfaction concerning the quality of key information exchanged between the team and key suppliers.
- They report greater reliance on suppliers to support directly the team's goals—thus making the supplier a resource.
- They report fewer problems coordinating work activity between the team and key suppliers.
- They report receiving greater supplier contribution across many performance areas, including cost-reduction and quality improvement ideas, process improvement suggestions, and material-ordering and delivery cycle time reductions.

Involving suppliers is not as easy as it sounds. Some of the challenges associated with working with external organizations include (1) determining who has responsibility for the supplier involvement process, (2) identifying which suppliers to involve (particularly if more than one supplier provides a good or service), (3) determining if involvement should be continuous or as-needed, (4) agreeing on how to share risks and rewards encountered during team projects, (5) motivating suppliers to be active and willing participants, and (6) managing different cultures and business practices.

An integrated approach to supply chain management should also begin to identify key customers to be part of sourcing teams (at least on an informal basis). Sourcing teams, with supplier involvement, can work to incorporate customer needs directly into sourcing strategies and practices.

Cross-functional sourcing teams offer all types of organizations, not just manufacturing firms, the opportunity to realize advantages across many performance areas. Underlying the development and use of sourcing teams must be a recognition that sourcing increasingly affects a firm's overall competitiveness along with the realization that cross-functional integration among purchasing, manufacturing, marketing, and technical groups can improve a firm's sourcing effectiveness.

PURCHASING, ENGINEERING, AND SUPPLIERS—A TEAM-BASED APPROACH TO NEW-PRODUCT DEVELOPMENT

Cycle-time reduction and new-product development are increasingly competitive factors today. A primary objective of cross-functional interaction, for example, is to reduce the time it takes to move a product from its concept to the final customer. As product life cycles become shorter within most industries, product and process innovation that focuses on cycle-time reduction becomes ever more critical. It is important to note that reducing time to market should never involve cutting corners, particularly in the area of product testing and safety.

The benefits of reducing development lead time include increased market share, heightened barriers to new competitors, and higher sales further into the future. One study revealed that a product marketed six months after its target introduction date earns on average 33% fewer projected profits over a five-year period. The study also concluded that a product that reaches the market at its projected time but as high as 50% over budget earns only 4% fewer projected profits.[16] An executive in charge of new-product development for a top U.S. company came to the conclusion that "if you get to the market sooner with a new technology, you can charge a premium until the others follow." The chief executive and chairperson of the Council of Competitiveness, a group dedicated to the competitiveness of U.S. industry, said, "We've [U.S. firms] ignored a critical success factor, speed. Our competitors abroad have turned new technologies into new products and processes more rapidly, and they've reaped the commercial rewards of the time-to-market race."[17]

The Team Approach to New-Product Development

Firms pursue time-based improvement during new-product development in a number of ways. One method, the focus of this section, is the team approach to new-product development. The use of teams often generates innovative new-product ideas while helping to speed the development and marketing of a new product. When implemented properly, the team approach can be an effective way to meet new-product goals. The traditional new-product approach simply does not support the development of innovative new products in reduced time.

EXHIBIT 5.5   *Gates in the Product Development Cycle*

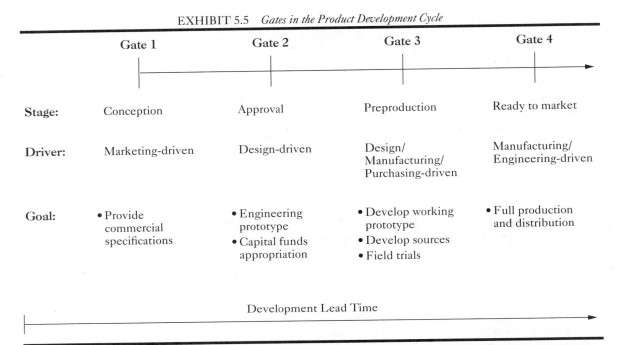

	Gate 1	Gate 2	Gate 3	Gate 4
Stage:	Conception	Approval	Preproduction	Ready to market
Driver:	Marketing-driven	Design-driven	Design/ Manufacturing/ Purchasing-driven	Manufacturing/ Engineering-driven
Goal:	• Provide commercial specifications	• Engineering prototype • Capital funds appropriation	• Develop working prototype • Develop sources • Field trials	• Full production and distribution

Development Lead Time

Source: Robert Handfield, "Effects of Concurrent Engineering on Make-to-Order Products," *IEEE Transactions on Engineering Management* 41, no. 4 (Nov. 1994): 1–11.

The traditional approach to product development stresses a rigid sequence of steps. A manager at Ford described the traditional product development process that Ford used to follow:[18]

Designers designed a car on paper, then gave it to the engineers, who figured out how to make it. Their plans were passed along to the manufacturing and purchasing people, who respectively set up the lines and selected the suppliers on competitive bids. The next step in the process was the production plant. Then came marketing, the legal and dealer-service departments, and finally the customer. In each stage, if a major glitch developed, the car was bumped back to the designer for changes. The further along in the sequence, however, the more difficult it was to make changes.

The business-as-usual approach excluded purchasing and manufacturing input during the product design phase. Product designers rarely communicated with process engineers who rarely communicated with manufacturing. Innovative ideas that often took years to develop never reached the customer. Product designers mistakenly assumed that process engineers and manufacturing could develop the process capability required for a new product. Early cooperation and communication could have eliminated some of the problems in this area.

This traditional approach is shown in Exhibit 5.5, where the product development cycle involves a series of "gates" that must be signed off by each of the functions.[19] The project cannot proceed until all requirements are completed at each gate. This approach clearly requires more time, because many of the decisions may occur

EXHIBIT 5.6   *The "Sachimi" Concurrent Development Schedule*

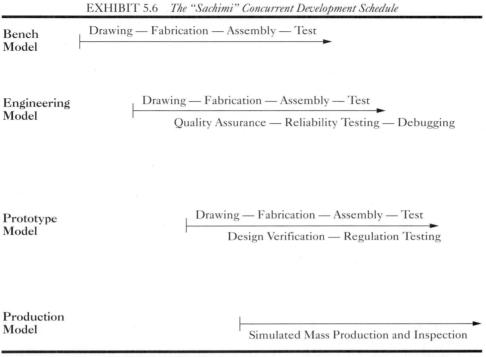

Bench Model

Drawing — Fabrication — Assembly — Test

Engineering Model

Drawing — Fabrication — Assembly — Test

Quality Assurance — Reliability Testing — Debugging

Prototype Model

Drawing — Fabrication — Assembly — Test

Design Verification — Regulation Testing

Production Model

Simulated Mass Production and Inspection

Source: Robert Handfield, "Effects of Concurrent Engineering on Make-to-Order Products," *IEEE Transactions on Engineering Management* 41, no. 4 (Nov. 1994): 1–11.

in isolation. Also, it is impossible to involve suppliers early in the process since purchasing does not even get involved until Gate 3.

The team approach can help remove communication barriers between functions during product development. Removing barriers allows a team to identify potential problems early in the design process. A team goal should be an average 30% to 50% reduction in total development cycle time compared with traditional product development times. The team approach should also contribute to lower total product cost through creative ways to design and manufacture products.

The most important way that cross-functional teams achieve reduced new-product cycle times is through a concurrent versus sequential approach to new-product development. *Concurrent engineering* is defined by the Institute for Defense Analysis (IDA) as "the systematic approach to the integrated concurrent design of products and related processes including manufacture and support. This approach causes developers, from the outset, to consider all the elements of a product's lifecycle from conception through disposal including quality, cost, and schedule and user requirements."[20] As shown in Exhibit 5.6, activities in the product development cycle are scheduled in parallel at the interface of different phases. The benefits of concurrent engineering at Fuji included faster speed of development, increased flexibility, and greater sharing of information.[21] This concurrent approach—which has been referred to as *sashimi development* by Fuji, because of the manner in which slices of raw fish overlap one another on a plate—also increases shared responsibility of project members. Members of sales, research and development (R&D), manufacturing, purchasing, and suppliers all work together as a team to solve the problems occurring during new-product design. Some of the disadvantages of the sashimi system include the amplification of ambiguity, tension, and conflict in the group.

What is it about a concurrent approach that supports reduced product development cycle times, particularly when compared with the traditional or sequential approach? A concurrent approach does the following:

- *It requires cross-functional agreement throughout the product development process concerning critical development issues.* This agreement can reduce costly and time-consuming design and product change requests by creating agreed-upon product specifications early in the development process.
- *It supports the interaction of a competent group of professionals, which should result in better decisions related to product design and manufacturability.* Better decisions should require less time to implement and require less rework later on, particularly where the team has the authority to make key decisions.
- *It supports early supplier involvement.* Suppliers can provide insight into design and manufacturing requirements that can save time and cost.
- *It accelerates learning throughout the new-product development process.* Functional team members must learn together simultaneously rather than separately as a project passes from one group or function to another. A team can spend a greater proportion of total development time on value-added activities than on separate learning across functions.
- *Requires up-front establishment and agreement on customer-oriented and competitive goals by the cross-functional team.*

The team approach to new-product development has the potential to provide significant time and cost savings. With cross-functional teams, Hewlett-Packard reduced the design and development time of computer printers from over four years to 22 months. AT&T reduced the time it takes to develop a phone from two years to one year. The team approach allowed Ford and Navistar to reduce new-vehicle product development time by 50%. Digital Equipment Corporation (acquired by Compaq in 1998) developed a new computer mouse in only 18 weeks. The new mouse required 54 parts compared to the 83 parts required for the previous version, required 277 seconds versus 592 for assembly, and had material costs 47% lower than previous models.[22]

Purchasing's Contribution on New-Product Development Teams

Purchasing should play a key role in new-product development. As the main contact with suppliers, purchasing is in a unique position to include suppliers early in the design process as well as to perform early evaluation of supplier capabilities. Think about how much easier it is for purchasing to support new-product development with the team approach versus the traditional approach. As a team member, purchasing has

John Deere Attacks Costs

At John Deere Harvester Works, the Cost Reduction Group's first undertaking was to initiate the Compare, Compare, Compare, and Share (CCCS) program—a six-stage process that consists of examining both physically and statistically, families of parts to find price variations that are not justified by engineering necessity. When CCCS teams find such variations, they look for ways to cut manufacturing costs by finding better sources or materials, or, in some cases, by modifying designs to enable more strategic sourcing of parts. Although simple in concept, the process can be very complicated in practice. Among the important tasks is making sure the units that undertake such analysis can handle the in-depth questioning of processes and decisions without getting defensive. For CCCS teams, how current parts design and sourcing came about is not important. What is important is finding cost-reduction opportunities. Deere's European office has logged almost $1.5 million in annual cost reductions from this seemingly simple exercise.

Source: Supply Management Linkages 1, no. 1 (October 1999): 1, published by Deere & Company.

early visibility to new-product requirements, which allows managers to contribute directly during the design and specification of material requirements. With the traditional approach, purchasing plays a reactive role after other functions have completed their tasks.

A product development manager provided a humorous metaphor during the early stages of a project regarding the integration of suppliers into the new-product development process:

Suppliers are like fish in the ocean. We [the buyers] are the fishermen. The key challenge facing us is how to put out the right bait, so that we can pull up the right suppliers at the right time and get them to help us develop our products. There are several problems associated with fishing. How do we know we're using the right bait? How do we know the right kind of fish are in the water? Most importantly, when we catch a fish, how do we know whether it's the right fish, and whether we should keep it or throw it back in the water? Finally, how do we know the fish will follow through with its commitments if we decide to keep it?

This metaphor illustrates the problems associated with supplier evaluation and selection for integration into new-product and -process development.

Reports and other information on supplier integration into new-product development can be found at http://gebn.bus.msu.edu. This site is maintained by the Global Procurement and Supply Chain Benchmarking Initiative.

In a recent study of 20 companies visited by the authors and other members of the research team, a number of critical success factors were identified that led companies to be more successful in integrating suppliers into the new-product development process.[23] These success factors included sharing information, identifying critical materials, identifying potential suppliers in the design phase, monitoring and forecasting changes in material markets, evaluating project timing, and bringing key suppliers directly into the process as needed. In the following section, we describe each of these critical success factors, and provide a set of "good practice" examples that illustrate how different companies implemented them within their new-product development process.

GOOD PRACTICE EXAMPLES
New-Product Development

■ ■ ■

Sharing Information A major responsibility of purchasing is to provide information to suppliers involved in a new-product development project. Sharing of information can help avoid unwelcome surprises throughout the life of a project, particularly if suppliers are brought in to design parts early in the concept stage. If purchasing selects capable and trustworthy suppliers, as NEC did in the vignette at the beginning of this chapter, it should be able to share product information early in the development process. For example, if a component for a new part requires a specific production process, it is important to make sure a supplier has the required process capability. Suppliers have delayed the launch of new products because they were unable to meet production requirements. Early visibility to product requirements allows purchasing to share critical information with suppliers that can help avoid delays. In turn, suppliers will be expected to share their information with the new-product development team.

Good Practice At Fujitsu, a manufacturer of hard drive technologies, information sharing is very informal during basic research in the laboratory stage, and it is conducted through joint meetings with suppliers, beginning with their top management in order to gain commitment. Suppliers are approached and asked if they are willing to work on development for a future product. This is a trust-based approach with no formal contracts. For such basic technologies, the R&D group is primarily involved in approaching and evaluating suppliers. R&D leads the discussions, with procurement "sitting in" but not taking an active role. For incremental products however, manufacturing and procurement are primarily involved in selection and negotiation.

Identifying Critical Materials for the New Product Purchasing's involvement allows it to determine at an earlier point the materials requirements for a new product and provide input during the design phase based on its knowledge of materials supply markets. Purchasing can recommend substitutes for high-cost or volatile materials, suggest standard items wherever possible, and evaluate longer-term materials trends.

A buying company seeks to discover a convergence in technology strategies with the supplier. The most common reference to this concept is a "technology roadmap," which refers to the set of performance criteria and undiscovered products and processes an organization intends to develop and/or manufacture within a specified or unspecified time horizon. Many companies define their technology roadmaps in terms of the next decade, while others employ a horizon of 50 years or even a century! While the exact form of a technology roadmap is somewhat industry-specific, it typically is defined in the following terms:

- Projected performance specifications for a class of products or processes (e.g., memory size, speed, electrical resistance, temperature, or pressure)
- An intention to integrate a new material or component (e.g., new form of molecule/chemical)
- Development of a product to meet customer requirements that is currently unavailable in the market (e.g., new television screen technology)
- Integration of multiple complementary technologies that results in a radical new product (e.g., a combined fax/phone/modem/copier, or combining television, cable, and computer technology)
- A combination of the above as well as other possible variations

Good Practice Honeywell has segmented their purchasing organization into three key groups and has carefully defined how supplier involvement with each group occurs. The first is the "blue sky" Advanced Technology Centers, a group that is tasked with long-range thinking—looking five to ten years out into the future. Any supplier involvement that occurs with this group focuses on technology, not specific product requirements (although the technology will eventually support specific requirements). The second group comprises Reuse Teams, who are responsible for promoting the use of standard, shelf application items over a one- to five-year planning horizon. The third group is the New Product Development Program Teams, who are involved in specific applications in which the company has won business over a two-year planning horizon. Buyers are responsible for 100% of these teams' needs. These are very focused teams that address specific customer requirements that need to be met.

Identifying Potential Suppliers During the Design Phase The evaluation and selection of suppliers requires a major time commitment by purchasing, the group that must evaluate and select suppliers regardless of the new-product development approach used. The team approach allows purchasing to anticipate product requirements earlier so it can identify the most capable suppliers.

Supplier selection can occur before a new part is actually designed or reaches production. The team approach helps eliminate a source of frustration for purchasing—a lack of time to evaluate, select, and develop suppliers to support new-product requirements. With the team approach, supplier selection can begin earlier in the development process, which allows purchasing to perform this critical task earlier in the process and with better information.

The following elements are important in considering new or existing suppliers for integration:

- *Targets:* Is the supplier capable of hitting affordable targets regarding cost, quality, conductivity, weight, and other performance criteria?
- *Timing:* Will the supplier be able to meet product introduction deadlines?
- *Ramp-up:* Will the supplier be able to increase their capacity and production fast enough to meet our market share requirements?
- *Innovation and technical:* Does the supplier have the required engineering expertise and physical facilities to develop an adequate design, manufacture it, and solve problems when they occur?
- *Training:* Do the supplier's key personnel have the required training to start up required processes and debug them?
- *Resource commitment:* If the supplier is deficient in any of the above areas, is management willing to commit resources to remedy the problem?

The supplier assessment should be systematically carried out based on both hard performance data, and subjective assessments by technical personnel. Performance data should be weighted in such a manner that they are aligned with customer performance requirements. All of the above criteria must be tied into the evaluation/measurement system in order to develop a comprehensive *risk assessment* that answers the following questions:

- What is the likelihood that this supplier has the ability to bring the product to market?
- How does this risk assessment compare to other potential suppliers (if there exist others)?
- At what point are we willing to reverse this decision if we proceed, and what are the criteria/measures for doing so?
- What is the contingency plan that takes effect in the event of the previous occurrence?

Good Practice Purchasing at Compaq Computers reiterates the importance of working with suppliers to determine their future design capabilities. In some cases, internal development groups will share early information about future technology roadmaps with just about any global supplier who will listen, in an attempt to ensure that the required technology will eventually be available. For instance, in one commodity, the manager has established a technology map with performance curves, and expected targets by date. The target area becomes the projected "sweet spot," which is shared with suppliers. Suppliers are told that if they can't hit the sweet spot by the target date, they won't get the business. This concept is somewhat different from conventional early involvement wisdom. Because of the volatility of this industry, the company does not have the time or the need to form alliances and go through an early involvement program. Rather, the strategy is to ensure the technology is available, by openly sharing technology roadmaps with any qualified supplier who will listen, and move the business around to take advantage of performance at the target price.

Monitor and Forecast Change in Material Markets Purchasing should always monitor and anticipate activity in its supply markets. For example, purchasing should forecast long-term supply and prices for its basic commodities. It should monitor technological innovations that impact its primary materials or make substitute materials economically attractive. It should evaluate not only its existing suppliers but other potential suppliers. Because team participation provides timely visibility to new-product requirements, purchasing can monitor and forecast change on a continuous basis.

Purchasing can also develop contingency supply plans, including end-of-life strategies to phase out obsolete components in order to avoid being stuck with the inventory. This is especially important in cases where component life cycles are much shorter than the actual product life cycle. It is not uncommon for high-tech firms who anticipate end-of-life situations to plan phase-out by first holding inventories of the soon-to-be obsolete part for some period of time after manufacture of the product or functional block is discontinued. The firm typically notifies customers that support will be phased out and one-time buys of the now obsolete component will be possible until some specified date. Finally, the component is written off and disposed of. Possible forms of disposition of the obsolete component include sale incentives for finished goods, disassembling and restocking nonobsolete components, returning to the supplier for credit, donation for a tax break, or scrap. In almost all of these cases, some loss will be incurred on the value of the component.

In the study of supplier integration, a variety of information-sharing mechanisms were employed to assess the alignment of technology roadmaps with potential suppliers. In most cases, no specific product or project was discussed at these meetings, only the potential for a "meeting of the minds." The sharing of technology roadmaps often strongly influenced the type of buyer-supplier relationship that resulted in the integration process. Very often, the buyer or supplier decided that this was not a company they were interested in doing business with due to a diverging technology roadmap. In cases when the supplier's current technology could be used but their long-term technology roadmap diverged, companies often "exploited" the technology for the current product or process but returned to the supply pool for future product cycles.

The actual process of sharing technology roadmaps occurred in a variety of forms, which in some cases influenced the type of relationship that emerged:

- Two-way information sharing between buyer and seller
- One way (information sharing from one buyer to many suppliers)
- Supplier councils tied to new-product development
- Technology "fairs"

In sharing roadmaps, purchasing companies paid particular attention to the relative rate of change for a particular technology.

Good Practice At NEC (the company in the opening vignette), technologies with short product life cycles and for which performance ceilings were rapidly rising were often delayed as much as possible in order to capture the latest technology in the product once released. For these types of products, the supplier was integrated on a "one-time" basis. In the next product cycle, the buyer often returned to the pool of suppliers to determine whether any new innovative technologies had evolved. In other cases, suppliers had technologies on their roadmaps that were not yet robust enough or cost-effective to be integrated into existing technologies. In such cases, the technology was "bookshelved" and revisited in the next new-product cycle.

Evaluate Project Timing Team participation allows purchasing to evaluate the timing of each phase of the product development project. Purchasing can assess whether project timing is realistic as it applies to a new part's sourcing requirements. If the timing is not realistic, purchasing should have enough visibility to reevaluate the timing requirements or come up with plans to meet the proposed time frame.

Good Practice Intel, a manufacturer of semiconductors, seeks to get new factories up and running from "dirt to finished product" in less than two years. There are literally hundreds of machine tools in a given facility. These are generally considered to be "islands of automation," as wafer fabrication is a continuous batch process. The company also does some assembly and test operations, which is more like straight manufacturing. The machine setups are highly expensive and sophisticated, much like an oil process industry.

Both product and process design are considered proprietary to Intel. Therefore, suppliers are only involved in a single unique stage of the process, *not* in process development. The product/process engineers help to select suppliers based on their ability to meet a specification, and then work to ensure that they meet the specification over time. The key strategy involves holding suppliers responsible for delivering, installing, servicing, and maintaining machine tools costing well over $1 million each. This involves supplier involvement in process ramp-up and maintenance of equipment in wafer fabrication facilities. While the company is also involved in supplier integration into new-product development, process integration represents a truly unique application in a nontraditional area. Suppliers are first fully responsible for the maintenance of these machine tools and the maintenance tasks are then gradually turned over to internal people. Each supplier is responsible for a single process, which is identically carried out at its three facilities in different parts of the world. The company has thus emphasized the exact replication of processes across all of its facilities as well as throughout all of its business strategies. The principle refers to the fact that any time a specification or task is transferred between functions or suppliers, the other party is responsible for exactly reproducing the requirements.

Bring Key Suppliers into the Process as Needed   Bringing suppliers into the product development process is different from simply sharing information, and it can involve including important suppliers early in the design process of a new product, perhaps even as part of the new-product team. The benefits of early supplier involvement include gaining a supplier's insight into the design process, allowing comparisons of proposed production requirements against a supplier's existing capabilities, and allowing a supplier to begin preproduction work early. A supplier can bring to the development process a fresh perspective and new ideas. If given the opportunity, suppliers can have a major impact on the overall timing and success of a new product. The type of involvement can also vary (see Exhibit 5.7). At one extreme, called the *white box design*, the supplier is given blueprints and told to make the product from them. At a more involved level often called a *gray box design*, the supplier's engineers work cooperatively with the buying company's engineers to jointly design the product. At the highest level of supplier involvement (*black box design*), suppliers are provided with functional specifications and are asked to complete all technical specifications, including materials to be used, blueprints, etc.

Good Practice   At Honeywell Microswitch (a division of Honeywell), a commodity team consolidated quantities in order to maximize leverage. By "piggy-backing" requirements for industrial and automotive divisions, the company established multiyear contracts with K-Tech, a plastics supplier that has proved to be very responsive. K-Tech has furnished a full-time in-house person responsible for ordering, scheduling, and expediting—who will be assigned a buyer's code, thereby eliminating a position in the purchasing area. K-Tech has reduced pricing and expanded capacity, and it wants to double its size and grow with Honeywell. It is a very open relationship. Honeywell provides a desk and computer for the supplier representative, who sits in on new-product development meetings and is considered "part of the team."

EXHIBIT 5.7   *Extent of Design Responsibility*

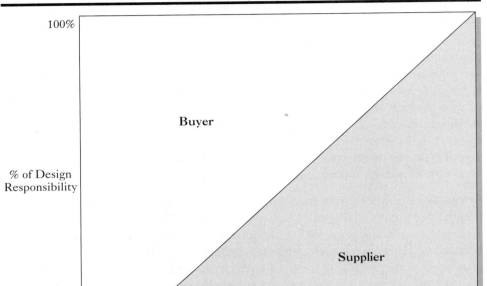

Source: R. Monczka, G. Ragatz, R. Handfield, D. Frayer, and R. Trent, *Integrating Suppliers into New Product/Process/Service Development* (Milwaukee, WI: ASQ Press).

Good Practice 3M is a diversified multibillion-dollar company selling products worldwide.[24] It is a company committed to product and technology innovation as a way to remain a world leader. The company also commits itself to a goal of having at least 25% of its total sales revenue come from newer products. Information on the latest technological advances from 3M Corporation can be found at http://www.mmm.com/us. Each of 3M's 40 operational units is responsible for managing its own global growth of sales and profit. This section reports on the specific process that one division—the 3M Industrial Specialties Division—uses to develop and market new-product ideas.

The Industrial Specialties Division uses cross-functional teams to manage families of products. These teams always include purchasing personnel, who are actively involved in each stage of the process. In addition, the teams are responsible for developing new products from new technologies and developing product extensions from existing products and technologies. The teams follow a general

EXHIBIT 5.8   *New-Product Evaluation at 3M*

Factor	Scale				
	1	2	3	4	5
Customer need	Low		Medium		High
Competitors	Many		Limited		None
Technology	None in 3M		Within 3M		Within division
Mkt. capability	None in 3M		Within business unit		Within division
Mfg. capability	None in 3M		Equipment modification		Existing equipment
Product price	Competitor advantage		Neutral		Strong 3M
Product performance	Competitor advantage		Neutral		Strong 3M
Total rating:_____					

Source: Adapted from McKeown, "New Products from Existing Technologies," *Journal of Business and Industrial Marketing* 5, no. 1 (Winter/Spring 1990).

four-step procedure designed to generate new-product ideas and streamline the new-product development process:

1. Opportunity identification
2. New-idea prioritization
3. Product development
4. Review of the development process

Opportunity identification involves the actual generation of new-product ideas. The team, with its different functional backgrounds, identifies ideas requiring new technologies as well as extensions of existing products and technology. In addition, a reward system encourages personnel to submit new-product ideas for the appropriate team to review. The cross-functional team accumulates the new-product ideas for further consideration during the second step of the process.

The first step involves prioritizing the new ideas. The team uses a subjective scale to evaluate ideas against a number of variables to arrive at an initial ranking of the ideas. Exhibit 5.8 shows the different variables used to evaluate product ideas at 3M. For any new product, the team rates the potential customer need for the product, the absence of competitors producing the product, the ability to harness existing technology capabilities within 3M, the ability to adequately manufacture and market the product, and the ability to meet competitors' pricing and performance features. These scores provide a good indication of the likelihood of new-product success. Products with higher ratings are more attractive for initial development. The second step involves the development of a ratio comparing the expected five-year cumulative sales to projected costs. 3M has found a strong correlation between the probability of technical and of marketing success. Each variable is estimated and placed into the opportunity-rating equation:

Opportunity Rating (in $) $= (CS \times TS \times MS)/(LB + OC)$

where CS = Five-year cumulative sales

TS = Probability of technical success

MS = Probability of marketing success

LB = Lab costs

OC = Other costs

The two rating systems allow the team to evaluate and compare new-product ideas. From this, the team identifies which ideas will move to the product development step.

The product development step involves the physical development of the new product. To assist the team in its development efforts, the division created an expediting system called FASTRACK. Each team selects a single product idea that does not require a new invention to expedite through the production system. Special stickers identify all documents and activities relating to a new product. This alerts all personnel to the item's special priority. Special priority for selected items does not mean the neglect of other items (such as the production of current items). This system simply serves as a notice that streamlining the product development process is a high priority at 3M.

The last step involves the periodic review of the new-product development process. If a product does not meet its timing or market objectives, the team determines the reasons for the shortfall. The objective of the review process is to improve the product development process in a nonthreatening and nonpunitive environment. 3M recognizes that a punitive process only stifles creativity. Falling short of product development objectives provides an opportunity to improve the development process by learning from past mistakes. The most common reasons for missing a product's development objectives are poor planning, technical difficulties, and poor support from outside functions. Teams meeting or exceeding their objectives receive recognition and a small reward as a team—not as individuals on a team. Team reward is a critical factor in maintaining a team effort versus an individual effort. ■

CONCLUSION

This chapter discussed the need for purchasing to develop closer relations with internal and external groups. To accomplish this, purchasing professionals must develop a working knowledge of the principles of engineering, manufacturing, cost-based accounting, quality assurance, and team dynamics. The days when purchasing operated in a confined area with an occasional visit to a supplier are over.

Firms are using the team approach to streamline and improve the product development process. This directly affects firms that rely on innovative new products for their continued success. Purchasing has a key role to play on these teams. Their role involves helping to select suppliers for inclusion in the process, advising engineering personnel of suppliers' capabilities, and helping to negotiate contracts once the product team has selected a supplier. Purchasing also acts as a liaison throughout this process, in facilitating supplier participation at team meetings and helping to resolve conflicts between the supplier and the team when they occur. Purchasing may also be involved in developing a target price for the supplier to aim at while planning the component/system, and helping the supplier to analyze costs and identify ways of meeting this target price. Finally, purchasing may also be involved in developing nondisclosure and confidentiality agreements in cases where technology sharing occurs.

Part of the increased interaction between purchasing and other functions is due to the need to compete in an environment driven by reduced product cycle times. Purchasing supports this effort by developing closer internal and external relationships and by participating on cross-functional teams. Those interested in a purchasing profession should learn as much as they can about what it takes to compete in today's markets, including expanding their knowledge about the team approach as well as understanding how firms compete on cost, quality, and time. The need to interact effectively with different groups plays a major role in how well purchasing can accomplish its tasks.

DISCUSSION QUESTIONS

1. What does it mean to say that purchasing is a boundary-spanning function?
2. Which internal purchasing linkages will become more important during the next ten years? Why?
3. Describe the types of information and data that purchasing and engineering may share with one another.
4. Why are engineers reluctant to share information with suppliers?
5. What are some of the possible ways that purchasing and engineering can strengthen their communication linkages?
6. Why is it necessary for purchasing to be the primary contact with suppliers? What are some drawbacks to non-purchasing functions contacting suppliers? Should purchasing control all contact with a supplier?
7. Engineers cite a variety of complaints or problems they sometimes have with purchasing. Select two of the problems and describe how purchasing can change engineering's perception.
8. Research with cross-functional sourcing teams revealed that teams that included suppliers as active team participants put forth greater effort, on average, than teams that did not include suppliers. Discuss why the involvement of external suppliers can affect a team's effort positively.
9. Why is goal setting so important to the success of the sourcing team process? What is the role of the team leader when setting team goals?
10. Relatively few individuals have the qualifications, experience, or training to immediately assume demanding sourcing team leadership positions. Do you agree or disagree with this statement? Why?

11. What are the pros and cons associated with concurrent sequential product design?
12. Describe the traditional model of buyer-seller relationships. How is the traditional model different from the collaborative model? What are the major characteristics of the collaborative model?
13. What are the advantages to a firm of successfully using a cross-functional team for different tasks?
14. Describe a typical "technology roadmap" for a manufacturer of PCs. How does this affect purchasing's activities in the new-product development cycle?
15. Why should a purchaser encourage early supplier involvement during new-product development? What types of information can a supplier provide that are useful during new-product development?
16. What is the difference between a gray box and a black box approach to early supplier involvement? Under what circumstances might each approach be appropriate?
17. What criteria are most important when considering whether a supplier should be involved in a new-product development effort?
18. Provide examples of some purchased components with a short product life cycle. How should purchasing manage such components differently from other components with long life cycles?

ADDITIONAL READINGS

Monczka , R. M., and R. J. Trent. *Cross-Functional Sourcing Team Effectiveness*. Tempe, AZ: Center for Advanced Purchasing Studies, 1993.

Monczka, R. M., and R. J. Trent. "Cross-Functional Sourcing Team Effectiveness: Critical Success Factors," *International Journal of Purchasing and Materials Management* (Fall 1994): 2–11.

Monczka, R. M., G. L. Ragatz, and R. B. Handfield. "Supplier Integration into New Product Development: Preliminary Results." In *Management of Organizational Quality*, vol. 2. Greenwich, CT: JAI Press, 1997, 87–138.

Monczka, R., D. Frayer, R. Handfield, G. Ragatz, and T. Scannell. *Supplier Integration into New Product/Process Development: Best Practices*. Milwaukee, WI: ASQ Quality Press, 2000.

Trent, R. J. "Understanding and Evaluating Cross-Functional Sourcing Team Leadership." *International Journal of Purchasing and Materials Management* (Fall 1996): 29–36.

———— "Individual and Collective Team Effort: A Vital Part of Sourcing Team Success." *International Journal of Purchasing and Materials Management* (Fall 1998): 46–54.

ENDNOTES

1. R. Monczka, R. Handfield, D. Frayer, G. Ragatz, and T. Scannell, *New Product Development: Supplier Integration Strategies for Success* (Milwaukee, WI: ASQ Press, January 2000).

2. Ernest Raia, "1989 Medal of Excellence," *Purchasing*, September 28, 1989, 67.
3. R. E. Spekman, "Strategic Supplier Selection: Understanding Long-Term Buyer Relationships," *Business Horizons* 31, no. 4 (July/August 1988): 76.
4. This model was developed by Schmitz, Frankel, and Frayer, "ECR Alliances." This report was based on case studies of several manufacturer-supplier and manufacturer-distributor alliance relationships.
5. J. M. Schmitz, R. Frankel, and D. J. Frayer, "ECR Alliances: A Best Practice Model," Joint Industry Project on Efficient Consumer Response, 1995, Proctor and Gamble, Cincinnati, OH.
6. Spekman, "Strategic Supplier Selection," 80–81.
7. Robert Monczka, Kenneth Peterson, Robert Handfield, and Gary Ragatz, "Determinants of Successful vs. Non- Strategic Supplier Alliances," *Decision Science Journal* 29, no. 3 (special issue on "Supply Chain Linkages), (Summer 1998): 553–77.
8. C. Larson, "Team Tactics Can Cut Product Development Costs," *Journal of Business Strategy* 9, no. 5 (Summer/October 1988): 22.
9. R. D. Russell, "Innovation in Organizations: Toward an Integrated Model," *Review of Business* 12, no. 2 (Fall 1990): 19.
10. I. D. Steiner, *Group Process and Productivity* (New York: Academic Press, 1972), 88.
11. I. L. Janis, *Groupthink: Psychological Studies of Policy Decisions and Fiascoes* (Boston: Houghton Mifflin, 1982), 9.
12. R. M. Monczka and R. J. Trent, *Cross-Functional Sourcing Team Effectiveness* (Tempe AZ: Center for Advanced Purchasing Studies, 1993).
13. L. H. Peters and E. J. O'Connor, "Situational Constraints and Work Outcomes: The Influences of a Frequently Overlooked Construct," *Academy of Management Review* 5, no. 3 (March 1980): 391–97.
14. John Zenger et al., *Leading Teams: Mastering the New Role* (Homewood, IL: Irwin, 1994), 14–15.
15. R. M. Monczka and R. J. Trent, "Effective Cross-Functional Sourcing Teams: Critical Success Factors," *International Journal of Purchasing and Materials Management* 30, no. 4 (Fall 1994): 7–8.
16. W. C. Musselwhite, "Time-Based Innovation: The New Competitive Advantage," *Training and Development Journal* 44, no. 1 (January 1990): 55.
17. Musselwhite, "Time-Based Innovation," 53, 55.
18. As quoted in Musselwhite, *"Time-Based Innovation,"* 54.
19. R. Handfield, *Reengineering for Time-Based Competition* (Westport, CT: Greenwood Publishing Group, 1995).
20. A. Kusiak and U. Belhe, "Concurrent Engineering: A Design Process Perspective," *Proceedings of the American Society of Mechanical Engineers* 59 (1992).
21. Ken-ichi Imai, Ikujiro Nonaka, and Hirotaka Takeuchi, "Managing the New Product Development Process: How Japanese Companies Learn and Unlearn," Colloquium on Productivity and Technology, Harvard Business School, March 27–29, 1989.
22. T. R. Welter, "Digital Builds a Better Mouse," *Industry Week* 23, no. 8 (April 16, 1990): 58.
23. R. Monczka, R. Handfield, G. Ragatz, D. Frayer, and T. Scannell, *Supplier Integration into New Product/Process Development: Best Practices* (Milwaukee, WI: ASQ Press, 2000).
24. This section summarizes a company study titled "New Products from New Technologies," *Journal of Business and Industrial Marketing* 5 no.1 (Spring 1990): 67–72.

6 Purchasing and Commodity Strategy Development

A Paradigm Shift in Purchasing—AlliedSignal Revisited

In 1992, Raymond Stark, the newly appointed vice president of materials management, walked into AlliedSignal (now known as Honeywell) prepared to make major changes.* Stark's mission, similar to the work he did at Xerox, was to revamp AlliedSignal's supply chain, with the goal of achieving productivity gains of 6% a year—forever! This would require drastically reducing the 9,500 suppliers who sold AlliedSignal $5.6 billion a year of raw materials, parts, and services.

During 1992, 1,500 U.S. suppliers were summoned to mass meetings at AlliedSignal to learn what Stark had in mind. At a meeting of aerospace suppliers, Stark bluntly asked participants to show up in January with plans to reduce their prices 10% to 15% and lead times 30%, while meeting stiff quality standards. AlliedSignal insisted it wanted to help its suppliers, not bully them, lest they end up cutting corners. To give suppliers a head start on cost reduction, AlliedSignal arranged to let them piggyback on its purchases of office supplies, tooling, and corporate travel; the volume discounts could mean major savings to smaller companies. More important, AlliedSignal formed "commodity teams"—cross-functional squads of manufacturing engineers, designers, and purchasing and finance experts in such areas as castings, electronic gear, machine parts, and raw materials. Each team was responsible for selecting the best suppliers in its specialty. Those chosen would receive long-term national contracts, become involved early in new-product design, get help in introducing total quality management at their own companies, and develop electronic links with AlliedSignal to reduce paperwork. In sum, it was a partnership that aimed to reduce costs for both sides rather than just prices.

Not all suppliers were surprised by this approach. Todd Haas, executive of Small Castings of Bechtelsville, Pennsylvania, which makes aluminum and zinc housings for the aerospace business, said, "We've been through this as a supplier to AMP, an electronic components maker, as well as AT&T. I'm delighted, not worried." But another supplier asked, "Isn't this more like a dictatorship than a partnership?" For the winners, however, the rewards were larger margins as costs fell and more sales as the "survivors" divided up the business that others lost.

One of the biggest changes made by AlliedSignal involved its long-term contracting practices. Now when AlliedSignal signs up a supplier, it requires a one-time reduction in price while also demanding that the supplier commit to lowering the component's total cost by 6%, adjusted for inflation, every year. Typically, suppliers have been able to hit this 6% target through a combination of price cuts and service improvements, such as increasing the frequency of deliveries, which helps lower inventory costs. Suppliers also pledge to eliminate defects. However, these agreements are not one-sided. AlliedSignal often enters into "partnering agreements" with suppliers. These agreements require that AlliedSignal purchase a certain volume from the supplier over an extended period of time in return for

→ → →

extra effort in improving productivity. Suppliers that exceed the new threshold, 7%, can either keep half of the cost savings or apply the savings to next year's target.

Since the early days of its procurement strategy development, AlliedSignal has expanded the scope of its strategy development efforts. It now provides free training to suppliers on improving designs, reducing defects, and finding ways to help lower costs without reducing the supplier's profitability. Suppliers are also actively part of new-product design teams, allowing suppliers to provide their expertise to such ventures. AlliedSignal is also expanding its global supplier network by forming partnerships with new suppliers in Europe and the Far East. It is also expanding its information systems so that all suppliers will be directly "on-line" with all AlliedSignal locations. Most recently, AlliedSignal has developed an "Onsite Supplier Delivery" program where suppliers have a full-time representative working at AlliedSignal's facilities, helping to manage the flow of materials and sharing information as required.

AlliedSignal is pushing a total supply chain philosophy throughout the organization with a mix of training and dedicated supply chain leaders in each business unit. These leaders, drawn from the materials group, work with the businesses to map their process, from sales through delivery, and identify opportunities to improve both the quality and cycle time of the supply chain. AlliedSignal is rolling all these tools into a corporate-wide initiative known as *Premier Business.* The heart of the program, which will include supply chain management, operational excellence, lean manufacturing, technical excellence, and delivery, are cross-functional teams comprised of members from manufacturing, finance, engineering, sales, human resources, and materials management. The current vice president of materials management, Fred McClintock, offers this observation: "If you believe in continuous improvement, you can *never* say 'We're there. We're as good as we'll ever be.'" One thing is clear—developing strong procurement strategies has helped make AlliedSignal one of the leading component and systems manufacturers in the world.

*In 1999, AlliedSignal acquired Honeywell, and the two merged enterprises were renamed "Honeywell."

Remaining competitive means that purchasing must contribute to profitability by focusing on the world-class coordination of activities related to the goals and objectives of the organization. World-class means that purchasing must adopt strategies that help a company compete with anyone, anywhere, anytime, and expect to win. This chapter focuses on the contribution that purchasing can make to corporate strategic planning, and how this contribution should filter down to lower planning levels. We begin by discussing the importance of purchasing and how purchasing executives can contribute to the strategic planning process at the corporate level. In order to contribute to corporate strategy, purchasing must be able to translate *corporate objectives* into specific *purchasing goals.* Purchasing goals serve as the driver for detailed *commodity strategies*—specific action plans that detail how goals are achieved through relationships with suppliers. To illustrate this, we provide a step-by-step process that purchasing executives can employ to translate corporate strategy objectives into purchasing commodity strategies. We also discuss the evolution of purchasing strategy while discussing the changes in management processes that must take place for this evolution to occur. The chapter provides an overview of the strategic planning process and illustrates how the purchasing decisions discussed in other chapters of this book are embedded within the concept of strategy development.

LINKING PURCHASING AND CORPORATE STRATEGY

Managers are familiar with many "buzzwords" that abound when the topic of business strategy is mentioned. Terms such as *downsizing, reengineering, best-in-class, benchmarking,* and many others reflect the fact that many organizations are in a state of dynamic change, which will continue throughout the twenty-first century. However, such terms often fail to capture the actual processes that occur when developing and implementing corporate strategies.

What is a corporate strategy? At its very roots, corporate strategy addresses the long-term mission of an organization, including long-term survival. The number of companies that have ceased operations or entered bankruptcy is not insignificant, even in periods of economic growth. Companies such as Studebaker, Packer, Eastern Airlines, PanAm, Kaiser Healthcare, and many other once-thriving companies were unable to withstand the market forces of competition. In many cases, this was due to poorly developed corporate strategies. A corporate strategy involves more than just survival. It requires a definition of how a company will compete in a changing competitive environment. We offer the following definition of corporate strategy. The strategy of an organization (or of a subunit of a larger organization) is a conceptualization of:

- Long-term objectives and purposes of the organization
- Broad constraints and policies that restrict activities
- A current set of action plans (also known as tactics) and near-term goals expected to help achieve an organization's objectives

Executive management must have a specific plan outlining how the company will differentiate itself from its competitors, achieve growth objectives, manage costs, achieve customer satisfaction, and maintain continued profitability in order to meet or exceed the expectations of stakeholders.

While it is beyond the scope of this chapter to go into detail regarding corporate strategies, the economics associated with corporate strategy are fairly straightforward. An organization must take in more revenues than it spends on operating costs in the long term to grow and increase profits. As shown in Exhibit 6.1, there are two fundamental ways of balancing this equation: increase revenues or decrease costs. Increasing revenues involves either raising prices, or keeping prices stable and increasing volume. Simultaneously, costs must be held steady or must increase at a rate smaller than the rate of increasing revenues. However, this option has become increasingly more difficult to realize over the last several years. Low inflation rates

EXHIBIT 6.1   *How Companies Make Money*

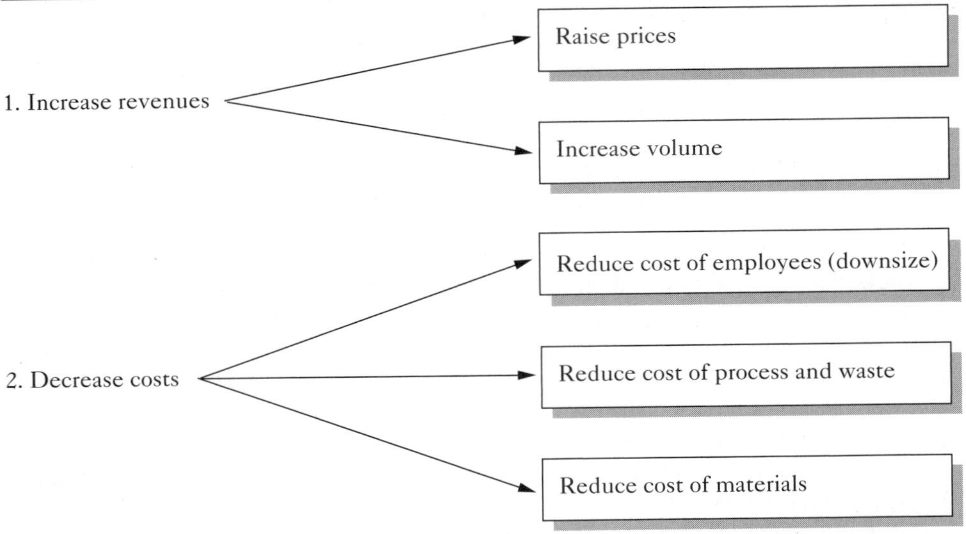

1. Increase revenues

> Raise prices
>
> Increase volume

2. Decrease costs

> Reduce cost of employees (downsize)
>
> Reduce cost of process and waste
>
> Reduce cost of materials

combined with increased productivity rates mean that prices cannot be raised without alienating customers. Customers also have a greater number of products and services to choose from, meaning that the number of lower-priced, higher-quality products is often increasing. Only a few markets in which a seller can increase or even hold prices steady exist today.

Reducing costs has become an area of intense interest. Faced with global competition, companies are constantly searching for ways to reduce costs and pass the savings on to customers while preserving their profit margins and maintaining a return to shareholders. Companies often begin addressing costs by reducing their workforce. This option was utilized extensively during the 1980s and 1990s when many larger organizations eliminated millions of jobs during corporate downsizing. To some extent, downsizing has reached its limits. Managers and workers today are required to perform more tasks and have greater responsibility with fewer resources and less time. The probability of obtaining significant cost savings through further downsizing is marginal.

Another way to reduce costs is through *process reengineering*. Any process contains a certain amount of non–value-added activity estimated to be as high as 80% to 90% of total process-cycle time.[1] Companies such as Hewlett-Packard, Toyota, Ford, Nortel Networks, Motorola, and many others have mapped their processes, identified significant non–value-added activities, and developed ways of reducing the time required to complete these processes.

Reducing the cost of materials and services has become an attractive option to most managers. Today, more and more managers are looking to purchasing to improve corporate profit margins. To some extent, purchasing is the last major opportunity area for achieving significant improvements in return on assets. Unfortunately, many

Electronic Data Systems (EDS) Partners in Software and Contract Labor Services

EDS, an information solutions provider located in Plano, Texas, recently partnered with its largest software supplier to develop a unique electronic linkage. The global agreement standardizes prices and eliminates individual billing for 120,000 EDS employees worldwide, and it also reduces order cycle time. "Through our efforts in strategic sourcing—just the beginning of EDS's supply advantage efforts—we have already reduced the firm's cost of goods on sourced items by approximately 10% annually," says Peter Quigney, EDS's vice president of global purchasing. "EDS is also working with a select group of suppliers to improve how we provide contract labor services to our internal customers," he adds. The goals of the contract labor alliance are to (1) categorize internal customers' requirements based on needs and marketplace availability, (2) standardize the products and services required, and (3) distribute labor-service requirements to approved suppliers. "In essence," says Quigney, "we're providing our internal labor-service recipients with qualified candidates while directing them to a preferred suite of suppliers. We're increasing efficiencies by better managing a human-resource commodity and saving time by eliminating unqualified undershoots or overshoots in meeting actual needs." The strategy relies on a "supplier management strategy," which Quigney describes as a "specific methodology of categorizing supplier relationships and managing them accordingly, with the lion's share of resources allocated to strategic partners."

Source: Presentation by Peter Quigney at North Carolina State University Graduate Research Symposium, November 3, 1999, Raleigh, NC.

companies in the United States do not perform well the task of strategic purchasing planning. The result is often a limited focus on functional strategic planning with minimal or no linkages to the corporate strategic plan. In some cases, this is caused by purchasing's limited understanding or awareness of company-wide strategies. In other cases, purchasing historically has not been included in the strategy development process. Perhaps the greatest problem is that executive management often fails to recognize the importance and contribution of supply-base management, and therefore has not focused on linking purchasing and corporate strategy. Without executive commitment to purchasing involvement in corporate strategy development, strategic sourcing results are unlikely to be successful.

Translating Corporate Objectives into Purchasing Goals

The need for purchasing to develop strategies that enhance an organization's competitive position through supply-base management is greater than ever. From this perspective, an effective purchasing strategy means more than simply promising "maximum efficiency" or "lowest cost." Given the diversity of available strategies, an effective purchasing strategy is one that fits the needs of the business and strives for consistency between the internal capabilities and the competitive advantage being sought, as defined in the overall business strategy. The term "strategic alignment" means that purchasing activities are consistent with the nature of the business strategy and make a proactive contribution to marketing effectiveness.

The concept of purchasing alignment with corporate strategy makes sense—but how does it happen? Before purchasing can align with corporate strategy, purchasing managers must be able to translate *corporate objectives* into *purchasing goals*. Goals and objectives differ across four major dimensions:

- *Time frame:* Objectives are timeless or open-ended, while goals are temporal or time phased and intended to be superseded by subsequent goals. For example, when John F. Kennedy stated that the United States was going to send a man to the moon, this was clearly an objective. When he added that it would be done "by the end of the decade," the objective became a goal.
- *Measurement:* Quantified objectives are often stated in "relative terms" (i.e., with respect to another entity or organization). Goals are much more specific, stated in terms of a particular result that will be accomplished by a specified date. The objective that "we will be the top automotive company in quality" is relative to other automotive companies. The goal that "we will reduce defects to 1,000 parts per million" is an absolute metric, which is a goal.
- *Specificity:* Objectives are stated in broad, general terms while goals are stated in terms of a particular result that will be accomplished by a specified date. For instance, the statement that "we will be the best in customer satisfaction" is a very broad statement that is an objective. The statement that "we will reduce warranty costs by 3% on part number 333 by the third quarter" is more specific.
- *Focus:* Objectives are often stated in some relevant external environment. Goals are internally focused and imply how resources shall be utilized in the future. For instance, the statement that "we will be regarded by the public as an environmentally conscious company" is externally focused; the statement that "we will invest 10% of our revenues in new environmentally friendly technology" is internally focused and states how resources will be used.

Notice that each of these examples couples an objective with a goal. This is an important part of the strategy development process. Executives often develop very broad, sweeping statements regarding where a company is headed, what the broad mission is, and where it will be in the future. However, it is up to managers to "translate" these broad objectives into actionable, realizable goals.

Integrative Strategy Development

The process of aligning purchasing goals with corporate objectives is especially important for purchasing and supply chain managers. These managers often face some very broad directives from corporate management—for example, to reduce costs or to improve quality. The strategy development process takes place on four levels:

EXHIBIT 6.2   *Components of Integrative Strategy Development*

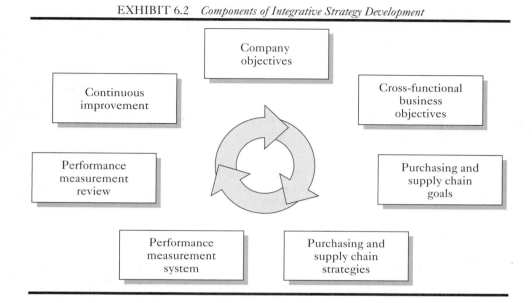

- *Corporate Strategies:* These strategies are concerned with (1) the definition of businesses in which the corporation wishes to participate and (2) the acquisition and allocation of resources to these business units.
- *Business Unit Strategies:* These strategies are concerned with (1) the scope or boundaries of each business and the links with corporate strategy and (2) the basis on which the business unit will achieve and maintain a competitive advantage within an industry.
- *Purchasing Strategies:* These strategies, which are part of a level of strategy development called *functional strategies*, specify how purchasing will (1) support the desired competitive business-level strategy and (2) complement other functional strategies (such as marketing and operations).
- *Commodity Strategies:* These strategies specify how a group tasked with developing the strategy for the specific commodity being purchased will achieve goals that in turn will support the purchasing-, business unit-, and finally the corporate-level strategies.

Companies that are successful in deploying supply chain strategies do so because the strategy development process is *integrative.* This means that the strategy is drafted (or has significant input) from those people responsible for implementation. Integrative supply chain strategies occur when corporate strategic plans are effectively "cascaded" into specific purchasing and commodity goals, through a series of iterative planning stages (shown in Exhibit 6.2). Corporate strategy evolves from corporate objectives, which effectively evolve from a corporate mission statement drafted by the chief executive officer (CEO), functional executives, and the board of directors. Corporate strategies are crafted by the CEO, taking into consideration the organization's competitive strengths, business unit and functional capabilities, market objectives, competitive pressures and customer requirements, and macro economic trends. What distinguishes an integrative strategy development process is that business unit executives, as well as corporate purchasing executives, provide direct input during the development of corporate strategy.

Corporate mission statements are often at the top of the strategy development process—they influence the scope and direction of the corporate strategy. The following are some examples of some corporate mission statements from manufacturing and service organizations.

- **Britax** (automotive mirror manufacturer): To lead the world in the design and manufacture of mirror component systems for the automotive industry.
- **Federal Express**: Our strategic actions and initiatives are summarized broadly by the FedEx "V3" strategy—Vision, Value, Virtual.
    - *Vision:* To satisfy worldwide demand for fast, time-definite, reliable distribution, FedEx continues to build and refine a uniquely integrated, all-cargo express network.
    - *Value:* To serve the world's largest express market with a wide range of premium and deferred express delivery services at competitive rates, FedEx continues to expand and enhance its integrated air-ground transportation network.
    - *Virtual:* FedEx remains our industry's premier innovator in developing information technologies that help customers manage and grow their businesses, which in turn helps fuel our own growth.

Additional information on FedEx's core values and mission can be found at http://www.fdxcorp.com/us/investorrelations/1999annualreport/

- **Honda Motor Company**: Maintaining an international view point, we are dedicated to supplying products of the highest efficiency yet at a reasonable price for worldwide customer satisfaction.
- **Honeywell (Microswitch Division)**: We supply customers with switches and sensors for applications that require precision and/or application-specific packaging.
- **L. G. Cook** (hardware distributor): We deliver quality service on a timely basis and provide a wide assortment of merchandise that can service the complete needs of the growing do-it-yourself home center segment. We guarantee 100% satisfaction, or your money back.
- **Sparrow Hospital**: The mission of the Sparrow Health System is to improve the health status of the people of mid-Michigan by providing quality, compassionate, comprehensive and cost-effective health services that are accessible to all.[2] As a nonprofit, community governed, comprehensive integrated health system this will be accomplished by
    - Providing excellent and responsible patient care;
    - Serving as a recognized leader and as a valued partner in developing and delivering a full continuum of services;
    - Improving health status through public education, professional education, research, public advocacy, and health plans;

SOURCING SNAPSHOT

Global Commodity Councils at IBM

Today, IBM purchases virtually every component that is shipped in their products—frames, covers, and memory to cards, packaging, and pallets. The company has become largely an "assemble-to-order" operation, focusing on complete solutions for the final customer. Purchases are organized around either production purchases (involving site-level execution) or general procurement (software, facilities, MRO, support services, trucking, transportation, etc.). Approximately 20 corporate councils exist across the divisions for the top 80% of dollar purchases. Each council includes a representative from every division that purchases the commodity and is headed by a global commodity council manager (also typically from one of the divisions). The councils meet quarterly or monthly, and establish preferred suppliers lists for cross-divisional use. In developing new suppliers, commodity councils study the industry and develop a commodity strategy, then develop corporate contracts that the sites execute under. The corporate councils are viewed as a staff function and have been in place since 1996. The sites execute against the contracts, or are responsible for developing contracts for parts that are not included in the commodity councils. In 1999, about 90% of purchases were on corporate contracts. For instance, items such as sheet metal parts are unique to each division, whereas power suppliers, memory, plastic resins, chemicals, monitors, keyboards, and tape drives are sourced via commodity councils. Typically, the commodity council may develop guidelines, strategies, and scorecards but may not actually develop specific contracts until they are approved by senior management. Gene Richter, the former vice president of procurement, has stipulated that to reach a decision in the commodity councils required only a majority agreement, not a 100% consensus. This is due to the need to move forward with supply-base improvement.

Source: Adapted from Daniel Krause and Robert Handfield, *Developing a World Class Supply Base* (Tempe, AZ:, Center for Advanced Purchasing Studies, 1999).

- Being accountable for the value of our services to all patients, health plan members, physicians, health care purchasers, and communities; and
- Living our values of excellence, service, people, responsibility, innovation and teamwork.
- **Van Keulen and Winchester Lumber Company:** Quality begins with top grade timber, properly felled, cut to length, skidded, hauled, sawn to proper thickness, inspected, stickered, air dried or predried, kiln dried, millwork as requested, packaged correctly . . . and then, delivered to you, our valued customer . . . with care!

As shown in Exhibit 6.2, a key feature of the strategy development process is the linkage, either directly or indirectly, between functional purchasing strategy development and other functional specialties. Business unit objectives span multiple functions and provide clear directions so that all functional strategies (purchasing, marketing, operations, finance, human resources) are *aligned*. This linkage recognizes the need to remove the barriers of cross-functional integration. A system that promotes integrative strategy development between functional specialties supports focusing limited corporate resources toward specific company-wide objectives and performance goals.

Translating Purchasing Objectives into Purchasing Goals

A major output of the strategy development process is a set of functional strategic objectives, including purchasing strategic objectives. As purchasing managers interact with other members within their business , as well as with corporate executives, a major set of strategic directives should begin to emerge. These strategic objectives may or may not provide details concerning how they are to be achieved. However, the process is not yet complete. Unless purchasing executives can effectively translate broad-level objectives into specific purchasing goals, these strategies will never be realized. Purchasing must couple each objective with a specific goal that it can measure and act upon. These specific goals become the initial step for a detailed commodity strategy formulation process. Remember—objectives drive goals, whether at the highest levels of an organization or at the functional or department level. Examples of corporate-wide purchasing goals associated with various purchasing objectives are shown in the parentheses below.

Cost-Reduction Objective
- Be the low-cost producer within our industry. (*Goal:* Reduce material costs by 15% in one year)
- Reduce the levels of inventory required to supply internal customers. (*Goal:* Reduce raw material inventory to 20 days' supply or less.)

Technology/New-Product Development Objective
- Outsource non–core-competency activities. (*Goal:* Qualify two new suppliers for all major services by end of the fiscal year.)
- Reduce product development time. (*Goal:* Develop a formal supplier integration process manual by the end of the fiscal year.)

Supply-Base Reduction Objective
- Reduce the number of suppliers used. (*Goal:* Reduce the total supply base by 30% over the next six months.)
- Joint problem solve with remaining suppliers. (*Goal:* Identify $300,000 in potential cost savings opportunities with two suppliers by year end.)

Supply Assurance Objective
- Assure uninterrupted supply from those suppliers best suited to filling specific needs. (*Goal:* Reduce cycle time on key parts to one week or less within six months.)

Quality Objective

- Increase quality of services and products. (*Goal:* Reduce average defects by 200 ppm on all material receipts within one year.)

   The next level of detail requires translating company-wide purchasing goals into specific commodity-level goals.

Bringing Goals and Objectives Together—The Purchasing Strategy Development Process[3]

While not always the case, companies often use commodity teams to develop purchasing strategies. Purchasing strategies often apply to commodities—general categories or families of purchased items. Examples of major commodity classifications across different industries include body side moldings (automotive), microprocessors (computer), steel (metalworking), cotton (apparel), wood (pulp and paper), petroleum products (chemicals), and office supplies (all industries). A commodity team is often composed of personnel from manufacturing, product design, process engineering, marketing, finance, and purchasing. The personnel involved should be familiar with the commodity being evaluated. For instance, if the team is tasked with purchasing computers, then users from information systems should be included. If the team purchases vehicles and vehicle parts, then it would be a good idea to include maintenance managers who are familiar with the characteristics of these commodities. In general, the more important the commodity, the more likely that cross-functional members and user groups will be involved. Together, the commodity team will develop a commodity strategy that provides the specific details and outlines the actions to follow in managing the commodity. Exhibit 6.3 highlights the commodity strategy development process, which the following section explains.

Step 1: Define Business Unit Requirements

As noted in previous sections and shown in Exhibit 6.2, purchasing derives its strategic direction from corporate objectives and the business unit strategy development process. The business unit functional strategy acts as the driver for the cross-organizational purchasing strategies that emerge for the major products and services purchased by the business unit. These in turn translate into purchasing goals. Once purchasing has identified a set of broad-level goals that it must achieve, another set of more detailed strategies should emerge at the commodity / service / product family level. The process of purchasing strategy *deployment* effectively begins at the commodity / product family level.

Step 2: Define the Strategic Importance of the Purchase Requirement (Portfolio Analysis)

The second step when developing a purchase strategy is to fully understand the purchase requirement relative to the business unit objectives. This is typically achieved

EXHIBIT 6.3 *Purchasing's Communications Flows and Linkages*

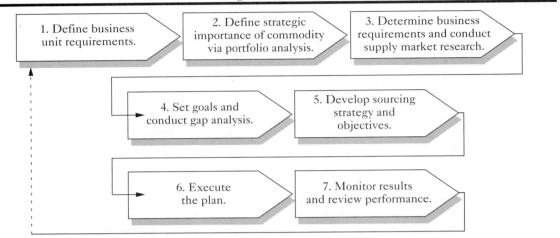

through a strategy segmentation tool known as *portfolio analysis* (shown in Exhibit 6.4). The premise of portfolio analysis is that every purchase or family of purchases can be classified into one of four categories or quadrants: (1) acquisition, (2) multiple, (3) leverage, and (4) strategic.

Acquisition Quadrant Acquisition items typically have few capable suppliers within a region and are of lower value. While many suppliers might conceivably be able to supply the item, the cost to search and compare supply alternatives often outweighs the value of the item. Generally, these items represent relatively low total dollars but may consume a disproportionate amount of time to acquire. Many acquisition items have standardized quality and technology requirements, and the "switching costs" of moving from one supplier to another supplier are low. The focus when acquiring these items should be on removing the effort and transactions required to obtain these items. Typical items that fall into this category include office supplies; maintenance, repair, and operating (MRO) supplies; and other items that users often need on short notice. Purchasing's contribution in this area is to "get out of the acquisition business." In other words, purchasing should try to establish systems such as procurement cards, electronic catalogs, direct ordering systems through the Internet (such as Ariba), and other automated transaction systems that eliminate unnecessary effort. This is not the quadrant where purchasing professionals want to focus their attention. The value that purchasing contributes in this category is assuring users that they can efficiently obtain these lower-value goods and services (in other words, Value = Possession of the good or service).

Multiple Quadrant The value of purchases in this quadrant is still low to medium, but there are a greater number of suppliers capable of providing the product or service.

EXHIBIT 6.4   *Example of a Functional Purchasing Policy*

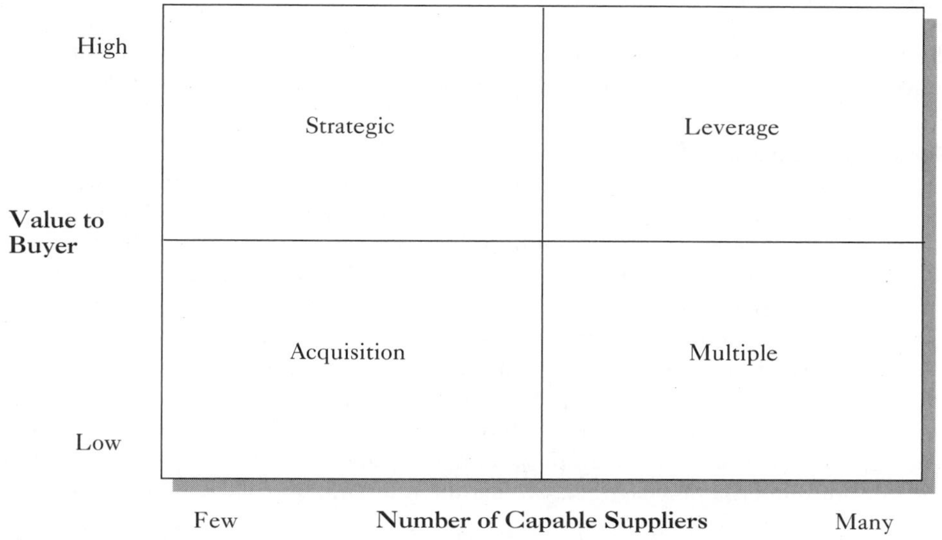

The technology characterizing these items is relatively standard and widely available. Switching costs are still relatively low, but because there are a greater number of suppliers available, purchasing should focus on price analysis as the primary tool for reducing costs. Price analysis effectively means "shopping around for the best deal" by sending out requests for bids or quotations to suppliers and accepting the most competitive bid. Historically, almost all items were purchased according to low price (particularly in government contracts). Bidding can be an effective strategy when conditions involve a standard item with many available sources of supply. Examples of such items might include personal computers, office furniture, steel castings and sheeting, and printers. Value in this quadrant is defined by achieving the lowest possible price (Value = 1 / Price), assuming that delivery and quality are acceptable.

Leverage Quadrant Items in this quadrant have a large number of capable suppliers with a medium to high annual expenditure. Furthermore, the item or service is often purchased across the entire organization. By combining the requirements of different units, purchasing can effectively negotiate a "better deal" with a select few suppliers. In analyzing the purchases in this quadrant, purchasers are often surprised to learn that they purchase the item from many different suppliers instead of concentrating their purchases with a few select suppliers. Consolidating purchases and reducing the supply base can yield an immediate and significant cost reduction. Steel and corrugated packaging are good examples. Remaining suppliers also benefit because average fixed costs decline as fixed costs are allocated over larger volumes.

Variable costs also decline due to improved productivity over a higher volume of product after consolidation. It is important for purchasing to ensure that the remaining suppliers have the capacity to handle additional business and that the quality of the product or service does not suffer (or indeed improves). Value in this quadrant is a function of the relationship between quality and price (Value = Quality / Price).

Strategic Quadrant The fourth quadrant includes items that are critical to success with few critical suppliers capable of supplying the good or service. Such items may be unique or customized, or they may simply represent a high-dollar item. Because of the small number of suppliers, it may be difficult to switch between suppliers. Items in this quadrant may be unique or involve technology that is unproven or in development. Examples include computer microprocessors, pharmaceuticals, new chemical compounds, catalytic converters, and aircraft engines.

By effectively classifying the goods and services being purchased into one of these categories, those responsible for proposing a strategy are able to comprehend the strategic importance of the item to the business. This begins to define the purchasing strategy that is best to employ. The implications of this task starts to become apparent through the process of classifying the item into one of the four categories, as illustrated in the following examples.

Items and services in the strategic and leverage quadrant will likely offer the greatest performance improvement opportunities. As such, the majority of purchasing's effort and resources should be spent on these types of commodities. However, organizations will still require lower-value, less critical items and services to operate. Steps must be taken to develop strategies to manage acquisition and multiple-type items so resources are available to manage value-added goods and services.

Once the commodity has been classified into one of these four categories, those responsible for developing the strategy must closely review the status of the commodity and match it to the objectives of the business unit as a whole. The objective here is to identify problems that the business unit has experienced with the commodity in the past, as well as identify future potential problems and opportunities (such as technology, cost, and quality improvements).

Step 3: Determine Business Requirements and Conduct Supply Market Research

The third major step in developing a purchasing strategy is to conduct a full commodity research analysis. This step is often overlooked or quickly done, but it is critical to understanding supply and demand. First, a business unit must accurately assess what it is currently spending for an item. Although this amount may be known in the aggregate, it is also important to understand where this spending is taking place, and with which suppliers. This can be a revealing analysis as it is often discovered that different business units are paying different amounts for the same product. In some cases the product is provided by the same supplier but at different prices.

EXHIBIT 6.5   *Data Collection Sources*

- Internet searches
  www.transportlink.com
  www.thomasregister.com
  www.bls.gov/datahome.htm
- Prior purchase files
- Discussions with users, customers, purchasing colleagues, and others

The analysis should also assess some of the important characteristics of the supply market as well as current and projected business requirements. The following items are among those that should be addressed:

- Determine the current strategy.
- Identify past expenditures for commodity and by supplier.
- Determine total expenditures for the commodity as a percentage of the total for the business unit.
- Identify currently used suppliers and potential suppliers.
- Define the marketplace (i.e., best price, average price, business unit's price, etc.).
- Determine expected trends in pricing.
- Perform supplier analyses.
- Identify the strategies of market leaders.
- Determine information technology requirements.
- Determine current and future volumes by using location requirements.
- Identify opportunities to leverage the commodity expenditures with similar commodities.

The commodity report should provide a basis for making sound purchasing decisions, and present management with information concerning future supply, price, and profit contribution of the purchased items. Potential information sources include supplier literature, government reports, trade magazines, the Thomas Register, and database searches. Much of this information is available through the Internet (see the list of the sites provided in Exhibit 6.5 and in the URL Appendix at the end of the book). In addition, benchmarking data may need to be generated through interviews with suppliers and other customers. Finally, a review of prior purchases may provide information on suppliers that were perhaps overlooked in the past but who are now potential candidates.

Step 4: Set Goals and Conduct Gap Analysis

The fourth step in the process is to establish specific targets for evaluating the progress of the strategy. Goals should relate directly to the objectives or requirements of a business. Effective goals all share certain characteristics:

- They are specific, measurable, and action oriented.
- They evaluate internal progress over time and compare performance to external competitors and benchmarks.
- They extend beyond price into other major total cost "drivers."
- They evaluate quality, customer service, availability, responsiveness, etc.
- They are established jointly with the supplier when appropriate.

Goals may be quantitative and "soft." They may be based on what external competitors are doing and may include external measures of supplier performance as well as internal integration issues. Regardless of how they are developed, they must be based on competitive analysis, comparison with market leaders, and future marketplace trends.

In addition to goals, the proposed strategy must include details on the specific actions required to realize those goals. For instance, the proposed strategy may specify the number of suppliers to do business with, as well as the dollar volume allocated to each supplier. The strategy proposal must also identify the type of contract it will use, whether it should pursue an alliance or partnership relationship, and whether a supplier requires further training and development. For each set of detailed actions, the proposal must provide an assessment of the possible risks and rewards associated with each action. An example of how one team might tie its business goals to product goals, system goals, and eventually commodity strategy goals is shown in Exhibit 6.6.

Step 5: Develop Sourcing Strategy and Objectives

The proposed strategy should consider the relevant criteria included in the research, including the best suppliers, the "risk" specified by the business unit requirements, and the "profit potential" associated with different options. The strategy presented to management should provide specific details, including

- Number of suppliers and amount of business to award to each supplier
- Recommended supplier(s)
- Length and type of contract
- Supplier involvement in product design (supplier provided designs or traditional designs?)
- Local or global suppliers
- Full-service distributor or original equipment manufacturer
- Supplier development activities
- Type of relationship (traditional or strategic alliance?)

Many of these criteria will be a function of the area of the matrix in which the commodity was classified using the portfolio analysis approach described in Step 2. For instance, a commodity that falls into the "acquisition" quadrant is not a suitable commodity for consideration of a strategic alliance. On the other hand, commodities with high purchased volumes have a high "upside" potential for significant savings, and a multiple/leveraged approach may be appropriate for such items. Those developing the strategy must provide a strong defense for why the chosen strategy is best.

EXHIBIT 6.6   *Purchasing at Different Organizational Levels*

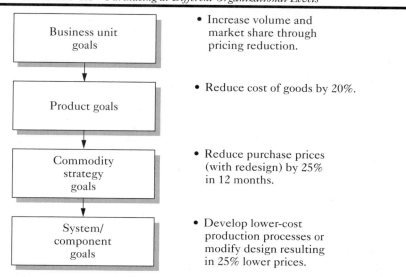

Business unit goals
- Increase volume and market share through pricing reduction.

Product goals
- Reduce cost of goods by 20%.

Commodity strategy goals
- Reduce purchase prices (with redesign) by 25% in 12 months.

System/ component goals
- Develop lower-cost production processes or modify design resulting in 25% lower prices.

Step 6: Execute the Strategy

Strategy execution requires ownership and documentation concerning timing and tasks. Affected parties should understand any changes brought about by the purchasing strategy. Key elements of strategy execution would include the following:

- Establish the tasks to be completed with timelines.
- Assign accountabilities and process ownership.
- Ensure adequate resources are made available to process owners.
- Explain the strategy to suppliers and internal customers and obtain full participation.
- Develop a negotiation plan prior to meeting with suppliers, as well as an "ideal contract."
- Communicate the strategy to all users and stakeholders.
- Develop a contingency plan if events do not occur as planned.

The individual or team responsible for implementation will then proceed to negotiate the contract, develop communication plans, and begin to execute the plan. Johnson & Johnson has initiated global contacts for providers of indirect items, such as services. A plant facilities contract required almost two years for transitioning from existing suppliers to the global supplier.

Step 7: Monitor Results and Review Performance

The final step of the strategy development process is to verify that a strategy is achieving its stated objectives. Regular reviews must be held to determine if the strategy is successful and whether the strategy requires modification. The review may include feedback and input from key suppliers. In any case, all suppliers should be advised of results along with future expectations. Purchasing personnel play a key role in this review because they are often the primary contact for the supplier with responsibility for supplier performance measurement. Earlier decisions may have to be revisited and reevaluated if suppliers do not perform as expected.

The key goals defined in Step 4 must be revisited periodically to identify modifications to the original strategy. Key elements of the results-monitoring process include the following:

- Conduct regular review meetings (at least annually) to determine if the strategy is well aligned with an organization's objectives.
- Share results with top management to provide additional momentum to the strategy; be sure to report the performance improvements achieved through the strategy.
- Assess internal customers and suppler perceptions. Are they satisfied with what has happened? If not—why not, and can the strategy be altered to improve the situation?
- Determine whether key goals are being achieved. If they are not achieved, what is the contingency plan? If the goals are achieved, are there any lessons learned?
- Provide feedback to those involved.

These strategy development steps are relatively general—they describe the steps to follow only when proposing and executing a strategy. However, the actual outcomes of the commodity strategy development process may vary considerably, depending on the specific commodity and the supply market.

Types of Purchasing Strategies

Organizations can employ a variety of different strategies that may be unique to each commodity. While we cannot cover all of the possible variations of strategies that may emerge, we will briefly review some of the most common and important purchasing strategies. As we will see later, certain strategies are used more often than others, depending on how advanced an organization is at the purchasing strategy development process. Each of these strategies or purchasing approaches is covered in greater detail in other chapters throughout the book.

Supply-Base Optimization

Supply-base optimization is the process of determining the appropriate number and mix of suppliers to maintain. While this term has also been referred to as *right-sizing*, it usually relates to reducing the number of suppliers used. Moreover, suppliers who are not capable of achieving world-class performance, either currently or in the near future, may be eliminated from the supply base. This process is continuous because the needs of the business unit may always be changing. Optimization requires an analysis of the number of suppliers required currently and in the future for each purchased item. Chapter 10 discusses supply-base optimization in detail.

Total Quality Management of Suppliers

Total quality management (TQM) requires suppliers to initiate statistical process control (SPC), design of experiments, process capability studies, and quality audits to focus on the elimination of process variability, improve immediate problem identification, and demonstrate corrective action capabilities. TQM also requires that suppliers develop a philosophy of zero defects while endorsing continuous improvement. Moreover, TQM emphasizes the need to meet and exceed the requirements of the customer (which in this case is the buying organization). In order to drive this change within the supply base, a purchaser must communicate to the supplier any expectations regarding quality. In particular, supplier evaluation and selection becomes crucial because of the need to select world-class suppliers. In some cases, a team from the buying company may have to work with a supplier to assess process capability, evaluate their quality philosophy, and recommend specific quality control techniques. Chapter 9 focuses on supplier quality management.

Global Sourcing

Global sourcing is an approach that requires purchasing to view the entire world as a potential source for components, services, and finished goods. It can be used to access new markets or to gain access to the same suppliers that are helping global companies become more competitive. Although true global sourcing is somewhat limited in most industries, more and more companies are beginning to view the world as both a market and a source of supply.

The major objective of global sourcing is to provide immediate and dramatic improvements in cost and quality as determined through the commodity research process. Global sourcing is also an opportunity to gain exposure to product and process technology, increase the number of available sources, satisfy countertrade requirements, and establish a presence in foreign markets. This strategy is not contradictory to supply-base optimization since it involves locating the best-in-class suppliers in the world for a given commodity. Some buyers also source globally to introduce competition to domestic suppliers.

There are several major barriers to global sourcing that must be overcome. Inexperience with global business processes and practices, along with few personnel qualified to develop and negotiate with global suppliers or manage long material pipelines, are serious issues. In addition, more complex logistics and currency fluctuations require measuring all relevant costs before committing to a worldwide source. Finally, organizations may not be prepared to deal with the different negotiating styles practiced by different cultures, and they may have to work through a foreign host national in order to establish contacts and an agreement. Chapter 11 addresses global sourcing in detail.

SOURCING SNAPSHOT

Toshiba's Partners Plus + Program

A new supply chain reengineering initiative that focuses on improving processes and cutting costs is expected to add 20% to the bottom line at Toshiba Toner Products Division in Mitchell, South Dakota. The Partners Plus + program sought to move past the adversarial relationships that purchasing had with suppliers. Instead of using strong-arm tactics to get suppliers to reduce prices, the program focuses on improvements suppliers can make in such areas as design, process/manufacturing, inventory, volume, business practices, materials handling, transportation/logistics, and tier-two secondary supply networks. It targets 21 priority U.S.-based suppliers responsible for 80% of Toshiba's Toner Products Division estimated $20 million in annual purchases. Big buys include packaging and raw materials. Managers at the company sought to create a program that would fit the Toshiba supply base. "We wanted a program that was tough, but not impossible," says Mona Ward, a buyer. The buyers also wanted to help suppliers meet cost-reduction goals. For instance, the program has resulted in two competing transportation companies working together to help reduce freight charges and improve service. Partners who meet targets can be rewarded with business guarantees, increased volumes, public recognition, an honors banquet, preference in new-product development, and performance awards. Those who do not participate receive no guarantees of existing volumes, no increased volumes, nonpreferential development status, and no trade/industry recognition. For each supplier involved in the program, goals using fiscal year 1997 as a benchmark call for a 6% first-year reduction, 5% reductions in both the second and third years, a 4% fourth-year cost reduction, and 3% in the fifth year. Reductions are accumulated from the base year and based on total dollar sales.

Source: Adapted from Susan Avery, "Toshiba Program Rewards Suppliers for New Ideas," *Purchasing* (May 20, 1999): 23.

Longer-Term Supplier Relationships

Longer-term supplier relationships involve the selection of and continuous involvement with suppliers viewed as critical over an extended period of time (e.g., three years and beyond). In general, the use of longer-term supplier relationships is growing in importance, and there will probably be greater pursuit of these relationships through longer-term contracts. Some purchasers are familiar with the practice, while for others it represents a radical departure from traditional short-term approaches to supply-base management.

Longer-term relationships are sought with suppliers who have exceptional performance or unique technological expertise. Within the portfolio matrix described earlier, this would involve the few suppliers that provide items and services that are critical or of higher value. A longer-term relationship may include a joint product development relationship with shared development costs and intellectual property. In other cases, it may simply be an informal process of identifying suppliers who receive preferential treatment. Chapter 15 discusses longer-term relationships and contracts.

Early Supplier Design Involvement

Early supplier design involvement and selection requires key suppliers to participate at the concept or predesign phase of new-product development. Supplier involvement may be informal, although the supplier may already have a purchase contract for the production of an existing item. Early involvement will increasingly take place through participation on cross-functional product development teams. This strategy recognizes that qualified suppliers have more to offer than simply the basic production of items that meet engineered specifications. Early supplier design involvement is a simultaneous engineering approach that occurs between buyer and seller, and seeks to maximize the benefits received by taking advantage of the supplier's design capabilities. This strategy is discussed in detail in Chapter 5, and the Good Practice Example at the end of this chapter also highlights how one company has successfully employed early involvement.

Supplier Development

In some cases, purchasers may find that suppliers' capabilities are not high enough to meet current or future expectations, yet they do not want to eliminate the supplier from the supply base. (Switching costs may be high or the supplier has performance potential.) A solution in such cases is to work directly with a supplier to facilitate improvement in a designated functional or activity area. Buyer-seller consulting teams working jointly may accelerate overall supplier improvement at a faster rate than will actions taken independently by the supplier. The basic motivation behind this strategy is that supplier improvement and success lead to longer-term benefits to both buyer and seller. This approach supports the development of world-class suppliers in new areas of product and process technology. Chapter 10 discusses supplier development in detail.

Total Cost of Ownership

Total cost of ownership (TCO) is the process of identifying cost considerations beyond unit price, transport, and tooling. It requires the business unit to define and measure the various cost components associated with a purchased item. In many cases, this includes costs associated with late delivery, poor quality, or other forms of supplier nonperformance. Total cost of ownership can lead to better decision making since it identifies all costs associated with a purchasing decision and the costs associated with supplier nonperformance. Cost variances from planned results can be analyzed to determine the cause of the variance. Corrective action can then prevent further problems. TCO is discussed in detail in Chapters 11 and 13.

EXHIBIT 6.7   *Stages of Supply Management Strategy Evolution*

1. Basic Beginnings	2. Moderate Development	3. Limited Integration	4. Fully Integrated Supply Chains
• Quality/cost teams • Longer-term contracts • Volume leveraging • Supply-base consolidation • Supplier quality focus	• Ad hoc supplier alliances • Cross-functional sourcing teams • Supply-base optimization • International sourcing • Cross-location sourcing teams	• Global sourcing • Strategic supplier alliances • Supplier TQM development • Total cost of ownership • Nontraditional purchase focus • Parts/service standardization • Early supplier involvement • Dock to stock pull systems	• Global supply chains with external customer focus • Cross-enterprise decision making • Full-service suppliers • Early sourcing • Insourcing/ outsourcing to maximize core competencies of firms throughout the supply chain

EVOLVING SOURCING STRATEGIES

If we compare the level of purchasing evolution to the strategies available, there is clearly an implementation sequence that emerges. Exhibit 6.7 presents the sequence of purchasing strategy execution based on research from multiple studies and interviews with many executives.[4] Organizations tend to evolve through four phases as they become mature and sophisticated in their purchasing strategy development.

Phase 1: Basic Beginnings

In the initial stages of purchasing strategy development, purchasing is often characterized as a lower-level support function. Purchasing adopts essentially a short-term, passive approach to purchasing and reacts to complaints from its internal customers when deliveries are late, quality is poor, or costs are too high. The only impetus for change here is the demand for change by management. The primary role of purchasing managers is to ensure that enough supply capacity exists, which usually means that suppliers are viewed in an adversarial manner. However, the amount of resources for improvement is limited, usually since the highest ranking purchasing manager likely reports to manufacturing or materials management. Performance measures focus on efficiency-related measures such as "number of purchase orders generated" or "dollars purchased per buyer." Information systems are location or facility focused and primarily transaction based; the primary form of communication is usually via mailed purchase orders, or occasionally a phone call when orders are misplaced.

In Phase 1, purchasing often focuses on supply-base optimization, and some attention is paid to total quality management at a greater rate than other progressive purchasing strategies. In this sense, these two strategies represent the building blocks from which to pursue increasingly sophisticated strategies. A reduced supply base is necessary due to the increased two-way communication and interaction necessary for successful execution of more complicated strategies. TQM also provides the fundamental focus on process that is required to implement purchasing strategies.

Phase 2: Moderate Development

The second phase of the strategy progression usually occurs as an organization begins to centrally coordinate or control some part of the purchasing function across regional or even worldwide locations. Purchasing councils or lead buyers may be responsible for entire classes of commodities, and company-wide databases by region may be developed to facilitate this coordination. The primary purpose of this coordination is to establish company-wide agreements in order to leverage volumes to obtain lower costs from volume discounts. Single sourcing with long-term agreements may eventually emerge as a policy for leveraged or consolidated purchase families. At this stage, limited cross-functional integration is occurring.

The approaches in Phases 1 and 2—supply-base optimization, TQM, and long-term contracting—have the potential, over time, to effect a steady increase in supplier contributions and improvements, but the performance change rate may not be dramatic. Purchasers must now begin to pursue strategic supplier relationships that focus on customer needs and the organization's competitive strategy. In Phase 2, buyers may begin to establish better relationships with critical suppliers while continuing to optimize the supply base. The purchasing department may now be evaluated on the achievement of competitive objectives, and suppliers are viewed as a resource. As such, there may be some informal channels of functional integration developing between purchasing, engineering, manufacturing, marketing, and accounting. Some of this may occur through infrequent cross-functional team decision making. The execution of purchasing strategy still takes place primarily at the business unit or local level.

Phase 3: Limited Integration

A number of purchasing initiatives discussed in this chapter, including concurrent engineering, supplier development, lead-time reduction, and early supplier involvement characterize this phase. In this environment, purchasing strategies are established and integrated early into the product and process design stage, and first- and second-tier suppliers are becoming actively involved in these decisions. Purchasing is evaluated based on strategic contribution, and resources are made available according to strategic requirements. Extensive functional integration occurs through design and sourcing teams that focus on product development, building a competitive advantage, and total cost analysis for new and existing products and services. Purchasing is viewed as a key part of the organizational structure with a strong external customer focus. As such, multiple customer-oriented measurements are used to identify performance improvements. Information systems include global databases, historical price and cost information, joint strategy development efforts with other functional groups, and the beginning of total cost modeling.

SOURCING SNAPSHOT

Paying Attention to Suppliers at Maytag

Consider these statistics: From 1991 to the end of 1998, the average price of household stoves and cooking equipment rose only 0.6%, says the U.S. Bureau of Labor Statistics. Meanwhile, according to analysis from Thinking Cap Solutions' industry cost escalation model, the direct costs of manufacturing cooking equipment in the United States jumped 9.1%. In the refrigerators and freezers sector, the data are even more startling. Here, average product prices dropped 4.6% while costs grew 9.2%. Moreover, household laundry equipment offered no respite either as average product prices fell 6.9% and costs rose 6.9% over the same period.

For procurement folks at appliance manufacturing companies, these price/cost trends set the stage for a pressure-cooker environment. "One of the biggest issues in the industry is the intense competitiveness," says Roy Armes, corporate vice president of global procurement operations for Whirlpool in Benton Harbor, Michigan. "Look at the price of an appliance today versus the price 20 to 30 years ago. Prices have remained the same even after inflation, giving the consumer a greater value for their purchase." The appliance companies, says Armes, will be able to provide the consumer with this value through greatly increased efficiencies, improved quality, and cost reductions. "We're not just offering another white box and competing on the basis of price alone," says Terry Carlson, vice president of procurement at Maytag in Newton, Iowa. "Our challenge is to continue differentiating our products through innovation." This means procurement must be more involved in product development, internally and externally.

"Purchasing has evolved to become an innovation search arm for Maytag," says Mike Rosberg, director of procurement. Thus, the purchasing function is

Phase 4: Fully Integrated Supply Chains

In the final and most advanced phase, purchasing has assumed a strategic orientation with reporting directly to executive management and a strong external, rather than simply internal, customer focus. Non–value-added activities such as purchase order follow-up and expediting have been automated, allowing purchasers to focus their attention on strategic objectives and activities. Organizations demand a higher performance standard from suppliers. Executives take aggressive actions that will directly improve supplier capability and accelerate supplier performance contributions. Examples of aggressive actions include developing global supplier capabilities, developing full-service suppliers, and adopting a "systems thinking" perspective that encompasses the entire supply chain. In such a mode, "insourcing" core activities that add the greatest value, while outsourcing components of their value chain to upstream or downstream parties that are more capable, often occurs. Such a system can directly affect the ability of the supply base to meet world-class expectations, and often involves direct intervention into the supplier's operating systems and processes.

responsible for choosing suppliers that not only meet cost and quality goal but also have innovative technologies and who can team closely with Maytag to develop next-generation appliances. Consequently, Maytag's procurement department is paying a lot more attention to fewer suppliers. From 2,700 direct materials suppliers five years ago, Maytag has whittled down its supplier ranks to 1,200 and aims to be down to around 300 in two more years. "We're developing long-term, three- to ten-year relationships with suppliers, and offering them more stability and a share of our growth," says Carlson. Maytag now teams with Emerson as its sole source for motors, Exxon Chemical as its sole source of polypropylene resins, Inland Steel Flat Products for steel, and Ferro Corporation for paints and coatings.

Inland Steel is one key supplier that has learned to work closely with Maytag. "Maytag does very rapid product development," says Steven J. Bowsher, vice president of sales and marketing for Inland Steel Flat Products in Chicago. "In order to be successful at this, they need the supplier to be sitting right there that has the same ethic. This changes the whole paradigm of the supplier/buyer relationship." This kind of partnership requires a high level of trust, says Bowsher, but the payoff can be great in terms of speed to market. For example, when one division was having trouble working with Inland, says Bowsher, Maytag allowed one of Inland Steel's people to take on an essential procurement job for Maytag, which in effect put Inland in charge of materials control.

Source: Adapted from Elizabeth Baatz, "How Purchasing Handles Intense Cost Pressure," *Purchasing* (April 8, 1999): 36.

Relatively few organizations have evolved to this phase. However, for those that succeed, a number of tangible and intangible benefits accrue from the progression of purchasing from a supportive to an integrated activity. These include price reductions across all product lines ranging from 5% to 25%, improved quality, cost, and delivery performance in the range of 75% to 98% in six to eight months, and a supply base that is better than the competition's. Purchasing is now in a position to influence rather than react to the supply base, and it can actually develop key suppliers in cases where a weak link exists. Moreover, all of these processes help establish the critical capabilities required of a global leader.

Observations on Purchasing Strategy Evolution

It is important that the purchasing student recognize an important point about the sequence shown in Exhibit 6.7 and the phases just discussed: *few organizations have executed the more complex strategies found in Phases 3 and 4.* This is due to a variety of factors including the relative complexity of complex or higher-level strategies, the resources and commitment necessary to execute the strategy, a lack of a supply-base optimization effort, and personnel who lack the skills and capabilities necessary for developing advanced sourcing strategies. However, those that successfully execute more sophisticated and comprehensive sourcing strategies should realize greater performance improvement over time. The following Good Practice Example illustrates how one company, BTR Engineering, developed a higher-level commodity strategy that integrates suppliers into its new-product development process. This strategy may be considered to be within the Phase 3–4 category of maturity.

GOOD PRACTICE EXAMPLE
Supplier Integration Strategies at BTR Engineering

■ ■ ■

BTR Engineering competes in the highly competitive global automotive industry as an original equipment manufacturer (OEM) for major automotive systems. To remain competitive, the company has developed a strategy to involve and integrate suppliers early during new-product/process/service development. Executive management views supplier integration as a critical strategy for remaining successful in a highly competitive industry. BTR's primary reasons for utilizing a supplier integration strategy include the following:

- *Ownership:* BTR attempts to integrate suppliers into the new-product development process to ensure that suppliers develop a sense of "ownership" for their part of the development process.
- *Design:* In many cases suppliers are more expert in a certain product or process. BTR's objective is to have suppliers share their design and/or process expertise in the new-product development process.
- *Long-term support:* Supplier integration provides a basis to negotiate long-term arrangements with suppliers and to use their skills on an ongoing basis.
- *Focus:* Historically, BTR has attempted to design, manufacture, and assemble its products. It expects to purchase complete product subassemblies from expert suppliers, and where possible, have those suppliers provide design and service product.
- *Cost reduction:* BTR requires that suppliers must agree to hold any required inventory in their own warehouses, thereby eliminating stock from BTR's plant. It is now establishing relationships with selected suppliers who will store and supply a range of products as required.

BTR Engineering relies on various practices, tools, and methods for developing and executing its early supplier involvement and integration strategies.

Cross-Functional Teams for Supplier Selection and Strategy Planning

The company recognizes the organizational importance of selecting the right suppliers for early involvement. It relies on cross-functional commodity teams to propose and execute its commodity and early involvement strategies.

Processes to Identify and Select Supplier Integration Candidates Currently, BTR has arrangements with suppliers who are capable of designing and producing parts or subsystems. The process, in simple terms, seeks quotations from selected suppliers that BTR believes and/or knows from past experience can design and manufacture a part. The quotation request document is a booklet used to collect information about the part and the suppliers. For many products BTR has no drawings. Instead, the company uses a performance specification that the supplier has to satisfy. Once BTR makes its supplier selection decision, the supplier becomes part of the product development team and is expected to serve as the design and engineering expert for that part or subsystem. The supplier provides the part according to this design after the part is approved for production.

Best Practice Manager BTR has appointed a "best practice manager" to each of its development teams. This individual ensures that all areas operate using the best tools possible to achieve maximum results. For example, one best practice approach is design for manufacture (DFM)/design for assembly (DFA) methodology used by development teams with supplier involvement. A benefit that BTR realized from adopting this methodology is that procedures that historically were performed as consecutive steps are now performed concurrently, leading to dramatically reduced development lead times.

Technology Sharing BTR provides suppliers with whatever information is needed during product development. This includes drawings, specifications, volume requirements, and more importantly, performance requirements. BTR's facilities are open to suppliers to provide them access to processes and expertise. Commodity teams expect suppliers to use, if needed, the latest technology that will provide the best parts. To protect all parties concerned, BTR insists that suppliers must sign a nondisclosure agreement prior to receiving any drawings or specifications.

Formal Trust Development Processes/Practices Every month BTR has several formal meetings with its key suppliers. These meetings bring together representatives from purchasing, quality, engineering, and senior management at BTR with sales, quality, engineering, and management groups from the supplier. Meetings rotate between BTR's plant and the supplier's facilities. While a large part of these meetings is taken up with discussion of current operating problems or projects, a significant amount of information also transfers from company to company—a process that helps highlight the fact that the success of both parties is linked.

Cost Information Sharing BTR utilizes a formal method of obtaining cost information from suppliers. The quotation booklets require suppliers to detail how they establish their costs. This detail allows BTR to determine if the supplier has provided a competitive quotation before the teams make a final supplier selection.

Colocation of Buyer-Seller Personnel Several major suppliers have placed people at BTR's plant on a permanent or semipermanent basis. For example, the "full-service" oil supplier has assigned a technical manager to the plant five days per week. BTR has provided the supplier's technical manager with office space, telephone lines, etc. The supplier controls BTR's total oil program within the plant. BTR also has a number of tooling suppliers who provide similar levels of support. BTR intends to have other suppliers join this program.

Performance Results BTR Engineering has realized some excellent results from its early supplier involvement and integration strategy:

*   Quality has improved by 5% over a 12-month period.
*   Total cost for product/process/service has improved by 20% over a 24-month period.
*   New-product/process/service development time has been shortened by 25% over a 12-month period.

BTR believes that suppliers have taken increased ownership in the product development and delivery process. The success of this strategy has demonstrated the importance of developing higher-level purchasing strategies that create advantages for the entire organization.

CONCLUSION

In reviewing the concepts outlined in this chapter, several points are clear regarding the role of purchasing in formulating sourcing strategies. The first is that purchasing must contribute to the formulation of corporate strategy by becoming an active participant in this process. Too many companies make decisions that profoundly affect their supply base while leaving purchasing personnel outside the decision-making process. The second point is that purchasing must become organized around critical commodities with dedicated personnel managing these commodities. Ideally, other functions such as engineering and production should also participate in the commodity strategy development process. The third major point involves the different types of purchasing strategies being developed by companies. Companies are increasingly shifting their attention from strategies such as supply-base optimization, purchase volume leverage, and TQM, and are focusing on long-term supplier relationships, early involvement of suppliers in new-product development, supplier development, and total cost of ownership. The final point is that all of this does not take place quickly. Strategic management is essentially a change process that evolves over time.

DISCUSSION QUESTIONS

1.   Select a commodity that you believe might be chosen for a strategic commodity analysis in the industries listed below. Justify why you believe the commodity is strategic to that industry, and the approach to be used in developing a commodity strategy.
>   Automotive
>   Computers
>   Plastic injected parts
>   Aeronautical equipment
>   Machine tools
>   Telecommunications
>   Paper

2.   Why has purchasing traditionally not been involved in the corporate strategic planning function?

3.   Describe a set of purchasing goals that might be aligned with the following corporate objective made by an automotive manufacturer: "To be the number one in customer satisfaction."

4.   Describe where you think the following commodities—paper clips, machine tools, castings, personal computers, fuel, computer chips, printers, styrofoam cups, paper, custom-designed networks—might fall within the portfolio matrix. Under what circumstances might one of these items fall into more than one quadrant of the matrix, or evolve from one quadrant to another?

5.   Under what conditions might you consider single sourcing an item in the "leveraging" category of the portfolio matrix?

6.   When conducting research, what are some advantages and disadvantages of the different types of information you might obtain from the Internet? Which types of Internet sites are likely to be more reliable?

7.   Why is it important to establish a document explaining the commodity strategy and share it with others? What are the possible consequences of not doing so?

8.   Why must organizations develop suppliers? Is supplier development a long-term trend or just a fad? Explain.

9.   Supply-base optimization must occur before long-term agreements can be put into place. What are the implications of this statement?

10. How long do you believe it takes a company to move from a Stage 1 phase to a Stage 4 phase of purchasing strategy development? In providing your response, consider all of the changes that must take place.

11. Provide a list of companies that, based on your reading of recent articles in the popular press, fit into the category of Stage 1 companies. What companies can you think of that might fall into the category of Stage 3 or 4? Provide some justification for your lists.

12. What do you think are the reasons why there are so few companies classified as Stage 4 companies? Do you think this is likely to change?

ADDITIONAL READINGS

"Anderson, Morgan Roll Out Systems Purchasing for the Next Century," *Purchasing* (April 8, 1999): 56.

Egelhoff, W. "Great Strategy or Great Strategy Implementation—Two Ways of Competing in Global Markets." *Sloan Management Review* (Winter 1993): 37–50.

Handfield, Robert, and Daniel Krause. "Think Globally, Source Locally." *Supply Chain Management Review.* (Winter 1999): 36–49.

Minahan, Tim, "OEM Buying Survey—Part 2: Buyers Get New Roles But Keep Old Tasks." *Purchasing* 125, no. 1 (July 16, 1998): 208.

Monczka, R. M., and J. P. Morgan. "Strategic Sourcing Management." *Purchasing* (August 13, 1992): 69–72.

Monczka, R., and R. Trent. *Purchasing and Sourcing Strategy: Trends and Implications* (Tempe, AZ: Center for Advanced Purchasing Studies, 1995).

Monczka, R. M., and R. J. Trent. "Evolving Sourcing Strategies for the 1990s." *International Journal of Physical Distribution and Logistics Management* 21, no. 5 (1991): 4–12.

Tan, Keah Choon, Robert Handfield, and Daniel Krause. "Enhancing a Firm's Performance Through Quality and Supply Base Management: An Empirical Study." *International Journal of Production Research* 36, no. 10 (1988): 2813–37.

Tyndall, Gene. "Ten Strategies to Enhance Supplier Management." *National Productivity Review* 17, no. 3 (Summer 1998): 31.

ENDNOTES

1. R. Handfield, *Reengineering for Time-Based Competition* (Westport, CT: Quorum Press, 1995).
2. Approved by the Sparrow Health System Board of Directors, December 20, 1997.
3. Based on a study carried out by the Global Procurement and Supply Chain Benchmarking Initiative, "Best Commodity / Purchase Family Strategy—Module 2," Michigan State University, East Lansing, MI, 1995.
4. This framework for the evolution of purchasing strategy was developed by the research team of the Global Procurement and Supply Chain Benchmarking Initiative through its comprehensive benchmarking studies from 1992 to 1999. Additional support for the four-phase model can be found in the following earlier research: C. A. Watts, K. Y. Kim, and C. K. Hahn, "Linking Purchasing to Corporate Competitive Strategy," *International Journal of Purchasing and Materials Management* (Fall 1992): 2–8; J. P. Morgan, "Are You Aggressive Enough for the 1990s?" *Purchasing* (April 6, 1989): 50–57; R. Reck and B. Long, "Purchasing: A Competitive Weapon," *Journal of Purchasing and Materials Management* (Fall 1988): 2–8; V. Freeman and J. Cavinato, "Fitting Purchasing to the Strategic Organization: Frameworks, Processes, and Values," *Journal of Purchasing and Materials Management* (Winter 1990): 6–10; Robert Monczka and Robert Trent, "Evolving Sourcing Strategies for the 1990s," *International Journal of Physical Distribution and Logistics Management* 21 (1991): 4–12.

Insourcing/Outsourcing 7

$\mathcal{T}$he Turnaround at IBM

Between 1991 and 1998, the world's largest information systems producer, International Business Machines (IBM) underwent a radical restructuring that affected every part of its business, including its supply chain. Between 1991 and 1995, IBM's primary business—producing computer hardware and peripherals—incurred major losses. During this period, the company's net profits were *negative $15 billion!* Moreover, IBM had become so large that it began to ignore what had made it successful: a strong focus on the needs of the customer and technology leadership.

Enter Louis Gerstner, IBM's new CEO. Gerstner, who was the CEO of a major consumer food company before coming to IBM, understood the importance of managing the supply chain with a customer focus. One of his first goals was to change IBM's focus from a computer producer to a customer solutions provider—satisfying a customer's needs rather than simply making products. As a solutions provider, IBM began to create integrated hardware and software solutions for customers and to purchase whatever products it needed to meet a customer's needs. In some cases, this might have meant purchasing and installing a competitor's product if that product was better suited to the customer's application. For instance, perhaps a customer required a network system to ensure that sales people could dial-in through a modem and upload orders to a central system. As a customer solutions provider, IBM would design the system, purchase the network hardware, develop and install customized software, and, when required, provide training to the users.

This model of total system development was a radical departure from what IBM had done in the past. It also had profound implications for IBM's future. It required a hard look at many "traditional core" businesses, such as mainframes and minicomputers. IBM was forced to conclude that it was no longer the world leader in all areas. Furthermore, some businesses were losing money as customers realized they no longer required some of the technology or products offered by IBM. In such cases, IBM closed down the business, sold them to other companies such as Solectron (a contract manufacturer that is discussed later in the chapter), or created new independent businesses. These changes required IBM to outsource many of the supply chain processes and products that it had created internally in the past. Almost every single process in IBM's supply chain was considered a candidate for possible outsourcing, including design, production, assembly, sourcing, software development, distribution, and testing.

IBM thus began to totally transform its culture and business. In the past, IBM purchased only 30% of its cost of goods sold from external suppliers; today external purchases represent 70% of cost of goods sold. Purchasing and logistics have suddenly become much more important from an executive perspective. In addition to purchasing raw materials and components, purchasing is involved with outsourcing key supply chain activities,

$\rightarrow\rightarrow\rightarrow$

including entire finished products. IBM's future certainly looks brighter today than it did in 1991. The company went from losing $15 billion over a five-year period to a $17 billion net profit between 1995 and 1998. Although the outsourcing decisions and restructuring that IBM confronted have been difficult, it is now positioned to withstand the competitive environment of the new century.

One of the most complex and important business decisions facing business today is whether to produce a component, assembly, process, or service internally (insourcing) or whether to purchase that same component, assembly, process, or service from an outside supplier (outsourcing). This decision is now being applied to virtually every process conducted within the traditional walls of an organization, and spans areas such as warehousing, distribution, transportation, production, assembly, sales, human resources, design, engineering, and even purchasing. The impact of such decisions is often felt for many years. Over the course of the twentieth century, the trend toward insourcing or outsourcing has shifted in both directions. For example, in the early 1920s, Henry Ford made a series of business acquisitions that went further and further up the automotive supply chain. He first began acquiring component suppliers for the Model T Ford and later acquired the steel mills to supply these same suppliers. He even acquired the mines that supplied coal to the steel mills. The process of insourcing all of these activities (also called "vertical integration") eventually proved to be too difficult and costly to manage.

Poor outsourcing decisions have also occurred. In the 1950s, the decision by U.S. television producers to outsource television components to Asian suppliers allowed the electronics industry in Asia to gain a foothold with this technology. The transfer of technology that took place allowed some suppliers to become major competitors who eventually captured many U.S. markets, putting the U.S. producers who originally developed the technology out of business. Today, not a single U.S-based producer of televisions exists.

We have also witnessed many excellent outsourcing decisions—decisions that allowed a company to enter and be successful in new markets. Consider the case of a mountain bike company that was interested in producing bicycles with titanium frames. Titanium, because it is light and strong, has many advantages over aluminum and alloy frames; customers wanted it. However, the material has many properties that make it difficult to work with, and the bicycle company did not have the equipment or the workforce skills to produce the frame. The company carried out an insourcing/outsourcing analysis and found a former arms producer in Russia that possessed excellent skills in working with titanium. With the arms market in Russia essentially gone, the arms producer was looking for new business. This match proved to be an excellent one, and the bicycle company now outsources its titanium frames from the former arms producer, who is also satisfied with the arrangement.

SOURCING SNAPSHOT

OEMs Outsource Value-Added Activities to Distributors

Electronics distributors are experiencing tremendous growth, which analysts expect to continue into the future. Supply channels are reshaping as more component suppliers want to sell through distributors and more OEMs want to purchase through distributors instead of buying direct. However, OEMs are requesting more services from distributors, and strategic alliances and an increased willingness to outsource are affecting electronic distribution. OEMs that outsource are seeking distributors capable of performing services such as battery and board assembly, integrated circuit programming, and kitting (placing separate components together to form a new package or kit). Buyers are also asking distributors to manage inventory, reduce procurement expenses through automated replenishment programs, manage in-plant stores, have EDI capability, and provide some design support. Value-added (VA) services are up to 27% of all services provided, compared with 17% five years ago, with an expected increase to 40% by the year 2000. Arrow Electronics says 50% of its $4 billion in annual sales already involve some form of value-adding service.

Source: Adapted from James Carbone, "Outsourcing, Alliances Change the Rules for Distribution," *Purchasing* (May 9, 1996): 52.

Insourcing/outsourcing (make-or-buy) decisions are often controversial. American workers are increasingly concerned over the fact that their employers are outsourcing production tasks to suppliers in developing countries with lower wage rates. These sentiments became especially evident during the North American Free Trade Agreement discussions in 1994 through 1999. In recent years, these issues have erupted, as members of the United Auto Workers union within the Big Three automotive companies have gone on strike to fight the increased outsourcing of components by these companies to nonunion or foreign suppliers. The World Trade Organization, a group dedicated to expanding the principle of free trade, had a stormy reception in Seattle during its 1999 meeting. Part of the debate centered around shifting business to countries that did not enforce child labor laws or comply with environmental standards.

Because of the importance of insourcing/outsourcing to organizational competitiveness, a number of variables and factors must be considered—from a firm's competency and specific costs to quality, delivery, technology, responsiveness, and desire for continuous improvement. Cross-functional teams are increasingly being used to make insourcing/outsourcing decisions. The outsourcing of major functions such as distribution, technology development, assembly, and even purchasing is being undertaken by companies (see Exhibit 7.1).

Recent benchmarking studies have found that organizations often make important insourcing/outsourcing decisions without fully understanding the strategic and total cost implications of these decisions. An "ad hoc" approach to this decision

EXHIBIT 7.1   *Product / Process Candidates for Outsourcing*

- Products
  - Technology
  - Manufacturing
- Processes
  - Design development
  - Process installation
  - Equipment service
  - Maintenance

can have devastating results, including a loss of a core capability, or worse, the outsourcing of a capability to a supplier who cannot meet performance expectations. The primary focus of this chapter is on a formal process that can be applied to any type of insourcing/outsourcing decision. The chapter concludes with a Good Practice Example that shows how one company confronted a difficult outsourcing decision.

THE INSOURCING/OUTSOURCING DECISION PROCESS

Due to the growing importance of services to the U.S. economy, insourcing/outsourcing analyses have broadened to include services and products. For example, the purchase of cafeteria and transportation services as well as payroll, distribution, and a variety of other areas are increasingly being considered as potential candidates for outsourcing (see Exhibit 7.2). The professional purchasing manager must bring a wide variety of knowledge and technical skills to bear on the insourcing/outsourcing decision, ranging from strategic thinking to in-depth cost analysis. In order to provide the most beneficial outcome to their organizations, purchasing managers must have a structured process in place that effectively considers all of the strategic and total cost implications of insourcing versus outsourcing. Exhibit 7.3 outlines the progression of steps involved in the insourcing/outsourcing decision process, starting with the use of cross-functional teams through the final deployment of the decision.

Step 1: Assess Technology and Demand Trends

The insourcing/outsourcing decision for any product, process, or service is made relatively infrequently: the level of investment required is usually significant, the amount of worker training needed to effectively implement a major decision is costly, and there are long lead times associated with the implementation of a decision. In many cases, this is not a decision that a single operation or purchasing manager can effectively reach. The long-term effects of these decisions as well as the shorter-term tactical effects of insourcing/outsourcing decisions must be considered using both objective and subjective criteria. All aspects of the decision must therefore be considered

EXHIBIT 7.2   *Service Candidates for Outsourcing*

• Workforce—security, janitorial, food service, etc.	• HMOs
• Information services	• MRO inventory
• Programming	• Utilities
• Human resource management	• Travel services
• Procurement	• Temporary labor
• Payroll	• Outplacement
• Third-party logistics	• Printing/copying
	• Customer satisfaction services

from a variety of perspectives, including finance, operations, design, engineering technology, marketing and sales, accounting, and purchasing. Not all of these individuals will play a major part on a cross-functional team assigned to reach a decision. However, the input of all functions should be solicited to some degree in every situation. Teams should collect as much information as possible from these different functions to prevent "straying down the wrong road."

Insourcing/outsourcing decisions, which often involve cross-functional teams, are affected by several factors.

New-Product Development   Insourcing/outsourcing decisions are often initiated during the new-product development cycle. Because the product, service, subassemblies, or components have not yet been designed, there may be minimal information available to guide the sourcing decision. The commodity under consideration may represent unfamiliar new technology or processes. In such cases, an outsource decision may be reached initially, unless the parts or technology under consideration are core competencies. The team should carefully consider the stability of the technology in question, the possible duration of the product life cycle, and the availability of reliable sources.

Strategy Development   An insourcing/outsourcing decision may also be driven by the business strategy development process. Top-level executives may decide that a change in sourcing patterns is necessary. For example, companies such as Spring, Union Pacific, Tenneco, Anheuser-Busch, and ITT have divested noncore businesses and are choosing to divest many product and process technologies formerly provided by those units.[1] In the 1990s, Jack Welch, the CEO of General Electric, implemented a radical policy of divesting any business unit that was not considered "number one or two" within its industry (even though many of these units were profitable at the time). Today, GE has record profits in the industries they chose to retain.

Poor Internal or External Performance   Insourcing/outsourcing decisions also stem from a failure of external suppliers to satisfy the business unit's requirements. If a supplier demonstrates an inability or unwillingness to provide a particular part or service, or shows an unwillingness to continuously improve, then the decision must be made whether to produce the part or component in-house or to develop another capable source. Likewise, if internal performance is not capable of meeting

EXHIBIT 7.3   *Insourcing/Outsourcing Decision Process*

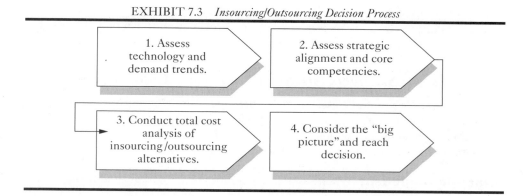

requirements, then the firm is faced with a decision to outsource with a capable supplier or spend time and resources to improve internal capabilities.

Changing Demand Patterns   Significant shifts in the marketplace stemming from changing sales demand or changing market economics caused by technological innovation often require a review of sourcing priorities. If demand for a product or service decreases dramatically, then there may be a need to shift production from internal to external sources to better utilize the buying firm's physical assets and intellectual capital. Certain types of suppliers specialize in lower-volume production or can combine business from other buyers to realize economic efficiencies. Likewise, if demand increases, then insourcing the part or service to realize economies of scale or scope might become an attractive option.

Shifting Technology Life Cycles   Changing technology may also affect insourcing/outsourcing decisions. Technology life cycles refer to the duration of a particular technology before it becomes outdated; this applies to product and process technology. For example, the Pentium II microprocessor replaced the Pentium, which replaced the 486, and so on. If a product technology is relatively mature or stable, then the technology life cycle will probably last a long while. In such cases, there is some reasonable assurance that investment in capital equipment to produce that technology will have a longer payback period and life. On the other hand, if the technology is changing rapidly, outsourcing effectively shifts the risk to external sources that specialize in a technology and are better able to manage the inherent risks.

Careful analysis of past life cycles of components and materials will provide insight into potential technology life cycles. In many technology-oriented firms, designers keep close watch on component technology and are usually in the forefront of anticipated change. Regular feedback and contact with designers can provide information on the potential life cycle of materials. Given the speed of introduction of new materials and products, managers may need to keep abreast of new developments on the Web, which is often quicker to respond to changes in specific technologies than printed matter. Examples of some Websites that provide insights into new technologies in a select group of areas include http://www.pddnet.com (product development and design) and http://www.ebnews.com (electronic buyers news), which provides insights into new materials in the electronics sector.

Step 2: Assess Strategic Alignment and Core Competencies

This step requires a detailed assessment of how the insourcing/outsourcing decision aligns or fits with an organization's strategic long-term plans, a determination of an organization's core competency, and, in the case of physical products, an assessment of the maturity of the process technology used to make an item.

Strategic Alignment   When assessing major trends in markets and technologies that affect the insourcing/outsourcing decision, purchasing must interact closely with the other functional groups and be aware of their functional strategies. As Exhibit 7.4 shows, a strategic planning process must consider the strategic plan for the specific business unit under consideration, as well as the plans for manufacturing/operations, technology/engineering, and the strategic sourcing. Several key questions should be asked at this stage of development:

- How will the supply base contribute to the goals of the strategic business unit?
- What is the current and future production/operations strategy?
- What is the long-term vision for what the supply chain of the organization will look like five years from now?
- What technology plans is engineering pursuing, both in the short and long term?

Those responsible for the insourcing/outsourcing decision or recommendation must ensure that the strategies of the major value-adding functions are essentially linked together. It is difficult to build a strategy to compete if every area has its own plan, and none of them are aligned. For instance, at one organization purchasing was attempting to develop an alliance with a supplier possessing a key technology while marketing was working with major customers to convince them to adopt a completely different technology. This is a clear case of poor strategic alignment.

Core Competence Alignment   Those responsible for insourcing/outsourcing decisions must also be keenly aware of an organization's core competence. What exactly is a core competence? In their classic *Harvard Business Review* article, Pralahad and Hamel define core competence as "the collective learning in the organization, especially how to coordinate diverse production skills and integrate multiple streams of technologies."[2] A manager or team responsible for making an insourcing/outsourcing decision must understand an organization's true core competence and whether the product or service under sourcing consideration is integral to that competence. A key product or service that is closely interrelated with the firm's core competence would more likely be reflected in a favorable insourcing (make) decision rather than an outsourcing (buy) decision. It could be a terrible mistake to outsource an organization's

EXHIBIT 7.4   *Strategy Alignment Through Business Planning*

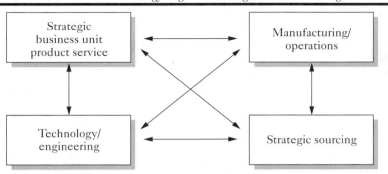

core competence (it may be lost forever) or to insource something that a firm is not qualified to make.

What really defines a core competence? This concept is often confused with *organizational capability*. An organization may be capable of providing a given product, service, or technology; however, a capability may not be a core competence. A capability is *also* a core competence when the following three conditions are true:

1. The capability is valued by the customer;
2. The capability can be applied to many products and services across multiple business units;
3. The capability is unique and cannot easily be imitated by competitors.

Consider the case of Polaroid. This company, until the 1990s, was highly vertically integrated—it produced internally almost all that it sold. Within the last five years, Polaroid has decided to aggressively outsource camera hardware to Asia while retaining the technology and production capability related to the film. Why? The film, rather than the physical camera, differentiates Polaroid's products and their performance. Retaining the technology involved with the development and production of film aligns directly with Polaroid's core competence, which is *image acquisition*. In fact, only two companies worldwide have the capability to make instant-photography film. Dozens of companies, on the other hand, have the capability to provide lower-technology cameras. Purchasing is now actively involved in identifying outsource partners.

Technological Maturity   A final insourcing/outsourcing consideration during Step 2 involves an analysis of process technology. Welch and Nayak, in their strategic sourcing model (shown in Exhibit 7.5), outline a three-way analysis of how the firm perceives its process capabilities in relationship to its competition (weak, tenable, or superior); the stage or maturity of the process involved (emerging/embryonic, growth, or mature); and the significance of the process technology for competitive advantage (low today, high today, or high in future).[3]

EXHIBIT 7.5   *Strategic Sourcing Model*

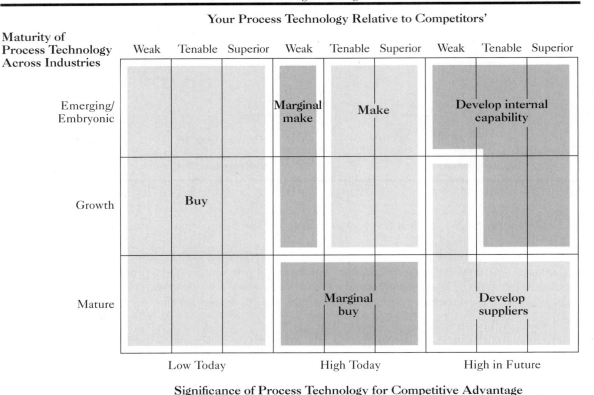

Your Process Technology Relative to Competitors'

Maturity of Process Technology Across Industries	Weak	Tenable	Superior	Weak	Tenable	Superior	Weak	Tenable	Superior
Emerging/ Embryonic				Marginal make	Make		Develop internal capability		
Growth		Buy							
Mature				Marginal buy			Develop suppliers		
	Low Today			High Today			High in Future		

Significance of Process Technology for Competitive Advantage

Source: Welch and Nayak, 1992 (see Endnote 3).

There are several possible outcomes within this framework. If the competitive advantage provided by a technology is low, then a "buy" decision allows the firm to leverage its own capabilities by focusing resources on high-value-added activities. A "marginal buy" situation involves mature technologies that provide significant competitive advantage, yet are better developed in other industries. If licensing of the technology is economically feasible, and the firm has demonstrated the ability to integrate and assimilate externally developed technologies, then it should purchase the technology.

In cases where a technology provides a competitive advantage but the technology is not yet mature, the technology should likely be internalized, which may then become a future core competence. Similarly, if the firm perceives that a technology may provide a future advantage but is still in an emerging or embryonic stage, it should be nurtured through research and development. The strategic sourcing model presented in Exhibit 7.5 allows an analyst to consider more than just the cost/price dimension of insourcing/outsourcing when determining whether to insource (vertically integrate) or outsource (purchase) a given product or service.

EXHIBIT 7.6   *Insourcing Versus Outsourcing Cost Factors Worksheet*

1. Insourcing		2. Outsourcing	
Operating Expenses:		Purchase costs	
Direct labor		Inbound freight/delivery	
Direct materials		Space	
Inbound freight		Administrative costs of control, contact with supplier	
Facilities		Continuing investment	
Depreciation		Costs of inventories	
Overhead		Working capital costs	
Direct management costs		*Total outsource costs* (2)	
Cost of inventories			
Working capital costs		*Net savings* (1) *minus* (2)	
		Less: Taxes on Savings	
Total insourcing costs (1)		*Net after-tax savings* (3)	

Source: Adapted from Joseph Cavinato, "How to Calculate the Cost of Outsourcing," *Distribution* (January 1988): 72–76.

Step 3: Conduct Total Cost Analysis of All Insourcing/Outsourcing Alternatives

In some respects, the economics of insourcing/outsourcing decisions resembles a capital budgeting problem. When considering a move from internal to external sourcing, a company must consider not only the obvious costs such as purchase price, direct labor, and materials, but also the estimated costs incurred in switching from insourcing to outsourcing (or vice versa). These extra costs may include idle equipment, loss of jobs, potential for union grievances, and other factors that may be difficult to estimate. These costs are then weighed against future monetary savings generated by making a change. For example, if switching from an internal to an external supplier costs $500,000 in switching and start-up costs and generates savings of $300,000 per year, the initial costs of making the switch will be recovered in less than two years. Exhibit 7.6 summarizes the key cost factors when conducting an insourcing/outsourcing analysis. Note that one of the most overlooked but important cost factors is the impact of federal, state, and local taxes.

In a typical insourcing/outsourcing decision, a worksheet such as the one in Exhibit 7.6 can be used to compare the savings between the current insourcing (1) and outsourcing operations (2). The difficult part of the analysis is adequately determining all of the relevant costs to the firm regardless of where they are incurred. Such costs may accrue across different departments, functions, personnel, or budgets.

It is usually easier to determine the costs involved with outsourcing a new item because most of the cost drivers are included in the purchase price shown on the supplier's invoice. (In cases when a global supplier is used, the cost of exchange rate fluctuations over the life of the contract must also be estimated.) Generally, the only additional costs that need to be included for the outsource decision are inbound freight,

EXHIBIT 7.7   *Costs Involved in the Insourcing Decision*

Total Variable Cost Elements

- Direct materials
- Variable fringes
- Expensed tooling

- Direct labor
- Variable overhead
- Variable overtime premiums

- Inbound freight
- Supplies

Total Factory Cost Elements

- Total variable costs
- Fees
- Research and development
- Indirect labor and fringe benefits

- Fixed overhead costs
- Property taxes
- Advertising
- Indirect materials costs

- Rent/building payments
- Support staff salaries
- Utilities
- Maintenance

Full Operating Costs

- Total factory costs
- Depreciation
- Expensed tooling

- Executive salaries
- Transfer pricing

- Corporate administration
- Commercial expenses

receiving, and inspection. These costs are relatively straightforward to determine. However, as discussed earlier, the hidden costs of discontinuing or switching from insourcing to outsourcing must be incorporated into the decision for existing parts or components, especially in the case of internal production costs.

Types of Insourcing/Outsourcing Costs   Identifying the costs involved in the insourcing decision are often difficult to identify. Exhibit 7.7 outlines the different categories that must be considered under the make option of the insourcing/outsourcing decision. The first is total variable cost elements, shown in the top section of the exhibit. These total variable cost elements are directly associated with the product and vary with the level of production. As production increases, the total variable costs increase (although average unit costs should decrease). Variable costs generally include direct materials, direct labor, variable fringes, freight, inbound supplies, and anything else that varies proportional to volume. Note that almost all direct costs are considered variable, and are normally the major portion of total costs.

The second cost element in Exhibit 7.7 is total factory costs, including all variable cots plus fixed overhead costs necessary to make a product in-house. Fixed overhead costs are directly attributable to the production process but cannot be as easily identified to a particular unit of product as can the direct costs included in total variable costs. They also do not vary over the short run with the level of production but remain relatively fixed. For this reason, they are often considered part of the "cost of doing business." Fixed costs may include rent/payment for buildings, grounds, fees, property taxes, support staff salaries assigned to a work center, research and development, advertising, and basic utilities. Other costs falling into this category are indirect costs involving fringe benefits, including health insurance, paid holidays and vacations, sick leave, social security contributions, and pension contributions. Indirect material costs include material handling, purchasing costs, packaging, storage, and so on.

Outsourcing Information Technology Services

Information technology (IT) managers at Warburg Dillon Read, the investment-banking arm of UBS AG of Switzerland, can no longer tap just any staffing service vendor to help hire contract staff. Instead, the bank has turned to another IT services vendor, Computer Horizons Corporation, to handle all details of hiring supplemental staff, from issuing requests for procurement to reviewing resumes to managing contracts. Centralizing the management of staffing vendors and contracts for the 75 IT managers who work with the bank's lines of business appears to be working well. These managers now have more time to work on projects, and economies of scale have been brought to staff sourcing. The system uses a Web browser that accesses Computer Horizon's systems, which provides details of all the vendor contracts available to Warburg Dillon Read. Contract employees represent about 20 percent of the 500 IT employees at the investment bank's U.S. operations. Michael Willis, the managing director of IT, says that now with the new system, "We have better bargaining leverage and a genuine temperature check on market rates."

Source: Adapted from Bruce Caldwell, "Outsourcing Helps in Staffing," *Computer Reseller News* (July 12, 1999): 12–13.

The third cost element in Exhibit 7.7 is full operating costs—all of the cost elements included in total factory costs plus all of the overhead costs not included in running a facility. Examples include executive salaries, bonuses, bid and proposal costs, claims and communication costs, custodial services, and industrial relations. Another important fixed cost is depreciation. Normally, the straight-line method of depreciation over the useful life of the equipment or product life cycle is used on capital expenditures. Overhead costs are assigned to individual products or families of products through an allocation process. This allocation process has typically been based on direct labor, but since direct labor has become a lower percentage of total cost of goods sold, other bases of allocation such as the proportion of purchased material have become more commonplace. More recently, new cost accounting techniques known as *activity-based costing* (ABC) have been developed to accurately reflect the proper allocation of overhead to different production activities (Chapter 13 discusses ABC). ABC uses "cost drivers" to determine the underlying reason for a cost occurring. These cost drivers are then used to allocate overhead costs. The bottom section of Exhibit 7.7 outlines the various cost elements included in full operating costs.

The last part of determining the total cost of internal production is deciding whether or not to include some level of profit to the in-house production cost. The transfer price (the price used between divisions of the same company) may or may not be different than the price used when the firm sells its output to an outside customer. For a truer representation of actual cost, the transfer price should include the same level of profit when output is used internally as when it is sold to outside

customers, particularly when the internal divisions have separate bottom-line responsibilities. However, many companies are hesitant to do this because they feel that
such internal pricing may adversely affect the insourcing/outsourcing decision and
bias it toward outsourcing. As a result, a given transfer price may or may not represent
the true cost of production.

The gray area of insourcing/outsourcing is the determination of what level of
costs (total variable, total factory, or full operating costs) should be included as the
proper cost figures during the insourcing/outsourcing decision. It is easy to recognize
that total variable costs are appropriately included because they are readily identifiable and vary directly with the level of production. However, is it appropriate to include all of the total factory costs or the full operating costs? The answer here is more
difficult to determine because it may not be readily apparent that all total factory
costs or full operating costs should be applied in a particular insourcing/outsourcing
decision. For example, how much of the firm's total electrical bill can be attributed to
the production of a particular part or family of parts? Proper allocation of overhead expenses is a difficult task. The assumptions underlying the allocation of overhead expenses can have dramatically different effects on total cost. The critical evaluation of
the underlying assumptions should be an ongoing process that always questions
whether the basis of allocation is appropriate or not. Fixed costs must be allocated,
but there are many different ways to accomplish the allocation of costs. As mentioned
earlier, this task can become even more difficult when production personnel attempt
to bias make-or-buy decisions by hiding costs.

One of the primary issues to address here is the time frame involved for the insourc-
ing/outsourcing decision. If the insourcing decision is expected to be relatively short in
duration, such as that encountered in a limited product life cycle, then perhaps only the
total variable costs and some proportion of the total factory costs should apply to the decision. However, if the make decision is to become part of the ongoing operation of a
facility, then the rule of thumb should be to include all relevant costs that would reasonably be incurred over the long term—that is, full operating costs plus some level of
profit. In the long run, a firm must recover all costs or go out of business. However, in
the short run, it is generally better for a firm to recover its variable costs and some portion of overhead rather than to undergo a significant decline in its business.[4]

Cost Analysis Example A Taiwanese supplier has bid on a new line of molded
plastic injected parts that are currently assembled internally within XYZ company's
facility. The supplier has bid $0.10 per part, given a forecasted demand of 200,000
parts in year 1, 300,000 in year 2, and 500,000 in year 3. Shipping and handling of
parts from the supplier's facility is estimated at $0.01 per unit. Additional inventory-
handling charges amount to $0.005 per unit. In addition, purchasing costs are esti-
mated at $20 per purchase order, with a purchase order being released every month
for the duration of the contract.

Although XYZ's facility already has an injection process capable of producing the
part, it is currently running at 95% capacity. Investing in another machine will cost
$10,000, with depreciation over the life of the product. Direct labor is estimated at
$.03 per unit, plus 50% fringe benefits. Direct materials purchased are $.05 per unit.

EXHIBIT 7.8   *Insourcing / Outsourcing Cost Analysis*

Insourcing

Operating expenses:		
Direct labor	$0.0300	
Fringe (50%)	$0.0150	
Direct materials	$0.0500	
Indirect labor	$0.0110	
Fringe (50%)	$0.0055	
Equipment depreciation	$0.0100	($10,000 depreciated over 1 million units)
Fixed overhead	$0.0300	
Engineering/design	$0.0300	($30,000 over 1 million units)
Total Insourcing Costs	**$0.1815 (1)**	

Outsourcing

Purchase costs	$0.1000	
Shipping and handling	$0.0100	
Inventories	$0.0050	
Administrative costs	$0.0072	($20 × 12 × 3/1,000,000)
Total Outsourcing Costs	**$0.1222 (2)**	

Savings

((1) − (2)) × 1,000,000	$59,300
Less taxes (40%)	$23,720
Total Savings **from Outsourcing**	$35,580

Indirect labor is estimated at $.011 per unit plus 50% fringe benefits. Upfront engineering and design costs will be $30,000. In addition, the comptroller has insisted that fixed overhead allocation at a rate of 100% of direct labor be included. Finally, current federal, state, and property tax rates are approximately 40%.

Given this scenario, one possible analysis is shown in Exhibit 7.8 where an outsourcing decision appears to provide significant savings of $35,580. However, many of the items included in the analysis are questionable and open to debate. For instance, should fixed overhead be included in the make costs? Are the assumptions regarding the supplier's ability to produce a quality product valid? What is the status of the exchange rate for the Taiwanese dollar vis-à-vis the U.S. dollar over three years? Many of these factors are not effectively captured in this analysis, yet they must be addressed within the framework of an insourcing/outsourcing analysis. In general, managers need to approach these major decisions from a total cost of ownership perspective, which attempts to integrate all of the relevant costs associated with a particular decision. Total cost and cost/price analysis are addressed in Chapter 13.

Step 4: Consider Non-Cost Factors and Reach Consensus on the Decision When making an insourcing/outsourcing decision, decision-makers must consider a variety of non-cost factors. This supports a balanced and complete picture of the advantages and disadvantages of the insourcing/outsourcing decision.

Insourcing Advantages There are a number of advantages to vertically integrating (insourcing) a product or service. First, the degree of control the buyer wishes to exert over the transfer of technology should be considered. If a high degree of control is desired so that proprietary designs or processes can be protected from unauthorized use, then vertical integration may be preferred over outsourcing. A vertically integrated firm increases its visibility over each step of the process by having more of the factors of production available under its control. A dedicated facility can also result in lower per-unit costs when economies of scale or scope provide the firm with higher efficiencies. Insourcing may also allow a firm to spread its fixed costs over larger volumes.

Insourcing Disadvantages The disadvantages of insourcing relate to the level of investment typically required when the insourcing decision is made. A high level of investment is required when new plant and equipment are purchased. The firm must ensure that adequate volume is present to justify purchasing the plant and equipment required for internal production. Another disadvantage is that if an investment is made in dedicated plant and equipment that cannot be utilized for other types of products, the risk associated with the insourcing alternative increases. A good example is the semiconductor industry. In 1995, at least a dozen new semiconductor plants were under construction in the United States, including three by Intel and two by Motorola. The average cost of a chip fabrication plant is currently about $3 billion. The life of process equipment is often as little as six months before newer technologies replace the chips. Plant expansions are made on the premise that investment in new capacity can provide rapid market-share gains. On the risk side, however, analysts worry that the chip business may fluctuate in future years, and the increasing cost of wafer-fabrication plants could soar beyond the reach of all but a few companies.[5]

Another disadvantage to insourcing occurs when a firm tries to change or alter the product in accordance with market needs or demand. Matching demand to requirements in the various parts of the supply chain is an intricate process. It is often easier to switch suppliers than to switch internal processes.

Outsourcing Advantages A major advantage to outsourcing is that it often provides a greater degree of flexibility. As market demand levels change, a purchaser can more easily make changes in its product or service offerings in response. Because there are lower levels of investment in specific assets, it is easier to make unexpected changes in its own production resources. There is a lower investment risk for the buyer as the supplier assumes the uncertainty inherent in plant and equipment investment. Ideally, both the buying and the supplying firms should concentrate on their own distinct core competencies while outsourcing other products and services that are not areas of expertise, yet are necessary for competing effectively. Also, outsourcing allows for improved cash flow because there is less upfront investment in plant and equipment. By using contract manufacturers, Dell Computer supported $3 billion in annual revenues with only $60 million of fixed assets in the mid-1990s.[6] This also made Dell's return on investment figures much higher than the industry average.

A firm may achieve reductions in labor costs by transferring production to an outsource location that pays lower wages or has higher efficiencies, resulting in lower per-unit production costs. As the high cost of providing retirement and medical benefits

SOURCING SNAPSHOT

Contract Production: A Tidal Wave of Opportunity

Michael Marks, CEO of Flextronics, a contract manufacturer (CM) based in San Jose, California, says that OEMs such as Cisco Systems, IBM, Hewlett-Packard, Sun Microsystems, Dell Computer, and others are flocking to contract manufacturers because it costs less for these organizations to build products than the OEMs. OEMs are not only using CMs, they are selling their production facilities to them and have them build not just boards but entire systems. For instance, Trimble sold its production assets to Solectron, and Ericsson sold its production facility in Sweden to Flextronics. It is also likely that other telecom companies such as Nokia, Nortel, and Lucent will outsource more in the near future. With this trend taking place, the electronics production services industry is forecast to grow from about $90 billion in 1998 to $178 billion in 2001, a 25% compound annual growth rate. Marks claims that many OEMs do not view production as a core competence. "There are OEM management teams saying 'we aren't good at production. It's not that important to us and there are five companies at $2 billion plus who can do a great job for us and are doing a great job for our competition.'" For instance, Cisco System says that 40% of their products never go into a Cisco facility; they are built by the contract manufacturer and shipped directly to the end customer. To date, few Japanese electronics OEMs outsource, but there are signs that this may change over the next few years. If that happens, the industry will grow at a breakneck pace for years to come. Solectron, Jabil, SCI, and Flextronics are the major players in this growing industry. In the near future, it is also likely that contract manufacturers will also handle purchasing for OEMs, by providing dedicated buying teams who do planning and procurement for the customer.

Source: Adapted from James Carbone, "High-Tech Buyers See Tidal Wave of Opportunity," *Purchasing* (June 17, 1999): 36–43.

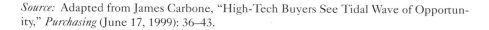

continues to escalate, firms are increasingly avoiding hiring more full-time personnel whenever possible.

Outsourcing Disadvantages Conversely, there is great risk if the purchaser chooses the wrong supplier to provide the product or service being outsourced. The supplier's capabilities may have been misstated, the process technology may be obsolete, or the supplier's performance may not meet the buying firm's expectations or requirements. In one case, a purchaser trusted a supplier to develop a component based on the supplier's claim that it had mastered the required process technology. By the time the purchaser realized that the supplier was incapable of producing the product, the market for the final product had already been captured by a competitor.

There is also the issue of loss of control. The buying firm may perceive that it has lost the ability to effectively monitor and regulate the quality, availability, confidentiality, or performance of the goods or services being bought because they are not produced under the firm's direct supervision. This may lead to concern over product/service performance. Ultimately, the buying firm may create costly safeguards to prevent poor performance by changing specifications, increasing inspection, or periodic audits to ensure that the supplying firm is meeting expectations.

Apple Computer provides an example of some of the risks associated with outsourcing. When demand for a new line of Macintosh computers increased dramatically during the mid-1990s, the company had a backlog of orders of more than $1 billion. Apple was unable to obtain timely deliveries of critical parts, including modems and custom chips, and was not able to capitalize on the demand for its products. The parts shortages occurred because most components were custom-designed and outsourced to a single supplier. Because managers failed to accurately predict the growth in sales (the actual increase was 25% instead of the 15% predicted), Apple alienated customers who were not willing to wait for the new product. This situation was especially risky because many customers switched to Microsoft's Windows 95 operating system instead of waiting for the Macintosh. In this situation, outsourcing and partnering provided technological benefits but resulted in a serious capacity shortfall and loss of market share.[7]

A final outsourcing disadvantage involves the potential for losing key skills, technology, or productive capacity. The phenomenon of North American firms outsourcing production to low-cost suppliers who later became global competitors has been described as the "hollowing out of the corporation." Indeed, some would argue that many U.S. firms are now only "shells" that no longer make anything but simply act as distribution and sales networks. While there is probably some truth to this statement, the outsourcing decision has to be balanced with the need to remain responsive, and to outsource those tasks over which the firm no longer has a competitive advantage.

A good example of this balance is Cisco Systems Inc., which uses outsourcing to achieve a significant competitive advantage in the webserver computer market. In fact, executives have found a way for custom production to be cheaper than mass production. If that seems hard to imagine, consider that Cisco outsources most production to contract manufacturers that operate 37 factories, all linked via the Internet. Suppliers not only make all components and perform 90% of the subassembly work, they even perform 50% of the final assembly. Suppliers regularly ship finished Cisco computers to Cisco customers without a Cisco employee ever touching the gear. The result is "savings of between $500 million and $800 million this year," compared to what it would cost to own and operate those plants, says Carl Redfield, Cisco's senior vice president for production.[8] One risk of outsourcing involves losing touch with the production expertise that contributes to continuing product improvements. To minimize this risk Cisco designs the production methods and uses the Internet to monitor operations at its contract manufacturers. "We develop the entire process, and we know what every supplier is doing every moment," says Redfield.

Exhibit 7.9 summarizes the advantages and disadvantages of either an insourcing or outsourcing decision. These are related to whether the supplier or the buyer enjoys a favorable position vis-à-vis the alternative. Issues related to cost, integration of operations, engineering capabilities, control over quality, capacity constraints, design secrecy, workforce issues, and availability of reliable suppliers must be considered.

EXHIBIT 7.9   *Advantages and Disadvantages of Insourcing and Outsourcing*

Insourcing	
Advantages	*Disadvantages*
• Higher degree of control over inputs	• High volumes required
• Visibility over the process increased	• High investment needed
• Economies of scale/scope	• Dedicated equipment has limited uses
	• Problems with supply chain integration

Outsourcing	
Advantages	*Disadvantages*
• Greater flexibility	• Possibility of choosing wrong supplier
• Lower investment risk	• Loss of control over process
• Improved cash flow	• Long lead times/capacity shortages
• Lower potential labor costs	• "Hollowing out" of the corporation

While many of these issues cannot be accurately translated into cost considerations, they must nevertheless involve specific cost analyses in order to arrive at the best decision. In the event that an outsourcing decision is made, the buying firm must be sure to include several key elements in the contract, and explore whether the supplier is open to these terms through negotiation. Typically, the insourcing/outsourcing decision is formally presented to executive management for approval. Whatever decision or recommendation is made, those responsible for the analysis must thoroughly justify their choice.

GOOD PRACTICE EXAMPLE
Insourcing/Outsourcing at Cummins Engine

■ ■ ■

As part of a routine competitive analysis (conducted much like that discussed earlier in the chapter), Cummins Engine noticed that several competing companies within the mature, capital-intensive heavy equipment industry, including John Deere, Navistar, and J. I. Case, seemed to demonstrate conflicting sourcing policies that tended to fragment the potential competitive advantages generated through strategic sourcing.[9] The insourcing/outsourcing decisions of these companies were frequently made using simplistic criteria. They tended to keep production in-house for high-volume items and items that were relatively easy to make. Most companies had no explicit analytical framework for distinguishing their essential core components from commodity-like items that many suppliers can provide.

Insourcing/Outsourcing Process Exhibit 7.10 diagrams the process used by Cummins Engine as it began to perform insourcing/outsourcing studies. When

EXHIBIT 7.10   *Insourcing/Outsourcing Process Example—Cummins Engine*

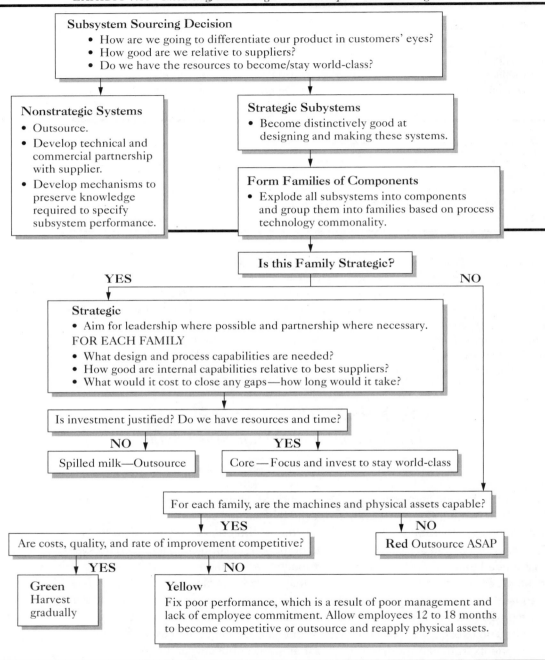

Subsystem Sourcing Decision
- How are we going to differentiate our product in customers' eyes?
- How good are we relative to suppliers?
- Do we have the resources to become/stay world-class?

Nonstrategic Systems
- Outsource.
- Develop technical and commercial partnership with supplier.
- Develop mechanisms to preserve knowledge required to specify subsystem performance.

Strategic Subsystems
- Become distinctively good at designing and making these systems.

Form Families of Components
- Explode all subsystems into components and group them into families based on process technology commonality.

Is this Family Strategic?

YES   NO

Strategic
- Aim for leadership where possible and partnership where necessary.
FOR EACH FAMILY
- What design and process capabilities are needed?
- How good are internal capabilities relative to best suppliers?
- What would it cost to close any gaps—how long would it take?

Is investment justified? Do we have resources and time?

NO   YES

Spilled milk—Outsource   Core — Focus and invest to stay world-class

For each family, are the machines and physical assets capable?

YES   NO

Are costs, quality, and rate of improvement competitive?   **Red** Outsource ASAP

YES   NO

Green
Harvest
gradually

Yellow
Fix poor performance, which is a result of poor management and lack of employee commitment. Allow employees 12 to 18 months to become competitive or outsource and reapply physical assets.

conducting competitive and insourcing/outsourcing analyses, Cummins Engine performed several critical tasks. The first was to determine the appropriate level of abstraction—that is, the proper unit of analysis. For example, due to the sheer number of individual components in most final products, it would be nearly impossible to make a sound insourcing/outsourcing decision on each and every individual component. Therefore, it was important to aggregate, or combine, the level of analysis from the individual component or subassembly level to the assembly or complete system level. Cummins managers, for example, considered a backhoe loader from the systems perspective, treating it as a system made up of a variety of assemblies and subassemblies (the drivetrain, chassis, cab, engine, and so forth). Using the backhoe loader's engine as an example of a subsystem, the engine could be further broken down into a series of complex assemblies and subassemblies like the fuel delivery system and the power cylinder.

Firms such as Cummins facing the strategic insourcing/outsourcing decision must painstakingly evaluate the entire hierarchy of components, subassemblies, assemblies, subsystems, and systems across major product lines to determine which subsystems and assemblies are essential to the firm's competitive position. This analysis should also include future product plans as well as an evaluation of its competitive priorities in terms of overall business strategies. The nature of the overall business strategy should dictate broad guidelines regarding how to conduct the insourcing/outsourcing analyses.

The Insourcing/Outsourcing Decision The internal insourcing/outsourcing analysis at Cummins Engine revealed that in order to meet emissions standards, the backhoe required a more advanced piston design. This meant that Cummins needed to invest heavily to upgrade its capabilities in this area. An emotionally charged debate occurred, lasting more than three years, over whether to continue insourcing or to outsource pistons, which are a key engine component. Many felt that Cummins should not surrender control of this critical component to a supplier. The debate was settled after management organized an interdisciplinary team to develop and implement an appropriate piston-sourcing strategy. (Refer to Chapter 6 for a discussion of developing commodity strategies.)

The team first identified the critical technologies and capabilities that would be required to specify, design, and build pistons for heavy equipment engines. Team members visited leading piston producers and performed a benchmarking analysis to measure Cummins's internal capabilities against those of the supply base. Their findings indicated that Cummins's internal capabilities in piston technology were inferior to at least two of the suppliers considered to be world-class competitors. These two piston suppliers were also aggressive innovators, and invested more than 20 times as much as Cummins did in product and process research and development of piston technology. In addition, higher production volumes at the suppliers allowed much quicker progression along the learning curve, thereby accelerating cost reductions. (See Chapter 12 for a discussion of the learning curve.) Given this apparent competitive disadvantage, Cummins made a difficult decision to outsource pistons to suppliers.

If a firm's insourcing analysis indicates a competitive disadvantage compared with a supplier, then management must make the decision whether to commit scarce resources to catch up or to source externally. Playing catch-up can be an expensive proposition that may adversely impact a firm's financial viability or restrict its ability to invest in other parts of the business. In pursuing the catch-up strategy, the firm must decide if it will seek competence in existing technologies or will attempt to leapfrog the competition through the use of new technology. Choosing the wrong technology development strategy will consume scarce resources with little or no payback in terms of creating a competitive advantage.

Implementing the Decision   Once the firm has committed to outsourcing a key subsystem, it should attempt to develop or enhance its competence in other critical subsystems, particularly if the technology involved is relatively new or not readily available outside the firm. Another alternative to the total outsourcing of key subassemblies is to develop a long-term partnering relationship with a highly capable supplier (such as J. I. Case has done in its engine joint venture with Cummins). This arrangement allows a higher level of management control over the supply base without having to invest in plant and equipment. That risk is transferred to the supplier, allowing the buying firm to become more flexible to changing demands in the marketplace.

Cummins has worked to gain effective control over the performance of outsourced components by overseeing design and production activities and keeping current on "architectural knowledge." Architectural knowledge is the intimately detailed and specialized power of translation required to capture customer requirements and reproduce them in the language of subsystem performance specifications. This body of knowledge is based on the interactions that occur between a customer's requirements and specifications and the producer's capabilities. One method of preserving this capability is for the buying firm's engineers to work closely with the supplying firm's engineers in order to perform several key functions:

*   Analyze product designs and review component performance.
*   Evaluate and substantiate the supplier's production process capabilities.
*   Oversee component-testing technology and procedures.

The grouping of individual parts and components into part families containing similar items is another task within the outsourcing process and moves the insourcing/outsourcing decision into a higher level of abstraction. Instead of determining whether a firm should insource or outsource a particular part number, the decision shifts to whether it is cost-effective to continue to invest in the capacity or capability to build each family of items. Managers must still analyze these families to identify if they are strategic in nature. In order to facilitate this process, Cummins developed a three-tier classification "stoplight" scheme for separating commodity part families into different categories based on common process characteristics, production processes, materials, volume, and so on.

- The green classification indicates that internal production is competitive with at least a 15% cost advantage over outsourcing. For these part and component families, internal production processes are highly capable, and the rate of performance improvement is high.
- The middle-range or yellow classification symbolizes those parts or families that are marginally competitive with about a 15% cost disadvantage compared to suppliers. Internal production capability is moderately high, but there is a need for improvement in labor productivity.
- For parts and families in the red classification, internal sourcing is at a clear cost disadvantage, with cost penalties exceeding 15%. In addition, moving parts families from the yellow zone to the green zone requires significant cooperation from the firm's employees because they must upgrade their work skills and utilize more efficient techniques. In the red zone, upgrading internal production capabilities may require prohibitive levels of capital spending and significant engineering expertise to make sufficient cost performance improvement to justify insourcing the item.

When outsourcing large numbers of parts that were formerly produced in-house, purchasing must upgrade its supplier control systems, such as supplier selection and qualification, performance measurement, and supply-base optimization processes. Volume discounts can be leveraged through the use of higher volumes provided by fewer, more capable suppliers. Sourcing decisions based on part families helps minimize the limitations of the traditional cost accounting system discussed earlier in the cost factors section of this chapter.

Today, Cummins Engine is pushing the boundaries of its core competencies to explore radical new data-mining technologies. Years ago it began building electronic components into its engines for gather information about performance, pollution control, and other diagnostic data. Only recently, Cummins has begun experimenting with collecting and mining that valuable data.[10] For example, Cummins found that one customer's trucks were idling three times as long as trucks at other companies, leading to more wear and tear on the engine, higher fuel consumption, and more pollution. This represents an important new competence that is being "insourced" and invested in for the future. "We're trying to do things we never thought of before," says Ron Temple, vice president of electronics technology at Cummins. "That's what data mining can do—show new relationships." In the end, this competence could help Cummins Engine achieve a new type of "insourced" competence that will provide better customer service, and in the end, a competitive advantage.

CONCLUSION

The insourcing/outsourcing decision is important to the economic success of an organization because the decision determines the firm's economic boundaries and its competitive character. The insourcing/outsourcing decision process has historically been conducted without a true strategic perspective. Typically, decisions were based on the purely economic issues of price, quality, and quantity of goods. Several factors will increasingly influence future insourcing/outsourcing decisions. Purchasing, operations, and technology managers will need to work together closely to identify activities where there is a distinctive competence. They must also identify those activities best performed by external sources. Managers must obtain clear insights into the relative long- and short-term economics associated with insourcing/outsourcing decisions, particularly from a total-cost perspective. Finally, organizations must conduct more accurate assessments of the technologies that are crucial to future success.

DISCUSSION QUESTIONS

1. What are the most typical situations that drive an insourcing/outsourcing decision?
2. Why is it important to employ a cross-functional team in reaching this decision? What would be the potential consequences if the decision were left to production or procurement alone?
3. What is meant by the term core competence?
4. What are some of the key advantages versus disadvantages that support an insourcing decision?
5. What are some of the key advantages versus disadvantages that support an outsourcing decision?
6. Why are insourcing/outsourcing decisions made relatively infrequently? When are they most likely to occur?
7. What is the process followed in carrying out an insourcing/outsourcing analysis?
8. What types of facility costs are most difficult to access accurately?
9. Describe the problems associated with allocating fixed overhead costs to an insourcing project. What criteria must be used to assign them?
10. In assessing the rate of technology change, how does this affect the insourcing/outsourcing decision?
11. Describe some examples of firms that are vertically integrated. Why are many firms now spinning off divisions instead of vertically integrating?
12. What are some of the various noncost factors affecting the insourcing/outsourcing decision?

ADDITIONAL READINGS

Hilmer, F., and J. Quinn. "Strategic Outsourcing." *Sloan Management Review* (Summer 1994): 43–55.

Handfield, Robert, Gary Ragatz, Robert Monczka, and Kenneth Peterson. "Supplier Integration into New Product Development." *California Management Review* (Winter 1999): 59–82.

McDermott, Christopher, and Robert Handfield. "Concurrent Development and Strategic Outsourcing: Do the Rules Change in Breakthrough Innovation?" *Journal of High Technology Management Research* (Summer 2000): 23–31.

Nishiguchi, Toshihiro. *Strategic Industrial Sourcing: The Japanese Advantage* (New York: Oxford University Press, 1994).

Venkatesan, Ravi. "Strategic Sourcing: To Make or Not to Make." *Harvard Business Review* (November–December 1992): 98–107.

Welch, James A. and P. Ranganath Nayak, "Strategic Sourcing: A Progressive Approach to the Make-Buy Decision." *Academy of Management Executives* 6, no. 1 (1992): 23–31.

ENDNOTES

1. "The Whirlwind Breaking Up Companies," *Business Week*, August 14,1995, 31.
2. C. K. Pralahad and Gary Hamel, "The Core Competence of the Corporation," *Harvard Business Review* (May–June 1990): 79–91.
3. James A. Welch and P. Ranganath Nayak, "Strategic Sourcing: A Progressive Approach to the Make-Buy Decision," *Academy of Management Executives* 6, no. 1 (1992): 23–31.
4. Cheryl Ransom, "The Six Categories of Costs," *NAPM Insights* (September 1995): 10–11.
5. "The Great Silicon Rush of '95," *Business Week*, October 2, 1995, 134–136.
6. Shawn Tully, "You'll Never Guess Who Really Makes . . . ," *Fortune*, October 3, 1994, 124.
7. "Is Spindler a Survivor?" *Business Week*, October 2, 1995, 62.
8. "The Internet Age," *Business Week*, October 4, 1999, 103–104.
9. Ravi Venkatesan, "Strategic Sourcing: To Make or Not to Make," *Harvard Business Review* (November–December 1992): 98–107.
10. Rick Whiting and Bruce Caldwell, "Data Capture Grows Wider," *Informationweek* (June 14, 1999): 12–13.

8 SUPPLIER EVALUATION, SELECTION, AND MEASUREMENT

Internet Database Supports Supplier Evaluation

A major challenge facing purchasers is the time and resources required to perform supplier evaluations prior to making selection decisions. Suppliers also face challenges when they are evaluated by three or more purchasers from the same industry—each with their own set of requirements. Now, imagine using the Internet to review quickly any evaluations that a supplier has already undergone, including when they were performed and who conducted them, and the results. For members of the Coordinating Agency for Supplier Evaluations (CASE), such a scenario is a reality. The Internet-based Supplier Performance Information Network (SPIN) furnishes members with interactive access to a shared database of suppliers and supplier assessment information.

CASE promotes itself as an "industry managed second-party organization of companies operating as a nonprofit, mutual benefit corporation," dedicated to (1) reducing redundant supplier audits or assessments, (2) sharing nonprejudicial supplier data, (3) standardizing supplier/procurement quality practices, and (4) achieving cost savings through expense avoidance. The second-party distinction (as opposed to a third party that works for a fee) means that CASE is run by volunteers from companies who are evaluating suppliers for the purpose of doing business with those suppliers. CASE has five associated industries:

- Aerospace and marine system
- Air carriers
- Aeronautical repair stations
- Electronics and computer manufacturers
- Automotive and heavy truck suppliers

An example from the air carrier industry illustrates how CASE has had great success in eliminating redundant audits. Each year, participating airlines submit to CASE their supplier lists with evaluation requirements for the coming year. The organization reported that it began a recent year with 5,200 scheduled evaluations, roughly 4,300 of which CASE identified as redundant. Ultimately, the exercise reduced the number of scheduled evaluations to just over 500. "This doesn't mean that the 53 airlines (that are part of CASE) can't go and visit their suppliers," says Richard Villeneuve, vice president and executive director of CASE. "It means simply that they may reduce their audit workload by accepting the surveillance activities performed by an auditor who is as equally skilled as their own."

CASE's jump to the Internet came faster when the electronics and computer manufacturers joined the organization. This industry segment was led by Digital Equipment Corporation (now part of Compaq computer) and AlliedSignal. The companies were interested in sharing noncompetitive information within their industry and suggested to CASE that its system would be ideally suited to an Internet application.

→→→

When CASE was originally formed, the vice president and executive director of CASE said the board of directors had resolved to move to the Internet. The addition of the electronic and computer companies helped push that resolve along.

CASE also offers a new feature called "supplier accounts." For a $600 annual fee, suppliers can list themselves in the CASE database so they will appear when members search SPIN. The supplier account option gives suppliers an opportunity to submit profiles to the system. While these profiles are designated as supplier provided, they will give suppliers an opportunity to list various awards or third-party accreditations. Members with access to SPIN can also search the entire CASE database with several options for narrowing their searches. This helps identify potential suppliers during the identification stage of the purchasing process.

Membership information, fees, and applications can be downloaded from www.caseinc. org. To participate in CASE, however, members must be capable of giving as well as taking. Purchasers cannot use the system to avoid performing supplier evaluations. They must also provide information.

Purchasers know that supplier evaluation and selection is one of the most important activities performed today. They also know that the innovative use of technology can help make the evaluation process faster, less expensive, and more effective.

Source: Adapted from Anne Millen Porter, "The CASE SPIN Database: A Who's Who of Quality Audits," *Purchasing* 123, no. 1 (July 17, 1997): 39–43.

One of the most important processes performed in organizations today is the evaluation, selection, and continuous measurement of suppliers. Traditionally, competitive bidding was the primary method for awarding purchase contracts. In the past, it was sufficient to obtain three bids and award the contract to the supplier offering the lowest price. Today, however, enlightened purchasers commit major resources to evaluate a supplier's performance and capability across many different areas. The supplier selection process has become so important that teams of cross-functional personnel are often responsible for visiting and evaluating suppliers. A sound supplier selection decision today can reduce or prevent a host of problems tomorrow.

This chapter focuses on different topics and issues pertaining to the evaluation, selection, and continuous measurement of suppliers. The first section provides an overview of the evaluation and selection process. The next sections present the various performance categories that are considered during the supplier evaluation and selection process. The third section focuses on an approach for developing a tool or instrument that can be used when conducting supplier evaluations. The chapter then highlights critical issues that confront a purchaser during the selection process. Finally, measurement systems that assess the continuous performance of suppliers are discussed.

The Supplier Evaluation and Selection Process

Experts agree that no one best way exists to evaluate and select suppliers, and organizations use a variety of different approaches. The overall objective of the supplier evaluation process is to reduce purchase risk and maximize overall value to the purchaser. An organization must select suppliers it can do business with over an extended period of time. The degree of effort associated with the selection is related to the importance of the commodity as reflected in the commodity portfolio matrix (discussed in Chapter 6). Depending on the supplier evaluation approach used, the process can be an intensive effort requiring a major commitment of resources (such as time and travel budget). Formal supplier evaluation can involve a team of experts from a purchaser spending several days at a supplier's workplace. This section addresses the many issues and decisions involved in effectively and efficiently evaluating, selecting, and maintaining a supply base. Exhibit 8.1 highlights the critical activities and decisions involved in the supplier evaluation and selection process.

Recognize the Need for Supplier Selection

The first step of the evaluation and selection process usually involves the recognition that a requirement exists to evaluate and select a supplier for an item or service. The reason we say *usually* is because it is possible that a purchasing manager begins the supplier evaluation process in anticipation of a future purchase requirement. Purchasing may have early insight into new-product development plans through participation on a product development team. In this case, engineering personnel may provide some preliminary specifications on the type of materials, service, or processes required, but will not yet have specific details. Nevertheless, this preliminary information may be enough to justify beginning initial evaluation of potential sources of supply in anticipation of a future material need.

The recognition of a purchase requirement often occurs by receiving a standard purchase requisition. As Chapter 2 highlighted, a purchase requisition is an internal document completed by a user of material informing purchasing of a specific need. The requisition is issued because no supplier is currently in the supply base that can satisfy the purchase requirement, or the user is unaware of any qualified suppliers that might currently be available. The complexity and value of a required purchase will influence the extent to which a buyer evaluates potential supply sources.

It is also possible that a supplier selection decision arises because existing suppliers are failing to perform as required. The term that describes changing suppliers for existing items is *supplier switching*.

Identify Key Sourcing Requirements

Throughout the supplier evaluation and selection process, it is important to understand the requirements that are important to that purchase. These requirements often differ widely from item to item, organization to organization, or industry to industry.

EXHIBIT 8.1   *Supplier Evaluation and Selection Process*

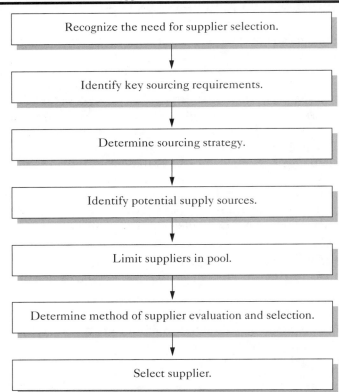

A later section on *key supplier evaluation criteria* discusses the various supplier performance areas where a purchaser should determine its critical sourcing requirements. While different requirements exist for each evaluation area, certain categories—supplier quality, cost, delivery performance, and technological capability—are at a minimum evaluated.

Determine Sourcing Strategy

No single sourcing strategy approach will satisfy the requirements of all purchases. Because of this, the purchasing strategy adopted for a particular item or service will influence the approach taken during the supplier evaluation and selection process. In this chapter, we will not go into great detail on the processes used to develop a commodity strategy. This subject was discussed extensively in Chapter 6, where we presented a formal process used when linking commodity strategies with overall business strategies. At this point, it is sufficient to say that a commodity sourcing strategy provides direction on the overall objectives to be achieved for the commodity, such as the number of suppliers that will be used, the type of contract (long-term versus

EXHIBIT 8.2   *Information Search for Potential Sources of Supply*

**Strategic importance/technical complexity
of purchase requirement**

	High	Low
High	Minor – moderate information search	Minor information search
	I	II
	III	IV
	Major information search	Minor – moderate information search
Low		

Capability of existing supply base to satisfy cost, delivery, technology, and service requirements

short-term), and the type of suppliers to be evaluated. Several strategy options will be available when reviewing the requirements for a purchase, including

- Single versus multiple supply sources
- Short-term versus long-term purchase contracts
- Choosing suppliers that provide product design support versus those that lack design support capability
- Developing a close working relationship versus traditional purchasing

The strategy option selected will influence greatly the supplier selection and evaluation process.

Identify Potential Supply Sources

Purchasers rely on various sources of information when identifying potential sources of supply. The degree to which a buyer must search for information about suppliers is a function of several variables. Exhibit 8.2 summarizes the intensity of an information search under various conditions.

Quadrants I and IV generally require a minor-to-moderate information search, while quadrant III requires a major search. In quadrant I, existing suppliers have the ability to satisfy a strategic or nonroutine purchase requirement. In this situation, a buyer may pursue additional information to verify he or she has considered the best possible sources of supply. Because the buyer has information about a current supplier or suppliers with the required capabilities, the information search will probably

SOURCING SNAPSHOT

Supplier Evaluation Tips When Selecting IT Sources

Buyers of information technology (IT) know that choosing the wrong supplier can create problems for many years. The rate of technological change can make the "perfect" supplier obsolete within months. Or the selected supplier may not have the capabilities to do the job. Unfortunately, it is usually next to impossible to switch to a new IT supplier quickly. For this reason, the selection process takes on added importance. *InfoWorld*, a magazine for IT professionals, offers these suggestions when making IT supplier selection decisions:

- *Don't put all your eggs in one basket.* Many companies try to complete all of their computer technology buying using one or two big suppliers. Take a portfolio approach by building a supply network that includes some smaller suppliers with some leading-edge and emerging technologies.
- *Make sure you and the supplier are headed down the same road.* Evaluate each supplier's technology and product roadmaps. Are both organizations working toward platforms, capabilities, features, and functions that are in synch?
- *Build your portfolio with the best.* Choose suppliers that add strength to your value proposition and your customer. Do not select the supplier simply because of a good purchase price.
- *Be a big fish in a little pond.* Sometimes sourcing from the biggest supplier may bring a great purchase price but limits your ability to leverage. A smaller supplier may be more encouraged to innovate in your direction.
- *Know the supplier's Internet strategy.* Understand how your suppliers are using the Internet to add value to what they develop, manufacture, service, or distribute.

Since information technology has become increasingly important to business success, making the right IT sourcing decision often means the difference between business success or business failure.

Source: Adapted from "Tips on Supplier Evaluation," *InfoWorld* 20, no. 43 (October 26, 1998): 72.

---

not be as intensive as in quadrant III. In quadrant IV, the purchase requirement is routine or less strategic but the buyer has no current access to suppliers capable of satisfying the purchase requirement. Given the nature of the purchase in this quadrant, the search requirements will be lower compared to quadrant III but greater than in quadrant II. The following sections discuss various sources of information used in the evaluation of potential suppliers of new purchase requirements.

Current Suppliers A major source of information comes from current or existing suppliers. Buyers often look to existing suppliers to satisfy a new purchase requirement. The advantage of this approach is that the purchaser does not have to add and maintain an additional supplier. Also, the buyer can do business with an already familiar supplier, which may limit the time and resources required to evaluate a new supplier's capabilities. On the negative side, using existing suppliers, while perhaps easier and quicker, may not always be the best long-term approach. A purchasing manager may never know if better suppliers are available without information on other sources. For this reason, most organizations are continuously seeking new sources of supply and are expanding this search to include suppliers from around the world.

Selecting an existing supplier for a new purchase requirement may be an attractive option if a list of *preferred suppliers* is maintained. Designation as a preferred supplier means that a supplier consistently satisfies the performance and service standards defined by the buyer. A preferred supplier status conveys immediate information about the supplier's overall performance and competency. However, the buyer must still determine if a preferred supplier is capable of providing a particular purchase requirement.

Sales Representatives   All purchasers receive sales and marketing information from sales representatives. These contacts can prove to be a valuable source of information about potential sources. Even if an immediate need does not exist for a supplier's services, the buyer can file the information for future reference. A visit to a purchasing manager's office would probably reveal a set of cabinets or drawers that contain sales and marketing information.

Information Databases   Some companies maintain databases of suppliers capable of supporting an industry or product line. NCR has compiled and maintains data on about 30,000 companies serving the computer industry. The company searches trade journals and financial newspapers for information about potential suppliers. This database serves as a source of information for NCR buyers at the plant level. Furthermore, purchasing sends a newsletter twice a month to buyers, engineers, and management at NCR plants worldwide reporting on market developments. The company also mails a quarterly overview to plants detailing supplier strengths, weaknesses, and technological capability. The use of automated databases can quickly identify suppliers potentially qualified to support a requirement.

Maintaining a supplier database is particularly important in industries where technology changes rapidly. The database may contain information on current products, the supplier's future technology roadmap, process capability ratios, and past performance.[1] Database users may quickly determine whether existing suppliers are capable of producing or supplying a given part or service requirement. It is important that supplier databases be updated on a regular basis.

Experience   Purchasing personnel may have knowledge about potential suppliers from experience. A buyer may have worked within an industry over many years and is familiar with the suppliers, perhaps including international suppliers. One argument against rotating buyers too frequently between product lines or types of purchases is that a buyer may lose the expertise built up over years. Because few purchasing organizations have put forth the effort to develop an intelligence database about suppliers, a buyer's experience and knowledge about a supplier market becomes valuable.

Trade Journals Most major industries have a group or council that publishes a trade journal or magazine, which routinely present articles about different companies. These articles often focus on a company's technical or innovative development of a material, component, product, process, or service. Suppliers also use trade journals to advertise their products or services. These advertisements target a specific audience and can provide information about sources of supply. Most buyers follow (or should follow) trade journals closely.

Trade Directories Almost all industries publish directories of companies that produce items or provide services within an industry. Such directories can be a valuable source of initial information for a buyer who is not familiar with an industry or its suppliers.

Industrial Trade Shows Trade shows may be an efficient way to gain exposure to a large number of suppliers at one time. Shows are often coordinated by associations such as the Chemical Manufacturers Association, American Society of Automotive Suppliers, and Sematech, which represents the semiconductor industry. Buyers attending trade shows can gather information about potential suppliers while also evaluating the latest technological developments. Many contacts between industrial buyers and sellers occur at trade shows.

Second-Party or Indirect Information This source of information includes a wide range of contacts not directly part of the purchaser's organization. For example, a buyer can gather information from other suppliers, such as knowledge about a noncompetitor that might be valuable. Another second-party information source includes other buyers. Attendees at meetings of the National Association of Purchasing Management (NAPM) can develop informal networks that provide information about potential supply sources. Other professional groups include the American Production and Inventory Control Society, the Council for Logistics Management, the American Manufacturing Engineering Association, and the American Society for Quality Control.

Some purchasers publicly recognize their quality-certified suppliers. Recognition may come in the form of a newspaper advertisement that highlights the achievement of superior suppliers. Delta Airlines periodically purchases a full-page advertisement in the *Wall Street Journal* expressing appreciation and recognition of its best suppliers. In the advertisement, Delta lists each supplier by name and why they are being recognized. Because of Delta's approach to recognizing its best suppliers, a buyer gains visibility to a group of blue-chip suppliers. Examples of other major corporations with supplier certification programs include Chrysler (Pentastar Award), Xerox, GM (Targets for Excellence), Ford (Q1 Award), Eastman Kodak (Quality First Supplier Award), and Cummins Engine (Preferred Quality Supplier Program).

Internal Sources Many larger companies divide business lines into units, each with a separate purchasing operation. The sharing of such information can occur across units through informal meetings, strategy development sessions, purchasing newsletters, or the development of a comprehensive database containing information about potential supply sources. Internal sources, even those from diverse business units, can provide a great deal of information about potential supply sources.

Internet Searches The Internet is a powerful search engine capable of providing reams of information. Buyers are increasingly using the Internet to help locate potential sources that might qualify for further evaluation. Sellers are increasingly using the Internet as a key part of their direct marketing efforts.

After collecting information about potential supply sources, the purchaser manager must begin to sift through and consolidate the information. This can be a huge task, depending on the number of suppliers and the information obtained. The first step in this process is to eliminate the suppliers who are not capable of meeting the buyer's needs or where a good fit is lacking.

Limit Suppliers in Pool

The result of this information gathering is that, depending upon the item under consideration, a purchaser may have many potential supply sources from which to choose. Unfortunately, the performance capabilities of suppliers vary widely. Also, limited resources preclude an in-depth visit to or evaluation of all potential supply sources. A first cut or preliminary evaluation of potential suppliers is often used to narrow the list before conducting an in-depth formal evaluation. This first cut eliminates those suppliers who are clearly not capable of meeting requirements based on the available information to date. Several criteria may be used in making the first cut.

Financial Risk Analysis Most purchasers perform at least a cursory financial analysis of prospective suppliers. While poor financial condition is not the only criterion upon which to evaluate a supplier, poor financial condition can indicate serious problems. A financial analysis performed during this phase of the supplier evaluation process is much less comprehensive than the one performed during final supplier evaluation. During this phase, a purchaser is trying to get a feel for the overall financial health of the supplier. Buyers often consult external sources of information such as Dun and Bradstreet reports to support the evaluation. The Sourcing Snapshot included here (see p. 232) highlights one source of information that may be of value during the evaluation process.

Evaluation of Previous (and Current) Supplier Performance A prospective supplier may have an established performance record with a purchaser. A purchaser may have used a supplier for a previous purchase requirement, or a supplier may currently provide material to another part of the organization. A supplier may also have provided other types of commodities or services to the purchaser than those under consideration. Based on prior experience, a purchasing manager may consider

SOURCING SNAPSHOT

D&B Makes Supplier Evaluation Data Available Through the Web

Imagine this scenario: You work for a small organization that simply does not have the financial or human resources to perform preselection supplier evaluations. Or perhaps you have a minor purchase requirement that does not justify a major search. Do you simply hope for the best when making your selection? Will you be reluctant to try new suppliers for fear that the risk of the unknown is simply too great? For many organizations and purchase situations, supplier evaluation is often a luxury when it should be a necessity.

What can you do when faced with these situations? One option is to use an external party to collect and disseminate supplier performance data. Dun & Bradstreet (D&B), a supplier of business information and receivables management services, now offers its Supplier Evaluation Report (SER) over the Internet. Users around the world can now purchase with a credit card the supplier evaluation report for any of the 10 million U.S. establishments contained in D&B's database (see http://www.dnb.com).

Designed for purchasing professionals, the SER provides an objective, third-party view of suppliers located in the United States and includes information and analyses that help purchasers evaluate established and prospective suppliers. The SER includes the business background of principals, payment trends (as reported to D&B), key financial ratios, plus an overall risk score ranging from one to nine. The SER also indicates if a supplier is ISO 9000 registered and/or a minority- or women-owned business. D&B maintains that the report is a tremendous resource for companies in every Internet-linked corner of the globe that want to confidently do business with U.S. suppliers.

Source: Adapted from "D&B's Supplier Evaluation Product Available Via Web," *Information Today* 14, no. 5 (May 1997): 58.

---

that supplier for a different type of commodity or service. Again, a centralized purchasing database can be useful in providing access to a supplier's performance record.

Evaluation of Supplier-Provided Information   Buyers often request specific information directly from potential suppliers. Requests for information (referred to as RFIs) involve sending a preliminary survey to suppliers. This can be a valuable tool when gathering information prior to formal supplier evaluations. The buyer uses this information to screen each supplier and to determine if the buyer's requirements appear to match the supplier's capabilities. Buyers can request information on a supplier's cost structure, process technology, market share data, quality performance, or any other area important to the purchase decision. It is not in the interest of the supplier to deceive the buyer when providing self-reported information. The buyer will eventually uncover a supplier's true performance capability either during a direct visit or during initial testing of a supplier's product.

Mack Trucks, for example, sends out several hundred RFIs when developing its worldwide purchasing contracts. Another company mandates that requests for information (which it calls presurvey questionnaires) be sent before conducting more detailed supplier surveys. Besides ownership, financial information, and type of business, this company attempts to determine how sophisticated the supplier's current practices are and how far along it is toward total quality.[2] The RFI is a way to gather information before committing to a formal supplier evaluation.

Determine the Method of Supplier Evaluation and Selection

Once an initial cut has eliminated suppliers that are not capable, the buyer or commodity team must decide how to evaluate the remaining suppliers, who may appear to be equally qualified. This requires a finer level of evaluation detail than that used in the initial process. A number of ways are available to evaluate and select suppliers from the remaining companies in the pool. These include evaluation from supplier-provided information, supplier visits, and the use of preferred supplier lists.

Evaluation from Supplier-Provided Information   Buyers often receive and evaluate detailed information directly from potential suppliers for the purpose of awarding a purchase contract. This information may come from *requests for quotes (RFPs)* or *requests for proposals (RFPs)*. Not too long ago buyers made almost all purchase decisions using this method. In recent years, however, many organizations have adopted a more direct and in-depth approach to evaluating potential suppliers. Increasingly, companies are also requesting that suppliers provide a detailed cost breakdown of their quoted price in the response to the RFQ, including details on labor, material, overhead, and profit.

Supplier Visits   A team of cross-functional experts may visit potential suppliers. The next section discusses the key supplier evaluation criteria, details the criteria often used by a cross-functional team during supplier visits. The use of teams for supplier evaluation and selection is increasing, particularly among larger organizations that have the resources to commit to this approach. The advantage to the cross-functional selection team approach is that each team member contributes unique insight into the overall supplier evaluation. For instance, one team member may be an expert in quality, engineering capabilities, or manufacturing techniques, and is uniquely qualified to assess the supplier in this regard.

Use of Preferred Suppliers   One advantage of measuring the performance of current suppliers is the opportunity to develop a preferred supplier list. Increasingly, purchasers are rewarding their best suppliers by creating preferred supplier lists, which can simplify greatly the supplier evaluation and selection process. A buyer can refer to the purchasing database to determine if a supplier currently exists that can satisfy the purchase requirement, and the buyer does not have to reevaluate a preferred supplier being considered as a source for a new purchase requirement. Buyers can also use a preferred supplier list as an incentive to improve the performance of existing suppliers. A purchaser should consider only its best suppliers as eligible for preferred supplier status, and should require them to go through a certification process. This is discussed in greater detail in the chapter on supplier management and development (Chapter 10).

External or Third-Party Information   The opening vignette highlighted one approach for making supplier-related information available to purchasers. The Sourcing Snapshot on Dun & Bradstreet highlights another approach for securing reliable third-party information. Using third-party information can be an efficient and effective way to gain insight into potential suppliers.

Select Supplier

The final step of the evaluation and selection process is to select the supplier(s). The activities associated with this step can vary widely depending on the purchase item under consideration. For routine items, this may simply require notifying and awarding a purchase contract to a supplier. For a major purchase, the process can become more complex. The buyer and seller may have to conduct detailed negotiations to agree upon the specific details of a purchase agreement.

*K*EY SUPPLIER EVALUATION CRITERIA

Purchasers usually evaluate potential suppliers across multiple categories using their own selection criteria with assigned weights. For example, requiring consistent delivery performance with short lead times to support a just-in-time production system may require emphasizing a supplier's scheduling and production systems. A high-technology buyer may emphasize a supplier's process and technological capabilities or research and development.

Most evaluations rate suppliers on three primary criteria: (1) cost/price, (2) quality, and (3) delivery. These three elements of performance are generally the most obvious and most critical areas that affect the purchaser. For many items, purchasers will be concerned with only these three performance areas. For critical items needing an in-depth analysis of the supplier's capabilities, a more detailed supplier evaluation study is required. An initial supplier evaluation will usually cover the following supplier performance categories to some extent:

- Supplier management capability
- Overall personnel capabilities
- Cost structure
- Total quality performance, systems, and philosophy

- Process and technological capability, including the supplier's design capability
- Environmental regulation compliance
- Financial capability and stability
- Production scheduling and control systems, including supplier delivery performance
- Information systems capability (e.g., EDI, bar coding, ERP, CAD/CAM)
- Supplier purchasing strategies, policies, and techniques
- Longer-term relationship potential

Management Capability

It is important for a buyer to evaluate a supplier's management capability. After all, management runs the business and makes the decisions that affect the future competitiveness of the supplier. There are a number of questions a buyer should ask when evaluating a supplier's management capability:

- Does executive management practice long-range planning?
- Has management committed itself to total quality management and continuous improvement?
- Is there a high degree of turnover among managers?
- What is the professional experience of the managers?
- Is there a vision about the future direction of the company?
- How many purchasing professionals are certified purchasing managers?
- What is the history of management/labor relations?
- Is management making the investments that are necessary to sustain and grow the business?
- Has management prepared the company to face future competitive challenges, including providing employee training and development?
- Does management understand the importance of strategic sourcing?

Many of these questions are difficult to answer using simple "yes or no" criteria. It may be challenging to identify the true state of affairs during a brief visit or questionnaire. Nevertheless, asking these questions can help the purchasing manager to develop a feeling for the professional capabilities of the managers in the supplying organization. When interviewing management at a supplier's facility, it is important to attempt to meet with as many people as possible in order to paint a "true picture" of management's attitudes. During such interviews, the team may often discover differing viewpoints on where the organization is truly headed in terms of management orientation.

Personnel Capabilities

This part of the supplier evaluation process requires an assessment of nonmanagement personnel. The benefit that a highly trained, stable, and motivated workforce can provide should not be underestimated, particularly during periods of labor shortages. A purchaser should evaluate these points:

- The degree to which employees support and are committed to quality and continuous improvement
- The overall skills and abilities of the workforce (especially with regard to education and training)
- The state of employee-management relations
- Workforce flexibility
- Employee morale
- Workforce turnover
- The opportunity and willingness of employees to contribute to improving a supplier's operation

A buyer should also gather information about the history of strikes and labor disputes. This can result in a general idea of how dedicated the supplier's employees are to producing products or services that will meet or exceed the buyer's expectations.

Cost Structure

Evaluating a supplier's cost structure requires an in-depth understanding of a supplier's total costs, including direct labor costs, indirect labor costs, material costs, manufacturing or process operating costs, and general overhead costs. Understanding a supplier's cost structure helps a buyer determine how efficiently a supplier can produce an item. A cost analysis also helps identify potential areas of cost improvement.

Collecting this information can be a challenge during the initial evaluation process. A supplier may not have a detailed understanding of its costs. Many suppliers do not have a sophisticated cost accounting system, and are unable to effectively assign overhead costs to products or processes. Furthermore, some suppliers view cost data as highly proprietary. A supplier may fear that the release of cost information will undermine its pricing strategy or that competitors will gain access to its cost data, which could provide insight into a supplier's competitive advantage. As a result of these concerns, buyers will often develop reverse pricing models that provide approximate estimates of the supplier's cost structure during the initial supplier evaluation (covered in Chapter 13). While these cost models are never completely accurate, they can be useful in obtaining more information and querying suppliers further on their cost structures. Once cost elements have been understood by both parties, a cost-based pricing approach can be used to derive mutual benefits. However, this requires a high level of mutual trust and commitment.

Total Quality Performance, Systems, and Philosophy

A major part of the evaluation process addresses a supplier's quality management processes, systems, and philosophy. Buyers not only evaluate the obvious topics associated with supplier quality (management commitment, statistical process control, number of defects) but also evaluate safety, training, and facilities and equipment maintenance. For example, Alcoa defines its supplier quality requirements in four broad areas: management, quality measurement, safety and training, and facilities.

Many purchasers are adopting supplier quality evaluation systems that are based on the Malcolm Baldrige National Quality Award or ISO 9000 criteria. In 1987, former President Ronald Reagan signed the Malcolm Baldrige National Quality Improvement Act, which established a national award to recognize quality improvement among manufacturing, service, and small businesses. Since then, the criteria, which have been revised, have become an operational definition of TQM. The wide distribution of the application guidelines has exposed many suppliers to the Baldrige definition of quality. Companies such as Honeywell, Motorola, Southwest Bell, Cummins Engine, and others are using modified versions of the Baldrige criteria for supplier quality measurement and evaluation. Chapter 9 discusses the Baldrige award in detail.

Process and Technological Capability

Supplier evaluation teams often include a member from the engineering or technical staff to evaluate a supplier's process and technological capability. Process consists of the technology, design, methods, and equipment used to manufacture a product or deliver a service. A supplier's selection of a production process helps define its required technology, human resource skills, and capital equipment requirements.

The evaluation of a supplier's technical and process capability should also focus on future process and technical ability, which requires assessing a supplier's capital equipment plans and strategy. In addition, a purchaser should evaluate the resources that a supplier is committing to its research and development effort. This information will indicate the emphasis that a supplier places on future process and technological improvement.

A purchaser may also assess a supplier's design capability. One way to reduce the time required to develop new products involves using qualified suppliers who are able to perform product design activities. Ford, for example, now requires almost all of its suppliers to have production and design capabilities. The company has transferred most of the design of its component and component system requirements to suppliers. The trend toward the increased use of supplier design capabilities makes this area an integral part of the supplier evaluation and selection process.

Environmental Regulation Compliance

The 1990s brought about a renewed awareness of the impact that industry has on the environment. Government regulations are increasingly harsh on polluters. The Clean Air Act of 1990, for example, imposes large fines on producers of ozone-depleting substances and foul-smelling gases, and the Clinton administration introduced laws regarding recycling content in industrial materials.[3] Furthermore, purchasers do not want to be associated with known environmental polluters from a public relations or potential liability standpoint.

Some of the most common environmental performance criteria to use in evaluating a supplier's performance in this area are shown in Exhibit 8.3. This list was developed through interviews of managers in several industries that are emphasizing environmental performance throughout their supply base.[4]

EXHIBIT 8.3   *Top Ten Environmental Performance Criteria*

1. Public disclosure of environmental record
2. Second-tier supplier environmental evaluation
3. Hazardous waste management
4. Toxic waste pollution management
5. On EPA 17 hazardous material list
6. ISO 14000 certified
7. Reverse logistics program
8. Environmentally friendly product packaging
9. Ozone-depleting substances
10. Hazardous air emissions management

At Herman Miller Inc., a manufacturer of office furniture, environmental concerns are integrated closely into the supplier evaluation and selection process. For instance, Herman Miller includes the supplier's packaging as an important evaluation criterion. Corrugated packaging is being used more often because it is easier to recycle. Standardized, reusable shipping containers are also favored over disposable ones; in fact, such containers can be used to support just-in-time deliveries. Labeling is also important. Herman Miller now requires its suppliers to label the chemical composition of its plastic procured items so that recyclers will know the exact content of the plastic found in the parts.[5]

Financial Capability and Stability

An assessment of a potential supplier's financial condition almost always occurs during the initial evaluation process. Some purchasers view the financial assessment as a screening process or preliminary condition that the supplier must pass before a detailed evaluation can begin. An organization may use a financial rating service to help analyze a supplier's financial condition. If the supplier is a publicly held company, other financial documents will be readily available. Because buyers rely on fewer suppliers today to support their purchase requirements, it is important to reduce risk by selecting financially sound suppliers expected to remain in business for the long term.

Selecting a supplier in poor financial condition presents a number of risks. First, there is the risk that the supplier will go out of business. This event can present serious problems if there are not other sources of supply readily available. Second, suppliers who are in poor financial condition may not have the resources to invest in plant, equipment, or research that is necessary for longer-term technological or other performance improvements. Third, the supplier may become too financially dependent on the purchaser. This can be constraining if the need arises to switch suppliers (the buyer may feel an obligation to the supplier). A final risk is that financial weakness is usually an indication of underlying problems. A buyer must understand why a supplier is financially weak. Is the weakness a result of poor quality or delivery performance? Is it a result of wasteful spending by management? Has the supplier assumed too much debt?

Circumstances may exist that support selecting a supplier in a weaker financial condition. A supplier may be developing but has not yet marketed a leading-edge technology that can provide a market advantage to the purchaser. Gaining access to new product and process technology before competitors is one indication of purchasing effectiveness. Also, a supplier may be in a weaker financial condition because of uncontrollable or nonrepeating circumstances.

If the supplier is a publicly traded company, specific financial ratios can be obtained from a variety of Websites providing detailed financial ratios, and industry averages to compare these ratios against. Dun and Bradstreet also provides a number of formula-based approaches that allow buyers without a detailed financial background to obtain an overall assessment of the financial health of suppliers. These ratios may help provide insight into the supplier's financial health. Many of these can also be calculated using income statements and balance sheets. Some common ratios used to assess supplier financial health appear in Exhibit 8.4. Some of the Websites available to obtain such information include the following:

- Yahoo! Financial section (http://www.biz.yahoo.com)
- Morningstar (http://www.morningstar.net)
- Marketwatch (http://www.marketwatch.com)
- 411Stocks (http://www.411stocks.com)
- The Street (http://www.thestreet.com)
- Dun and Bradstreet (http://www.dnb.com)

Procurement specialists should become familiar with financial ratios because they can provide quick and valuable insights into a supplier's financial health. Moreover, purchasing managers should track such ratios for possible "red flags" that may signify potential financial difficulty. If at any point the purchasing manager has reason to believe that the supplier is facing a financial crisis of some sort, the supplier should be consulted for an explanation before any immediate action is taken.

Production Scheduling and Control Systems

Production scheduling includes those systems that release, schedule, and control a supplier's production process. Does the supplier use a material requirements planning (MRP) system to ensure the availability of required components? Does the supplier track material and production cycle time and compare this against a performance objective or standard? Does the supplier's production scheduling system support a purchaser's just-in-time requirements? How much lead time does the supplier's production scheduling and control system require? What is the supplier's on-time delivery performance history? The purpose behind evaluating the production scheduling and control system is to identify the degree of control the supplier has over its scheduling and production process. The benchmark for this element of evaluation is whether the supplier has a certified Class A material requirements planning system. As defined by Oliver Wight, a Class A MRP user

. . . is one that uses MRP in a closed loop mode. It has material requirements planning, capacity planning and control, shop-floor dispatching, and vendor scheduling systems in place and being used; and management uses the system to run the business. They participate in production

EXHIBIT 8.4   *Interpreting Key Financial Ratios*

Liquidity Ratios	**Interpretation**
Current ratio = Current assets/Current liabilities	Should be over 1.0, but look at industry average; high—may mean poor asset management.
Quick ratio = (Cash + Receivables)/Current liabilities *Note:* Calculation includes marketable securities	At least .8 if supplier sells on credit; low—may mean cash flow problems; high—may mean poor asset management.

Activity Ratios	**Interpretation**
Inventory turnover = Costs of goods sold/Inventory	Compare industry average; low—problems with slow inventory, which may hurt cash flow.
Fixed asset turnover = Sales/Fixed assets	Compare industry average; too low may mean supplier is not using fixed assets efficiently or effectively.
Total asset turnover = Sales/Total assets	Compare industry average; too low may mean supplier is not using its total assets efficiently or effectively.
Days Sales Outstanding = (Receivables × 365)/Sales	Compare industry average, or a value of 45–50 if company sells on net 30; too high hurts cash flow; too low may mean credit policies to customers are too restrictive.

Profitability Ratios	**Interpretation**
Net profit margin = Profit after taxes/Sales	Represents after-tax return; compare industry average.
Return on assets = Profit after taxes/Total assets	Compare industry average; represents the return the company earns on everything it owns.
Return on equity = Profit after taxes/Equity	The higher the better; the return on the shareholders' investment in the business.

Debt Ratios	**Interpretation**
Debt to equity = Total liabilities/Equity	Compare industry average; over 3 means highly leveraged.
Current debt to equity = Current liabilities/Equity	Over 1 is risky unless industry average is over 1; when ratio is high, supplier may be unable to pay lenders.
Interest coverage = (Pretax Inc. + Int. Exp.)/Int. Exp.	Should be over 3; higher is better; low may mean supplier is having difficulty paying creditors.

planning. They sign off on the production plans. They constantly monitor performance on inventory record accuracy, routing accuracy, attainment of the master schedule, attainment of the capacity plans, etc. In a Class A company, the MRP system provides the game plan that sales, finance, manufacturing, purchasing, and engineering people all work to. They use the formal system.[6]

Suppliers can formally claim to have a Class A production system once they have undergone a formal review of their system by a professional external reviewer who has verified that the requisite criteria are satisfied.

In some cases, companies who are considering sourcing high volumes of product with a supplier that has multiple facilities may also want to consider whether the supplier has any plans to implement an enterprise resource planning (ERP) system. ERP systems effectively provide a single information system linking accounting, operations, purchasing, logistics, finance, marketing, and sales. Such information systems provide a higher level of accuracy on cost tracking, delivery, and scheduling across multiple facilities.

E-Commerce Capability

The ability to communicate electronically between a buyer and seller is becoming a requirement for entering into a purchase contract. In the past, electronic data interchange (EDI) was considered a primary condition for doing business. However, more and more companies are moving to Web-based platforms for their transactions. Such systems are often referred to as business to business (B2B) electronic commerce. In early 2000, relatively few companies had implemented B2B electronic commerce platforms, but the rate of technology change in this area has been escalating rapidly. For instance, IBM stated that the majority of its purchases (by dollar spent) occured via the Web in 2000. However, such statements assume that suppliers have the required ability to adopt to an e-commerce approach. In contrast to EDI, electronic commerce requires a relatively low investment on the part of suppliers. Ford Motor Company has offered to provide their suppliers with a computer, modem, and Web software for as little as $5 a month, and expects to significantly reduce its cost of transactions with suppliers as a result. Besides the efficiencies that B2B e-commerce provides, these systems support closer relationships and the exchange of all kinds of information. (Chapter 19 discusses purchasing information systems and e-commerce.)

Purchasing managers should also evaluate other dimensions of the supplier's information technology. Does the supplier have computer-aided design (CAD) and computer-aided manufacturing (CAM) capability? Does the supplier have a Web-based supplier measurement system in place? Is bar coding used where appropriate? Can the supplier send advance shipping notices (ASNs) or accept payment by electronic funds transfer? Is the supplier able to communicate via e-mail? Are managers networked throughout the company? Evidence that the supplier is using these technologies can provide reasonable assurance that the supplier is staying current with new e-commerce technologies.

Supplier Sourcing Strategies, Policies, and Techniques

The concept of understanding a supplier's suppliers is a key part of integrated supply chain management. Unfortunately, organizations do not have the resources or personnel to investigate all of the suppliers within their supply chain. However, there are ways to indirectly obtain information on the performance capabilities of tier-two and even tier-three suppliers. Exhibit 8.5 illustrates how it is possible for a purchaser to develop an understanding of the purchasing approaches and techniques of suppliers three tiers below the primary buyer.

Assume that during the supplier selection process, a purchaser (Level 0) evaluates the sourcing strategies, approaches, and techniques of its first-tier supplier

EXHIBIT 8.5   *A Firm's Supply Chain*

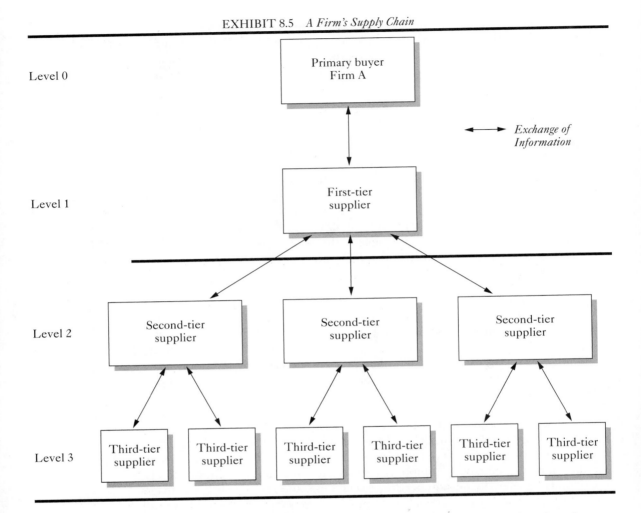

(Level 1). Through discussions with the purchasing department of the first-tier supplier, the purchaser can gain insight about its second-tier suppliers (Level 2). If the supplier at Level 1 (the purchaser's first-tier supplier) also evaluates the sourcing strategies, approaches, and techniques of its first-tier suppliers (Level 2 suppliers to the purchaser), then this can provide information about third-tier suppliers (Level 3). The original purchaser has an opportunity to gain information, with support from first-tier suppliers, about suppliers three tiers below.

Evaluating a potential supplier's sourcing strategies, policies, and techniques is one way to gain greater insight and understanding of the supply chain. Because few purchasers understand their second- and third-tier suppliers, those that do can gain an important advantage over competitors. Integrating information systems across multiple tiers of suppliers can improve planning and forecasting, reduce lead time throughout the supply chain, reduce in-transit inventory, and significantly reduce costs. On the technology side, engineers can obtain advance information on new in-novations being developed by second- and third-tier suppliers, thereby improving the design of their own products.

Chrysler, now part of DaimlerChrysler, has developed a concept it refers to as the extended enterprise. This process requires Chrysler to map its supply chain for its purchased materials all the way to raw materials. Part of the process requires Chrysler to enlighten suppliers far up the supply chain by letting those suppliers know how their products are used in Chrysler vehicles. This process also helps Chrysler under-stand its total supply chain.

Longer-Term Relationship Potential

Assessing a supplier's willingness to develop longer-term relationships that may evolve into alliances or partnerships is increasingly becoming part of the evaluation process. Robert Spekman presents a number of questions that a buyer should ask when evaluating the potential of a longer-term relationship. He argues that ap-proaches emphasizing supplier efficiency, quality, price, and delivery are sometimes incomplete. Although these performance areas are important, they do not necessarily cover the issues upon which to base a longer-term relationship or partnership.[7]

- Has the supplier indicated a willingness or commitment to a longer-term or part-nership arrangement?
- Is the supplier willing to commit resources that it cannot or will not use in other relationships?
- How early in the product design stage is the supplier willing or able to participate?
- What does the supplier bring to the relationship that is unique?
- Will the supplier immediately revert to a negotiated stance if a problem arises?
- Does the supplier have a genuine interest in joint problem solving?
- Is the supplier's senior management committed to the processes inherent in strategic relationships?
- Will there be free and open exchange of information across the two companies?
- How much future planning is the supplier willing to share?
- Is the need for confidential treatment of information taken seriously?
- What is the general level of comfort between the two parties?
- How well does the supplier know our industry and business?
- Will the supplier share cost data?
- Is the supplier willing to come to us first with innovations?
- Is the supplier willing to commit capacity exclusively to our needs?
- What will be the supplier's commitment to understanding our problems and concerns?
- Will we be special to the supplier or just another customer?

This is not a complete list of questions when evaluating the possibility of a longer-term relationship. However, this does provide a framework regarding the types of is-sues that are important. It is relatively straightforward to create a numerical scale to assess these questions as part of the supplier evaluation and selection process.

DEVELOPING AN INITIAL SUPPLIER EVALUATION AND SELECTION SURVEY

Supplier evaluations often follow a rigorous, structured approach through the use of a survey. An effective supplier survey should have certain characteristics. First, the survey should be *comprehensive* and include the performance categories considered important to the evaluation and selection process.

A second characteristic is that the survey process must be as *objective* as possible. This requires the use of a scoring system that defines the meaning of each value on a measurement scale. If a performance item rates a supplier along a 10-point scale, the individual or team conducting the rating must understand what a value of a 10 versus a 9 means. Objectivity means creating a quantitative scale to evaluate performance items and categories that are often subjective.

A third characteristic is that the items and the measurement scales are *reliable*. Reliability refers to the degree to which different individuals or groups reviewing the same items and measurement scales will arrive at the same conclusion. In other words, if two individuals evaluated the same supplier under the same conditions, a reliable item is one that results in basically the same evaluation from the two individuals. Reliable supplier evaluations require well-defined measures and well-understood items. The items and scales must be clearly written and unambiguous so the user understands exactly what each means. Perhaps one of the best methods of obtaining objective and reliable scales is effective training of those who conduct the survey.

A fourth characteristic of a sound supplier survey is *flexibility*. While an organization should maintain a structure to its supplier survey, the format of the evaluation should provide some flexibility across different types of purchase requirements. The requirements when evaluating a service provider may differ substantially from a highly engineered subsystem purchase. The easiest way to include flexibility within the supplier evaluation process is to adjust the performance categories and weights assigned to each category. The performance categories that are most important will receive a higher weight within the total evaluation score.

Finally, the supplier survey should be *mathematically straightforward*. The use of weights and points should be simple enough so that each individual involved in the evaluation understands the mechanics of the scoring and selection process. To ensure that a supplier survey has the right characteristics, we recommend the use of a step-by-step process when creating this tool. Exhibit 8.6 presents the steps to follow when developing such a system. The following section discusses this framework in detail and develops a sample supplier evaluation survey.

Step 1: Identify Key Supplier Evaluation Categories

One of the first steps when developing a supplier survey is deciding which performance categories to include. Recall from an earlier section of this chapter that many possible performance evaluation categories exist. Typically, a purchaser may evaluate a supplier's cost structure, expected delivery performance, technological and process capability, quality systems, and management capability.

EXHIBIT 8.6   *Initial Supplier Evaluation and Selection Audit Development*

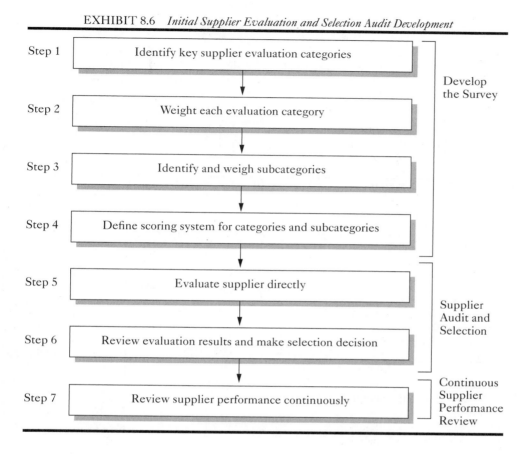

For illustrative purposes, assume that a purchaser selects quality, management capability, financial condition, supplier cost structure, expected delivery performance, technological capability, systems capability, and a general category of miscellaneous performance factors as the categories to include in the evaluation. These categories would reveal the performance areas the purchaser considers most important.

Step 2: Weight Each Evaluation Category

The performance categories usually receive a weight that reflects the relative importance of that category. For example, if quality performance is important, a purchaser may assign a greater weight to that category. The assigned weights reflect the relative importance of each category. The total of the combined weights must equal 1.0.

Exhibit 8.7 shows the weight assigned to each selected performance category. Notice that the quality systems category receives 20% of the total evaluation while systems capability receives 5%; this simply reflects the difference in relative importance to the purchaser between the two performance categories. An important characteristic

EXHIBIT 8.7   *Initial Supplier Evaluation*

Supplier: Advanced Micro Systems

Category	Weight	Subweight	Score (5 pt.scale)	Weighted Score	
1. Quality Systems	20				
Process control systems		5	4	4.0	
Total quality commitment		8	4	6.4	
Parts per million defect performance		7	5	7.0	
					17.4
2. Management Capability	10				
Management/labor relations		5	4	4.0	
Management capability		5	4	4.0	
					8.0
3. Financial Condition	10				
Debt structure		5	3	3.0	
Turnover ratios		5	4	4.0	
					7.0
4. Cost Structure	15				
Costs relative to industry		5	5	5.0	
Understanding of costs		5	4	4.0	
Cost control/reduction efforts		5	5	5.0	
					14.0
5. Delivery Performance	15				
Performance to promise		5	3	3.0	
Lead-time requirements		5	3	3.0	
Responsiveness		5	3	3.0	
					9.0
6. Technical/Process Capability	15				
Product innovation		5	4	4.0	
Process innovation		5	5	5.0	
Research and development		5	5	5.0	
					14.0
7. Information Systems Capability	5				
EDI capability		3	5	3.0	
CAD/CAM		2	0	0	
					3.0
8. General	10				
Support of minority suppliers		2	3	1.2	
Environmental compliance		3	5	3.0	
Supplier's supply-base management		5	4	4.0	
					8.2
			Total Weighted Score		80.6

of an effective evaluation system is flexibility. One way that management achieves this flexibility is by assigning different weights or adding or deleting performance categories as required. A dynamic approach to supplier evaluation recognizes that different purchase requirements may require different performance categories or weights.

Step 3: Identify and Weigh Subcategories

Step 2 specified broad performance categories included within our sample evaluation. Step 3 of this process requires identifying any performance subcategories, if they exist, within each broader performance category. For example, the quality systems category may require the identification of separate subcategories (such as those described in the Malcolm Baldrige Award criteria). If this is the case, the supplier evaluation should include any subcategories or items that make up the quality systems category. Equally important, the purchaser must decide how to weigh each subcategory within the broader performance evaluation category. In Exhibit 8.7, the quality systems category includes an evaluation of a supplier's process control systems, total quality commitment, and parts per million defect performance. The sum of the subcategory weights must equal the total weight of the performance category. Furthermore, the purchaser must clearly define the scoring system used within each category. This becomes the focus of Step 4.

Step 4: Define Scoring System for Categories and Subcategories

Step 4 defines each score within a performance category. If an evaluation uses a 5-point scale to assess a performance category, then a purchaser must clearly define the difference between a score of 5, 4, 3, etc. A major U.S. company scored each category and subcategory in its supplier evaluation program on a 10-point scale where 1–2 = poor, 3–4 = weak, 5–6 = marginal, 7–8 = qualified, and 9–10 = outstanding. The scoring values did not have any further definition detailing what each means. The company has since revamped its system to include a 4-point scale that is easier to interpret and is based on the language and principles of total quality management:

- *Major nonconformity (0 points earned):* The absence or total breakdown of a system to meet a requirement, or any noncompliance that would result in the probable shipment of a nonconforming product.
- *Minor nonconformity (1 point earned):* A noncompliance (though not major) that judgment and experience indicate is likely to result in the failure of the quality system or reduce its ability to ensure controlled processes or products.
- *Conformity (2 points earned):* No major or minor nonconformities were noted during the evaluation.
- *Adequacy (3 points earned):* Specific supplier performance or documentation meets or exceeds requirements given the scope of the supplier's operations.

A clearly defined scoring system takes criteria that may be highly subjective and develops a quantitative scale for measurement. Scoring metrics are effective if different individuals interpret and score similarly the same performance categories under review. A scoring system that is too broad, ambiguous, or poorly defined increases the probability of arriving at widely different assessments or conclusions.

Step 5: Evaluate Supplier Directly

This step requires that the reviewer visit a supplier's facilities to perform the evaluation. Site visits require at least a day and often several days to complete. When factoring in travel time and post-visit reviews, we begin to realize that an organization must select carefully those suppliers it plans on evaluating. In many cases, a cross-functional team will perform the evaluation, which allows team members with different knowledge to ask different questions.

Purchasers often notify suppliers beforehand of any documentation required to support the initial evaluation. This can save time once the evaluation begins. If a purchaser has no previous experience with a supplier, the reviewer might require a supplier to provide documentation of performance capability. For example, a supplier will have to present evidence of its process capability studies, process control systems, or delivery performance.

In the example shown in Exhibit 8.7, the total score for the quality category is calculated as follows. The evaluator assigned the process control systems a score of 4 out of 5, the supplier's quality commitment received a score of 4 out of 5, and the parts per million defect performance received a 5 out of 5. Next, the evaluator divided each score by five to obtain a ratio (because each score is based on a 5-point scale). The ratio is multiplied by the subweight to produce the subweight score. Finally, the subweight scores are added to form the category score for this particular supplier, as shown next.

Quality Systems Performance Category (Weight = 20)

Subcategories:

Process control systems (4 points out of 5 possible points) = 0.8×5 subweight = 4.0 points

Total quality commitment (4 points out of 5 possible points) = 0.8×8 subweight = 6.4 points

PPM defect performance (5 points out of 5 possible points) = 1.0×7 subweight = 7.0 points

Total for category 17.4 points
or 87% of total possible points (17.4/20)

As shown in Exhibit 8.7, Advanced Micro Systems received a total overall evaluation of 80.6%. A purchaser can compare objectively the scores of different suppliers competing for the same purchase contract or select one supplier over another based on the evaluation score. It is also possible, based on the evaluation, that a supplier does not qualify at this time for further purchase consideration. Purchasers should have minimum acceptable performance requirements that suppliers must satisfy before they can become part of the supply base. In this example, the supplier performs acceptably in most major categories except delivery performance (9 out of 15 possible points). The reviewer must decide if the shortcomings in this category are correctable or if the supplier simply lacks the ability to perform.

Step 6: Review Evaluation Results and Make Selection Decision

At some point a reviewer must decide whether to recommend or reject a supplier as a source. What actually happens is a function of the particular situation under review. An organization may review a supplier for consideration for expected future business and not a specific contract. Evaluating suppliers before there is an actual purchase requirement can provide a great deal of flexibility to a purchaser. Once an actual need materializes, the purchaser is in a position to move quickly because it has a prequalified supplier.

It is important to determine the seriousness of any supplier shortcomings noted during the evaluation and assess the degree to which these shortcomings might affect performance. Evaluation scales should differentiate between various degrees of supplier shortcomings. Alcoa, for example, explicitly defines the difference between a performance problem and a deficiency. A problem is "a discrepancy, nonconformance, or missing requirement that will have a significant negative impact on an important area of concern in an audit statement." A deficiency is "a minor departure from an intended level of performance, or a nonconformance that is easily resolved and does not materially affect the required output."[8]

The primary output from this step is a recommendation about whether to accept a supplier for business. A purchaser may evaluate several suppliers who might be competing for a purchase contract. The initial evaluation provides an objective way to compare suppliers side-by-side before making a final selection decision. A purchaser may decide to use more than one supplier based on the results of the supplier survey. The purpose of the evaluation is to qualify potential suppliers for current or expected future purchase contracts.

The authority for the final supplier selection decision varies from organization to organization. The reviewer who evaluated the supplier may have the authority to make the supplier selection decision. In other cases, the buyer or team may present or justify the supplier selection decision or findings to a committee or a manager who has final authority.

Step 7: Review Supplier Performance Continuously

The supplier survey or visit is only the first step of the evaluation process. If a purchaser decides to select a supplier, the supplier must then perform according to the purchaser's requirements. The emphasis shifts from the initial evaluation and selection of suppliers to evidence of continuous performance improvement by suppliers.

CRITICAL SUPPLIER SELECTION ISSUES

A number of important issues arise during the supplier evaluation and selection process. Each has the potential to affect a final decision.

Size Relationship A purchaser may decide to select suppliers over which it has a relative size advantage. A buyer may simply have greater influence when it has a relative size advantage over the supplier or represents a larger share of the supplier's total business. For example, Allen-Edmonds Shoe Corporation, a 71-year-old maker of premium shoes, tried unsuccessfully to implement just-in-time methods to speed production, boost customer satisfaction, and save money. Unfortunately, Allen-Edmonds had difficulty getting suppliers to agree to the just-in-time requirement of matching delivery to production needs. While domestic suppliers of leather soles agreed to make weekly instead of monthly deliveries, European tanneries supplying calfskin hides refused to cooperate. The reason? Allen-Edmonds Shoe was not a large enough customer to wield any leverage with those suppliers.

Use of International Suppliers The decision to select a foreign supplier can have important implications during the supplier evaluation and selection process. For one, international sourcing is generally more complex than domestic buying. As a result, the evaluation and selection process can take on added complexity. This is often true, for example, in the electronics industry where many component suppliers are located in the Far East. In addition, it may be difficult to implement JIT with international suppliers, as lead times are frequently twice as long as those for domestic suppliers.

Competitors as Suppliers Another important issue is the degree to which a buyer is willing to purchase directly from a competitor. A major supplier to Chrysler is Saginaw Steering Gear, a unit of General Motors. Purchasing from competitors often limits information sharing between the two parties. The purchase transaction is usually straightforward and the buyer and seller do not develop a working relationship characterized by mutual commitment and confidential information sharing.

Countertrade Requirements The need to satisfy countertrade requirements can also influence or affect the supplier evaluation and selection decision. Countertrade is a broad term that refers to all trade where buyer and seller have at least a partial exchange of goods for goods or face some restrictions on their commercial activities. Boeing, a producer of commercial aircraft, purchases a portion of its production requirements in markets where it hopes to do business or where it must satisfy the countertrade requirements of international governments. An organization involved in extensive worldwide marketing may have to contend with countertrade requirements before it can sell to international customers, which can have a direct impact on the supplier evaluation and selection process. Chapter 11 addresses international purchasing and countertrade.

Social Objectives Most purchasers are attempting to increase their volume of business with traditionally disadvantaged suppliers, including suppliers with female, minority, or handicapped owners. Buyers may also want to conduct business with suppliers that commit to the highest environmental standards. The influence of social objectives on purchasing will continue to remain strong.

SUPPLIER MEASUREMENT AND EVALUATION

Once a supplier is selected, the focus must shift from supplier evaluation to the continuous measurement of supplier performance. An organization must have the tools to measure, manage, and develop the performance of its supply base. Without a system to evaluate supplier performance, how do purchasers really know how well a supplier is satisfying its performance obligations over time? Supplier performance measurement includes the methods and systems to collect and provide information to measure, rate, or rank supplier performance on a continuous basis. The measurement system is a critical part of the sourcing process—essentially serving as a supplier's "report card." Supplier performance measurement differs from the process used to initially evaluate and select a supplier. It is a continuous process as opposed to a one-time or sporadic event.

Supplier Measurement Decisions

Organizations face some key decisions when developing a supplier measurement system. These decisions are critical to the final design and implementation of the system.

What to Measure Central to all measurement systems is the decision about what to measure and how to weigh the performance categories. An organization must decide which performance criteria are objective (quantitative) measures and which criteria are subjective (qualitative). Most of the objective, quantitative variables lie within the following three categories:

- *Delivery performance:* Orders or material releases sent to a supplier have a quantity and a material due date. A buyer can track how well a supplier satisfies the quantity and due-date commitment. A buyer can also track a supplier's material lead time. Quantity, lead-time requirements, and due-date compliance help define a supplier's delivery performance.
- *Quality performance:* Almost all supplier measurement systems include quality performance as a critical component. A buyer can compare a supplier's quality against some previously specified performance objective, track improvement rates, and compare similar suppliers. It is important for a purchaser to define supplier quality requirements.
- *Supplier cost reduction:* Buyers often rely on suppliers for cost-reduction assistance. An organization can measure cost reduction in a number of ways. One common method is to track a supplier's real cost after adjustment for inflation. Another way is to compare a supplier's cost against other suppliers within the same industry.

Buyers can also use a number of qualitative factors to assess supplier performance. Exhibit 8.8 details some of the qualitative service factors available to buyers. Although these factors are usually subjective, a buyer can still assign each factor a score or rating. A buyer might evaluate five different qualitative factors (assume equal

EXHIBIT 8.8   *Possible Qualitative Service Factors*

Factor	Description
Problem resolution ability	Supplier's attentiveness to problem resolution
Technical ability	Supplier's manufacturing ability compared with other industry suppliers
Ongoing progress reporting	Supplier's ongoing reporting of existing problems or recognizing and communicating a potential problem
Corrective action response	Supplier's solutions and timely response to requests for corrective actions, including a supplier's response to engineering change requests
Supplier cost-reduction ideas	Supplier's willingness to help a buyer find ways to reduce purchase cost
Supplier new-product support	Supplier's ability to help a buying firm reduce new-product development cycle time or to help with product design
Buyer/seller compatibility	Subjective rating concerning how well a buying firm and a supplier work together

weighing for simplicity) along a 5-point scale. The system adds the five scores and divides by the total possible points to arrive at a percentage of total points, so that a buyer can rank suppliers by the percentage of total possible points earned. A purchaser may have minimum levels of acceptable supplier performance on each factor. If a supplier falls below any one minimum, then the buyer must work closely with the supplier to approve the rating.

Frequency of Measurement and Reporting   Two critical aspects relate to the frequency of measurement—reporting frequency to the buyer and reporting frequency to the supplier. A buyer (or someone responsible for the day-to-day management of suppliers) should receive a daily report summarizing the previous day's incoming activity. This report allows the purchaser to scan incoming receipt activity. The report should also highlight past-due supplier receipts. A buyer should receive additional reports summarizing supplier performance on a weekly, monthly, and quarterly basis.

Routine reporting of supplier performance usually occurs monthly or quarterly. Weekly reporting is usually too often and once or twice a year is not enough. Most buyers try to meet with suppliers at least on an annual basis to review performance results. A buyer should never delay reporting a supplier's poor performance, particularly when it affects day-to-day operations.

Use of Measurement Data   An organization can use the data it gathers from its measurement system in a number of ways. The data support an organization's continuous supply-base management efforts by helping to identify those suppliers that are capable (or not capable) of performing at world-class levels (discussed in Chapter 10). The system also helps identify suppliers who qualify for longer-term partnerships or designation as preferred suppliers because of exemplary performance. Measurement data also support supply-base optimization efforts. If suppliers do not improve performance to a minimum acceptable level by a specific date, then it is likely they will be eliminated from the supply base.

Another use of supplier performance data includes determining a supplier's purchase volume based on its performance rating. Some companies adjust purchase volumes periodically and reward better-performing suppliers with a slightly higher share of their purchase requirement. Adjusting volumes between suppliers provides a financial incentive for a supplier to exceed performance expectations. At Honda of America, the vice president of purchasing has been known to personally sign every supplier report card on a quarterly basis. This sends a very strong signal to suppliers that someone is watching.

A major measurement benefit is that supplier performance data allow an organization to identify areas requiring improvement. It is difficult to track an organization's supply-base performance improvement without a formal measurement system. Purchasers also use the data when making future sourcing decisions. Future sourcing decisions become clearer when a buyer has a system that rates and ranks supplier performance against other suppliers or against established performance standards.

Types of Supplier Measurement Techniques

Every supplier measurement system is subjective to some degree. Even the implementation of a computerized measurement system requires subjective decisions. What data to analyze, what type of measurement system to use, what performance categories to include, how to weight different categories, how often to generate performance reports, and how to use the performance data are all subjective decisions to some degree. Moreover, no hard rules exist regarding the specific attributes to include in supplier measurement systems.

Organizations typically use one of three supplier measurement techniques or systems. These systems differ in their ease of use, level of decision subjectivity, required resources to use the system, and implementation costs. Exhibit 8.9 compares the advantages and disadvantages of these three systems.

Categorical System A categorical system is the easiest and most basic measurement system to implement and use, and it is also the most subjective as far as determining supplier performance. This system requires the assignment of a rating to each selected performance category. Examples of possible ratings include excellent, good, fair, or poor. Internal users often provide input when determining the rating. Receiving personnel may provide input about a supplier's delivery performance while quality personnel provide input about quality performance.

The categorical approach is common for smaller organizations or those just starting their formal supplier measurement efforts because this approach is easy and relatively inexpensive to implement. While the categorical approach provides some structure to the measurement process, it does not provide detailed insight into a supplier's

EXHIBIT 8.9   *Comparison of Supplier Measurement and Evaluation Systems*

System	Advantages	Disadvantages	Users
Categorical	Easy to implement Requires minimal data Different personnel contribute Good for firms with limited resources Low-cost system	Least reliable Less frequent generation of evaluations Most subjective Usually manual	Smaller firms Firms in the process of developing an evaluation system
Weighted-Point	Flexible system Supplier ranking allowed Moderate implementation costs Quantitative and qualitative factors combined into a single system	Tends to focus on unit price Requires some computer support	Most firms can use this approach
Cost-Based	Total cost approach Specific areas of supplier nonperformance identified Objective supplier ranking Greatest potential for long-range improvement	Cost accounting system required Most complex so implementation costs high Computer resources required	Larger firms Firms with a large supply base

true performance. Furthermore, because categorical systems often rely on manually collected data, an organization generates supplier performance reports less frequently than if an automated or structured approach existed. The reliability of the categorical method is the lowest of the three measurement systems discussed here, which limits the value of this approach for ranking suppliers based on performance.

Weighted-Point System   This approach overcomes the primary disadvantage of the categorical system—its subjectivity. A weighted-point system weighs and quantifies scores across different performance categories. This approach to supplier measurement usually features higher reliability and moderate implementation costs. Weighted-point systems are also flexible—users can change the weights assigned to each performance category or change the performance categories.

Lockheed Martin Brings a Method to Supplier Measurement

Few organizations have created measurement systems that provide information about how well suppliers really perform. Lockheed Martin's Aeronautics Material Management Center (LM-AMMC), however, has demonstrated that with time, patience, commitment, and a proper method, the creation and refinement of a comprehensive supplier measurement system is possible.

Methodical is a good way to describe Lockheed Martin's evolution toward supplier improvement. LM-AMMC began its process in the early 1990s with a requirement that all production suppliers must become certified users of statistical process control. This quickly drove out many suppliers that did not want to get involved in this program. What remained was a proactive supplier base.

The second step was to endorse the process of preventing nonconformance and to move away from inspection to detect nonconformance. Lockheed Martin no longer routinely uses inspectors at its facilities. Now, it employs 65 field engineers to work directly at supplier facilities to help them better manufacture parts. The company has shifted from inspection to what it calls source surveillance.

The third step has been the implementation of a supplier certification program. The program sets forth and measures a set of stringent performance requirements in cost, quality, and delivery. If a supplier continuously meets those requirements, Lockheed Martin performs no oversight and no inspection.

Supporting the supplier certification program is a company-wide continuous supplier performance rating system. The rating system captures data from three points in the supply chain—information about rejections at each supplier's site, rejections that occur in receiving, and rejections on the assembly line. The system allows users to evaluate a supplier's performance by delivery location and for the company as a whole.

Has the supplier measurement system revealed any performance improvement results? Consider that in 1991, the firm's Fort Worth site outsourced 9,000 part numbers for the F-16 fighter. In 1997, it outsourced 46,300. Still, total assembly line rejections were down even though the number of part numbers provided by suppliers quadrupled.

Where is Lockheed Martin evolving in its supplier measurement efforts? The company has plans for what it calls the lowest evaluated price (LEP). This system will allow the company to assign costs of poor supplier performance and to use this information in its bidding processes to more accurately represent the true cost of doing business with suppliers.

Source: Adapted from "Lockheed Martin Brings Method to Metrics Madness," *Purchasing* 124, no. 1 (January 15, 1998): 26–30.

EXHIBIT 8.10   *Weighted-Point Supplier Measurement and Evaluation of*
Davis Industries for Third Quarter 2001

Performance Category	Weight	Score	Weighted Score
Delivery			
On time	.10	4	.4
Quantity	.10	3	.3
Quality			
Inbound shipment quality	.25	4	1.0
Quality improvement	.10	4	.4
Cost Competitiveness			
Comparison with other suppliers	.15	2	.3
Cost-reduction ideas submitted	.10	3	.3
Service Factors			
Problem resolution ability	.05	4	.2
Technical ability	.05	5	.25
Corrective action response	.05	3	.15
New-product development support	.05	5	.25
Total Rating			**3.55**

1 = Poor, 3 = Average, 5 = Excellent

Several important issues underlie the use of weighted-point systems. First, users must select the performance categories to measure. Second, an organization must decide how to weight each performance category. An organization can assign equal weights to each category or weight some categories more heavily than others. While assigning weights is subjective, an organization can reach a consensus about how to weight the performance categories through careful planning and involvement from different functions. Third, a set of rules must exist that compares a supplier's performance against a performance objective to provide a score for each category.

Exhibit 8.10 illustrates a sample weighted-point system based on a 5-point scale. A value of 5 is the highest possible score. The weighted-point plan should provide a higher level of objectivity for most performance categories compared with the categorical approach. This system also evaluates supplier performance in somewhat more detail than the categorical approach.

Cost-Based System   The most thorough and least subjective of the three measurement systems presented here is the cost-based system. This approach quantifies the total cost of doing business with a supplier. The lowest purchase price is not always the lowest total cost for an item or service. Chapter 13 discusses total cost of ownership in detail. Here, we discuss how calculating the total cost associated with each supplier nonperformance provides a rational method for evaluating key supplier performance factors.

EXHIBIT 8.11   *Supplier Performance Comparison Through Third Quarter 2001*

Commodity: Integrated Circuit

Part Number	Supplier	Unit Price	SPI	Total Cost
04279884	Advanced Systems	$3.12	1.20	$3.74*
	BC Techtronics	$3.01	1.45	$4.36
	Micro Circuit	$3.10	1.30	$4.03
04341998	Advanced Systems	$5.75	1.20	$6.90*
	BC Techtronics	$5.40	1.45	$7.83
	Micro Circuit	$5.55	1.30	$7.21

Service Factor Ratings:

Advanced Systems	78%
BC Techtronics	76%
Micro Circuit	87%

*Lowest total cost supplier for item (Unit price × SPI = Total cost)

Source: Robert M. Monczka and Steven J. Trecha, "Cost-Based Supplier Performance Evaluation," *Journal of Purchasing and Materials Management* (Spring 1988): 1–4.

Most companies with computer system capability can implement a cost-based supplier measurement system. The major challenge involves identifying and recording the costs associated with supplier nonperformance. To use the system, an organization must calculate the additional costs that result whenever a supplier fails to perform as expected. The basic logic of the system lies in the calculation of a supplier performance index (SPI).[9] This index, with a base value of 1.0, is a total cost index calculated for each item or commodity provided by a supplier:

SPI = (total purchases + Nonperformance Cost)/total purchases

An organization must perform a number of tasks when developing a cost-based supplier measurement system, such as the supplier performance index. System development involves not only purchasing but also other departments that are affected by supplier performance. Development requires identifying the items and/or commodities to evaluate; identifying key performance categories (i.e., delivery, service, cost); identifying key functional areas or activities affected by supplier nonperformance; identifying events that create nonperformance costs; identifying the costs associated with each nonperformance event; and calculating the SPI index for each item or commodity. The costs associated with each nonperformance can be an actual or average cost.

Exhibit 8.11 illustrates a total cost-based approach for supplier measurement. The cost-based approach can also include an assessment of qualitative service factors to provide a complete picture of supplier performance. This exhibit compares the total cost of ownership for each supplier for the two items in the integrated circuit commodity. It also compares suppliers based on their service factor ratings. The lowest price supplier, BC Techtronics, is not the lowest total cost supplier. BC Techtronics also has a lower service rating score compared with the other two suppliers.

EXHIBIT 8.12   *Supplier Performance Report for First Quarter 2001*

Supplier: Advanced Systems
Commodity: Integrated circuit
Total part numbers in commodity: 2

A. Total purchase dollars this quarter: $5,231.67

Nonperformance Costs:

Event	Number of Occurrences	Average Cost per Occurrence	Extended Cost
Late delivery	5	$150	$750
Return to supplier	2	$45	$90
Scrap labor costs	3	$30	$90
Material rework cost	1	$100	$100
B. Total nonperformance costs			$1,030
C. Purchase + nonperformance cost	(Line A+B)		$6,261.67
D. Supplier performance index	(Line C/A)		1.20
E. Service factor rating			78%

Exhibit 8.12 summarizes supplier performance for a group of items comprising a single commodity. It details the total number of nonperforming events, the cost of each event as identified by the purchaser, and the total nonperformance cost for the quarter. Lines C and D include the figures required to calculate the SPI. Line E is the ratio of points earned to the total possible points for the qualitative or service factors. The service factor rating, while not reflecting a supplier's performance on any one item, is still considered a measure of a supplier's strengths and weaknesses in servicing a buyer's account.

In many cases, the cost per event may be difficult to estimate. For instance, the average cost of a late delivery may vary widely, depending on the impact on the customer's order, potential lost sales, line shutdown costs, etc. Many organizations get around this by assigning a standard charge each time a nonperformance event occurs.

The SPI sometimes provides an incomplete or misleading assessment of supplier performance. Consider a supplier that delivers $100,000 of material with one late delivery charged at $5,000. That supplier will have an SPI of ($100,000 + $5,000)/$100,000, or 1.05. This looks much better than a supplier that delivers $30,000 of material with one late delivery charged at $5,000. The second supplier has an SPI of ($30,000 + $5,000)/$30,000, or 1.17. Although both suppliers committed the same infraction, the smaller supplier was penalized more severely. The Q adjustment is a normalization factor that eliminates a favorable bias toward higher-dollar-volume suppliers. Exhibit 8.13 illustrates how to calculate the SPI with the Q adjustment factor to allow an apples-to-apples comparison between suppliers.

Management has many uses for the data from a cost-based measurement system. This system provides the information a buyer needs to justify purchasing a higher-

---

EXHIBIT 8.13   *Supplier Performance Index Calculation with Q Adjustment Factor*

Q is a normalization factor that eliminates high-dollar lot biases.

Q = (Average cost of a lot of material for an individual supplier)/(Average cost of a lot of material for all suppliers)

Consider the following information for Suppliers A, B, and C, each with a single late delivery nonconformance calculated at $4,000. **Assume the average cost of all lots for suppliers of this commodity is $2,500.**

	Supplier A	Supplier B	Supplier C
3rd quarter shipments	20 lots @ $500 each	20 lots @ 1,000 each	20 lots @ $10,000
Total value of shipments	$10,000	$20,000	$200,000
Average lot cost	$500	$1,000	$10,000
Nonconformance charges	Late delivery $4,000	Late delivery $4,000	Late delivery $4,000
3rd Quarter SPI	($10,000 + $4,000)/ $10,000 = 1.40	($20,000 + $4,000)/ $20,000 = 1.20	($200,000 + $4,000)/ $200,000 = 1.02
Average cost of a lot from all suppliers	$2,500	$2,500	$2,500
Q calculation	$500/$2,500 = .2	$1,000/$2,500 = .4	$10,000/$2,500 = 4

Notice how different the SPI values are for the three suppliers, even though they each committed the same nonconformance. Supplier C, due to the high lot bias, has the lowest SPI.

SPI calculation with Q adjustment = Cost of material + (Nonconformance Costs x Q factor)/Cost of Material

Supplier A: $10,000 + ($4,000 x .2)/$10,000 = 1.08

Supplier B: $20,000 + ($4,000 x .4)/$20,000 = 1.08

Supplier C: $200,000 + ($4,000 x 4)/$200,000 = 1.08

The Q adjustment now allows a fair comparison.

---

quality product from a supplier despite a difference in unit price. The system also allows a buyer to communicate the cost of specific nonperformances to a supplier, which supports the development of joint performance improvement programs. Quantifying nonperformance costs can also result in charging a supplier for unplanned costs. Finally, a buyer can use the data to identify longer-term sources of supply based on a supplier's total cost performance history.

Each of the three types of measurement approaches featured in this chapter, while differing in their complexity and scope of use, raises a buyer's awareness about supply-base performance. Supplier measurement is a powerful tool for managing the supply base. What follows is one company's successful attempt to systematically measure supplier performance.

GOOD PRACTICE EXAMPLE
Scorecards Help FedEx Stay on Top of Supplier Performance[10]

■ ■ ■

FedEx, a worldwide leader in package delivery with annual revenues over $17 billion, has built a solid reputation for on-time package delivery service. Throughout its history (the company is just over 25 years old), FedEx has focused on operational excellence and the ability to pick up, sort, and deliver packages on time to their final destination.

Over the last ten years, the package delivery industry has become highly competitive. Besides FedEx, customers can select UPS, Airborne, DHL, or the U.S. Postal Service to deliver their packages. Even electronic mail is a source of new competition—senders simply attach large files with their electronic messages instead of sending paper copies via the overnight letter pack. As a result, FedEx is looking to provide new services to customers, expand into new markets worldwide, and control costs if it expects to meet its growth targets.

FedEx purchases billions of dollars of goods and services annually, making purchasing a major value-adding activity. Furthermore, FedEx realizes that its suppliers greatly affect total costs and the ability of FedEx to serve its final customers. For example, if a supplier of aircraft replacement parts misses a delivery or ships defective parts, this impacts FedEx's ability to keep its planes flying safely and on time. To help in its supply chain management efforts, the company has created a detailed supplier scorecard to continuously evaluate supplier performance for goods, services, and fuels.

The FedEx supplier scorecard, which is available internally through an Intranet, establishes a level of uniformity among the many diverse purchasing groups at FedEx. Buyers or supply chain specialists maintain scorecards for the suppliers for which they have responsibility. Completed scorecards are forwarded to a central source so they can be reviewed for procedural compliance and maintained in a central file. Exhibit 8.14 is an example of the scorecard template that FedEx uses for products. There are also templates with scoring guidelines for service and fuel suppliers.

The scorecard is flexible and can be tailored to meet the unique needs of a purchase requirement. Users can adjust the weights within each performance category as well as determine which categories and subitems within a category to include. While the system offers the user flexibility in selecting categories and weights, several scorecard rules apply. First, the performance category titled *Diverse Supplier Development* must be included in each evaluation per corporate requirements. Second, the selected performance category weights must sum to 100. Third, all subitems within a category must be scored on a 0–5 scale, which are added together and divided by the number of category subitems to arrive at

EXHIBIT 8.14   *FedEx Strategic Sourcing and Supply Supplier Scorecard for Products*

Supplier Number	Eval. Period: From
FSC Code	To
Supplier Name	Date:
Address	FedEx Rep:
	Manager:
Representative	Department:

CATEGORY				Weight	Score	Total
1. On-Time Delivery Performance	6 mths	3 mths	1 mth	25		
No. of on-time deliveries						
Total deliveries						
Pct. On-Time						
(100–95% = 5 // 94–90 = 4 // 89–80 = 3 // 79–70 = 2 // 69–60 = 1 // less than 60 = 0)						
2. Cycle Time Improvement (Yes / No)				5		
3. Quality				10		
A. Discrepancy rate	6 mths	3 mths	1 mth			
No. of problem receipts						
Total receipts						
Discrepancy rate (rec.)						
No. of problem invoices						
Total invoices						
Discrepancy rate (inv.)						
Total discrepancy rate						
(0–1% = 5 //2–3 = 4 // 4–6 = 3 // 7–9 = 2 // 10–12 = 1 // greater than 12 = 0)						
B. MTBF						
C. Bad from stock						
D. No. of customer / quality complaints						
E. No. of warranty claims						
F. Turn time on warranty claims						
G. Certification (yes / no)						
(Average score for quality)						
4. Service				15		
A. Flexibility						
B. Customer service responsiveness						
C. Operational compatibility / coverage / accessibility						
D. Sales person product knowledge						
E. Sales person knowledge of FedEx						
F. Post sales support						
G. Technology upgrades / enhancements						
(Average score for service)						
5. Financial Stability (measured by D&B)				5		
6. Cost				20		
A. Price competitiveness						
B. Cost trends						
C. Add-ons						
D. Frequency / value of cost-reduction ideas						
E. Supplier savings sharing						
F. Gratis service (no incremental costs)						
G. FedEx cost of quality (or benefit)						
(Average score for cost)						
7. Diverse Supplier Development (DSD) — contact DSD for scoring				10		
A. Direct reporting						
B. Indirect tier reporting (completed by DSD & Prime)						
C. Use of local suppliers						
(Average score for DSD)						
8. Optional or Supplier / Product specific				10		
A.						
B.						
C.						
(Average score for optional)						
9. TOTAL SCORE				100		

Scoring Scale: 5 = Excellent // 4 = Above average // 3 = Average // 2 = Below average // 1 = Poor // 0 = Unacceptable
Performance Level: 500–450 = Platinum // 449–400 = Gold // 399–350 = Silver // 349–300 = Bronze // <300

an average category score. This score is multiplied by the category weight to yield the total score for that category. When all selected categories are scored, the category totals are added to arrive at a *Performance Level* ranging from 0–500 points, with the following designation:

- 500–450   Platinum
- 449–400   Gold
- 399–350   Silver
- 349–300   Bronze
- <300 Requires special attention

A detailed user's manual provides guidance for subitem scoring. For example, the first performance category listed in Exhibit 8.14 is on-time delivery performance. The score is based on the number of deliveries that were on time divided by the total number of deliveries. The following scale is used to arrive at a delivery performance score:

On-Time Delivery %	Score
100–95	5
94–90	4
89–80	3
79–70	2
69–60	1
<60	0

Buyers or supply chain specialists must communicate with internal customers to get insight into each supplier's performance. Ideally, feedback from internal customers is incorporated into the scorecard so results can be shared with suppliers on a regular basis. Since most supplier scorecards include some qualitative assessments or judgment, suppliers may question or even disagree with parts of their score. This is not a major drawback to the system. In fact, any disagreements should be viewed positively since they open up channels of communication between FedEx and suppliers.

With any system, improvements are expected. Users will soon have the ability to weight the subitems within a category rather than providing a single weight for the entire category. Also, products, services, and fuels will be combined into one robust template rather than the three templates that are now used. The information will be available to everyone in the company and can be used to award or deny new business as it becomes available. FedEx also expects to expand scorecard use to include a greater number of suppliers. Currently, scorecards are maintained primarily for higher-volume suppliers. FedEx understands that supplier performance is critical to future success. Progressive FedEx supply chain managers also realize that something as important as supplier performance must be rigorously measured and reported.

CONCLUSION

This chapter discussed one of the most important functions of business—the evaluation, selection, and continuous measurement of suppliers. Performing these activities well establishes the foundation upon which to further develop and improve supplier performance. In his book *Purchasing in the 21st Century*, John Schorr maintains that a buyer should look for certain characteristics when evaluating and selecting suppliers:[11]

- A good supplier will build quality into the product, aiming for zero-defect production.
- Delivery performance is a key measure of a good supplier. This involves a willingness to make short and frequent deliveries to point-of-use areas within a purchaser's facility, along with a willingness to package items according to a purchaser's specifications.
- A good supplier will demonstrate responsiveness to a purchaser's needs by ensuring that qualified and accessible people are in charge of servicing the purchaser's account.
- Long lead times are the enemy of all businesses; a good supplier will work with a purchaser to reduce lead times as much as possible.
- A good supplier willingly provides a purchaser with information regarding capability and workload.
- The best suppliers create the future rather than fear its coming. Look for suppliers on the cutting edge of technology.
- A leading-edge supplier reinvests part of its profits in R&D; a good supplier takes a long-term view and is willing to spend for tomorrow.
- Good suppliers can meet the stringent financial stability criteria used when evaluating potential new customers for credit.

A focus on selecting only the best suppliers possible will make a major contribution to the competitiveness of the entire organization. The ability to make this contribution requires careful evaluation, selection, and continuous measurement of the suppliers that provide the goods and services that help satisfy the needs of an organization's final customers.

DISCUSSION QUESTIONS

1.   Why do organizations commit the resources and time to evaluate suppliers before making a supplier selection decision?
2.   Discuss the possible ways that purchasing becomes aware of the need to evaluate and select a supplier.
3.   Discuss why purchasers should measure supplier performance on a continuous basis.
4.   Discuss the sources of information available to a buyer when seeking information about potential sources of supply. When do you think it is appropriate to use different sources?
5.   What are the various methods for evaluating and selecting suppliers?

6. Why is it important to assess the capability of a supplier's management when performing a supplier evaluation? What are some possible indicators on a supplier visit that might cause you to question whether the managers in the company are forward-looking or whether the company is capable of becoming a best-in-class supplier?
7. Discuss the reasons why suppliers are sometimes reluctant to share cost information with buyers, particularly during the early part of a buyer-seller relationship.
8. Discuss the logic behind a purchaser trying to understand its total supply chain (i.e., the need to understand its supplier's suppliers).
9. What are the issues or questions purchasing needs to address when evaluating whether a supplier is a candidate for a longer-term relationship?
10. Define and discuss the characteristics of an effective supplier survey.
11. How can a purchaser build flexibility into a supplier survey?
12. What are the advantages of assigning numerical scores to the categories and subcategories included in a supplier survey?
13. Why is it important for a reviewer to discuss promptly the results of a supplier visit or survey with the supplier? Given that a supplier has a weak area, when do you think supplier development is appropriate?
14. Discuss a situation in which a purchaser might select a supplier that is having financial difficulties.
15. Discuss the following statement: *If a purchaser decides to select a supplier based on the results of the initial evaluation, the supplier must then meet the purchaser's continuous performance requirements.*
16. When using a cost-based approach to supplier measurement, discuss how a smaller-volume supplier can have a higher SPI compared to a higher-volume supplier even though both suppliers committed the same infractions. How can we correct for this small-volume bias?

ADDITIONAL READINGS

Brown, Mark Graham. *Keeping Score: Using the Right Metrics to Drive World-Class Performance.* New York: Quality Resources, 1996.

Gustin, Craig M., Patricia J. Daugherty, and Alexander E. Ellinger. "Supplier Selection Decisions in Systems/Software Purchases." *Journal of Supply Chain Management* 33, no. 4 (Fall 1997): 41–46.

Przirembel, Janet L. *How to Conduct Supplier Surveys and Audits.* West Palm Beach, FL: PT Publications, 1997.

Woods, John A. (editor). *The Purchasing and Supply Yearbook: 2000 Edition,* National Association of Purchasing Management. New York: McGraw-Hill, 2000.

ENDNOTES

1. Robert Handfield and Ronald Pannesi, "Managing Component Life Cycles in Dynamic Technological Environments," *International Journal of Purchasing and Materials Management* (Spring 1994): 20–27.

2. Janet L. Przirembel, *How to Conduct Supplier Surveys and Audits* (West Palm Beach, FL: PT Publications, 1997): 40.

3. "How Green Is Green Paper?" *Business Week*, November 1, 1993, 60–61.

4. Robert Handfield, Robert Sroufe, Steven Walton, and Steven Melnyk, "A Decision Framework for Integrating Environmental Factors into Purchasing Decisions," submitted to special issue on Environmental Decision Making, *European Journal of Operations Research* (June 1999).

5. Lisa Seegers, Robert Handfield, and Steven Melynk, "Environmental Best Practices in the Office Furniture Industry," *Proceedings of the National Decision Science Institute Conference* (November 1995).

6. Thomas E. Vollman, William Lee Berry, and Clay D. Whybark, *Manufacturing Planning and Control Systems*, 2nd ed. (Homewood, IL: Richard D. Irwin, 1988).

7. Robert E. Spekman, "Strategic Supplier Selection: Understanding Long-Term Buyer Relationships," *Business Horizons*, July-August 1988, 80–81.

8. From Alcoa's Supplier Certification Guidelines.

9. Robert M. Monczka and Steven J. Trecha, "Cost-Based Supplier Performance Evaluation," *Journal of Purchasing and Materials Management* (Spring 1988): 1–4.

10. Used with the permission of FedEx.

11. John Schorr, *Purchasing in the 21st Century* (New York: John Wiley & Sons, 1998).

9 SUPPLIER QUALITY MANAGEMENT

$\mathcal{A}$ Sad But True Story

Several years ago a retired couple purchased a top-of-the-line, Class A motor home for cross-country travel. During their 5,000-mile inaugural trip, the travelers experienced more than 25 quality-related problems with the unit, some quite serious. Before they left their home state, the power steering failed, making the motor home difficult and even dangerous to drive. Soon after, the camera that provided visibility to traffic and obstacles behind the vehicle stopped working. Eventually, the water pump broke, leaving the travelers with no use of their shower, toilet, or sink. Later, the internal electrical system failed, leaving them in the dark and rendering the refrigerator useless. One of the most difficult problems occurred when the steps that allowed passengers to enter and exit the motor home failed to retract. This required the travelers to drive with the steps extended away from the vehicle. Eventually, the transmission began to fail during the last several hundred miles of the trip. After limping home (with frequent stops for less than responsive service), the weary travelers concluded, quite dejectedly, that a recreational vehicle was probably not the best travel option for them. They eventually sold the motor home several months later at a significant loss.

Were the quality-related problems in this story solely the fault of the company whose name is on the final product? Invariably, customers will blame the final producer since, in the owner's mind, the producer has ultimate responsibility for the product. To be sure, some problems were due to poor product design and assembly at the factory. However, in this case external suppliers provided most of the components and subunits that failed within the final product. Are these quality defects really part of a broader problem concerning how this company manages its supply chain? Can supplier quality, which many firms take for granted and do not systematically measure, cause serious market *disadvantages*?

In situations when externally sourced components and subassemblies significantly affect cost, quality, and performance, or when suppliers provide value-added activities through design, engineering, and testing, supplier quality becomes absolutely necessary. Furthermore, any company that is serious about total quality management cannot ignore the importance of supplier quality management. Since *quality at the source* is central to the total quality philosophy, executive managers are realizing that their supply chains are a primary source of value to their products, processes, and services. The ability of suppliers to affect end customers makes supplier quality essential to long-term market success.

This chapter approaches the issue of supplier quality from two perspectives. The first considers the actions that an individual buyer can take to ensure that suppliers provide a quality product or service. The second perspective explores how purchasing can ensure the receipt of quality goods and services. The chapter contains five major sections: an overview of supplier quality management, the role of the individual buyer in managing supplier quality, the role of the purchasing function in managing supplier quality, a discussion of ISO 9000 certification and the Baldrige Award, and a good-quality practice example about supplier certification at Alcoa. Appendix E located on the Website reviews various total quality management tools and approaches.

An Overview of Supplier Quality Management

What Is Supplier Quality?

What do we mean by quality? One quality expert, Arman Fiegenbaum, defines quality as the "total composite product and service characteristics of marketing, engineering, manufacturing, and maintenance through which the product or service in use will meet the expectations of the customer."[1] Prior to this view 20 years ago, quality was defined as *conformance to requirements.* The problem with conformance is that it is dependent on who defines the requirements for which goods and services must conform. In every case, users (i.e., customers) define product or service requirements. They define, sometimes in very precise terms, the qualities or features that an item or service must have to be acceptable. The user may be a consumer purchasing an end product, an industrial buyer purchasing raw materials, components, or finished assemblies from external suppliers, or an internal customer receiving output from a "supplier" within the same company. As the Sourcing Snapshot titled "Who Is the Customer?" shows, supply chains have different customers, sometimes with conflicting demands, and different conformance requirements.

In recent years, the concept of quality has changed radically, largely because of Colby Chandler, the former CEO of Eastman Kodak. He redefined quality as *exceeding customer expectations.* This concept has been reemphasized by other organizations, who define quality in terms of "customer delight" and "quality equals survival."

Competition also creates new quality expectations on the part of users. Not surprisingly, many actions by competitors are aimed at driving a change in customer perceptions. For example, a customer may be satisfied with two-day package delivery service until another company offers one-day service with guaranteed delivery at a competitive cost. Changes due to competition can redefine the requirements that customers eventually accept as their standard of quality performance.

From these various quality perspectives, we can begin to define what we mean by *supplier quality*—the ability to consistently meet or exceed current and future customer (i.e., buyer and eventually end customer) expectations or requirements within critical performance areas. There are three major parts to this definition:

1. *Ability to consistently meet or exceed:* This means that suppliers satisfy or exceed buyer expectations or requirements each and every time. Inconsistent supplier performance, whether in physical product quality or on-time delivery, is not a characteristic of a quality supplier.

2. *Current and future customer expectations or requirements:* Suppliers must meet or exceed today's demanding requirements while having the ability to satisfy future requirements. Suppliers must be capable of continuous performance improvement. A supplier who can satisfy today's requirements but cannot keep pace with future requirements is not a quality supplier.

3. *Within critical performance areas:* Supplier quality does not apply only to the physical attributes of a product. Quality suppliers satisfy a purchaser's expectations in many areas, including the following:

   • *Product or service delivery:* This involves the physical delivery of a product or service as well as the delivery of required information (i.e., documentation). A late delivery is an indication of supplier nonperformance, regardless of how well the physical product meets the buyer's needs.

   • *Product or service conformance:* This reflects the ability of the physical product or service to meet physical expectations or requirements, which may be stated in terms of measures, tolerances, grades of material, functionality, specifications, or any other product or service attribute considered important.

   • *After-sale service:* After-sale service, such as maintenance and repair, is important for many items, particularly capital equipment purchases or durable goods.

   • *Technology and features:* A supplier's ability to keep pace with leading technology, including the development of process technology, is another important area where purchasers have requirements. The ability to develop leading technology and then to incorporate that technology into product or service features is critical if a purchaser's end items are to remain competitive.

   • *Cost management:* A direct relationship exists between improved quality and lower cost. As suppliers improve their processes, they can eliminate non–value-added costs and pass on part of these savings to the buying company in the form of lower prices.

Within supply chains, purchasing does not buy parts or service from suppliers—it buys (and sometimes must help manage) supplier capabilities. Purchasers should focus not only on a supplier's physical output (the end result) but also on the systems and processes that create that output. This includes the supplier's expertise and capabilities in logistics, engineering, and management of their own supply chain.

Why Be Concerned with Supplier Quality?

As the opening vignette made clear, any firm that does not manage quality throughout its supply chain is making a serious mistake. Why should a company take an active interest in the quality performance of suppliers?

Supplier Impact on Quality   Quality expert Philip Crosby estimates that suppliers are responsible for 50% of a firm's product-related quality problems. Furthermore, the average manufacturing firm spends over 55% of its sales dollar on purchased goods and services. A firm that focuses only on internal quality issues will fail to recognize the true cause of many quality-related problems. Poor supplier quality can quickly undermine a firm's total quality improvement effort.

SOURCING SNAPSHOT

Who Is the Customer in a Supply Chain?

Total quality management requires a complete understanding of customers and their requirements. However, most supply chains have multiple tiers of suppliers and multiple tiers of customers, sometimes with different expectations and needs. Consider the airline industry. Boeing is a major supplier of aircraft while the airlines are major customers. But aren't passengers a key part of the supply chain? Airlines are now flying a new version of Boeing 737s, Boeing's smallest jet, coast to coast, sometimes with flights up to six hours long. Big carriers have invested the spoils of the current travel boom in a new generation of equipment they are counting on to fatten their profits. "This airplane [the 737] gives you the opportunity to grow markets. It's a killer airplane," said the chairman and chief executive at Continental Airlines. Unfortunately, passengers see it differently. With seats that are one inch narrower than other planes, with less legroom, and a plane that is one lavatory short of what it really needs, it is obvious that the needs of one customer (the airlines) do not exactly align with the needs of another customer (the passengers). One Continental pilot proudly announced to his passengers that they were aboard one of the airlines' newest aircraft. At the end of the flight, he was shocked to be blistered with complaints that the plane was too small. "We love it—it's a great plane to fly," says the captain. "But passengers hate it."

Source: Adapted from Scott McCartney, " Feeling Confined? You May Be Flying in One of Boeing's New 737s," *Wall Street Journal,* August 2, 1999, A1.

Current Performance Levels Exhibit 9.1 reports on the perception that purchasing managers have of supplier performance within three quality-related areas: supplier responsiveness to design or schedule changes, physical product quality, and materials/product delivery. Supplier performance is currently closer to *average* than *excellent,* even though longer-term competitiveness requires a much higher performance level from suppliers. By 2003, purchasers expect a significantly higher level of supplier performance, which is not surprising given the intense level of global competition.

Continuous Improvement Requirements Exhibit 9.2 reveals that most firms plan to achieve continuous quality improvements in all aspects of their business. One way to do this is through the effective management of supplier quality. Quality improvement requirements are a function of a company's industry along with how well its performance compares to that of its competitors. Companies in high-technology industries, such as Intel or Texas Instruments, face intense competitive pressure to achieve rapid quality improvement rates that approach perfection. Other industries, such as

EXHIBIT 9.1   *Current Supplier Performance and Expected Performance*

Performance Area	Current Performance	Expected Performance for 2003	Percentage Change
Responsiveness to design or schedule changes	4.88	6.02	+23
Product quality	5.13	6.23	+21
Material/product delivery	5.09	6.15	+21

1 = Poor performance
4 = Average performance
7 = Excellent performance
N = 68 firms

Source: Executive Purchasing and Supply Chain Management Seminar, Michigan State University, East Lansing, MI, 1999.

EXHIBIT 9.2   *Planned Quality Performance Improvements by 2003*

Anticipated Improvement (%)	Percentage of Firms	Anticipated Improvement (%)	Percentage of Firms
No improvement planned	5	51–60	6
1–10	22	61–70	0
11–20	25	71–80	0
21–30	24	81–90	2
31–40	6	91+	6
41–50	4		

N = 68 firms

Source: Executive Purchasing and Supply Chain Management Seminar, Michigan State University, East Lansing, MI, 1999.

furniture making, experience a slower and less dramatic rate of change. Regardless, all industries experience some pressure to achieve continuous quality improvement.

Outsourcing Complex Purchase Requirements   Many firms are willing to purchase entire subassemblies or even finished products from suppliers. It is no longer considered an advantage in many industries to make most of a product or provide all of your own service. As a result, buyers are relying on suppliers who have design and build capabilities, even for highly technical or complex part requirements. For example, Dell Computer is primarily an assembly operation that purchases almost all of its components (monitor, hard drive, keyboard, microprocessors, power unit, etc.) from external suppliers. The larger the proportion of the final product that suppliers provide, the greater the impact they have on overall product cost and quality.

SOURCING SNAPSHOT

Supplier Quality Matters on the Ground—and in the Air!

Pratt & Whitney told 16 major airline buyers of its engines that it improperly serviced thousands of jet-engine blades, and that they should immediately remove engines with the suspected parts from their aircraft. A company service bulletin had reported that the blades may be prone to cracking, and a spokesman for the supplier said 8,200 blades are affected. Federal Aviation Administration officials said they couldn't recall a service bulletin being issued by an engine maker that called for immediately taking jetliners out of service. The problem stemmed from a machine used to clean the blades. The machine was improperly set, and the resulting cleaning was "overaggressive." Some blades were left to sit in a cleaning solution for 24 hours instead of the 20 minutes recommended by engineers. This problem came at a time when federal regulators have expressed increasing concern about engine problems and failures.

Source: Adapted from Frederic Biddle and Andy Pasztor, "United Technologies Unit Tells Airlines Certain Jet Engines Should Be Removed," *Wall Street Journal*, April 7, 1998, A3.

$\mathcal{M}$ANAGING SUPPLIER QUALITY—THE ROLE OF THE BUYER

Buyers play an important role in managing supplier quality. In this respect, the job requirements of a purchasing manager or buyer have changed dramatically over the last five to ten years. Many difficult and new tasks are now a routine part of the buyer's job, including an active involvement in managing supplier quality. What can individuals do to ensure total supplier quality?

Clearly Communicate Specifications and Expectations

Specifications are characteristics that are detailed by performance, drawings, commercial standards, or a combination of these. Providing clear, firm, meaningful, and mutually acceptable specifications that define requirements or expectations is an important part of supplier quality management. In determining specifications, the buyer is essentially defining the level of quality required. Conformance quality refers to the ability of an item to perform the necessary function at the lowest total cost. Keki Bhote, an expert on supplier quality, argues that suppliers must have a clear understanding of product specifications:

At least half or even more of the quality problems between customer (i.e., the buyer) and supplier are caused by poor specifications, for which the buying company is largely responsible. Most

---

EXHIBIT 9.3   *XYZ Company Statement of Expectations of Suppliers*

XYZ company expects suppliers to commit to the following:

- Work with new-product development teams to achieve supplier product performance targets as agreed upon by the buyer and supplier.
- Be proactive in working with XYZ company in all phases of your business.
- Support value analysis/value engineering programs.
- Put forth a continuous emphasis on quality, cost minimization, and continuous improvement in the design and development of your respective components.
- Provide the necessary resources including personnel from engineering, design, and manufacturing, to support XYZ new-product development teams.
- Respond in a timely manner to any requests from XYZ company for information or support.
- Actively support the requirements of second-tier suppliers.
- Maintain confidentiality of information exchanged with XYZ company.
- Notify XYZ company immediately if the supplier requires information or support from XYZ company or if certain XYZ actions or policies inhibit supporting XYZ company at the expected performance level.
- Commit to the active use of systems and tools that focus on the prevention of supplier nonperformance. Insist that your suppliers also commit to use of systems and tools that focus on the prevention of nonconformance.
- Provide cost-effective material that is defect-free and on time.

---

specifications are vague or arbitrary. They are generally determined unilaterally by engineering, which lifts them from some boiler-plate document and embellishes them with factors of safety to protect its hide. When bids go out to suppliers, suppliers are seldom consulted on specifications, and most suppliers are afraid to challenge specifications for fear of losing the bid. . . . So, the first cure for poor supplier quality is to eliminate the tyranny of capricious specifications.[2]

Another important form of communication involves expectations or requirements. The clear understanding of buyer expectations and requirements has two dimensions. The first is the ability of the buying company to quantify or specify its requirements. The second dimension is the buyer's ability to communicate these requirements to the supplier. This means that both parties understand the requirements, whether these involve physical product specifications, raw material grades, supplier delivery compliance, or specific supplier tasks and responsibilities. The ability of a supplier to meet its requirements is partly a function of the buyer clearly informing the supplier about what the buyer expects. Exhibits 9.3 and 9.4 provide examples of communicating a purchaser's requirements or expectations to a supplier.

Service quality can be much more difficult to measure or convey in terms of requirements. Very often, service quality is defined as the difference between the perception of what the service provided versus what was actually provided. As a consumer, you have different expectations regarding the quality of the experience from a fast food restaurant. Buyers must be as explicit as possible in communicating their expectations when purchasing a service from a supplier.

EXHIBIT 9.4   *Statement of Responsibility*

The following details specific responsibilities of XYZ Company project team and ABC supplier during the design and development of light truck J300.

Responsibility	XYZ Project Team	Supplier
• Agree on performance targets for product cost, weight, quality, and improvement.	X	X
• Work directly with XYZ project team to meet product performance target levels.	X	X
• Provide design support for component requirements.		X
• Develop total project timing requirements.	X	
• Provide build schedules as needed.	X	
• Support vehicle launch at assembly plant.	X	X
• Report project status to executive steering committee.	X	
• Attain manufacturing feasibility sign-off.	X	
• Provide technical/engineering project support.	X	X
• Develop final product concept.	X	
• Provide prototype parts according to agreed-upon schedule.		X
• Identifying critical and significant product characteristics.	X	X
• Prepare final detail drawings and transmit to XYZ.		X
• Provide material and product test results.	X	X

Be a Good Customer

Suppliers enjoy working with good customers. Supplier quality performance requires that a buyer be a good customer by understanding the supplier's needs and expectations. Some of the expectations that suppliers have of buyers within a supply chain relationship include

- Minimal product design changes once production begins
- Visibility to future purchase volume requirements to assist in planning
- Early visibility to future new-product requirements
- Adequate production lead time
- Ethical treatment
- Payment in a reasonable time
- Minimal or no changes to purchase volumes after receiving a purchase order
- Clear understanding of physical product specifications and delivery requirements

A buyer cannot expect to receive the highest level of supplier performance when the supplier must respond to frequent changes. Stability allows a supplier to plan based on information provided by the buyer. Change limits a supplier's ability to meet buyer expectations in a timely and consistent manner. Being a good customer also means that the supplier is treated fairly, ethically, and with respect. Organizations must not tolerate unethical behavior toward suppliers.

SOURCING SNAPSHOT

Poor Supply Chain Quality Takes the Fizz Out of a Great Brand

In 1999, hundreds of consumers of Coke in Europe became ill, prompting European officials to ban for a period the sale of Coke products. Anton Amon, Coca-Cola's chief scientist, says that a major culprit was quality lapses at a Belgian bottling plant. These lapses allowed contaminated carbon dioxide, the gas that creates the soda's fizz, to enter into Coke's products. A Coke spokesman confirmed that the Belgian plant did not test the CO_2 received from the supplier. The company also did not request a certificate of quality analysis from the supplier of the gas. The supplier says that Coke never asked for a certificate of analysis for any shipment. Hoping to prevent future problems, Amon says he has given strict instructions prohibiting the receipt of CO_2 without a certificate of analysis. Furthermore, each plant must now perform its own testing of every CO_2 receipt. Unfortunately, lapses in managing supply chain quality tarnished the reputation of one of the world's greatest brand names.

Source: Adapted from Nikhil Deogun, James Hagerty, Steve Stecklow, and Laura Johannes, " Anatomy of a Recall: How Coke's Controls Fizzled Out in Europe," *Wall Street Journal,* June 29, 1999, A1.

Provide Feedback

Providing supplier performance feedback is a primary responsibility of buyers. This assumes that a firm has the ability to measure supplier quality performance, which may not be the case. It is difficult to provide the highest levels of quality when a supplier is unaware of a buyer's current perception of supplier performance.

Effective supplier feedback is *timely*. For example, if a supplier sends a shipment with incomplete documentation, the buyer, or someone in materials management representing the buyer, must provide immediate notification to prevent future occurrences. Supplier feedback must also be *specific and accurate*. A buyer should not communicate in vague or general terms. The more specific the feedback, the greater the likelihood the supplier can respond.

Many organizations send a corrective action request (CAR), a form that demands actions to be taken by a supplier to ensure that a problem does not occur again. ISO 9002—an internal quality certification standard—requires suppliers to complete a corrective action request in the event of a supplier-caused nonconformance. A good supplier will treat these corrective action requests seriously. Exhibit 9.5 is an example of a corrective action request form used at a major company.

In some cases, buyers do not get involved with suppliers on a day-to-day basis. Operations or materials managers are responsible for conveying feedback. In some

EXHIBIT 9.5   *Sample Corrective Action Form*

Supplier Corrective Action Request

Section A: To be completed by buyer

Corrective action request log #:

Date:

To:

From:

Subject:

Type of defect / nonconformance:

Description of defect / nonconformance:

Estimated total cost of defect / nonconformance:

Charge to supplier?   ☐ Yes   ☐ No

                              If yes, indicate amount: _____

Section B: To be completed by supplier

Supplier corrective action response: (Please use back of page if additional space is required.)

Date corrective action response will be fully implemented:

Buyer sign-off: _____   Supplier sign-off: _____

Date: _____   Date: _____

cases, involving the purchasing department slows down the communication process by adding an extra communication channel. Purchasing should still monitor performance through the supplier measurement system.

Purchasing's Role in Managing Supplier Quality

The purchasing function must take an active role in managing supplier quality throughout the supply chain. A number of factors and constraints influence how much attention a buying firm commits to managing supplier quality performance:

1. *The ability of a supplier to affect a buying firm's total quality.* Clearly, certain suppliers will provide items that are critical to a firm's success. Purchasing must manage the suppliers of critical items differently from those providing items of less importance.

2. *The resources available to support supplier quality management and improvement.* Firms with limited resources available for supporting and managing supplier quality must carefully select where to budget those resources. Resource availability will influence the scope of the supplier quality management effort. Resources may include personnel, budget, time, and information technology.

3. *The ability of a buying firm to practice world-class quality practices.* A buying firm should work with suppliers on the proper use of quality concepts, tools, and techniques only after the buying firm itself understands and uses the concepts and tools correctly.

4. *A supplier's willingness to work jointly with a buying firm to improve quality.* Not all suppliers are willing to work closely with a buying firm. Instead, some suppliers may prefer a traditional purchase arrangement characterized by limited buyer involvement.

5. *A supplier's current quality levels.* A supplier's current performance influences the amount and type of attention required from a buying firm. World-class suppliers will require minimal active management while suppliers providing less-than-desirable quality will require greater attention.

6. *A buying firm's ability to collect and analyze quality-related data.* Purchasing must keep track of how well a supplier is meeting key quality performance measures. For most firms, this means having an automated system that collects and distributes supplier-related quality data on a timely basis.

7. *A buyer's ability to quantify quality expectations and requirements.* A buying firm's quality requirements will reflect the requirements of the buyer's customers. A number of sources can define component and subassembly quality requirements, including industry standards, end-customer requirements, or product engineers specifying design tolerances and specifications.

Exhibit 9.6 presents a hierarchy of activities that, when executed properly, supports world-class supplier quality performance and will help ensure the achievement of current and future quality expectations. These activities are presented across three dimensions: (1) implementation complexity, which refers to the skill, time, and resources required to successfully execute a particular activity, (2) the expected rate of

EXHIBIT 9.6   *Realizing World-Class Supplier Quality*

High		Accelerated
	Supplier early design involvement Supply performance development	
Implementation Complexity	Supplier certification Performance improvement rewards Aggressive supplier improvement targets	**Expected Rate of Quality Improvement**
Low	Supplier performance measurement Supply-base optimization	Gradual
	Basic Moderate Advanced	

Procurement / Supply Chain Management Activity

quality improvement, which results from successfully executing a particular activity, and (3) whether the procurement/supply chain management activity is basic, moderate, or advanced.

Optimize the Supply Base

A prerequisite for realizing world-class supplier quality involves optimizing or rationalizing the size of a supply base, which is the process of determining the right mix and number of suppliers to maintain. Historically, this process has required most companies to reduce the number of suppliers they used, often drastically and in a brief period. In fact, a dramatic supply-base restructuring took place during the late 1980s and early 1990s within the United States. Companies such as Xerox and Northern Telecom have emphasized supply-base reduction as a preliminary step in the implementation of their just-in-time and total quality programs. However, supply-base quality improvement requires more than simply reducing the size of the supply base.

Why does optimization affect supplier quality? Simply stated, pursuing value-added activities is easier with 300 suppliers than with 3,000. Furthermore, optimization should lead to higher *average* supplier quality if a company has reduced its supply base correctly. Remaining suppliers should provide higher levels of overall performance. Who would eliminate their best suppliers?

Supply-base optimization remains a continuing activity across most industries. The supplier-reduction efforts carried out during the early 1990s resulted primarily in a smaller group of suppliers selected from the original supply base, thereby ignoring the evaluation of new suppliers. Part of this resulted from the urgent need to reduce the supply base quickly in response to threats from overseas producers, beginning for some companies in the early to mid-1980s. The resulting improvement in supplier quality was probably not as great as it might have been if purchasers had broadened their supply search.

Optimization is only a first step toward world-class supplier quality. Advanced sourcing strategies requiring closer interaction between the purchaser and seller simply are not feasible with a large supply base. Executive management must question whether supplier optimization has created a foundation for pursuing more complex activities that will further *accelerate* supplier quality improvement. Chapter 10, which focuses on supplier management and development, discusses supply-base optimization and optimization techniques in greater detail.

Measure Supplier Performance

An often neglected area involves the continuous measurement of supplier performance. Most organizations, large and small, have failed to recognize the need for supply chain measurement, which has resulted in diverting systems development resources to more "important" areas. Wide differences still exist in the quality and capability of supplier measurement systems. Some firms perform a monthly qualitative assessment of supplier performance while others assess performance against stringent performance targets daily or calculate the *total* cost of supplier-caused quality nonconformances. Other companies fail to assess supplier performance at all.

Why measure supplier performance, and what is the relationship with quality? It is how organizations use the data rather than the act of measurement that makes these systems valuable. Procurement managers use supplier measurement systems to identify (1) supplier improvement opportunities, (2) performance trends, (3) the best suppliers to select, both for routine purchase requirements and for critical items that would benefit from longer-term purchase agreements, (4) where to commit limited supplier development resources, and (5) the overall effectiveness of supply chain improvement efforts. A formal measurement system is also an efficient way to convey customer (i.e., purchaser) requirements throughout the supply chain. Delivery and quality requirements become definable performance elements.

Measuring continuous supplier performance is not the only time firms should evaluate suppliers. The supplier evaluation and selection process also provides opportunities for assessing supplier performance and capabilities. Executive managers, while recognizing the importance of performance measurement throughout other parts of their organization, must question where and when formal supply chain measurement occurs and how the data are used to help improve supplier quality performance.

Establish Aggressive Supplier Improvement Targets

Some supply chain managers believe that incremental supplier improvement fails to create the performance and quality advantages expected from their sourcing practices. Aggressive improvement targets reflect a major shift in thinking at most firms, particularly as it relates to supply chain management. Incremental goals, however worthy, invite suppliers to perform the same comfortable processes incrementally better, with mediocrity often the result. Establishing aggressive performance targets (sometimes called "stretch targets") means that a purchaser expects supplier performance to improve at a rate faster than the improvement competitors realize from their suppliers. Firms often use benchmarking to verify that stretch targets, while challenging, are possible to achieve.

Executive management plays a key role in setting the expectation that the supply base must achieve the same performance improvements expected of the purchaser. Motorola, for example, has decreed that suppliers must pursue the same aggressive goals that it establishes for itself. Company executives aim for a great deal more than merely fine-tuning existing supplier performance. Its suppliers must satisfy stringent improvement expectations in four critical areas: (1) keeping pace in attaining perfect product quality; (2) remaining on the leading edge of product and process technology; (3) practicing just-in-time manufacturing and delivery; and (4) offering cost-competitive service. A comprehensive measurement system allows Motorola to verify progress against these ever-changing goals. Motorola, noted for attaining 3.4 parts per million quality levels, is now pursuing quality defect levels measured in parts per *billion*.

Performance measurement systems, combined with aggressive supplier improvement targets, are essential for promoting supply chain improvement. Once a supplier proves it can satisfy current performance expectations, then more demanding objectives take effect, reflecting the need for continuous improvement.

Provide Rewards for Superior Supplier Performance and Improvement

Offering performance-related rewards recognizes that a direct link exists between rewards and supplier improvement. Traditionally, purchasers sought supplier improvement but were reluctant to share the resulting benefits, which often encouraged self-promoting behavior by suppliers. Suppliers who improved internally avoided notifying the purchaser, thereby retaining all the benefits. These same suppliers might also be unwilling to commit the time or resources required to improve the product or the buyer-seller relationship. An incentive to invest in longer-term improvements simply did not exist. As a result, minimal innovation or improvement originated within the supply chain.

Chrysler provides a best-case example of rewarding supplier improvement efforts. Suppliers enter improvement suggestions electronically through Chrysler's on-line SCORE (Supplier Cost Reduction) system, which in 1999 saved the company and suppliers an estimated $1.5 billion in current and future costs. Many of these savings involve quality improvement suggestions leading directly to cost reductions. Chrysler shares the savings from these suggestions directly with suppliers, which provides the incentive to participate. Suppliers also know that Chrysler seriously evaluates each idea put forth, which is critical to the success of this program.

Purchasers have many options available for rewarding superior supplier performance and improvement:

- Share the benefits resulting from supplier-initiated improvements.
- Award longer-term purchase contracts.
- Offer a greater share of total volume.
- Publicly recognize superior suppliers.
- Provide new opportunities across the business.
- Provide "Top 10" supplier awards, including a supplier of the year award.
- Provide access to new technology from the purchaser.
- Offer opportunities for early involvement in new-product design, which can provide an advantage when pursuing a contract for the new product.

For example, consider what a longer-term contract offers a supplier and how these agreements affect quality. Most suppliers, especially smaller ones, rely on external funds for financing inventories and capital equipment purchases. Longer-term agreements are evidence of a commitment between the buyer and seller, which enhances the likelihood that suppliers will get the financing required for the purchase of quality-improving capital equipment. These contracts strengthen the supply chain in ways that may not have occurred without the rewards offered by the agreement. Additionally, longer-term agreements often stipulate continuous improvement requirements, which further encourages quality-improving capital investment. Improvement rewards of all kinds can accelerate the rate of quality improvement and is one way to directly influence supplier quality. They can also foster a greater commitment by the supplier toward satisfying the purchaser's unique needs.

Certify Supplier Quality

Supplier certification is the formal process of certifying, usually through an intensive site audit performed by a cross-functional team, that a supplier's processes and methods lead to consistent quality. Certification indicates that a supplier's processes and operating methods are in total control and that incoming material, components, or subsystems usually do not require inspection upon receipt. The process usually applies to a specific part, process, or site rather than an entire company or product. Certification affects material quality because of the process used to assess supplier performance. Purchasers usually rely on cross-functional teams and rigorous audits when performing certification visits. During these visits, the teams often identify performance improvement opportunities that will affect product quality. The Good Practice Example at the end of this chapter outlines Alcoa's quality certification process. Other companies with extensive supplier quality certification awards based on multiple quality criteria include Honeywell, Motorola, Southwest Bell, Cummins Engine, Eastman Kodak, Chrysler, General Motors, and many others.

While certification should contribute to higher levels of supplier quality, the process also exposes the supplier and purchaser to certain risks. Supplier risk involves not meeting the purchaser's quality performance requirements. While certified suppliers often become *preferred* suppliers, suppliers who fail to receive certification or do not show meaningful improvement risk losing the purchaser as a customer. Also, a supplier may find that each of its larger customers has a different set of quality requirements, which can create inefficiencies as the supplier attempts to conform to differing requirements. Suppliers are becoming receptive to a standard set of requirements such as ISO 9000 standards, the Malcolm Baldrige criteria, or the automotive industry's QS 9000 standards.[3]

For purchasers, the resources required to develop and execute a certification program, such as personnel, time, and travel budget, can be extensive. Larger firms are clearly more likely to have a supplier certification process in place compared with smaller firms. Also, purchasers may become complacent once a supplier receives certification. This reflects a belief that certification guarantees consistent quality from certified suppliers. In reality, supplier processes, management, and workforce change over time. Certification, *which applies to a specific point in time with no guarantee of future performance*, demands a continuous commitment of resources for regular reassessment. Ford Motor Company withdrew Q1 quality certification and its business from 44 suppliers due to quality-related problems at certified facilities. Ford excluded these suppliers from bidding on new work for six to nine months as the suppliers attempted to correct internal quality problems. Industry experts say Ford's move was significant because it marks the first time an automaker had moved to take action against so many suppliers at once.[4]

The certification process benefits from, and most often requires, a comprehensive measurement system that identifies any deterioration in certified supplier performance. A lack of continuous measurement increases the risk that certification will not lead to the longer-term quality improvements sought from the certification process.

Perform Supplier Development

Perhaps one of the most significant changes over the last several years involves an increased willingness of firms to help develop supplier performance capabilities. Various types of supplier development activities and resources exist, some of which require an intensive commitment of resources. Major growth has occurred in the number of U.S. firms willing to pursue development activities, particularly those requiring a direct sharing of resources. While there has been an overall growth in the number of firms practicing some form of supplier development, most firms admit they expend only *limited* to *moderate* resources, on average, to develop supplier capabilities (average 3.69 where 1= limited resources, 4 = moderate resources, and 7 = significant resources expended).[5] Supplier development is an area that begins to separate basic and moderately complex supply chain practices from more advanced ones. Development activities represent a conscious effort to identify, integrate, and develop key supply chain members.

Companies pursue supplier development either to improve an existing supplier performance capability or to develop a new performance capability. In the latter case, an organization may wish to create new competition within a market in order to avoid a sole-source situation or to reduce the total number of suppliers a firm maintains. One automobile manufacturer, through the sharing of process technology, helped a supplier begin producing exterior automotive mirrors, which were in addition to the interior mirrors already produced. This supplier now does work that previously required two suppliers.

Honeywell's Corrective Action Reporting System

Honeywell recently developed a quality system that allows traceability of quality problems. Whenever a quality problem occurs, the division corrective action system (DCAS) initiates a quality corrective action report (QCAR) or a NCAR (nonconforming action report). The DCAS initiates these reports in order to track and solve problems when they occur. Once initiated, a QCAR comes to the product maintenance and modification manager and then is routed to purchasing if it is a supplier problem. This then becomes part of the automated follow-up system. The purchasing person can either assign a responsible person in his or her department to follow through, or pass it on to a responsible person. In most cases, a hard copy of the QCAR is printed and forwarded to the supplier. If not resolved in a timely manner, the QCARs show up on the purchasing manager's computer screen and flash annoyingly until resolved.

Source: R. Monczka, R. Handfield, D. Frayer, G. Ragatz, and K. Petersen, *Supplier Integration into New Product / Process Development: Best Practices.* (Milwaukee, WI: ASQ Quality Press, 2000).

Once a firm fully rationalizes its supply base, improvement will occur primarily through the development of existing supplier capabilities rather than large-scale supplier switching. However, firms must target their development resources carefully since not all suppliers qualify for assistance. Some suppliers will never achieve world-class performance, despite the resources committed to the effort. Others may not require attention simply because they currently deliver exceptional performance and will continue to do so. Still others may choose not to participate in any development projects.

Supplier development commands a total commitment of resources at Honda of America. Because Honda sources 80% of its part requirements from suppliers, more than any other major automotive producer, supplier performance improvement is crucial to continued success. Consider just some of the resources and activities Honda commits to supplier development—two full-time employees help suppliers develop employee involvement programs; 40 full-time engineers in the purchasing department work to improve supplier productivity and quality; suppliers receive technical support in areas such as plastic technology, welding, stamping, and aluminum die casting; special teams help suppliers resolve problems as needed; a "Quality Up" program involves working directly with the executive supplier management at suppliers with lower quality; Honda personnel regularly visit supplier facilities; and an executive exchange program between Honda executives and supplier executives allows key managers to appreciate the issues each party faces. Chapter 10 discusses supplier management and development in greater detail.

Pursue Early Supplier Involvement in Product and Process Development

Early product and process design involvement seeks to maximize the benefit received from a supplier's engineering, design, testing, manufacturing, and tooling capabilities. This approach recognizes that competent suppliers have more to offer a purchaser than simply producing an item according to buyer-provided specifications.[6]

Allowing a supplier to apply its full experience to a development project can lead to better quality and designs. Suppliers may provide suggestions concerning how to simplify a product's design, which impacts product cost and quality. Early involvement allows a supplier to anticipate and begin preproduction work, which can lead to reduced product development cycle time and reduced early-production problems. A supplier can also work with engineering personnel early to establish component tolerances that improve process consistency and product manufacturability.

U.S. industry is starting to recognize the value of including suppliers during new-product and -process development. An "America's Best Plants" competition conducted by *Industry Week*, for example, found that almost 90% of competition finalists emphasized early supplier involvement during product and process development. According to our research, only 29% of firms emphasized early involvement in 1990 as a key supply chain strategy; by 1993 this increased to 34%; and by 1999 over 70% of firms emphasized early involvement. John Deere, a manufacturer of construction and farm equipment, maintains that early-involvement, along with supplier development activities, are the two most critical supply chain activities the company must pursue to remain competitive globally.[7]

Although the logic behind early involvement is straightforward, factors or barriers are present that limit supplier participation in product design and development. The two most cited factors are the purchaser's (and sometimes the supplier's) view regarding confidentiality and a lack of accepted means or understanding of the process to involve suppliers. A third factor is that current suppliers are not qualified to be part of early-involvement efforts. Firms must work actively to overcome any barriers limiting the use of this leading-edge approach.

Determining which quality-related activities to pursue presents a serious challenge for supply chain managers. The activities presented in Exhibit 9.6 require varying degrees of resource support and expertise. In reality, few organizations have put together a full range of basic to advanced sourcing strategies featuring supplier quality improvement as a central focus. Some firms lack the personnel, have a structure that supports plant-level purchasing only, or face resource limitations. Others simply have a limited need for more advanced supplier quality approaches.

SUPPLIER EVALUATION SYSTEMS: ISO 9000 AND THE BALDRIGE AWARD

Within the United States, relatively few companies apply a uniform set of quality standards to their supplier certification process, which can result in duplication of effort and other inefficiencies. In measuring and assessing their suppliers' quality management systems, purchasing managers are increasingly turning to established quality auditing and measurement systems. Two audit frameworks often applied are the ISO (International Standards Organization) 9000 criteria and the Malcolm Baldrige National Quality Award criteria.

The ISO 9000 criteria are recognized as the required quality standard for the European Union (EU), and many other parts of the global marketplace have already adopted these standards. However, ISO 9000 has some limitations. The criteria address only standards related to quality assurance, which include variables related to process control, design, documentation, and supplier control and assessment. Such factors, while critical, represent only a single dimension of total quality management. Another criticism of the ISO 9000 standards is that although they provide an indicator that a supplier has complied with process requirements, they in no way guarantee that the supplier produces quality products or services that actually meet customer requirements.[8] Registration ensures that a quality system is in place but provides no absolute measures of quality results or customer satisfaction. These issues were recently addressed when the International Standards Organization completely overhauled the ISO 9000 process in 2001.

A more comprehensive set of quality-related criteria for North American–based firms is provided by the Malcolm Baldrige National Quality Award. The award is a competition and implies that an organization excels not only in quality management but also in quality *achievement*. The application for the award provides a broad framework for implementing a quality program and establishes benchmarks suitable for monitoring quality progress. It is worthwhile to examine both of these supplier quality measurement systems, as each can be used for different purposes.

ISO 9000 Registration

A process gaining rapid acceptance throughout the world is the ISO 9000 registration process. Developed in Europe in 1987, ISO 9000 consists of a series of process quality standards—not product quality standards—that recognize that product quality is a result of a process. Exhibit 9.7 reveals that ISO 9000 is actually a series of standards: ISO 9001, ISO 9002, ISO 9003, and ISO 9004. ISO 9000 simply provides guidelines for using the ISO standards while ISO 9004 is an internal quality management document that provides help in implementing ISO 9001 through ISO 9003.

ISO 9003 is the least restrictive of the three primary standards, requiring conformance only to final inspection and test standards within a production environment. ISO 9002, while requiring the same standards as ISO 9003, also includes standard requirements for purchasing, production, and installation capabilities. ISO 9001, which requires everything that ISO 9003 and 9002 require, also includes standard requirements to ensure conformance in design and servicing a full range of manufacturing and support activities.

Perhaps the best way to recognize the character of the ISO 9000 process is to relate it to the concept of total quality management (TQM). ISO 9000 describes and defines the fundamental nature of work processes necessary for an organization to achieve the objectives of TQM. Therefore, ISO 9000 is a critical first step in implementing a TQM system. ISO 9000 implementation forces managers to reexamine all

EXHIBIT 9.7   *Comparing ISO 9000 Standards*

ISO 9003	*ISO 9002*	*ISO 9001*
Least restrictive standard— requires conformance to final inspection and test standards	Includes ISO 9003 requirements plus standard requirements for purchasing, production, and installation capabilities	Includes ISO 9002 and 9003 requirements plus standard requirements for designing and servicing a full range of manufacturing and support activities
Requirement Areas: • Use of statistical methods • Personnel and training • Quality documentation and records • Handling and postproduction functions • Control of nonconforming product • Control of measuring and test equipment • Product verification (inspection and testing) • Material control and traceability • Quality system principles • Management responsibility	*Requirement Areas:* ISO 9003 requirements plus • Purchaser-supplied product • Corrective action • Quality in procurement • Contract review • Auditing the quality system (internal)	*Requirement Areas:* ISO 9002 and 9003 requirements plus • Quality in specification and design (design control) • After-sales servicing

Note: ISO 9000 provides guidelines for using the ISO standards. ISO 9004 is an internal quality management document that provides guidance for implementing ISO 9001, 9002, and 9003.

of their business processes, and recognize discrepancies between what employees are doing and what the documentation states is being done. In cases where a discrepancy exists, there are three possible actions: retrain the employee with regard to his or her actions, change the documentation to reflect what the employee is doing, or reengineer the process.

It is in the best interests of suppliers to pursue ISO 9000 certification, particularly if customers (i.e., buyers) value the certification. Suppliers can receive many benefits from pursuing ISO registration:

• Buyers have immediate visibility that a supplier has received registration according to internationally accepted quality process standards. The supplier can use registration as a marketing tool.
• Buyers may be willing to recognize ISO 9000 registration in place of individual certification programs, resulting in lower costs for the buyer and supplier. Even if a buying firm is not willing to eliminate its own certification requirements, it may still be able to reduce the scope of its certification because of probable overlap with the ISO 9000 standards.

SOURCING SNAPSHOT

Making Certification Part of the Customer's Requirements

For years the Big Three carmakers (Ford, GM, and now DaimlerChrysler) have required suppliers to meet stringent quality standards and requirements. Unfortunately, the standards were unique to each company. The result? Suppliers spent too much time trying to conform to varying and sometimes conflicting requirements. Now, suppliers are trying to meet one agreed-upon standard: QS 9000, an expanded version of the ISO 9000 group of standards adopted by firms worldwide. What sets this standard apart from the individual certification programs is that QS 9000 requires periodic reviews to verify that a supplier still conforms and that any shortcomings have been corrected. "With mandatory audits every six months, you can't drift too far, or you will lose your certification," says the director of quality at Peterson Spring. A manager at Laser Specialist maintains, "I'm a strong advocate of QS 9000 as a management tool: Forget that the Big Three are shoving it down your throat, because it creates objective standards to follow and makes everything traceable." At least now suppliers to the automotive industry have a consistent set of requirements provided by their customers—the Big Three.

Source: Adapted from Stuart Brown, "Detroit to Suppliers: Quality or Else," *Fortune,* September 30, 1996, 134C–H.

- Each supplier that earns ISO 9000 registration is included on a master list of companies satisfying the ISO 9000 standard. Inclusion on this list may lead to interest from potential customers wanting to do business with ISO 9000–registered companies.
- Suppliers earning ISO registration will be in a better position to satisfy corresponding U.S. ANSI standards.
- U.S. suppliers may be able to do business in certain parts of the world that they would be excluded from without ISO 9000 registration.

Buying firms can also benefit from ISO 9000 registration. First, few buying firms have the size or resources to develop and conduct comprehensive supplier certification audits. ISO 9000 certification provides insight into a supplier's quality system conformance that a buyer may otherwise lack. The buying firm receives the benefit of a supplier quality certification without actually having to conduct quality certification audits.

Another potential benefit for buyers is that the supplier must assume responsibility for meeting the standards and paying ISO registration fees. With individual supplier certification, the buying firm assumes most, if not all, of the expenses related to certification. ISO 9000 registration requires suppliers to contract with a recognized independent registrar certified to perform ISO 9000 audits.

Because ISO 9000 is accepted as a common standard of quality assurance, it has been adopted by various industries as a prequalifying criterion for awarding business. For instance, the Big Three automotive companies have joined forces to create QS

9000, which has replaced the Pentastar Award (Chrysler), Targets for Excellence (GM), and Q1 Audit (Ford). QS 9000 certification includes the 20 categories contained within ISO 9001, along with requirements that are specific to the automotive industry. An independent third-party registrar conducts certification, which is the same party that registers companies for ISO 9000 certification. (See the Sourcing Snapshot "Making Certification Part of the Customer's Requirements" for further discussion of QS 9000 requirements.)

The Malcolm Baldrige National Quality Award

In 1987, President Ronald Reagan signed the Malcolm Baldrige National Quality Improvement Act, which established a national award to recognize quality improvement among manufacturing, service, and small businesses. Malcolm Baldrige was the former Commerce Secretary in the Reagan administration. The award criteria were developed by a group of recognized quality professionals, including Dr. Joseph M. Juran, who helped create the award through congressional testimonies. Since then, the criteria have become an operational definition of TQM, and the wide distribution of the application guidelines has exposed many managers to the Baldrige definition of TQM. The Baldrige criteria are often used as a template for a thorough TQM system, and one of the important outputs of the award is the creation and diffusion of useful TQM practices. The U.S. government has distributed several hundred thousand award applications, although the number of companies actively pursuing the award has decreased over the last several years.

While the process to receive the award lasts one year from the time of application to the time of award announcement, it typically takes a company eight to ten years to develop a quality system that is competitive for the award.[9] The Baldrige Award is composed of seven separate and weighted categories—leadership, strategic planning, customer and market focus, information and analysis, human resource focus, process management, and business results—which are described in Exhibit 9.8. A total of 1,000 points are possible; to be a contender for the award, a company should be capable of scoring above 700 points. The top companies, with scores of 700 or more, have balanced and outstanding performance across the board. The highest score to date on the application has been in the mid-800-point range.

Continuous improvement is the most basic and important tenet of the Baldrige criteria. In each of the major criteria items, companies are asked how they plan to improve in that area. The criteria are both process and results oriented and they are intended to address many company operations, processes, strategies, and requirements.

Many companies are using the Baldrige Award criteria in designing systems for supplier quality assessment. For instance, companies such as Cummins Engine, Motorola, Pacific Bell, Alcatel, and Honeywell all use modified versions of the Baldrige Award to conduct in-depth studies of their major suppliers' quality systems. A similar scoring system is used, and trained assessors may spend several days visiting the supplier's facilities to rate their continuous improvement efforts.

EXHIBIT 9.8   *Malcolm Baldrige National Quality Award*

Score Summary Worksheet — Business Criteria

Examiner Name _____   Application Number _____

Summary of Criteria Items	Total Points Possible A	Percent Score 0-100% (Stage 1–10% Units) B	Score (A x B) C
1 Leadership			
1.1 Organizational Leadership	85	_____ %	_____
1.2 Public responsibility and citizenship	40	_____ %	_____
Category Total	125		_____
			SUM C
2 Strategic Planning			
2.1 Strategy development	40	_____ %	_____
2.2 Strategy deployment	45	_____ %	_____
Category Total	85		_____
			SUM C
3 Customer and Market Focus			
3.1 Customer and market knowledge	40	_____ %	_____
3.2 Customer satisfaction and relationships	45	_____ %	_____
Category Total	85		_____
			SUM C
4 Information and Analysis			
4.1 Measurement of organizational performance	40	_____ %	_____
4.2 Analysis of organizational performance	45	_____ %	_____
Category Total	85		_____
			SUM C
5 Human Resource Focus			
5.1 Work systems	35	_____ %	_____
5.2 Employee education, training, and development	25	_____ %	_____
5.3 Employee well-being and satisfaction	25	_____ %	_____
Category Total	85		_____
			SUM C
6 Process Management			
6.1 Product and service processes	55	_____ %	_____
6.2 Support processes	15	_____ %	_____
6.3 Supplier and partnering processes	15	_____ %	_____
Category Total	85		_____
			SUM C
7 Business Results			
7.1 Customer focused results	115	_____ %	_____
7.2 Financial and market results	115	_____ %	_____
7.3 Human resource results	80	_____ %	_____
7.4 Supplier and partner results	25	_____ %	_____
7.5 Organizational effectiveness results	115	_____ %	_____
Category Total	450		_____
			SUM C
GRAND TOTAL (D)	1000		_____
			D

Source: U.S. Department of Commerce, National Institute of Standards and Technology (www.quality.NIST.gov).

EXHIBIT 9.9   *Comparing the Baldrige Award and ISO 9000 Criteria*

Baldrige Items Not Covered by ISO 9000	*Baldrige Items Covered by ISO 9000*
• Public responsibility • Competitive comparisons and benchmarks • Analysis and uses of company-level data • Strategic quality and company performance planning process • Quality and performance plans • Employee involvement • Employee well-being and morale and services • Quality assessment • Product and service quality results • Company operational results • Business process and support service results • Customer relationship management • Commitment to customers • Customer satisfaction determination, results, and comparison • Continuous improvement	• Senior executive leadership • Management for quality • Scope and management of quality • Performance data and information • Human resource management • Employee education and training • Employee performance and recognition • Design and introduction of quality products • Process management—product and service delivery processes • Production and delivery processes • Process management—business processes and support services • Supplier quality and results • Future requirements and expectations of customers

Comparing ISO 9000 and the Baldrige Award as Supplier Assessment Tools

A study comparing the two supplier quality evaluation systems was carried out at Michigan State University in 1995.[10] The major results shown in Exhibit 9.9 suggest that ISO 9000 is indeed a stepping-stone for establishing process conformance, but is not in itself a foundation for the integration of total quality management. Although many of the Baldrige criteria are not included within the ISO 9000 audit, use of the ISO 9000 criteria should not be summarily dismissed by purchasing organizations seeking to evaluate supplier quality. Moreover, ISO 9000 criteria can be useful as a prequalifying instrument for documenting processes of suppliers who are beginning their quality efforts. Prequalifying is an important initial step in the supplier selection process, as shown by the application of QS 9000 in the automotive industry.

Both the ISO standard and the Baldrige Award criteria can be useful as supplier evaluation tools at different stages of a supplier's progression toward total quality. For noncritical suppliers, a prequalification audit may suffice. In such cases, ISO 9000 measures can document the supplier's conformance to process documentation. This tool can help to ensure that all processes are well understood, and that all employees are well trained and understand management's expectations regarding these processes. For instance, in cases where the item procured from the supplier is of low-dollar usage or purchased in low volumes, it may not be necessary to conduct a full-scale quality audit on the level of the Baldrige criteria. Moreover, ISO 9000 registration may provide sufficient evidence that quality system documentation is in place, as assessed by a third-party assessor.

Once a supplier is prequalified and the processes are established, purchasing managers may want to use measures contained within the Baldrige framework to establish a baseline for continuous improvement. Moreover, as a supplier seeks to progress toward the quality improvement objectives, the Baldrige criteria can provide an indication of the effectiveness of suppliers' efforts to reengineer processes and ensure that initiatives are carried across functional boundaries. Such assessments are particularly important for high-dollar/high-volume critical items. Organizations such as BellSouth and Honeywell have adopted modified versions of the Baldrige Award to perform detailed quality audits of their supply base. Purchasing managers seeking to establish long-term partnerships and strategic alliances with key suppliers may want to integrate these measurements into their long-term contracts as a safeguard for assurance of continuous process improvement and dedication to customer satisfaction.

GOOD PRACTICE EXAMPLE
Supplier Certification at Alcoa

■ ■ ■

Alcoa, a manufacturer of aluminum, has developed a straightforward yet comprehensive supplier quality audit to certify that its key suppliers satisfy its quality expectations. A primary objective of the audit, besides resulting in a decision about supplier quality certification, is to encourage and help Alcoa suppliers achieve continuous quality improvement. One way this happens is by identifying specific areas of supplier deficiency in order to provide opportunities for improvement. The Alcoa supplier quality improvement process

- Evaluates quality systems and locations rather than individual products
- Involves suppliers directly in the quality improvement process
- Helps suppliers make meaningful improvements with Alcoa providing support as required
- Measures supplier quality improvement progress
- Formally recognizes supplier quality achievement

The Alcoa supplier quality improvement process has several key features. First, the process applies to internal and external suppliers. An internal supplier is an Alcoa facility that supplies another Alcoa facility with a product. Including internal suppliers demonstrates that Alcoa practices and follows its own quality prescriptions. Second, a trial audit of the supplier's facility occurs before the official quality audit. The trial audit minimizes the possibility of surprise and gives the supplier a fair opportunity to prepare and improve (where necessary) before the official audit. Third, Alcoa relies on a cross-functional team of experts to perform supplier audits. These teams provide a level of expertise that a single individual cannot provide. Finally, suppliers receive a quantified numerical rating after the official audit. This provides immediate visibility about how the team perceives and rates a supplier's quality systems.

Alcoa divides its quality improvement process into a series of steps. Each step represents a progression toward Alcoa's final objective—a supply base capable of world-class quality and continuous improvement. Exhibit 9.10 presents an overview of Alcoa's supplier quality improvement process.

Step 1: Meet and Plan Once Alcoa identifies the suppliers that it plans to evaluate for certification, the company conducts a one-day overview meeting with the suppliers' key managers. A representative from Alcoa then meets with each targeted supplier to plan a schedule of initial contact between Alcoa and the supplier.

Step 2: The Supplier Self-Survey Each supplier scheduled for a certification audit has an opportunity to perform a self-survey. The self-survey covers the same four sections as the formal audit (Step 5): management, quality measurement, safety and training, and facilities. The supplier rates itself on each survey item on a scale of 0 to 10. During the supplier self-survey, suppliers become aware of the score required to satisfy Alcoa's requirements.

Step 3: Strategy Planning Alcoa and the supplier use the results of the self-survey to identify supplier strengths and weaknesses. Where necessary, Alcoa will assign an employee to work directly with a supplier to assist in developing an improvement strategy. This individual lends personal support and guidance where required. The supplier must commit to improvement and not rely on Alcoa personnel to achieve any necessary changes. It is during this phase of the process that the supplier initiates the necessary quality improvement activities to correct deficiencies.

Step 4: The Trial Audit The support person assigned by Alcoa conducts a trial audit once it appears that the supplier has improved in each deficiency area. The trial audit serves two purposes. First, it reveals the status of the supplier's improvement effort. Second, it prepares the supplier for the formal audit conducted by the cross-functional audit team.

Step 5: The Formal Audit The formal review process includes information from two separate sources. First, each Alcoa location that has direct contact with a supplier evaluates the supplier's performance on a 10-point scale. The user evaluates the supplier for material quality, delivery, paperwork, nonconformance resolution (i.e., how the supplier resolves problems), and sales and marketing service. The user evaluation is for a specific supplier location. An Alcoa location that receives material from multiple supplier locations evaluates each of the supplier's locations separately.

The most comprehensive part of the certification process is the formal supplier audit. If the results of the trial audit indicate that a supplier is likely to achieve the

EXHIBIT 9.10   *Alcoa Supplier Quality Improvement Process*

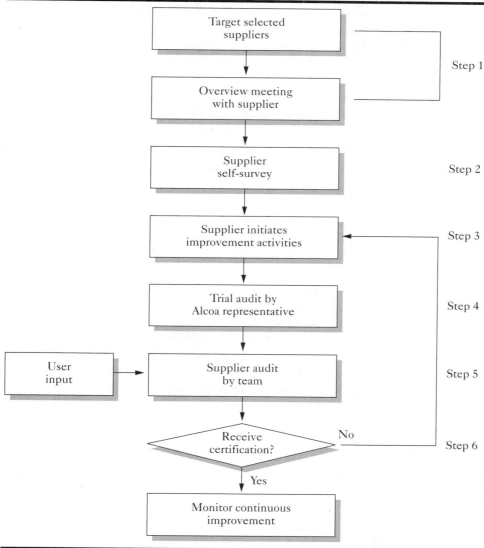

Source: Adapted from a presentation ot the Executive Purchasing and Supply Chain Management Seminar, Michigan State University, East Lansing, MI, 1993.

minimum required for certification, Alcoa schedules a formal audit. The company tries to conduct the formal audit within 90 days of the trial audit.

To make the audit as objective as possible, the audit team evaluates those items included in the corporate supplier quality audit survey. This survey defines each area of interest within four categories: management, quality measurement, safety and training, and facilities. It is critical to define, as precisely and concisely as possible, the meaning of each value so the audit team can accurately and fairly evaluate a supplier. The scoring system for each item includes a minimum score that a supplier must achieve to qualify for certification.

The audit team records its score for each audit statement, adds all the item scores together, notes if the supplier meets all minimum scoring requirements, and makes a certification recommendation. The audit team recommends certification, certification after corrective action, or no certification. Furthermore, a supplier that does not receive certification must have a full re-audit before any future certification attempt.

Step 6: Recommendation Review An audit review committee evaluates the certification recommendation of the audit team before reaching a final decision. The committee also reviews the user evaluations completed during the review process. The review committee weighs the audit team's score as 80% of the total rating and the user evaluation as 20% of the total. Supplier certification occurs at three levels. The initial level is a "Certified Supplier," the middle level is a "Preferred Supplier," and the top level is a "Supplier of Excellence." Each level receives different forms of Alcoa recognition and rewards.

Alcoa maintains the information from all audits and user evaluations in a database, which allows the company to assess supplier progress, particularly in areas of initial deficiency. The audit and certification are not the end of the quality process. Rather, these activities represent part of the effort to strengthen the relationship between Alcoa and its suppliers. As Alcoa and suppliers work together to improve quality, a mutual trust and respect can develop that supports even greater joint improvement activities.

Alcoa's supplier quality certification and improvement process illustrates the effort put forth as part of the quest for total quality. Although supplier certification requires a major resource commitment, the longer-term benefits that can result from consistently high supplier quality are worth the effort—both to Alcoa and to the supplier. ■

CONCLUSION

Improving supplier quality involves much more than providing clear specifications and maintaining open communication. The purchasing and sourcing process can effectively improve supplier quality practices and set a standard for excellence. Supplier quality excellence can be achieved through a number of approaches:

- Being a good customer
- Providing feedback

- Measuring performance and eliminating poor suppliers
- Certifying and rewarding performance
- Setting targets and helping suppliers reach their goals

In order to reach these goals, purchasing must have people who understand the principles and tools of total quality management and can effectively work with suppliers to ensure that zero supplier defects is the norm rather than the exception.

DISCUSSION QUESTIONS

1. Why should a buyer be concerned with supplier quality performance?
2. Discuss the following statement: *Purchasing not only buys parts or services from suppliers—it buys supplier performance capability.*
3. Do suppliers each have the same impact on product quality? Discuss the conditions under which one supplier may have a greater impact on a firm's final product quality compared with another supplier.
4. Why is it important for a buyer to "be a good customer"? How can a buyer be a good customer to a supplier?
5. Is it important to measure the cost of quality at a firm? What should the cost of quality include?
6. How can early supplier design involvement contribute to higher levels of product quality?
7. Discuss the benefits to a supplier of achieving ISO 9000 certification.
8. Some purchasing experts argue that suppliers should not receive rewards for doing something that is already expected (i.e., continuously improving quality). Do you agree with this position? What are some examples of rewards that a supplier can receive?
9. Discuss the benefits to a buying company of quality certifying its suppliers. Discuss the benefits to a supplier of being certified.

ADDITIONAL READINGS

Bossert, James, ed., *Supplier Management Handbook*. Milwaukee, WI: ASQC Quality Press, 1999.

Brown, Mark Graham. *Baldrige Award Winning Quality: How to Interpret the Baldrige Criteria for Performance Excellence*, 9th ed. Milwaukee, WI: ASQC Quality Press, 1995.

Duncan, William L. *Total Quality: Key Terms and Concepts*. New York: AMACOM, 1995.

Fernandez, Ricardo R. *Total Quality in Purchasing and Supplier Management*. Delray Beach, FL: St. Lucie Press, 1995.

Juran, J. M., ed. *Juran's Quality Handbook*, 5th ed. Milwaukee, WI: ASQC Quality Press, 1999.

———. *A History of Managing for Quality: The Evolution, Trends, and Future Directions for Managing Quality*. Milwaukee, WI: ASQ Quality Press, 1995.

ISO 9000 Quality Management. Geneva, Switzerland: International Organization for Standardization, 1998.

Lindsay, William M., and Joseph A. Petrick. *Total Quality and Organization Development*. Delray Beach, FL: St. Lucie Press, 1997.

Maass, Richard, John O. Brown, and James L Bossert. *Supplier Certification: A Continuous Improvement Strategy*. Milwaukee, WI: ASQ Quality Press, 1999.

Merrill, Peter. *Do It Right the Second Time: Benchmarking Best Practices in the Quality Change Process*. Portland, OR: Productivity Press, 1997.

Moss, Marvin A. *Applying TQM to Product Design and Development*. New York: M. Dekker, 1996.

Smith, Gerald F. *Quality Problem Solving*. Milwaukee, WI: ASQ Quality Press, 1995.

ENDNOTES

1. Arman V. Fiegenbaum, *Total Quality Control*, 3rd ed. (New York: McGraw-Hill, 1983), 7.
2. Keki Bhote, *Supply Management: How to Make U.S. Suppliers Competitive* (New York: American Management Association, 1987), 87.
3. For further discussion, see Stuart Brown, "Detroit to Suppliers: Quality or Else," *Fortune*, September 30, 1996, 134C–J.
4. Rebecca Blumenstein, "Big Three Pare Design Time for New Autos," *Wall Street Journal*, August 9, 1996, A3.
5. From data collected at the Executive Purchasing and Supply Chain Seminar, Michigan State University, East Lansing, MI, 1999.
6. For a complete discussion, see R. Monczka, R. Handfield, D. Frayer, G. Ragatz, and K. Petersen, *Supplier Integration into New Product / Process Development: Best Practices* (Milwaukee, WI: ASQC Press, 2000).
7. From the John Deere Supply Management Conference, Moline, IL, September 1997.
8. R. W. Peach, "Creating a Pattern of Excellence," *Target* 6, no. 4 (1990): 15.
9. Robert Handfield and Soumen Ghosh, "Creating a Total Quality Culture Through Organizational Change: A Case Analysis," *Journal of International Marketing* 2, no. 4 (1994): 15–30.
10. Robert Handfield and S. Curcovic, "The Use of ISO 9000 and Baldrige Award Criteria in Supplier Quality Measurement and Evaluation," *International Journal of Purchasing and Materials Management* (Spring 1996): 2–11.

SUPPLIER MANAGEMENT AND DEVELOPMENT: CREATING A WORLD-CLASS SUPPLY BASE

10

Supplier's Perspective on Supplier Development

Plastics Engineering, a small privately owned supplier located in Warwickshire, England, provides plastics injected parts to the automotive industry. A key customer, Standard Products, uses Plastics Engineering's parts to produce seat latches for a seat manufacturer, which eventually end up in a Ford-UK product. In 1997, Standard Products was pushing Plastics Engineering to improve their production process by creating a manufacturing cell. Standard Products wanted a large number of latches produced and realized this would work better with just-in-time production and daily deliveries (4,000 units per day). When a Standard team visited the Plastics Engineering plant, it found additional quality problems and more material than was desirable. To help Plastics Engineering achieve the sought-after performance improvements, Standard Products deployed a supplier development approach known as a "Kaizen breakthrough."

Mike Hart, the manufacturing director of Plastics Engineering, described what happened next:*

> Standard Products appointed team leaders who helped us to do it. They sent over six people at their expense who stayed for a week and showed us step by step how to create a manufacturing cell. At first, things went very badly, and we produced many bad parts. Eventually, the cell started working very well.

> In implementing the Kaizen breakthrough, we first explained to everyone what was going on, and guaranteed to them that there would be *no job losses* as a result of their cooperation, even with the implementation of a new information system. This was a critical success factor. Next, two people came in and had a meeting with our people. A team leader from our facility was appointed. In this case, it was Paul Collins, a young special projects production supervisor who was well respected in the shop. He then chose people that he thought would be suitable from the shop floor.

> The whole process took one week, and involved relatively simple concepts. We began with problem-solving sheets and process maps, then studied the process and went about changing it. Afterward, the group made a presentation to the Managing Director and the Manufacturing Director. What was unique about it was that they pushed the changes through to a time scale they set. At the end of the day, it was their success that was being celebrated, not ours.

> Afterward, photographs were used to document the exercise and the group went around describing it to other suppliers in the Standard Products Supplier Association. What also happened as a result of this was that we recognized that we had only touched the tip of the rest of the factory. We then went about breaking the factory down into manageable segments that could be focused on. We took different people from each segment to a Standard Products factory so that they could see what was expected of them (e.g., an ideal factory). This was very important, as many people

→ → →

thought the whole idea was stupid initially. We are now in the process of implementing our fourth Kaizen breakthrough team. There has even been some internal competition created between the teams!

A side effect of the entire process has been that our successes have been brought to the attention of various boards which make decisions on the group of companies that we are a part of. They are finally listening to what some of us at the bottom have been proposing. As a result of our participation, we are now helping Standard Products to develop new products, and they are continuing to help us on our production line. They realized they needed good suppliers and weren't happy with their current ones. We were low volume, but had great potential. Both parties ended up winners.

The key success factor in the case of Standard Products was that they supplied us with something that we didn't have, rather than the other way around. Other companies tell you to improve, then give you a list of consultants to call up. Another important factor is how the cost reductions were shared: in an equitable manner on a product-by-product level that is fair to both parties. They are also very honest with us. When we go to meetings, they begin with a "good news / bad news" approach. With many of our other customers, we don't really know where we stand.

*Daniel Krause and Robert Handfield, *Developing a World-Class Supply Base* (Tempe, AZ: Center for Advanced Purchasing Studies, National Association of Purchasing Management, 1999).

Supplier management and development includes the actions a purchaser takes to manage and improve its suppliers effectively and efficiently. The primary objective is the continuous development and performance improvement of suppliers. Supply-base management involves purchasing, engineering, quality assurance, and suppliers working together to achieve a closer working relationship and reach mutual goals. Business history has shown that unless companies are able to bring their supply-base performance up to world-class levels, they are at the mercy of competitors who can take market share within a matter of two to three years.

This chapter focuses on how organizations manage, develop, and improve the performance of suppliers. While a number of approaches to supplier management exist, most fall into the sets of activities described in this chapter. The first section discusses supply-base optimization, which is the process of identifying the proper mix and number of suppliers to maintain. The second section discusses supplier development and a strategy for improvement. In the third section, we discuss some of the many barriers faced by organizations that attempt to improve supplier performance through supplier development. This section also summarizes some best practices of companies who have successfully overcome the barriers to supplier development. Finally, we conclude with a Good Practice Example of a supplier development strategy from Honda of America.

Supply-Base Optimization: The Foundation for Supplier Management and Development

Effective supplier management and development begins with a determination of the appropriate number of suppliers an organization should maintain. This usually means relying on a smaller number of suppliers than has historically been the case. *Supply-base optimization* (also known as *supply-base rationalization*) is the process of identifying how many and which suppliers a purchaser will maintain. It often involves eliminating suppliers who are not capable of achieving purchasing performance objectives, either currently or in the near future.

It became clear during the 1980s that the costs associated with having multiple suppliers for each purchased item outweighed any perceived reduction in supply risk. Furthermore, competition from offshore producers, new technological innovations, and a compression in product life cycles have forced buyers to rely on a smaller but more competent group of suppliers.[1] Most purchasers have moved aggressively to reduce the total number of suppliers with whom they do business.

Supply-base optimization is a continuous process for most large organizations today. The elimination of marginal suppliers and those from whom few purchases are made is usually the first phase of the optimization process. Subsequent optimization requires the replacement of good suppliers with better suppliers. Organizations must develop supplier evaluation and performance management methods to identify the best-performing suppliers and then develop stronger business relationships with those suppliers. In many cases, U.S. companies must search globally (not just domestically) for the best suppliers.

During the early phases of supply-base optimization, the process usually results in a reduction in the total number of suppliers that are maintained. A reduction, however, is not always the end result for every single family of items. For instance, consider this example of a U.S. automobile producer. At a truck assembly plant, tires and wheels were received from separate suppliers. The wheel and tire were joined and balanced inside the assembly plant in a labor- and space-intensive operation. The company established a new supplier near the assembly plant who received both the tires and wheels, assembled the two items into a finished product, stored the assembled wheel, balanced the wheel, and shipped it to the assembly plant in smaller quantities on a just-in-time basis. Although the company added an additional supplier to its supply base, overall system efficiency increased and total cost declined. In this instance, optimization resulted in the net addition of a supplier.

Advantages of an Optimized Supply Base

Supply-base optimization should result in improvements in cost, quality, delivery, and information sharing between buyer and seller. Because supplier optimization identifies the best suppliers in terms of number and quality, remaining suppliers are often capable of performing additional tasks that improve performance or add value to the

Guess Who's Getting into Supplier Development: The Air Force!

In the fall of 1998, the Air Force Research Laboratory's Manufacturing Technology Division (ManTech) convened a meeting of 30 high-level purchasing officials from aerospace and defense organizations to discuss plans and initiatives for supply-base development. The meeting was an important initial step in a major ManTech initiative (dubbed the SME Initiative) that set a goal for prime and subprime Air Force contractors to foster improvements among the small- or medium-sized enterprises (SMEs) within their supply bases. Underpinning the SME Initiative has been research by a ManTech team indicating that up to 80% of production for most weapons systems is now performed by suppliers, many of which are small- or medium-sized companies. The report found that two common denominators were found in the world-class companies they studied: (1) Most of the commercial companies allowed and even encouraged their suppliers to offer improved capabilities to other customers (including competitors), and (2) most tended to use long-term agreements, typically with single-source suppliers. The ManTech team also identified a set of mechanisms these companies typically employed (in order of popularity): (1) supplier training, (2) supplier rating, certification, and awards, (3) customer technical expertise available to suppliers, (4) integrated customer/supplier teams to reduce supplier process waste and solve supplier problems, (5) supplier symposia and suggestion programs, (6) supplier continuous improvement programs, (7) supplier access to customer's volume discount rates, (8) organized methodology for problem solving, (9) integrated customer/supplier technology roadmaps, and (10) customer development of a capability prior to outsourcing. Under the SME Initiative, ManTech will identify critical small suppliers for direct development by either themselves or third-party consultants, and will identify incentives for prime contractors and subsystem producers to pursue supplier development policies.

Source: Adapted from Anonymous, "Air Force Pushes Its Supplier Development Program Forward," *Purchasing* 126, no. 7 (May 6, 1999): 34–37.

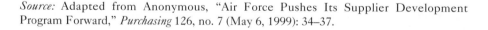

buyer-seller relationship. Examples of additional functions include early product design involvement and supplier quality self-certification of incoming shipments made to the buying company. Suppliers in an optimized supply base often develop longer-term relationships with purchasers, which can lead to further joint improvement efforts.

Buying from World-Class Suppliers Because suppliers play an important role in an organization's overall success, it is not difficult to see why choosing only the best suppliers supports higher performance. Instead of being responsible for hundreds or even thousands of suppliers and not doing an adequate job managing most of them, purchasing can concentrate on developing closer relationships with a core group of qualified suppliers. Some of the benefits of doing business with world-class suppliers include fewer quality and delivery problems, visibility to leading-edge technology, opportunities to develop closer relationships with leading suppliers, and a lower total product cost as purchasing and engineering gain supplier input during new-product design.

Use of Full-Service Suppliers The remaining set of suppliers in an optimized supply base are often larger (on average) and are capable of offering a range of services. When a purchaser uses full-service suppliers, it expects to receive benefits in the form of access to the supplier's engineering, design, testing, production, service, and tooling capabilities. The full-service supplier approach places a greater burden on a supplier to manage an entire system of components, activities, and services, as well as to manage its own suppliers. A purchaser can use a full-service supplier to perform complete design and build work instead of performing the work internally or using several different suppliers. Over 70% of Ford's purchase dollars for automotive production, for example, go to suppliers capable of providing engineering and design support. Honda of America's purchasing managers estimate that within their pool of 500 major suppliers in the United States, approximately 40 engineering, production, and purchasing people at each supplier are providing suggestions regarding how to reduce cost and improve quality. This represents an additional 20,000 people who are trying to think of better ways to build Honda products. This example illustrates why Honda considers its major suppliers as "family members."

The automobile industry provides many examples of how full-service suppliers can provide benefits. Producers rely on suppliers to develop entire subassemblies for new cars. (A related concept is that of modular design, where a supplier develops an entire system or "module" for the original customer or producer.) A supplier receives the functional requirements of a system from its customer and then engineers, designs, and coordinates the production of the entire assembly. For example, all cars have extensive electrical wiring systems. Traditionally, automobile producers designed each individual wiring harness and sent the design specifications to suppliers. It was not unusual for ten different suppliers to work on wiring systems for final connection into a car. Electrical problems have historically been a major source of quality problems for North American producers. Now, a single supplier or only several suppliers might design and produce the entire wiring system for a new car or truck. The result is lower cost, improved quality, and reduced product development time. A supplier can design the wiring systems concurrently with the design of the car.

Reduction of Supply-Base Risk At first glance, it does not seem possible that using fewer suppliers results in reduced supply-base risk. After all, what if the only source for an item goes on strike or has a fire at its production facility? The risk of supply disruption has been the primary argument against supply-base reduction or single sourcing of purchased items.

Most purchasers have now concluded that if they select suppliers carefully and develop close working relationships with fewer suppliers, supply risk can actually decrease. Risk does not only include supply disruption. Other supply risks include poor supplier quality, poor delivery performance, or paying too high a price for purchased items. Maintaining large numbers of suppliers can actually increase the probability of increased risk in these areas. As a purchasing executive involved in the optimization process at his company commented, "Supply-base optimization reduces risk because it creates a win-win situation. We benefit but so do our suppliers. They become stronger because of larger and longer-term contracts, which reduces supply risk to our company."

Lower Supply-Base Maintenance Costs It requires resources to maintain an active supplier because of the interaction required between buyer and seller. Purchasers must interact with suppliers in a number of ways, including contacting suppliers about design and material specifications; communicating quality and other performance requirements; negotiating purchase contracts with suppliers; periodically visiting supplier facilities; evaluating supplier performance; contacting suppliers if performance problems occur (i.e., a quality problem or a late delivery); working with suppliers to improve performance; requesting supplier input about product design; contacting suppliers about design engineering changes; and transmitting material releases. Each of these activities has an associated cost in terms of time, effort, and potential miscommunication. Clearly, the cost of maintaining 5,000 suppliers will be dramatically higher than the cost of maintaining a core group of 500 qualified suppliers. Furthermore, qualified suppliers require fewer problem-related contacts. The contacts between a buyer and seller should be those that add value (such as information sharing) rather than resolve problems.

Lower Total Product Cost During the 1980s, purchasers began to recognize the true cost of maintaining multiple suppliers for each purchased item. Costs increased due to inconsistent product quality and delivery and because of the smaller production volumes offered to each supplier. Short-term purchase contracts that awarded too little business to a supplier increased production costs. With small contracts, a supplier cannot spread its fixed production costs over large enough volumes or generate enough revenue to invest in new plants and equipment. If a single supplier or several suppliers receive larger purchase volumes, lower production costs can be attained due to the economies of scale possible with larger contracts, along with increased investment in plant and equipment. Supply-base optimization provides the opportunity to achieve lower product costs by awarding larger volumes to fewer suppliers.

Ability to Implement Complex Purchasing Strategies Implementing complex purchasing strategies requires a manageable supply base. The implementation of more complicated activities with suppliers requires a reduced supply base due to the increased two-way communication and interaction requirements between a buyer and seller. Examples of complex purchasing strategies include supplier development, early supplier design involvement, and the development of cost-based pricing with suppliers.

SOURCING SNAPSHOT

Supply-Base Optimization—Isuzu Axes Its Keiretsu Ties

To get an idea about the tough time Japanese producers have had keeping pace in cost cutting, consider the struggle of Isuzu Motors. Isuzu's chairman, Kazuhira Seki, took over as president in 1992 and quickly began cutting procurement costs and trimming the product lineup. Weak demand for trucks among construction companies and other core buyers in Japan and Southeast Asia has not allowed Isuzu to economize fast enough to keep up with falling sales. However, this is not due to a lack of trying. Seki was one of the first auto executives in Japan to eliminate models and start dismantling his company's *keiretsu* family of suppliers—a process that Nissan Motor Company has also been embarking upon under its new bosses from France's Renault SA. Upon becoming Isuzu's president, Seki "froze" a project to develop a new version of its only passenger car, the Gemini. This move shocked Isuzu insiders, as the chairman now fully intends to formally eliminate the model and exit the passenger-car business altogether. Seki also turned his attention to what he calls "keiretsu destruction"—trimming the number of suppliers Isuzu uses and selling off stakes in members of the corporate family. The move, he said, angered some former Isuzu executives who had joined Isuzu's keiretsu suppliers after retiring, but it freed Isuzu to go to any supplier in search of better purchase contracts. In a case that raised eyebrows, Seki visited Denso Corporation, a key parts affiliate of rival Toyota Motor Corporation, and quickly established ties to meet Isuzu's needs for core components. Amid tough times for Japan's auto industry, Seki said, "allergies for tough corporate restructuring are disappearing."

Source: Adapted from Norihiko Shirouzu and Michael Williams, "Isuzu Endures Pangs of Cost Cutting," *Wall Street Journal*, November 15, 1999, A30.

Potential Risks of Maintaining Fewer Suppliers

Few purchasing executives would argue in favor of maintaining many suppliers for every purchased item. Currently, the debate centers around maintaining a limited number of qualified suppliers for each major item versus using a single source. Some organizations use several suppliers for most purchased items. They believe this approach promotes a healthy competition between suppliers while providing the benefits of a reduced supply base. Others, however, believe that a single source can still deliver cost and quality improvements over the life of a contract. The best approach is the one with which a purchaser or commodity team feels most comfortable and that works within the particular purchasing system. Although most purchasers recognize the benefits of supply-base optimization, potential risks from relying on a dramatically reduced supply base still exist.

Supplier Dependency Some puchasers fear that a supplier can become too dependent on a purchaser for its economic survival. This situation can occur if a buyer combines purchase volumes for an item with a single supplier. A smaller supplier with limited capacity may eliminate some of its own customers to meet the purchase requirements of its larger customer. As a result, the supplier may become too dependent on a purchaser for its financial well-being. Although supply-base optimization can lead to a healthy mutual commitment between buyer and seller, it can also result in an unhealthy dependence of one party on the other.

Absence of Competition Competition is the foundation of North American business systems. By relying on only one or a limited number of suppliers, some purchasers fear losing the benefit of a competitive system. The proponents of this view argue that becoming too dependent on a single supplier invites problems. A supplier may raise prices or try to dominate the purchase relationship. Organizations with supply-base optimization experience argue that careful supplier selection and the development of contracts that address any risks should prevent reliance on suppliers who try to take advantage of a single-source situation.

Supply Disruption Supply disruption is a potential risk when sourcing from a single-location supplier. Supply can be disrupted due to a union strike, fire, acts of nature, production or quality problems, or a disruption with the supplier's sources of supply. Purchasers minimize the possibility of this risk by sourcing from a supplier with multiple production facilities. If a disruption occurs, a supplier can shift production to another facility.

Another method to minimize supply disruption risk is to select suppliers with multiple capabilities—a practice referred to as *cross-sourcing*, a method in which the supply base is expanded without increasing the total number of suppliers.[2] With this approach, a buyer selects and/or develops suppliers with multiple or duplicate capabilities. If difficulty arises with a primary source of supply, the back-up, which is the supplier for another purchased item, assumes ownership of the process. This approach requires identifying suppliers capable of producing different items or performing different functions throughout the production process.

Honda of America utilizes an interesting form of cross-sourcing.[3] The company uses a single source for all of its major commodity items. Within the commodity family, however, different suppliers support different product models. For example, supplier A is the only source for transmissions for the Prelude, while supplier B is the only source of transmissions for the Accord. When Honda develops a new vehicle, the transmission contract will be single sourced to either supplier A or B, based on who has the best performance record in terms of cost, quality, delivery, etc. In this manner, both suppliers strive to remain competitive because both want to increase their business.

Overagressive Supply Reduction Purchasers can move too aggressively when reducing the supply base. If this occurs, the remaining suppliers may not have the production capacity to meet purchase requirements if demand increases. This is what happened to some companies during the 1980s when demand for certain products exceeded the capacity of remaining suppliers. The companies were forced to add suppliers to their supply base to meet the increased demand.

Formal Approaches to Supply-Base Reduction

In his discussion of strategic supply management, Bhote offers several possible supply-reduction methods.[4] Bhote's framework for managing the supply base contains three primary steps: (1) initial supply-base reduction, (2) the selection of finalist suppliers, and (3) the selection of partnership suppliers. This section focuses on the various methods to reduce the supply base.

Twenty/Eighty Rule This approach identifies the 20% of suppliers receiving the majority of purchase dollars, or the minority of suppliers causing the majority of quality problems. Purchase dollars and supplier quality are two possible decision criteria used to identify suppliers for elimination. The use of this approach requires information generally available from company records. Organizations often use this approach when they require a rapid reduction in the supply base. A disadvantage to the 20/80 approach is the possible elimination of competent suppliers simply because they received fewer purchase dollars. This approach assumes the best suppliers receive the majority of the purchase dollars, which may not necessarily be true.

"Improve or Else" Approach This approach provides all suppliers, regardless of their performance history, a chance to remain in the supply base. It involves notifying all suppliers that they have a specified period of time to meet new purchase performance requirements—from improved quality levels and delivery performance to lead-time and cost reductions, or any other key performance indicator. Suppliers who fall short of the stated goals may soon become ex-suppliers. While this approach has the potential for driving improvement in the supply base, it can also be a heavy-handed way of dealing with supplier selection.

Triage Approach This approach requires the careful evaluation of the performance records of suppliers and placing them into one of three categories. The first category, and most likely the largest, includes those suppliers incapable of meeting purchase performance requirements, either currently or in the future. The purchaser targets these suppliers for immediate deletion from the supply base. The second category includes those suppliers who currently do not meet purchase requirements but demonstrate performance potential. The best of these suppliers often receive supplier assistance and development. The third category includes the near-perfect suppliers requiring no improvement assistance. These suppliers are immediate candidates for closer buyer-seller relationships, which includes offering longer-term contracts in exchange for continuous performance improvement. The distribution of suppliers across these categories may vary across industries.

Competency Staircase Approach This method requires suppliers to pass a successive series of cuts to remain in the supply base. First, all suppliers must meet a buyer's quality standards for consideration as a potential supplier. Suppliers must then pass a series of hurdles similar to climbing a staircase. Each hurdle brings a supplier one step closer to remaining in the supply base.

The next hurdle may be a supplier's ability to meet a purchaser's technical requirements. Subsequent hurdles can include production competency, delivery capability (such as just-in-time requirements), willingness to share information, supplier size, and a supplier's physical proximity. Different purchase requirements will present a different set of hurdles. Each hurdle results in fewer and fewer remaining suppliers. The end result is a supply base comprised of the strongest suppliers.

Summary of Supplier Optimization

We can reach several major conclusions about supplier optimization. First, different approaches to supply-base reduction exist. This chapter provided only a sample of those approaches. Furthermore, an organization can combine more than one approach to meet its optimization goals. Second, we do not have to limit our evaluation only to the suppliers currently in the supply base. A purchaser should always be open to the possibility of using new suppliers if their use offers some benefit. Third, the benefits of supply-base optimization are real while the potential drawbacks are manageable. Fourth, optimization is a critical first step toward the management and development of suppliers. It is difficult, if not impossible, to manage many suppliers as efficiently as a small core group of suppliers. It is also virtually impossible to pursue progressive purchasing activities with too many suppliers. A large supply base also means the duplication of a wide range of purchasing activities.

SUPPLIER DEVELOPMENT: A STRATEGY FOR IMPROVEMENT

Supplier development is any activity undertaken by a purchaser to improve a supplier's performance and/or capabilities, to meet the purchaser's short- and long-term supply needs. Organizations rely on a variety of activities to improve supplier performance, including supplier assessment, providing incentives to suppliers for improved performance, instigating competition among suppliers, and direct involvement of personnel with suppliers through activities such as training.[5]

Direct involvement of personnel is undoubtedly the most challenging part of supplier development. Not only must internal management and employees be convinced that investing company resources in a supplier is a worthwhile risk, but the supplier must also be convinced it is in their best interest to accept direction and assistance. Even if a mutual understanding of the importance of supplier development is reached, there is still the matter of making it happen. Effective supplier development

EXHIBIT 10.1   *Process for Implementation of Supplier Development Strategy*

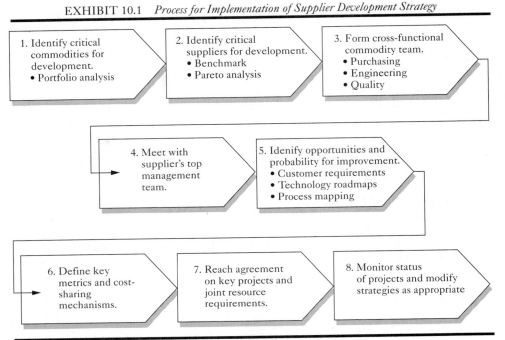

Source: Adapted from Robert Handfield, Daniel Krause, Thomas Scannell, and Robert Monczka, "An Empirical Investigation of Supplier Development: Reactive and Strategic Processes," *Journal of Operations Management* 17, no. 1 (December 1998): 39–58.

requires the commitment of financial, capital and human resources, skilled person-nel, sharing of timely and accurate information between the purchaser and supplier, and timely performance measurement.

In the remainder of the chapter, we discuss supplier development using survey data and several case studies from the electronics and automotive industries in the United States, United Kingdom, Japan, and South Korea.[6] First, a process model is introduced that identifies suppliers requiring development. While many companies are able to identify which suppliers require assistance, relatively few are completely successful in their supplier development efforts. The next section identifies and de-scribes the most common barriers to supplier development. Finally, ways to overcome these barriers are presented in a later section in this chapter.

A Process Map for Supplier Development

After scanning the strategies for more than 60 organizations, a group of researchers developed a generic process map for deploying a supplier development initiative, as shown in Exhibit 10.1.[7] While many organizations are able to successfully deploy the first four stages of the process, some are less successful in the latter four stages.

Step 1—Identify Critical Commodities for Development

Not all organizations need to pursue supplier development. For example, an organization may already be sourcing from world-class suppliers due to effective insourcing/outsourcing decisions and supplier selection, or they may buy external inputs in a very small proportion to total costs or sales so that investment in suppliers is neither strategically nor financially justifiable. Therefore, managers must analyze their own situation to determine if supplier development is warranted, and if so, which purchased commodities and services require attention.

Senior managers should consider the following questions to determine if a supplier development effort is warranted.[8] Answering "yes" to the majority of these questions would lead to supplier development efforts:

1. Do externally purchased products and services account for more than 50% of turnover by value?
2. Is the supplier a source or potential source of competitive advantage?
3. Do you currently purchase or plan to purchase on the basis of total cost versus initial purchase price?
4. Will your existing suppliers be able to meet your competitive needs five years from now?
5. Do you need suppliers to be more responsive to your needs?
6. Are you willing and able to become more responsive to your suppliers' needs?
7. Do you plan to treat suppliers as partners in your business?
8. Do you plan to develop and maintain open and trusting relations with your suppliers?

A corporate-level executive steering committee should develop an assessment of the relative importance of all goods and services purchased by the company to identify where to focus any development efforts. The result of this assessment is a "portfolio" analysis of critical commodities (products or services) that are essential for success in the targeted industry segment. This discussion is an extension of the company's overall corporate-level strategic planning function and should therefore include participants from other critical functions affected by sourcing decisions, including finance, marketing, technology, accounting, production, and design. Each case requires analysis of the strategic importance of suppliers and/or purchased goods. For example, Exhibit 10.2 presents a matrix to assess the relative importance of all goods and services purchased by a company. Using this process, a company separates low-opportunity/low risk commodities from high opportunity/high risk commodities, and low-volume from high-volume purchases. Using this approach helps identify the strategic set of commodities, which form the target group for study on an individual basis by a dedicated commodity team.

Step 2—Identify Critical Suppliers for Development

As a direct extension of commodity portfolio analysis, supply-base performance assessment identifies the suppliers within any commodity group requiring development. A common approach involves a Pareto analysis of current supplier performance, as shown in

EXHIBIT 10.2   *Comodity Portfolio Matrix*

	Low-Volume Purchases	High-Volume Purchases
High-Opportunity Higher-Risk Commodities	**Bottleneck Supplies** • Substitution difficult • Monopolistic markets • High entry barriers • Critical geographic/political situation	**Critical Strategic Supplies** • Strategically important • Substitution/alternate supplier difficult • Major importance for purchasing overall
Low-Opportunity Lower-Risk Commodities	**Noncritical Supplies** • Availability adequate • Standard specifications of goods/services • Substitution possible	**Leverage Supplies** • Availability adequate • Alternative suppliers • Standard product specifications • Substitution possible

Source: Robert Handfield, Daniel Krause, Thomas Scannell, and Robert Monczka, "Avoid the Pitfalls in Supplier Development," *Sloan Management Review* 41, no. 2 (Winter 2000): 37–49.

Exhibit 10.3. Many leading companies monitor supplier performance on a facility-by-facility basis, and suppliers are ranked from worst to best. Suppliers failing to meet minimum performance objectives in the areas of quality, delivery, cycle time, late deliveries, total cost, service, safety, or the environment are targeted for analysis and eventual development. The purchaser meets with supplier representatives to determine the cause of the problem(s) and the required corrective action(s). After a period of time, if improvement is not forthcoming, the purchased item may be sourced from an alternate supplier. The Pareto analysis may also help the buying company rationalize its supply base by identifying underperforming low-volume suppliers to be eliminated. Assuming that the strategic analysis indicates that supplier development is warranted, an organization must then harness the resources to drive the required improvements.

Step 3—Form Cross-Functional Commodity Team Before approaching suppliers and asking for improvements, it is important to develop internal cross-functional consensus for the initiative. Purchasing executives continually emphasize that improvement begins from within through "buyer focused" activities—that is, the buying company must have its "own house in order" before expecting commitment and cooperation from suppliers. Team members may come from engineering and quality, not just purchasing.

Step 4—Meet with Supplier's Top-Management Team Once the mission for the team is established, and an appropriate supplier identified for improvement, the team should approach the supplier's top-management group and establish three

EXHIBIT 10.3   *Supplier Performance—Pareto Analysis*

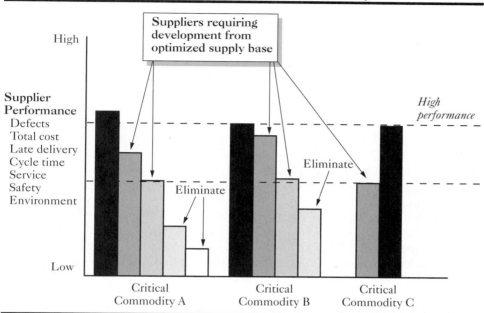

Source: Robert Handfield, Daniel Krause, Thomas Scannell, and Robert Monczka, "Avoid the Pitfalls in Supplier Development," *Sloan Management Review* 41, no. 2 (Winter 2000): 37–49.

key building blocks upon which to seek supplier improvement: strategic alignment, measurement, and professionalism. Strategic alignment requires not only an internal business and technology alignment, but alignment with key suppliers and a focus on customer requirements throughout the supply chain. Supplier measurement requires a total cost focus, credibility and participation of not only purchasing, but key technical functions such as engineering, quality, information systems, and production, in both the buying and supplying organizations. By approaching the supplier's top management with a good business case for improvement, the demonstrated professionalism of all parties involved sets a positive tone and reinforces relationships, fosters communication, provides specialized expertise, and develops trust, all of which enable continuous improvement throughout the supply chain.

Step 5—Identify Opportunities and Probability for Improvement At meetings with the supplier's top management, executives should identify areas for improvement. Companies adopting a strategic approach to supply-base development are able to identify a wide variety of areas for improvement. Such areas are in some cases driven by customer expectations.

Step 6 – Define Key Metrics and Cost-Sharing Mechanisms Once potential opportunities have been identified, the opportunities are evaluated in terms of feasibility, resources, and time required to carry out the project, and the potential return on

SOURCING SNAPSHOT

Supplier Management and Development: Delphi Steering Helps Suppliers

Means Industries Inc., a large stamping company in Saginaw, Michigan, was having trouble meeting its supply commitments to its customer for three different brackets, even though it had a dedicated press running parts seven days a week. A quick-changeover workshop, which included a videotaping and analysis of a complete changeover cycle to remove non–value-added time, reduced changeover from 16 hours to less than one hour. Means gained press capacity to meet demand, was able to cancel an order for a new press, and saved the customer some $400,000 for an additional die set. The quick-changeover workshop was run by a Means *customer*—Delphia Saginaw Steering Systems (DSSS), a global steering-column producer.

Through its purchasing department, DSSS makes available 18 specific workshops to its suppliers (and customers), based on its own lean-manufacturing best-practices strategy. Four dedicated DSSS supplier development specialists travel to conduct the workshops. Examples of other workshops include maximizing throughout via capacity constraints, minimizing material movement via plant layout/cell design, and improved manufacturability via value analysis. "What we try to do with our suppliers is to help them understand the value stream for the entire part, all the value added from the time they start processing the right part through until it gets to our customer in our product," says Rick Schneider, business-team purchasing manager. "After participating in one of our programs, a supplier invariably ends up saving time or money, and many times gives us a higher-quality product."

Source: Adapted from Tim Stevens, "Do Unto Others," *Industry Week* (December 6, 1999): 18.

---

this investment. At this stage, the two parties are interested in identifying whether the project can be achieved, and what are realistic goals for the future. Some of the other criteria used to evaluate opportunities include cost/benefit analysis, willingness and ability of buyer and supplier to implement changes, duration of product/service life, total cost of production related to potential savings, strategic importance of the product/service and its impact on the business, return on investment, impact analysis, and standardization.

Step 7—Reach Agreement on Key Projects and Joint Resource Requirements Once a potential improvement project has been identified with a supplier, the parties must come to an agreement on the specific measures that will indicate success. These measures may include percentage of cost savings shared, percentage of quality improvement, percentage of delivery or cycle time improvement, key product or service performance targets, technology availability, or system implementation targets. The most critical portion of these agreements is that they contain visible milestones and time horizons for improvement. The agreement should also

EXHIBIT 10.4   *Degree of Satisfaction with Supplier Development Outcomes*

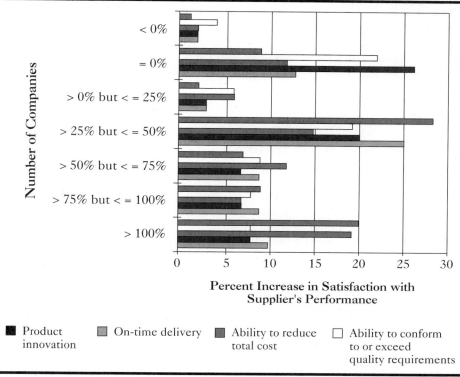

Source: Robert Handfield, Daniel Krause, Thomas Scannell, and Robert Monczka, "Avoid the Pitfalls in Supplier Development," *Sloan Management Review* 41, no. 2 (Winter 2000): 37–49.

specify the role of each party, who is responsible for the success of the project, and manner and timing for deploying allocated resources. Once an agreement is reached, the project is rolled out, hopefully according to schedule.

Step 8—Monitor Status of Projects and Modify Strategies as Appropriate Once a development project has been initiated, progress must be monitored and tracked over time. Moreover, an ongoing exchange of information is needed to maintain momentum of such projects. This can be achieved by creating visible milestones for objectives, updating progress, and in turn creating new or revised objectives based on progress to date. Project planning may require modifications to the original plan, additional resources, information, or priorities depending on events.

Supplier Development Efforts That Sometimes Don't Work

Evidence indicates that supplier development works—at least some of the time. Exhibit 10.4 presents the percentage increase in the level of satisfaction with supplier performance in a variety of performance areas.[9] The distribution in this exhibit clearly indicates that not all supplier development efforts are equally successful. Some efforts are quite successful, leading to increased satisfaction with the supplier's performance in the areas of total cost, quality, and delivery performance, product innovation and product, process or service development cycle times. However, supplier development may have led to *decreased* satisfaction—in the most successful effort. The next section describes some of the techniques and tools used by leading-edge companies to address the problems or barriers that contribute to reduced supplier development effectiveness.[10]

OVERCOMING THE BARRIERS TO SUPPLIER DEVELOPMENT

The barriers to supplier development fall into three categories: (1) buying firm-specific barriers, (2) barriers that focus on the interface between the purchaser and the supplier, and (3) supplier-specific barriers. Companies use a variety of approaches to overcome barriers to supplier development. In general, these approaches fall into one of three categories:

- *Direct-involvement activities* ("Hands-on"): Companies often send personnel to help suppliers. These efforts are characterized as hands-on activities, where buying-company representatives are directly involved in fixing supplier problems and increasing capabilities. These hands-on efforts include performing continuous improvement workshops at a supplier's premises and providing training and education for the supplier's personnel.
- *Incentives and rewards* ("The Carrot"): Companies also use incentives to encourage suppliers to improve, largely on their own. For example, a purchaser may increase order volumes if improvement takes place within a specific time frame or hold annual award ceremonies to recognize the best suppliers. These actions serve as "carrots" to strive for—that is, rewards to be gained for progress achieved.
- *Warnings and penalties* ("The Stick"): In some cases, companies may withhold potential future business if a supplier's performance is poor, or a lack of improvement is evident. Purchasers may also use competition to provide a competitive threat to a poorly performing supplier.

In many cases, organizations employ a combination of these three strategies to elicit improvement as quickly as possible, applying the strategies judiciously in response to a particular supplier's needs.

The following sections address barriers that are internal, external, or interface based, and provide examples of how to overcome these barriers. In each example below, ask yourself whether the approach used by the company falls into the category of a "hands-on," "carrot," or "stick" approach (or a combination in some cases).

Buying Firm-Specific Barriers

As shown in Exhibit 10.5, a buying company will not engage in supplier development if management does not recognize the need or the benefits from the supplier

EXHIBIT 10.5   *Buying Firm-Specific Barriers to Supplier Development*

Barrier	Mean Response*
Size of our purchase from the supplier does not justify development investment.	2.82
No immediate benefit is evident to our organization.	2.72
Importance of commodity purchased does not justify development investment.	2.67
Executives within our organization do not support supplier development.	2.60

*Where 1 = not a barrier, 2 = limited barrier, 3 = moderate barrier, 4 = significant barrier, and 5 = very significant barrier. The larger the mean response, the greater the barrier.

Source: Robert Handfield, Daniel Krause, Thomas Scannell, and Robert Monczka, "Avoid the Pitfalls in Supplier Development," *Sloan Management Review* 41, no. 2 (Winter 2000): 37–49.

development effort. Moreover, if purchasing personnel have not consolidated purchased volumes with fewer suppliers, the size of the company's purchase with any particular supplier may not justify the investment. In addition, there is sometimes a lack of executive support for financing a supplier development effort.

Barrier: The Buying Company's Purchase Volume from the Supplier Does Not Justify Development Investment *Solution: Standardization and Single Sourcing.*

Parts standardization is a way to increase volume orders with key suppliers, and thereby justify the development effort. This was true even for "design-to-order" operations. For example, IBM's Networking Hardware Division, which produces customized networking solutions for customers, is constantly striving to increase parts commonality. Currently over 50% of purchased components for each major network hardware project are unique items. If IBM personnel believe customized componentry will provide a market advantage, then they will continue to use it. However, standardization remains a key strategy to leveraging worldwide purchases.

Concurrent with the drive to standardize parts, many purchasing managers plan to optimize their supply base and to use single suppliers, wherever possible, to achieve economies of scale. For example, Daewoo Corporation uses single sourcing wherever possible, using two or more suppliers only in situations with high potential for labor disputes. Similarly, NCR, Doosan Corporation of Korea, Honda of America Manufacturing, and Rover have made or are planning moves toward single sourcing within a product line but maintaining multiple sources across product lines. This strategy provides opportunities to leverage purchase volumes while simultaneously reducing supply risk.

Barrier: No Immediate Benefit Is Evident to the Buying Organization

Solution: Pursue Small Wins. Varity Perkins is a producer of diesel engines that are used in automotive and construction vehicles. The company's initial supplier development efforts were relatively unsuccessful, which resulted in lowered expectations internally and dampened enthusiasm for future efforts. However, Varity personnel realized that part of the problem was that they were trying to accomplish too much. Thus, the company focused on a smaller group of suppliers for "Kaizen" (continuous improvement) efforts to gain a series of small wins. Kaizen efforts originated in Japan, and involve studying a process and making changes to improve performance. In this case, Varity's Kaizen approach was rewarded with incremental improvements that ultimately gained renewed commitment from all impacted parties.

Barrier: Importance of Commodity Purchased Does Not Justify Development Effort *Solution: Take a Longer-Term Focus.* Solectron, a contract manufacturer in the computer industry, has a competitive strategy that relies heavily on its supply chain management competencies. The company thus looks beyond the price of purchased inputs and examines how its most important suppliers impact the quality and technology of its products. Suppliers are expected to provide designs offering integrated solutions that can be used by Solectron designers. Total costs and long-term strategic impact are used as criteria to justify investments in suppliers.

Barrier: Lack of Executive Support Within the Buying Organization for Supplier Development *Solution: Prove the Benefits.* Top-management support for supplier development is gained when management becomes convinced that company profits can improve if supplier performance improves. For companies that spend nearly 80% of the cost of goods sold on purchased inputs, such an argument is easy to make—for companies with lower percentages, the argument may be more difficult. Although proving a specific relationship between supplier performance improvement and increased profits can be difficult to prove, somebody within the purchasing organization must make that argument. Managers also note that efforts to optimize their companies' supply bases combined with part standardization can free up resources over the long term, making supplier development more plausible. In addition, the total cost approach to supplier performance measurement should also prove to be an effective communication tool for demonstrating the cost of poor supplier performance. Thus, many of the strategies used by companies to overcome internal barriers to supplier development may be complementary.

Interface Barriers to Supplier Development

Barriers may also originate in the interface between the purchaser and supplier in areas such as communication, alignment of organizational cultures, and interorganizational trust. Exhibit 10.6 reveals that supplier reluctance to share information on costs/processes was the most significant interface barrier to supplier development.

Barrier: Supplier Is Reluctant to Share Information on Costs and/or Processes *Solution: Create a Supplier Ombudsman Position.* Honda of America has supplier ombudsmen who deal with the "soft side of the business—primarily the human resource issues that are not associated with cost, quality, or delivery. Because an ombudsman is not involved in contract negotiations, suppliers are often much more willing to talk with the ombudsman. One ombudsman emphasized that it takes a long time to build trust with suppliers, and that this period varies with different suppliers. If a supplier approaches the ombudsman with a problem that is the result of poor communication or misunderstanding between Honda and the supplier, the ombudsman

EXHIBIT 10.6   *Interface Barriers to Supplier Development*

Barrier	Mean Response*
Supplier is reluctant to share information on costs/processes.	3.17**
Confidentiality inhibits sharing information.	2.77
Supplier does not trust us.	2.66
Poor alignment of our organizational culture with that of supplier's organization.	2.61
Not enough inducements to participate are provided to supplier.	2.58

*Where 1 = not a barrier, 2 = limited barrier, 3 = moderate barrier, 4 = significant barrier, and 5 = very significant barrier. The larger the mean response, the greater the barrier.

Source: Robert Handfield, Daniel Krause, Thomas Scannell, and Robert Monczka, "Avoid the Pitfalls in Supplier Development," *Sloan Management Review* 41, no. 2 (Winter 2000): 37–49.

communicates the supplier's perspective within Honda. He does so while maintaining as much confidentiality as possible. Over time, suppliers have come to trust the ombudsman, and appear to be more willing to share information in all areas, including cost data.

Barrier: Confidentiality Inhibits Sharing Information *Solution: Confidentiality Agreements.* Perhaps one of the biggest challenges in developing suppliers is sharing confidential information, especially when dealing with new suppliers in high-technology areas. Thus, many companies require nondisclosure agreements and even exclusivity agreements (i.e., the supplier provides a specific product to only one purchaser) in development efforts, especially when dealing with technologically advanced products that contribute to the buying company's competitive edge. Motorola has made confidentiality a key part of its supplier development agenda. The company is helping suppliers segregate Motorola's production from the rest of their operations to prevent competitors from seeing Motorola's parts. (Nondisclosure agreements are covered later in the contracts chapter.)

Barrier: Supplier Does Not Trust the Buying Organization *Solution: Spell It Out.* The driving forces behind Kaizen events at Varity Perkins indicate that the company will not run a Kaizen without a signed agreement between the company and supplier. Although there are some procurement personnel at Varity Perkins who prefer a "gentleman's agreement," Kaizen leaders believe the only way to gain a supplier's trust is to have the terms written and signed, especially when conducting the first few Kaizen events. Recently it took Varity Perkins eight months to convince a key supplier to consider a Kaizen workshop because the supplier felt that a similar event with a different company failed to yield any significant improvements. The trust problem was compounded at Varity Perkins because the company previously had a reputation for "arm's-length" relationships with suppliers, which were manifested by frequent switching of suppliers based on price. The company has moved aggressively to reverse this perception through a revised purchasing philosophy emphasizing well-defined purchasing objectives that go beyond purchase price and cooperative relationships with key suppliers.

Barrier: Organizational Cultures Are Poorly Aligned *Solution: Adapt Approach to Local Conditions.* When setting up production in South Carolina, Bavarian Motor Works (BMW) quickly realized it would have to change its supplier development approach to conform to North American supply conditions. BMW uses a "Process Consulting" approach to supplier development in Germany, which involves analyzing suppliers' processes and telling them what is wrong. This approach works well in a mature supplier relationship, where the supplier intuitively understands what the customer wants because the parties have worked together over a number of years. In the United States however, a very different approach was required.

When BMW started U.S. production, suppliers had difficulty understanding what would be required of them in terms of quality and continuous improvement. This misunderstanding resulted in several strained relationships. Consequently, BMW spent a lot of time communicating with suppliers and showing them what was needed. A major difference between the U.S. and German approach to supplier development was that BMW could not simply tell suppliers where to improve, but needed to provide technical support. Furthermore, BMW had to change the message they sent to suppliers by emphasizing that "your problems are our problems!" They also said, "You have good products, but you have to do better, and we are here to help you!"

BMW strives to be 20% above the industry average in a number of quality performance categories and believes supplier development to be a key contributor in this effort. BMW managers believe one of the most important ways to achieve this is to effectively communicate expectations. Thus BMW recently published a Supplier Partnership Manual that clearly delineates supplier responsibilities and expectations. The company also held seminars to present their "Roadmap to Quality" to suppliers. These efforts are geared toward better alignment of corporate cultures.

Barrier: Not Enough Inducements to Participate Are Provided to the Supplier *Solution: Designed in Motivation.* Although Solectron is now generally able to offer large order volumes to suppliers, that was not always the case. To gain supplier cooperation in the "low-volume years," Solectron emphasized that a supplier could become "designed in" to its products and thus have a greater potential for future business. Allowing suppliers to be designed in to the product has motivated most suppliers to participate in supplier development efforts. Solectron still uses this approach as a motivational force.

Solution: Financial Incentives. Hyundai Motor Company uses financial incentives as one motivational tool for suppliers to improve. The company rates supplier performance from 1 (highest) to 4 (lowest). Class 1 suppliers are paid in cash, Class 2 suppliers are paid net 30 days, Class 3 suppliers are paid net 60 days, and Class 4 suppliers receive no new business. Because suppliers know how their performance is evaluated, they can take the steps necessary to ensure high levels of performance.

EXHIBIT 10.7   *Supplier-Specific Barriers to Supplier Development*

Barrier	Mean Response*
Supplier's top management lacks commitment.	2.90
Supplier's top management agrees to proposals but fails to implement them.	2.87
Supplier lacks engineering resources to implement solutions.	2.77
Supplier lacks required information systems.	2.74
Suppliers are not convinced development will benefit their organization.	2.71
Supplier lacks employee skill base to implement solutions.	2.70

*Where 1 = not a barrier, 2 = limited barrier, 3 = moderate barrier, 4 = significant barrier, and 5 = very significant barrier. The larger the mean response, the greater the barrier.

Source: Robert Handfield, Daniel Krause, Thomas Scannell, and Robert Monczka, "Avoid the Pitfalls in Supplier Development," *Sloan Management Review* 41, no. 2 (Winter 2000): 37–49.

Supplier-Specific Barriers

Exhibit 10.7 shows the relative importance of barriers to supplier development that may exist within the supplier. Just as lack of recognition of benefits by the purchaser prevents the inception of supplier development, a lack of recognition of potential benefits may keep the supplier's top management from committing to the effort. This lack of commitment may be evidenced by failure to implement improvement ideas, and/or the failure of the supplier to provide the necessary technical and human resources to support the development process.

Barrier: Lack of Commitment on the Part of Supplier's Top Management *Solution: Implement After Commitment.* Varity Perkins's supplier development efforts are closely integrated with the Kaizen, or continuous improvement, workshops. Perkins's managers state that they will not engage in a Kaizen event with a supplier unless the supplier is fully committed to the process prior to the event. A buyer at Varity Perkins arranges an initial contact meeting with the supplier's managing director to obtain direct involvement. To secure commitment, Perkins's quality managers persuade the managing director of the impact of Kaizen efforts by first explaining the Kaizen process, then asking him or her to participate in one of the weekly internal Kaizen events at Perkins. After the presentation and Kaizen event, the supplier's commitment is solicited. If the managing director is positive, a Kaizen Awareness Session for the supplier's senior management takes place at the supplier's facility. The supplier is advised of the project and is asked to commit its workforce to the project, which typically involves eight to ten operators for one week.

Barrier: Supplier's Top Management Agrees to Improvement Proposals But Fails to Implement Them *Solution: Supplier Champions.* JCI Corporation, a first-tier automotive supplier to the Big Three and other manufacturers, has instituted a Supplier Champions Program (SCP) with strategic suppliers that is designed to ensure suppliers are proficient in areas that are important to JCI's customers.

The program was initiated because many of the suppliers that had attended JCI's training sessions failed to implement any of the tools and techniques that had been provided. The SCP identifies what suppliers' personnel need to implement after they return from training and requires verification. The program designates a Supplier Champion, a supplier employee who understands JCI's expectations, has consistently demonstrated an acceptable level of competence, and is expected to disseminate this knowledge throughout his or her organization. A certification process requires that the Champion submit to JCI a number of examples of actions that the supplier has taken to improve. These actions might include process flow mapping, failure mode effects analysis, quality control planning, best-practice benchmarking, and process auditing.

Barrier: Supplier Lacks Engineering Resources to Implement Solutions *Solution: Direct Support.* Honda of America (HAM) has invested a significant number of resources in its supplier support infrastructure. For example, of 310 people working in HAM's purchasing department, 50 are engineers who work exclusively with suppliers. In one case, a small plastics supplier did not have the capacity to keep up with volume, resulting in quality deterioration. HAM sent four people to the supplier for ten months at no charge to the supplier, with additional services offered on an as-needed basis. The supplier improved and today is a well-established Honda supplier. Although engineering support plays a large role in the success of HAM's supplier development program, the company generally does not invest directly in suppliers' equipment. However, in some cases they will own a percentage of the supplier equipment for capitalization purposes and allow the supplier to pay the investment back over time. The Good Practice Example at the end of this chapter details Honda of America's extensive supplier development efforts.

Barrier: Supplier Lacks Required Information Systems to Implement Solutions *Solution: Direct Electronic Data Interchange Support.* At NCR Corporation, a manufacturer of ATMs, managers note that timely and accurate information is critical to decision making and ultimately to improved performance. An important focus of their supplier development efforts has been to get suppliers to make a commitment to electronic data interchange (EDI) with a significant amount of money committed to getting suppliers on-line. Suppliers producing lower-level components that do not have resources to get on-line themselves are provided help. In addition, NCR provides training for suppliers and will help make recommendations on hardware and software.

Barrier: Suppliers Are Not Convinced Development Will Provide Benefits *Solution: Let Suppliers Know Where They Stand.* Varity Perkins recently revamped its supplier evaluation system to show suppliers where they could improve. Previously, a 100-point weighted report was sent to suppliers once a quarter that assessed performance in the areas of quality, delivery, and price competitiveness. At that time, Perkins did not utilize the data in any manner and suppliers did not take the assessments seriously. In revamping the system, the company decided to keep the same criteria and continue to provide it via quarterly reports. However, the "granularity" of measures was changed to capture the impact of supplier performance on daily operations.

For example, delivery performance had previously been measured using a weekly time bucket performance, and average performance had been 90% to 95% on time. With a daily time bucket, performance dropped to 26% on time. Since the new measure has been in place, daily on-time delivery has improved to 90%. In addition to increased granularity, the supplier's history, its performance against Varity's other suppliers, and the deviation from mean performance for each area as well as overall by quarter, are shown on the new report. Another change was to make the report more visual and to use graphs to make the data more meaningful.

This system has become the foundation for the company's supplier development program. Although the new system does not explicitly address warranty and service issues, it does concentrate on results. By allowing suppliers to view their performance relative to competitors, the company expects that suppliers will realize the potential benefits of supplier development.

Barrier: Supplier Lacks Employee Skill Base to Implement Solutions

Solution: Establish Training Centers. JCI Corporation realized that some suppliers would lack the skills required to implement improvement ideas. With this problem in mind, JCI built a training facility dedicated to providing extensive training to their internal groups, suppliers, and customers. Their Supplier Principles Program is required for all potential suppliers, and hundreds of people have been through the program. For the first 11 months of 1997, 765 hours were spent by suppliers in classes at JCI's facility; 1,283 hours were spent by JCI supplier development engineers involved in management and process training at suppliers' facilities; and supplier development personnel spent 573 hours on technical problem-solving activities at suppliers' sites.

Solution: Industry and Government Cooperation. Hyundai Corporation recognizes that smaller suppliers with limited resources cannot consistently recruit and retain the most skilled engineers. Therefore, the majority of improvement efforts focus on smaller suppliers. Hyundai selects engineers from its own shops to spend time with suppliers. The engineers "live" at suppliers, performing time/motion studies, teaching layout design, and improving productivity. Suppliers are consistently encouraged to learn, apply, and eventually teach themselves and second-tier suppliers the transferred knowledge.

The Korean government strongly encourages such industry collaboration. Hyundai has a domestic training center that provides supplier personnel with training in areas such as specialized welding. This cost of the effort is shared evenly between Hyundai and the suppliers. The Korean government also supports these training centers by providing tax benefits for building training centers and making the training fees shared by Hyundai and suppliers tax-deductible.

Lessons Learned

A theme that underlies each of these examples is that many of the barriers to supplier development are related. Thus it appears that as companies work toward solving one barrier, they may make concurrent progress toward solving other barriers. Several lessons are learned from studying supplier development processes and efforts:

1. *Managerial attitudes are a common and difficult barrier to overcome.* A purchasing executive at Honda of America noted that although quality problems always have a solution, the attitudes of suppliers' managers must be "right" if the problem is to be truly solved. Many managers note that suppliers are sometime not willing to accept help in the form of supplier development, perhaps because they are too proud to accept help, or because they do not see the value in improving quality or delivery performance. Management attitudes can significantly affect the success of the supplier development effort.

2. *Realizing comparative and competitive advantage from the supply chain requires a strategic emphasis on purchasing and supply chain management, and the alignment of purchasing objectives with business unit goals.* A strong purchasing mission statement reflects and drives this strategic emphasis and alignment. Consider a U.K. auto parts manufacturer's purchasing mission statement: "We are committed to procure goods and services in a way that delivers our aims and objectives of becoming the most successful auto parts business in the world." The company pursues this mission through (1) development of a world-class supplier base capable of meeting current and future needs; (2) obtaining the highest quality, most cost-effective goods and services in a timely manner; and (3) establishing long-term relationships with supply partners who meet company standards and are committed to the manufacturer, and strive for continuous improvement in all areas.

3. *Relationship management is critical to success.* By using specific tools and processes such as total cost analysis, volume leveraging, resource support, formal and informal communication, linked information systems, business "incentives," and agreement on goals and objectives, the relationships between buying companies and their suppliers can be developed and strengthened, and barriers to improved supplier performance overcome.

Instigating supplier performance improvement is not an easy task. The objective, of course, is to transform suppliers such that continuous improvement becomes an integral part of suppliers' capabilities. Such an accomplishment is achieved only over time, and by those companies that are patient and tenacious enough to make follow-up visits to suppliers and continue with a strong program of supplier evaluation and feedback of suppliers' performance.

GOOD PRACTICE EXAMPLE
Putting It All Together at Honda of America[11]

■ ■ ■

Honda of America, with production locations in Ohio, strongly commits to longer-term relationships and supplier development. Honda purchases 80% of the total cost of its car from outside suppliers—the highest percentage for an automaker in the world. It also has a policy of developing sources of supply near its plants. This policy supports a close relationship between Honda and its suppliers, makes supplier development more likely, and supports just-in-time delivery. Honda's plants keep less than three hours' worth of inventory on hand for most items.

In 1982, 27 U.S. suppliers sold $14 million worth of parts and components to Honda of America. By 1990, 175 U.S. suppliers provided over $2.2 billion worth of parts and components. Most suppliers are within 150 miles of the assembly plants. In 1999, a Honda built in Ohio had over 90% local U.S. purchase content, although some material come from Japanese transplant suppliers.

A strong, local supply base has been important to Honda's success. Honda commits a significant amount of resources toward developing local suppliers, an approach that ensures that Honda has access to suppliers capable of meeting the company's stringent performance standards. Honda's goal is that its purchase volume be at least 30%—and sometimes 100%—of a supplier's total output. The company tries to create a sense of mutual dependence between itself and its suppliers. It has, on occasion, pursued small equity ownership with suppliers as a way to demonstrate commitment and be recognized as an important customer.

Honda has high respect for its suppliers. As a result, long-term mutual loyalty exists between Honda and its suppliers. A supplier who meets Honda's performance standards becomes a lifetime supplier. Honda will remain loyal to a supplier even if the supplier experiences temporary performance problems. Supplier development and improvement, which covers a wide range of areas, has one primary objective: to create and maintain a dedicated supply base that supports Honda's U.S. requirements. Honda commits varied resources to support and develop its supply base into world-class performers:

- Two full-time employees help suppliers develop their employee involvement programs.
- Forty full-time engineers in the purchasing department work to improve supplier productivity and quality.
- The quality-control department has 120 engineers dealing with incoming parts and supplier quality issues.
- Honda provides technical support to suppliers in a number of technical areas, including plastics technology, welding, stamping, and aluminum die casting.
- Honda forms special teams to help suppliers on an as-needed basis. For example, one supplier experienced problems resulting from rapid growth. Honda formed a four-person team that moved to the supplier's town for nine months to help correct the problems.
- A "Quality-Up" program targets suppliers with lower quality. Honda works directly with the highest executives at the supplier to make sure the supplier produces a 100% quality product.
- Honda's representatives regularly visit a supplier's facilities. Among other things, Honda examines each supplier's financial and business plans.

- Honda has a loaned executive program where it sends its executives to work at the supplier's location. This supports greater understanding and communication between Honda and its suppliers.

Most companies are not willing to provide this level of commitment to supplier development and performance improvement. A company that maintains a hands-off approach to supply-base management is probably not willing to provide the resources necessary to support supplier development. Furthermore, some suppliers are not willing to expose themselves to the level of scrutiny required by Honda. For example, Honda conducts minimal price negotiation. Instead, the company identifies a target cost and then works with a supplier to meet that cost. Honda must have a detailed understanding of a supplier's cost structure. Detailed cost sharing, however, is a difficult area for independent U.S. suppliers, which is one reason Honda has developed its own sources of supply in the United States for some purchased items.

The relationship between Donnelly Corporation and Honda of America provides an example of the success of this effort. Honda selected Donnelly in 1986 to produce all the interior mirrors for its U.S.-built cars. At that time, Donnelly's expertise involved the production of interior mirrors. Over the years, the two companies developed a closer relationship, partly due to their similar cultures and values. Honda approached Donnelly to discuss building exterior mirrors—a process Donnelly was not familiar with. With Honda's assistance, Donnelly built a brand-new plant to produce Honda's exterior mirrors. Donnelly's business with Honda, which involved $5 million in sales the first year, grew to $60 million by 1997. A development effort such as this one requires a commitment between two entire corporations, not just between purchasing and sales managers.

Most large U.S. purchasers fall somewhere between providing minimal supplier development support and Honda's level of support. The Honda example provides some major points for those considering purchasing careers. First, suppliers play a critical role in the success of most organizations. It makes sense to pay real attention to a supplier's performance improvement needs. It also makes sense to develop loyalty and trust between buyer and seller, particularly with suppliers who provide critical items. Honda has realized the benefits that a local world-class supply base provides. Second, too large a supply base usually prohibits providing adequate supplier development support. There are not enough resources available to support and develop thousands of suppliers at once. Finally, a successful supplier development effort requires more than slogans and increased performance standards. It requires actually committing the resources to make the process successful.

While the Honda approach seems extreme to some observers, few can argue with the company's success in the U.S. car market. The cars produced at the Ohio assembly plants have consistently been the best-selling cars in the United States with high customer loyalty. In fact, Honda now exports a portion of its U.S. production back to Japan. The success of Honda's supplier development and improvement effort is one reason the company has such loyal customers. ■

CONCLUSION

Managing and improving supplier performance is a primary purchasing and business function. Supplier management and development have become the new model of purchasing behavior. No longer does a buyer simply purchase parts from the lowest price source. The activities that best describe today's purchaser include planning, coordinating, managing, developing, and improving the performance capabilities of the supply base. For many items, purchasers no longer buy parts from suppliers; they manage supplier capabilities.

Purchasing must select and manage a proper mix of suppliers. To accomplish this, managers must have the proper resources for supplier management, including a supplier performance measurement system, contracts with preferred suppliers, and a wide range of supplier development resources. A well-supported supplier management program helps maximize the contribution received from suppliers.

DISCUSSION QUESTIONS

1.   Why is it critical to have a smaller supply base before committing to a supplier management and development program?
2.   Discuss the advantages and disadvantages of an optimized supply base. How can the disadvantages be overcome?
3.   Discuss the logic behind maintaining multiple suppliers for each purchased item. Discuss the logic behind maintaining a reduced number of suppliers for each item.
4.   What is a full-service supplier? What are the benefits of using full-service suppliers?
5.   Why is the Honda approach to supplier development and improvement not widespread among U.S. firms?
6.   Many companies are now using the World Wide Web to share performance information with suppliers, thereby allowing suppliers to compare their performance to other suppliers within the buying company's supply base. Discuss the potential benefits of this strategy to both buyers and suppliers.
7.   Discuss the different types of supplier development and support that a firm can offer. Which are the most common? Why?
8.   Research has revealed that no single unique approach to supplier development is effective in achieving performance goals. Rather, a mix of the "carrot," "stick," and "hands-on" approaches seems to work best. Explain why you think this is the case.
9.   Why do some firms receive better service, quality, and price from a supplier than do other firms within the same industry?
10. Consider the following statement: *Increased specialization has resulted in greater reliance on external suppliers.* What does this mean? Why does specialization result in greater

external reliance? What steps should a firm that is becoming more highly specialized take with regard to its supply base?

11. A common statement made in some purchasing organizations is "We can't be spending money on supplier development—we're not in business to train suppliers and do their job for them!" What type of barrier does this statement represent? How would you respond to such a statement?

12. Of the barriers to supplier development mentioned in this study, which are the most difficult to overcome in your opinion?

13. A DaimlerChrysler executive made the following statement: "Only about one in five supplier development efforts are truly 100% successful." Why do you think this is the case? What makes supplier development such a challenging effort?

14. Discuss the reasons why top-management commitment is essential to the success of supplier management and development.

ADDITIONAL READINGS

Burt, D. N. "Managing Suppliers Up to Speed." *Harvard Business Review* (July-August, 1989): 15–28.

Fitzgerald, K. R. "For Superb Supplier Development–Honda Wins!" *Purchasing* 21 (September 1995): 32.

Galt, Major J. D. A., and B. G. Dale. "Supplier Development: A British Case Study." *International Journal of Purchasing and Materials Management* 27 (Winter 1991): 16–22.

Giunipero, L. C. "Motivating and Monitoring JIT Supplier Performance." *Journal of Purchasing and Materials Management* 26 (Summer, 1990): 19–24.

Hahn, C. K., Watts, C. A., and Kim, K. Y. " The Supplier Development Program: A Conceptual Model." *International Journal of Purchasing and Materials Management* 26 (Summer 1990): 2–7.

———. "Supplier Development Program at Hyundai Motor." Paper presented at annual conference of the National Association of Purchasing Management, Tempe, AZ, 67–81.

Handfield, Robert, and Daniel Krause, "Think Globally, Source Locally." *Supply Chain Management Review* (Winter 1999): 36–49.

Handfield, Robert, Daniel Krause, and Tom Scannell. "Avoid the Pitfalls in Supplier Development," *Sloan Management Review* (Winter 2000): 37–49.

Hartley, J., and T. Choi. "Supplier Development: Customers as a Catalyst of Process Change." *Business Horizons* (July-August, 1996): 37–44.

Helper, S. "How Much Has Really Changed Between U.S. Automakers and Their Suppliers?" *Sloan Management Review* 32 (1991): 15–28.

Hines, P. *Creating World-Class Suppliers: Unlocking Mutual Competitive Advantage.* London: Pitman, 1994.

Hunter, L., P. Beaumont, and D. Sinclair. "A 'Partnership' Route to Human Resource Management?" *Journal of Management Studies* 33, no. 2 (March 1996): 235–57.

Krause, D. R. " Supplier Development: Current Practices and Outcomes." *International Journal of Purchasing and Materials Management* 33, no. 2 (1997): 12–19.

Krause, D. R., & Ellram, L. M. "Success Factors in Supplier Development." *International Journal of Physical Distribution and Logistics Management* 27, no. 1 (1997): 39–52.

————. Krause, D. R., & Ellram, L. M. (1997). "Critical Elements of Supplier Development: The Buying Firm Perspective." *European Journal of Purchasing and Supply Management* 3, no. 1 (1997): 21–31.

Lascelles, D. M., and B. G. Dale. " The Buyer-Supplier Relationship in Total Quality Management." *International Journal of Purchasing and Materials Management* 25 (1989): 10–19.

Leenders, M. R. " Supplier Development." *International Journal of Purchasing and Materials Management* 25 (1989): 47–55.

Leenders, M. R., and D. L. Blenkhorn. *Reverse Marketing: The New Buyer-Supplier Relationship.* New York: Free Press, 1988.

Monczka, R. M., R. J. Trent, and T. J. Callahan. "Supply Base Strategies to Maximize Supplier Performance." *International Journal of Physical Distribution & Logistics Management* 23, no. 4 (1993): 42–54.

Newman, R. G., and K. A. Rhee. "A Case Study of NUMMI and Its Suppliers." *International Journal of Purchasing and Materials Management* 26 (1990): 15–20.

Watts, C. A., , K. Y. Kim, and C .K. Hahn. "Linking Purchasing to Corporate Competitive Strategy." *International Journal of Purchasing and Materials Management* 28 (1992): 15–20.

ENDNOTES

1. R. E. Spekman, "Strategic Supplier Selection: Understanding Long-Term Buyer Relations," *Business Horizons* 31, no. 4 (July/August 1988): 75.
2. R. G. Newman, "Single Sourcing: Short-Term Savings Versus Long-Term Problems," *International Journal of Purchasing and Management* 25, no. 2 (Summer 1989): 24.
3. This approach was discussed by David Curry of Honda of America Manufacturing.
4. K. R. Bhote, *Strategic Supply Management* (New York: American Management Association, 1989), 75.
5. Krause and Handfield, *Developing a World-Class Supply Base* (Tempe, AZ: Center for Advanced Purchasing Studies, 1999), 7.

6. Ibid, p. 8.
7. Robert Handfield, Daniel Krause, Thomas Scannell, and Robert Monczka, "An Empirical Investigation of Supplier Development: Reactive and Strategic Processes," *Journal of Operations Management* 17, no. 1 (December 1998): 39–58.
8. C. K. Hahn, C. A. Watts, and K. Y. Kim, "The Supplier Development Program: A Conceptual Model," *International Journal of Purchasing and Materials Management* 26, no. 2 (Spring 1990): 2–7.
9. Robert Handfield, Daniel Krause, and Tom Scannell, "Avoid the Pitfalls in Supplier Development," *Sloan Management Review* (Winter 2000): 37–49.
10. Robert Handfield, Daniel Krause, Tom Scannell, and R. Monczka. "Avoid the Pitfalls in Supplier Development," *Sloan Management Review* 41, no. 2 (Winter 2000): 37–49.
11. Krause and Handfield, *Developing a World-Class Supply Base*, 102.

WORLDWIDE SOURCING 11

Global Sourcing and Design at Santek Chemicals

Santek Chemicals,* a worldwide industrial gas and chemical company headquartered in New York, recently launched a globally integrated approach to engineering and procurement. During 1999, Santek Chemicals implemented a global process that proactively integrates and coordinates common items, processes, designs, technologies, and suppliers across two worldwide buying and engineering centers (North America and Europe).

As a designer and operater of chemical facilities, Santek Chemicals had operated historically as an engineer-to-order company, which implied that a great deal of engineer and design work was customized to each new project. New plants were largely engineered without considering previous designs or leveraging commonality across design and procurement centers. Even if the United States and Europe used a similar or the same item (which was often the case) or designed the same facility in terms of process and technology, each would have component specifications that were developed by engineers who did not coordinate their efforts. As a result, design specifications differed unnecessarily with little coordination of purchasing across regions.

The global process at Santek Chemicals evolved as a senior engineering manager expressed a desire to gain advantages from "globalizing" engineering and procurement but was not sure what that meant or required. The director of project and logistics supply assembled a leadership team to develop, sell internally, and launch a global engineering and procurement process.

Part of the process development involved several procurement managers working together to define the concept of globalization. These managers then assumed responsibility for developing the process, which required three to four months of effort. Broadly, the definition of global sourcing has involved Santek Chemicals identifying opportunities that provide synergy between a minimum of two worldwide engineering offices during the development of a new facility.

Today, Santek's global process involves more than identifying similar items or commodities that have a global application. Each project involves an extensive analysis between the U.S. and European design centers to determine areas of commonality and synergy. Cross-functional/cross-locational (CF/CL) teams, with members from the United States and England, work jointly to develop specifications that satisfy both design centers. Although the process began with very focused commodities, the projects have become broader in scope as the cost-saving possibilities have become apparent. Although the primary focus of the global sourcing effort involves commodities associated with plant and technical processes, Santek Chemicals is now looking at telecommunications, travel, and some purchased chemicals.

$\rightarrow \rightarrow \rightarrow$

Santek Chemicals had certain organizational advantages that increased the success of global engineering and procurement. The company organizes its purchasing effort by commodity and maintains a strong centralized project focus. Although it operates facilities around the world, the practice of making decisions at one or several locations, which characterizes this global process, is not unusual or resisted. Decentralization, which could impede the acceptance of global sourcing contracts, is not an issue at Santek Chemicals.

The global engineering and procurement opportunities identified by a steering committee are assigned to cross-functional/cross-locational teams. Each project follows a series of steps as it progresses toward a global procurement agreement that satisfies the needs of Santek's design and procurement centers:

- Step 1: Identify global sourcing opportunities.
- Step 2: Establish and charter a global sourcing development team.
- Step 3: Propose a procurement strategy.
- Step 4: Develop request for proposal (RFP) specifications.
- Step 5: Release RFPs to suppliers.
- Step 6: Evaluate bid or proposals.
- Step 7: Negotiate face-to-face.
- Step 8: Award contract.
- Step 9: Implement and manage the project.

Perhaps the major reason Santek Chemicals has enjoyed success with its global projects is due to the organizational support mechanisms put in place to guide the process. This includes the creation of an executive steering committee and globalization manager to oversee the process, placing the process and supporting documents on the company's Intranet, and extensive use of cross-locational/cross-organizational teams.

Senior managers are positive about the future of global engineering and procurement at Santek Chemicals. Completed projects have delivered dramatic cost savings averaging 20% compared with previous agreements. Executive management considers global engineering and sourcing to be one of the key internal processes in place at Santek Chemicals today. This has elevated senior management's expectations, which helps explain the aggressive performance targets established for 2001 and beyond.

*This company has requested that its actual name not be used.
Source: Interviews with company managers.

As world markets become increasingly competitive and open to trade, purchasers must identify suppliers that are capable of providing world-class performance at the lowest total cost. As a result, most purchasing professionals must be familiar with domestic and international sources of supply. A challenge arises when we consider that worldwide sourcing requires an entirely new set of competencies and skills within the materials management function. Companies must improve their logistics capability to accommodate longer material pipelines, manage the complex set of transactions that occur as materials move across international borders, and appreciate the cultural and legal differences between countries. Purchasers must manage and negotiate with international transportation carriers and suppliers and stay abreast of the complex and dynamic rules that govern international trade.

Fundamental differences exist between international buying and global sourcing. *International buying* refers to a commercial purchase transaction between a buyer and a supplier located in different countries. This type of purchase is typically more complex than a domestic purchase. Purchasing must contend with lengthened material pipelines, increased rules and regulations, currency fluctuations, customs requirements, and a host of other variables such as language and time differences. *Global sourcing* requires a firm to integrate and coordinate information, purchasing strategy, and common purchase requirements across worldwide business units or divisions. It differs from international buying in its sophistication and complexity.

As the opening vignette highlighted, companies seek major performance improvements from globally coordinating the design and purchase of common items, technologies, and production processes. Companies that actively pursue global sourcing often have a strong centralized or coordinated purchasing function to manage the process. The division or plant level can carry out international purchasing because of the lack of specialized coordination required between purchasing units. Because of the differences between international buying and global sourcing, we will use the terms *worldwide* or *foreign sourcing* for general discussions of the process of purchasing from other countries.

There are three primary objectives to keep in mind in this chapter. First, it is important to become familiar with the basics of worldwide sourcing, including an overview of the process and an understanding of how to organize for it, recognizing the costs associated with worldwide sourcing, and managing currency risk. Second, an understanding of countertrade is important because of its growth as a form of international trade and the role purchasing plays in managing countertrade arrangements. Finally, an understanding of the evolutionary process that occurs is important, as firms progress from domestic purchasing to the global coordination of sourcing strategy.

An Overview of Worldwide Sourcing

The level of foreign purchasing by U.S. companies has increased dramatically during the past several decades. Between 1973 and 1975, the percentage of companies sourcing worldwide doubled from 21% to 45% due to a variety of factors.[1] The first was that the oil embargo of the 1970s coupled with shortages of other basic materials forced purchasing to search overseas for suppliers. As a result, the number of companies engaged in foreign sourcing increased dramatically. Another factor was that many worldwide producers were becoming quality and cost leaders within a number of industries.

For example, the most sought-after foreign items in 1975 were production machinery and equipment followed by chemicals and mechanical/electrical components.

The percentage of U.S. companies sourcing worldwide increased from 45% to 56% from 1975 to 1982. This increase reflected the continuing inability of domestic suppliers and manufacturers to compete in terms of quality, price, and even delivery—problems that still afflict some U.S. companies. Foreign suppliers could often provide higher-quality parts at a lower total cost. For some, survival against foreign competitors required sourcing from the same suppliers who supported the competition.

The period from 1982 through 1987 saw a sharp rise in the number of companies sourcing worldwide—from 56% to 71%. During this period the value of the U.S. dollar increased dramatically against other major currencies due to high government budget deficits. As a result, U.S. imports became less expensive while U.S. firms found it difficult to export and compete in world markets. The huge trade imbalances of the 1980s reflected the strength of the U.S. dollar in world currency markets along with a lack of competitiveness of many U.S. suppliers.

In the period since 1987, the level of global sourcing and global sales growth has accelerated rapidly. First, the end of the Cold War led to the opening of trade with emerging markets such as Russia, Eastern Europe, and China, which in turn led to the development of new markets and new sources of supply. Second, import and export restrictions began to lessen, partly as a function of the General Agreement on Tariffs and Trade (GATT) signed in Uruguay. Third, the North American Free Trade Agreement (NAFTA), passed in 1993, resulted in a dramatic increase in trade between the United States, Canada, and Mexico. Finally, trade talks between the United States and countries such as Japan have reduced the number of trade restrictions existing between countries. In particular, American companies are making intriguing inroads into Japan's high-tech, automobile, consumer goods, and retailing markets, and they are also using Japanese distribution channels.[2]

Purchases from foreign sources have increased from 9% of total purchases in the late 1980s to 27% in 1997, to more than 30% in 2000.[3] The trend toward increased worldwide purchasing is clear. However, the need to manage currency risk, extended logistics pipelines, global databases, and cultural and language differences creates complexity within the supply chain. The question becomes whether organizations have the resources and capabilities required to coordinate their worldwide purchasing activities.

Why Source Worldwide?

Although the previous discussion provided some reasons for purchasing internationally, let's discuss formally the reasons that companies pursue worldwide sourcing. While every company will have its own reasons, the four most predominant reasons are (1) to achieve cost/price benefits, (2) to ensure better quality, (3) to gain access to technology, and (4) to access the only source available. Other reasons cited less frequently but still important include introducing competition to the domestic supply base, satisfying countertrade requirements, reacting to the sourcing patterns of competitors, establishing a presence in a foreign market, and increased supplier responsiveness.

Cost/Price Benefits After considering all the costs associated with international purchasing, savings of 20% to 30% may be available. Cost differentials between countries arise because of lower labor rates, different productivity levels, a possible willingness to accept a lower profit margin, exchange rate differences, lower-cost inputs for materials, or perhaps even government subsidies. Purchasing should consider only suppliers who are capable of meeting rigid quality standards, although far too often price differentials become the primary criterion behind a foreign sourcing decision.

It is important to note that in assessing the cost benefits of sourcing internationally, purchasers should include all of the relevant costs associated with sourcing the item beyond piece price as well. This is the only way to effectively compare a quote from a domestic and an international producer. For example, international sourcing should also include the following costs:

- Freight
- Import duties
- Warehouse charges
- Quality costs
- Damage in travel
- Obsolescence
- Factory yield
- Freight-forwarding fees
- Other administrative costs

Quality Some countries, such as Japan and Germany, are obsessed with product quality. As a result, producers in these countries have been able to capture an increasing share of world markets across a range of industries. During the 1980s, U.S. purchasers were faced with a need to improve end-item quality or risk losing even more domestic and world market share to aggressive competitors. Many began to purchase foreign components with the hope of improving end-product quality. The combination of consistently high quality and lower overall price has been a major contributor to the growth of U.S. foreign buying.

Access to Technology The United States is no longer the undisputed product and process technology leader in the world. Other countries have developed leading-edge technologies in a number of areas, such as electronic components. Purchasers that require these components know that Asian suppliers are technology leaders. Gaining access to the most current technology leaves many companies with little choice except to pursue worldwide purchasing.

Access to Only Source Available The economic recession of the early 1980s resulted in the permanent closing of many suppliers across a wide range of industries. For example, U.S. copper producers closed many mines during the early and mid-1980s because of low copper prices (low demand coupled with high supply) and inefficient process technology. As a result, some copper buyers turned to overseas producers to meet raw material and semifinished material requirements. A loss of supplier capability and availability in the automotive, machine tool, and electronics industries often left domestic buyers with no viable supply alternative except international sources. In many industrial sectors today this is still a factor—no domestic supplier can adequately meet the requirements of purchasers.

Introduce Competition to Domestic Suppliers Companies that rely on competitive forces to maintain price and service levels within their industry sometimes use worldwide sourcing to introduce competition to the domestic supply base. In industries characterized by limited domestic competition, this can diminish a supplier's power and break certain practices unfavorable to purchasers. For example, Paradyne, featured in the Good Practice example at the end of the chapter, historically has sourced many chemical and substrate products with a single large U.S. supplier. However, Paradyne is now qualifying suppliers in emerging countries as a way to counteract the domestic supplier's pricing power. A more competitive supply market will shift power away from U.S. suppliers as well as shift power from sellers to buyers. In Korea and Japan, manufacturers such as Hyundai and Sony are sourcing more from U.S. and European suppliers, in order to introduce competition into their (traditionally) protected supply base. This is causing many Japanese and Korean suppliers to take notice, and improve their price and quality performance.

Satisfy Countertrade Requirements Countertrade agreements specify that a company must source a specified amount of goods from a foreign country if it sells to that country. This often requires purchasing to evaluate and select suppliers in the foreign country where it has a countertrade agreement. This is typically done in close cooperation with the marketing department, which may be seeking to increase sales within a particular market. While this is not a major reason to source worldwide, countertrade can be a greater factor in international business.

React to Sourcing Patterns of Competitors This is probably the least mentioned reason for worldwide sourcing because most firms do not want to admit they are reacting to the practices of competitors. Imitating the action of competitors is the "fashion and fear" motive. A purchaser may try to duplicate the factors that provide an advantage to a competitor, which may mean sourcing from the same suppliers or regions of the world that a competitor uses. There may be a belief that not sourcing in the same region(s) may create a competitive disadvantage.

Establish a Presence in a Foreign Market Marketing may have plans to sell to a foreign market where it currently does no business. As a way of developing goodwill with a foreign country, purchasing may first choose to source certain items from that country. The business relationship with members of the foreign country may later support an expanded marketing presence.

There are three major reasons why establishing a local supply base is a critical component of international market expansion.[4]

SOURCING SNAPSHOT

Thinking Globally and Buying Locally at Sony

Countless organizations today are facing this scenario: They are expanding production facilities or distribution networks in a new country, and they must develop localized sources of supply to meet local content regulations or minimize transportation costs. An alternative to this scenario is to develop suppliers with the ability to supply multiple global facilities equally well. The configuration of the supply base must be carefully considered through a detailed risk assessment that takes advantage of leveraging opportunities, without exposing production facilities to inordinate levels of supply risk. At Sony, the basic global procurement strategy has been to procure local parts (PLP) whenever possible, and to produce in those countries where the countries' products are sold. In Europe, approximately 90% of the company's product value is localized; in Asia 30% to 50% is localized. The company also has two factories in China and one in Korea. The PLP approach accounts for more than 90% of U.S. business. When production is shifted to a new area, local suppliers are developed whenever possible. As a backup, Sony often negotiates with Japanese suppliers to ship parts to the new production facilities. If no suitable local supplier can be found, purchasing may negotiate with the Japanese supplier to set up local production in the new country of operation. Sony does not contribute capital to suppliers to set up offshore production facilities but will help them with training of personnel at new locations. Thus the general policy is to produce as many parts locally at each location as possible. The only exception involves optical parts and semiconductors, which are shipped from Japan to its worldwide production locations.

Source: Adapted from: Robert Handfield and Daniel Krause, "Think Globally, Source Locally," *Supply Chain Management Review* (Winter 1999): 36–49.

- The total cost to import products from the United States, Japan, or Europe to emerging countries is often prohibitive. Managers have claimed that the cost of shipping heavy and bulky goods is often twice the value of the part itself. If one also considers the cost of warranty, field service, and other important factors, the costs become even more difficult to manage. From a cost standpoint, developing a local source becomes imperative.
- In order to encourage technology transfer and increase employment levels, governments are increasingly enforcing domestic content laws requiring that manufacturers purchase a significant percentage of their parts and components domestically. Senior management has begun to understand that if "the world is your market, then the world must be your supplier."
- Competition is perhaps the most obvious but often overlooked reason. In order to gain access to the lowest costs, cutting-edge technology, and best capabilities, organizations must scan the global landscape in search of the best suppliers. By aligning

EXHIBIT 11.1   *International Versus Domestic Supplier Performance*

Performance Criteria	Firms Using International Sources	Firms Using Domestic Sources Only
Percentage using JIT	32.0%	61.5%
Quality (% nondefective lots)	94.5%	96.7%
Delivery (% on-time delivery)	84.7%	91.2%
Lead time (weeks)	10.7 weeks	5.5 weeks
Delivered lot size (day's supply)	36.5 days	21.8 days
On-hand inventory at buyer's plant (week's supply)	5.6 weeks	3.3 weeks
Number of alternate suppliers	2.2	2.3
Percentage of requirements from single source	61.3%	75.1%

Source: Robert Handfield, "Global Sourcing: Pattens of Development," *International Journal of Operations and Production Management* 14, no. 6 (1994): 40–51.

technology roadmaps with leading-edge suppliers, designers can ensure that their products and services will truly be "world-class," not just "the best in the region."

While the exact reasons each company sources internationally will vary, they surely include some of those discussed here. Without access to worldwide sources of supply, companies may not remain competitive. A domestic company that purchases a portion of its material requirements worldwide is better than a domestic company that is no longer in business due to its inability to meet global competition.

Even with the reasons presented here, worldwide sourcing presents trade-offs that must be managed, as illustrated in Exhibit 11.1. Of the companies using domestic sources only, 62% were also implementing just-in-time (JIT) programs. Of the companies using international sources, only 32% were implementing JIT programs. JIT involves daily (or sometimes hourly) deliveries, elimination of receiving and inspection, and quick response through an electronic ordering system. It also requires a responsive logistics system that is capable of making regular pick-ups of smaller lot sizes so that less inventory is kept on hand. JIT purchasing programs are difficult to implement with foreign sources, largely due to the difficulty of coordinating logistics systems. Exhibit 11.1 also shows that companies using domestic suppliers performed better in on-time delivery, lead times, delivered lot sizes, and on-hand inventory of critical material.

Barriers to Worldwide Sourcing

Companies with little or no international experience often face obstacles or barriers when beginning worldwide sourcing. The major barrier is the lack of understanding of international purchasing procedures. This includes a lack of knowledge about potential sources of supply and/or a lack of familiarity about the additional documentation required with international purchasing. International documentation requirements include letters of credit, multiple bills of lading, dock receipts, import licenses, certificates of origin, inspection certificates, certificates of insurance coverage, packing lists, and commercial invoices.

Resistance to change from an established, routine procedure or shifting from a long-standing supplier is also a major barrier. It is natural to resist changes that represent a radical departure from existing ways of doing business. Domestic market nationalism has also sometimes presented itself as a barrier. Buyers are sometimes reluctant to shift business from domestic sources to unknown foreign sources. Home market nationalism, while not the obstacle it was 15 or 20 years ago, can still be an issue. The riots in Seattle protesting the World Trade Organization in December 1999 highlighted the resentment of several groups toward free trade and global sourcing. The decision to purchase domestically versus overseas should not be made on an emotional basis but should be based on solid analysis that weighs the quantitative and qualitative advantages and disadvantages of each alternative.

Another barrier involves the changes required to accommodate longer lead times and lengthened material pipelines. With longer lead times, accurate material forecasts over extended time periods become critical. Buyers must manage delivery dates closely because of the possibility of in-transit or customs delays. International sourcing also introduces an additional degree of logistical, political, and financial risk.

Other barriers relate to a lack of knowledge about foreign business practices, language, and cultural differences. Negotiations with foreign suppliers can be more difficult. Simple engineering or delivery change requests can become frustrating experiences.

U.S. companies have been creative in overcoming such barriers to worldwide sourcing. The following is only a small sample of the approaches used to overcome worldwide sourcing barriers:

- The most common method for overcoming barriers involves education and training, which can generate support for the process as well as help overcome the anxiety associated with change.
- Publicizing success stories can show the performance benefits that worldwide purchasing provides.
- Communication problems in engineering have been reduced by using globally linked computer-aided design (CAD) systems. With these systems, engineers and purchasing managers can look at a drawing and understand the universal language of design without having to translate words.
- Some companies work with only those foreign suppliers who have U.S.-based support personnel.
- Some companies have created a measurement and reward system that encourages sourcing from the best suppliers worldwide. For example, firms can measure and reward buyers based on their ability to realize performance benefits from the selected use of international sources.
- The use of third-party or external agents can prove valuable, particularly when first beginning worldwide sourcing. Using brokers can be an efficient way to "get your feet wet" in worldwide sourcing. Over time, companies may wish to

WESCO Helps Customers Outsource International MRO Buying

WESCO International has formed a new business unit to support global customers interested in outsourcing their international procurement requirements. The new division, Bruckner International Group, specializes in sourcing, negotiating, purchasing, and delivery of a wide range of maintenance, repair, and operating (MRO) supplies. Bruckner International has established operations worldwide directed from three procurement centers staffed with experienced multinational procurement professionals. The company has customer relationships with international oil and gas firms, and is currently providing sourcing and procurement services in support of operating units located in 34 countries. Business is transacted in multiple currencies with an established base of more than 15,000 suppliers.

"We use a unique global procurement network, maintaining continuous contact between our three procurement centers, to offer worldwide 24-hour customer support," says Russ Lambert, general manger and director of Bruckner International. "Since products are sourced from a large number of local and multinational suppliers," he adds, "we maintain extensive records on the cost and availability of thousands of products in different parts of the world to make sure we deliver the lowest cost of procurement and ownership regardless of location."

Source: Adapted from "WESCO Forms New Unit for Global Customers," *Purchasing* 124, no. 8 (May 20, 1999): 111.

insource this function as the volume of overseas purchases increases. For example, FedEx acquired Tower, a major international broker firm, in 2000 due to the high volume of customer transactions it performs in its daily operations that were previously outsourced.

Regardless of the technique used to overcome worldwide sourcing barriers, the effort will fail unless top management demonstrates its support for international procurement. Management must send the message that international sourcing is a means to remain competitive by using only world-class suppliers and does not represent an effort to force domestic suppliers out of business.

THE INTERNATIONAL SOURCING PROCESS

Companies often follow a structured approach when pursuing international sourcing, as shown in Exhibit 11.2. This section discusses key portions of the international sourcing process in greater detail. Although the sequence of this process may vary from organization to organization, each step must be completed at some point to successfully complete an international purchase.

EXHIBIT 11.2   *The International Sourcing Process*

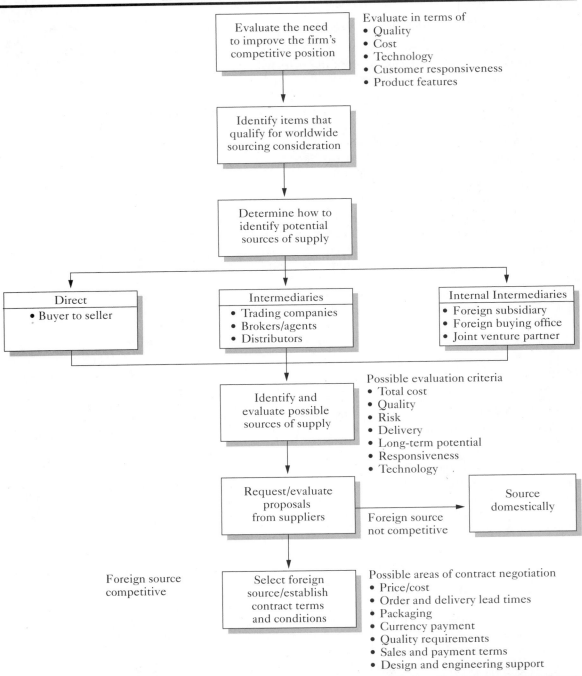

Selecting Items to Get Started

For those unfamiliar with international sourcing, getting started for the first time is a learning experience. The initial attempt at foreign buying can influence the success or failure of the overall international sourcing process. Almost any item purchased locally is available internationally, especially basic, commodity-type items. Companies should select items for foreign purchase evaluation that offer an opportunity for quality, cost, or delivery benefits yet do not represent an unusual level of risk. A good first step involves selecting one or more items to evaluate. Here are some suggestions about how to select initial items if a manager is considering international sourcing for the first time.[5]

- Select items that are noncritical to ongoing operations. Commodity-type items or items available from multiple sources are good candidates. Once enough experience has been developed with such an item, other types of items can be included.
- Select items with standard or easily understood specifications.
- Select items with sufficiently high purchase volumes to justify the effort associated with international sourcing.
- Select items at a stage in the product life cycle that will provide sufficient benefit for longer-term sourcing.
- Select items that require relatively standard equipment.
- Identify items that are not competitive along some key performance criterion such as cost or quality.

These criteria are important because if the international source fails to meet the buyer's expectations, domestic alternatives must be found on relatively short notice. Another factor contributing to initial success includes keeping other departments informed about the items being considered for international sourcing. Also, potential suppliers should receive extended schedules of quantity and delivery requirements.

Obtaining Information About Worldwide Sources

After identifying potential items to source worldwide, a company must gather and evaluate information on potential suppliers or identify intermediaries capable of that task. This can prove challenging if a company is inexperienced or has limited outside contacts or sources of information. The following sources can provide valuable leads when identifying potential suppliers or trade intermediaries.

International Industrial Directories Industrial directories, which are increasingly available through the Internet, are a major source of information about suppliers by industry or region of the world. Hundreds of directories are available that identify potential international contacts. Here are some examples:

- *Principal International Businesses: The World Marketing Directory:* Covers 50,000 major businesses in all lines having high sales volume and at least an interest in foreign trade; published by Dun and Bradstreet. Entries include the company's line of business and industry code.

- *Marconi's International Register:* Details 45,000 firms worldwide conducting business internationally; lists products geographically under 3,500 product headings.
- *ABC Europe Production:* Covers 130,000 European manufacturers who export their products.
- *Business Directory of Hong Kong:* Details Hong Kong firms, including manufacturers, importers, exporters, banks, construction, transportation, and service companies.
- *Japan Yellow Pages:* Provides information about manufacturers, traders, service firms, and other businesses in Japan and classifies them by line of business and city.

Trade Shows   Trade shows are often one of the best ways to gather information on many suppliers at one time. These industrial shows occur throughout the world for practically every industry. Most business libraries have a directory that lists worldwide trade shows. Internet searches will also reveal the time and place of industrial trade shows, including how to register. Examples include the Detroit Auto Show (every January) and the Computer World show held annually in Silicon Valley. With a minimal amount of research, purchasers can identify trade shows related directly to their purchasing needs.

Companies interested in foreign purchasing should not ignore U.S. trade shows. The larger and more established shows will feature suppliers from around the world as exhibitors. These shows provide an opportunity to establish sourcing contacts and to gather information about many products and producers at one time.

Trading Companies   Trading companies offer a full range of services to assist purchasers. These companies will issue letters of credit and pay brokers, customs, dock fees, insurance, ocean carrier, and inland freight bills. Clients usually receive one itemized invoice for the total services performed. One U.S.-based trading company offers more than 20 services including finding qualified sources, performing product quality audits, supplier evaluations, contract negotiations, total logistical management, preshipment inspection, expediting, and duty classifications. The use of a full-service trading company may actually result in a lower total cost for international purchases compared with performing each activity connected individually. Foreign trading companies, such as Mitsubishi and Mitsui of Japan, maintain offices worldwide. Most of these companies have a long history of trade and have the expertise to provide full-service support throughout the world.

External Agents   Experts are available to provide international sourcing assistance. Independent agents, working on commission, will act as purchasing representatives in a foreign country. They locate sources of supply, evaluate the source, and handle the required paperwork and documentation. Some agents also provide full-service capability or can arrange for full-service capability. Agents are an option when a company lacks foreign expertise or a presence in a foreign market.

Import brokers are also an option. They help locate foreign suppliers and act as intermediaries between the buyer and seller. Direct manufacturer's representatives or sales representatives can also be a source of valuable information. Such individuals work directly for sellers as their representatives in a country. Purchasers can deal directly with the representative without leaving their home country. Many international banks and financial institutions also have personnel capable of providing information about foreign sources. Finally, different state and federal agencies encourage and promote international trade. Services provided by these agencies are usually reasonable in cost.

Trade Consulates Purchasers can contact foreign trade consulates located in major cities across the United States for information. Almost all consulates have trade experts who are eager to do business with American buyers. Purchasers can also contact U.S. embassies located overseas to inquire about suppliers located in a particular country. The U.S. Department of Commerce also has offices staffed by trade specialists that offer several good services at a nominal fee. There are several free Websites and sources for obtaining information:

*   International Trade Association
    8383 E. Evans Road
    Scottsdale, AZ 85260
    Tel: (602) 483-0001
    Fax: (602) 998-8002
    http://ami.org/ita.html
    http://www.ita.doc.gov
*   World Trade Organization
    http://www.unicc.org/wto
*   Organization for Economic Cooperation and Development (OECD)
    OECD Washington Center
    2001 L St. NW Suite 650
    Washington, DC
    20036-4922
    Tel: (800) 456-OECD
    http://www.oecdwash.org

Internal Sources These sources include the use of foreign subsidiaries, foreign buying offices a company may have established, or international joint venture partners. Foreign partners will have greater experience with suppliers in their part of the world or have contacts who can get the required information.

Other Sources Other potential sources include yellow page directories for a country or city, trade journals, and sales brochures and catalogs.

The amount and type of information required is partly a function of how a purchaser chooses to handle the foreign purchase. Purchasers who use intermediaries, such as trading companies and external agents, must search for information that identifies the best intermediaries. Purchasers who control the buying must obtain information about suppliers through trade directories, trade shows, embassies, supplier representatives, and other sources of international information.

SOURCING SNAPSHOT

Ford Motor Company—Creating a Global Supply Base

Ford Motor Company is one of the world's leading manufacturers of automobiles and trucks. Purchased materials and parts account for approximately 60% of its average total cost of manufacturing. Ford purchases in Canada, Japan, Mexico, Germany, Brazil, and many other countries. Although Ford has been purchasing internationally for years, increased emphasis has been placed on evaluating worldwide suppliers since the late 1970s to identify world-class quality, cost, and technology providers. In recent years, Ford has sought to extend this program into an integrated "Ford 2000" procurement strategy. The objective of this approach is to develop a common set of automotive platforms to be manufactured worldwide—that is, components for automobiles are designed, manufactured, and purchased worldwide, but integrated into a common set of platforms, which are also assembled worldwide.

To create a lean supply chain, Ford has developed a system of dedicated daily deliveries, which has been implemented in all of its assembly plants. The daily deliveries consist of one day's worth of production materials from suppliers in close proximity to the demand location. Although Ford does not require its international suppliers to open warehouses in the United States, the ability of a supplier to make JIT deliveries from a local warehouse is considered during the supplier selection decision. The most frequent delivery from an international source is once a week, due to transportation economics.

Ford works with and trains foreign suppliers as needed; the effort required varies by country and type of company. In general, suppliers in developed countries require less support than suppliers in less-developed countries. A number of Ford's foreign suppliers assign engineering and design staffs to the United States to facilitate working relationships. Ford is also developing a fully integrated information system to further link the company with its worldwide suppliers.

Source: Interviews with company manager.

Evaluating Sources of Supply

Whether the purchaser or an external agent coordinates the international purchase, foreign suppliers must be subject to the same performance evaluation and standards as (or perhaps even more rigorous than) domestic suppliers. Do not assume that a foreign company can automatically satisfy a buyer's performance requirements or expectations. Here are some of the questions to ask when evaluating foreign sources:

- Does a significant total cost difference exist between the domestic and foreign source?
- Will the foreign supplier maintain these differences over time?

- How stable is the foreign supplier's price?
- What is the effect of longer material pipelines and increased average inventory levels?
- What are the supplier's technical and quality capabilities?
- Can the supplier assist with new designs?
- Does the supplier employ rigorous quality control techniques?
- Is the supplier capable of consistent delivery schedules?
- How much lead time does the supplier require?
- Can we develop a longer-term relationship with this supplier?
- Are patents and proprietary technology safe with this supplier? Is the supplier trustworthy?
- How will foreign purchasing affect relations with domestic suppliers?

Sometimes trial orders are used to evaluate foreign sources. Purchasers are usually not willing to rely initially on a foreign source for an entire purchase requirement. A buyer can use smaller or trial orders to begin to establish a supplier's performance track record.

Awarding the Purchase Contract

After identifying what it believes are qualified suppliers, the purchaser can solicit detailed proposals. If a foreign source is not competitive (as determined by a review of the proposals), then a purchaser can select a domestic source. If the foreign supplier satisfies a buyer's criteria for initial supplier selection, then the buyer can begin to negotiate contract terms and conditions. As with any supplier, a buyer must continuously measure the supplier's performance throughout the life of the agreement.

ORGANIZING FOR WORLDWIDE SOURCING

An organization's current structure strongly influences how it will organize for worldwide sourcing. Exhibit 11.3 highlights how worldwide sourcing fits into a highly decentralized organization. In this exhibit, each strategic business unit (SBU) is organized as an individual profit center and is responsible for managing its own activities. Organizations are often structured by product line or the characteristics of major-customer market segments. Consider, for example, a high-tech electronics manufacturer. One business unit may be responsible for military production and sales, another unit for the manufacture of electronic components to the computer industry, while a third business unit manufactures and markets consumer electronics. Each unit has a different market focus and product line. Accordingly, each exists almost as its own business with individual support functions. A decentralized organizational structure is a fairly common approach for companies with highly differentiated product lines or market segments with few common characteristics. Within a

EXHIBIT 11.3   *International Sourcing in a Decentralized Firm*

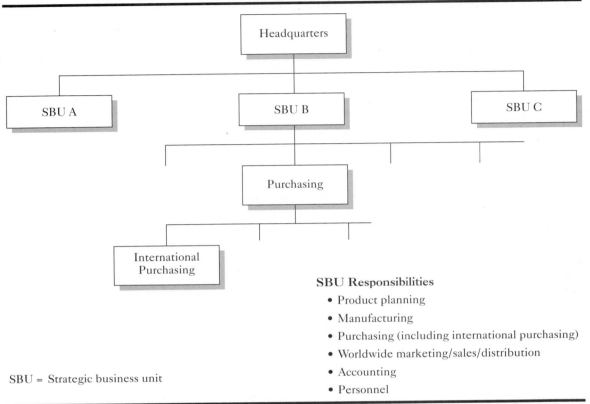

SBU Responsibilities

- Product planning
- Manufacturing
- Purchasing (including international purchasing)
- Worldwide marketing/sales/distribution
- Accounting
- Personnel

SBU = Strategic business unit

decentralized structure, each business unit is responsible for both domestic and international purchasing.

How does worldwide sourcing fit within a centralized purchasing structure? Exhibit 11.4 diagrams one possible organizational structure. In a centralized or coordinated environment, commodity managers are responsible for commonly purchased items across the organization. International purchasing managers work alongside the commodity managers, and report to the corporate executive responsible for purchasing. In this exhibit, regional buying offices cover South America, the Far East, and Europe.

When evaluating whether a company is ready for global sourcing, four major elements should be considered:

1. *Corporate global vision: Does the organization create an effective global vision as a primary driver for investing resources and effort in seeking global suppliers?* Without an "ideal" vision of what the organization is attempting to accomplish, managers at different locations throughout the world will have difficulty coordinating strategic

EXHIBIT 11.4   *International Sourcing in a Centralized Firm*

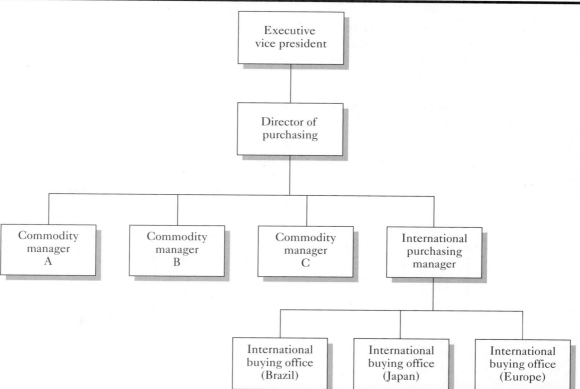

business unit strategies and functional goals. As organizations seek to expand their global operations, an effective vision serves as the primary force for development and deployment of a global supply base.

2. *Management structure and systems: Is the company effectively organized to promote coordination among the different global strategic business units?* Best-in-class companies have invested in enabling structures and systems to deploy their global vision. These enablers include the following: (1) global commodity councils and reporting systems to facilitate communication among the different business units; (2) international purchasing offices (IPOs) and contacts with government agencies to promote sharing of expertise and knowledge regarding regional sourcing opportunities; (3) improved total cost models for decision making; and (4) global information systems capable of providing sourcing information to global production and design sites.

3. *Sourcing strategy: Configuring the global supply base: Are sourcing strategies developed to optimize the mix of local suppliers and transplant suppliers?* As organizations set up production in new regions, they often discover that some mix of local and global

suppliers is optimal. However, the mix may change as they gain experience with local suppliers.

4. *Supplier development: Is the sourcing organization deploying resources to ensure that suppliers' capabilities are aligned with the competitive and manufacturing strategies?* Supplier development approaches vary in different regions according to the specific types of problems encountered. Approaches focus on either using process specialists to attack isolated technical problems or applying a full-scale intervention when systemic problems are traced to poor management practices within the supplier's organization.

A logical approach toward meeting a company's growing worldwide sourcing requirements has been the establishment of IPOs in selected areas around the world. Foreign nationals, who usually report directly to a centralized corporate procurement office, staff the IPO. IPOs can support the sourcing needs of the entire organization, not just a single division or buying unit. The IPO has several major functions:

1. Identify foreign suppliers for company operations.
2. Solicit quotes from foreign sources.
3. Expedite and trace shipments.
4. Negotiate supply contracts.
5. Make sure the buyer and seller understand all communications.
6. Obtain product samples.
7. Manage technical problems.
8. Be a firm's sole representative to a foreign supplier.
9. Manage countertrade activities.
10. Obtain design and engineering support.

A centralized structure allows the domestic buyer and commodity manager to concentrate on the activities they perform best. Commodity managers develop corporate contracts for common goods and services. The division or plant purchasing managers concentrate on identifying capable domestic suppliers for the items for which they are responsible. The international purchasing offices search their region of the world to identify potential foreign sources. The end result of this process is a purchasing structure that is able to choose among the world's best suppliers to meet an organization's purchase requirements.

Companies may also create a hybrid structure that contains elements of decentralized and centralized decision making. Exhibit 11.5 shows a structure with decentralized purchasing at the divisional or business unit level with a centralized international purchasing office that supports the different operating or business units.

A company that gains little from worldwide sourcing will not establish international offices or create worldwide information networks. Simply stated, not all organizations require specialized international purchasing expertise. The organizational structure and capabilities of Hewlett-Packard (high-technology electronics) will be different from Ralston Purina (pet food) because of a different emphasis on international sourcing. The international purchasing structure of these two firms will reflect this difference.

EXHIBIT 11.5   *Decentralized Purchasing with Centralized International Purchasing*

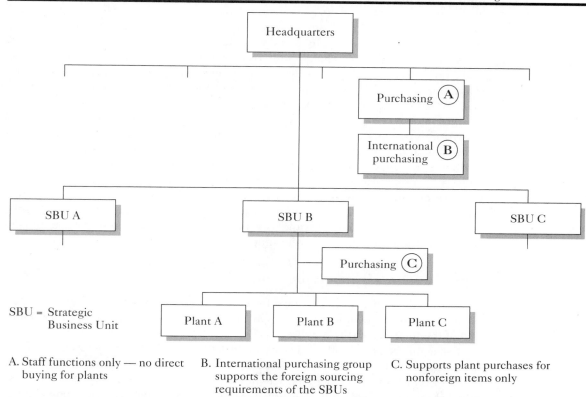

SBU = Strategic
Business Unit

A. Staff functions only — no direct
buying for plants

B. International purchasing group
supports the foreign sourcing
requirements of the SBUs

C. Supports plant purchases for
nonforeign items only

Costs Associated with Worldwide Sourcing

Purchasers must examine closely the additional costs associated with worldwide
sourcing. This is one area that requires a *total cost perspective*. The case study focusing
on Guava Puree, located at the back of this book, illustrates the point that unit cost
does not equal total cost, particularly as it relates to worldwide sourcing.

Whether the purchase transaction is with a domestic or foreign producer, certain
common costs exist. The difference between domestic and foreign purchasing, however, is that foreign purchasing must include the additional costs associated with conducting overseas transactions. If price is a major factor, then a buyer must compare
the total cost of the foreign purchase to the total cost of the domestic purchase.

Common Costs

Certain costs are common between domestic and foreign purchasing. These costs include the unit purchase price quoted by a supplier, tooling charges, and transportation

from the supplier (common costs does not mean the costs are equal). If the item requires tooling, purchasing must compare the benefit of owning versus not owning the tooling. Unit price evaluation must consider the effect of quantity breaks, minimum buys necessary for shipping efficiency, the effect on price due to rush shipments, and any supplier-specified surcharges or extras. Transportation costs also require critical evaluation. For example, what is the effect on transportation costs if the purchaser controls a shipment directly from the supplier instead of having the supplier arrange shipment? What is the effect on transportation costs due to longer distances?

International transportation often requires assistance from personnel with special expertise. A transportation group can review carrier quotations, evaluate shipping alternatives, and recommend the most efficient course of action, which may include combining international shipments with other purchasers to realize favorable freight rates. A firm may also contract with international carriers for dedicated delivery services. International transportation is usually a major part of the total cost of international purchasing. Allowing a supplier to arrange transportation may not result in the most cost-efficient method possible. It will, however, usually represent the most convenient method of shipment for the supplier.

International Transaction Costs

International purchasing can create additional costs that are not part of domestic purchasing. Failure to include these costs in a total cost analysis can lead to a miscalculation of the total cost of the purchase.

Packaging requirements and costs are usually higher with foreign purchases due to the longer distances traveled and increased handling of shipments. Packaging engineers may be able to develop packaging designs that minimize this cost on international shipments. Each item entering a country is also subject to a customs duty or tariff. A purchaser can hire a customs broker to help move the material through customs at the lowest legal rate. Duty rates vary widely over seemingly small differences between items. A knowledgeable customs broker may lower duty costs as well as expedite the shipment through customs. Total cost analysis must include any duty and broker fees incurred during the international transaction.

International shipments often have insurance protection. This issue is important, since unlike domestic transportation, oceangoing carrier liability is generally limited. Insurance is usually required when a third party is financing the inventory or shipment, and is provided by large firms such as Lloyd's of London.

Other costs include port terminal and handling fees. Depending on the exact terms of the purchase contract, a purchaser can expect charges for unloading of cargo, administrative services of port authority personnel, and general use of the port; these are U.S. port terminal and handling charges. Exhibit 11.6 provides a general list of costs that can increase the total cost of international purchasing.

A critical factor in international purchasing is keeping the surprises that affect total cost and customer service to a minimum. For example, if a shipment arrives in Los Angeles without proper documentation, customs will place the shipment in warehouse storage awaiting documentation. Whether a buyer or seller pays the storage charges should be clear in the event this issue arises.

EXHIBIT 11.6   *Elements of Total Cost for International Sourcing*

Base Price
- Ascertain quantity breaks, minimum buys for shipping efficiency, and any surcharges.
- Determine price for rush shipments of smaller than planned quantities, which are often more.

Tooling
- Ideally, the purchaser should own the tooling and pay for it only once.
- Consider shipping tooling from a domestic source if transferable.

Packaging
- This is a hidden cost (may be expensive for long distances and multiple handlings).
- Consult a packaging supplier or internal engineer for methods to minimize cost on international shipments.
- Don't forget about disposition of packaging materials—it can be expensive in certain countries.

Escalation
- Determine for how long the quoted price is firm.
- Determine components of escalation (i.e., ensure that price increases are not hidden in other costs).

Transportation
- Obtain assistance from logistics personnel who have expertise in international transportation.
- Consider consolidation of shipments with other corporations from the same geographical area.
- Use multinational carriers or freight brokers to manage shipments and cost where required.
- Consult the foreign supplier as a source of information regarding freight sources.

Customs Duty
- Duties paid any time a shipment crosses international lines—can vary widely over range of goods, and often change on short notice.
- Provided by U.S. Published Tariff Schedules.
- Items may fall into more than one classification.
- May be best to discuss this with a customs agent/broker.

Insurance Premiums
- Not typically included in an ocean shipment price (need marine insurance).
- Don't pay for extra coverage that your company may already carry for international transactions.

Payment Terms
- Foreign suppliers often grant longer payment terms such as net 60.
- If dealing with intermediaries, the payment may be requested upon shipment.

Additional Fees and Commissions
- Keep surprises to a minimum.
- Ask supplier, customs broker, and transportation personnel if other costs may be incurred, and who is responsible for these costs.
- If your shipment is held at the port of entry due to a lack of documentation and customs officials place it in storage, a storage fee will be billed to the customer. (Who will pay for this?)

Port Terminal and Handling Fees
- U.S. port and handling charges (unloading cargo, administrative services of port personnel, and use of port).

(continued)

EXHIBIT 11.6   *(continued)*

Customs Broker Fees
- Flat charge per transaction.

Taxes
- Consider any additional taxes that may be paid.

Communication Costs
- Higher phone, travel, mailing, telex, fax, e-mail charges.
Payment and currency fees.
- Bank transfers, bills of exchange, hedging and forward contracts.

Inventory Carrying Costs
- Higher levels of inventory will have to be held due to longer lead times.
- Costs include the interest rate forgone by investing funds, insurance, property taxes, storage and obsolescence (check with controller).
- Internal carrying costs are typically 15% to 25%.

Total carrying cost = Average inventory in units × unit price × carrying cost per year

Source: Adapted from Robert M. Monczka and Larry C. Giunipero, *Purchasing Internationally: Concepts and Principles* (Chelsea, MI: Bookcrafters, 1990).

MANAGING INTERNATIONAL CURRENCY RISK

A major concern with international purchasing is managing the risk associated with international currency fluctuations. Because of this risk, companies often take steps to reduce the uncertainty associated with fluctuating currencies.

The following example illustrates the principle of currency fluctuation and risk. Suppose a U.S. company purchased a machine from Canada in June. The purchase is denominated in Canadian dollars at $100,000 paid upon delivery in November. For simplicity, assume the exchange rate in June is $1 U.S. equals $1 Canadian. By November, however, the Canadian dollar has strengthened to the point where $1 U.S. equals $.90 Canadian (it now takes less than a Canadian dollar to purchase a U.S. dollar; the Canadian currency is now relatively stronger). Now, $100,000 U.S. only equals $90,000 Canadian. This firm needs $100,000 Canadian to pay for the machine, or $100,000 U.S./.9 exchange rate = $111,111 U.S. If the purchaser does not protect itself from fluctuating currencies, the machine would cost $11,111 more than originally planned. On the other hand, if the U.S. dollar strengthened against the Canadian dollar during this period, the purchase would require fewer U.S. dollars in November to buy $100,000 Canadian dollars.

Approaches to Currency Risk Management

Companies use a variety of measures to address the risk associated with currency fluctuations. These range from very basic measures to the sophisticated management of international currencies involving the corporate finance department.

Purchase in U.S. Dollars Buyers who prefer to pay for international purchases in U.S. dollars are attempting to eliminate currency fluctuations as a source of risk by shifting the risk to the seller. In the previous example, the purchaser would have paid for the Canadian machine in November with $100,000 U.S. funds regardless of the exchange rate. It would have been up to the Canadian firm selling the machine to manage the exchange rate risk.

While this appears to be an easy method of risk management, it is not always the best or most feasible approach. The foreign supplier, who is also aware of currency risks, may be unwilling to accept the risk of currency fluctuations by itself. Also, many foreign suppliers anticipate exchange rate fluctuations by incorporating a risk factor into their price. A purchaser willing to accept some of the risk may obtain a favorable price. While purchasing in U.S. dollars is sometimes an alternative, it does not apply to all international purchasing transactions.

Sharing Currency Fluctuation Risk Equal sharing of risk permits a selling firm to price its product without having to factor in the acceptance of risk costs. Simply stated, sharing of risk requires equal division of a change in an agreed-upon price due to currency fluctuation. In the Canadian machine example, the U.S. firm realizes over $11,000 in additional costs due to currency fluctuations. With equal risk sharing, the Canadian and U.S. firms would divide evenly the additional cost.

Currency Adjustment Contract Clauses With currency adjustment clauses, both parties agree that payment occurs as long as exchange rates do not fluctuate outside an agreed-upon range or band. If exchange rates move outside the agreed-upon range, the parties can renegotiate or review the contract. This provides a mutual degree of protection because firms do not know with certainty in which direction exchange rates will fluctuate.

Purchase contracts often contain one of two types of currency adjustment clauses: *delivery-triggered clauses* and *time-triggered clauses*. Delivery-triggered clauses stipulate that the parties will review an exchange before delivery to verify the rate is still within the agreed-upon range. If the rate falls outside the range, the buyer or seller can ask to renegotiate the contract price. Time-triggered clauses stipulate that both parties will review a contract at specified time intervals to evaluate the impact of fluctuating exchange rates. The parties review the exchange rate at scheduled intervals and a new contract is established if the rate falls outside the agreed-upon range. Exhibits 11.7 and 11.8 show examples of a delivery- and time-triggered renegotiation clause.

To summarize, a currency adjustment clause offers some attractive features:

- Allows the buying firm to pay in its own currency
- Eliminates settlement problems on minor currency fluctuations
- Allows for renegotiation of contract payment terms due to major currency fluctuations
- Saves the cost of purchasing forward contracts
- Saves the cost of hedging foreign purchases

EXHIBIT 11.7   *Example of a Delivery-Triggered Renegotiation Clause*

A contract for 3,000 castings with Nippon Steel is issued on June 1, with delivery of 1,000 castings to be on June 30, July 30, and August 30. A currency adjustment clause was written into the contract establishing an exchange rate of 100 yen per dollar (spot rate), ± 4%. The quoted price is $20 per unit.

1. Fixed currency rate is established.
2. Upper and lower boundaries are established (±4%).
3. If currency exceeds upper or lower bound, renegotiation may be requested by either party.

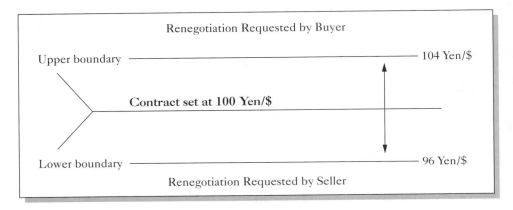

June 30: Yen appreciates to 90 yen per dollar; price renegotiated to $20.50 per unit.

July 30: Yen is at 97 yen per dollar; no reopening required.

August 30: Yen has depreciated to 100 yen per dollar; no reopening required.

Source: Robert M. Monczka and Larry C. Giunipero, *Purchasing Internationally: Concepts and Principles* (Chelsea, MI: Bookcrafters, 1990).

- Enables a buyer to offer a flexible payment mechanism during negotiations
- Is attractive to suppliers and therefore helps stimulate competition for a purchase

Currency Hedging   Hedging involves the simultaneous purchase and sale of currency contracts in two markets. The expected result is that a gain realized on one contract will be offset by a loss on the other. Hedging is a form of risk insurance that can protect both parties from currency fluctuations. The motivation for using hedging is risk aversion, not monetary gain. If the purpose of buying currency contracts is to realize a net gain, then the purchaser is speculating and not hedging.

Hedging involves entering into an agreement to purchase a set amount of a currency after a specified period of time. This period is usually between the time the parties enter into a contract for foreign goods and when delivery occurs and payment is due. Hedging can be undertaken by purchasing a futures exchange contract or a forward exchange contract. Both types of contracts involve currency purchases on the spot currency market.

EXHIBIT 11.8   *Example of a Time-Triggered Renegotiation Clause*

An annual contract with Nippon Steel for 1,000 castings per month to be delivered is issued. Nippon Steel will be paid in yen. A time-triggered currency clause is negotiated with adjustments to be made quarterly.

1. Currency exchange rate is set on purchase order.
2. Rate may fluctuate within a range (±4%).
3. Payment is made in amount not in excess of lower or upper boundary.
4. Rate is readjusted quarterly for all new purchases at set time intervals.

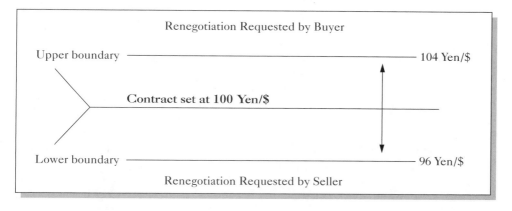

April 1: Yen appreciates to 99 yen per dollar; no readjustment of the contract occurs.

July 1: Yen further appreciates to 97 yen per dollar; no readjustment of the contract occurs.

October 1: Yen appreciates to 93 yen per dollar, which is below the lower boundary; readjustment of the contract may occur.

Source: Robert M. Monczka and Larry C. Giunipero, *Purchasing Internationally: Concepts and Principles* (Chelsea, MI: Bookcrafters, 1990).

Buyers and sellers trade *futures exchange contracts* (also referred to as *futures contracts*) on commodity exchanges open to anyone needing to hedge or with speculative risk capital. In fact, the exchanges encourage speculation because speculators help create markets for buyers and sellers of futures contracts. Traders sell futures contracts in fixed currency amounts with fixed contract lengths.

Forward exchange contracts have a different focus than futures exchange contracts. Issued by major banks, these contracts are agreements by which a purchaser pays a preestablished rate for a currency in the future as well as a fee to the bank. Trading participants include banks, brokers, and multinational companies. The use of forward exchange contracts discourages speculation. Forward exchange contracts meet the needs of an individual purchaser in terms of dollar amount and time limit. Institutions trade these contracts worldwide.

A simple example illustrates the use of forward contracts. Let's assume a buying firm purchases 300,000 French motors on September 1 at a cost of four francs each (1,200,000 total francs). Delivery and payment will occur on December 1. The September 1 exchange rate between dollars and francs is $.1530 and the 90-day forward exchange rate is $.1545. (The reason for the difference between the current rate of $.1530 and the 90-day rate of $.1545 is not important in this example.) The purchaser wants protection against possible unfavorable future exchange rate fluctuations. He or she accomplishes this by purchasing a forward contract that locks in the exchange rate at the forward rate of $.1545. The total cost of the contract is $185,400 (300,000 motors × four francs per motor × the forward exchange rate of $.1545) plus the bank's commission. The only cost before December 1 is the forward contract fee or commission. On December 1, the seller delivers the motors and expects payment of 1,200,000 francs (as agreed in the original purchase contract). On December 1, assume the exchange rate has become $.1565 dollar per franc. If the purchaser did not purchase the forward contract locking in the 90-day forward rate, it would cost $187,800 (1,200,000 francs × $.1565) to purchase the 1,200,000 francs required for payment. Purchasing the forward contract helped avoid $2,400 (not counting commissions) in costs, which is the difference between the $187,800 required on December 1 without a forward contract to purchase 1,200,000 francs and the $185,400 required to fulfill contract obligations with the forward contract.

The purchase of the forward contract would actually have resulted in a lost opportunity if exchange rates had fluctuated in the opposite direction. Locking in the exchange rate on September 1 prevented a possible gain from favorable exchange rate fluctuations between September and December. The reason for purchasing a forward contract, however, is to avoid exchange risk by locking in a specified rate. Hedging is simply the transfer of risk to another party who is seeking a gain from exchange rate fluctuations.

Finance Department Expertise   Companies with extensive international experience usually have a finance department that can support international currency requirements. Finance can identify the currency a firm should use for payment based on projections of currency fluctuations. The finance department can also provide advice about hedging, currency forecasts, and whether to seek a new contract or renegotiate an existing one due to currency changes, and it can act as a clearinghouse for foreign currencies to make payment for foreign purchases.

Tracking Currency Movements   Purchasing managers should track the movement of currencies against the dollar over time to identify longer-term changes and sourcing opportunities due to changing economics. For example, the weakening of the U.S. dollar against the Japanese yen and German mark during the late 1980s made U.S. exports more attractive to those countries. Purchases from Japan became more expensive to U.S. buyers in the early to mid-1990s as the Japanese yen strengthened in value from 200 yen to 100 yen per dollar. As a result, a financial incentive existed to source domestically or from countries where exchange rates were more favorable.

COUNTERTRADE

One form of international trade that has increased worldwide during the last 20 years is *countertrade*— a broad term that refers to all international and domestic trade where buyer and seller have at least a partial exchange of goods for goods. This exchange can involve a complete trade of goods for goods or involve some partial payment to a firm in cash. Here are some examples of countertrade:[6]

- General Electric won a $150 million contract over Siemens and Hitachi in Romania because it agreed to market $150 million worth of Romanian products.
- Chrysler finalized a truck sale to Jamaica during the 1980s by arranging for intermediaries to export Jamaican alumina in exchange for the vehicles.
- Under a $20 billion, 20-year contract, Occidental Petroleum agreed to market Soviet ammonia in the West in order to guarantee a long-term market for its phosphate fertilizer in Russia.

Compared with earlier periods, the U.S. government now takes a realistic view of world trading practices. The government no longer opposes all countertrade agreements by U.S. corporations. In fact, the U.S. government itself has entered into several agricultural countertrade agreements involving foreign trading partners. Since 1988, the U.S. government has maintained an interagency group on countertrade through the Office of Barter within the International Trade Administration of the U.S. Department of Commerce.[7]

While most companies have established a countertrade office or department, purchasing is often involved in negotiating and managing countertrade agreements, including determining the market or sales value of countertrade deals or selecting appropriate products to fulfill countertrade requirements.

A country imposes countertrade demands for a number of reasons. First, some countries simply lack the hard currency to purchase imported goods. During the 1970s, rapidly rising oil prices drained the cash reserves of many poorer countries. Many Third World countries required Western multinationals to accept goods as at least partial payment for sales to their country. Once this practice started, it was difficult for countries to cease countertrade requirements. Another reason for countertrade requirements is that countertrade provides a means to sell products in markets in which a country may have otherwise lacked access. A country may rely upon the marketing expertise of multinational companies to market or arrange for marketing of the country's products.

Countertrade demands often arise when several factors are present. Items involving large dollar amounts are prime candidates for countertrade, such as military contracts. Companies can also expect countertrade demands from a country when that country's goods have a low or nondifferentiated perception in the world marketplace. This may include items that are available from many sources, commodity-type items, or items not perceived as technologically superior or having higher quality compared with other available products. Highly valued items or those sought after by the buying country are less susceptible to countertrade demands.

Types of Countertrade

The decision about an acceptable form of countertrade is a major part of the counter-trade process. The five predominant types of countertrade arrangements include (1) barter, (2) counterpurchase, (3) offset, (4) buy-back, and (5) switch trading.

Barter The oldest and most basic form of trading is barter, a process that involves the straight exchange of goods for goods with no exchange of currency. It requires trading parties to enter into a single contract to fulfill trading requirements. Despite its apparent simplicity, barter is one of the least-practiced forms of countertrade to-day. It is perceived as highly restrictive because countries rarely offer their most mar-ketable goods in a barter arrangement. If a company receives goods for payment that it does not want or cannot use, it often turns the countertrade goods over to a trading company that will, for a fee, market them.

Barter differs from other forms of countertrade along several dimensions. Barter involves no exchange of money between parties. Next, a single contract formalizes a barter transaction while other forms of countertrade require two or more contracts. With nonbarter agreements, one contract formalizes the sales agreement between buyer and seller while the second contract details the seller's commitment to pur-chase that country's goods. Finally, barter arrangements usually relate to a specific transaction and cover a period of time shorter than that covered by other arrange-ments. Some nonbarter countertrade arrangements allow the parties to fulfill their contractual obligations over a period of years.

Counterpurchase Counterpurchase requires a selling firm to purchase a speci-fied amount of goods from the country that purchased its products. The amount of goods to be counterpurchased is a percentage of the amount of the original sale. This requirement usually ranges from 5% to 80% of the total value of the transaction but can actually exceed 100% under some circumstances.

This form of countertrade requires a company to fulfill its countertrade require-ment by purchasing products within a country unrelated to its primary business. The countertrading government identifies a list of possible purchase items that will fulfill the countertrade requirement. The purchaser must market the unrelated goods or use a third party to assume those duties, which introduces increased complexity and cost into the transaction.

Let's look at a simple counterpurchase agreement. U.S. company A wants to sell $1 million worth of goods to country B, which practices countertrade. Country B agrees to the purchase if company A agrees to counterpurchase $500,000 of specified goods from country B. This represents a 50% counterpurchase requirement. Both parties sign a contract detailing these obligations. Country B pays company A $1 million in cash for the purchased goods. Company A later fulfills its requirement by purchasing $500,000 worth of goods from country B in cash over an agreed-upon period of time.

Offset Offset agreements, which are closely related to counterpurchase, also require the seller to purchase some agreed-upon percentage of goods from a country over a specified period of time. However, offset agreements allow a company to fulfill its countertrade requirement with any company or industry in the country. The selling firm can purchase items related directly to its business requirements, which offers the purchaser greater flexibility.

Most transactions involving offsets are of high value, and the terms and value of offset deals vary from country to country. Between 1993 and 1995, there were close to 1,700 offset transactions involving U.S. firms. In 1995, of the $7.4 billion in total value of offset deals, the offsets accounted for $6 billion. Over 80% of offsets involve manufactured goods such as electrical machinery, equipment, and aircraft parts.[8]

Buy-Back   Some countertrade authorities also refer to this type of countertrade as *compensation trading*. Buy-back occurs when a firm physically builds a plant in another country or provides a service, equipment, or technology to support the plant. The firm then agrees to take a portion of the plant's output as payment. Countries lacking foreign exchange for payment but rich in natural resources can benefit from this type of countertrade arrangement. For example, Russia has vast reserves of oil, gas, and mineral resources but lacks the technology and infrastructure for mining, refining, and marketing. Opportunities exist for Western companies to provide the plant, equipment, and expertise to bring these resources to market. Aggressive firms can often gain favorable access to a usable or marketable resource by pursuing buy-back arrangements.

Switch Trading   This form of countertrade involves the use of a third-party trader to sell earned counterpurchase credits. Switch trading occurs when a selling company agrees to accept goods from the buying country as partial payment. If the selling company does not want the goods from the country, it can sell, at a discount, the credits for these goods to a third-party trader who sells or markets the goods. The trader charges a fee for handling the transaction. The original selling company must consider the discount and third-party fee when evaluating the total cost of a countertrade arrangement with a country.

Issues to Consider When Evaluating Countertrade

How to Implement Countertrade   Implementing countertrade usually involves a multiple-phase process when evaluating countertrade opportunities. First, the benefits or opportunities gained from countertrade must be assessed. If countertrade opportunities are present, then a countertrade strategy is developed. The strategy, which requires top-management approval, must detail how countertrade will help achieve organizational objectives. If executive management approves the use of countertrade, a firm then organizes for countertrade, including deciding whether to manage countertrade in-house or by a third-party trading company.

Organizing for Countertrade   Existing in-house capability as well as the particular preference of management will influence the structure required for countertrade. One company may insist on total control and be unwilling to rely on outside help. This company will likely establish a specialized internal countertrade group. Another company may lack the personnel or desire to manage the process internally.

A third may manage certain tasks or types of countertrade internally but not others. The final decision about how to organize is a function of existing and potential countertrade capabilities, the operating philosophy of management, the type of countertrade being pursued, and the volume of countertrade proposals.

PROGRESSING FROM DOMESTIC TO GLOBAL SOURCING

As companies develop international sourcing experience, an internationalization of the procurement process takes place. This involves five phases, progressing from domestic purchasing only to the global coordination and integration of common items, processes, designs, technologies, and suppliers across worldwide buying and engineering centers.

Phase 1: Domestic Purchasing Only A Phase 1 company engages in no direct foreign purchasing activities, either because they do not perceive the need or lack the expertise. Domestic sources provide all purchased requirements. This does imply, however, that the purchaser does not use foreign-produced goods to support its operation. Many companies purchase from a domestic supplier or distributor involved in foreign sourcing. Such suppliers are responsible for conducting the international transactions.

During the 1960s and 1970s, most U.S. firms, small and large, operated in this stage. Although the trend was toward increased international business on the marketing side, the global emphasis characterizing the 1990s was not yet a factor. Firms could successfully operate in a Phase 1 mode. And, depending on the industry, some still do today.

Phase 2: Foreign Buying Based on Need A company progresses to Phase 2 because it is confronted with a requirement for which no suitable domestic supplier exists, or because competitors are gaining an advantage due to foreign sourcing. Phase 1 firms often find themselves being driven toward Phase 2 because of triggering events in the supply market. Such an event could be a supply disruption, rapidly changing currency exchange rates, a declining domestic supply base, or the sudden emergence of foreign competitors.

International procurement in this phase is usually limited or performed on an ad hoc basis. A major requirement is the need for information. Buyers often rely on foreign distributors to supply not only material but also information. The international procurement structure and capabilities of the buying unit are usually quite limited.

Phase 3: Foreign Buying as Part of Procurement Strategy Phase 3 represents a realization that a focused international procurement strategy results in significant performance gains. Discussion of proactive international sourcing strategies does not occur until a purchaser reaches this point in the evolutionary process.

SOURCING SNAPSHOT

Bose Works with Carriers and Suppliers to Manage International Purchasing

Companies have different experiences and approaches when developing their worldwide sourcing strategies. Bose Corporation, a manufacturer of some of the world's best-known high-fidelity speakers, is committed to just-in-time manufacturing, even though it has suppliers located in North America, the Far East, and Europe. The company has had to find a way to blend low inventory with buying from distant sources.

Controlling transportation is a central part of Bose's international purchasing strategy. Bose controls its inbound and outbound transportation by taking control of shipments when the supplier turns goods over to a carrier and then relinquishing control only when finished goods are delivered to Bose's customer. To accomplish this task, Bose relies on a limited number of transportation suppliers, with whom it has developed mutually beneficial "partnership" agreements. Bose has a contract with PIE Nationwide, a national less-than-truckload carrier based in Jacksonville, Florida, to handle North American transportation requirements. W.N. Proctor Company, a Boston-based freight forwarder and customs broker, plays a central role in Bose's critical international shipping. Bose also has established an extensive EDI system called "Shipmaster" that allows the company to contact every one of PIE's 230 terminals. If a shipment must be expedited, a message is quickly sent directly to the terminal. What Shipmaster does for domestic freight, ProctorLink does for international cargo. When a shipment goes on a plane or a boat, it goes into the Proctor system. All of the specifications—the boat, customs clearance, etc.—are included, providing the information needed to control the inventory. Proctor also provides hands-on service to Bose, such as selecting overseas agents who help move goods from the Far East to the United States.

Source: Adapted from Bose Corporation sources and public information.

International sourcing strategies developed in this phase view the supply market from a worldwide perspective. The shift from Phase 2 to 3 occurs because of the realization that lower purchase prices and other performance improvements can be derived from foreign sourcing. During this shift, a purchaser develops a worldwide attitude and an awareness of alternate sources that can support the achievement of business goals. Executive management support is critical to the development and implementation of an international procurement strategy.

Phase 3 companies tend to (1) designate certain buyers to manage international purchasing, (2) solicit international help from foreign subsidiaries, and/or (3) rely on international purchasing offices for assistance. Companies that compete in intensely competitive industries should exhibit behavior that is characteristic of Phase 3 firms.

SOURCING SNAPSHOT

Saving Big with Global Buying Agreements

Based on the success of implementing a worldwide sourcing agreement for office suppliers, buyers at Elsag Bailey Process Automation (now part of ABB) are purchasing personal computers, electronic components, and transportation services from global suppliers for sites located throughout North America and Europe. These global buying agreements have helped to reduce purchasing costs at the automation systems and products manufacturer by $15 million annually. Most of these savings are due to consolidating the buys across a number of Elsag Bailey locations worldwide, says Rich Heider, regional procurement director for the Americas. Future cost savings, he says, will come from increased efforts at standardizing these buys and specification changes. About 40 operating companies located in 20 countries make up Elsag Bailey Process Automation.

Global sourcing has been anything but easy for Elsag Bailey. In the past four years, the company has tripled in size. Like many global companies, Elsag Bailey's recent growth is due mainly to acquiring a number of smaller businesses. Working for a company that grows by acquisition can be challenging for a corporate purchasing manager. Businesses that are acquired are accustomed to operating autonomously—they have in place their own purchasing strategies, information systems, and supply base. Gathering data, working across multiple purchasing systems, a reluctance to change from local suppliers, nationalistic buyers, different measuring systems (metric versus U.S.), and different product specifications all combine to make integrated worldwide sourcing a lot harder than it sounds. To overcome these challenges the company has formed a global buying team made up of U.S. and European representatives to manage the global process.

Source: Adapted from Susan Avery, "Office Supplies: First Step in a Global Buying Strategy," *Purchasing* 126, no. 4 (March 25, 1999): 81–84.

The need for a global perspective will force even new firms to adopt a proactive attitude toward worldwide procurement.

Phase 4: Integration of Global Procurement Strategy This phase of the internationalization process occurs when a purchaser realizes greater benefit through the integration and coordination of procurement requirements on a global basis. It represents true global sourcing efforts, as opposed to basic international buying.

Phase 4 represents a highly sophisticated level of global procurement strategy development. As such, the requirements for managing the sourcing process are great. Operating in this phase requires worldwide information systems, personnel with advanced skills and knowledge, coordination mechanisms, an effective organizational structure, and the highest level of executive management support. A later section in this chapter discusses these requirements in greater detail.

The Japanese steel industry provides a good example of how an integrated and coordinated global procurement strategy can provide a competitive advantage.[9] A single Japanese trading company coordinates and conducts negotiations for the procurement of raw materials for the entire steel industry, which provides maximum price/volume leverage. Japanese steel companies rely on long-term contracts, develop supplier capabilities, and promote buyer/supplier partnership arrangements. Accumulating large procurement volumes and using longer-term contracts encourage suppliers to invest in equipment, expand facilities, and develop techniques to increase productivity and reduce costs. As a result of combining integrated procurement and logistics strategies, a country devoid of natural raw materials is able to source, manufacture, and sell a finished product at some of the lowest prices in the world. Coordinated and integrated procurement can begin to provide the same benefits at the firm level that the Japanese have realized at an industry level.

Phase 5: Global Coordination Between Buying and Engineering Design Centers   Phase 5 organizations have all the capabilities of those in Phase 4. In addition, Phase 5 participants proactively integrate and coordinate common items, processes, designs, technologies, and suppliers across worldwide buying and engineering centers. In this phase global sourcing strategy is linked closely to the global strategies of other functional groups, particularly engineering and operations. Also, the design, build, and sourcing functions are assigned to the most capable unit. The vignette opening this chapter featured a company that for many years operated in Phases 3 and 4 but is now aggressively moving to Phase 5.

Assessing the Need for Global Sourcing

Sophisticated global sourcing (Phases 3–5) is not for every company. A smaller manufacturer competing in regional markets against other regional producers probably does not have the need or capability to pursue anything beyond basic international purchasing. An enterprise with a single design and manufacturing facility will not require sophisticated global sourcing systems. The level of international or global sourcing required to remain competitive is a function of four variables: (1) competitive forces, (2) customer requirements, (3) level of worldwide business activity, and (4) the location of the best suppliers for the specific purchase requirement. Once the desired level of worldwide sourcing has been identified, a company should determine the operating requirements to support that level and identify its current sourcing capabilities. Identifying the operating requirements and current capabilities helps highlight any potential gaps between where a firm is and where it should be.

Competitive Forces   Competition is becoming more intense within most industries as a result of stronger domestic and foreign competitors. This creates pressure for continuous improvement in five performance areas: (1) technology, (2) cost, (3) quality, (4) availability and delivery of products and services, and (5) new-product development cycle time. Because suppliers are critical to a purchaser's success in these areas, it is easy to see why competing in intensely competitive industries encourages the development of worldwide purchasing strategies designed to capture the benefit of a world-class supply base.

Customer Requirements Today's customers, both industrial and consumer, are becoming very sophisticated and demanding. They can also pressure firms to improve continuously on a worldwide basis in the five performance areas just discussed. Customer pressure requires sourcing strategies that help satisfy demanding customer requirements.

Level of Worldwide Business Activity A company that produces and sells throughout the world and maintains a global perspective within other functions, such as finance and engineering, should likely develop a stronger worldwide procurement perspective. As a result, it should pursue globally oriented purchasing strategies.

Location of Suppliers for Specific Purchase Requirements The greater the geographic dispersion of qualified suppliers, the more likely it is that a company must develop the systems and structure to coordinate a global sourcing effort. Suppliers of the various components and subassemblies required to support end-item production may be located throughout the world. If this is the case, the systems and structure required to support a geographically diverse supply base will be different than what is required to support local or domestic suppliers.

Global Sourcing Enablers

The advanced integration and coordination of global sourcing strategy requires certain enablers before a company can expect to capture the benefits that global sourcing potentially offers.

Worldwide Information Systems Access to information is perhaps the most important enabler to global sourcing. A purchaser must have the ability to identify the requirements of diverse geographic production and buying centers. A worldwide purchasing information system must have the following characteristics:

- A common part number coding system or a means to identify common part requirements across all operating units
- The capability to accumulate needed volumes by part number or part family
- Calculation of usage requirements over time for the entire system and by each using location
- A time-phased schedule of material requirements by part number for each using location
- Packaging, labeling, and shipping requirements for each market
- Easy access to the global database
- Supplier delivery performance to each of the buying company's locations

Developing a global system with these capabilities is complex and can present many obstacles: justifying a large investment in the network, dealing with unreliable or nonexistent public networks in many countries, dealing with uncertain technical standards, dealing with cultural and language gaps, and confronting regulatory obstacles concerning the transfer of data across borders. Competition against global companies, however, requires a worldwide system to coordinate procurement activities.

Coordination Mechanisms A series of coordination mechanisms help ensure that the worldwide coordination process is successful. One common mechanism is the use of cross-functional/cross-locational teams composed of members with different areas of expertise. These teams are responsible for identifying high-volume common purchase items across a company, identifying suppliers for these items, performing supplier evaluation and selection, and perhaps even negotiating a global contact. A second coordination mechanism is periodic review meetings of business unit or divisional procurement managers. These meetings allow managers to discuss concerns and opportunities about the global sourcing process. A third mechanism is the use of liaisons between operating units. The liaisons ensure that no sourcing problems exist between the operating units as related to global sourcing. Companies also rely on global sourcing contracts as a coordination mechanism. These contracts specify in detail a supplier's contractual requirements with respect to the requirements of individual purchasing units throughout the world.

A final coordination mechanism is the continuous evaluation of supplier performance. An ideal global supplier evaluation system monitors performance by commodity or part, the supplier's service to each using location, the supplier's performance by geographic region of the world, and performance at each of the supplier's production or distribution sites. A global supplier must provide consistent quality and service to all locations. If a supplier favors one region or location over another, then the various purchasing centers will be tempted to work outside the global sourcing process.

Executive Management Support A higher-level executive should have responsibility for managing the integration and coordination of global purchase requirements. A corporate-level position is often required because procurement executives within a decentralized operating unit usually cannot create the systems and structure required for global sourcing. A corporate-level executive must provide an unbiased perspective that supports the integration of purchase requirements between operating units. In the opening vignette, Santek Chemicals created a globalization manager's position to oversee the global engineering and procurement process. Executive management provides not only the commitment to the process but also the resources required to establish global information networks and structures.

Personnel Capabilities Those responsible for global sourcing should have certain traits and skills that match the requirements of the assignment. Research has found that these traits include a commitment to the process, a global focus to procurement, an understanding of other cultures, knowledge of global information systems, and an understanding of currency and international risk management.[10] A balanced perspective of not favoring one geographic region over another is also highly desirable. Managers who favor their own region or market over other regions of the world are exhibiting a home-market bias. A true global perspective requires coordinating purchase requirements worldwide, sourcing with the best suppliers, and maintaining an open-minded approach to the process.

The integration and coordination of worldwide sourcing is not an easy task. It requires the highest level of executive management commitment, complex information systems, worldwide coordination mechanisms, and the proper personnel capabilities. However, companies that successfully pursue integrated worldwide sourcing when required will be in a position to realize greater performance gains in cost, quality, technology, and responsiveness throughout the supply chain.

GOOD PRACTICE EXAMPLE
Global Sourcing at Paradyne

■ ■ ■

Paradyne,[11] a U.S.-based electronics company with $1.85 billion in annual sales, is a company in transition. The early 1990s, which began the longest period of industrial expansion in U.S. history, were not rewarding for the company. Paradyne experienced eroding profit margins due to intense global competition and mature product lines (with some of their products being 20 to 25 years old, making them vulnerable to cost-reduction pressure and lower profit margins). The company suffered through several costly product-launch failures and lost market share as new competitors and technologies encroached on core markets. And, with some difficulty, the company was forced to change its culture to respond to the demands of a new marketplace and CEO. Paradyne has thus had to change from being an R&D-driven company to a flexible market-focused company. In the process the company has had to focus on cross-functional interaction and the coordination of global operations like never before.

This example summarizes the global sourcing approaches taken by the three primary procurement groups at Paradyne: (1) indirect purchasing (nonproduction goods and services), (2) raw materials purchasing (any material that is required directly for production), and (3) contract or finished goods purchasing (outsourced finished goods).

Indirect Purchasing Of Paradyne's $1.8 billion in revenue, $1.3 billion is committed to purchased goods and services. Of this $1.3 billion, $700 million is committed to indirect purchases, or items that are not directly part of Paradyne's products. Previous efforts at managing indirect purchases were U.S. focused, even though Paradyne has a manufacturing presence in the United Kingdom, Mexico, the United States, Japan, and China. The question facing Paradyne procurement executives is how to globalize indirect purchasing, including the human resources that are involved with worldwide indirect purchasing.

One of the major initiatives at Paradyne involves the development of a global sourcing process called *Sourcing Vision 2000*. The goal is to systematically review the company's entire global indirect spend. The indirect purchasing director is committed to annual cost savings of 7% to 15%. The pressure to produce these savings is strong—managers include expected savings in their financial projections.

The Sourcing Vision 2000 process has three primary phases:

1. *Discovery and kick off:* This phase involved eight weeks of analysis and a review of existing agreements and Paradyne's total procurement expenditures. The primary output from this phase was the identification of high-potential opportunities. A major challenge during this phase involved determining what Paradyne spends globally by category or commodity.
2. *Identify high-impact areas and select commodities:* Paradyne pursues five commodity projects at a time, each lasting four to six months. These projects have a corporate officer, who is a steering committee member, assigned as a sponsor. Cross-functional teams, working with their steering committee sponsor, will develop milestones and timelines.
3. *Recycle and move to the next level or group of projects:* Management expects to continuously have an array of in-process projects.

Paradyne's CEO elevated the importance and visibility of global indirect sourcing by stating that Sourcing Vision 2000 was one of the company's three primary initiatives for 2000. An executive steering committee was created to oversee the process. This committee consists of the vice president of research, the vice president of supply chain management, the corporate controller, the vice president of marketing and sales, and the vice president of information technology. Each member resides at the executive vice president level, and each champions a specific project.

Cross-functional teams are an integral part of the Sourcing Vision 2000 process. Team membership includes a representative from engineering, finance, purchasing (the individual responsible for the commodity), and one or two other internal participants. Team members are expected to commit 25% of their professional effort to team activities.

Executive management has assigned goals to each project team:

1. Analyze the industry and identify the strengths and weaknesses of the key buyers and sellers.
2. Redefine the goals that were established in the first phase of the process.
3. Identify potential suppliers.
4. Work through the RFP process. (Paradyne has developed an electronic RFP for nonproduction purchases.)
5. Determine the criteria for supplier selection (including criteria weights).
6. Make supplier selection decisions.

Teams have the authority to make sourcing strategy decisions rather than simply making recommendations. They are working within a structured analytical process that requires each team to support all decisions. After selection, the internal participants, rather than the project teams, manage the transition to the new contracts.

Raw Materials Purchasing A second major procurement group at Paradyne, and the one that is most experienced with worldwide sourcing, is raw materials purchasing. Raw materials refer to any component or item that is used during production. The director of raw materials purchasing has broad responsibilities—overseeing a staff that is responsible for sourcing all materials and components that go directly into Paradyne products while accountable for annual material cost reductions. As part of its global procurement strategy, the raw materials group has focused on (1) identifying and qualifying sources worldwide and (2) aggregating volumes with leveraged agreements. This group also has responsibility for finished goods planning (which includes aggregate product planning).

The most profound changes in raw materials sourcing are occurring in electronic component procurement. Certain components that are central to Paradyne's core competency are manufactured in the United States, Scotland, Holland, and Mexico. Until five years ago the sourcing decisions to support component production occurred at the plant level. No process or authority was in place to centrally control or coordinate global raw materials procurement.

The first major change with raw materials procurement involved technical personnel, operations (those making the components), and procurement working together globally to refine component materials. This cross-functional approach, which is coordinated at the corporate level, examines systems trade-offs to arrive at an expected lowest total component cost.

The second major change emphasized a commodity approach to global strategy development with leadership roles assumed by personnel from different sites. A centrally coordinated commodity management approach, which differs dramatically from Paradyne's previous decentralized approach, requires the support of personnel from different locations or sites. Purchasing and technical resources across Paradyne's production sites are now assigned to commodity management teams. Paradyne is also in the process of establishing lead buyers at sites for items that are not part of the coordinated commodity approach. One individual at each plant will be responsible for a procurement area and become Paradyne's resident expert.

A coordinated approach to commodity management has required some purchasing resources to be physically located at corporate headquarters to oversee the process. The raw materials purchasing director, for example, has assigned worldwide responsibility for sourcing to a single manager.

Contract Purchasing The global outsourcing of finished products at Paradyne, also called *contract purchasing,* represents a 180-degree shift from finished product outsourcing in the 1970s and 1980s. A key driver behind the outsourcing of non-core hardware products was the realization that vertical integration could not support 20 to 40 new-product launches a year. Almost all outsourcing involves non-U.S. suppliers.

Many products at Paradyne use self-contained electronic components, which Paradyne refers to as *media*. The physical housing of the product is referred to as *hardware*. Paradyne has decided to insource media and outsource hardware since most of the innovation that customers value occurs within media rather than hardware. Furthermore, the margins for media products are higher than the margins for hardware products.

Beginning in 1996, Paradyne began to actively search for outsourcing partners. Unfortunately, there was no organization in place to formally support that effort. In 1997, Paradyne formed a contract manufacturing organization with primary responsibility for hardware outsourcing. The contract manufacturing group now has responsibility for procurement (identifying and qualifying outsource partners), product quality, and working with contract manufacturers during new-product development.

As part of the contract manufacturing organization, the outsourcing director has responsibility for two Asian purchasing groups. The primary mission of these groups, which are international purchasing offices (IPOs), is to identify and work with potential and existing partners. The IPOs help identify potential contract manufacturing suppliers or identify available suppliers for a specific application (including support for the indirect and raw materials purchasing groups discussed earlier in this case).

A direct involvement and linkage of the outsourcing group with marketing and technical groups is critical to the success of global outsourcing. An operations and a technical representative, reporting to the vice president of new-product delivery, are assigned to each of Paradyne's marketing categories. These individuals act as liaisons with marketing to make sure the operations and technical voices are represented and considered during new-product development. Participation with marketing also ensures that operations and technology groups have early insight into new-product requirements. The outsourcing director converses with the operations and technical people weekly, who also report to the same vice president. These discussions provide early insight into Paradyne's product development plans that affect the development of strategic outsourcing plans.

Paradyne has also created a futures group, an advanced technology development group that meets weekly. Being part of this group provides the outsourcing director with early insight into future product and technology requirements. Furthermore, one of this director's key objectives involves pursuing greater early supplier involvement. Participation with the futures group is one way the outsourcing director can pursue greater early involvement, both for his own department and with suppliers.

This example illustrates how a major corporation, faced with new competitive threats and declining markets, was forced to transform from a slow, functionally driven organization into a responsive, market-driven, cross-functional enterprise. The example also illustrates how three procurement centers, each taking very different approaches, have endorsed worldwide sourcing as a way to help achieve Paradyne's corporate objectives. ■

CONCLUSION

International purchases for raw materials, components, finished goods, and services will continue to increase. Purchasing personnel at all levels must become familiar with the nuances of worldwide purchasing. Benefiting from worldwide sourcing requires the proper structure and systems, which often means having an executive with the vision to coordinate and integrate purchasing operations on a global basis. While most organizations prefer to purchase from suppliers who are geographically close, this is not always possible. Firms operating in competitive industries must purchase from the best sources worldwide.

Perhaps one of the biggest barriers to international sourcing involves the cultural differences that arise when doing business with other countries. For instance, the standard procedures for negotiation and contracting are distinctly different in Asia, Europe, and the United States. Dealing with these issues requires purchasing personnel and organizations to develop the skills and capabilities required to manage the international purchasing process.

DISCUSSION QUESTIONS

1. Discuss whether the growth in worldwide sourcing will have a positive or negative effect over the long run in the United States. Why? What alternatives exist to worldwide sourcing?
2. What are the most important reasons for pursuing worldwide sourcing today?
3. What are the obstacles to worldwide sourcing? Do the same obstacles exist now as were present during the early 1980s or 1990s? Why or why not?
4. Discuss what is meant by the following statement: *Leading-edge companies must develop personnel who have global perspectives.* Should personnel from organizations of all sizes have a global perspective? Why?
5. What are the advantages of establishing an international purchasing office?
6. How does the international part-sourcing process differ from the domestic-sourcing process?
7. Discuss the reasons why a firm would use a third-party external agent for worldwide sourcing.
8. Why do a majority of companies favor the use of forward contracts over futures exchange contracts when hedging international purchases?
9. Discuss some of the sources of information a buyer can use to identify potential foreign sources of supply.

10. How do international sourcing and global sourcing differ? Do you think the differences are meaningful? Why?

11. During the 1980s, many U.S. firms pursued worldwide sourcing on a reactive basis. What does this mean? What might cause a firm to shift from reactive worldwide sourcing to a proactive approach to worldwide sourcing?

12. What is the role of coordination mechanisms within the global sourcing process?

13. Refer to the barriers to worldwide sourcing that many firms confront. For each barrier, discuss one or more ways that a company can overcome the barrier.

14. What form of countertrade appears to offer the most purchase flexibility? Why?

15. Some purchasing personnel regard countertrade as an infringement on purchasing's authority. Why might some purchasing personnel not view countertrade favorably?

16. Do you believe countertrade demands made by countries will increase or decrease in the future? Why? What are some of the unknown factors that could influence your answer?

17. Discuss what is meant by the following statement: *Companies and the U.S. government must recognize and confront the realities of countertrade requirement.*

ADDITIONAL READINGS

Biederman, David. "Offset and Countertrade." *Traffic World* 259, no. 6 (August 9, 1999): 18.

Herbig, Paul, and Bradley S. O'Hara. "Broadening Horizons: The Practice of Global Relationships in Procurement." *Management Decision* 33, no. 9 (1995): 12.

Kroll, Karen M. "Corporate Barter: Out of the Dark?" *Industry Week* (May 18, 1998): 44–47.

Handfield, Robert, and Daniel Krause. "Think Globally, Source Locally." *Supply Chain Management Review* (Winter 1999): 36–49.

Monczka, Robert M., and Larry C. Giunipero. *Purchasing Internationally: Concepts and Principles.* Chelsea, MI: Bookcrafters, 1990.

Monczka, Robert M., and Robert J. Trent. "Global Sourcing: A Development Approach." *International Journal of Purchasing and Materials Management* (Spring 1991): 2–8.

Monczka, Robert M., and Robert J. Trent. "Worldwide Sourcing: Assessment and Execution." *International Journal of Purchasing and Materials Management* (Fall 1992): 2–9.

Murphy, Paul R., and James M. Daley. "Logistics Issues in International Sourcing: An Exploratory Study." *International Journal of Purchasing and Materials Management* 30, no. 3 (Summer 1994): 22.

Murray, Janet Y., Albert R. Wildt, and Masaaki Kotabe. "Global Sourcing Strategies of U.S. Subsidiaries of Foreign Multinationals." *Management International Review* 35, no. 4 (1995): 307.

Stevens, John. "Global Purchasing in the Supply Chain." *Purchasing and Supply Management* (January 1995): 22.

ENDNOTES

1. Dowst Somerby, "International Buying—the Facts and Foolishness," *Purchasing* 25 (June 1987): 52–57.
2. B. Brenner, "Made in American Isn't the Kiss of Death Anymore," *Business Week*, November 13, 1995, 62.
3. From data collected at the Executive Purchasing and Supply Chain Management Seminar, Michigan State University, East Lansing, MI, 1999.
4. Robert Handfield and Daniel Krause, "Think Globally, Source Locally," *Supply Chain Management Review* (Winter 1999): 36–49.
5. Robert M. Monczka and Larry C. Giunipero, *Purchasing Internationally: Concepts and Principles* (Chelsea, MI: Bookcrafters, 1990): 19.
6. D. B. Yoffie, "Profiting from Countertrade," *Harvard Business Review* 62, no. 3 (May-June 1984): 8–12.
7. Laura B. Forker, *Countertrade: Purchasing's Perceptions and Involvement* (Tempe, AZ: Center for Advanced Purchasing Studies, 1991): 37.
8. David Biederman, "Offsets and Countertrade," *Traffic World* 259, no. 6 (August 9, 1999): 18.
9.
10. Monczka and Giunipero, *Purchasing Internationally*.
11. This company has requested that its actual name not be used.

PURCHASING AND SUPPLY CHAIN TOOLS AND TECHNIQUES

12

Project Management Supports New-Product Development

Getting to market on time and before competitors can make the difference between a successful and an unsuccessful product launch. Within the past several years, more and more companies have started using project management software to shorten development cycles, reduce costs, and streamline business processes. As one senior consultant states, "Having the ability to understand where your products are, what the deliverables are, what tasks need to be completed, what critical path is not being addressed and being able do so in a much shorter time frame allows companies to be proactive instead of reactive in getting products to market."

In a recent survey, the majority of respondents said they planned to use or are currently using project management software. When this software is used in the conceptual and early stages of a product design cycle, it helps development teams determine if they have enough personnel, time, and other key resources required to complete a project in a timely manner. The software helps to reduce time and cost by keeping track of all of the steps or tasks required to complete a product launch or construction project on time and on budget.

Understanding how to use project management tools is critical not only for engineers, but for anyone assuming the role of project leader or project team member and, of course, for purchasing and supply chain management specialists. Mack Trucks, for example, relies extensively on a project management approach when developing global sourcing strategies with its European partner, Renault. Global sourcing strategies are developed within a structured project management approach that introduces discipline to each cross-functional project team. The teams rely on project management software to report their progress and to manage budget and timing.

There are many different human factors that are a part of project management. The stumbling block to introducing a rigorous or structured approach to projects is that it requires a cultural change by internal users. However, one of the reasons for the high rate of project failures today is due to a lack of a disciplined use of the best organizational practices and the effective management of resources. Project management software brings together all the relevant information about a project's resources, time, and costs, and thus supports the move toward a more integrated approach to the entire work process.

Source: Adapted from Lisa Kempfer, "First to Market: The Power of Managing Products," *Computer-Aided Engineering* (February 1999): 34–40.

Having the right tools and applying the right techniques is an essential part of supply chain management. As the opening vignette illustrated, purchasers and supply chain specialists rely on various tools and techniques to perform their jobs effectively. For example, purchasing team leaders must be skilled in managing team assignments involving multiple tasks and team members. Buyers must understand how to analyze competitive bids or negotiate favorable prices due to learning improvements that occur at a supplier. Process mapping helps identify and eliminate waste throughout the supply chain. Value analysis supports continuous quality improvement.

This chapter presents a set of tools and techniques that support effective purchasing and supply chain management. It will focus on project management, learning curve analysis, value engineering/value analysis, quantity discount analysis, and process mapping.

PROJECT MANAGEMENT

Project management is a valuable skill for supply chain managers to have since more and more work is being structured as projects. Projects have certain characteristics that make them unique compared with other forms of work. A *project* is a series of tasks that require the completion of specific objectives within a certain time frame; has defined start and stop dates; consumes resources, particularly time, personnel, and budget; and operates with limited resources. Examples of projects involving purchasing and supply chain personnel include developing new products, developing new management information systems, implementing value analysis recommendations, and initiating performance improvement plans at a supplier. Project management can be crucial in applications across organizations—from implementing enterprise resource planning systems and construction projects to developing a marketing plan and creating a Website.

Roles and Responsibilities of a Project Manager

Most projects have a manager who has primary responsibility for planning, organizing, directing, and controlling the project as well as coordinating the tasks and personnel working on the project. Project managers have four broad responsibilities:

- *Ensure customer satisfaction:* Almost all projects are undertaken at the request of an external or internal customer. An important part of ensuring customer satisfaction involves reporting on project status, which prepares the internal or external customer for the final result or outcome and helps avoid surprises.
- *Direct and control day-to-day activities:* Project control is a major responsibility of project managers, who must make sure tasks are assigned and completed as scheduled. Directing and controlling also involve effectively delegating tasks to project team members, and can be a challenge when projects are complex and/or members have other nonproject assignments for which they are accountable. A later section discusses several tools and techniques available to help control and coordinate project tasks.

- *Secure resources and confront project obstacles:* This responsibility includes acting on behalf of the project team to make sure that required resources, including personnel, equipment, time, budget, or information resources are available. The project manager also works to overcome any obstacles confronting the team.
- *Perform duties inherent to project leadership:* Project managers must perform certain duties as a formal part of that role:
    1. Coordinate the development of a project implementation plan, including timing and task assignments.
    2. Define, negotiate, and secure resource commitments as required.
    3. Manage and coordinate the interfaces created by subdividing the project into separate tasks.
    4. Monitor and report progress and problems on a continuous basis to project customers.
    5. Alert executive management of difficulties beyond the project's control.
    6. Maintain high performance standards within the project team.
    7. Organize and present reports and reviews as required.
    8. Motivate and develop all personnel as required to complete the project.

The project manager is an important position with great influence over project success. For purchasing and supply chain personnel serving as project managers, the position often involves working with representatives from other functional areas.

Defining Project Success

Since projects usually have a defined scope with agreed-upon tasks and responsibilities, it is often easier to measure project success compared with other types of work. Did a supplier quality improvement project improve supplier quality by the intended amount? Was a new product developed within the time and budget constraints? Did the new product achieve its initial sales goals? Successful projects are completed

- Within the allocated time period and budget
- At the proper performance or specification level as determined by the stated goals and objectives of the project
- At a level accepted by the customer, user, or management
- With minimal or only mutually agreed-upon changes
- Without disturbing the main work flow of the organization

Project Phases

Projects move through various phases from conception to completion. Exhibit 12.1 summarizes six phases along with the characteristics defining the activities comprising each phase. The phases become increasingly detailed as projects progress from concept through completion.

Concept Early in the project management process, project planners must develop a broad concept or definition of the project. A broad project objective may include

EXHIBIT 12.1   *Project Phases and Characteristics*

Abstract		Start

Concept
- Initiate broad discussion of project

Project Definition
- Develop project description
- Describe how to accomplish the work
- Determine tentative timing
- Identify broad budget, personnel, resource requirements

Planning
- Develop detailed plans identifying tasks, timing, budgets, and resources
- Create organization to manage the project

Preliminary Studies
- Validate the assumptions made in the project plan through interviews, data collection, literature search, experience

Performance
- Execute the project plan and perform work
- Use project control tools and techniques here

Postcompletion
- Confirm project results
- Reassign personnel
- Restore equipment and facilities
- Document project files for future reference

Concrete		Finish

developing a new product for a certain market within a specified time and budget. Project planners also identify any broad constraints facing the project. Budget estimates made during the concept phase are usually accurate to approximately 30% compared with final budget targets.

Project Definition   If a project is initially feasible, it proceeds to the definition phase. This phase requires the development of a project description that provides greater detail than the concept phase. The project description identifies how to accomplish the work, how to organize for the project, the personnel required to support the project, tentative timing schedules, and tentative budget requirements. Budget estimates begin to become more exact with a target of approximately 5% to 10% compared with the actual final budget.

Planning   Planning involves preparing detailed plans that identify the tasks, timing milestones, budgets, and resources required to support each task. This phase also includes creating the organization that will carry out the project, often through the use of project teams. The planning phase is particularly critical because there is a strong correlation between effective planning and successful project outcomes.

The project plan developed during the concept or project definition phase is usually not detailed enough to provide guidance during project implementation. Detailed planning provides an opportunity for discussing each person's role and responsibilities throughout the project. An organization must also define how the different tasks and activities comprising the project will come together to complete the project.

Preliminary Studies A final phase before actually executing the project involves verifying the assumptions in the project plan, including performing literature searches, conducting field interviews, and gathering any required data. This phase confirms (or does not confirm) the planning work performed to date. Once the project manager or team confirms the assumptions made during detailed planning, then the actual performance of the project begins.

Performance The performance phase involves carrying out the project's plan and reporting the work results on a continuous basis to management or customers. Effective planning increases the likelihood that actual performance outcomes will meet expectations. Project managers play a particularly important role here in coordinating and directing the work effort. Depending on the type of project, this may be the longest of the six phases in terms of time and resources consumed.

Postcompletion Project managers or teams perform several important tasks during the postcompletion phase:

- Confirm that the final project meets the expectations of management or customers. This usually involves a comparison of the project performance outcome compared with the expected outcome established during earlier planning.
- Conduct a postimplementation meeting to discuss the strengths and weaknesses of the project. An effective organization learns from the experiences of its project teams. Any lessons learned should be communicated to other project teams.
- Reassign project personnel to other positions or other projects. One of the primary characteristics of projects as a form of work is the movement of personnel from project to project.
- Restore any equipment or facilities used to their original status. Also, make sure all files are in good order and are available for future reference.

Project Planning and Control Techniques

Various tools and techniques are available to plan, control, and coordinate work activities. These tools allow a project manager to track what requires completion, by whom, and by when as specified in the project plan. These tools also allow performance tracking over time, particularly in the areas of time and budget. Two popular planning and control techniques include Gantt charts and project networking (CPM and PERT).

Implementing an ERP System

One of the most important types of projects a company undertakes is implementing an enterprise resource planning (ERP) system. This effort can take many years, and requires the input of multiple participants in the company. Price Waterhouse, an ERP consultant and accounting firm, has a four-step process they use to help clients implement these systems. The first step is to identify the strategic imperative and desired outcomes for the system. The second is to assess against the business realities and define the constraints implicit in implementing the system. The third step is to develop possible change program alternatives. A change program is a specific combination of process, technology, and change management efforts. The fourth step is to finalize the program architecture and business case, documenting the savings and identifying future requirements. Price Waterhouse estimates that the total time required for such a project, optimistically, is several months. Through this structured project management approach, Price Waterhouse has helped many of its clients to successfully deploy this very complicated process.

Source: Adapted from: A presentation by Jacob Seidelman, Price Waterhouse, March 1998.

Gantt Charts A Gantt chart visually displays the tasks and times associated with a project. Named after Henry Gantt, the chart is a horizontal bar chart with activities listed vertically and times or dates displayed horizontally. The advantage of Gantt charts is that they are relatively inexpensive to develop and use and can convey a great deal of information. The primary disadvantage is that for larger projects, they become increasingly difficult to use or to keep up-to-date. In such cases, users can use project management techniques such as CPM/PERT. Exhibit 12.2 illustrates a Gantt chart for a project involving the transfer of equipment to a supplier during an outsourcing project.

CPM/PERT Critical Path Method (CPM) and Program Evaluation and Review Technique (PERT) are two popular project control techniques, particularly for projects that are complex or involve many activities or tasks. These techniques require the user to identify the activities or tasks that make up a project and to determine the sequence of those activities.

Users apply CPM to projects where there is a single known time (referred to as a *deterministic time*) for each activity with no variance. PERT applies to projects where time estimates are variable or uncertain. Each activity in PERT has three time estimates: (1) a most likely, (2) a pessimistic, and (3) optimistic. Project managers combine these estimates to arrive at a single estimate of the expected activity time for each activity within the network.

EXHIBIT 12.2   *Gantt Chart for a Supplier Development Technology Transfer Project*

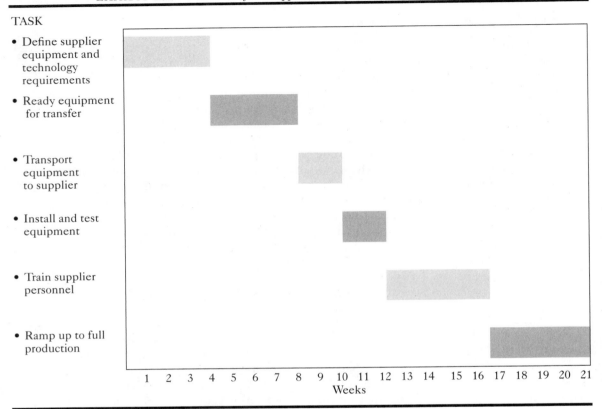

Project control techniques allow project managers to monitor progress over time while managing costs across all activities. Users can also determine the probability of completing projects by certain target dates using normal distribution statistics. Readers requiring in-depth detail of probability analysis or time/cost trade-offs are urged to consult an operations research or project management textbook.

Rules for Constructing a Project Management Network

A graphical network can be used to represent each PERT or CPM project. A network is a graphical representation that shows how each individual activity relates in time and sequence to all other activities. Network illustrations are powerful because they show how separate activities come together to form an entire project. The construction of CPM and PERT project networks follow generally accepted rules or conventions. Later in this section we will use a purchasing project example to demonstrate the use of these rules, which apply only to constructing the network and do not yet involve the use of time estimates.

Network Rules

1. Identify each unique activity within a project by a capital letter that corresponds only to that activity.
2. A unique branch or arrow represents each activity in the project. Circles or nodes represent events. For example:

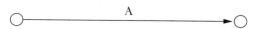

This is the branch for activity A. Sometimes we also number the events, which represent points in time. The events associated with this activity (the circles) represent the start and completion of this activity.

3. This diagram means only that B cannot start until A is complete. Branches show only the relationships between different activities; the length of the branches has no significance.

The sequence of the branches, however, is important.

4. Branch direction indicates the general progression in time from left to right.
5. When a number of activities end at one event, no activity starting at that event may begin before all activities ending at that event are complete.

Activity D can start only after all activities preceding it in the network are complete. In this example, activities B and C must both be complete before beginning D. Activities B and C are predecessors of D (activities that must be complete before work on D can begin).

6. Two or more activities cannot share graphically the same beginning and ending events.

Not allowed:

K

L

Allowed:

K

L

This rule may require the use of a dummy activity, which is simply an extension of the activity that precedes it. In this case, the dummy activity is an extension of activity L. Dummy activities have no expected activity time—they simply carry forward the time from the preceding activity.

7. Networks start and finish at only a single event.

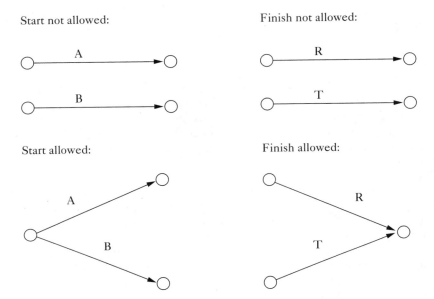

Start not allowed: Finish not allowed:

A   R

B   T

Start allowed: Finish allowed:

A   R

B   T

In this example, the project starts and ends with two activities (A and B at the start and R and T at the end). This rule requires each network to start and stop on a single event. There is no limit to the number of activities that can begin or end at a single event.

Project Management Illustrated A cross-functional team is responsible for managing a supplier selection and systems development project. The project has three primary objectives: (1) develop a set of performance criteria along with the evaluation system to assess potential supplier performance; (2) identify, evaluate, and select suppliers for a critical commodity; and (3) develop an information technology system that will evaluate the performance of selected suppliers on a continuous basis.

The project manager has identified the unique tasks shown below that are required to meet the primary objectives of this project.

Activity	Designation	Preceding Activity
Assemble project team	A	
Identify potential commodity suppliers	B	A
Develop supplier evaluation criteria	C	A
Develop supplier audit form	D	C
Perform preliminary supplier financial analysis	E	B
Conduct supplier site visits	F	E, D

EXHIBIT 12.3   *Project Network Illustration for the Supplier Selection Project*

Activity	Designation	Preceding Activity
Compile results from site visits	G	F
Identify requirements for computerized supplier performance system	H	A
Perform detailed systems analysis and programming	I	H
Test computerized system	J	I
Select final suppliers	K	G

Exhibit 12.3 illustrates the network for this project. There are three paths of activities through this project: A–B–E–F–G–K; A–C–D–F–G–K; and A–H–I–J. (A path is a continuous or connected flow of activities from project start to finish.) The project manager must evaluate the progress of all three paths to ensure meeting the original project objectives. After reviewing Exhibit 12.3, one of the primary benefits of networking should become clear: the ability to see the relationships among all the tasks in a project.

Three observations are important at this point. First, the project manager has not identified the time associated with each task, only the tasks and their sequence. The manager does not yet know which set of activities will make up the longest path (the critical path) within the project. Second, projects continuously change over time. As the project team progresses on its assignments, it must update the network to reflect that progress. The network only looks like it does in Exhibit 12.3 *at the beginning of the project*. PERT and CPM require regular updating with the most current information available. Third, computer software, such as Microsoft Project, is available that will construct the network and allow the user to perform various analyses. The most challenging part of project management is defining the activities that make up a project, the relationship between those activities, and the time and budget required for completing the activities.

Project Management with Time Estimates The following steps describe how to develop a PERT network with variable time estimates.

1. Identify each activity requiring completion during the project and the relationship between those activities. This is a critical step. The activities should not be too broad or too narrow in scope. They must be definable tasks with a start and stop point whose completion supports the objectives of the project.

2. Construct the network reflecting the proper precedence relationships using the rules discussed earlier.

3. Determine the three time estimates for each activity (optimistic = a, pessimistic = b, and most likely = m). The optimistic and pessimistic estimates should reflect the end points on the time estimate continuum. These times should have only a 10% to 20% chance of actually occurring. Accurate time estimates are critical. Inaccurate time estimates or those with a great deal of variability will lessen the validity of the control process.

4. Calculate the expected activity time for each activity using the following formula:

$$\text{Expected Activity Time} = (a + 4m + b)/6$$

If activity G has an optimistic time of five weeks, a most-likely time of six weeks, and a pessimistic time of thirteen weeks, then its expected activity time is $(5 + 24 + 13)/6 = 7$.

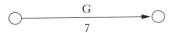

5. Place the expected activity times on the network under their respective activity branches and identify the critical path. The critical path is the longest path of continuous activities through the network (in time). Any delay for activities on the critical path will delay the entire project. There can be more than one critical path in a project.

6. Identify the early start (ES), late start (LS), early finish (EF), and late finish (LF) times. These times also appear on the activity branch and provide a great deal of information to the project manager:

Early Start: The earliest point in time an activity can begin.

Late Start: The latest point in time an activity can begin without delaying the entire project.

Early Finish: The earliest time a project can finish given the expected activity time. Early finish time equals ES + expected activity time.

Late Finish: The latest time an activity can finish without delaying the entire project. Latest finish time equals LS + expected activity time.

Project Management Illustrated with Time Estimates

Using the project presented earlier, we can now include time estimates (in weeks) and calculate the expected time for each activity. Project planners calculate these estimates during the planning phase of project management.

Task	Optimistic	Most Likely	Pessimistic	Expected Activity Time
Assemble project team (A)	1	2	3	2
Identify potential commodity suppliers (B)	3	6	9	6
Develop supplier evaluation criteria (C)	2	4	5	3.8
Develop supplier audit form (D)	2	3	4	3
Perform preliminary supplier financial analysis (E)	1	2	4	2.2
Conduct supplier site visits (F)	4	8	12	8
Compile results from site visits (G)	2	5	8	5
Identify requirements for computerized supplier performance system (H)	2	4	8	4.3
Perform detailed systems analysis and programming (I)	8	10	16	10.7
Test computerized system (J)	2	3	5	3.2
Select final suppliers (K)	1	2	3	2

Exhibit 12.4 shows this project with all times displayed. When calculating times, the user always completes the early start (ES) and early finish (EF) times moving left to right across the top of the network. Next, complete the bottom half of the network, which includes the late finish (LF) and late start (LS) times, by moving right to left through the network. Notice that all projects start at time 0, and not time 1.

Activities E and D converge at the same event, which means that activity F, in this case, requires the completion of both E and D before it can begin. It is common for two or more activities to conclude at the same event. When this happens, the early start (ES) time for the next activity (activity F) is the *larger* of the early finish (EF) times for the preceding activities. This makes sense because the subsequent activity cannot start until all preceding activities are complete. Working right to left to arrive at the late finish and late start times on the bottom half of the network, we notice that three activities (B, C, and H) originate from the same event. In this case, the *smaller* of the late start (LS) times becomes the late finish (LF) time for activity A. In this case, two weeks is the late finish time for activity A.

The longest path (in time) through the network is the *critical path*. It is also the path on which the connected activities each have no slack. In our example, the critical path of this project consists of activities A–B–E–F–G–K. Any delay beyond the estimated times for each activity will result in a delay to the entire project. Project managers must always be aware of the status of critical path activities since they have no time slack.

EXHIBIT 12.4   *Project Network Illustration for the Supplier Selection Project with All Times Displayed*

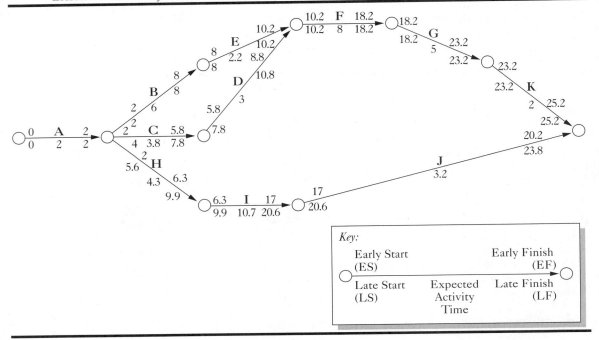

Key:

Early Start (ES)		Early Finish (EF)
Late Start (LS)	Expected Activity Time	Late Finish (LF)

The difference between the late start and early start (LS – ES) or the late finish and the early finish (LF – EF) times is *slack*—the maximum amount of leeway in an activity that will not delay the entire project. Activities without any slack (activities A, B, E, F, G, and K) are by definition on the critical path. Activities not on the critical path will have slack.

Of special interest to project managers is a project's *path slack*—the amount of time that activities along the path can be delayed without delaying the entire project. Notice in our example there are three continuous paths throughout the project. Exhibit 12.5 details the paths and their total time. Of the three paths, A–B–E–F–G–K is the longest path at 25.2 weeks. None of the activities on this path have any slack.

The length of the path equals the sum of the expected activity times for each activity on that particular path. Note that the length of path A–C–D–F–G–K is 23.8 weeks. We must further notice that the slack for this path resides in only two activities—C and D each have two weeks of slack. However, this does not mean there are a total of four weeks of slack. There are only two weeks between the two activities. If activity C finishes at week 7.8 instead of 5.8, then activity D no longer has any slack because it now cannot start until week 7.8.

Project management tools are critical when managing large-scale projects. Purchasing professionals are managing an increasing number of projects involving more than one functional area and large amounts of resources. To do this effectively, they must have an understanding of project management control tools and techniques.

EXHIBIT 12.5   *Supplier Selection Project Paths*

Path	Length
A-B-E-F-G-K	25.2 weeks
A-C-D-F-G-K	23.8 weeks
A-H-I-J	20.2 weeks

$\mathcal{L}$ EARNING CURVES

Learning curves establish the rate of improvement due to learning as producers realize direct-labor cost improvements as production volumes increase. When referring to learning improvement, the learning rate represents the improvement as production doubles from a previous level. For example, with an 85% learning rate, the direct labor required to produce a single unit declines by 15% each time production doubles. With a 90% rate, direct-labor requirements decrease by 10% each time production doubles. The fundamental principle of the learning curve is that as production doubles, direct-labor requirements decline by an observed and predictable rate. The rate of improvement varies from situation to situation.

Why should purchasers be concerned with learning curves? If learning occurs at a supplier during the performance of a purchase contract and the buyer does not take that into account, then the supplier will reap the financial benefits that result from learning. If learning occurs, the benefits must go somewhere.

Learning curves apply to the average direct labor required to produce a unit of output. The labor component is usually the easiest data to gather because companies assign direct-labor hours to specific items or projects. Historically, the term *learning curve* refers to the reduced direct-labor requirement per unit of output due to the effects of learning. This empirically derived concept was first noted by Boeing Corporation, which noticed the amount of time required to build the same model aircraft over time decreased. The term *experience curve* refers to the longer-term factors of production that systematically reduce production costs. These factors include the shorter-term labor component along with longer-term product and process modifications.

Components of the Learning or Experience Curve

What drives the expected cost reductions, which are the basis of the learning curve and the broader experience curve? Different factors combine to produce a learning effect. The first factor is the workforce. This includes the ability of the worker on the job to learn and improve through repetitive effort and increased efficiency, and the effort by management to pursue productivity gains.

The next factor includes modifications to the production process. Because labor improvements quickly reach the point of smaller and smaller return, management often relies on process changes to realize continuous improvement. Management may introduce new production methods, substitute increased automation for labor, or pursue vertical integration that results in greater cost control. Some firms also update their process technology during the life of a product to take advantage of improvements offered with newer equipment. Offering a supplier a longer-term contract with guaranteed volumes, for example, encourages investment in equipment that results in lower production costs.

When to Use the Learning Curve

Not all processes or items benefit from or exhibit improvement from learning. In fact, when used incorrectly, this approach can result in a significant underestimation of true production costs. The learning curve approach applies when certain operating conditions are present.

Learning-curve analysis is appropriate when a supplier uses a new production process or produces an item for the first time. Production efficiency usually increases as a supplier's workforce becomes familiar with a new process. The learning curve is also appropriate when a supplier produces a technically complex item for the first time. The approach is also appropriate when an item has high direct-labor content.

The human factors present at the beginning of production must remain fairly constant over time to apply the learning curve. If an organization experiences high turnover, then the workforce may not demonstrate the anticipated rate of learning. For example, in the 1960s the Douglas Aircraft Company experienced high turnover due to a tight labor market during the initial production of its DC-9. The company was unable to realize the labor efficiencies it had factored into the sales price of the aircraft. The resulting higher-than-planned costs created a financial strain on the company.

Learning curves require the accurate collection of cost and labor data, particularly during the early stages of production. A buyer must have confidence that learning occurs at a uniform rate and that any improvements resulted from employee learning. Initial production data often provide the basis for negotiation regarding expected improvement rates and scheduled price reductions.

Learning Curve Illustrated

Exhibit 12.6 provides direct-labor data for a purchased item over increasing levels of output. Learning-curve examples can become quite complex, especially when using logarithmic scales to show the relationship between units produced and labor requirements. This simple example illustrates the effect on the average labor requirement due to a fairly consistent rate of learning.

Each column in Exhibit 12.6 provides data needed to estimate the cumulative learning rate for this supplier:

- *Column A:* The total units produced over a period of time. In this example, a total of 64 units were produced.
- *Column B:* The cumulative total labor hours (TLH) required to produce a given level of units. This supplier used 288 total labor hours to produce 32 total units but only 493 total labor hours to double production to 64 total units.

EXHIBIT 12.6   *Supplier Learning-Curve Data*

(A) Units	(B) Total Labor Hours	(C) Average Labor Hours Per Unit	(D) Learning Rate
1	20	20.0	—
2	34	17.0	15.0%
4	58	14.5	14.7%
8	100	12.5	14.8%
16	168	10.5	16.0%
32	288	9.0	14.3%
64	493	7.7	14.4%

Average improvement rate: 15% or 85% learning curve

- *Column C:* The total labor hours for a given level of output divided by the units produced. The figure represents the cumulative average labor per unit of output.
- *Column D:* The associated learning rate for each doubling of production. The learning rate from one to two units of production equals

$$(20 \text{ TLH} - 17 \text{ TLH})/(20 \text{ TLH}) = .15 \text{ or } 15\%$$

The learning rate from two to four units equals

$$(17 \text{ TLH} - 14.5 \text{ TLH})/(17 \text{ TLH}) = .147 \text{ or } 14.7\%$$

Each level can be calculated in a similar way.

This analysis reveals that the supplier has an approximately 85% learning curve for this item, which means that as production doubles, the direct labor required to produce a unit should decrease 15% on average. A producer realizes the most dramatic learning improvements over early volumes when the effect from learning is the greatest.

The successful use of the learning curve requires knowing when and how to apply the technique. A buyer's objective must be to use the tool to identify anticipated labor costs for increasingly larger production volumes. An analyst often cannot identify a learning rate until some preliminary production data are available. If data are not available, one approach is to rely on historical learning rates or previously observed rates at a supplier.

Learning-Curve Problem

A buyer does business with a supplier who uses a production process that historically demonstrates an 80% learning curve; that is, as production rates double, there is a 20% reduction in the average direct-labor hours required to produce a unit. Given this learning rate, a buyer hopes to capture this reduced labor requirement through a lower purchase price.

Exhibit 12.7 outlines one use of the learning curve in purchasing. In this example, the buyer expects the per-unit price on a 600-unit order due to learning to lower from $228 to $170. Whether the buyer actually receives a $170 unit price will probably be subject to negotiation. The supplier may argue that overhead did not change since the original order and should remain at $50 per unit. The supplier's profit is affected as both direct and overhead costs decline and profit remains at 20% of total costs. The buyer may counter that material costs should decline due to larger volumes. The key point is that the buyer now has a price range for negotiation with the supplier.

Learning-curve analysis highlights a key reason why many purchasers consolidate purchase volumes with fewer suppliers. Astute buyers know that an even lower purchase price may be obtained if the buyer correctly factors in the effects of learning as production volumes increase.

VALUE ENGINEERING/VALUE ANALYSIS

Value analysis (VA) involves examining all elements of a component, assembly, end product, or service to make sure it fulfills its intended function at the lowest total cost. The basic component of value analysis is *value*—the lowest total cost at which an item, product, or service achieves its primary function while satisfying the time, place, and quality requirements of customers. While value analysis traditionally applies to tangible products, there is no reason that companies cannot apply VA techniques to services.

The primary objective of value analysis is to increase the value of an item or service at the lowest cost without sacrificing quality. In equation form, value is the relationship between the function of a product or service and its cost:

$$Value = Function/Cost$$

There are many variations of function and cost that will increase the value of a product or service. The most obvious ways to increase value include increasing the functionality or use of a product or service while holding cost constant, reducing cost while not reducing functionality, and increasing functionality more than increasing cost. For example, offering a five-year warranty versus a two-year warranty with no price increase raises the value of a product to the customer.

Value analysis is a way to achieve continuous performance improvement in an item, product, or service. It is not a technique to cheapen a product or service by lowering quality or other performance attributes below what customers expect. Many firms realize that VA is a powerful technique that can help a firm achieve its continuous cost and quality improvement targets.

Who Is Involved in Value Analysis?

Value analysis, certainly not exclusively a purchasing tool, involves many organizational functions. However, because most products and services require major inputs from suppliers, purchasing should take an active role in coordinating value analysis

EXHIBIT 12.7   *Learning-Curve Problem*

XYZ Corporation is buying a new item produced by a process that historically demonstrates an 80% learning curve. A buyer has placed an order for 200 pieces and receives a quote of $228 per unit. The buyer has accumulated the following per-unit cost data:

Material	$90	
Direct labor	$50	(5 hours on average per unit at $10 per hour)
Overhead	$50	(Assume 100% of direct labor)
Total costs	$190	
Profit	$38	(Difference between per-unit price and total costs, which equals 20% of total costs)
Total per unit	$228	(Quoted price)

The buyer wants to place a second order for an additional 600 pieces, or a combined total order of 800. How much should the buyer expect to pay per unit *given the expected benefit of the learning curve* (which affects direct-labor requirements)?

1. Calculate the average labor hours for the entire combined order of 800 units:

    From the first order, 200 units required an average of 5 hours labor per unit. Therefore, 400 units should require only 80% as much as the original 200, or an average 4 hours of labor per unit given an 80% learning rate. 800 units should require an average of 3.2 hours of labor per unit (80% of 4 hours is 3.2 hours). One of the guidelines of learning curve is that labor costs decrease by a predictable rate each time production doubles.

2. Calculate the hours required for the total combined order of 800 units less the labor incurred for the original 200-piece order:

    $$800 \text{ units} \times 3.2 \text{ average hours/unit} = 2{,}560 \text{ total hours}$$
    Less:

    $$200 \text{ units} \times 5 \text{ average hours per unit} = 1{,}000 \text{ (direct labor required for original 200-piece order)}$$

    $$1{,}560 \text{ total labor hours required for the next 600 units}$$

3. Calculate the additional total and per-unit labor cost for the additional 600-unit order:

    $$1{,}560 \text{ hours} \times \$10 \text{ per direct-labor hour} = \$15{,}600 \text{ total additional labor cost}$$

    $$\$15{,}600 \text{ divided by 600 units} = \$26 \text{ per unit}$$

4. Calculate the expected new per-unit price for the additional 600-piece order:

    Additional 600 pieces per-unit cost

Material	$90	(Remains unchanged, although higher quantities may reduce the per-unit material cost)
Direct labor	$26	
Overhead	$26	(Assume 100% of direct labor)
Total costs	$142	
Profit (20%) of total costs	$28.40	
Total per unit	$170.40	

SOURCING SNAPSHOT

Value Analysis Is Not Only for Manufacturing

HealthEast, a three-hospital system based in St. Paul, Minnesota, has participated in a process standardization and supply chain management improvement program for the past ten years. Called the Value Analysis Program, it has paid off over the years with annual savings of almost $7 million. Originally established to counter financial downturns resulting from the expansion of managed care in the area, along with reduced reimbursement, the Value Analysis Program recently was used to reduce nonsalary expenses by almost 3%. In its cost-reduction effort, HealthEast received help from staff members of its group purchasing organization, VHA, and VHA's new supply company, Novation. In recognition of the program's success, HealthEast received a leadership award at VHA's leadership conference in Orlando, Florida.

Source: Adapted from: "Value Analysis Effort Continues to Pay Off for Small Minnesota Hospital System," *Hospital Materials Management* (June 1999): 4.

activities. A common approach for using value analysis involves creating a VA team composed of professionals with knowledge about a product or service. Many functional groups can contribute to the value analysis team:

- *Executive management:* Executive management provides overall guidance and support for the VA process. Functional groups will commit to VA at a higher level if they see that executive management expects that commitment. Executive management can also provide support by providing the time, budget, and personnel to work actively on VA projects.
- *Suppliers:* Because much of what value analysis examines involves the cost and design of component parts, it is logical to request input from suppliers, a group that can propose alternative materials, provide insights into what other firms are doing, and identify lower-cost production methods. Buyers motivate suppliers to participate in the process in a number of ways. Supplies may provide cost-reduction ideas if they can share in the savings.
- *Purchasing:* Purchasing often takes a primary role in organizing the VA effort by coordinating and disseminating relevant information. Purchasing may be responsible for bringing suppliers directly into the process, and it may also evaluate any component or material changes that result from VA or help suppliers establish their own VA projects.
- *Design engineering:* Design engineers evaluate any proposed changes to the design of an item. They also help define product function, establish quality and engineering standards, and evaluate the effect of VA changes on other parts within the product.
- *Marketing:* The marketing group provides insight about the impact that VA changes may have on customers. Just as purchasing may involve suppliers during value

analysis, marketing may involve customers. Marketing can also help establish price ranges and provide information about competitor actions and responses.

- *Production:* The production group has the responsibility of producing final items or products, and it can also propose better ways to produce an item or service to achieve higher quality and/or lower total cost. It is essential that this group is informed about any changes proposed by other functional groups.
- *Industrial/process engineering:* This group can contribute extensively, particularly when discussing methods of producing and delivering a product or service. Industrial/process engineers can evaluate proposed manufacturing methods, material handling and flow, the effect of alternative materials on the production process, and packaging requirements.
- *Quality control:* Quality control can evaluate the impact on quality that proposed changes may have. Quality control can also establish how and where to evaluate quality performance levels for a proposed production method. This group can also work with purchasing to support quality control efforts at suppliers.

Value analysis works best when the process involves different functional groups.

Tests for Determining Value in a Product or Service

Value analysis teams ask a number of questions to determine if opportunities exist for item, product, or service improvement:

1. Does the use of this product contribute value to our customers?
2. Is the cost of the final product proportionate to its usefulness?
3. Are there additional uses for this product?
4. Does the product need all its features or internal parts?
5. Are product weight reductions possible?
6. Is there anything else available to our customers given the intended use of the product?
7. Is there a better production method to produce the item or product?
8. Can a lower cost standard part replace a customized part?
9. Are we using the proper tooling considering the quantities required?
10. Will another dependable supplier provide material, components, or subassemblies for less?
11. Is anyone currently purchasing required materials, components, or subassemblies for less?
12. Are there equally effective but lower-cost materials available?
13. Do material, labor, overhead, and profit equal the product's cost?
14. Are packaging cost reductions possible?
15. Is the item properly classified for shipping purposes to receive the lowest transportation rates?
16. Are design or quality specifications too tight given customer requirements?
17. If we are making an item now, can we buy it for less (and vice versa)?

The most likely VA improvement areas include modifying product design and material specifications, using standardized components in place of custom components, substituting lower-cost for higher-cost materials, reducing the number of parts that a product contains, and developing better production or assembly methods.

Selecting Items for Value Analysis

A number of guidelines exist that help identify where to start the value analysis effort. First, likely VA candidates often provide most of a firm's revenue and can have the greatest impact resulting from a formal value analysis. Other likely candidates include products that are complex in design. These products offer opportunities to simplify design or production methods, thereby creating cost savings. Another group may be products or items that are not currently competitive because of changing market conditions or other factors. Other selection criteria include items, parts, or products with

- High scrap or rework costs
- Large purchased quantities from suppliers
- Many nonstandard parts
- Relatively difficult production requirements

Many organizations create a list of most likely VA candidates given a set of objectives. Also, a number of VA teams can work on different products or product lines simultaneously.

The Value Analysis Process

Value analysis projects follow a systematic approach consisting of five stages:

1. Gather information
2. Speculate
3. Analyze
4. Recommend and execute
5. Summarize and follow up

These stages occur after identifying an item or product as a VA candidate.

Gather Information The first stage for any value analysis project requires agreement about an item or product's primary and secondary functions to customers. VA participants should ask "What does this product do for the customer?" and "Why does a customer buy this product?"

It is important to understand a product's primary and secondary functions. Value analysis experts recommend naming each function of an item or product with two words—a verb and a noun. After this is complete, the team must agree on which functions are primary versus secondary. For example, the primary function of an industrial pump may be to move fluids at a rate required by the customer. A secondary function may be to minimize noise in the customer's facility. In this case, the VA team must recognize that moving fluids is the primary function of the industrial pump. Minimizing noise, a secondary consideration of industrial pumps, still must receive consideration during analysis.

During this stage, detailed information about the item or product is collected. This includes sales trends, supplier performance data, costs to make and sell, design drawings, quantity estimates, and production method analyses.

Speculate This stage calls for wide-open or creative thinking on the part of the VA team. Brainstorming is ideal as the team evaluates an item or product against the various tests or questions presented earlier. The primary objective of this phase is to develop as many improvement ideas as possible while withholding judgment on any one alternative. A VA team moves to the analysis stage after it exhausts its ideas about how to improve a particular item or product.

Analyze This stage evaluates critically the different ideas put forth during the speculation phase. Analysis can include cost/benefit calculations or assessment of the feasibility of implementing an idea. The result is a set of ideas that satisfy the original goals and objectives of the VA effort. This phase is very specific and no longer involves generalities.

Recommend and Execute Up to this point the VA process has generated only a prioritized list of ideas. The team may have to present its proposals to executive management for approval. Moving an idea from the team to the organization requires an ability to motivate others; creativity; good communication skills; ability to think analytically; solid product knowledge; commitment; and salesmanship.

Once a team receives approval, it must implement its ideas. Some ideas will be quite simple to carry out while others are more complex. The team must develop a project plan with timings, budget requirements, and responsibilities. The team often has to generate support outside the team for its proposals and help during implementation.

Summarize and Follow Up This step is common during the implementation of any idea or plan. It may be the responsibility of the VA team or group to follow up and track implementation progress. The team may also track the gains achieved by the VA effort.

Value Analysis or Value Engineering—Which One?

The terms *value analysis* and *value engineering* are often used interchangeably. While the concepts are similar, there is a fundamental difference. Value analysis techniques are applied to existing items or products, usually after introducing the item or product to the marketplace. In one sense it is an after-the-fact activity. Value engineering is the application of VA techniques during product design and development.

Is the application of VA techniques too late to provide a benefit? Absolutely not. World-class firms apply value-engineering techniques during new-product development. They then emphasize value analysis as a way of achieving continuous improvement. The only way to maintain customers and demonstrate market leadership is to offer improved products and services on a continuous basis.

QUANTITY DISCOUNT ANALYSIS

Quantity discount analysis (QDA) is a technique used to examine the incremental costs between quantities within a supplier's price quotation. This tool allows the user to verify that quantity discounts are reasonable. Using this technique, a buyer may be able to negotiate price improvements through a better understanding of incremental unit costs. There are two primary types of quantity discount analyses. The first involves prices at specific quantities while the second examines discounts over quantity ranges.

Quantity Discount Analysis Illustrated

Exhibit 12.8 demonstrates how to use QDA when a buyer has price breaks at specific quantities. Exhibit 12.9 illustrates how to use QDA when a buyer has price breaks in ranges of quantities. The exhibits explain how to perform the appropriate calculations.

When using quantity discount analysis, the key calculation is the incremental cost of each additional unit at different quantity levels. In Exhibit 12.8, even though the original quote at the three quantity levels moves lower on a per-unit basis, the incremental cost for units 7–10 ($67.50) is actually higher than for units 4–6 ($60). The same type of situation occurs in Exhibit 12.9. A buyer faced with this quote would want to know why incremental unit costs increase rather than decrease. Often, the supplier is unaware why the incremental costs are higher.

QDA provides the buyer with information for questioning and negotiating improvements in the discount schedule. The analysis often reveals an up-and-down roller-coaster effect between incremental price differences. Questions asked because of a QDA often produce additional discounts and a better understanding of the quotation by the buyer and seller. The buyer should not accept a quote that features higher incremental costs as volumes increase unless the supplier can provide a valid explanation.

PROCESS MAPPING

Process mapping is a tool that reduces processes to their component parts or activities and helps identify and then eliminate non–value-added activities (waste) or delays within a process. Process mapping is valuable in purchasing, for example, when attempting to streamline the flow of material or information between suppliers and a purchaser.

Organizations have many processes that, when taken together, define the organization's primary work. A process is essentially an outcome composed of a set of tasks, activities, or steps. How well an organization performs these tasks determines how efficient and effective it is at that process. The following supply chain processes are among those that most businesses perform:

- Supplier evaluation and selection
- Supply-base management

EXHIBIT 12.8   *Quantity Discount Analysis (Price Breaks at Specific Quantities)*

1. Quotation from Avco at Specific Quantities

       1 unit @ $85 each
       3 units @ $80 each
       6 units @ $70 each
      10 units @ $69 each

2. Instructions

Line 1: Place specific quantities from the quotation on line 1 in the appropriate column. Each column represents a specific quantity. Assume that ordering 0 is an option. This will support the quantity discount calculation.

Line 2: Place the quoted price from the supplier for each specific quantity on line 2 in the appropriate column.

Line 3: Multiply line 1 by line 2 for each column to arrive at a total price per order.

Line 4: Take the difference between the total price per order (line 3) and each successive order. For column A, it is the difference between $85 and ordering zero pieces, or $0.00. For column B, it is the difference between column B/line 3 and column A/line 3, or $240 – $85 = $155.

Line 5: This is the difference between each quantity break specified on line 1.

Line 6: This equals line 4/line 5 for each column.

3. Price Breaks at Specific Quantities

Supplier _____Avco_____   Part Name & No. ____Compressor 04273999____   Date ____10/24/01____

		A	*B*	*C*	*D*	*E*	*F*	*G*	*H*
1. Number units per order	0	1	3	6	10				
2. Price per unit (quoted price)	0	85	80	70	69				
3. Total price per order	0	85	240	420	690				
4. Price difference between orders		85	155	180	270				
5. Quantity difference between orders		1	2	3	4				
6. Price per unit per order quantity difference		$85	$77.50	$60	$67.50				

4. Quantity Discount Analysis

Quantity	Total Cost	Incremental Quantity	Incremental Cost
1	$85	1	$85
		2	$77.50
3	$240	3	$77.50
		4	$60
		5	$60
6	$420	6	$60
		7	$67.50
		8	$67.50
		9	$67.50
10	$690	10	$67.50

EXHIBIT 12.9   *Quantity Discount Analysis (Price Breaks in Ranges of Quantities)*

1. Quotation from Dynamic Industries at Ranges of Quantities

Range	Price per Unit in Range	Range	Price per Unit in Range
1–5	$10.00 each	21–100	$7.60 each
6–10	$8.00 each	101–499	$7.00 each
11–20	$7.80 each	500+	$6.90 each

2. Instructions

Line 1: Place specific quantity ranges from the supplier quotation on line 1 in the appropriate column. Each column represents a specific quantity range provided by the supplier.

Line 2: Place the price per unit within each quantity range in the appropriate column. This is information provided by the supplier on the quote.

Line 3: "Total price per order" equals the lowest quantity in a range from line 1 times the "Price per unit" in line 2 for each column. For example, for column C (quantity range 11–20), "Total price per order" equals 11 × $7.80 = $85.80.

Line 4: Take the "Total price per order" from the next-highest quantity range (line 3) and divide this by "Price per unit" for the column being calculated. For example, for column A, the maximum units to order equals 48/10 equals 4.8. For column B, the maximum units to order equals 85.80/8 = 10.7 and so on. Round down to the nearest whole number.

Line 5: This equals line 2 times line 4 for each column.

Line 6: Calculate the difference between the "Total price maximum order" for successive quantity ranges. For example, the "Total price per maximum order" for column B (6–10 quantity range) is $80, while the "Total price per order" for column A (1–5 quantity range) is $40. The difference is $40, which appears in column A on line 6. Calculate all other columns on line 6 accordingly.

Line 7: This is the difference between line 4 and the preceding column value on line 4. It is the difference between the maximum units to order from one quantity range to the next.

Line 8: This equals line 6 divided by line 7 for each column. It represents the incremental cost for each unit within that quantity range.

3. Price Breaks in Ranges of Quantities

Supplier ___Dynamic Industries___   Part Name & No. _____Wedge 04336280_____   Date ____9/14/01____

		A	B	C	D	E	F	G	H
1. Number of units per order	0	1–5	6–10	11–20	21–100	101–500	500+		
2. Price per unit (quoted price)	0	10	8	7.80	7.60	7.00	6.90		
3. Total price per order (use minimum quantity)	0	10	48	85.80	159.60	707	3,450		
4. Maximum units to order	0	4	10	20	93	492	——		
5. Total price per maximum order		40	80	156	706.80	3,444	——		
6. Price difference between maximum order		40	40	76	550.80	2,737.20	——		
7. Quantity difference between maximum units to order		4	6	10	73	399	——		
8. Price per unit per order quantity difference		$10	$6.67	$7.60	$7.54	$6.86			

(continued)

EXHIBIT 12.9   *(continued)*

4. Quantity Discount Analysis

Quantity	Quoted Price	Quantity Range	Incremental Cost
1–5	$10.00	First 5 units	$10.00 each
6–10	$8.00	Next 5 units	$6.67 each
11–20	$7.80	Next 10 units	$7.60 each
21–100	$7.60	Next 80 units	$7.54 each
101–500	$7.00	Next 400 units	$6.86 each
500+	$6.90	——	——

- New-product design and development
- Accounts receivable/accounts payable
- Inventory control and management
- Customer service support
- Training and education
- Inbound logistics
- Outbound logistics and physical distribution
- Research and development
- Customer order fulfillment

Most processes cross more than one functional boundary. When this happens, a risk exists that no one actually owns or takes responsibility for the entire process. In fact, some departments may actually have goals that are in conflict with one another. A transportation department evaluated on cost may use the least expensive method possible, such as rail. Customer service, on the other hand, may want to make material available to customers as soon as possible, which implies speed. Rapid delivery will likely increase transportation costs. These two groups may thus have goals that conflict.

Organizations use process mapping to redesign or reengineer processes. There are two basic types of processes: sequential and concurrent. *Sequential processes* are those in which the set of steps or activities comprising the activity occur one after the other.

Activity B does not begin until A is complete while C does not begin until B is complete. When mapping processes, we may place time estimates of the activity along with the sequence of the activities. A primary goal of process mapping is to eliminate waste from a process. Activity times are important to this goal.

Concurrent processes consist of activities or steps performed concurrently during the main flow of work. For example, many organizations are attempting to develop new products concurrently rather than sequentially, which not only saves time and money but also allows agreement on major issues early in the process.

Cross-functional teams often use process mapping. Since most processes move across functional boundaries, it is logical to have those groups connected with the process involved with mapping and improving the process. This involvement will help generate buy-in from different groups concerning any proposed changes while keeping all impacted groups informed of those changes.

Process Mapping Illustrated

Perhaps the best way to describe process mapping is with an example. Exhibit 12.10, taken from the automobile industry, describes the receiving process at a physical distribution facility. This process is critical because the speed at which a facility receives and moves material defines the flow for downstream work centers. If the receiving process is slow, it can create a bottleneck affecting the entire facility as well as other facilities requiring material from that location. The process itself may also contain non–value-adding tasks or waste.

Exhibit 12.10 reveals that seven different employees take part in the physical receipt and movement of material. The average time to unload, process, and move material from a truck is 215 minutes, which means that, on average, each receiving line can process and move two trailer loads of material a day. With eight receiving lines, this process averages 16 truckloads per eight-hour shift.

As volumes at this company increased, the company faced two options: add a second shift or improve the receiving process to make it more efficient. In the short run it added a second shift as a fix to the receiving capacity problem. A longer-term solution required a total revamping of the process, which Exhibit 12.11 illustrates.

The new system combined physical system changes with information technology. The redesigned system generates move-control tickets automatically once the front gate of the plant acknowledges the arrival of a truck. Furthermore, the new process operates concurrently versus sequentially. The employee unloading the trailer now has expanded duties. The employee not only unloads the material but also hangs control tickets and resolves receiving discrepancies, which illustrates the benefit of flexibility versus specialization. These changes reduced the time required to process an inbound trailer by over 50%, which means that a single shift can now process over twice as many trailers a day. Material moves faster and the process requires fewer total resources. Until an organization maps its processes, it cannot realize major improvements. The following steps are critical to process mapping:

- Search for better ways and methods to perform the tasks comprising a process, which often involves using information technology to automate transactions within the process.
- Replace sequential activities with concurrent activities wherever possible.
- Identify those activities that contribute to waste or add minimal value to the process and target those for elimination.
- Identify the time associated with each part of a process and identify how much of that time is waste.
- Involve the functional groups that impact a process.
- Represent graphically the process so those involved have a clear understanding of the process steps.

EXHIBIT 12.10   *Physical Receipt of Purchased Material as a Sequential Process*

Step Description and Average Required Time per Trailer

- Employee 1 physically places trailer at receiving dock (*15 minutes*)
- Employee 2 unloads the trailer with material handling equipment (*30 minutes*)
- Employee 3 checks load quantity from the trailer against shipping documents for accuracy[*] (*30 minutes*)
- Employee 4 acknowledges receipt of the material on the computer and prints control tickets to move material to required warehouse locations (*60 minutes*)
- Employee 5 attaches control tickets to individual loads (*20 minutes*)
- Employee 6 inspects inbound material[*] (*30 minutes*)
- Employee 7 moves material to required warehouse location, freeing up the receipt line for another trailer (*30 minutes*)
- Employee 4 files copy of shipping documents and forwards copies to Accounts Payable at the end of the day. This does not impact the physical movement of material (*15 minutes*)

Total inbound trailer processing times: 215 minutes (excludes Step 8), or 3 hours and 35 minutes

[*]Non-Value-Added Activity: As purchasing works with suppliers to improve material and delivery quality, it is not necessary to check each inbound load.

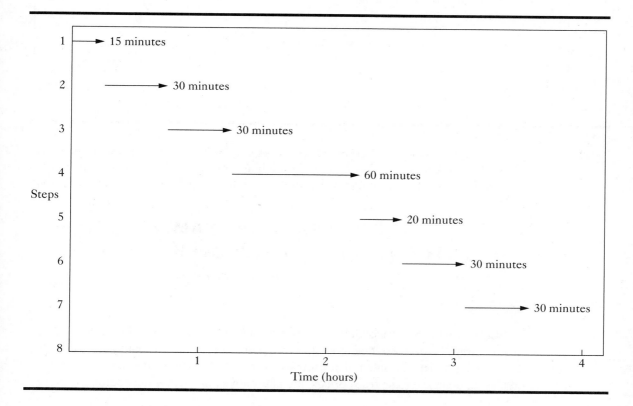

EXHIBIT 12.11   *Physical Receipt of Purchased Material, Revised Process*

Step description and average required time

- Employee 1 physically places trailer at receiving dock. Move-control tickets are printed concurrently and automatically as facility guard acknowledges the arrival of the trailer electronically at the front gate (*15 minutes*)
- Employee 2 picks up printed control tickets for the trailer, unloads the trailer with material handling equipment, performs a cursory check of the loads as they are unloaded, and hangs load tickets as material comes off the truck (*60 minutes*)
- Employee 3 physically moves material to required warehouse location, freeing up the receipt line for another trailer (*30 minutes*)
- Receipt information stored electronically with information forwarded to Accounts Payable (*0 minutes*)

Total inbound trailer processing times: 105 minutes, or 1 hour and 45 minutes

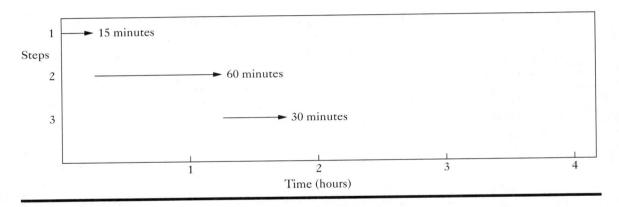

There are many ways to represent a process graphically. One popular approach is *flow-charting*, a technique in which different symbols represent different stages or parts of a process. Exhibit 12.12 shows the different symbols commonly used during flowcharting.

GOOD PRACTICE EXAMPLE
VCI/Ellison Trucks Apply Project Management to Global Sourcing

■ ■ ■

VCI/Ellison*—the consolidation of the truck-making unit of VCI with Ellison—is facing intense product-pricing pressure from customers and competitors. The ability to meet financial targets has presented a major challenge for the company. With limited ability to raise truck prices, the alternatives facing the new company were

EXHIBIT 12.12   *Common Symbols Used During Flowcharting*

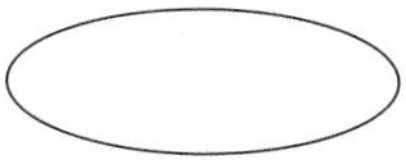

Denotes the start and end of a process

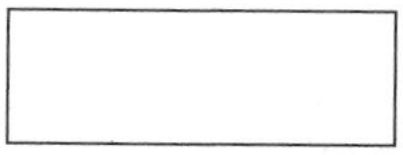

Denotes an activity

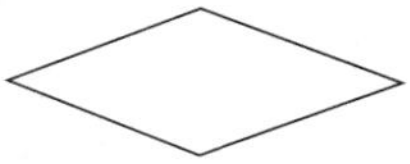

Denotes a decision point

Denotes the delivered product or service

Denotes the direction or flow of work within a process

to manage material costs better or to absorb price increases through lower profit margins and profitability.

From the day VCI assumed ownership of Ellison, both companies sought to leverage the commonality between them on a global basis. In fact, a recent corporate reorganization has integrated engineering and procurement from both companies in a major attempt to achieve global purchasing and product design advantages. VCI/Ellison has concluded that procurement offers excellent opportunities for global synergy across the two continents. The company has implemented a global sourcing process that takes a project management approach to leverage the volumes available across the combined truck units. All projects move through nine steps, with project teams managing the first four steps:

*   Step 0: Select global sourcing projects.
*   Step 1: Launch project.
*   Step 3: Develop requests for proposals.
*   Step 2: Develop the sourcing strategy.
*   Step 4: Recommend and negotiate with suppliers.
*   Step 5: Certify suppliers.
*   Step 6: Formalize the sourcing contract.
*   Step 7: Test and approve samples.
*   Step 8: Implement production readiness.

Formal team leaders and business analysts are critical to project team success. Two teams, one from VCI and one from Ellison, work simultaneously on the same sourcing opportunity, each with a formal team leader, two functional members (usually from engineering and purchasing), and a business analyst who supports both teams. Each project consists of seven combined positions across two teams. The team leader and business analyst are full-time while the buyer and engineer provide a part-time commitment. The two teams may come together physically two or three times over a project's duration.

With any team-based approach to projects, the role of the team leader is vital to project success. VCI/Ellison always has nine projects progressing at one time in a wave. Team leaders work simultaneously with three global sourcing project teams. The team leader is responsible for planning team meetings, which are held once or twice a week depending on the phase of the project, and reporting project status to an executive steering committee. Planning includes setting the meeting agenda, ensuring the global sourcing process is followed, and working with team members to meet time lines and achieve project goals. The leader also communicates with each member's management when necessary to ensure commitment. The team leader is critical to project success, particularly when the leader must work with members to balance their priorities and challenge the teams to achieve demanding performance improvement targets.

Executive management looks for people who are regimented and have project management skills to be team leaders. They must have the ability to manage projects, including follow-up with members and reporting to executive management. The executive steering committee also looks for team leaders who are open-minded, can listen to and value the contribution of others, enjoy the challenge that global sourcing projects present, and are fluent in English (almost all of the global sourcing process is conducted in English).

Each pair of teams that is working on three projects simultaneously also has a business analyst assigned to support the effort. The work required for sending requests for information (RFIs) and requests for proposals (RFPs) across two continents is extensive. VCI/Ellison created the position of full-time business analyst to help manage the tasks required within the first four steps of the global sourcing process and to record and report all data collected. This individual attends all team meetings and is present at negotiations to provide information or data as required. Management views the business analyst position as an ideal way for high-potential individuals to gain exposure to purchasing and sourcing. The position is somewhat like a training assignment before the analyst progresses to other purchasing or sourcing responsibilities.

A key part of the analyst's responsibilities involves maintaining a software database that has been developed to manage the global sourcing projects. The analyst inputs the sourcing categories and subcategories that a team is pursuing, establishes RFI and RFP records, and eventually inputs individual part numbers as they are received from engineers. Analysts compile and send RFI and RFP packages to suppliers, track and report response rates, input RFI and RFP response information into the project database, and follow up with those suppliers who are late with their submission. The business analyst also answers any questions that suppliers have or forwards their inquiries to the appropriate procurement or engineering representative.

Analysts also have responsibility for providing feedback to suppliers concerning the competitiveness of their initial quote. At times the analyst "invites" suppliers to resubmit their quotation. The project software system provides a report that compares a supplier's quote with the best quote received.

When managers describe the value that global sourcing provides to the company, a number of themes emerge. Perhaps most important, taking a project approach has demonstrated that VCI and Ellison could work jointly to capture the benefits offered through that global sourcing. In addition, the process has demonstrated that a disciplined project approach to sourcing can lead to significant material savings, which have averaged 7% to 10% over previous contracts. ■

*Company name changed at the request of the companies.

CONCLUSION

Purchasers and supply chain specialists rely on various tools and techniques to support and improve the purchasing and sourcing process. The development of software, which Appendix B at the end of the book illustrates, has greatly expanded the capabilities of purchasing and supply chain specialists to analyze costs and manage the supply chain. The need to routinely apply the techniques and tools presented in this chapter is critical to world-class purchasing and supply chain management. Wherever possible, decisions should be based on quantitative analysis rather than qualitative information.

DISCUSSION QUESTIONS

1.   Why does the learning curve apply mainly to direct rather than indirect labor?
2.   If each time production volume doubled and direct-labor requirements decreased by 5%, what would be the appropriate learning rate?
3.   Discuss why it is important for buyers to have knowledge of a supplier's learning rate when preparing to negotiate a purchase contract.
4.   Why is it sometimes easier to evaluate the success or failure of a project than of other forms of work?
5.   Describe the concept of value as it relates to value analysis. Provide examples of how an organization can increase value to itself or to its customers.
6.   Why do progressive firms actively practice value analysis?
7.   Discuss why different functional groups often work together when value analyzing a product or service.

8.   Assume you are the leader of a value analysis team. Discuss how you would go about identifying value analysis opportunities.

9.   In general, do you believe a project manager's responsibilities are challenging? Why or why not?

10. When are users most likely to use Gantt charts for project management? When are they likely to use CPM or PERT?

11. What does it mean for a path to have three weeks of slack? Does each activity necessarily have three weeks of slack? Why or why not?

12. Discuss the information gained from flowcharting a process.

13. What are the various parts or phases of the sourcing process? Can any of these parts be made more efficient? Discuss.

ADDITIONAL READINGS

Brown, James. "Value Engineering: A Blueprint." New York: Industrial Press, 1992.

Cavinato, Joseph L., and Ralph G. Kauffman, eds. *The Purchasing Handbook: A Guide for the Purchasing and Supply Professional*. New York: McGraw-Hill, 2000.

Farrington, Brian. *The Services Buyer in the Role of Project and Cost Management*. London: International Thomson Business Press, 1997.

Greico, Peter L. *Supply Management Toolbox: How to Manage Your Suppliers*. West Palm Beach, FL: PT Publications, 1995.

Miles, Larry. *Techniques of Value Analysis and Engineering*. New York: McGraw-Hill, 1972.

Westney, Richard, ed. *The Engineer's Cost Handbook: Tools for Managing Project Costs*. New York: M. Dekker, 1997.

STRATEGIC COST MANAGEMENT 13

$\mathscr{H}$ow IBM Transitioned to Cost-Based Purchasing

During the latter months of 1993, international high-tech giant IBM needed to trim billions from its overall operation. After a painful workforce reduction initiative, "Big Blue" looked at its procurement system and cost management for even more savings. Purchasing professional Gene Richter was brought on board and promptly changed IBM's procurement models, which were based on an antiquated and fragmented system of individual divisions and departments, and adopted a dynamic, forward-thinking approach that saved the organization more than $5 billion over a five-year period. In 1999, IBM was awarded one of the highest honors in purchasing, *Purchasing* magazine's Medal of Professional Excellence.*

"In the past, our purchasers kept suppliers at arm's length," says Javier Urioste, director of policy, strategy, and international operations for IBM Global Procurement, and one of Richter's chief reengineering architects. "We had 60 or 70 disconnected procurement organizations around the world. We weren't leveraging volume or coordinating efforts. We would take three bids and choose the lowest. We are now more open and direct [with suppliers]. We went away from bids and looked at the market and internal and external processes. We looked to understand suppliers' businesses, the industry, and market trends. We saved our suppliers money, which saved us money. Some things were over-designed. We had multiple suppliers in a lot of areas but now have the right supply base."

So what happened? "What happened is we woke up. We realized that we couldn't be expert in everything," Richter says. IBM also realized that outside suppliers had technology that IBM needed, and that competitors were reducing their costs by outsourcing. In 1986, 28% of IBM's revenue was spent with outside suppliers. In 1996, that percentage grew to 49%. In 1998, it was 51%. To take advantage of IBM's huge purchasing volumes globally, Richter centralized IBM's purchases, setting up commodity councils to buy parts rather than having individual sites buy their own components. In 1993, IBM had about 4,900 production suppliers. Now about 85% of IBM's $17.1 billion in production purchases is with 50 suppliers.

Part of IBM's methodology has been to analyze cost drivers, with each cost element identified and addressed. Urioste explains their approach: "How many man-hours are spent on a particular function during a set period of time? Will the costs of transportation increase? What costs are moving ahead of the market? These are a few of the questions posed during their research." Urioste also says that in the past, IBM's suppliers were asked to hold too much inventory, and that too many warranties existed for just one part. Trimming these elements, as minor as they may seem, saved millions for both suppliers and IBM. IBM has 17 commodity councils for such items as DRAM, microprocessors, logic, passives, monitors, electronic card and test among others. Richter says, "We have one global contract with a supplier. So a logic chip supplier would supply logic to all IBM divisions.

→→→

IBM will commit to buying a percentage of its component requirements from a supplier."
These efforts have paid off. For instance, while the cost for memory-integrated circuits decreased by 44% in the market, IBM was able to shave costs by 49%. In technical service
subcontracting, market prices went up by 7.8% in 1998; while IBM actually reduced costs
by 1.7 % in this same period.

Source: "IBM Takes It," *Purchasing* (September 16, 1999): 18–22.

In the new century ahead, the concept of customer value will determine the difference between those organizations that succeed and those that fall by the wayside.
The ratio of customer value can be simply stated:

$$\text{Value} = \frac{(\text{Quality} + \text{Technology} + \text{Service} + \text{Cycle Time})}{\text{Price}}$$

Although purchasing has a major impact on all of the variables in the numerator in
this equation, this chapter focuses on the denominator: price, and its immediate driver, cost.

A major responsibility of purchasing is to ensure that the price paid for an item is
fair and reasonable. The price paid for purchased products and services will have a direct impact on the end customer's perception of value provided by the organization.
Evaluation of a supplier's actual cost to provide the product or service, versus the actual purchase price paid, is an ongoing challenge within all industries. In many situations, the need to control costs requires a focus on the costs associated with producing an item or service, versus simply analyzing final price. In these cases, innovative
pricing approaches involve cost identification as a process leading to agreement on a
final price. In other cases, however, purchasing may not need to spend much effort
understanding costs, and will focus instead on whether the price is fair given competitive market conditions.

Purchasing and supply chain specialists must understand the principles of price
and cost analysis. *Price analysis* refers to the process of comparing supplier prices
against external price benchmarks, without direct knowledge of the supplier's costs.
Price analysis focuses simply on a seller's price with little or no consideration given to
the actual cost of production. In contrast, *cost analysis* is the process of analyzing each
individual cost element (i.e., material, labor hours and rates, overhead, general and
administrative costs, and profit) that together add up to the final price. Ideally, this
analysis identifies the actual cost to produce an item so the parties to a contract can
determine a fair and reasonable price and develop plans to achieve future cost reductions. Finally, *total cost analysis* applies the price/cost equation across multiple processes that span two or more organizations across a supply chain.

This chapter presents a traditional discussion of price and cost fundamentals
along with a number of innovative price and cost management tools that can be applied using available information on the Internet and simple spreadsheet analysis.

Some of these tools include learning-curve analysis, value analysis (both presented in Chapter 12), price analysis, reverse price analysis, and total cost analysis. By applying such tools, purchasers can evolve toward a system of *strategic cost management* that seeks to reduce costs across the entire supply chain. While not all of these tools are appropriate for every situation, supply chain managers must learn to recognize when and how such tools can be applied. Before moving on to this discussion, we will begin by reviewing the fundamental types of costs encountered in supply chain situations.

Cost Fundamentals

Knowledge of costs is essential to effective purchasing. As organizations strive to reduce expenditures, an understanding of cost allows a purchaser to recognize major cost components. Knowledge of costs and their behavior is also necessary when evaluating the product and process capability of potential suppliers. More often than not, supplier cost analysis is a major portion of a purchase quotation evaluation. The ability to identify and understand the components of cost can mean the difference between successful and unsuccessful control of the "cost of goods sold" component of any financial statement.

This section discusses various types of costs. Readers requiring an in-depth analysis of different costs are urged to refer to a managerial accounting textbook.

Types of Costs[1]

Fixed Costs Fixed costs remain constant or stable over different levels of volume, at least during the short term. To stay in business over the long term requires pricing at a level that covers fixed costs (and makes some contribution to profit). Examples of traditional fixed costs include:

- Property taxes
- Depreciation expense
- Salaries of some employees
- Pension obligations
- Rent
- Insurance payments
- Interest on outstanding loans
- Equipment lease payments and charges

Technically, these costs are present even if there is no material output. However, during slower economic conditions a producer can partially reduce fixed costs by closing a section of a plant to realize lower insurance premiums, for example. *Avoidable costs* are the portion of fixed costs reduced during slower economic periods.

Most organizations attempt to maintain fixed costs at the lowest level possible because these costs represent financial obligations. During slower business conditions, some sellers take on business simply to increase the utilization of production facilities and generate some fixed-cost contribution. The logic behind this is that the fixed cost per unit becomes lower as sales increase. For example, if a seller has $10,000 in fixed costs and a current sales volume of 5,000 units, the average fixed cost per unit is $2.00 ($10,000/5000 units = $2 per unit). If volume doubles to 10,000 units, the average fixed cost per unit lowers to $1.00 ($10,000/10,000 units = $1 per unit). This illustrates why suppliers are sometimes willing, in the short run, to take on business that actually appears unprofitable. The seller can recover its variable costs while making at least some contribution to fixed costs.

Variable Costs Variable costs change proportionally with output. In particular, these costs vary directly and proportionally with the production of a particular product or service. As production or use increases, the costs increase. As production or use decreases, so do the costs. Traditional accounting practices depict variable costs as varying directly with volume, which means the relationship of variable costs to production output is perfectly linear. If volume doubles, then variable costs also double. In reality, few costs have a perfectly linear relationship with volume. Consider, for example, material costs. The per-unit material cost for an item at 10,000 units may not be the same per-unit cost at 30,000 units. Larger production volumes tend to generate lower per-unit costs (a relationship often referred to as *economies of scale*).

By definition, a producer incurs variable costs only during the production of an item or service. Examples of variable costs include the materials used directly in production, some types of labor, transportation, material-ordering costs, and packaging supplies. Direct-labor and direct-material costs usually account for the bulk of variable costs.

Semivariable Costs These costs have both a fixed and a variable component (and are therefore often called *mixed costs*). For example, the base salary of an executive manager is a fixed expense while an earned bonus is a variable expense. Telephone expenses are another example of a semivariable cost. Regardless of usage, a customer still receives a fixed charge each month for basic phone service. As long-distance usage increases, costs increase. Another example would be a basic equipment rental or lease (such as a car rental or lease). A monthly payment is due regardless of volume. As equipment usage increases, however, so do the operating expenses associated with the equipment.

Total Cost Total cost is the sum of variable, fixed, and semivariable costs. Total costs increase as the volume of production or service increases, while the cost to produce each unit or provide each service decreases. Several points can be made specifically about costs:

- Total fixed costs do not change with volume.
- Per-unit fixed costs decrease as volume increases.
- Total variable costs increase with volume.
- Per-unit variable costs may or may not change with volume.

Exhibit 13.1 shows the relationship between fixed, variable, semivariable, and semifixed costs across different volumes. Total cost is simply the sum of the various

EXHIBIT 13.1   *Cost Behaviors*

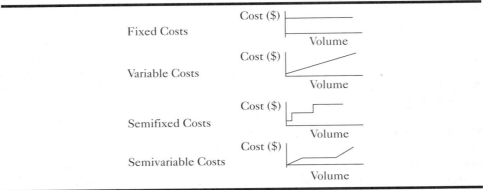

costs at different volumes. This exhibit illustrates several important principles. First, variable costs equal zero when production equals zero. When no production occurs, a producer has only fixed costs. Furthermore, the variable cost line indicates the proportional relationship between variable costs and volume. Next, all cost lines in the exhibit are straight, which suggests that a linear relationship exists between all costs and volume. (This is probably not the true relationship between costs and volume.) Finally, this type of analysis usually applies to a seller's entire cost structure and does not portray the cost structure for an individual product or product line. This is an important distinction when trying to analyze the costs associated with producing a particular item. Exhibit 13.2 shows how average costs vary on a per-unit basis. In this case, the fixed cost is linear with respect to volume, while variable per-unit costs may vary in a nonlinear fashion, as economies of scale and learning-curve effects take place.

A Different System of Classifying Costs

The fixed, variable, and semivariable cost categories can be reclassified according to their origin or association with a process.

Direct Costs These costs can be directly traced and allocated to an item or are the direct outcome of an operation or process. Common direct costs include the material and labor that directly support the production of an item. Cost managers who perform detailed cost analysis typically focus on the direct and indirect costs required to produce an item.

One area of confusion concerns the difference between direct and variable costs. At first glance, it appears that little difference exists between the terms. After all, if no production occurs, then no direct or variable costs occur. When production begins, both direct and variable costs rise. The difference lies in the context of how to use the costs. Direct costs are of interest when we need to calculate item-specific costs.

EXHIBIT 13.2   *Behaviors of Unit Costs*

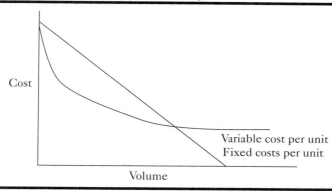

We refer to variable costs when describing the behavior of a cost over a range of production volumes. Variable costs are usually not identified with a specific item or operation, but they often apply to an entire facility or plant and are aggregated over multiple product lines. This information is useful for summarizing performance for financial reporting purposes but is of little value for decision-making on specific processes. For instance, a manager requiring detailed cost data for a make-or-buy analysis would require data on the direct cost to produce an item along with some allocation for indirect or overhead costs. Variable costs for the entire facility would not be appropriate for this type of decision.

Indirect Costs This category includes costs not assigned directly to a specific process or production item. Consider a materials handler who supports two separate machines producing multiple items. The cost analysis must include the materials-handling costs associated with production. It is impractical in traditional cost accounting to assign the materials handler's labor to a specific unit of production because this employee shifts from machine to machine and from item to item. In this case, the cost accounting system usually allocates the materials-handling expense between machines or production items based on an allocation formula. Other allocated costs include the energy required for the machine, managerial and administrative expenses, and shipping containers. Some producers account for indirect or nontraceable costs by assigning a single expense, often called a *burden expense*, to the item when calculating the total cost of production. The burden expense is typically some percentage of the direct costs to produce an item. Organizations with advanced cost accounting systems are able to segregate overhead costs along specific product lines, instead of "throwing everything into the pot" and allocating a burden rate to products according to direct costs. Such advanced systems are often called activity-based costing (ABC), a topic discussed in the Appendix F located on the Website.

Now that we understand the basics of different costs, let's move on to the implications of costs for supply chain management.

EXHIBIT 13.3   *Cost Management Approaches*

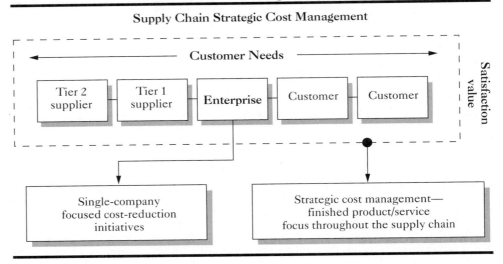

STRATEGIC COST MANAGEMENT: A STRUCTURED APPROACH TO COST REDUCTION

Managers are increasingly considering the implications of price and cost management from a total supply chain perspective, as shown in Exhibit 13.3. In the past, many companies focused their cost efforts on internal cost management initiatives. Today, organizations wanting to fully capture the benefits of cost-reduction initiatives must begin to consider cost-reduction initiatives that include both upstream and downstream members of their supply chains.

Such a change requires a fundamental shift in thinking in the minds of managers and employees. This shift may take several years to be fully realized due to the pervasive types of "price-based" thinking that are ingrained in traditional financial managers. As Exhibit 13.4 illustrates, most companies are undertaking initiatives that focus on internal cost-reduction efforts. Many of these initiatives have been discussed in other sections of this book, and include efforts such as value engineering, value analysis, commodity strategies, process improvement, and cost modeling. However, a "new generation" of cost management initiatives is also evolving that includes both upstream and downstream members of the supply chain. Such initiatives, shown in Exhibit 13.5, often involve direct involvement of two or more supply chain partners working together to identify process improvements that reduce costs across the supply chain. Examples include team-based value-engineering efforts, supplier development, cross-enterprise cost improvement, joint brainstorming efforts, supplier suggestion programs, and supply chain redesign. Such initiatives are only beginning to evolve between supply chain parties.

EXHIBIT 13.4   *Supply Chain Strategic Cost Management Processes–Single-Company Focus*

```
                        ┌──────────────────┐
                        │   Supply chain   │
                        │  strategic cost  │
                        │   management     │
                        └────────┬─────────┘
                                 │
                        ┌────────┴─────────┐
                        │  Single-company  │
                        │      focus       │
                        └────────┬─────────┘
                                 │
   ┌──────────┬───────────┬──────┴──────┬───────────┬──────────┐
┌──────┐  ┌──────┐   ┌──────────┐  ┌──────────┐  ┌──────┐
│Value │  │Value │   │Commodity │  │ Process  │  │ Cost │
│engin-│  │analy-│   │strategies│  │improve-  │  │model-│
│eering│  │sis   │   │          │  │ment      │  │ing   │
└──────┘  └──────┘   └──────────┘  └──────────┘  └──────┘
```

Value engineering	Value analysis	Commodity strategies	Process improvement	Cost modeling
• Initiate new-product development process • Achieve target pricing and other performance targets	• Design/ specification elimination/ changes	• Negotiation • Volume leveraging • Supplier switching/threat • Supply-base structuring • Longer-term agreements • Globalization • Outsourcing • Supplier "partnering"	• Elimination of non–value-added activities	• Should-be cost determination • Part, process, subsystem, module

Strategic cost management approaches will vary according to the stage of the product life cycle. As shown in Exhibit 13.6, various approaches are appropriate at different product life cycle stages. In the initial concept and development stage, purchasing will often act proactively to establish cost targets. Target costing/target pricing is a technique developed originally in Japanese organizations in the 1980s to combat the inflation of the yen against other currencies. Target pricing, quality function deployment, and technology sharing are all effective approaches for cost reduction used at this stage. As a product or service enters the design and launch stages, supplier integration, standardization, value engineering, and design for manufacturing can improve the opportunity to use standard parts and techniques, leverage volumes, and create opportunities for cost savings. During the product or service launch, purchasing will adopt more traditional cost-reduction approaches, including competitive bidding, negotiation, value analysis, volume leveraging, service contracts focusing on savings, and linking

EXHIBIT 13.5   *Supply Chain Strategic Cost Management Processes–Supply Chain Focus*

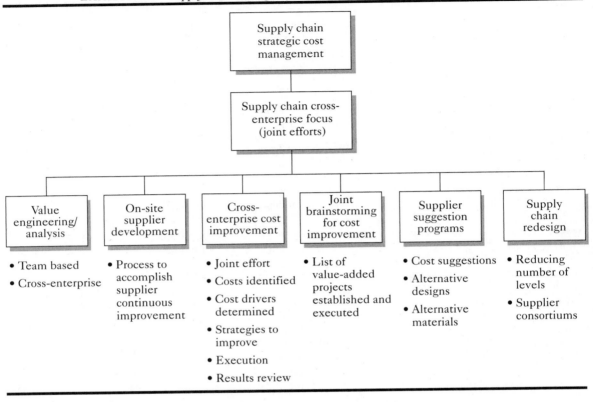

- Team based
- Cross-enterprise

- Process to accomplish supplier continuous improvement

- Joint effort
- Costs identified
- Cost drivers determined
- Strategies to improve
- Execution
- Results review

- List of value-added projects established and executed

- Cost suggestions
- Alternative designs
- Alternative materials

- Reducing number of levels
- Supplier consortiums

EXHIBIT 13.6   *Managing Life-Cycle Costs*

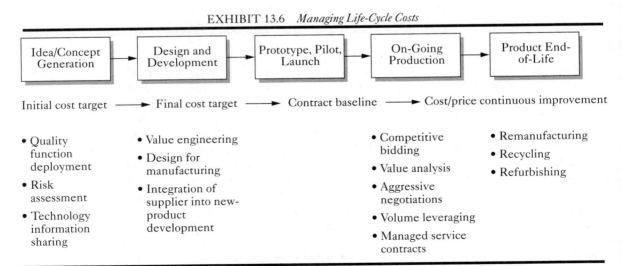

Initial cost target ⟶ Final cost target ⟶ Contract baseline ⟶ Cost/price continuous improvement

- Quality function deployment
- Risk assessment
- Technology information sharing

- Value engineering
- Design for manufacturing
- Integration of supplier into new-product development

- Competitive bidding
- Value analysis
- Aggressive negotiations
- Volume leveraging
- Managed service contracts

- Remanufacturing
- Recycling
- Refurbishing

EXHIBIT 13.7   *Framework for Price/Cost Management*

High	Unique products	Critical products
Low	Generics	Commodities

Risk (vertical axis)

Low   High

Value (cost, service, administration)

longer-term pricing to extended contracts. As a product reaches its end of life, purchasing cannot ignore the potential value of environmental initiatives to remanufacture, recycle, or refurbish products that are becoming obsolete. For instance, print cartridge manufacturers such as Xerox and Hewlett-Packard have developed innovative technologies that allow customers to recycle laser toner cartridges, which are subsequently refurbished and used again, eliminating landfill costs.

As noted in Chapter 5, the major benefits from cost-reduction efforts occur when purchasing is involved early in the new-product/service development cycle. When sourcing decisions are made early in the product life cycle, the full effects of a sourcing decision over the product's life can be considered. When purchasing is involved later in the product development cycle, efforts to reduce costs have a minimal impact because the major decisions regarding types of materials, labor rates, and choice of suppliers have already been made. A manager in a major automotive company described this situation as follows: "In the past, we allowed engineering to determine the specifications, the materials, and the supplier. In fact, the supplier already produced the first prototype! That's when they decided to call in purchasing to develop the contract. How much leverage do you have in convincing the supplier to reduce costs when the supplier already knows they are guaranteed the business, and they have already sunk money into a fixed design and tooling for the product?"[2]

When prioritizing efforts to reduce costs, companies often apply a structured framework for cost reduction similar to the one illustrated in Exhibit 13.7. This framework is consistent with the portfolio analysis framework developed in Chapter 6 and should be integrated into an organization's commodity strategy development

EXHIBIT 13.8   *Price/Cost Management Approaches*

Unique Products
- High-risk, low-value
- Strategies
    Preferred suppliers
- Critical factors
    High costs when cost/quality problems occur
- Metrics
    Unit price cost reduction—actual prices for same items
    Target prices achieved, "should cost" $
    Total delivered cost reduction

Generics
- Low-value, low-risk
- Strategies
    Standardize / consolidate
- Critical factors
    Reduce cost of acquisition
- Metrics
    Total delivered cost reduction
    Percent of cost of goods sold improvement
    Transportation cost reduction

Critical products
- High-risk, high-value strategies
    Strategic supplier partnerships
- Critical factors
    High costs when cost/quality problems occur
- Metrics
    Target prices achieved
    Unit price cost reduction—actual to actual prices for same items
    Joint cost savings

Commodities
- High-value, low-risk
- Strategies
    Leverage preferred suppliers
- Critical factors
    Reduce cost of materials
- Metrics
    Price change improvement to market index

process. As shown in Exhibit 13.8, each approach requires a different strategic focus in terms of price versus cost. In general, low-value generics in which a competitive market exists should emphasize total delivered price. There is no need to spend time conducting a detailed cost analysis for low-value items that do not produce significant returns. Commodities that are high value but that offer a competitive market situation, can be sourced through traditional bidding approaches. Unique products present a different challenge: companies must strive to reduce costs for products having few suppliers, yet that are still low value. Examples include suppliers of unique fasteners, specialty papers, and specialty MRO items. For such items, purchasers should focus on achieving lowest delivered cost, and may also wish to identify suppliers that are charging too high a price.

The major focus of a purchaser's efforts to reduce costs should be on critical products where relatively few suppliers exist but the items are higher value. Managers should commit time to exploring opportunities for value analysis/engineering, cost-savings sharing, joint identification of cost drivers, and supplier integration early in the product development cycle.

The remainder of this chapter presents a number of price-based and cost-based techniques that can be applied to help control the costs associated with these different purchased goods and services. We will begin by focusing on price analysis, which is appropriate for items in the "generic" and "commodity" sections of the matrix. Such items are generally mature with less dramatic opportunity for cost savings.

EXHIBIT 13.9   *Market Analysis*

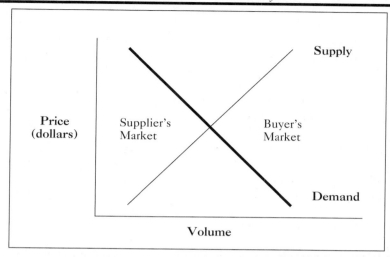

However, purchasing should track these items to ensure that the price being paid is consistent with current pricing trends in the open market. In the price analysis section, we will discuss types of market structures, economic conditions, pricing strategies, product specifications, volume discounts, and the product price index. Following this, we will present cost analysis, which involves breaking down a supplier's price into its cost elements to uncover potential cost savings, and hence, price reductions. Cost analysis is used for items in the "unique" and "critical" sections of the matrix.

PRICE ANALYSIS

In order to understand the factors affecting pricing levels in a given market, it is crucial to employ a *market analysis*—an analytical tool that identifies the primary external forces that are causing prices to either increase or decrease. As shown in Exhibit 13.9, prices are driven to a large extent by the degree of competition in a market, as well as by conditions of supply and demand. The resulting market prices are indicated by a heavier line, depending on the volume of supply in a given situation. When demand exceeds supply, a seller's market exists, and prices generally increase. The reverse situation, a buyer's market, occurs when supply exceeds demand, and prices generally move downward. There should be an appreciation for the variety of variables that directly and indirectly influence an item's price. Let's take a closer look at some of these different factors driving prices in different market and environmental conditions.

Types of Market Structures

A supplier's market structure has a major influence on price. Market structure refers to the number of competitors in an industry, the relative closeness of their products, and any existing barriers of entry for new competitors.[3] The different competitive market structures represent a continuum ranging from *perfect competition* at one end to *perfect monopoly* at the other. In between the two extremes are *monopolistic competition* and *oligopolistic competition*. The market structure of a seller's industry can directly affect how a supplier determines price.

Perfect Competition This structure is characterized by identical products (standardized) with minimal barriers for new suppliers to enter the market. Price is solely a function of the forces of supply and demand. No single seller or producer controls enough of a market to affect the market price. Of course, a seller could reduce its price with the hope of selling additional products. In the long run, however, this simply results in lost revenue.

Monopolistic Competition Monopolistic competition is characterized by many producers selling similar yet somewhat differentiated products. This is the structure for a large portion of U.S. industrial producers. (Gas stations are a good example.) In theory, so many producers offer so many different items that the actions of a single seller have limited or no impact on the overall market. Because no single player dominates an industry, a purchaser can influence a seller based on the size of its purchase requirement.

Oligopolistic Competition An industry with only a few large competitors is classified as oligopolistic. The market and pricing strategies of one competitor directly influence others within the industry. Examples of oligopolies in the United States historically included the steel, automobile, appliance, and large-scale computer-manufacturing industries. Within an oligopolistic industry, a firm may assume the role of a price leader and raise or lower prices, which can result in all other firms changing their prices or choosing to maintain existing price levels. If others do not follow, the initiating firm might be forced to reverse the change. The growth of international trade and competition has created additional choices in many industries, shifting market power away from the producer and toward the purchaser.

Perfect Monopoly Monopolies represent the other extreme of the market structure spectrum. While we often think of monopolies as large producers who face no competition, few pure monopolies actually exist. Government or quasi-government agencies regulate the natural monopolies, such as utilities, that exist. Historically, the barriers to entry in a monopolistic industry are so great that the entrance of new competitors is not a practical reality. However, industries typically thought of as monopolies are increasingly facing competition because of government deregulation or the invention of substitute materials, products, or services.

Purchasers have the least amount of price leverage in purely competitive and monopolistic markets. In the former, the forces of supply and demand determine price,

---

Using the Producer Price Index to Track Packaging Costs

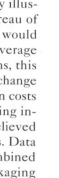

Purchasers of packing supplies face both opportunities and risks. In paper-related packing and packaging supplies, opportunities abound for buyers to enjoy a deflationary economy. The corrugated and solid fiber box industry illustrates a perfect example of a buying opportunity. In May 1999, the Bureau of Labor Statistics (BLS) producer price index data suggested that buyers would be hit with yet another sharp price increase of 1.5%. By November, average product prices had increased 4.1%. According to Thinking Cap Solutions, this rate of escalation was roughly five times faster than the estimated rate of change in the cost of manufacturing the typical box. With prices rising faster than costs over the previous six months, inflation-adjusted profit margins (excluding investments in new capital equipment, power costs, and overhead) were believed to be at a 1987–1999 record high. Therein lay the opportunity for buyers. Data from Thinking Cap Solutions' Industry Cost Escalation (ICE) model combined with an analysis of BLS price data presented a good road map for packaging buyers. Questions to ask included which industries have suppliers who have room to negotiate for lower prices? Which industries have suppliers that are preparing to increase prices? ICE data, for instance, suggested that suppliers of paper and paperboard had large profits in this area. Yet box buyers were going away from the negotiation table more than a little bit hungry—over the previous three years, the price of the average product rose 7.4% despite a 5% decline in the cost to manufacture a unit of output. Buyers thus had to become more aware of these opportunities and not let them slip by.

Source: Adapted from Elizabeth Baatz, "Price/Cost Trends Reveal Opportunities for Buyers," *Purchasing* (August 12, 1999): 51–52.

---

while in the latter the producer controls price. The best example of this is electric utilities in Pennsylvania in 1998 and 1999. Formerly a monopoly, the introduction of deregulation and consumer choice allowed consumers to choose their source of power, resulting in reductions in the price of electricity. Fortunately, the vast majority of industrial or commercial purchases occur between the two extremes. The more knowledgeable purchasers are about a supplier's competitive market structure, the better prepared they can be when developing pricing and negotiating strategies.

Economic Conditions

Economic conditions often determine whether a market is favorable to the seller or to the purchaser. When capacity utilization at producers is high (supply is tight) and demand for output is strong, supply and demand factors combine to create pricing conditions favorable to the seller. When this occurs, buyers often attempt to keep prices or price increases below the industry average. When an industry is in a decline, purchasers can take advantage of this to negotiate favorable supply arrangements.

The macroeconomy influences prices—for example, interest rate levels influence the internal rate of return at a supplier—the overall cost of capital that drives productive investment. Even the level of the dollar in relation to other currencies influences price, particularly for international purchasing. Also, tight labor markets can create cost increases resulting in higher purchase prices.

Knowledge of economic conditions is helpful when identifying the market factors affecting the supply and demand for a product or commodity. Awareness of current and forecasted economic conditions assists in the development of purchase budgets and material forecasts, and also provides valuable insights when developing future price negotiating strategies. One good source of information is the Website for the National Association of Purchasing Management, http://www.napm.org which presents key data on pricing trends for a variety of commodities.

Pricing Strategy of the Seller

Sellers pursue different strategies or approaches that affect the pricing of their products or services. Some sellers rely on a detailed analysis of internal cost structures to establish price while others simply price at a level comparable to the competition. The pricing strategy of the seller has a direct impact on quoted prices. In many cases, however, the price charged by a seller may have little or no relationship to actual costs. As strange as this seems, pricing strategies are often based on other factors that are important to the seller. A seller may quote an unusually low price to secure a purchase contract with the intention of raising the price once it drives competition from the marketplace. In other cases, the seller may exploit their position when they sense they have the purchaser "over a barrel" by charging an excessive price. In still other cases, the seller may simply not understand its own costs.

Several questions should be asked when analyzing a seller's pricing strategy. These include:

- Does the seller have a long-term pricing strategy, or is it short-term in nature?
- Is the seller a price leader (e.g. sets new pricing levels in the market), or a price follower (only matches price increases/decreases when the competition does so)?
- Is the seller attempting to establish entry barriers to other competitors by establishing a low price initially, then preparing to raise prices later in the future?
- Is the seller using a cost-based pricing approach, which develops price as a function of true costs, or a market-based pricing approach? The last question is most important of all. Purchasers must understand when sellers are pricing based on their actual costs versus using a market-based approach to pricing.

Seller pricing strategies can be grouped into four major categories: (1) demand pricing, (2) cost-plus pricing, (3) rule-of-thumb pricing, and (4) buy-in pricing.[4]

Demand Pricing This is a "skimming" approach to pricing. A seller who relies on a demand pricing policy attempts to earn as much as possible as quickly as possible from a product. This strategy is common for innovative products that reach a market before the competition, and it is often used in the introductory stages of the product life cycle. Some product managers admit that a producer with a technically innovative product must price to maximize return before the inevitable influx of competition occurs. This approach is also common when a seller has a proprietary patent that provides a market monopoly. Demand pricing can invite increased competition because of the higher rates of return realized by sellers, and it is typically short-lived. Examples of products that went through this cycle were Intel's series of personal computer microchips. Each time a new, faster chip went on the market, prices were initially high then gradually decreased as volumes increased. This trend occurred even more rapidly when Advanced Micro Devices entered the PC chip market and provided competition to Intel.

Cost-Plus Pricing Once volumes increase and greater competition enters the market, sellers will generally switch from a demand pricing strategy to a cost-plus pricing strategy. Cost-plus pricing establishes a price to cover variable production costs for an item while providing some contribution to fixed costs and profit. This approach, also referred to as *penetration pricing*, is an aggressive pricing approach for efficient producers because price is a direct function of cost. Penetration pricing can lead to faster market penetration for a product because of the lower profit margins a seller is willing to accept. Generally speaking, the seller is willing to take a lower price because of the potential "mass market" appeal of the product, resulting in substantially higher sales volumes. It can also discourage future competition from entering the market or can drive out existing competition. A word of caution is in order here: purchasers should question whether the seller is the most efficient producer willing to accept lower margins to win market share, or is the real intention to drive competition from the marketplace and later raise prices to exorbitant levels? Asian semiconductor manufacturers, who were later accused of dumping chips in the United States at below cost prices in the 1980s, used this technique.

Rule-of-Thumb Pricing This is the most conservative of the four pricing approaches. Many sales agents have little information on their firm's true costs of producing the product, so the seller often employs some general rule of thumb when establishing price. In some situations, a seller may prepare a price quote by calculating the direct costs associated with an item and then increasing that figure by a certain percentage. The seller may add the firm's direct-labor cost and direct-materials cost, then add an additional 40%. The 40% mark-up contributes to the indirect and fixed costs to produce an item while providing some contribution to profit. This simplified approach ignores a great deal of information and does not take into consideration the seller's true costs of producing the item. A purchaser who spots a seller using this approach may receive a favorable price by effectively gathering better cost data about the seller than what the seller has.

Buy-In Pricing Users of this approach establish a price covering variable costs, which contributes only a small portion to fixed costs and profit. Buy-in pricing is similar to cost-plus pricing but is driven by a different motivation—to generate revenue in periods of low demand, or to "steal" market share from competitors. Sellers often resort to this approach during slower economic conditions. For this reason it is sometimes also called *survival pricing.* Buy-in pricing is commonly used by airlines during fare wars to fill excess seats on individual lanes. In addition, buy-in pricing is also called the "foot-in-the-door" approach, as sellers will use the price to get business without any intention of maintaining this lower price in the long run.

Another pricing strategy that is less well known is *social responsibility pricing,* a technique used in cases of natural or personal crises, such as a hurricane or death in the family. Sellers will reduce prices and put profit considerations aside to accommodate these situations. A good example of this was the contributions of businesses to public support during the flooding in North Carolina following Hurricane Fran in 1999.

Most sellers usually use a specific strategy approach when establishing price. Knowledge of a seller's pricing approach and longer-term motivation can help to arrive at a better decision when evaluating seller quotations or when directly negotiating price.

Product Specifications

Whether they realize it or not, purchasers impact price at the time they set the specifications for the product or service. Specifying products or services requiring custom design and tooling affects a seller's price, which is one of the reasons purchasers try to specify industry-standard parts whenever possible. Cost (and hence price) becomes higher as firms increase the value-added requirements for an item through design, tooling, or engineering requirements. Purchasers should specify industry-accepted standard parts for as much of their component requirements as possible and rely on customized items when they provide a competitive product advantage or help differentiate a product in the marketplace. An example of a company that experienced problems because it did not use standard parts is Apple Computer. Although demand for a new line of Macintosh computers was booming, the company had an order backlog of more than $1 billion. The company was unable to obtain timely deliveries of critical parts, including modems and custom chips, and it was therefore unable to meet product demand. These parts shortages occurred because many of the components were custom-designed and sourced from one supplier.[5]

Purchase Volume and Quantity Discounts

Purchase volume has a direct relationship with the per-unit cost and price of an item. Combining purchase requirements across separate operating units can yield savings in tooling, setup, and operating efficiencies. A major benefit of reduced or single sourcing is a lower price that results from the higher volumes offered to a supplier. In return for a purchase contract with higher volumes, a buyer expects favorable pricing because a supplier should realize lower per-unit costs. The willingness of a supplier to offer quantity discounts also affects the final selling price. Although a number of different discounts exist, the two most common are quantity and cash discounts. Recall that Chapter 12 presented a quantitative technique for analyzing quantity discounts.

Quantity Discounts Sellers often provide incentives to purchase larger quantities. While a quantity discount has a positive effect on the purchase price, a purchaser must be cautious about the net impact on the total cost of the item. Buying in larger-than-normal quantities requires additional storage of purchased goods. At a time when most firms are reducing or even eliminating inventory, the additional inventory-carrying costs must be evaluated against the benefit of the quantity discount.

Cash Discounts The practice in most industries is to offer incentives to pay invoices promptly. One way to encourage this is to offer cash discounts for payment within a certain period of time. For example, a seller may offer a discount of 2% for invoice payment within 10 days of receipt. The seller usually expects full payment within 30 days. (This is often expressed as *2% 10/net 30*).

Unlike quantity discounts, it is usually worthwhile to take advantage of cash discounts. Purchasers can rarely earn the equivalent return within a ten-day period of transactions offered with a cash discount. The opportunity cost of not taking the discount is almost always higher than the opportunity cost of taking the discount. Well-managed firms take advantage of cash discounts and arrange payment within the specified time frame.

Using the Producer Price Index to Manage Price

As noted earlier, price analysis is appropriate for certain types of commodities. Specifically, monitoring price instead of cost is appropriate for market-based products where pricing is largely a function of supply and demand. Examples include steel, paper, plastic, and other types of bulk commodities. When assessing whether the price charged is fair compared with the market, managers can compare price changes for a purchase family to an external index. An important factor when conducting a price analysis is the producer price index (PPI), which is maintained by the U.S. Bureau of Labor Statistics. This information can easily be downloaded from the Bureau of Labor Statistics Web page (http://www.bls.gov/datahome.htm). The index tracks material price movements from quarter to quarter. It is scaled to a base year (1988), and tracks the percentage increase in material commodity prices based on a sample of industrial purchasers. By converting price increases paid from quarter to quarter into a percentage increase, and comparing the changes to the PPI for a similar type of material, the purchaser can determine whether the price increases paid to the supplier of that material are reasonable.

To use this tool, users will first need to identify the supplier's standard industrial code (SIC). This can be found on http://www.FreeEDGAR.com. Next, look at the price index for the SIC and product that you are interested in. Consider the following example for steel castings:

Price paid to supplier on March 30, 2000: $52.50/unit
Price paid to supplier on June 30, 2000: $53.20/unit
Percentage price increase = ($53.20 − $52.50)/$52.50 = 1.33%
Steel castings PPI (March 30, 2000) = 120.55
Steel castings PPI (June 30, 2000) = 124.55
Percentage inflation for steel castings = (124.55 − 120.55)/120.55 = 3.32%

EXHIBIT 13.10   *Producer Price Index*

Data

Year	Jan	Feb	Mar	Apr	May	Jun	Jul	Aug	Sep	Oct	Nov	Dec	Ann
1999	107.1	105.7	105.4	105.3	104.6	105.2	104.7	104.7	104.7	105.4(P)	105.6(P)	106.0(P)	105.4(P)
2000	106.2(P)												

Data extracted on March 14, 2000 (11:19 AM)
Series Catalog
Series ID: WPU1017

Not seasonally adjusted
Group: Metals and metal products
Item: Steel mill products
Base Date: 8200

In this case, the price increase paid by the purchaser is reasonable (about 2% less than inflation for steel castings).

Examples of recent indices for metals and metal products are shown in Exhibit 13.10. In addition to PPI data, the Bureau of Labor Statistics Website also contains information on labor rates in different regions of the country, and updates on pricing and market conditions. Information on employment cost data is also available in *Purchasing* magazine's "Buying Strategy Forecast," a semimonthly newsletter (http://www.manufacturing.net/magazine/purchasing) and the Direct-ICE report prepared by Thinking Cap Solutions (http://www.ice-alert.com). Other sources of commodity price information are the "Pink Sheets" published by the World Bank (http://www.worldbank.org/prospects).

Some companies set an objective of consistently bettering price inflation with suppliers. That is, they expect that performance should be better than the market. As shown in Exhibit 13.11, this can provide the company with a relative "competitive advantage" in terms of pricing. Caution should be used when applying PPI data that match the commodity being purchased. The buyer should carefully study the history of the index to ensure that it has a strong correlation with the price history of the commodity being purchased. Several questions should be asked in this situation:

- How did the purchasing situation affect the price fairness and reasonableness at the time?
- How have conditions (e.g., delivery requirements) changed?
- What is the effect on price of changes in the quantity of a material or service purchased?
- Was the purchasing situation a sole source or competitive source?
- Are the index comparisons driving purchasing strategies?

A real benefit of using this price analysis approach is to track price changes across different commodities and compare performance. For example, consider the following. Three sourcing teams are discussing their cost results for the past year:

EXHIBIT 13.11   *Actual Price Change Versus Market Index Change*

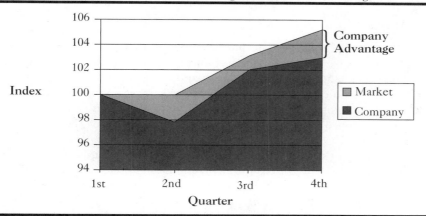

EXHIBIT 13.12   *Actual to Index Comparison*

	PPI 6/97	PPI 6/98	(%) Change	Act. 6/97	Act. 6/98	(%) Change
Gasoline	71.2	57.3	−19.5	100.0	90.5	−9.5
Paperboard	146.8	152.6	4.0	100.0	101.3	1.3
Aircraft parts	141.5	141.3	0.0	100.0	100.0	0.0

Source: PPI Data from U.S. Bureau of Labor Statistics: (http://stats.bls.gov/ppihome.htm).

Gasoline team: 9.5% cost reduction
Paperboard team: 1.3% cost increase
Aircraft parts team: no change

Which team has been most effective at managing costs for the year?

At first glance, it would appear that the gasoline team is doing the best since they have the greatest cost reductions (−9.5%). However, in comparing the results with the PPI data shown in Exhibit 13.12, the picture is markedly different. The gasoline team has failed to capture savings in a rapidly declining price market (−19.5%), while the paperboard team has limited price increases to only 1%, when prices actually rose in the market by 4%. This analysis can help identify different price changes in markets where a fair and open market is present.

COST ANALYSIS TECHNIQUES

As noted earlier, more and more organizations are shifting their attention away from price management and toward cost management. In so doing, opportunities to reduce costs may exist that are not available when the discussion focuses only on price. The

SOURCING SNAPSHOT

When Market Changes Affect Purchase Price

It was beginning to look like another blockbuster Christmas for makers of personal computers. With slick new products, low prices, and Internet service rebates that promised "free" PCs, record sales seemed certain. That's when Taiwan was rocked by a horrific earthquake that disrupted America's big PC makers and other electronics firms from vital sources of supply. The disruptions in supply lines helped to tighten the vise in which the PC industry found itself. On one side, consumers were expecting lower prices and couldn't remember the last PC price hike. On the other, suppliers were suddenly commanding higher prices for key components such as memory chips, due to the shortage caused by the earthquake. A worldwide shortage of computer parts, from 3-cent capacitors to $400 flat-panel displays, had been driving costs up for months. The price of a 64-megabit DRAM chip skyrocketed from less than $5 to almost $20 in a matter of months. With the Taiwan disaster tying up supplies, PC makers were scrambling to secure the motherboards, chipsets, and other parts they needed to meet demand—even if it meant paying more to get them. And that undid the formula that allowed PC makers to thrive, despite falling prices. Before, they could use dropping component costs to help underwrite lower prices and make up for shrinking margins with higher volumes. Today the options are less attractive: absorb the rising costs and sacrifice earnings, or try to increase prices and risk losing sales. The latter seems risky, considering that the driving force behind surging PC volume has been falling prices that bring new shoppers into the market.

Source: Adapted from: Peter Burrows, "The Vise Trapping PC Makers," *Business Week*, October 25, 1999: 40-41.

---

ability to perform a cost analysis is a direct function of the quality and availability of information. If a purchaser and seller maintain a distant relationship, cost data will be more difficult to identify due to the lack of support from the seller. An obvious approach that can help in obtaining necessary cost data is to require a detailed production cost breakdown when a seller submits a purchase quotation. The reliability of self-reported cost data must be considered. Another approach or option involves the joint sharing of cost information. A cross-functional team composed of engineers and manufacturing personnel from both companies may meet to identify potential areas of the supplier's process (or the purchaser's requirements) that can potentially reduce costs. One of the benefits of developing closer relations with key suppliers is the increased visibility of supplier cost data. The following section details some techniques that focus on cost.

Estimating Supplier Costs Using Reverse Price Analysis

Often suppliers will not be forthcoming in sharing cost data. In these situations, the purchaser must resort to a different type of analytical approach called *reverse price analysis*. A seller's cost structure affects price because, in the long run, the seller must price at a level that covers all variable costs of production, contributes to some portion of fixed costs, and contributes to some level of profit. As discussed later in the chapter, many suppliers are reluctant to share internal cost information. This information, however, is valuable to a purchaser, particularly when evaluating the reasonableness of a supplier's price. In the absence of specific cost data, a supplier's overall cost structure must be estimated. This type of analysis is often called a *reverse price analysis* or a *"should cost analysis"*—meaning that if the supplier is assigning costs in an appropriate manner, what should the product cost based on these calculations?

Information about a specific product or product line is often difficult to identify. A purchaser may have to use internal engineering estimates about what it costs to produce an item, rely on historical experience and judgment to estimate costs, or review public financial documents to identify key cost data about the seller. The latter approach works best with publicly traded small suppliers producing limited product lines. Financial documents allow estimation of a supplier's overall cost structure. The drawback is that these documents do not provide much information about a specific breakdown of cost by product or product line. Also, if a supplier is a privately held company, cost data become difficult to obtain or estimate.

Despite these difficulties, there are tools available that can be used to estimate a supplier's cost using some publicly available information. When evaluating a supplier's costs, the major determinants of a supplier's total cost structure must be taken into consideration. Let's assume a purchasing manager is buying a product or service for the first time without experience of what fair pricing might be. Because they don't have the tools at hand, or because they're too busy, many purchasers' usual technique is to go with their "gut feel" or to evaluate competitive bids. It may be worth the time and effort, however, to perform some additional research using data from an income statement or from Internet sites. In doing so, the purchaser may perform a reverse price analysis—which essentially means "breaking down" the price into its components of material, labor, overhead, and profit.

Let's start the process with a supplier-provided price of $20.00 per unit. The first component to consider is the price contribution toward profit, and sales, general, and administrative (SGA) expenses. For publicly traded companies, this can be estimated by looking at a variety of Websites that provide information on financial reports, including balance sheets, income statements, cash flow statements, and annual reports shown in Exhibit 13.13 under the "Financial Reports" section.

Exhibit 13.13 provides a list of available data sources for other components of cost. Assume the purchaser determined that for this example the supplier is a privately held company. This is still not a problem, assuming the buyer can look up the supplier's SIC code (http://www.FreeEDGAR.com). Another useful resource is Robert Morris Associates (RMA), which publishes the gross profit margin for this SIC overall, as well

EXHIBIT 13.13   *Data Sources*

- Labor: Annual Survey of Manufacturers—total direct labor and material for SIC codes
- Overhead:
    150% for labor intensive
    As high as 600% for capital intensive
- Materials and Profit: Robert Morris Associates data broken out by SICs including:
    Breakout of income sources
    Gross profit margins
    Percentages for operating expenses
    Percentages for "all other expenses"
    Before-tax profit percentages

Other Sources of Data
- Financial Reports (Profit and SGA estimates):
    Ward's Industrial Directory
    Census of Manufacturers
    Yahoo! Financial section (http://biz.yahoo.com)
    Morningstar (http://www.morningstar.com)
    Marketwatch (http://cbs.marketwatch.com)
    411Stocks (http://www.411stocks.com)
    The Street (http://www.the street.com)
    Buying Strategy Forecast (http://www.manufacturing.net/magazine/purchasing)
    Thinking Cap Solutions (http://www.ice-alert.com)

as before-tax profit percentages. While this is a rough estimate, it does offer a good starting point. In Exhibit 13.14, the gross profit and SGA expense percentage for this supplier's SIC code is 15%. Thus on a price of $20 the estimated profit is $3. Next, the purchaser will need to understand the labor and material cost components of price. Material costs can often be estimated by consulting with internal engineers. Using an estimate of required material, as well as external information on current pricing of these materials (as shown in the previous section), a rough estimate can be made of the amount of material in the product. In our example, we discovered that an approximation of the amount of material included is 20% of the price, or $4.00.

To find out how much labor is included, the best place to look is the Annual Survey of Manufacturers, published by the U.S. Department of Commerce and available at http://www.census.gov/prod/www/abs/industry.html. This site allows the user to download information on total direct-labor costs and total material costs for any SIC number. Using this information supports calculating a material to labor ratio. For the analysis shown in Exhibit 13.11, suppose that the purchaser discovered that the ratio of materials to labor based on the SIC code was 1.333. Thus, if material costs were previously estimated at $4, then direct-labor costs should be approximately $3 (4/1.333). After subtracting the estimates for profit/SGA, material, and labor from the price, the remaining portion of cost is considered "manufacturing burden" or "overhead."

At this point, the purchaser must determine whether $10 per unit paid on a price of $20 per unit is a reasonable amount for overhead costs. Typically, overhead is expressed as a percentage of labor costs. For labor-intensive industries, the ratio could be

EXHIBIT 13.14   *Reverse Price Analysis*

Hypothetical price	$20
Profit / SG&A allowance (15%)	$ 3
Subtotal	$17
Direct material	$ 4
Subtotal	$13
Direct labor	$ 3
Manufacturing burden	$10

as low as 150%. For capital-intensive industries, it could be as high as 600%. In our example, the overhead rate is 333% of labor ($10/$3). Using other data from Robert Morris Associates, the purchaser can also estimate the percentages for operating expenses and for "all other expenses." With this cost estimate in hand, the purchaser should now be able to approach the supplier in a negotiation and initiate a discussion that addresses price and cost. While these estimates may not be 100% accurate, they provide a baseline for discussion of the supplier's cost structure.

In discussing the supplier's cost structure with the supplier and how it applies to the price paid, the purchaser should attempt to initiate discussion in the following areas to discover opportunities for cost reductions.

- *Plant Utilization:* The cost impact of additional business on the operating efficiency of a supplier should be evaluated. Is a supplier currently operating at capacity? Will additional volume actually create higher costs through overtime? Or will a supplier be able to reduce its cost structure through additional volume? The utilization rate of productive assets contributes directly to a supplier's cost structure.
- *Process Capability:* A firm should also consider if projected volume requirements match a supplier's process capability. It may be inefficient to source smaller lot sizes with a supplier who requires long runs to minimize costs. On the other hand, suppliers specializing in smaller batches cannot efficiently accommodate volumes requiring longer production runs. A supplier's production processes should match a purchaser's production requirements. Purchasing should also evaluate production processes to determine if they are state-of-the-art or rely on outdated technology. Production and process capability influences operating efficiencies, quality, and the overall cost structure of a seller.
- *Learning-Curve Effect:* Learning-curve analysis indicates whether a seller can lower its cost due to the repetitive production of an item. Chapter 12 discussed this topic in detail.
- *The Supplier's Workforce:* A supplier's labor force affects the cost structure. Issues such as unionized versus nonunionized, motivated versus unmotivated, and the quality awareness and commitment of employees all combine to add another component to the cost structure. When visiting a supplier's facility, representatives from the purchaser should take the time to talk with employees about quality and other work-related items. Meeting with employees provides valuable insight about a supplier's operation.

- *Management Capability:* Management affects costs by directing the workforce in the most efficient manner, committing resources for longer-term productivity improvements, defining a firm's quality requirements, managing technology, and assigning financial resources in an optimal manner. Management efficiency and capability have both a tangible and intangible impact on a firm's cost structure. In the end, every cost component is a direct result of management action taken at some point in time.
- *Purchasing Efficiency:* How well suppliers purchase their goods and services has a direct impact on purchase price. Suppliers face many of the same uncertainties and forces in their supply markets that purchasers face. Supplier visits and evaluations should evaluate the tools and techniques suppliers use to meet their material requirements.

Production Cost Schedules

Another valuable technique for analyzing cost is a *production cost schedule.* Such a schedule identifies a supplier's cost to produce an item and then determines cost behavior across a range of volumes. This analysis is useful for several reasons. First, it identifies a supplier's most efficient production level, which is useful when performing a make-or-buy analysis comparing a purchaser's production cost schedule (make) against a supplier's cost schedule (buy). Second, the technique provides insight about whether a supplier can efficiently produce at a level that meets a purchase requirement. Suppliers who are efficient at low volumes may be capacity constrained at higher volumes. Capacity constraints usually result in higher per-unit costs of production.

Exhibit 13.15 illustrates a production cost schedule for supplier XYZ. Production cost schedules focus on total and average costs and do not include price or total revenue. This schedule identifies the production level that provides the lowest total cost per unit of production. Price determination is separate from production cost schedules. Each column of this schedule contains important information used to arrive at the average total cost per unit of production. (For simplicity, we will assume that any semivariable costs that exist have the fixed portion added to the fixed costs and the variable portion added to the variable costs.) The schedule includes only those costs pertinent to the purchase decision:

- *Column A:* This is the output production schedule, which lists the volume of product purchased. Schedules normally begin at zero and continue to a point that covers the range of volumes of interest, or includes volume ranges where accurate information is available.
- *Column B:* For this example, total fixed costs are constant at $500 over each level of output. These are not the fixed costs for the entire firm but rather the fixed costs allocated to the production of a particular item.
- *Column C:* Total fixed costs divided by output equals the average fixed cost per unit. Notice that fixed costs per unit decrease as production increases.
- *Column D:* This is the average variable cost per unit. Notice that the relationship between variable costs and output is not linear. At lower output, the supplier has

EXHIBIT 13.15   *A Production Cost Schedule for Supplier XYZ*

A. Output	B. Total Fixed Cost	C. Average Fixed Cost	D. Average Variable Cost	E. Total Variable Cost	F. Total Cost	G. Average Total Cost	H. Price
0	$500.00	—	$(0.00)	$(0.00)	$500.00	—	$80.00
10	500.00	$50.00	19.00	190.00	690.00	$69.00	80.00
20	500.00	25.00	17.00	340.00	840.00	42.00	80.00
30	500.00	16.67	15.00	450.00	950.00	31.67	80.00
40	500.00	12.50	13.00	520.00	1,020.00	25.50	80.00
50	500.00	10.00	13.00	650.00	1,150.00	23.00	80.00
60	500.00	8.33	13.00	780.00	1,280.00	21.33	80.00
70	500.00	7.14	13.00	910.00	1,410.00	20.14	80.00
80	500.00	6.25	15.00	1,200.00	1,700.00	21.25	80.00
90	500.00	5.56	17.00	1,530.00	2,030.00	22.56	80.00
100	500.00	5.00	19.00	1,900.00	2,400.00	24.00	80.00

higher material costs while at higher output capacity becomes strained and variable labor costs increase.
- *Column E:* Total variable cost equals the average variable cost times the output level.
- *Column F:* Total cost is the sum of column B (fixed cost) plus column E (total variable cost) for each level of output.
- *Column G:* This is the key column used in the purchase decision. Total cost divided by output equals average total cost per unit of output.

From this schedule, the most efficient level of output is 70 units. The lowest average total cost per unit of production occurs at that output level. A buyer must determine if the anticipated purchase volume supports the supplier's most efficient production level. It is possible that volumes are so high that more than one supplier must produce the item. Production cost schedules are useful when a cost behavior can be accurately predicted at different levels, competitive bidding is not used to purchase the item, and there is a willingness to commit the time and resources to perform a proper analysis. Like all cost analysis tools, this tool is only as good as the quality of the data used during the analysis.

Graphical Analysis of Cost

Graphical displays provide a visual means to present production cost data. It is useful to include graphical analyses of cost data because graphs are often easier than data tables to interpret. Exhibit 13.16 graphs the total cost data from Exhibit 13.15 (columns B, E, and F). The graph illustrates the fixed component of the cost structure along with the relationship of total costs over different volumes. Notice that the slope of the total cost line begins to accelerate upward after 70 to 80 units, indicating diminished efficiencies and higher per-unit total costs.

EXHIBIT 13.16   *Average Cost Curve*

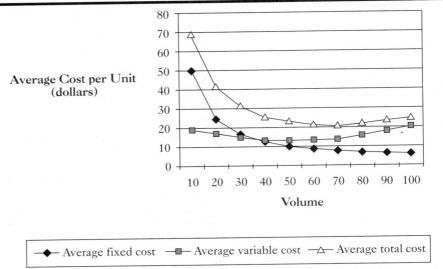

Exhibit 13.17 graphs the average costs from Exhibit 13.15 as a function of volume (columns C, D, and G). The graph in Exhibit 13.17 illustrates, without providing line after line of detailed cost data, that the most efficient or optimal production level for supplier XYZ is 70 units, which is the lowest point of the average total cost curve. It also illustrates that over a range of 60 to 80 units, average total costs flatten to a point that indicates some supplier volume flexibility.

Break-Even Analysis

Break-even analysis includes both cost and revenue data for an item to identify the point where revenue equals cost, and the expected profit or loss at different production volumes. Firms perform break-even analysis at different organizational levels. At the highest levels, top management uses this technique as a strategic planning tool. For example, an automobile manufacturer can use the tool to estimate expected profit or loss over a range of automobile sales. If the analysis indicates that the break-even point in units has risen over previous estimates, cost-cutting strategies can be put in place. Divisions or business units can use the technique to estimate the break-even point for a new product line.

Purchasing and supply chain specialists use break-even analysis to develop the following insights:

- Identify if a target purchase price provides a reasonable profit to a supplier given the supplier's cost structure.
- Analyze a supplier's cost structure. Break-even analysis requires detailed analysis or estimation of the costs to produce an item.

EXHIBIT 13.17   *Total Cost Curve*

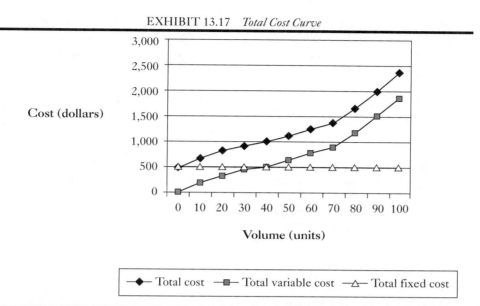

Cost (dollars)

Volume (units)

—◆— Total cost   —■— Total variable cost   —△— Total fixed cost

- Perform sensitivity (what-if) analysis by evaluating the impact on a supplier of different mixes of purchase volumes and target purchase prices.
- Prepare for negotiation. Break-even analysis allows a purchaser to anticipate a seller's pricing strategy during negotiations. Research indicates that a direct relationship exists between preparation and negotiating effectiveness. The software tool SDS NoteBooks, which is discussed in Appendix B at the end of the book, supports the development of break-even analyses.

Break-even analysis requires the user to identify the important costs and revenues associated with a product or product line. Graphing the data presents a visual representation of the expected loss or profit at various production levels. Cost equations also express the expected relationship between cost, volume, and profit. When using break-even analysis, certain common assumptions are typically used: [6]

1. Fixed costs remain constant over the period and volumes considered.
2. Variable costs fluctuate in a linear fashion, although this may not always be the case.
3. Revenues vary directly with volume. This is represented graphically by an upward-sloping total revenue line beginning at the origin.
4. The fixed and variable costs include the semivariable costs. Thus no semivariable cost line exists.
5. Break-even analysis considers total costs rather than average costs. However, the technique often uses the average selling price for an item to calculate the total revenue line.

6. Significant joint (i.e., shared) costs between departments or products limits the use of this technique if these costs cannot be reasonably apportioned among users. If shared costs cannot be apportioned, then break-even analysis is best suited for the entire operation versus individual departments, products, or product lines.
7. This technique considers only quantitative factors. If qualitative factors are important, management must consider these before making any decisions based on the break-even analysis.

Break-Even Analysis Example   The following example assumes that fixed costs, variable costs, and target purchase price for a single item are reasonably accurate. The construction of a break-even graph requires these three pieces of information. Exhibit 13.18 shows the required cost and volume data along with the break-even graph for this example. Because a buyer is estimating the break-even analysis for a supplier, the price is a target purchase price established by the purchaser. A range of prices can be analyzed to estimate a supplier's expected profit or loss given the fixed and variable costs.

In this example, the purchaser wants to determine if the anticipated volume of 9,000 units provides an adequate profit for the supplier at the target purchase price. Exhibit 13.18 indicates that the supplier requires at least 7,500 units to avoid a loss with this cost structure and target purchase price. The following equation identifies the profit or loss associated with a given volume:

$$\text{Net income or loss} = (P)(X) - (VC)(X) - (FC)$$

where: P = Average purchase price

X = Units produced

VC = Variable cost per unit of production

FC = Fixed cost of production for an item

The supplier's expected profit for the anticipated 9,000 units is calculated as follows, using $10 per unit as the average purchase price:

$$\text{Net income} = (\$10)(9,000) - (\$6)(9,000) - (\$30,000)$$
$$= \$6,000 \text{ Profit}$$

We can also calculate the number of units the supplier needs to produce to break even (i.e., cover fixed costs). This is calculated as follows:

$$\text{Total revenue} = \text{Variable cost} + \text{Fixed cost}$$
$$\$10(X) = \$6(X) + \$30,000$$
$$\$4\,X = \$30,000$$
$$X = 7,500 \text{ Units}$$

If the cost data are accurate, then the anticipated purchase volume provides a profit to the supplier, since it exceeds 7,500 units. Whether this is an acceptable profit level given the cost structure is an issue both parties may have to negotiate. If the

EXHIBIT 13.18   *Break-Even Analysis for Supplier XYZ*

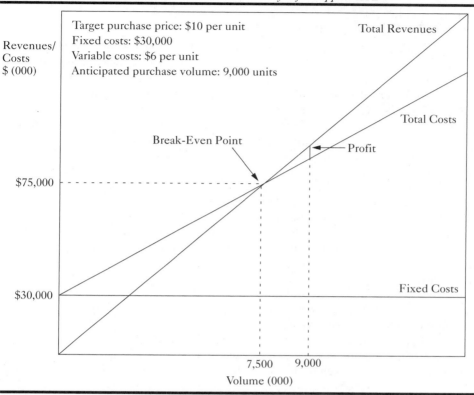

analysis indicates that the purchase volume results in an expected loss to the seller, then a purchaser must consider several important questions:

- Is the target purchase price too optimistic given the supplier's cost structure?
- Are the supplier's production costs reasonable compared with other producers in the industry?
- Are the cost and volume estimates accurate?
- If the cost, volume, and target price are reasonable, is this the right supplier to produce this item?
- Will direct assistance help reduce costs at the supplier?

This method allows an evaluation of a supplier's expected profit over a range of costs, volumes, and target purchase prices. The break-even technique, however, often provides only broad insight into a purchase decision.

Learning-Curve Analysis

Users of learning-curve analysis recognize that the cost to produce certain items decreases over larger and larger volumes. The more often a firm produces an item, the

SOURCING SNAPSHOT

GE Pushes Suppliers to Move South

A major component of a supplier's cost is due to labor. While labor costs are often considered an uncontrollable element determined by the local job market, General Electric doesn't believe this is the case. In fact, they are taking the unprecedented step of demanding deep price cuts, and prodding suppliers to move to low-cost Mexico, where the industrial giant already employs 30,000 people. This is taking place in several of GE's business units—including aircraft engines, power systems, and industrial systems. GE even puts on a "supplier migration" conference to help them make the leap. Rick Kennedy, a spokesman at GE Aircraft Engines, says "We're aggressively asking for double-digit price reductions from our suppliers. We have to do this if we're going to be part of GE." This is causing GE's 14 unions to argue that it's paving the way for a new wave of job shifts. GE's U.S. workforce has been shrinking for more than a decade as CEO Jack Welch has lowered costs by shifting production and investment to lower-wage countries. In his annual pep talk to GE's top managers in January 1999, he again stressed the need to globalize production to remain cost-competitive but also insisted that GE prod suppliers to follow suit. GE Aircraft Engines moved quickly, and told dozens of suppliers that it wants to cut costs up to 14%. An internal report stated that "GE set the tone early and succinctly: 'Migrate or be out of business.' This is not a seminar just to provide information. We expect you to move and move quickly." Although this seems tough, GE Aircraft Engine officials argue that heightened competition leaves them no choice. Jet engines now sell for less than they did four years ago.

Source: Adapted from Aaron Bernstein, "Welch's March to the South," *Business Week,* December 6, 1999, 74–75.

greater the likelihood that direct labor becomes efficient and management develops effective production and control systems. This approach requires identifying a learning rate of improvement and then applying this rate into a supplier's cost structure to reflect anticipated improvement. Please refer to Chapter 12 on quantitative purchasing tools and techniques for a detailed discussion of this important concept.

$\mathcal{T}$OTAL COST OF OWNERSHIP

Total cost of ownership requires a purchaser to identify and measure costs beyond the standard unit price, transportation, and tooling when evaluating purchase proposals or supplier performance. Formally, total cost of ownership is defined as the sum of all expenses and costs associated with the purchase and use of equipment, materials, and services. To use a total cost approach, a firm must define and measure a purchased item's major cost components.

Most large firms base purchase decisions and evaluate suppliers on cost elements beyond unit price, transportation, and tooling. Research indicates, however, that companies differ widely about what cost components to include in a total cost analysis. Exhibit 13.19 details the frequency of use of different cost components at a large semiconductor manufacturer. An inverse relationship exists between the complexity of a cost component and its use in a total cost analysis system. For example, unit price data are low on complexity of data collection and are also typically included. On the other hand, firms categorize field failure data as highly complex and difficult to identify with the exact product, and therefore use these data less frequently. Field failures are still a cost, however, affecting total cost of ownership.

A problem with total cost analysis is either an absence of data warehouse systems to collect total cost data or a lack of accounting systems to capture cost data in the required format. Furthermore, an exact definition of total cost requirements can vary widely—even within the same company. Traditional accounting methods simply do not focus on quantifying the costs associated with a total cost activity system. With the development of enterprise resource planning (ERP) systems, the ability of organizations to identify total cost elements will improve. Also, the emerging data warehouse systems being deployed by companies will allow users to efficiently extract and compile cost data.

Total cost data come from a number of different areas within the supply chain. Activities as diverse as finance, accounting, quality assurance, manufacturing, receiving and inspection, and purchasing all contribute cost information. It can be difficult to coordinate the collection of data from diverse organizational functions, particularly with a manual data collection system. Purchasing plays a critical role in total cost analysis. It is the logical function to manage a total cost system because of its close interaction with functions inside and outside the firm, and its reliance on total cost data to support the sourcing process.

Developing a Total Cost System

When a supplier fails to meet its delivery, price, and quality commitments, the buying company often absorbs these additional costs because it lacks the means to identify nonperformance costs. For a company to develop a total cost of ownership measurement system, it should follow a structured approach to system development.

1. *Identify Total Cost Items to Evaluate:* Not all purchase items require total cost measurement. Typically, 20% of purchased items contribute 80% of total costs. The best total cost candidates include those items having the highest dollar impact on the purchasing budget. Problem items contributing high nonperformance costs are another logical choice, as are families of similar items. Similar items from the same supplier can be grouped into a composite index of total cost.

2. *Map Processes and Identify Affected Functions or Activities and Associated Costs:* Certain functions or activities are affected when a supplier does not meet its performance

EXHIBIT 13.19   *Total Cost Management—Pyramid Perspective*

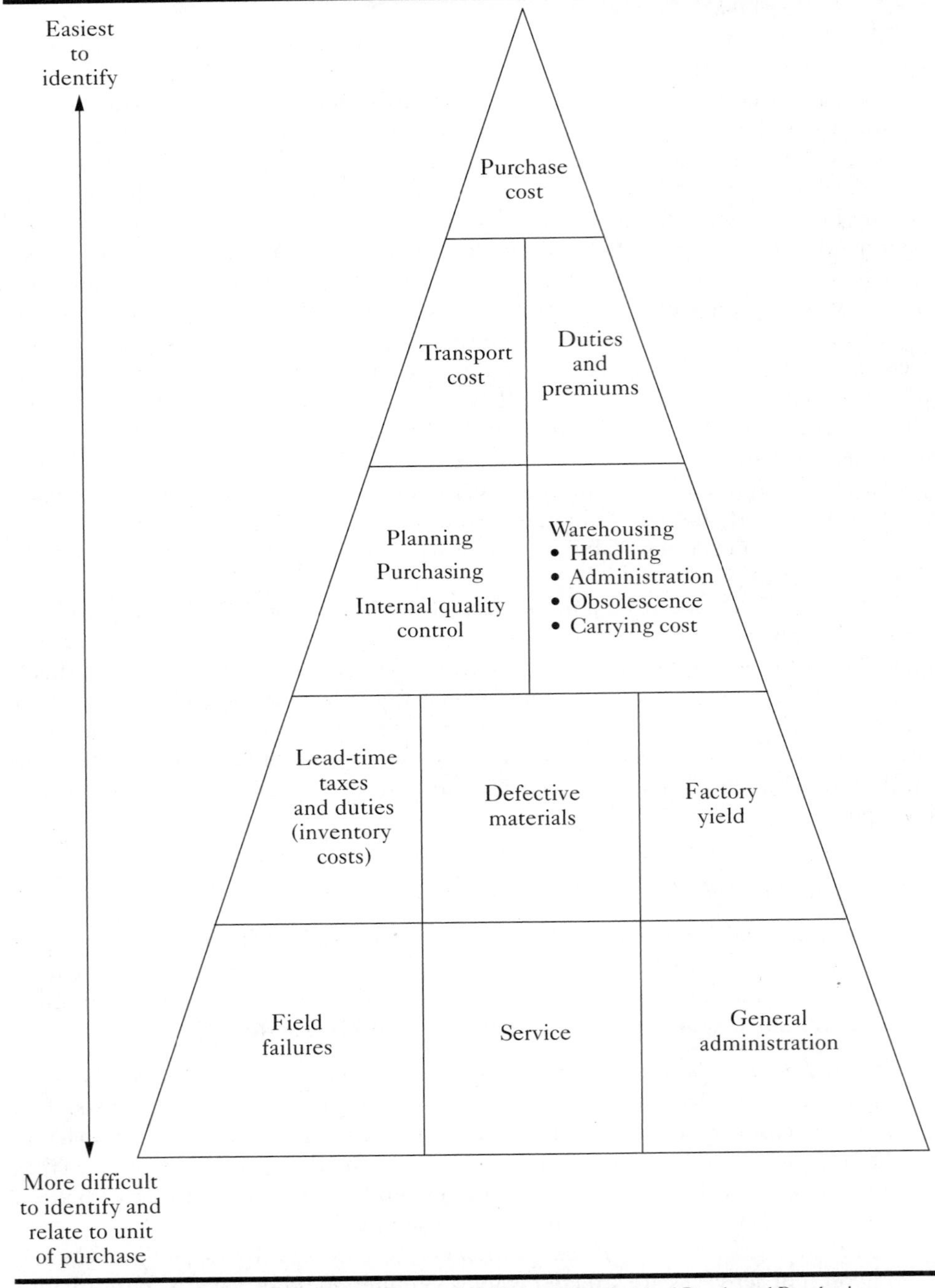

Easiest
to
identify

More difficult
to identify and
relate to unit
of purchase

Purchase
cost

Transport
cost

Duties
and
premiums

Planning
Purchasing
Internal quality
control

Warehousing
• Handling
• Administration
• Obsolescence
• Carrying cost

Lead-time
taxes
and duties
(inventory
costs)

Defective
materials

Factory
yield

Field
failures

Service

General
administration

Source: L. Ellram, *Total Cost of Ownership* (Tempe, AZ: Center for Advanced Purchased Purchasing Studies, 1993).

standards. In order to understand this, the total cost team should identify the actual steps in a process that occur when an order is transmitted to the supplier and the item is shipped, inspected, put into inventory, used in the internal process, and then shipped on to the customer. In mapping out this sequence of events, total cost measurement requires departments or functions to record the time and resources committed to resolving a supplier-caused problem.

3. *Identify Scope of the Model and Cost Elements:* Once the process of material flowing through the supply chain is understood, the team should focus on the major costs identified in the process. At this point, the team should check to ensure that the scope of the model is not too broad, that it is relevant to internal customers, and that the elements are controllable.

4. *Identify Performance Criteria, Collect Data, and Establish Model:* This step establishes the categories and criteria used to compare actual versus anticipated supplier performance. A company can also include other performance areas and parameters unique to its operating requirements. In addition, the relevant equations that link these performance criteria to actual cost dollars are important. This step requires the establishment of a structured measurement and recording system to monitor the total cost of an item or family of items. Larger and complex systems will require a computerized system to collect data and generate total cost reports.

5. *Document Model and Use It:* Total cost data allow performance comparisons between suppliers. It is not enough to say supplier A had a total cost of $10,000 while supplier B had a total cost of $15,000, because this does not compare the relative efficiency (as measured by the total cost to the purchase cost) of the two suppliers. The development of a standardized ratio or index supports direct comparisons or supplier ranking based on total cost. A standardized index allows comparisons of overall performance between suppliers. The index relates total cost to contract purchase price:

Total cost index = (Purchase price + Nonconformance costs) / Purchase price

The index allows a comparison of one supplier's total cost performance index against another supplier's regardless of the actual dollar values. If supplier A has an index rating of 1.3 and supplier B has a rating of 1.1, then supplier B is clearly the lower-cost supplier. For every $1 paid to supplier A for purchased material, the total cost of doing business with that supplier is $1.30. Total cost measurement identifies the suppliers with the potential to provide the lowest total sourcing cost. It requires time and effort to identify the items to track and to identify performance criteria and the costs of nonperformance.

Using of Total Cost of Ownership Data

Total cost of ownership measurement is increasingly important as supply chain managers strive to select the lowest total cost sources of supply (not the lowest price!). Total cost of ownership applies not only to items sourced from external suppliers but also to internally manufactured items. Companies implement total cost systems to realize very specific benefits.[7] A total cost of ownership approach allows a firm to do several things:

- Select supply sources based on total cost considerations.
- Increase supplier performance by identifying areas of nonperformance with responsibility for corrective action.
- Clearly define performance expectations and communicate those expectations to suppliers. Total cost systems should have a feedback mechanism that provides positive and negative supplier feedback.
- Increase supplier accountability and control. Total cost requires purchasing to develop an awareness of nonprice factors that are under the control of suppliers that contribute to total cost.
- Select preferred suppliers based on performance merit. The practice of developing partnerships with suppliers over an extended period of time requires comprehensive performance data. Total cost data allow a firm to rank suppliers and select only the best.
- Introduce measurement discipline throughout the organization by relying upon an equitable and consistent evaluation tool.

Total cost measurement information can be used in a number of managerial applications. The data provide the ability to quantify and communicate areas of nonperformance to concentrate supplier performance improvement efforts. Total cost information is also used during negotiations with suppliers to identify areas requiring contractual performance improvement. The information also assists in the overall supplier selection process by providing historical performance data and a means to rank supplier performance, which is especially useful if a firm is reducing its supply base. Finally, a structured approach to total cost may allow a buying company to recoup nonperformance costs through charge-backs to nonperforming suppliers. In the future we may see many more innovative applications of total cost data.

TARGET PRICING WITH COST-BASED PRICING: AN INNOVATIVE APPROACH TO STRATEGIC COST MANAGEMENT

Competitive demands have forced most purchasers to develop closer relationships with key suppliers and to pursue continuous performance improvement. Along with closer relationships has come a willingness to share cost information. Today, more companies are using target-based pricing to determine the relevant price that must be achieved for new-product success. Target pricing is then followed by cost-based pricing to drive continuous cost reductions throughout the product life cycle, yet allow suppliers to benefit from suggested cost-savings ideas. The combination of these innovative strategic cost management approaches relies on a critical component: the identification and sharing of cost information.

The last frontier of information exchange between firms is the detailed sharing of supplier cost data. Most North American supply firms have been reluctant to share this information. Some suppliers simply do not have a good idea about their true cost structure. Other suppliers may view cost data as proprietary information that provides insights into areas that the supplier wants kept confidential. A supplier may be reluctant to reveal how much it actually earns from a contract for fear of a price-reduction demand. For whatever reason, the detailed sharing of cost data has been a step many North American suppliers have not yet been willing to take. Although these fears may have been justified to some extent, target and cost-based pricing are increasingly being viewed as ways for both parties to benefit from detailed information sharing.

Target Pricing Defined

Target pricing is an innovative approach used in the initial stages of the new-product development cycle to establish a contract price between a buyer and seller. Japanese manufacturers, in an effort to motivate engineers to select designs that could be produced at a low cost, originated target pricing. These manufacturers came up with a simple concept to address cost: the cost of a new product is no longer an *outcome* of the product design process; rather, it is an *input* to the process. The challenge is to design a product with the required functionality and quality at a cost that provides a reasonable profit. In a new car, for example, the development team may work with marketing to determine the target price of the vehicle for the product's market segment. Using final price as a basis, the product is disaggregated into major systems, such as the engine and powertrain. Each major system has a target cost. At the component level (which represents a further disaggregation from the system level), the target cost is the price that a purchaser hopes to attain from a supplier (if the item is externally sourced).

The following contrasts traditional and target pricing. With target pricing, a product's allowable cost is strictly a function of what a market segment is willing to pay less the profit goals for the product. Under traditional pricing: Product cost + Profit = Selling price. However, using a target-pricing approach, the Selling price − Profit = Allowable product cost.

Generally speaking, the target cost is not always achievable by the supplier upon first discussion. Moreover, the supplier's current price to provide a product or service today is probably greater than the target price set forth by the buying company. The difference between these two figures becomes the *strategic cost-reduction objective*. This gap must be reduced by both parties working together, through such efforts as value engineering, quality function deployment, design for manufacturing/assembly, and standardization. Setting product-level target costs that are too aggressive may result in unachievable target costs. Setting too low a strategic cost-reduction challenge leads to easily achieved target costs but a loss of competitive position. In setting target prices and target costs, the new-product development team should bear in mind the cardinal rule of target costing: *the target cost can never be violated*. Moreover, even if engineers find a way to improve the functionality of the product, they cannot make the improvement unless they can offset the additional cost. Once a purchaser has established a target price with a supplier for the first year of a contract, additional cost reductions over the life of the product can be made through cost-based pricing.

SOURCING SNAPSHOT

Honda's Target-Pricing Approach.

Honda of America Manufacturing uses target pricing to identify cost-saving opportunities. The company breaks product costs down to the component level. Suppliers are asked to provide a detailed breakdown of their costs, including raw materials, labor, tooling, and required packaging as well as delivery, administrative, and other expenses. The breakdown of costs is helpful in suggesting ways that suppliers can seek to improve and thereby reduce costs. Cost tables are jointly developed with suppliers and used to find differences (line by line) across all elements of cost. A potential area of disagreement involves the supplier's profits and overhead. A fair profit is required but may be dependent on the level of investment. No fixed profit level is used in negotiations. Purchasing must then aggregate the parts costs and compare them with the target costs. If total costs exceed target costs, the design must change or costs must be reduced. While the supplier's profit margins might be an easy place to look for cost savings, Honda realizes that doing so would squander the trust it worked hard to develop with suppliers.

Source: Adapted from Daniel Krause and Robert Handfield, *Developing a World Class Supply Base* (Tempe, AZ: Center for Advanced Purchasing Studies, National Association of Purchasing Management, 1999).

Cost-Based Pricing Defined

Cost-based pricing differs from traditional market-based pricing in several ways. First, cost-based pricing requires joint identification of the full cost to produce an item, which is not the case with market-based pricing. Second, profit is a function of the productive investment committed to the purchased item and a supplier's asset return requirements (i.e., return on investment). Profit is not a direct function of cost (which is usually the practice with market-driven prices). The cost-based approach provides a supplier with incentives to pursue continuous performance improvement to realize shared cost savings and invest in productive assets. A later example illustrates these concepts.

An important feature of cost-based pricing is the financial incentives offered to a seller for performance improvements above and beyond the improvements agreed to in the purchase contract. This differs from the traditional market-based pricing approach where one party (usually the purchaser) seeks to capture all cost savings resulting from a supplier's improvement effort. Traditional pricing practices have been a deterrent to cooperative efforts to make design, product, and process improvements. A cost-based pricing approach recognizes the need to provide financial incentives to a supplier while enhancing closer relationships.

Prerequisites for Successful Target and Cost-Based Pricing

In order for target and cost-based pricing to occur, joint agreement must exist on a supplier's full cost to produce an item. Identification of all costs provides the basis for establishing joint improvement targets. The total cost to produce an item includes labor, materials, other direct costs, any costs due to start-up and production, and administrative, selling, and other related expenses.

Besides total cost components, the parties must jointly identify and agree upon product volumes, target product costs at various points in time, and quantifiable productivity and quality improvement projections. Each firm must also agree on the asset base and return requirement at the supplier that determines an item's profit. There must also be agreement on the point in time when mutual sharing of cost savings takes place, as well as the formula used to share the rewards. Mutual sharing of rewards usually occurs for savings above and beyond the performance improvement targets agreed to in the purchase contract, and savings on any items incidental to joint performance improvement targets.

This approach requires a high degree of trust, information sharing, and joint problem solving. This process will fail if one firm takes advantage of the other or violates confidentiality of information sharing. There must also be a willingness to provide the resources necessary to resolve problems affecting overall success.

The ability to manage the risks associated with target pricing is another key prerequisite. Perhaps the major risk concerns volume variability. Because volume affects cost levels, both parties must carefully consider and manage the impact of changes from planned volume projections. Higher-than-projected volumes will result in a supplier achieving greater economies and lower per-unit costs. These lower costs are not the result, however, of a supplier's performance improvement. Conversely, lower-than-projected volumes may raise a supplier's average costs. Contractually, the parties must determine how to manage changes from the buying plan.

Cost-Based Pricing Applications

A cost-based approach to determining price is clearly not appropriate for most purchased items. Many items do not warrant cost analysis or the marketplace determines price. Products that are readily available from multiple sources, standardized instead of customized, and heavily influenced by the market forces of supply and demand do not fit a profile of items appropriate for cost-based pricing.

What types of items are feasible for a cost-based cooperative approach? A cost-based approach is feasible when the seller contributes high added-value to an item through direct or indirect labor and specialized expertise. This approach is particularly appropriate for complex items customized to specific requirements. Also, products requiring a conversion from raw material through value-added designs at a supplier are possible candidates. Examples of such items include a specially designed antilock brake system or dashboard for an automobile. These items require a high value-added conversion from raw materials into a semifinished product. The supplier also likely contributes design and engineering support.

EXHIBIT 13.20   *Key Data for the Cost-Based Pricing Example*

First-Year Target Price $61.00

Negotiated/Analyzed Cost Structure

Material	$20 per unit
Labor rate	$8.50 per unit
Burden rate*	200% of direct labor
Scrap rate	10%
Selling, general, and administrative expense rate	10% of manufacturing cost
Effective volume range	125,000 units per year +/- 10%
Projected product life	2 years
Return on investment agreed to	30%

	Year 1	Year 2
Supplier investment	$3 million	$2 million
Total supplier investment	$5 million	
Supplier improvement commitment		
Direct labor	10% reduction annually	
Scrap rate	50% reduction annually	

Improvements incidental to agreed-upon performance improvements: Shared 50/50

*Burden is a term used in accounting to describe costs of manufacture or production not directly identifiable with an exact product or unit of production. They are indirect or apportionable costs.

An Example of Target and Cost-Based Pricing

While actual target and cost-based pricing agreements can be lengthy and complex, the following example demonstrates the fundamental principles of this strategic cost management approach.

A purchaser seeks to purchase a designed component that is part of a final end product. The final selling price of the product has been determined through discussions with marketing, and this figure has been rolled down (or disaggregated) to the component level. As such, both parties have agreed to target a purchase (or selling) price of $61 for the component for the first year. The purchaser has targeted this price as one that will support meeting the overall target price of the final end product.

Cost-based pricing uses the most efficient processes to produce a product as the basis for the cost structure. This approach does not reward inefficient processes or practices. Throughout this example the supplier's costs and return requirements serve as the basis for determining a fair and competitive price. Both parties agree to a negotiated cost-based approach because the parties have developed a close working relationship supporting the sharing of detailed cost data, and because the supplier's cost structure is relatively efficient.

The following two exhibits outline a cost-based agreement. Exhibit 13.20 details the costs and investment data needed to develop a cost-based purchase contract. Both firms must identify the costs and supplier investment associated with the

EXHIBIT 13.21   *Cost and Profit Breakdown for the Cost-Based Pricing Example*

	Year 1	Year 2	
Materials	$20.00	$19.24	Materials reduction of $1.50 plus an overall materials increase of 4% (($20.00 − $1.50) × 1.04)
Labor	8.50	7.88	Reduction of 10% − Contractual target improvement plus 3% increase ($8.50 × .9 × 1.03)
Burden (200% × labor)	17.00	15.76	
Total materials, labor, burden	$45.50	$42.88	
Scrap (10%)	4.55	2.14	Scrap reduced from 10% to 5% − Contractual target ($42.88 × .05)
Manufacturing cost	$50.05	45.02	
Selling and administrative expenses (10%)	5.00	4.50	
Total cost	$55.05	$49.52	
Profit*	6.00	6.75	Includes $.75 share for joint material reduction ($6 + ($1.50 ÷ 2))
Selling price	$61.50	$56.27	New selling price after year 1 events

*Profit is based on the 30% return on investment figure agreed to between buyer and seller.
Profit = ($5 million total two-year investment × .3)/250,000 total units
   = $6.00 profit per unit

purchased component, identify and agree on the supplier's asset return requirements, and identify supplier commitments to annual performance improvement targets. These exhibits provide the basis for evaluating cost and price throughout the life of the contract.

Exhibit 13.21 details the cost breakdown and subsequent price of the component for each year of this contract. Data for year 1 include the negotiated/analyzed information presented in Exhibit 13.20. During the first year, the following events affected the selling price at the start of year 2:

- Overall material costs rise by 4% due to raw material increases.
- Joint value analysis team identifies a substitute material that reduces material costs by $1.50 per unit.
- Labor rates increase by 3% per unit due to a scheduled contractual increase at the supplier.
- Supplier meets the agreed productivity improvement targets for reduced scrap and improved labor productivity.

Year 2 data include these events. The supplier received 50% of the $1.50 material reduction identified by the value analysis team. The profit figure for year 2 includes the supplier's share of the material reduction. The selling price at the start of year 2 becomes $56.27. By focusing on joint and continuous performance improvement, the purchase price was reduced at a time when material and labor costs actually increased.

This example, based on an actual case in the computer industry, illustrates the potential for improvement that can occur through joint price/cost analysis.

Establishing agreement on cost and price early in design and development supports the reduction of material costs through cooperative efforts. The use of cost-based pricing can provide inducements to work together to achieve mutual goals. The purchaser reduces its cost curve for purchased items, and also establishes a basis for continuous cost-improvement initiatives. The supplier benefits from longer-term contracts, a fair profit based on its asset investment, and increased competitiveness due to improvements occurring from the purchaser's insights and contributions.

GOOD PRACTICE EXAMPLE
Solectron's Total Supply Chain Cost Model

■ ■ ■

Solectron, founded in 1977 as the "Solar Energy Company," originally produced solar energy products. Today it is a worldwide provider of electronics manufacturing services to original equipment manufacturers (OEMs). The company provides customized, integrated manufacturing services that span all three stages of the product life cycle, including premanufacturing, manufacturing, and postmanufacturing. These services are integrated to the point where Solectron is now responsible for all supply chain processes associated with sourcing parts, producing, and distributing electronics and systems for almost every major OEM in the telecommunication, networking, computer systems, peripherals, semiconductors, consumer electronics, industrial equipment, medical electronics, avionics, and automotive electronics industries.

Managing supply chain inventories is one of the most formidable tasks at Solectron. Because the company deals with so many different market segments (computers, networking, workstations, etc.), each major sector/customer has a dedicated customer supply chain manager who is tasked with serving their product needs. Each industry sector has different life cycles, cost constraints, and market windows. Some customers must bring new products to market faster while others emphasize cost reductions. This makes the role of inventory planning even more complex with a significant amount of speculative planning and risk management required.

The major requirement for successful inventory management in this industry is rapid flexibility. For instance, a single customer can ask for a different product configuration involving a complete product change overnight, with increased capacity and plant requirements. To help achieve this flexibility Solectron is pursuing a strategy of increasing standardization through a "design for supply chain strategy."

One of the major drivers underlying Solectron's competitive strategy is its Total Supply Chain Cost Model. Steve Ng, Solectron's former senior vice president

EXHIBIT 13.22   *Analyzing Total Supply Chain Costs*

Buy Price

+ Supplier performance cost (delivery, quality)
+ Cost of acquisition
+ Out of sync planning
   (delays between schedule changes)
− Speculation Returns
+ Speculation costs (buffer cost inventory, capacity)
+ Manufacturing cost
+ Selling cost
+ Distribution cost
+ Profit
= Selling Price

---

and chief materials officer, discussed four major challenges associated with deploying supply chain management strategies at Solectron:

1. Where is the value created in the supply chain and who controls the value? Further, if one controls the value, where should one invest next to improve value?
2. How can we get the attention of executive management at our customers so that they understand our supply chain management strategy? Unless the customer understands the benefits of the strategy and its execution, it is very difficult to execute it down the line.
3. How can U.S. companies evolve from a "partnership" mode to a cross-enterprise decision-making mode? Cross-enterprise decision making involves decisions made to optimize value across organizations in the supply chain. While Japanese keiretsus have operated in this mode to some extent, U.S. companies are very unfamiliar with this type of competitive strategy.
4. How can we simplify our supply chain strategy and capture it in a quantitative model so that all supply chain decisions flow down from this model?

The new Total Supply Chain Cost Model currently being developed by Solectron addresses the last challenge. The model is continuing to evolve, but will be used as a basis for making future supply chain decisions. Exhibit 13.22 features the key elements of the model. The model expands decision making from a simple "buying price" perspective to one that emphasizes total supply chain cost improvements and joint competitive advantages as materials and information pass from the supplier to Solectron and on to the customer. This is reflected in the bottom-line selling price to the customer. Note that in Exhibit 13.22, the speculation returns and speculation costs reflect the fact that growth margins can be increased through greater responsiveness, which is achieved by positioning inventory, capacity, etc., strategically throughout the supply chain.

This model will help Solectron understand (1) customer requirements regarding what needs to be delivered, (2) the variables and constraints to doing so, (3) how to minimize excessive exposure to obsolescence due to engineering change orders, and (4) how to optimize direct material cost, cost of acquisition, and plant-to-plant and plant-to-volume flexibility. The model can also be used in "what-if" analysis to help set customer expectations, especially with regard to product introduction, time to volume, margins, and liability to exposure.

On the supply end, the structure will help to organize "value partnerships" with key strategic suppliers. Such partnerships will eliminate the need for negotiation and pricing because the Total Cost Model will be the basis for making supply chain decisions. Maximizing return on assets and cash flow will be the primary drivers underlying these relationships. Each supplier relationship should increase value, reduce cost, and remove uncertainties preventing the increase of market share.

The Total Supply Chain Cost Model acts as an important bridge between customers and suppliers. Customers may often make extraordinary demands that require major investments in upside capability (lead time, cost, capacity, inventory, etc.). Customer requirements are used as a baseline for creating innovative solutions by working backward with the supply management group. Solectron must be able to leverage its preferred suppliers to create solutions. They can then go to the customer and offer potential solutions by considering a different set of suppliers, technologies, etc. The Total Cost Model thus serves as the integrating mechanism for driving supply chain relationships backward and forward in the chain. ■

Source: Adapted from Robert B. Handfield and Ernest L. Nichols, Jr., "*Introduction to Supply Chain Management*" (Upper Saddle River, NJ: Prentice-Hall, 1998).

CONCLUSION

An awareness of cost fundamentals, cost analysis techniques, and innovative approaches to product costing is simply another area for the purchasing and supply chain professional to master. Buyers and supply chain specialists involved with nonstandard, technically complex items must have the ability to evaluate a supplier's cost structure and match supplier capabilities and product requirements from a cost perspective. The ability to practice price and cost analysis techniques, such as those outlined in this chapter, can make the difference between creating value and creating waste.

DISCUSSION QUESTIONS

1.   Why should a purchaser evaluate the cost of making an item instead of simply evaluating the purchase price? Is this true for all types of products? Why or why not?
2.   List some of the reasons suppliers are reluctant to share detailed cost information. What can purchasers do to convince suppliers that shared cost data will not be exploited?

3.   Explain what is meant by the following statement: *In the long run, all costs are variable.*
4.   What is the difference between a fixed cost, a semivariable cost, and a variable cost? Provide several examples of each type of cost.
5.   Why is a graphical analysis of cost relationships sometimes better than a numerical presentation?
6.   Under what types of market structures does a purchaser have the greatest price flexibility? The least flexibility? Why?
7.   Discuss the different pricing strategies a seller can use along with the key features of each.
8.   What types of cost information are available on the Internet? What types of price information are available on the Internet? Is this information reliable?
9.   Under what conditions does a buyer have the most purchasing leverage over a seller? When does a seller have the most leverage over a buyer?
10. What is the total cost of ownership concept? What are some of the challenges that must be overcome when implementing a total cost measurement system?
11. What are the benefits from measuring the total cost of ownership for a purchased item? Are there any potential disadvantages of this approach? If so, what are they?
12. How is the price of an item established in a cost-based pricing contract? What makes cost-based pricing attractive to a buyer and seller?
13. If a buyer and seller do not have a close working relationship, how can a buyer obtain cost data to perform a cost analysis for a supplier before awarding a purchase contract?
14. What happens if a supplier cannot meet a purchaser's initial target price? How is this issue resolved?
15. Why does a supplier have an incentive to invest in production plant and equipment with a cost-based approach to price determination?

ENDNOTES

1. R. S. Schmidgall, *Managerial Accounting* (East Lansing, MI: Educational Institute, 1986), 271–72.
2. Personal interview by Robert Handfield with John Calabrese, VP of Advanced Purchasing, General Motors, August 16, 2000.
3. B. T. Allen, *Managerial Economics* (New York: Harper & Row, 1988), 115.
4. D. V. Lamm and L. C. Vose, "Seller Pricing Strategies: A Buyer's Perspective," *International Journal of Purchasing and Materials Management* (Fall 1988): 10.
5. "Is Spindler a Survivor?" *Business Week*, October 2 1995, 62.
6. Schmidgall, *Managerial Accounting.*
7. R. M. Monczka and S. J. Trecha, "Cost-Based Supplier Performance Evaluation," *International Journal of Purchasing and Materials Management* (Spring 1988): 3; Lisa Ellram, *Total Cost of Ownership* (Tempe, AZ: Center for Advanced Purchasing Studies, 1993).

14 NEGOTIATION

*L*earning About Negotiation the Hard Way

John Williamson, a purchasing manager at Technatron, a U.S.-based electronics company, was sent to Japan to negotiate a major purchase contract.* Although John had some experience in handling a variety of transactions, he had never negotiated overseas. John was determined, however, to do well, particularly since the last words he heard from his manager were, "Make sure you come home with an agreement!"

Upon arriving in Japan, John's hosts met him at the gate. While walking to the luggage carousel, they graciously asked for his plane ticket, saying they wanted to verify that everything was satisfactory with his departure arrangements. Although the buyer was tired after 20 hours of travel, his hosts insisted that he join them for a large dinner and drinks. When the American indicated that he wanted to begin negotiations, his hosts politely suggested that it was important to take the time to get to know one another.

The negotiations formally began the next afternoon. John was surprised to find that he was negotiating against a team from the Japanese company. Furthermore, the Japanese appeared to have several well-respected and senior members of the company taking part. There was no denying that John felt intimidated at the negotiating table. He also felt at a disadvantage when the Japanese talked among themselves in their own language. They seemed to know a great deal about him and his company. The negotiations were also abruptly cut short when his hosts insisted that he visit some of the local cultural attractions, which included a late night in a karaoke bar.

John soon realized that he had severely underestimated the time it would take to negotiate. Every phrase and word had to pass through a translator. While he could not prove it, John suspected that at least one of the Japanese could speak English quite well. By the end of the second day, John began to get apprehensive. The two parties still had not reached agreement on several major issues and his flight was leaving the next day. He could not miss that flight, particularly since it was difficult to reschedule flights to the United States. John found himself increasingly making concessions to speed the process along. He realized that the Japanese knew his deadline time, since they had "graciously" verified his departing flight arrangements.

On the long flight home, John had time to think about the negotiations. Yes, he did reach agreement with the Japanese. However, he settled for a price that was 10% higher than his target, although it was still in the top end of his range. He also failed to reach favorable agreement on several other issues. While he did not believe he failed, he also knew he did not succeed. He was concerned how his company would accept the agreement, particularly since his manager did not seem too enthusiastic when he outlined the agreement over the phone. John realized he now knows what it means to be a stranger in a strange land.

→ → →

This vignette highlights many of the topics presented in this chapter: the use of tactics; the importance of planning; the challenge of international sourcing; and managing time, information, and power. We start this chapter by defining the concept of *negotiation*, with the second section presenting negotiation as a five-phase process. Next, the most important part of the negotiation process, planning, is described in detail. We then present sources of negotiating power, the use of concessions, and negotiating tactics. We follow with the important topics of win-win negotiation and international negotiation. Finally, a good practice example highlights how one organization uses negotiation to support the development of longer-term systems contracts.

*The names of the purchasing manager and electronics company have been changed.

What Is Negotiation?

One of the most important activities performed by purchasers is negotiating purchase agreements or contracts with suppliers. Purchasing is certainly not the only function or group within a company that negotiates. Negotiation, however, is a vital part of the purchasing process. We define *negotiation* as a process of formal communication, either face-to-face or via electronic means, where two or more people come together to seek mutual agreement about an issue or issues. More than ever, negotiation is becoming a team rather than an individual activity. So, in addition to the knowledge and skills required to be an effective negotiator, participants must also learn to work as a group when planning and executing a negotiation.

The negotiation process involves the management of time, information, and power between individuals and organizations who are interdependent. Each party has a need for the other yet recognizes that compromises or concessions are often required to satisfy that need. Without a willingness to compromise, most negotiations result in deadlock or a failure to agree. However, a deadlock does not necessarily mean that a negotiation failed. It is possible that the parties in a negotiation are so far apart that an agreement cannot be reached. In such cases, it may actually be better not to agree than to accept a poor agreement.

An important part of negotiation is realizing that the process involves relationships between people, not just organizations. Managing personal relationships in a negotiation is an important part of the negotiation process. A central part of negotiation involves each party trying to persuade the other party to do something that is in their best interests. The process involves skills that individuals, with the proper training and experience, can learn and improve upon. Good negotiators are not born; they develop their skills through practice.

Viewing Negotiation as a Value-Creating Activity

An alliance between General Motors and Fiat began as a series of vague, lower-level exploratory discussions on how to share investments and costs in emerging markets. But the talks picked up momentum and importance in February and March of 1999, when the two companies began discussing the possibility of setting up a common purchasing organization for Europe and Latin America. At that point, the meetings began to involve senior executives from both companies: GM President Rick Wagoner and Fiat Chairman Paolo Fresco and/or CEO Paolo Cantarella.

As talks proceeded, the areas of possible cooperation moved from joint purchasing to a single company to run powertrain operations and the creation of common platforms. Several times, Fiat executives say, honorary chairman Giovanni Agnelli attended meetings to discuss his hopes and goals for an alliance.

As negotiations between Wagoner, Fresco, and Cantarella continued through the fall, the realization grew that a wider alliance involving equity was justified. The final round of negotiations began in mid-January, culminating in talks in Detroit. GM delivered its final and formal offer to Fiat Auto headquarters in Turin. The next day Wagoner arrived in Milan, where he began talks with Fresco and Cantarella that lasted until 3 A.M. The Italian government was officially informed early Sunday, and GM Chairman Jack Smith arrived in Milan early Sunday afternoon to conclude the negotiations.

Source: Adapted from Luca Ciferri, "The Deal," *Automotive News*, March 20, 2000: 47.

Negotiation Framework

Perhaps the best way to approach this topic is by presenting negotiation as a process involving five major phases:

1. Identify or anticipate a purchase requirement.
2. Determine if negotiation is required.
3. Plan for the negotiation.
4. Conduct the negotiation.
5. Execute the agreement.

Exhibit 14.1 summarizes the negotiating process.

Identify or Anticipate a Purchase Requirement

The purchasing cycle begins with identifying or anticipating a purchase requirement. Chapter 2 addressed how firms identify or anticipate purchase requirements (the

EXHIBIT 14.1　*Five-Phase Negotiation Process*

Identify or anticipate a purchase requirement	Determine if negotiation is required	Plan for the negotiation	Conduct the negotiation	Execute the agreement
1	2	3	4	5

1
- Prepare purchase requisitions
- Update inventory counts
- Establish reorder point systems
- Support new-product development
- Plan for new facilities

2
- Is bid process inadequate?
- Are many nonprice issues involved?
- Is contract large?
- Are complex technical requirements involved?
- Does contract involve capital-intensive plant and equipment?
- Does contract involve a partnership?
- Will supplier perform value-added activities?
- Will there be long lead times?
- Will there be high risk and uncertainty?

3
- Identify participants
- Develop objectives
- Analyze strengths and weaknesses
- Gather information
- Recognize counterpart's needs
- Identify facts and issues
- Establish positions
- Develop strategies and tactics
- Brief personnel
- Practice the negotiation

4
- Perform fact finding
- Recess or caucus as necessary
- Work to narrow differences
- Manage time pressures
- Maintain informal atmosphere
- Summarize progress periodically
- Employ tactics
- Keep relationships positive

5
- Provide performance feedback
- Build on the success of the negotiation

purchasing process). The purchasing cycle begins with identifying (or anticipating) a material need or requirement for a component, raw material, subassembly, service, piece of equipment, or finished products. Two categories of purchases include requirements for existing items and requirements for new items, which are often identified during new-product development. For existing items, there may not be a need to identify a supplier since a purchase agreement may already exist. New requirements, however, require purchasing to identify potential suppliers.

Determine If Negotiation Is Required

Not all purchase requirements require buyers and sellers to enter into detailed negotiation. For many items, the competitive bidding process will satisfy a buyer's purchase requirements, as may be the case for items that are low value, or widely available or have established standards. Negotiation is often appropriate when issues besides price are important or competitive bidding will not satisfy the buyer's purchase requirements on those issues. A buyer can still use competitive bidding to identify potential sources of supply. After identifying a likely supplier through bidding, the buyer may negotiate to discuss other issues affecting the purchase agreement. The following are areas or issues besides price that may require purchase negotiation:

- Agreement on a supplier's allowable costs
- Delivery schedules and requirements
- Expected product and service quality levels
- Technology support and assistance
- Contract volumes
- Packaging requirements
- Liability for damage
- Payment terms
- Progress payment schedules
- Mode of transportation/transportation responsibility
- Warranties
- Capacity committed to the purchaser
- Responsiveness to buyer needs
- Material lead times
- Nonperformance penalties
- Contract length and renewal
- Protection of proprietary information
- Ownership of intellectual property developed jointly
- Items related to developing closer relationships, such as committing personnel specifically to the buyer-seller relationship
- Continuous improvement requirements in quality, delivery performance, lead time, cost, etc.
- Improvement incentives or nonperformance penalties
- Resolution mechanisms for contract disputes

This list, while not exhaustive, highlights the range of topics that negotiators can address. As buyers pursue closer relationships and longer-term agreements with suppliers, we expect less pure competitive bidding and more purchase negotiation, or a combination of competitive bidding with some negotiation. There may be several other reasons for negotiating with suppliers:

- *The contract value is large:* It is not unusual for purchasers to negotiate contracts worth hundreds of millions of dollars. Nonperformance on large contracts can cause unusually severe problems. The purchaser may want to negotiate special safeguards to make sure the supplier recognizes the importance of performing exactly as required.
- *The purchase involves complex technical requirements, perhaps even requirements that are still evolving:* Under this condition, it is difficult for the parties to reach specific agreement on a purchase requirement. However, there are times when a purchaser will want a supplier to begin work early during a project, even though final product requirements are not yet established.

- *The purchase involves capital-intensive plant and equipment:* Suppliers often customize capital-intensive plant and equipment to a purchaser's specific needs. Parties must address design responsibility along with payment terms.
- *The agreement involves a partnership-type arrangement:* Under such an agreement, all parties involved must address special considerations beyond those of a traditional or conventional purchase agreement. For one, these agreements are longer term and often contain automatic renewal clauses if the supplier achieves specified performance targets.
- *The supplier will perform important value-added activities:* Increasingly, buyers are asking suppliers to perform activities such as product design and testing. Additional activities performed by a supplier often require negotiation to determine the supplier's responsibilities and how to compensate for those efforts.

Exhibit 14.1 identifies other times when negotiation may be warranted.

Plan for the Negotiation

Negotiation planning involves identifying who will negotiate, what are the key issues in the negotiation, when and where negotiation will occur, and how to conduct the negotiation. Specifically, negotiation planning involves multiple steps that prepare the parties for a forthcoming negotiation. Many negotiations are relatively straightforward and require only basic preparation and planning. Other negotiations may be complex and require months of preparation. Regardless, purchasers who plan and prepare for a negotiation usually experience better outcomes. Planning is so central to effective negotiation that a later section focuses on this topic.

Conduct the Negotiation

Negotiations with a supplier should occur only when a purchaser feels confident about the level of planning and preparation put forth. However, planning is not an open-ended process; buyers must usually meet deadlines that satisfy the needs of internal customers within the purchaser's firm. Thus, the buyer faces pressure to conduct the negotiation within some sort of time frame. A negotiation should not be conducted until the negotiator has attempted to do certain things:[1]

- Understand the nature and purpose of the negotiation.
- Clarify the goals and objectives sought from the negotiation.
- Understand and prioritize the key issues of the negotiation.
- Understand the predictability of the negotiation process so the negotiator can strategically plan how to achieve his or her goals and objectives.
- Understand the personality, history, negotiating style, and important issues of the negotiator's counterpart.
- Manage the time pressures imposed by users who require an item or service.

Deciding where to negotiate can be an important part of the planning process. A home location can provide a great advantage to a negotiator, particularly during international negotiations. Advances in telecommunication technology now allow for some negotiations to occur electronically rather than face-to-face. Most experts agree that the atmosphere surrounding a negotiation should be less formal wherever possible. Excessive formality can constrain the parties and restrict the free exchange of ideas and solutions. It is also a good idea to summarize positions and points of agreement throughout the negotiation, which helps reduce misunderstanding between the parties while helping track progress against the negotiation agenda. It is also wise to have a dedicated note taker or scribe throughout the negotiation whose responsibility it is to record what was said, who said it, what the reaction was, and areas of agreement.

It is during the negotiation that the parties play out their strategy with *tactics*—the skill of employing available means to accomplish or achieve a desired end. Tactics are the action plans designed to help achieve a desired result. A later section reviews various tactics that negotiators may employ.

A sequence of four phases often characterizes face-to-face negotiating sessions. The first consists of fact finding between the parties. This part of the process helps clarify and confirm information provided by the buyer and seller. During the second phase, the parties often take a recess after fact finding. This allows each party to reassess relative strengths and weaknesses, review and revise objectives and positions if necessary, and organize the negotiation agenda. Next, the parties again meet face-to-face and attempt to narrow the differences on the issues on the agenda. Finally, the parties seek an agreement and conclusion to the negotiation.

Effective negotiators display certain behaviors or characteristics when conducting a negotiation. Students and managers should understand why each of these characteristics relates to more effective negotiators. Effective negotiators will compromise or revise their goals, particularly when new information becomes available that challenges a negotiator's position. More effective negotiators will also view issues independently without linking them in any particular sequence. Linking risks undermining an entire negotiation if the parties reach an impasse on a single issue. Effective negotiators also establish lower and upper ranges for each major issue, in contrast to a single, rigid position that limits the number of options available.

Effective or skilled negotiators explore twice as many options per issue than do average negotiators. Furthermore, effective negotiators make almost four times the comments about the common ground between the parties (rather than the differences) than do average negotiators. Finally, compared with average negotiators, effective or skilled negotiators make fewer irritating comments about the other party, give fewer reasons for arguments they advance (too many supporting reasons can dilute an argument), and make fewer counterproposals. Effective negotiators are willing to make counterproposals, though not as many as an average negotiator. A willingness to make too many counterproposals means the negotiator is probably compromising or offering too many concessions to the other party.

Execute the Agreement

Reaching agreement is not the end of the negotiation process. Rather, an agreement represents the beginning of the contract's performance for the item, service, or activity covered by the agreement. A key part of executing a negotiated agreement between parties is providing performance feedback. A purchaser must let a supplier know if the supplier is meeting its contractual requirements. Conversely, it is a supplier's responsibility to let the buyer know if the buyer is meeting its responsibilities within the negotiated agreement. Both parties should work to build upon the success of a negotiation. Executing the agreement should reaffirm the commitment of the parties to work together to pursue future opportunities.

NEGOTIATION PLANNING

Experts on negotiation agree that planning is perhaps the most important part of the negotiation process. Unfortunately, many negotiators fail to properly prepare before entering into formal negotiation. A *plan* is a method or scheme devised for making or doing something to achieve a desired end. *Planning*, therefore, is the process of planning or devising methods to achieve a desired end. Once purchasers develop a plan, they can begin to develop the tactics to carry out that plan. Without planning, a negotiator cannot possibly have the information required to support a complex negotiation or argue positions persuasively.

Negotiators frequently fall short of their goals because of the following failures in their planning process:[2]

- *Failing to commit sufficient time to the planning process:* Committing adequate time specifically to negotiation planning is probably the main hurdle that negotiators must overcome. Effective planning requires an up-front time commitment on the part of the negotiator or negotiating team.
- *Failing to establish clear objectives:* Not only do negotiators need to establish clear objectives concerning what they want from a negotiation, they need to establish a range for those objectives. Failure to establish clear objectives beforehand can result in a disorganized negotiation, agreeing to something that is not in a company's best interest, or delaying the negotiating process.
- *Failing to formulate convincing arguments or support for positions:* Preparing convincing arguments requires a negotiator to understand the strengths and weaknesses of his or her positions. The negotiator can also identify areas of flexibility within those positions.
- *Failing to consider a counterpart's needs:* To reach agreement, it is important to understand the needs of a counterpart. Such a process will clarify the critical issues that will move the parties toward an agreement.
- *Believing quick and clever is enough:* Individuals who believe they can bluff or talk their way through a complex negotiation will almost always fail when negotiating with someone who has prepared thoroughly. At least 90% of the success of any negotiation is determined by effective planning. Preparing at the last minute before a negotiation meeting is a sure recipe for disaster.

Successful negotiating planning consists of the following steps:

1. Develop specific objectives.
2. Analyze each party's strengths and weaknesses.

3.   Gather relevant information.
4.   Recognize your counterpart's needs.
5.   Identify facts and issues.
6.   Establish a position on each issue.
7.   Develop a negotiating strategy and tactics.
8.   Brief other personnel.
9.   Practice the negotiation.

Develop Specific Objectives

The first step of the planning process involves developing specific objectives sought from the negotiation. An *objective* is an aspiration or vision to work toward in the future. The primary objective in a purchasing negotiation is to reach an agreement covering the purchase of a good or service. A buyer or seller would not commit scarce resources if the goal were to see a negotiation fail. This does not mean that all negotiations will be successful. Many negotiations end in deadlock when there is no overlap in positions on key issues. Before actual negotiations begin, however, the parties usually believe they can reach an agreement. If the parties believed otherwise, they would not put forth the time and effort to prepare for a negotiation.

An important objective during a negotiation is to reach agreement on a fair and reasonable price between buyer and seller. Examples of objectives for a specific buyer preparing for a negotiation might include the following:

- Achieve a unit price of $10.
- Achieve a delivery lead time of four weeks.
- Improve quality from 500 parts per million defects to 50 parts per million defects.
- Exert some control over the way in which the parties execute the contract.
- Persuade the supplier to give maximum cooperation to the purchaser, even better cooperation than competitors receive from that supplier or other suppliers with whom competitors do business.
- Develop a sound and continuing relationship with competent suppliers.

Not all objectives may be equally important, so the purchaser must begin to identify the importance of each objective. One company separates its objectives into "must have" and "would like to have" categories. This begins to differentiate the importance of each objective.

Analyze Each Party's Strengths and Weaknesses

Experienced negotiators understand their counterpart through research and experience. This means understanding what is important to them. It also means coming to the negotiating table with an understanding of personalities and histories. When a purchaser negotiates with a supplier for the first time, a buyer must put forth additional research before fully understanding that supplier.

Analyzing each party requires an assessment of relative strengths and weaknesses. This process can influence the strategy and tactics taken at the bargaining table. The buyer does not always have power or influence over the supplier. Many times a supplier holds a power position over the buyer due to financial size or perhaps the supplier does not have a great need for the contract. A later section details various sources of power that are part of the negotiating process.

Understanding a supplier's production system is important. With this understanding, a buyer can determine if a supplier is using efficient process technology. A buyer can also estimate a supplier's cost structure, which leads to identifying a fair and reasonable price. The buyer might be able to determine how sensitive a supplier is to changes in volumes, material yields, and material and labor costs.

Gather Relevant Information

The ability to analyze yourself and your counterpart requires the gathering of information. This process is not as complex if the buyer and seller have previously negotiated a purchase agreement. When this is the case, the buyer may already have the answer to a number of important questions. What happened between the parties? Are we negotiating with the same or different people? What are the important issues to this supplier? What were the areas of disagreement? Is there anything about the rules of the negotiation we would like to change?

Where does a purchaser who has no experience with a supplier gather the required information? One possible source is others within the organization who are experienced with that supplier. These sources may help identify what is important to that supplier, provide background information, or even address the personalities of those involved in the negotiation. Sources of information may come from an organization's engineers, sales, purchasing, or manufacturing personnel, to name a few.

Published sources of information may also be available. These sources include trade journals, other business publications, trade association data, government reports, annual reports, financial evaluations such as Dun and Bradstreet reports, commercial databases, inquiries directly to personnel at the supplier, and information through the Internet. A buyer may already have information from quotations provided by the supplier before the negotiation.

Recognize Your Counterpart's Needs

The buyer and seller in a purchasing negotiation are, in many ways, mirror images of each other. Each side wants to reach an agreement that is favorable to longer-term success. As a buyer gathers information about a supplier, it is important to identify those issues that are particularly critical to the supplier. For example, a supplier may want to maintain market share and volume in its industry. Therefore, receiving an entire purchase contract, rather than a portion of a contract, may be an important objective to that supplier.

The issues that are most critical to a supplier may not be the most critical to a buyer (and vice versa). When one party has an issue or requirement that is not important to the other, then the parties will likely reach agreement. For example, a supplier's production scheduling system may require the supplier to produce a buyer's requirement late in the day with delivery during the evening. If a buyer has an evening work crew that can easily receive late deliveries, the buyer can satisfy the supplier's requirement for later deliveries so the parties should reach agreement on that issue. In return, the buyer may now expect the supplier to be accommodating on one or more issues that are important to the buyer. Give and take is essential to negotiation, and each party should not expect to prevail on all issues.

Identify Facts and Issues

Negotiation planning requires differentiating between facts and issues. The two parties will want to reach agreement early concerning what is a fact versus an issue. A fact is a reality or truth. In negotiation, these are not the items to be debated. A fact can be clearly stated: A buyer wants to purchase a piece of capital equipment. There is no negotiating with a supplier whether the buyer actually needs a piece of equipment (although the specific type of equipment may be an unanswered question requiring discussion). Issues, on the other hand, are items or topics to resolve during the negotiation. For example, the resolution of price and of equipment delivery date are both issues. Identifying the expected major issues for a negotiation is important because these are the topics on which the parties must reach agreement. The parties to a negotiation can debate many issues besides price. Part of the planning process requires identifying the critical issues that each party seeks from the negotiation.

Establish a Position on Each Issue

The parties to a negotiation must establish a position for each issue to be addressed, a position that should have some flexibility. Negotiators should therefore develop a range of positions— typically, a minimum acceptable position, a maximum or ideal outcome, and a most likely targeted position. If the issue is price, a seller may have a target price for which it wants to sell a product. Of course, the seller will be willing to take a higher price if the buyer is willing to offer one. The critical part of the range will be the seller's minimum price. This is the lowest price at which the seller is willing to sell to a buyer. Each party must carefully determine this range before beginning a negotiation.

This area of overlapping positions is termed the *bargaining* or *settlement zone*.[3] It is the heart of the negotiating process. Exhibit 14.2 demonstrates this zone for a purchase price negotiation. With example A, the parties will probably not reach agreement unless one or both parties modify their original range or position. The minimum selling position of the seller is far above the buyer's maximum position. With example B, an overlap exists between buyer's and seller's positions that should lead to an agreement. The buyer is willing to pay up to $11.45 per unit. The supplier is willing to sell as low as $11.15 per unit. The two parties will likely reach an agreement somewhere between those two figures. The buyer may open with an offer to purchase at less than $11 as a tactic (i.e., start out very low). However, if the seller remains with its original plan, the negotiation will likely conclude within the overlap range.

Several factors influence whether a party modifies or even abandons an original position on a negotiating point. This includes the party's desire for the contract, new

EXHIBIT 14.2   *Developing Negotiating Ranges for a Purchase Price*

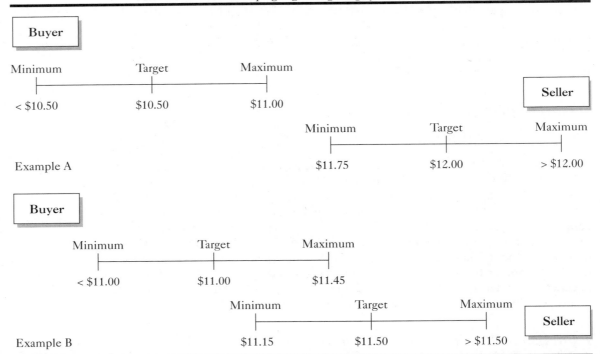

Example A

Example B

or improved information that becomes available and challenges the accuracy of the original position or range, a major concession made by one party on an issue that supports other modifications or compromises by the other party, or a shifting power relationship between the two parties.

Develop a Negotiating Strategy and Tactics

Negotiating strategy refers to the overall approach used to reach a mutually beneficial agreement with a supplier who holds different points of view than the buyer. Strategy implies a longer-term focus. Another major part of the strategic planning process involves *tactics*—the art or skill of employing available means to accomplish an end, objective, or strategy. They include the current set of action plans and processes adopted to achieve the negotiating objectives and strategy.

Strategic negotiating issues involve the broader questions regarding who, what, where, when, and how to negotiate. We can think of strategy and tactics as two dimensions of the negotiating process. The ideal situation is to have a well-developed negotiating strategy with the tactics to support that strategy. As an analogy, think of a military battle. The best-developed strategy will fail unless a commander has the tactics and the resources to implement the strategy. The same is true in negotiation—it is a process that requires attention to the plans and tactics required to carry out the strategy. The strategy in turn supports the original objectives of the negotiators.

Brief Other Personnel

Purchase negotiation usually affects other parties within a company. The individual or team conducting the negotiation should brief these parties to make sure they are aware of and in agreement with the objectives of the negotiation. This briefing can also address the major issues of the negotiation and positions on these issues. Briefing personnel prior to a negotiation helps eliminate unwanted surprises during face-to-face negotiation.

Practice the Negotiation

Experienced negotiators practice or rehearse before commencing the formal negotiation. One way to do this is to hold a mock or simulated negotiation. For instance, a marketing or sales person might represent the supplier. The counterpart in a practice negotiating session may be able to raise questions and issues that the buyer had not originally addressed or considered. When using simulation, it is important for each party to play its roles as realistically as possible.

Taking shortcuts when planning for a negotiation can have disastrous effects—effects that a firm may have to live with for years. Effective planning means that a purchaser addresses critical issues and needs and works to reach an agreement that is more creative than one available to competitors. It also means managing relationships that support future negotiation.

POWER IN NEGOTIATION

An important part of the negotiation process involves the power relationship between parties. *Power* is the ability to influence another person or organization. Party A has power over party B if A can get B to do things that directly benefit A. Throughout history, we have seen both positive and destructive uses of power. Within negotiation, the use of power employed by the parties can influence the outcome of a negotiation. A buyer's ability to reward or punish a supplier represents a use of power that can influence the outcome of a negotiation.

Individuals and organizations bring different sources of power to the negotiating table, and the use of power can be part of the negotiating strategy. We must recognize, however, that different sources of power can have varying short- and long-term effects on a negotiation and a relationship. Some types of power are detrimental to a continued relationship while other types come about as a result of expertise or access to information. Purchasers must understand the advantages and disadvantages of using power. They must also understand the possible effect that using a particular source of power will have on a relationship.[4]

Sources of Negotiating Power

Researchers have identified six major types of power exercised by individuals or organizations: (1) informational, (2) reward, (3) coercive, (4) legitimate, (5) expert, and (6) referent.[5] A negotiator may resort to using power when persuasiveness and information fail to make the other party agree to a position. Other negotiators, given the right circumstances, may make the use of power an up-front part of their negotiating strategy.

Informational Power Having access to information is the most common form of power used in a negotiation. It relies on persuasion through the use of facts, data, and other arguments. The use of information in negotiation does not necessarily mean open and complete sharing of that information. One party can manipulate a situation by presenting only favorable information that supports a position. The other side may present only negative information to refute a position. When used as a source of power, one party often manipulates information to control or restrict the options available to the other party.[6]

Reward Power Reward power means that one party is able to offer something of value to the other party. A large purchase contract is an example of reward power, particularly if the supplier values that business. Rewards are a source of power only if the other party values the reward. A purchase contract totaling 1/20 of 1% of a supplier's total business is probably not enough to persuade the supplier to accept certain positions put forth by the buyer.

Using rewards represents a direct effort to exert control, particularly compared with the use of informational power, which relies more on persuasion. The basis of reward power is the belief that individuals respond and behave accordingly when rewards are available. An important risk of reward power is that a counterpart becomes conditioned to respond only when offered rewards.

Coercive Power Coercive and reward power are somewhat related. If one party can give (reward power), then that party can also take away (coercive power). Coercive power, however, has a more negative connotation than reward power. It includes the ability to punish—financially, physically, or mentally. An example of this involves a purchaser threatening to withhold business or reduce a price unilaterally if a supplier does not agree to certain demands.

The decision to use coercive power often relates to the power holder's perception of the willingness of the other party to comply.[7] Repeated use of coercive power can have damaging effects on longer-term relationships. There is also a strong likelihood that retaliation becomes an option for the other party if the power structure shifts in the future. When supply markets begin to tighten during an economic recovery, suppliers may retaliate by pursuing large price increases, not providing excellent service to certain buyers, or even denying materials. Each of these actions is a form of retaliation.

Legitimate Power The position that an individual holds, rather than the individual, is the basis of legitimate power. Parents, ministers, managers, and political office-holders are examples of positions with legitimate power. When individuals exercise legitimate power, they are doing so because they feel their position allows them that right. Individuals often respond to legitimate power because they respect a position. In purchasing, a buyer may have legitimate power simply because he or she represents a prominent company. It is not the case that individuals with legitimate power necessarily have reward or coercive power (e.g., a church minister).

Expert Power   Expert power is a related and special form of informational power. Informational and expert power involve the retention of knowledge. Information power is present when someone has researched and prepared for a discussion, such as a negotiation. On the other hand, an expert is recognized as having accumulated and mastered vast knowledge about a subject, often with credentials to verify that mastery. If a well-respected heart specialist tells a patient to reduce fat intake, that patient will likely listen to the doctor. If that doctor begins to dispense financial advice, individuals will probably not seriously consider it (unless the doctor also happens to be a financial expert). Expert power can influence others in a negotiation by reducing the likelihood that another party will refute a position. Furthermore, nonexperts are less likely to challenge an expert due to the expert's depth of knowledge.

Referent Power   This power source comes from attraction based on personal qualities and attributes of an individual. These qualities could be physical but likely include characteristics such as honesty, charisma, friendliness, and sensitivity. The power holder—the referent—has some attributes or qualities that attract another party or make another person want to be like the power holder. The basis of referent power is that the nonreferent wants the referent to look favorably upon him or her. As such, the referent may have power that can be used during negotiation. What one party in a negotiation feels toward a referent may have no relationship to how another party feels toward that referent. Someone with referent power may not even be aware that power exists. Referent power is most successful in negotiation when the referent is aware that a counterpart identifies with or has an attraction to the referent.

Parties with power will likely use their sources of power to some degree during a negotiation. Negotiators must be careful not to abuse that power or risk damaging relationships, inviting retaliation at a later date, or diminishing the value of the power. In most negotiations, the sources of power that are usually the most effective are *legitimate*, *informational*, and *expert*. These are the primary sources of power that purchasing professionals should strive to achieve. They are also the sources of power that will allow the parties to work together after reaching agreement.

CONCESSIONS

A fundamental part of every negotiating process is the *concession*—a movement away from a negotiating position that offers something of value to the other party. For example, a buyer's willingness to offer $8.50 per unit instead of $8.25 is a concession that favors the supplier. To make the negotiating process work, each party

EXHIBIT 14.3   *Offering Concessions*

		Round				Continue to Round 5 or stop?
		1	2	3	4	
Supplier	1	$50	$50	$50	$50	_____
	2	$110	$75	$0	$15	_____
	3	$35	$45	$55	$65	_____
	4	$200	$0	$0	$0	_____
	5	$0	$0	$0	$200	_____
	6	$80	$60	$40	$20	_____

Concessions received per
negotiation round

must be willing to demonstrate flexibility. Recognizing that concessions are a necessary part of negotiation, purchasers still want to minimize how much they concede on each point.

The manner in which a negotiator approaches concessions is an important part of negotiating strategy. A purchaser who opens with a low initial offer (on price, for example) with a relatively small opening concession is signaling a reluctance to be flexible by taking a firm position. Conversely, a cooperative opening position or moderate offer with a relatively strong concession signals a willingness to be flexible.

Exhibit 14.3 illustrates possible ways that a seller might offer total concessions and how this influences the ways the other party responds. If a seller continues to offer concessions during each round of negotiation, a buyer will likely be conditioned to ask for further concessions. Examine Exhibit 14.3 and ask yourself if you would continue to a fifth round of negotiation with each supplier given the pattern of concessions presented. Remember that continuing a negotiation results in additional costs. How a negotiator presents concessions affects the length of the negotiation and the other party's expectations.

Suppliers or buyers who open with their best and final offers with no concessions are practicing *boulwarism*—a negotiating style named after Lemuel R. Boulware, the former CEO of General Electric. Boulware believed that the most efficient way to approach a negotiation was to quickly place the final offer on the negotiating table with no discussion or concessions. More often than not this approach creates an unrealistic expectation because negotiators expect concessions to follow. When concessions fail to follow, the other side often becomes angry or believes the counterpart is not bargaining in good faith. In fact, boulwarism now means bad faith or no-concession bargaining.[8] Negotiations featuring boulwarism often end in deadlock.

Frank Haluch, an expert on buyer-seller negotiation, offers the following advice about concessions:

- *Regardless of a negotiator's opening position, leave room to maneuver.* If you take a flexible position, make sure your counterpart is also taking a flexible position or you will be offering the majority of the concessions.
- *As a negotiation progresses, the frequency and value of concessions need to diminish.*
- *During a negotiation, remove the audience (nonparticipants, employees, or managers) to increase the potential of obtaining a concession.* The larger the audience, the more difficult it becomes to offer concessions. A natural tendency exists to want to appear firm and tough at the negotiating table. This appearance, however, can hurt the negotiating process.
- *Smaller and smaller concessions indicate a likely resistance to further concessions.*

While concessions are an important part of the negotiation process, a willingness to offer large concessions is not in the best interests of a purchaser. Purchasers should pursue strategies and tactics that provide as much protection as possible to their original target positions while still recognizing the need for compromise. The level of planning and the relative power of each party will influence how much each party concedes during a negotiation.

Negotiation Tactics: Trying to Influence Others

Negotiating tactics are the short-term plans and actions employed to execute a strategy, cause a conscious change in a counterpart's position, and influence others to achieve negotiating objectives. Negotiators can choose many possible tactics during the course of a negotiation. Negotiators develop tactics to try and persuade (ethically) a counterpart to endorse a certain position. Furthermore, a negotiator must understand what type of tactics a counterpart is using. An awareness of a counterpart's tactics may diminish the effectiveness of those tactics during the negotiation.

According to Robert Cialdini, we can cluster hundreds of negotiating tactics into six categories, which represent fundamental social psychology principles that guide human behavior.[9]

- *Reciprocation:* Virtually every society on earth adheres to the principle of reciprocation, which means we feel an obligation to give something back to someone after we have received something. In negotiation, this principle creates an obligation to return something in kind when the other party offers a concession. Effective negotiators understand the powerful influence that reciprocity has on most individuals.
- *Consistency:* This principle directs us to be consistent in our beliefs and actions. In a negotiation, if we can get others to agree to something, then not following through on their part would be inconsistent and irrational. Skilled negotiators also

understand that after someone agrees to something, he or she feels better about that decision than before they agreed. Furthermore, once a small commitment is in place, it becomes easier to request larger commitments later.

- *Social proof:* According to this principle, we look to the behavior of others to determine what is desirable, appropriate, and correct.[10] This can work against us in negotiations if we look to others to determine our behavior. For example, a seller may state that a well-respected company uses the seller's product, providing social proof of the purchase to the buyer.

- *Liking:* This principle states that we work well and are more agreeable with people we like. Effective negotiators take time to get to know their counterparts, knowing that concessions are more likely when a favorable level of familiarity exists.

- *Authority:* This principle states that we are more likely to accept the positions, arguments, and direction from authority figures. In a purchase negotiation a senior salesperson may be able to influence an inexperienced buyer.

- *Scarcity:* Sellers learn early in their career the influence that scarcity can have on a buyer. Who wants to close a plant because supply will be short next month (unless purchasers act now)? The same argument applies to price increases. If the product will be scarce at this price, purchasers better buy before the price increases. Sellers know that scarcity often creates its own demand.

The following represents only a small sample of specific negotiating tactics. Some are really ploys or tricks—they are not recommended for use—but we present them so purchasers are aware of them. However, those tactics presented here that are legitimate and ethical are the best approaches for persuading others to endorse a point of view.

Low Ball This tactic involves one party, often the seller, offering an unusually low price, for example, to receive a buyer's business. This tactic is also known as the "foot in the door" approach. Suppliers know that once a buyer makes a commitment to a seller, it is often difficult for that buyer to switch to another supplier.

Honesty/Openness Parties with a close working relationship have a level of trust that allows them to share information freely. The objective of open and honest information sharing is to make each party aware of the relevant information needed to craft an agreement that is acceptable to both parties.

Questions Open-ended questions serve dual purposes during negotiation. First, insightful questions can result in revealing new information, such as a negotiator's true position or real concerns. Second, questions provide a period of relief as the other party takes time to consider an answer.

Caucus This involves taking time out to process new information, take a needed break when a negotiation is going poorly, or when a negotiator feels he or she is making too many concessions.

Trial Balloon A negotiator using this tactic might ask, "What if I can persuade my manager to endorse this option. Would you go along?" Trial balloons are ideas being tested for acceptance. The reaction to the idea influences whether the parties will pursue the idea further.

Price Increase Sellers sometimes argue that if a buyer does not agree to a certain price, the price will soon increase. Unsuspecting buyers may agree to the seller's terms to avoid the increase. A well-informed negotiator can tell the difference between a real price change and a tactic used by the seller merely to get a purchase contract.

Limited Stock This tactic involves scarcity as a means of persuasion. Again, unsuspecting or ill-prepared buyers may agree to buy at a certain price because they do not want to close down an operation, particularly after the seller "warned" the buyer of the scarcity.

High Ball This tactic involves taking an initial high or low position on an issue. A buyer may offer an extremely low purchase price or the seller may put forth an extremely high selling price. The logic is that once a party actually makes a concession from the extreme position, the new position may appear quite acceptable to the other party. This is a process of contrasting one position (the extreme position) to another position so the new position looks favorable.

Best and Final Offer This tactic may signal the end of a negotiation on an issue. The person making the best and final offer must be prepared to end the discussion if the other party does not accept the offer. If the best and final offer is rapidly amended to a new best and final offer, this tactic quickly loses its effectiveness.

Silence This tactic involves not immediately responding when a counterpart makes an offer. Most individuals, particularly in our culture, are extremely uncomfortable with silence. Silence can be used, at select times, as an effective negotiating tactic. For instance, when the other party makes a point that weakens our position, it may be better to remain silent than to admit the other party is correct.

Phantom Quotes/Offers A phantom quote or offer involves one party lying or deliberately misleading the other party. For example, a buyer may inform a seller that it has a quote from another supplier that is $5.00 less per unit. If the seller does not match that quote, it can forget about doing business with the buyer. Sellers also use this approach. A seller might inform buyer A that buyer B has offered to purchase the same material (which is scarce) at a higher price. Buyer A must match or exceed buyer B's price or else no sale will occur. This tactic is unethical and risky. If one party does not respond to the phantom quote or offer, then that party has effectively counteracted that tactic.

Planned Concessions This tactic uses concessions to influence the other party's behavior. As mentioned earlier, a buyer who opens with a low initial offer (on price, for example) with a relatively small opening concession signals a reluctance to move

SOURCING SNAPSHOT

Effective Negotiators Are Always on Guard

Integrated supply relationships and win-win long-term deals might be gaining popularity, but that doesn't mean hard-nosed, adversarial negotiators have suddenly become extinct. As supply managers look to place their volumes with fewer and fewer first-tier suppliers, the risks of locking into long-term deals have never been so high. Buyers who are aware of dirty negotiating tactics might be able to avoid costly long-term mistakes. Buyers who employ dirty tactics might damage their firm's ability to establish long-term supply relationships with the best available suppliers. Here are some common dirty tricks to watch out for:

- *Escalation:* This tactic sets the other party up to think a deal is in the works, wears them down with extra work or delays, then asks the other party to take less than originally bargained. The escalator is counting on others to relent because they've invested work and emotional equity in closing the deal.
- *Devil in the details:* Hidden in an obscure attachment, specification, or boilerplate document lies an administrative or technical nightmare. Devils in the details are designed to be overlooked.
- *Figure finaglers:* Numbers presented in negotiations are apt to be biased. Even when parties have worked together for a long time, they'll still have different viewpoints.
- *White hat/black hat:* A subtle version of good cop, bad cop. Black hat always says "no," making white hat appear infinitely more reasonable.
- *The switch:* One of the most dangerous assumptions made is that the agreement everyone shakes hands on is the one that will be written up. A simple one-word switch—for example, use of the word *net* versus *gross*—could make a huge difference in the outcome of a contract. Skilled negotiators are always on guard to spot any questionable tactics displayed by their counterparts.

Source: Adapted from Chester L. Karass, "Dirty Tricks Persist Despite Era of Win-Win Relationship," *Purchasing,* September 2, 1999: 24.

---

from the initial position. Conversely, a cooperative opening position or moderate offer with a relatively significant concession signals a willingness to be flexible. The use of planned concessions also signals that it is now the other party's turn to reciprocate and make a concession on an important issue.

Use of Power   The type of power used is dependent on the purchase situation. If a buyer wants a longer-term relationship with a supplier, for example, then using coercive power is not recommended. The conscious use of power as a tactic was addressed during the negotiating planning process.

A tactic used for one issue may not be successful or applicable to other issues. When conducting a negotiation, an effective negotiator must be willing to modify tactics that are not effective. Tactics are most effective when the other party is unprepared, stressed, under severe time deadlines, inexperienced, fatigued, or disinterested.

$\mathcal{W}$IN-WIN NEGOTIATION

Many purchasers believe that the primary objective of negotiation is to win at the expense of a counterpart. We call this *win-lose negotiation* (also called *competitive* or *distributive bargaining*). Win-lose negotiation means that two or more parties are competing over a *fixed* value with the winner taking the larger share. Characteristics of win-lose negotiation include rigid negotiating positions, arguments over fixed value, and the strict use of power by one party over the other. It is adversarial competition being played out at the negotiating table. It is also a zero-sum game—if one party gains it is at the expense of the other party. Every increase in the purchase price benefits only the seller, and every decrease in price benefits only the buyer. The level of competition in a win-lose purchase negotiation rarely makes a supplier anxious to cooperate with a buyer to provide advantages that are not available to other customers. A second type of negotiation, *lose-lose,* occurs when parties fail to capitalize on compatible interests and suboptimize an agreement.[11] Neither party has their needs satisfied in lose-lose negotiation.

Win-win negotiation, also called *integrative bargaining,* seeks to *expand* the value or resources available to participants through cooperative negotiation. The parties will still negotiate to determine how to divide a bigger and expanded value pie. Increased value to the buyer may mean receiving a better purchase price than a competitor, a shorter material-ordering lead time from the supplier, joint efforts to reduce waste between the parties, or assistance in developing new technology or product designs. On the supplier's side, increasing value may mean additional volume from the purchaser, preferential treatment in the awarding of future business, or technical assistance provided by the purchaser to help reduce operating costs (which can make the supplier more competitive to all customers). Exhibit 14.4 summarizes the characteristics of win-lose and win-win negotiation.

Certain conditions are necessary for win-win negotiation to be successful:[12]

- Common, shared, or joint goals and objectives
- A faith in one's own problem-solving ability
- Motivation and commitment to work together
- Mutual trust
- Open and accurate communication
- A belief in the validity of the other's position

Parties rarely state to each other that they are taking a win-win negotiation approach. Rather, it is through their actions that the desire to pursue a cooperative negotiating approach is revealed. One party may open a negotiation by clarifying what it perceives are the goals and priorities of each party, and then offer a cooperative negotiating position. This conveys a willingness to work together and to recognize each

EXHIBIT 14.4   *Characteristics of Win-Lose/Win-Win Negotiation*

Characteristics of win-lose negotiation (distributive bargaining)	Characteristics of win-win negotiation (integrative bargaining)
• Rigid negotiating positions • Competition over a fixed amount of value • Strict use of power by one party over another • Adversarial competition played out at the negotiating table	• Understanding each other's needs and wants • Focusing on common rather than personal interests • Conducting joint efforts to problem solve and develop creative solutions that provide *additional* value • Engaging in open sharing of information

other's needs during the negotiating process. When areas of disagreement arise between the buyer and seller, win-win negotiators develop solutions that accommodate both parties.

A fundamental question is how a buyer and seller, through the negotiation process, can achieve their integrative bargaining objectives. Previous research has identified five different methods for achieving integrative (win-win) agreements:[13]

- *Expand the pie:* Working together, the parties identify ways to expand the resources or value obtained through a negotiated agreement. For example, a seller that offers a buyer early access to new technology for inclusion in new products can expand the value pie. If the market endorses the new product, presumably sales will increase and the supplier will receive larger purchase orders. Both sides realize higher volume and, hopefully, higher profit.
- *Logroll:* Successful logrolling requires the parties to identify more than one issue where disagreement exists. The parties agree to "trade off" these issues so each party has a top-priority issue satisfied. (In win-lose the parties would not concern themselves with the needs of the other.)
- *Cost cut:* With cost cutting one party (usually the buyer) gets a lower price as the parties work to reduce the seller's costs or work to reduce the costs of doing business (transactions costs). This is win-win because the buyer satisfies his or her objective (a competitive price) while the seller becomes more competitive in the marketplace due to a reduced cost structure.
- *Bridge:* Bridging involves inventing new options that satisfy each party's needs. While bridging solutions will likely not totally satisfy each party, they are usually satisfactory to each side.
- *Offer nonspecific compensation:* With this approach one party achieves his or her objective on an issue while the other receives something of value as a "payoff" for going along.

The win-win approach works best for items or services that are important to the buyer's product or business, involve high-dollar items or services where cost control is critical to remaining competitive, or where the supplier adds value to the product or service. When variables such as technology, cycle time, quality, and price/cost are important, win-win negotiating may be the best approach.

$\mathcal{I}$NTERNATIONAL NEGOTIATION

With the growth in international purchasing over the last 20 years, the need to negotiate across cultures has increased greatly. Negotiation with suppliers takes on added complexity when the parties have different languages, customs, laws, and cultures. When preparing for an international negotiation, extra planning must occur to accommodate translation, travel, and other foreign business requirements.

Previous research focused on the barriers to effective international negotiation and the characteristics of effective international negotiators.[14] In order of importance, the major obstacles to effective international negotiation were (1) miscommunication due to language, (2) time limitations, (3) cultural differences, and (4) limited authority of the international negotiator. This same research revealed that (1) patience, (2) knowledge of the contract agreement, (3) an honest and polite attitude, and (4) familiarity with foreign cultures and customs characterized effective international negotiators.

Beyond the natural barriers of language differences, it is still possible to fail to understand and to be understood. Culture plays a significant role in communication. For example, during international negotiation an interpreter enables verbal communication to take place but may not convey the significance of "unspoken" actions, signals, and customs. International negotiation requires additional planning and preparation to be successful. Not only must purchasers perform normal supplier analysis and fact finding, they must also understand the customs and traditions of their counterpart. As buying and selling increases between countries, the need for international negotiation skills will also increase.

The following presents a broad and somewhat stereotypical profile of various cultures and their negotiators, admittedly from an American perspective. However, understanding these profiles can prove beneficial when developing negotiating strategies and tactics.

British The British appear to be polite, reserved, and friendly (particularly to Americans), but they can also be tough negotiators when required. Americans must understand that the British view their relationship with the United States as special. However, Americans often do not view this relationship differently from relationships with other countries. The British are quite sensitive to comparisons with other European cultures, particularly the Germans.

British negotiators tend to be deliberate and less prepared than their counterparts, yet they will be open and forthright in their negotiations. They do not "play games" at the negotiating table. The British are often risk averse and tend to focus and debate small contractual items, especially the terms and conditions of the transaction. Be aware that while Americans and British both speak English, many words are unknown or have different meanings across the cultures.

German Germans perceive that titles are important in terms of "expertise"; therefore it is important to involve individuals in the negotiation who have the right skills and credentials. They are the most similar to Americans in terms of entrepreneurial spirit yet are somewhat more risk averse. Germans are more willing to seek compromise rather than risk confrontation or controversy. They are somewhat slow to reach a decision due to their hierarchical nature and the need to analyze situations thoroughly. In fact, committees usually make decisions, with several signatures required on all documents. Because of the historical strength of German engineering, they are often not receptive to external technical suggestions. Other characteristics of German negotiators include being sensitive to comparisons with the French and British, responding well to logic and thoroughness, being concerned with the precision of the written word or contract, and not responding to attempts at humor.

Chrysler has extensive experience working with Germans (and vice versa) through the merger of Chrysler and Daimler Benz. A Chrysler executive differentiates the two cultures with an analogy of playing a new board game. He said that when Americans begin a new game they immediately want to start playing. Americans figure out the instructions and rules as they proceed. The Germans, however, will want to study the instructions and rules thoroughly before beginning play. Play will begin "several days later." These differences in style can affect how negotiations are conducted.

French   Of all European cultures, the French are the least like the Americans. International competitiveness is not necessarily an important motivator to them if the sacrifice involve compromises to French culture or lifestyle. While the French are friendly and humorous, they show no real need to be "liked." In fact, they often find disagreements more interesting than common views, and they have gained a reputation by thinking and acting against others. They are aware that some positions are irreconcilable and that people must learn to deal with these differences.

The French do not respect the work ethic as much as Americans, and welcome long lunches and breaks. Furthermore, Americans should not plan on conducting negotiations during August, since most industry shuts downs for holiday (what we call vacations). However, the French take pride in work well done, take a direct stake in their work, and are concerned with quality as a matter of personal pride. Decisions may take longer than normal due to centralized decision making.

French negotiators may be very difficult to negotiate with—in many situations not accepting facts, no matter how convincing those facts may be. They are status conscious—the French negotiator should have the same status as his or her counterpart. Common negotiating tactics on their part include emotionalism and theatrics. They tend to be secretive in negotiations, and Americans will find it difficult to obtain data and information from them and about them. The French appreciate the "finer things in life," so perhaps the most effective way to conduct business is over a fine dinner and a vintage bottle of wine.

Japanese   The Japanese culture is vastly different from American culture. Despite such differences, the extra effort needed to develop mutually satisfying negotiations can result in an excellent relationship—Japanese firms are dependable and loyal suppliers. They will treat their customers like valuable family members. Entertainment is an important part of the process of developing personal relations and goodwill. Small gifts are ideal for showing good faith before conducting business. However, personal relations are conducted away from the negotiating room.

The negotiating process is unique with Japanese companies. For example, the Japanese are comfortable with extended silence, which is not true with Americans. Japanese are team players concerned with the well-being of their country and firm rather than themselves as individuals. Politeness is valued above all else. Instead of saying no, Japanese often say yes, which really means they hear rather than agree. The Japanese go to considerable lengths to conceal their emotions and are quite uncomfortable when others lose control or show anger.

When negotiating with the Japanese, a great deal of time is required to reach a decision. Decisions are reached by consensus with proposals circulated among all concerned members. When negotiating, keep in mind that it is necessary to convince the whole group rather than a single individual. Avoid placing the Japanese in a position in which they must admit failure or "lose face." Japanese do not like the appearance of having to make forced concessions. Splitting the difference is often a good way of reaching a compromise.

During complex negotiations, a crisis may develop when one member of a Japanese negotiating team voices disagreement over a proposal. When this happens, it is critical for Americans to keep communication channels open. One strategy is to keep in contact with those who favor a proposal and seek advice on how to get negotiations back on track.

GOOD PRACTICE EXAMPLE
The Railroads of Bethlehem Steel

■ ■ ■

Several years ago executive management at Bethlehem Steel directed its operating units to concentrate on return on net assets (RONA) as a key financial performance indicator. As a corporation, all operating units were to achieve at least a 16% return on net assets. The RONA formula applied across each profit center or subsidiary was:

Return on net assets =

$$\frac{\text{Earnings before interest and taxes}}{((\text{Inventory} + \text{Accounts receivable} + \text{Plant property equipment}) - \text{Accounts payable}) + \text{Other current liabilities}}$$

The subsidiary railroads of Bethlehem Steel include six railroads, a trucking company, and an intermodal carrier. Each operates as a separate business entity (by law), and the parent company measures the financial performance, including net return on assets, of each unit. This good practice case focuses on how Wayne Dilliplaine, a corporate procurement director, uses negotiation to represent the interests of six separate railroads while striving to achieve corporate return targets.

The corporate decree to improve RONA forced different functional groups at the railroads to search for ways to increase earnings while simultaneously reducing assets and other current liabilities. The centralized purchasing group, negotiating on behalf of the subsidiary railroads, decided to focus extensively on the denominator of the RONA equation. As such, this group knew it had to develop creative ways to *manage purchased inventory*, which is its primary area of responsibility. Locomotives, railroad cars, and the material to maintain railroad tracks comprise the main components of inventory.

The purchasing group's approach to increase RONA involves negotiated longer-term systems contracts that feature consignment inventory from suppliers. (Systems contracts include many different part numbers, such as a contract with a distributor.) Inventory consignment involves deferring payment for an item until a user physically takes an item from a railroad yard or warehouse and receives or "posts" the material into the railroad's inventory. Each year, purchasing works with field managers to identify potential items to add to existing systems contracts, identify items for new contracts, and develop estimates of annual demand requirements for systems contract items at each railroad. Suppliers deliver all items by truck during the first quarter of each year and are responsible for unloading and physically placing the inventory in a yard or warehouse. These services are part of the negotiated price.

The five railroads currently have 25 to 30 negotiated systems contracts in place with six suppliers. Each contract covers approximately 25 items, with renewal or renegotiation occurring every three years. The contracts are subject to review earlier than three years if suppliers fail to meet expectations. While early contracts involved higher-value items, purchasing is beginning to apply systems contracting to lower-unit-value items (less than $500) that have higher volume requirements.

Although the five railroads operate as separate entities, Dilliplaine is responsible for working directly with users at each railroad to develop and negotiate systems contracts. Specifically, purchasing identifies potential items for systems contracts, determines the requirements of each railroad for those items, identifies and analyzes potential systems contract suppliers, coordinates the calculation of annual demand estimates, and represents the interests of each railroad during negotiation with suppliers. This allows purchasing to coordinate and consolidate the combined purchase requirements of the railroads. This also simplifies the negotiation process, since suppliers can negotiate with a single representative.

Users at each railroad participate during the development of annual purchase requirements but not the negotiation itself. Local managers have the best idea concerning planned maintenance projects and expected usage, so they are responsible for developing local demand forecasts. Furthermore, all sites have an opportunity to present their comments before purchasing enters a new negotiation or renegotiation. Before each negotiation, internal purchasing customers receive an interoffice correspondence with a sample "boiler plate" systems contract attached. Each railroad has an opportunity to identify the contractual options they prefer, and users can expand the contract by listing any items they would like to see addressed in the final agreement.

Negotiated Systems Contracting Benefits   Negotiating systems contracts on behalf of the six independent railroads has resulted in direct benefits for the railroads. First, negotiating these longer-term agreements has helped purchasing achieve its primary goal of reducing inventory investment. Over a three-year period, average inventory has decreased over 50%. The railroads expect further reductions as they expand their use of systems contracts. Cash flow has increased more than $1 million annually due to reduced inventory investment. The railroads have also avoided or deferred price increases due to the fixed three-year negotiated agreements. Systems contracts have also allowed for some downsizing because suppliers assumed responsibilities such as delivering and placing physical inventory in storage. Finally, acquisition costs are lower because users submit only an annual order for items covered by systems contracts.

Critical Success Factors   Purchasing has identified certain factors that are critical to the successful planning and negotiation of systems contracts.

Accurate Demand Estimates   Accurate demand estimates are essential for planning, and then negotiating, systems contracts. Each railroad must accept any unused consigned material into its inventory in January. The railroads agreed to this condition as an incentive for suppliers to participate. Suppliers know that inventory cannot be on consignment for more than a year, and at the end of the calendar year the railroads pay for any excess consigned inventory. Because the items covered by these contracts are standard to the rail industry and are usually readily available, purchasing requires that suppliers agree to deliver any systems contract item for which the railroad has a shortage within 24 hours.

Because each railroad must assume ownership of unused consignment inventory, the temptation might exist to underestimate annual requirements, particularly with 24-hour guaranteed delivery for items with no on-hand inventory. This would reduce the inventory the railroads have to assume at the end of each year due to overestimating demand requirements. Purchasing has instructed each railroad to provide accurate and reasonable demand estimates for items. Using 24-hour deliveries to cover shortages applies to exceptions rather than normal operations. Purchasing reports that underestimating demand has not been an issue, and suppliers have not voiced any concerns about abusing the 24-hour delivery requirement. Railroads will shift inventory when one railroad has available material and another has a need.

Continuous Communication Purchasing engages in continuous communication with user groups at each railroad, particularly during the planning phase when the calculation of annual demand estimates for consigned items occurs. Purchasing managers argue that negotiating these agreements has also resulted in improved relationships with suppliers due to the face-to-face sharing of requirements and needs. Suppliers also receive performance feedback from user groups at least twice a year.

Willingness to Negotiate a Broad Range of Issues Because systems contracts are longer-term agreements, negotiations often involve many nonprice issues. Besides identifying which items to include and their prices, a systems contract may address how each railroad wants items delivered or unloaded, particularly for items that the supplier must deliver on a just-in-time basis. Purchasing's request to user groups is to "tell purchasing what you want in the contract." All negotiation with suppliers occurs at the headquarters of the corporate parent (Bethlehem Steel), where purchasing leases office space.

Various negotiated contractual options include the industry specification the item must meet, pricing requirements, delivery schedule time frames, invoice details and information, payment terms, and inventory management requirements. As Dilliplaine explains, "Anything in these contracts is open to negotiation." Negotiation has taken on increased importance as systems contracts cover most of the railroads' inventory investment.

Executive Commitment Purchasing conducts frequent meetings with the president of the subsidiary railroads to inform him of the progress of the negotiating process. This has proven valuable when some suppliers attempted to contact the president directly to challenge the validity of negotiating systems contracts with consignment inventory. The railroad president agreed fully with the systems-contracting goals and supported the negotiation efforts. Meeting with executive management also served to protect the president from being caught unaware or being influenced when contacted by suppliers.

Determine Preconsignment Prices Before Pursuing Systems Contracting Early in the planning process purchasing decreed that it would not accept higher unit charges due to inventory carrying costs assumed or calculated by the supplier. During negotiation planning, purchasing uses past costs as a basis for price negotiation, although some suppliers initially attempted to add consignment costs into purchase prices.

Why would suppliers agree to a systems contract that required them to assume additional inventory-carrying costs? The railroad has agreed to a three-year fixed systems contract, which typically resulted in greater purchase volumes for each systems contract supplier. Furthermore, agreeing to take ownership of unused consigned material at the end of the year reduced some risk exposure for the suppliers.

Systems contract suppliers receive a guaranteed three-year contract with fixed prices. The only prices that fluctuate are for items that have a high raw material content, such as wood products. The suppliers and the railroad have negotiated a pricing adjustment formula based on published commodity prices.

Planning and Analysis Purchasing relies on spreadsheets during the planning process to analyze purchase requirements in detail. Tying into the railroad's automated inventory databases, purchasing calculates actual usage and company-wide requirements, identifies potential systems contract candidates, and determines inventory investment data. Spreadsheets are also used to analyze supplier-provided data before formal negotiation. Procurement executives argue that computerized spreadsheets using the company's databases have been invaluable toward the development of systems contracts.

An example shows the importance of prenegotiation planning and analysis. Purchasing sent a request for quotation to several suppliers for items that were to be part of a negotiated systems contract. When the RFQs arrived, a detailed analysis showed that neither supplier was pricing competitively across all items. Purchasing decided to create two systems contracts covering only those items where each supplier was competitive. Extensive planning highlighted the need for a change during the execution phase of negotiation.

Future Enhancements While the current emphasis is on maintaining existing systems contracts, purchasing plans to negotiate additional contracts. Future contract areas include brake shoes, locomotive parts, and air brake hoses. Although these items are not as high dollar as those covered by earlier contracts, they can help further reduce the denominator of the RONA equation.

Purchasing is also beginning to renegotiate some three-year agreements. Because systems contracting is a continuing process, renegotiation is an opportunity to further strengthen these agreements. Purchasing is trying to convey to suppliers that only those who accept the basic objectives of a systems contract should continue to the renegotiation phase.

This good practice highlights how one firm uses negotiation to help achieve its corporate goals. The ability to improve return on net assets was possible only through extensive planning, negotiation, and the use of longer-term contracts that consolidated the purchase requirements of geographically diverse operating units. ■

SOURCING SNAPSHOT

Will E-Procurement Change Negotiation?

As the number of people buying online continues to grow exponentially, certain changes are in store for purchasing professionals who have traditionally prided themselves on their people skills. The ability to conduct negotiations may take a backseat, especially in repetitive, low-cost transactions dealing with high volumes that are obtained through e-procurement systems. Kevin Rohan, a purchasing specialist at JP Cannon Associates in New York, says that "Being a strong negotiator is not enough in today's market. Candidates need to continue to develop their skills and be familiar with the latest technology such as how to utilize the Internet, market changes, and strategic planning and client development."

Does this widespread acceptance of e-procurement and technology into the framework of the purchasing industry indicate an abandonment of the tried and true method of purchasing negotiation? The chances that e-procurement will completely replace one-on-one negotiation in the near future are slim. Emery J. Zobro, president of the John Michael Personnel Group in Chattanooga, Tennessee, is confident that while the characteristics of a successful purchasing professional might be changing, there are certain qualities that will survive e-procurement's infiltration of the industry. "In five years a person who hasn't established a track record with e-commerce and e-procurement will definitely be left behind." Nevertheless, he remains firm in the assessment that "buying things over the computer will never take the place of one-on-one negotiations."

Source: Adapted from Damon Francis, "The Decline of the Negotiator?" *Purchasing,* August 24, 2000: 160.

CONCLUSION

An organization's success is partly due to the skill of its negotiators. Regardless of the industry, successful purchasing negotiators share some common traits.

- They know they are not born with negotiating knowledge and skills. They practice and train to become effective negotiators.
- They have higher negotiating goals than do their counterparts, which they generally achieve; they have high expectations or aspirations.
- They are destined to be among an organization's most valued professionals.

Professional purchasers must become effective negotiators by participating in training, simulations, and workshops that develop negotiating skills. The difference between a good purchase agreement and an excellent one is often a function of the preparation and skill of the negotiator or negotiating team.

DISCUSSION QUESTIONS

1.   Why is negotiation such an important part of the purchasing process?
2.   Planning for and conducting a negotiation requires a commitment of resources. What resources are required to support negotiation planning and execution?
3.   This chapter identified various ways that purchasing becomes aware of purchase requirements. Which of these ways do you think are most likely to result in a need to negotiate with a supplier?
4.   The parties to a purchase negotiation can discuss many issues besides price. Select five nonprice issues over which a buyer and seller can reach agreement and explain why each issue might be important to the buyer or seller.
5.   Develop a profile of a skilled or effective negotiator.
6.   What are some of the important objectives that a purchaser tries to satisfy through negotiation?
7.   Discuss different strengths and weaknesses that a buyer and seller might bring to the negotiating table.
8.   What information should a purchaser gather about a supplier prior to a negotiation?
9.   Contrast a win-win with a win-lose negotiating approach.
10. Why is compromise during a purchase negotiation so important? How do the parties to a negotiation demonstrate their willingness to compromise?
11. What is the risk of relying on national negotiator profiles? Is there a benefit to using these profiles?
12. Discuss the various sources of power that parties can bring to a negotiation. Are there risks to using power?
13. Why does a negotiator that practices boulwarism risk sending a negotiation into deadlock (failure to reach agreement)?

ADDITIONAL READINGS

Bazerman, Max H., and Margaret A. Neale. *Negotiating Rationally*. New York: Free Press, 1992.

Fuller, George. *The Negotiator's Handbook*. Englewood Cliffs, NJ: Prentice Hall, 1991.

Ghauri, Pervez N., and Jean-Claude Usunier, eds. *International Business Negotiations*. Tarrytown, NY: Pergamon, 1996.

Jandt, Fred. *Win-Win Negotiating: Turning Conflict into Agreement*. New York: Wiley, 1985.

Kublin, Michael. *International Negotiation: A Primer for American Business Professionals*. New York: International Business Press, 1995.

Moran, Robert T. *Dynamics of Successful International Negotiations*. Houston, TX: Gulf Publishing, 1991.

Ramundo, Bernard A. *The Bargaining Manager: Enhancing Organizational Results Through Effective Negotiation*. Westport, CT: Quorom Books, 1994.

Thompson, Leigh. *The Mind and Heart of the Negotiator.* Saddle River, NJ: Prentice Hall, 1998.

Tirella, O. C., and Gary D. Bates. *Win-Win Negotiating: A Professional's Playbook.* New York: American Society of Civil Engineers, 1993.

Warne, Thomas R. *Partnering for Success.* New York: ASCE Press, 1994.

Zeckhauser, Richard J., Ralph L. Keeney, and James K. Sebenius. eds. *Wise Choices: Decisions, Games, and Negotiations.* Boston: Harvard Business School Press, 1996.

ENDNOTES

1. Roy J. Lewicki and Joseph A. Litterer, *Negotiation* (Homewood, IL: 1985), 45–47.
2. Lewicki and Litterer, *Negotiation*, 47–48.
3. Leigh Thompson, *The Mind and Heart of the Negotiator* (Upper Saddle River, NJ: Prentice Hall, 1998), 19-20.
4. Lewicki and Litterer, *Negotiation*, 241–57.
5. Thompson, *Mind and Heart*, 23–24, citing original work by French and Raven, *The Bases of Social Power*, in *Studies in Social Power*, 1959, University of Michigan Press.
6. Lewicki and Litterer, *Negotiation*, 251.
7. Lewicki and Litterer, *Negotiation*, 244.
8. Lewicki and Litterer, *Negotiation*, 13.
9. Thompson, *Mind and Heart*, 34–38; Robert Cialdini, *Influence: The New Psychology of Modern Persuasion* (New York: Quill, 1984).
10. Thompson, *Mind and Heart*, 35.
11. Thompson, *Mind and Heart*, 49.
12. Lewicki and Litterer, *Negotiation*, 109–114.
13. Lewicki and Litterer, *Negotiation*, 119–121.
14. Hokey Min and William Galle, "International Negotiation Strategies of U.S. Purchasing Professionals," *International Journal of Purchasing and Materials Management* (Summer 1993): 46.

MANAGING CONTRACTS 15

An Automotive Manufacturer Contracts a New Technology

Recently, a major U.S. automotive manufacturer was preparing to negotiate a long-term contract with a key electronics supplier. The supplier had developed a new technology that would enable customers to access the World Wide Web from their vehicle through voice activation capabilities. This technology was considered "cutting edge" and would result in a major competitive advantage for the automotive company. Talks between the two companies had been underway for several months, but had reached an impasse. For one thing, the electronics manufacturer held the only patent for the technology. This had made discussions difficult. The negotiations had reached a breaking point when the supplier sent a team of lawyers rather than sending in a team of sales personnel and engineers to discuss the contract.

The lawyers promptly began making specific demands regarding exclusivity clauses, nondisclosure agreements, and technology ownership in language that the automotive technology team did not fully understand. Rather than continue, the automotive team promptly stood up and left the room. Upon hearing this, the director of purchasing at the automotive company called up the vice president of technology at the electronics supplier and demanded that a team of engineers and sales people represent the company's interests during the negotiations. Sending lawyers in was not only adversarial but would likely end the deal altogether if it continued. The vice president apologized for this situation and claimed he was unaware that the lawyers had been sent in to represent the company.

At the next meeting a group of engineers arrived from the supplier to discuss implementing the technology in future new-model vehicle platforms. The negotiation was successful and resulted in a very interesting contract. The contract stipulated that the automotive producer would have sole use of the electronic technology through an exclusivity clause. Further, the contract contained wording describing the joint ownership of the intellectual property contained in the technology. The final point in the contract also stated that the electronics supplier was required to continue to update this technology into the future. If the supplier failed to do so and a competing electronics company developed a similar technology that had superior performance, it was required to license this technology from the competitor and sell it to the automotive company at the previously negotiated price. Upon looking at this situation, one wonders if perhaps the lawyers should have been present at the meeting after all.

Source: Interviews by Robert Handfield with anonymous executives.

Because purchasing professionals buy products and services as a career, it is not surprising that they deal regularly with contracts. It is therefore critical for purchasing managers to understand the underlying legal aspects of business transactions and develop the skills to manage those contracts and agreements on a day-to-day basis. Once a contract has been negotiated and signed, the real work begins. From the moment of signing, it is the purchasing manager's responsibility to ensure that all of the terms and conditions of the agreement are fulfilled. If the terms and conditions of a contract are breached, purchasing is also responsible for resolving the conflict. In a perfect world, there would be no need for a contract, and all deals would be sealed with a handshake. However, contracts are an important part of managing buyer-supplier relationships as they explicitly define the roles and responsibilities of both parties, as well as how conflicts will be resolved if they occur (which they almost always do!). The importance of understanding contracts is even more important in the Internet age. President Clinton signed a law in early 2000 that recognizes electronic signatures as equivalent to hard copies. This law facilitates the full integration of business transactions via the Internet and was a major stepping-stone to future developments in electronic commerce. However, the importance of understanding contracts and "reading the fine print" should not be overshadowed by this event. In fact, it makes the role of contracts even more important in e-commerce.

This chapter addresses contracting from several perspectives. The first section addresses the different types of contracts available to purchasing managers. The next section deals with an important type of contract being used more in purchasing scenarios: long-term contracts and alliance agreements. In the third section, we discuss a number of unique contracts, involving information systems deployment, construction, consulting, and minority supplier contracts. In the fourth section, we discuss some of the basic requirements for writing contracts, and conclude with an important element: how to settle contractual disputes in a buyer-supplier relationship when they arise.

Types of Contracts

Purchasing contracts can be classified into different categories based on their characteristics and purpose. Almost all purchasing contracts are based on some form of pricing mechanism and can be categorized as a variation on two basic types: fixed-price and cost-based contracts. The major types of contracts are shown in Exhibit 15.1.

Fixed-Price Contracts

Firm Fixed Price   The most basic contractual pricing mechanism is called a *firm fixed price*. In this type of purchase contract, the price stated in the agreement does not change, regardless of fluctuations in general overall economic conditions, industry competition, levels of supply, market prices, or other environmental changes. This

EXHIBIT 15.1   *Types of Contracts*

Type of Contract	Description	Buyer Risk	Supplier Risk
Firm fixed price	Price stated in the agreement does not change, regardless of any type of environmental change	Low	High
Fixed price with escalation/ deescalation	Base prices can increase or decrease based on specific identifiable changes in material prices		
Fixed price with redetermination	Initial target price based on best-guess estimates of labor and materials, then renegotiated once a specific level or volume of production is reached		
Fixed price with incentives	Initial target price based on best-guess estimates of labor and materials, then cost savings due to supplier initiatives are shared at a predetermined rate for a designated time period		
Cost plus incentive fee	Base price is based on allowable supplier costs, and any cost savings are shared between the buyer and supplier based on a predetermined rate for a designated time period		
Cost sharing	Actual allowable costs are shared between parties on a predetermined percentage basis and may include cost productivity improvement goals		
Time and materials contract	Supplier is paid for all labor and materials according to a specified labor, overhead, profit, and material rate		
Cost plus fixed fee	Supplier receives reimbursement for all allowable costs up to a predetermined amount, plus a fixed fee, which is the percentage of the targeted cost of the good or service	High	Low

contract price can be obtained through any number of pricing mechanisms—i.e., price quotations, supplier responses to the buying organization's requests for proposal (RFP), negotiations, or any other method. Fixed-price contracts are the simplest and easiest for purchasing to manage because there is no need for extensive auditing or additional input from the purchasing side.

If market prices for a purchased good or service rise above the stated contract price, the seller bears the brunt of the financial loss. However, if the market price falls below the stated contract price due to outside factors such as competition, changes in technology, or raw material prices, the purchaser assumes the risk or financial loss. If there is a high level of uncertainty from the supplying organization's point of view regarding its ability to make a reasonable profit under competitive fixed-price conditions, then the supplier may add to its price to cover potential increases in component, raw materials, or labor prices. If the supplier increases its contract price in anticipation of rising costs, and the anticipated conditions do not occur, then the purchaser has paid too high a price for the good or service. For this reason, it is very important for the purchasing organization to adequately understand existing market conditions prior to signing a fixed-price contract to prevent contingency pricing from adversely affecting the total cost of the purchase over the life of the contract.

Fixed-Price Contract with Escalation   A number of variations on the basic firm fixed-price contract exist. If the item being purchased is to be supplied over a longer time period and there is a high probability that costs will increase, then the parties may choose to negotiate an escalation clause into the basic contract, resulting in *a fixed-price contract with escalation*. Escalation clauses allow either increases or decreases in the base price depending on the circumstances. A greater degree of price protection is therefore provided for the supplier while the purchaser enjoys potential price reductions. All price changes should be keyed to a third-party price index, preferably to a well-established, widely published index (such as the Producer Price Index for a specific material).

Fixed-Price Contract with Redetermination   In cases where the parties cannot accurately predict labor and/or materials costs and quantities to be used prior to the execution of the purchase agreement (e.g., an unproven technology), *a fixed-price contract with redetermination* may be more appropriate. In this scenario, the buying and selling parties negotiate an initial target price based on best-guess estimates of the labor and materials to be used in manufacturing a new product. Once a contractually agreed-upon volume of production has been reached, the two parties review the production process and redetermine a revised firm price. Depending on the circumstances surrounding the contract, the redetermined price may be applied only to production following the redetermination, or it may be applied to all or part of the units previously produced.

Fixed-Price Contract with Incentives   A final type of fixed-price contract is the *fixed-price contract with incentives*. This contract is similar to the fixed-price contract with redetermination except that the terms and conditions of the contract allow cost-savings sharing (CSS) with the supplier. As in the redetermination contract, it is difficult for the buying and selling parties to arrive at a firm price prior to actual production. If the supplier can demonstrate actual cost savings through production efficiencies or substitution of materials, the resulting savings from the initial price targets are shared between the supplier and the purchaser at a predetermined rate. This type of purchase contract is typically utilized under conditions of high unit cost and relatively long lead times. The sharing of cost savings may be 50/50 (or some other split), and is typically a negotiated part of the contract.

Cost-Based Contracts

Cost-based contracts are appropriate for situations in which there is a risk that a large contingency fee might be included using a fixed-price contract. Cost-based contracts

SOURCING SNAPSHOT

Audit Blasts Oversights in Military Contracts

An internal audit of $6.7 billion in military contracts for professional, adminis-trative, and management services uncovered what it called inadequate govern-ment oversight in 105 contracts examined. The Pentagon spent $51.8 billion in 1999 on all kinds of services contracts—from trash collection to engineering studies—up from $39.9 billion in 1992. While spending is rising, the amount of oversight isn't, the Pentagon's inspector general said in a report. In 81 of the 105 contracts reviewed, "contracting officers either failed to prepare cost esti-mates or developed estimates that were inadequate or lacked detail," the re-port said. "Deficiencies in estimating clearly left the government vulnera-ble—and sometimes at the mercy of the contractor to define the cost." In addition, "Contract-ing officers essentially used contractor-prepared status re-ports as evidence of surveillance to determine how well the contractor was performing." A major problem, according to the audit, is the frequent use in services contracts of "cost-plus" deals, in which the government reimburses all the contractors' costs and then pays an award fee on top of that. Typically, cost-plus deals are used on technically challenging, new programs, where the government assumes most of the financial risk. In "fixed-price" contracts, which the government usually prefers, the contractor gets paid a set amount negotiated beforehand. These are generally used when a program's cost his-tory and technology are well known. The inspector general found that the armed forces frequently buy support services from the same company for years using cost-plus contracts. Instead of making the company stick to a fixed price, the military covers all the costs as if it were buying a cutting-edge fighter plane. In one instance, the Army in 1997 awarded Raytheon Corporation a $36.2 million contract for engineering services for the Hawk air-defense system without any competition. Though this system was first fielded in 1958, the Army still chose to cover the contractors' costs, even after 39 years of history with the same contractor.

Source: Adapted from Associated Press, March 14, 2000.

---

typically represent a lower risk level of economic loss for suppliers, but they can also result in lower overall costs to the purchaser through careful contract management. It is important for the purchaser to include contractual terms and conditions that require the supplier to carefully monitor and control costs. The two parties to the agreement must agree what costs are to be included in the calculation of the price of the goods or services procured.

Cost-based contracts are generally applicable when the goods or services procured are expensive, complex, and important to the purchasing party or when there is a high degree of uncertainty regarding labor and material costs. Cost-based contracts are generally less favorable to the purchasing party because the threat of financial risk is transferred from the seller to the buyer. There is also a low incentive for the supplier to strive to improve its operations and lower costs (and hence price) to the purchaser.

Cost Plus Incentive Fee   A third cost-based contract is the *cost plus incentive fee contract*. This contract is similar to the fixed-price plus incentive fee contract except that the base price depends on allowable supplier costs rather than on a fixed-price basis. As before, if the supplier is able to improve efficiency and/or material usage as compared with the initial target cost, then the buying and selling parties will share any cost savings at a predetermined rate. This type of contract is appropriate for cases where both parties are relatively certain about the accuracy of the initial target cost estimates.

Cost-Sharing Contract   With pure *cost-sharing contracts*, allowable costs are shared between the parties on a predetermined percentage basis. The key to successful negotiation is the identification of a firm set of operating guidelines, goals, and objectives for the contract. When in doubt, the two parties to a cost-sharing contract need to spell out their expectations in as much detail as possible to avoid confusion and misunderstanding regarding their respective roles and responsibilities.

Time and Materials Contract   Another cost-based contract is the *time and materials contract*. This type of contract is generally used in plant and equipment maintenance agreements where the supplier cannot determine accurate costs prior to the repair service. The contract should spell out the appropriate labor rate (generally computed on a per-hour basis), plus an overhead and profit percentage, resulting in a "not-to-exceed" total price. With these terms and conditions, the purchaser has little control over the estimated maximum price. Thus labor hours spent should be carefully audited over the life of the contract.

Cost Plus Fixed-Fee Contract   In a *cost plus fixed-fee contract*, the supplier receives reimbursement for all of its allowable costs up to a predetermined amount plus a fixed fee, which typically represents a percentage of the targeted cost of the good or service being procured. Although the supplier is guaranteed at least a minimal profit above its allowable costs, there is little motivation for the supplier to dramatically improve its costs over the life of the contract. The U.S. military has been highly criticized for using such contracts on a routine basis with suppliers who are making above-normal profits for commonly used goods and services at the expense of taxpayers.

To be most effective, cost-based contracts should include cost productivity improvements in order to drive continuous cost reduction over the life of the contract.

Considerations When Selecting Contract Types

Among the more important factors to consider when negotiating with a supplier over contract type are the following (see Exhibit 15.2):

1. Component market uncertainty
2. Long-term agreements

EXHIBIT 15.2   *Desirability of Using Contracts Under Different Conditions*

Environmental Condition	Fixed-Price Contract	Incentive Contract	Cost-Based Contract
		Desirability of Use	
High component market uncertainty	Low	←————————————————→	High
Long-term agreements	Low	←————————————————→	High
High degree of trust between buyer and seller	Low	←————————————————→	High
High process/technology uncertainty	Low	←————————————————→	High
Supplier's ability to affect costs	Low	←————————————————→	High
High dollar value purchase	Low	←————————————————→	High

3. Degree of trust between buyer and seller
4. Process or technology uncertainty
5. Supplier's ability to impact costs
6. Total dollar value of the purchase

The first of these factors, component market uncertainty, refers to the volatility of pricing conditions for major elements of the product, such as raw materials, purchased components, and labor. The more unstable the underlying factor market prices, either upward or downward, the less appropriate a fixed-price contract will be for the two parties. Increasing factor market prices will place more risk on the supplying organization, while decreasing such prices will shift the contract economic risk to the purchasing party. (This condition also applies in the case of unstable currency exchange rates in contracts with international suppliers.)

The length of the purchase agreement can also have a significant impact on the desirability of different contract types. The longer the term of the purchase agreement, the less likely firm fixed-price contracts will be acceptable to the supplier. For ongoing purchase arrangements, suppliers will generally prefer to employ fixed price with escalation or any of the cost-type contracts, since they incur less economic risk for the selling party. Purchasing managers must therefore evaluate the economic risk of the different contract types and make a decision as to the acceptability of each type for the entire length of the agreement. For most short-term contracts and in conditions of stable component factor markets, firm fixed and fixed-price with redetermination contracts can safely be applied.

The choice of contract type is also dependent on the nature of the buyer-seller relationship. If the relationship has been mutually beneficial in the past and has existed for a considerable period of time, a greater degree of trust may have developed between buying and selling parties.[1] In such cases, both buyer and supplier are more likely to cooperate in the determination of allowable costs, thereby preferring cost-type purchase agreements.

For products and services characterized by high process or technological uncertainty, fixed-price contracts are less desirable for the seller. However, if the purchaser has a reasonable estimate of the supplier's cost structure, then cost-type contracts may be preferable because they allow the price to be adjusted either upward or downward depending on the efforts of the supplier. If the supplier can potentially reduce costs through continuous improvement, then an incentive-type contract may prove beneficial to both contracting parties.

As the total dollar value/unit cost of the contract increases, purchasers must spend more effort creating effective pricing mechanisms. The contracting parties must consider each of the factors in Exhibit 15.2 in detail, as well as the total impact of the contract over the lifetime of the agreement. It is important to remember that both parties in a contract must benefit (although not necessarily in the same proportion).

LONG-TERM CONTRACTS IN ALLIANCES AND PARTNERSHIPS

The number of strategic alliances and partnerships between buyers and sellers has increased greatly in the last five years. The negotiation and execution of unique types of agreements that specify the requirements and responsibilities of the parties is more important than ever in these types of relationships. In the words of the vice president of purchasing at a Fortune 500 company, "Our two organizations prefer to think of our relationship being governed by a 'covenant' rather than a 'contract.' A covenant implies a greater commitment than a contract, and implies a promise that is enduring. It provides a means to manage expectations. The shared goal that is necessary to succeed in this type of relationship is to satisfy the end consumer more than any other competitor or alliance. The reason that this works is very simple: each party perceives that the benefit received outweighs the risks or problems incurred."[2]

A common method of classifying industrial buying contracts is based on the length of the contract term. *Spot contracts* are defined as those purchases that are made on a nonrecurring or limited basis with little or no intention of developing an ongoing relationship with the supplier. *Short-term contracts* are defined as contract purchases that are routinely made over a relatively limited time horizon, typically one year or less. *Long-term contracts* are contract purchases that are made on a continuing basis for a specified or indefinite period of time, typically exceeding one year. Because long-term contracts involve greater commitments into the future, the contractual terms and conditions must be carefully developed. In this section we focus primarily on long-term contracts, but a number of the considerations covered may apply to shorter-term agreements as well.

Benefits of Long-Term Contracts

As noted in earlier chapters, the terms "strategic alliances" and "partnerships" are often used in industry without truly understanding the implications of these agreements. Regardless of the terminology used, almost all buyer-seller relationships have

EXHIBIT 15.3   *Advantages and Disadvantages of Long-Term Contracts*

Potential Advantages

Assurance of supply
Access to supply technology
Volume leveraging
Supplier receives better information for planning

Potential Disadvantages

Supplier opportunism
Selecting the wrong supplier
Supplier volume uncertainty
Supplier foregoes other business
Buyer is unreasonable

a contract (even if it is implied) that governs them. The contract itself is a formal symbol that these joint responsibilities and expectations exist. What distinguishes supplier alliances and partnerships is that in most cases, the contracts are long term in nature (i.e., greater than one year). Effective long-term contracts generally have specific and measurable objectives clearly stated in them, including pricing mechanisms, delivery terms, quality standards and improvements, productivity improvements, cost-savings sharing, evergreen clauses, risk sharing, conflict and dispute resolution, and termination of the relationship. Because long-term contracts are increasingly being used in industry, it is worthwhile to discuss the attributes, advantages, and risks of this approach in detail.

Why would a buying organization consider a long-term contract with a supplier? In a general sense, the buyer usually expects a greater level of commitment from a supplier involved in a long-term contract. Long-term contracts can also result in the opportunity for creating joint value between the contracting parties. Joint value can be enhanced through the sharing of information, risk, schedules, costs, needs, and even resources. In addition, a long-term contract serves as a blueprint or guide for the relationship between the buyer and the supplier. It typically delineates initial price, mechanisms for price adjustments, cost-reduction expectations, intellectual properties such as patents and copyrights, currency adjustment procedures as well as any other responsibilities.

There are many reasons why both buyers and suppliers would want to consider a long-term contract (see Exhibit 15.3). These are discussed in more detail here.

Assurance of Supply   Perhaps the most compelling reason to consider a long-term contract, from the buyer's perspective, is that such contracts may reduce the level of risk incurred if shorter-term contracts are employed. By committing to a well-thought-out long-term agreement, buyers can reasonably assure themselves of a continued source of supply, particularly important if the material, product, part, or component being procured is subject to potentially severe supply disruptions or extreme variations in quality, price, availability, or delivery. For example, in the 1970s maintaining consistent supply was often more important than the actual price of the material purchased because many goods were subject to routine shortages. Examples of commodities that have experienced supply or price swings include steel (1950s and 1960s), petroleum (1970s), semiconductors (1980s), lumber (1990s), and catalytic converters (2000).

Access to Supplier Technology   Long-term contracts can help the buyer to gain exclusive access to proprietary supplier technology, as the opening vignette highlighted. Blocking competitor access to this supplier technology through a long-term exclusivity contract can result in at least a short-term competitive advantage for the buyer. Tying up a supplier in the initial introductory stage of a new or dramatically improved technology product life cycle forces competitors to spend valuable time and effort searching for a comparable technology elsewhere or developing it themselves. The buying firm therefore can reach the marketplace first and establish a "first-mover" advantage. The potential risk here is that the buyer must be forward-looking enough to choose suppliers with the most promising or most marketable technology, at the peril of locking themselves into the wrong technology and losing their expected competitive advantage.

Access to Cost/Price Information   Agreeing to a long-term contract frequently allows the buyer to have access to more detailed cost and price information from the supplier in exchange for the extended contract term. Longer-term contracts create greater incentives for suppliers to improve or expand their processes through capital improvements because they are able to spread their fixed costs over a larger volume. Long-term contracts should be written to include incentive or cost-sharing arrangements that reward the supplier for making improvements in their processes while passing some of the cost savings along to the buyer. This additional supplier investment can also result in higher product quality as well as lower costs. Joint buyer-seller teams may work together to improve the suppliers' process and divide the resulting savings. The cost-savings sharing terms should be explicitly negotiated and written into the contract (do not assume that the savings will automatically be divided 50/50).

Volume Leveraging   A final benefit of developing a long-term contract is that the buyer can leverage his or her enhanced position to drive the supplier toward a higher rate of performance improvement. Using the added leverage of a long-term, multi-year agreement with the supplier, the buyer can require the supplier to increase his or her rate of progress up the learning curve and pass along the savings to the buyer at an accelerated rate. This performance improvement can be driven by additional capital investment as described earlier, an accelerated learning curve effect, and a higher level of commitment on behalf of the supplier. Long-term contracts with incentives are based on the notion that as purchase volumes increase, cost structures change.

Long-term agreements in cases of increasing volumes should establish productivity improvement goals and cost-savings sharing, where both buyer and seller share in cost reductions achieved. If suppliers are not forthcoming with labor and material cost

SOURCING SNAPSHOT

General Dynamics, EDS, IBM, and CSC Bid on Navy Contracts

General Dynamics and software giants EDS, IBM, and CSC survived the first elimination round for a Navy information technology contract worth as much as $10 billion, the largest in Pentagon history. The Navy told General Dynamics and the three software companies that their initial bids and service proposals were acceptable. The firms will now compete to be top contractor for a Navy in-house communications system serving sailors and Marines in the United States, including Hawaii, and Alaska, Puerto Rico, and Guantanamo Bay, Cuba. "It's one of the biggest outsourcing contracts in the history of the industry," said Steve McClellan, an IT analyst for Merrill Lynch. The winner will sign a fixed-price contract through 2005 that requires the firm and its subcontractors to absorb any cost overruns. On the plus side, the team could earn up to $150 million in performance bonuses based on customer satisfaction from Navy and Marine users. The winning contractor will manage a system providing voice, e-mail, and video services to 360,000 users. This came about as a result of the 1991 Persian Gulf War, when the Pentagon recognized the need to link systems electronically for "network centric warfare" that transfers information such as target data and intelligence. The program still faces a major hurdle though. The Navy has yet to persuade Congress, or its auditing arm, the General Accounting Office, that it has a sound acquisition and oversight strategy or an adequate long-range budget for the project. Representative Jerry Lewis, a chairman of the House Defense Appropriations Subcommittee, wrote that the Navy's latest six-year budget "apparently does not accurately reflect the costs, appropriations or personnel impact of this acquisition strategy." The Navy is already spending millions of dollars on many separate information technology contracts supporting more than 100 different data and communications networks.

Source: Adapted from Bloomberg Business News, "Navy Holds Bid Elimination," April 2, 2000.

---

data, cost models can be developed to improve the buyer's negotiating position using material/labor ratios available from industry databases (see Chapter 13). For instance, Nortel Networks uses such models to estimate a variety of commodity cost structures, enabling reasonable component cost targets for new products. While such models are never 100% accurate, they provide a stronger buyer negotiating position and tend to lower supplier expectations. In cases when prices are increasing due to escalating raw material costs, the price should be linked to the cost of a raw material that constitutes the largest percentage of the total cost to the supplier.[3]

Supplier Receives Better Information for Planning A supplier may have several reasons for preferring a long-term contract. First, the supplier receives better scheduling information, which in turn helps the supplier's production area improve efficiency and materials planning. With less uncertainty in production schedules, the supplier's purchasing departments can buy material in larger quantities, thereby obtaining volume discounts. Second, detailed projections of volumes and delivery dates allow the supplier to better budget the flow of funds and investment stemming from the expectation of continued future volume. In turn, the supplier's organization lowers unit costs, since fixed costs are spread out over a larger number of units. Third, the supplier can realize lower administrative costs over the term of the contract. Less effort is required to seek out and develop replacement volume on an ongoing basis. In addition, a long-term contract may result in reduced customer turnover. The risk associated with this decision is that the supplier becomes increasingly dependent on a smaller number of customers. This risk must be weighed against the potential benefits (reduced production and administrative costs, and higher profitability).

Risks of Long-Term Contracts

A buyer or seller must consider a number of risks when evaluating whether a long-term contract is necessary or even desirable. Three primary questions must be asked when developing a long-term contract and considering the risks:

1. What is the potential for opportunism? In other words, how likely is the supplier to take advantage of the purchaser (or vice versa)?
2. Is this the right supplier to engage in a long-term contract?
3. Is there a fair distribution of risk and gains between the parties involved?

Supplier Opportunism From the buyer's perspective, there is a major risk that the supplier will become too complacent and lose motivation to maintain or improve performance as the contract progresses. Performance deterioration can be observed in a variety of ways; higher price, deteriorating quality and delivery, lagging technology, and increased cycle times. It is important for buyers to build appropriate incentive clauses into their long-term agreements that serve to motivate suppliers to adequately perform as expected over the term of the agreement. It requires a tremendous degree of insight on the part of a buyer to determine exactly what levels of supplier performance are necessary, how they will be measured, and the corrective actions that must be taken if the supplier fails to execute its responsibilities and expectation. Best-in-class benchmarking to ensure that suppliers are pursuing continuous improvement along all performance dimensions must augment supplier performance measurement.

Selecting the Wrong Supplier An additional risk associated with long-term contracts is the possibility that the best available supplier may not be recognized or chosen to participate in the long-term agreement. It is the buyer's responsibility to conduct adequate research that documents the supplier's past performance, capabilities, financial health and stability, technology roadmap, and commitment to the relationship. Once a long-term agreement with a given supplier has been executed, it is much more difficult (and expensive) to switch suppliers. In order to ensure a successful future relationship, sufficient time and effort must be invested prior to signing a long-term contract.

Supplier Volume Uncertainty   To be successful, a good long-term contract considers the needs of both parties. The buyer must consider a number of issues from the supplier's perspective. The first and foremost is volume uncertainty, particularly when dealing with a new product or a new customer. Although the prospective buyer may indicate to the supplier that a certain purchased volume level may be expected, there are many reasons why that volume might never be achieved. Possible reasons include overforecasting of requirements, lack of marketability of the end item, intense competition in the marketplace, and other environmental considerations such as government regulation. A related reason is that the item being supplied may be in the mature or decline phases of the product life cycle. A long-term contract that indicates volume growth under these circumstances is unlikely ever to be fully realized.

Supplier Foregoes Other Business   Agreeing to a long-term contract that limits the supplier's ability to service the buyer's competitors might lock the supplier out of several profitable business opportunities. Also, when companies agree to supply a particular customer's needs, this precludes them from taking on more profitable business with other customers later on due to a lack of available capacity. This is particularly true in industries that are approaching full capacity.

Buyer Is Unreasonable   Another risk that the supplier must consider is the likelihood of the buyer making extraordinary demands once the contract has been executed. Unforeseen customer demands typically result in higher costs that the supplier may or may not be able to recover under the terms of the agreement. An example of this situation occurred during the tenure of Jose Ignacio Lopez at General Motors in the 1990s; many long-term suppliers decided to give up their business with GM when demands for cost reductions exceeded their ability to make a profit.[4]

Contingency Elements of Long-Term Contracts

Effective long-term contracts contain a number of elements that allow for contingencies that may arise during the course of the contract.

Initial Price   A buyer must focus intently on determining an acceptable initial price because over the course of a long-term contract the price adjustment mechanism will use the initial price as the base for future adjustments. An initial price that is too high will cause all following prices to be too high. A buyer needs to be aware that some suppliers often front-load their initial price by including excess profits, which inflates all future prices. Likewise, if the initial price is too low, then the supplier may not be motivated to perform as expected because all future prices will be too low and unprofitable. In a long-term contract the relationship between the parties is immaterial unless both parties gain something during the course of the exchange. In a major long-term agreement, it is important that high-level managers from the buyer and the supplier recognize the mutual benefits and drive the development of the relationship.

Price-Adjustment Mechanisms   Selecting an appropriate price-adjustment mechanism is also a key consideration in a long-term contract. If future price adjustments are linked to an outside index or the price of a related product, then care should be exercised in selecting which index or related product is to be used. Choice of the wrong index or related product can also result in higher prices over the term of the agreement.

Supplier Performance Improvements   Buyers should use long-term agreements to obtain specific supplier performance improvements over time. Again, this compels the buyer to conduct extensive research regarding the supplier's capabilities and past performance, as well as determining the types and levels of risk that might be associated with a particular long-term supply contract. Managers must decide whether the contract should be written for a specific period such as three or five years, or whether the contract should be a series of rolling contracts with an evergreen clause, which renews the agreement at the end of every period.

Evergreen, Penalty, and Escape Clauses   An effective evergreen clause should be based on a periodic joint review period, typically one year or shorter, and should incorporate a point system that rewards the supplier for acceptable performance. In cases when expectations are not met, the purchasing manager may request specific corrective action and may even charge back lost time and expenses to the supplier. For instance, major automobile manufacturers such as Honda of America and Ford Motor Company charge the supplier a rate of $10,000 for every minute that the assembly line is held up due to a late just-in-time delivery.

Associated with the evergreen clause is an escape clause, which allows the buyer (and possibly the supplier) to terminate the contract if either side fails to live up to contractual requirements. However, a long-term contract will usually contain terms and conditions that call for a corrective action process when the supplier continually fails to meet its contractual performance requirements. In such a scenario, the buyer must first notify the supplier within a particular time period if the supplier's performance has not met expectations. The supplier will have a specific time to take corrective action to bring quality, delivery, and responsiveness to acceptable levels. If the supplier has not achieved contractually acceptable levels of performance within the specified time period, then the buyer can terminate the contract without recourse. Long-term contracts should thus contain appropriate clauses covering conflict resolution, termination of the agreement, and handling of unanticipated requirements. Such contingency planning may prolong the contract negotiation period up front but may prove to be invaluable later on down the line should problems occur.

$\mathcal{U}$NIQUE TYPES OF CONTRACTS

In addition to long-term contracts, companies must also create special types of contracts with information systems providers, consultants, minority business contracts, and services. All of these purchases require unique contractual approaches.

IT Systems Contracts

Systems contracts, also known as *systems outsourcing,* are designed to provide access to expensive computer networks and software that single companies are unable to afford on their own. Examples of systems contractors include SAP, Oracle, IBM, EDS, Hewlett-Packard, Nortel Networks, Lucent Technologies, and many others. Subcontracting information technology (IT) requirements to an outside service provider is a major contractual issue for companies. Both legal and purchasing executives from the company should bring their expertise to the table on such issues that represent a major cost and commitment for the enterprise. Unfortunately, IT departments often enter into such agreements on the basis of technical evaluation without the benefit of input from purchasing or legal, and later pay in the form of higher costs or poor service requirements contained in the "fine print." Prior to committing to an outsourcing contract with such a service provider, a systems outsourcing team should consider the length of the proposed agreement, the role of company growth or downsizing, service provider defaults or contract amendments, data security, control of outsourcing costs, and control of information systems operations. A number of other issues pertain to IT systems contracting.

Systems Contracting Risks   One of the leading causes for failure of systems contracts is that purchasers become locked into price structures that do not adequately reflect changes occurring since the agreement was originally signed. Examples of such changes include dramatic shifts in user demand patterns, dramatically reduced costs for services provided, and quantum leaps in software and hardware technology.

Level of Service   The extent that an IT supplier becomes involved in the buying firm's operation is determined by three basic levels of service: (1) turnkey, (2) modular, and (3) shared. In the *turnkey approach,* the client company essentially turns over the entire outsourced service at a given point in time. The outsource service provider performs 100% of that function for the buying organization. In the *modular approach,* the outsource service provider takes on only two or three small functions from the client using a stepping-stone approach. As the service provider and the client company become more at ease with each other and a higher level of trust develops, additional services are shifted from the client to the service provider. In the *shared approach,* the service provider and the client company share resources and operational control over the outsourced service. Under the best of conditions, outsourcing systems contracts remains a risky proposition due to the nature of uncertainty associated with the transaction. Purchaser negotiations should focus on price, performance, and procedures.

Price   Purchasers should consider negotiating a fixed, all-inclusive fee instead of relying on a flexible pricing system that may or may not accurately reflect changing business conditions. If future changes are anticipated, then the purchaser should carefully think how contract prices should be set to reflect those changes. Critical pricing issues include the payment method and timing, scheduling of workloads, and reporting.

Performance Criteria   Performance considerations for a systems contract should, at a minimum, include specification of the overall business requirements required by the service provider. The acceptance test criteria should be specified before issuing the contract so that both parties completely understand how the outsourcing system is expected to perform. A primary concern for the purchaser is the development of a measurement system for evaluating the service provider over the course of system development. The more specific the purchaser can be in providing clear goals and objectives for the service provider to meet, the less likely it is that misunderstandings and conflicts will result.

Procedures   In addition to acceptance criteria, systems contracts should also provide a complete conversion plan that details the steps to be taken in converting from in-house data processing to the outsource system. Again, the more specific the purchaser can be in providing this information, the less likely it is that serious problems will occur later. Also, the purchaser should be careful in detailing how to handle technological changes. A service provider that fails to keep up with recent technological advances is actually providing a disservice to its clients. It is the joint responsibility of the purchasing manager and the supplier to ensure that the technology provided remains current with future needs. Various types of information requirements planning techniques can be beneficial in the earliest systems-planning stages to determine that the system will actually meet user needs.[5]

Other Service Outsourcing Contracts   The use of outsourcing contracts is not always limited strictly to information processing. Other potential applications include:

- Facility management services
- Research and development
- Logistics and distribution
- Order entry and customer service operations
- Accounting and audit services

For example, a third-party logistics provider can support a centralized point of contact for the client's customers to provide traffic management, customer service, and order entry services. Such providers can also offer a simpler, more responsive and reliable supply chain system, thereby lowering a client's final customer costs as well as their own.

Minority-Owned Supplier Contracts

Programs to stimulate growth of minority-owned businesses have existed in the United States since the late 1960s. The term *minority-owned suppliers* is used by the U.S. federal government to describe a company that is at least 51% owned by minorities such as a African Americans, Hispanic Americans, Native Americans, or Asian-Pacific Americans.

Women-owned businesses and firms that are owned by physically disabled people are separate classes of firms with unique designations.[6] The following federal actions were carried out to promote minority-owned businesses:

- *Executive Order 11485 (1969):* Established by the U.S. Office of Minority Business Enterprise within the Department of Commerce, for the purpose of mobilizing federal resources to aid minorities in business.
- *Executive Order 11625 (1971):* Gives the secretary of commerce the authority to implement federal policy in support of minority business enterprise programs, to provide technical and management assistance to disadvantaged businesses, and coordinate activities between all federal departments to aid in increasing minority business development.
- *Public Works Employment Act (1977):* Requires that at least 10% of federal construction contracts be awarded to businesses owned by minorities.
- *Public Law 95–507 (1978):* Mandates that if a buyer's firm is awarded a federal contract that exceeds $10,000, the buyer is required to make "maximum efforts" in awarding subcontracts to small minority businesses. If the federal contract exceeds $500,000 ($1,000,000 for construction projects), prior to contract award the buyer's firm must submit an acceptable buying plan that includes percentage goals for the utilization of minority businesses. The plan must also detail procedures for identifying and dealing with minority businesses.

Minority suppliers are a special class of supplier. As such, they face many problems that are unique to their special status, while also facing many of the same problems that confront nonminority suppliers. Several factors lie at the core of these problems: lack of access to capital; large firms' efforts to optimize their supply bases; inability to attract qualified managers and other professionals; and minority suppliers' relatively small size, which may lead to overreliance on large customer firms.[7] Many companies often deploy supplier diversity programs that are aimed at increasing the representation of minority-owned suppliers in their supply base. For some companies, supplier diversity programs are based on social considerations. However, an increasing number of companies have focused on supplier diversity simply because it is good business. Minorities now represent the largest sales growth markets, especially in consumer goods, and companies realize that increasing the amount of business with minority businesses may mean increased sales for their own firm over the long term.[8]

Consultant Contracts

A knowledgeable consultant can often provide an objective point of view and contribute to an analysis of a situation that is not biased in favor of a predetermined solution. An important factor to consider when hiring an outside consultant to perform contract services for a company is that such a person is the purchasing company's agent, not its employee. The distinction is critical because as an agent, the consultant will maintain ownership of any intellectual properties developed during the consultation. There is an automatic determination of copyright ownership unless the consultant and the client company execute an agreement specifically assigning the copyright to the client company. If the consultant were considered an employee, then the firm—not the individual because of the "works made for hire" concept under U.S. copyright law—would own the copyright. One of the legal means to distinguish an independent contractor consultant from an employee is the presence of a written contract that describes the consultant's expected services and the ability to produce the results of the consultation.

Consultants will typically consider the following six goals when negotiating a consulting contract for their services:[9]

- Avoidance of misunderstanding
- Maintenance of working independence and freedom
- Assurance of work
- Assurance of payment
- Avoidance of liability
- Prevention of litigation

Perhaps the most important clause of a consulting contract is the assurance of payment. Typical consulting contracts will demand a large down payment, perhaps as much as one-third of the total amount. Payment of the balance due can exist in a range of options including percentage of work accomplished or time elapsed. Due to the extensive litigative climate in the business world, contracts written by the consultant will seek to minimize the consultant's exposure to liability and subsequent potential litigation. Language in this section of the contract should spell out exactly what the consultant is and is not liable for. Consultants will try to identify those circumstances that may cause the project to fail and for which they will disavow any responsibility.

There are two general causes for litigation arising from a principal-client relationship. The first concerns belief on the purchaser's part that the consulting work was not completed in full, within a reasonable time, or properly. The second concern is when the consultant fails to receive the entire fee that he or she believes was due and proper. Consultants will typically avoid litigation whenever possible to avoid negative public relations. Payment clauses, down payments, and installment payments usually include the following terms and conditions:

- Payment on delivery of the final report
- Late-payment penalties
- A negotiable promissory note or a collateralized promissory note

Construction Contracts

Many construction contracts involve the owner/purchaser seeking bids from approximately four or five contractors. A typical sequence of events starts with the owner/purchaser determining a base of preferred contractor bidders. The bidders are then contacted prior to distribution of the bid package to ascertain if they are interested in preparing a competitive bid for the proposed construction project. Following the distribution of the bid requests, the purchaser usually holds a pre-bid meeting with interested bidders to answer any questions that they may have regarding the initial bid documents. All future questions are then submitted to the purchaser in writing to prevent any misunderstanding.

All final bid submissions should consider the stated completion period. The purchaser should require that all bid submissions break the total price into different costs by type, phase, or area. The purchaser should also provide guidance to the bidders regarding how the bidders' indirect costs are to be applied. Contractor overhead costs can be segregated into several categories based on the chosen method of cost allocation or recovery. The most common categories are

- Payroll taxes and insurance premiums
- Field project overhead
- Home office overhead

Construction safety requirements are an important aspect of any construction contract. In selecting from a group of bidders who have already qualified because of past safety performance for the project, the following guidelines should be followed:[10]

1. Make a thorough review of each bidder's written construction safety plan.
2. Before the final selection is made, refer to each bidder's previous injury experience to determine if it is current and if any areas need improvement because of an excessive number of one type of injury from the same hazard. Check with OSHA to see if there have been any recent citations of the bidder and what corrective measures are required.
3. Make a site visit to current projects on which bidders are working to see firsthand the day-to-day quality and functioning of each bidder's construction safety program. References from past clients should also be researched in detail.

In all of these cases, the purchaser is seeking to determine whether senior managers in the firm have established an accountability system under which supervisors at all levels are held accountable for their subordinates' accidents. Previous research about the effect of top management on safety in construction has found that safety had to be a goal of top management in order for others in the firm to take it seriously. A buyer of construction services who maintains a "hands-off" policy through the use of "hold-harmless" clauses is in for a surprise if an accident occurs; the only way to guarantee reduced liability for accidents is to ensure that fewer accidents occur.[11]

Once a construction contract has been completed, a monthly job cost summary can be used to identify the contractor's total costs. An actual cost system records the amounts actually expended, while a standard cost system estimates what the cost should be based on known parameters. Any claims presented by the contractor must be carefully scrutinized, as the claimed costs may not actually be incurred costs. Contractors must be able to substantiate their costs by producing records consistently maintained in the normal course of business.

Purchasers can minimize the likelihood of contractor claims through a number of actions. The first is the presence of a realistic timetable that takes into account foreseeable delays due to factors beyond the control of either the contractor or the purchaser. A second action involves setting clear specifications that define exactly what is to be constructed. Last, the design documents created by the architect should be complete and up-to-date reflecting any and all changes as they occur. If the contractor presents a claim against the purchaser, the purchaser should insist on the following information, at a minimum, to help determine the accuracy and appropriateness of the contractor's actual costs in the claim:

- A breakdown of the claim by dollar amounts into the greatest possible number of components
- A detailed outline of the derivation of all hourly rates, equipment costs, overhead, and profit
- The underlying assumptions on which the claim is based to help ensure that the claim is not inflated

Contract administrators for construction projects may also wish to employ penalty clauses to avoid prolonged delays in the construction schedule. For instance, a penalty fee of $100 to $1,000 per day for every day late can provide strong incentives to the construction firm to meet schedules. For example, the construction company building a new parking ramp for the Raleigh-Durham airport in North Carolina was assessed a late fee of $6.00 per day per parking space. With 1,000 parking spaces, and a project that ran six months past the scheduled completion date, the contractor paid $1 million to the airport authority according to the contract penalty guidelines. Needless to say, the company did not express an interest in bidding on the second phase of parking ramp construction.

Other Types of Contracts

Some of the other types of contracts that may be encountered by purchasers include the following:

Purchasing Agreements   Agreements that group similar items together for procurement help to reduce the amount of paperwork for numerous and repetitive small orders. Purchasing agreements also increase the buyer's negotiating clout with the supplier by leveraging their volume of business. A number of variations of purchasing agreements exist:

- *Annual contracts:* Generally run for a 12-month period and may or may not come up for renewal at the end of the year.
- *National contracts:* Specify that the purchaser will buy a certain amount of goods and services for the duration of the agreement.
- *Corporate agreements:* Specify that business units within a corporate organization must buy from specific suppliers during the term of the agreement.
- *National buying agreements:* Nonbinding on either the purchaser or the supplier; typically provide discounts to corporate buyers based on total volume for the corporation as a whole, not for any subunits individually.
- *Blanket orders:* Typically cover many different items that can be purchased under the same purchase order number, thereby minimizing repetitive paperwork in the purchasing department for relatively low-cost items (e.g., office supplies).

- *Pricing agreements:* Occur in situations in which a buyer is allowed to automatically discount the published purchase price by a negotiated percentage for all purchases from a given price list or catalog during the contract period.
- *Open-ended orders:* Similar to blanket orders but allow the addition of items not originally included in the blanket order; may also allow the original purchase order to be extended for a longer term.

National Account Marketing Suppliers with strong marketing efforts have developed a new concept called *national account marketing,* which focuses on providing special attention to their most important customers.[12] Benefits of national account marketing include improved relationships and communications between buyers and sellers, increased sales for the supplier, improved problem solving for the purchaser, and reduced administrative efforts for both parties.

Online Catalogs and E-Commerce Contracts Coupled with the growing trend toward longer-term agreements and consolidated purchasing agreements, many firms have turned to electronic commerce in order to further reduce their administrative overhead. The use of automated online catalogs by major suppliers of MRO items such as Staples, Grainger, OfficeMax, and others allows users to buy directly from blanket orders and national contracts from their desktop. Such transactions are facilitated by operating resource management systems (ORMS) such as Ariba and Commerce One.

Despite the recent laws validating electronic signatures on contracts, many firms are wary of using electronic contracts and related documents because of a perceived lack of control regarding who is authorized to represent the firm. A major legal issue that arises in electronic contracts is how to record sufficient evidence of an electronic message, to permit later proof of its existence, origin, and content in a court of law or with an arbitrator. Purchases of small quantities of items can often be made through purchasing credit cards. For detailed information on technology, cyberlaw, and the Internet, visit the course Website of cyberlaw expert Dr. David Baumer from North Carolina State University at http://www4.ncsu.edu/~baumerdl/bus504.htm.

How to Write a Contract

Most commonly used contracts are developed from earlier contracts that are subsequently modified to fit the situation at hand. Although this procedure minimizes the amount of administrative effort required each time a purchase contract is written, there is a danger in blindly assuming that all past contracts will be appropriate, particularly in dynamic environments where technology changes occur rapidly or where there are few legal precedents. Purchasing managers should keep a contract file and refer to portions of previous contracts to create a contract that uniquely fits the situation at hand.

The most appropriate method of drafting a new contract is to start with a general form (or forms) and samples of past contracts for similar situations. Some of the specific types of legal language and organization of the different sections of the contract are discussed in greater detail in the Appendix C at the end of this book. Purchasing managers will often get advice from the legal department or appropriate counsel and create several different general forms for the various types of purchase situations that may be routinely encountered. Verifying the following information will help ensure that the contract is appropriate:[13]

- The contract identifies clearly what is being bought and the cost.
- The contract specifies how the purchased item is going to be shipped and delivered.
- The contract covers the question of how the items are to be installed (if installation is to be a part of the contract).
- The contract includes an acceptance provision detailing exactly how and when the purchaser will accept the products.
- The contract addresses the appropriate warranties.
- The contract spells out remedies.
- The contract does a good job on the "boilerplate," which includes the standard terms and conditions common to all contracts and purchase agreements.

The purchasing manager should consider arbitration or other dispute resolution mechanisms for inclusion in the contract. It is always a good idea to double-check all attachments to the contract, since many of the technical details are included here. Technical sections of the contract are typically the greatest source of misinterpretation of terms and conditions. For instance, if the contract contains a clause that says, "this is the entire agreement," remember that this means exactly what it says; there are no other additions or modifications to the agreement that are enforceable.

SETTLING CONTRACTUAL DISPUTES

All contracts, no matter how carefully worded and prepared, can be subject to some form of dispute or disagreement. It is virtually impossible to negotiate a contract that anticipates every potential source of disagreement between buyer and seller. Generally speaking, the more complex the nature of the contract and the greater the dollar amounts involved, the more likely it is that a future dispute over interpretation of the terms and conditions will occur. Purchasing managers must therefore attempt to envision the potential for such conflicts and prepare appropriate conflict resolution mechanisms to deal with such problems should they arise (see Exhibit 15.4).

The traditional mechanism for resolving contract disputes is grounded in commercial law, which provides a legal jurisdiction in which an impartial judge can hear the facts of the case at hand and render a decision in favor of one party or the other. Due to the uncertainty, cost, and length of time required to settle a dispute in the U.S. legal system, most buyers and sellers prefer to avoid the problems associated with litigation and deal with the situation in other ways. Taking a dispute into the jurisprudence system should be viewed as a last resort, not an automatic step in resolving contractual disputes.

EXHIBIT 15.4   *Means of Settling Contractual Disputes*

Action	Description
Legal action	File a lawsuit in a federal/state/local court
Nonlegal actions	
Arbitration	Use of an impartial third party to settle a contractual dispute
Mediation	Intervention by a third party to promote settlement, reconciliation, or compromise between parties involved in a contractual dispute
Minitrial	An exchange of information between managers in each organization, followed by negotiation between executives from each organization
Rent-a-judge	A neutral party conducts a "trial" between the parties and is responsible for the final judgment
Dispute prevention	A progressive schedule of negotiation, mediation, arbitration, and legal proceedings agreed to in the contract

Legal Alternatives

New methods of settling buyer-seller disputes have evolved in the last several years. These techniques, although diverse in form and nature, have a number of similar characteristics.[14]

- They exist somewhere between the polar alternatives of doing nothing or of escalating conflict.
- They are less formal and generally more private than ritualized court battles.
- They permit people with disputes to have more active participation and more control over the processes for solving their own problems than traditional methods of dealing with conflict.
- Almost all of the new methods have been developed in the private sector, although courts and administrative agencies have begun to borrow and adapt some of the more successful techniques.

Perhaps the simplest method of resolving a contractual disagreement involves straightforward, face-to-face negotiation between the two parties involved. Frequently, there are other factors surrounding the dispute that can be brought into consideration by the parties, even though these factors are not directly involved in the dispute at hand. For example, if the buying and selling parties to a contract disagree on the interpretation of the contract's terms and conditions regarding delivery, then perhaps they might be able to collaborate on other terms and conditions such as price or scheduling.

When this alternative is exhausted, both parties may become aware of the fact that it is infeasible to agree on suitable alternatives. In such cases, it may be virtually impossible for the parties to negotiate an acceptable resolution of the dispute on a good faith basis without additional assistance from outside parties.

Arbitration

The use of an outside arbitrator, or third party, to help settle contractual disputes is the fastest growing method of conflict resolution among contracting parties, both in the United States and overseas. Because of the parties' inability to reach a negotiated settlement, emotional reactions to the problem (frustration, disappointment, and anger) may prevent rational examination of the true underlying causes of the source of disagreement. The only solution in such cases may be *arbitration*, which is defined as "the submission of a disagreement to one or more impartial persons with the understanding that the parties will abide by the arbitrator's decision."[15] If set up and handled properly, arbitration can serve to protect the interests of both parties to the dispute because it is relatively inexpensive, less time consuming, private, and typically a reasonable solution for all involved.

When writing and negotiating purchase contracts, many purchasing managers include an arbitration clause in the boilerplate terms and conditions contained on their purchase orders and other contract documents. Such a clause typically spells out how the disputing parties will choose an appropriate arbitrator and the types of disputes for which arbitration will be considered. A good source for commercial arbitrators is the American Arbitration Association, which can also handle the administrative burden of the entire process from an impartial point of view. It is important to ensure that the arbitrator's opinion will be binding on both parties to the dispute. A key point to remember here is that adequate advance planning for potential disputes can prevent significant problems later should an unforeseen conflict arise. Also, it is a good idea to spell out the location and method of conducting the arbitration hearings, particularly if the dispute involves companies or individuals from different states or countries.

When preparing the purchase contract or purchase order, contract managers should consider two factors (in conjunction with the organization's legal counsel), to ensure that the ruling of an arbitrator will be legally binding:[16]

- State statutes must be reviewed to determine whether the state or states in question do in fact have such legal provisions allowing arbitration.
- Wording of the arbitration clause should be developed carefully in accordance with state law and the guidelines published by the American Arbitration Association.

Purchasing managers wishing to take advantage of the process in their dealings with suppliers should understand several caveats regarding binding arbitration. Purchasers cannot rely on an arbitration clause contained in their forms, particularly if the supplier's forms do not contain such a clause. If the supplier's forms contain an arbitration clause that is not in the buyer's forms, and the buyer does not want to follow it, the supplier cannot rely on the presence of such a clause. Finally, if both the buying and selling organizations' forms contain arbitration clauses, arbitration will become an enforceable part of the overall agreement.

Other Forms of Conflict Resolution

Along with the rising popularity of arbitration between buyers and sellers, a number of different forms of conflict resolution have been introduced. When people think of the arbitration process, the process that generally comes to mind is *mediation*—an intervention between conflicting parties to promote reconciliation, settlement, or compromise. The mediator's responsibilities include listening to the facts presented by both parties, ruling on the appropriateness of documents and other evidence, and rendering judgment on a solution that reconciles the legitimate interests of both disputing parties. Mediation varies from arbitration in that the arbitration is binding on the parties. In the mediation process, however, the disputing parties preserve their right of final decision on the solution proffered by the mediator.

A second type of dispute resolution mechanism is called a *minitrial*, which is not actually a trial at all.[17] The minitrial is a form of presentation, involving an exchange of information between managers from each organization involved in the dispute. Once the executives hear both sides of the presentation, they then attempt to resolve the dispute through negotiation with their executive counterparts. Because minitrials are generally more complicated than other forms of negotiation, they are typically used when the dispute between the parties is significant and highly complex. One of the benefits of such a process is that it turns a potential legal conflict into a business decision and promotes a continuing relationship between the parties.

Another related conflict-resolution mechanism is the *rent-a-judge*, which is a popular name given to the process by which a court refers a lawsuit pending between the parties to a private, neutral party. The neutral party (often a retired judge) conducts a "trial" as though it were conducted in a real court. If one or both of the parties is dissatisfied with the outcome of the rent-a-judge decision, then the verdict can be appealed through normal appellate channels. In this process, the parties agree to hire a private referee to hear the dispute. Unlike the binding arbitration process, rent-a-judge hearings are subject to legal precedents and rules of evidence.

A final alternative to dispute litigation and dispute resolution that is gaining popularity is *dispute prevention*, a key factor in the concept of collaborative business relationships such as long-term contracting, partnering, and strategic alliances. When contracting parties initially agree to dispute-prevention processes, a progressive schedule of negotiation, mediation, and arbitration followed by litigation as a last resort can be defined and delineated in the agreement. The "baring of souls" involved in this type of close, collaborative relationship dictates that the two parties fully recognize and agree upon the mechanisms for dispute resolution that are to be utilized under certain conditions.

There are a number of factors to consider when deciding which dispute-resolution mechanism to use. The first and, perhaps, foremost consideration is the *status of the relationship between the parties* in the dispute. In cases where the relationship between the parties is ongoing and expected to continue for the foreseeable future, the disagreeing parties will prefer to resolve the contract dispute through means that will hopefully preserve the relationship.

The choice of mechanism should also be based on the *type of outcome desired* by the purchaser. There may be a need to establish an appropriate precedent to govern the purchaser's actions in future disputes as well as the one at hand. Another consideration is whether the disputing parties *need to be directly involved in generating the outcome or resolution*. The presence of the disputing parties is important to successfully resolving disputes using techniques such as negotiation, arbitration, mediation, minitrials, and rent-a-judge proceedings. Active participation by all parties involved in a dispute generally results in a more equitable and harmonious resolution (as opposed to having third parties such as attorneys involved).

The *level of emotion* displayed by the principals is another important consideration. If emotions such as anger and frustration are high, the total cost of litigation, in terms of time, money, and management effort may be more significant than originally anticipated. The harsh experience of a prolonged court battle has convinced more than one set of potential litigants to consider less costly and more timely dispute-resolution alternatives.

The *importance of speed in obtaining resolution* can be a factor determining whether to litigate, mediate, or arbitrate. In many instances the alternatives to court adjudication are quicker than litigation. Time pressures may force the disputing parties to be more creative and understanding in reaching an appropriate resolution short of meeting in court. There is a direct relationship between the time involved in settling a dispute and the cost involved. Quicker resolution is generally cheaper.

The *information required to reach a settlement* may dictate the mechanism preferred. The closer the parties come to having the courts settle their dispute, the more formal the information requirements. Strict rules of evidence in the courtroom may not be desirable to parties because of publicity. Companies involved in the dispute may not be willing to spread out their dirty linen or trade secrets in public. In addition, the credibility of experts and other witnesses may be more difficult to achieve or maintain in a trial. All of the conflict-resolution mechanisms or settlement options presented here allow a greater degree of privacy to the parties involved than that which can be attained in a court.

GOOD PRACTICE EXAMPLE
Intel's "Copy Exactly" Facility Maintenance Contracts

■   ■   ■

Intel is a global manufacturer of high-tech semiconductor products (computer chips). Because of the short duration of product life cycles and increasing cost pressures experienced in this industry, all production downtime is immediately reflected in lost revenue. The company has a number of facilities located in the major high-tech centers of the world. A physical building has an average life of 20 years, while process equipment has a life of five to seven years before it becomes obsolete. This results in a turnover of process equipment three times over each 20-year plant cycle. Every new facility costs over $1 billion to construct. However, a new product generation is introduced every month, resulting in hundreds of product life cycles over the life of a plant.

A key organizational objective at Intel is to get factories from "dirt to finished product" in less than two years. There are literally hundreds of machine tools in a given facility. These are generally considered to be "islands of automation," as wafer fabrication is a continuous batch process. The company also does some assembly and test operations. Machine setups are highly sophisticated and expensive, much like an oil/process industry.

Both product and process design are considered proprietary. Therefore, suppliers are involved only in a single unique stage of the process, *not* in the total process. The entire process involves approximately 800 steps. A supplier is capable of developing a single process, but it is the integration of all the 800 steps in design that is Intel's core competency. The supplier has expertise in only a single area and is required to meet a target specification for a baseline process.

A key strategy within Intel involves developing detailed contracts holding suppliers responsible for delivering, installing, servicing, and maintaining machine tools that each cost well over $1 million. This involves supplier involvement in process ramp-up and maintenance of equipment in wafer fabrication facilities. Suppliers are fully responsible for the maintenance of these machine tools. Maintenance tasks are gradually turned over to internal employees as Intel becomes increasingly familiar with a specific piece of equipment and machine tool. Each supplier is responsible for a single process, which is identically carried out at its facilities around the world. Intel emphasizes the exact replication of processes across all facilities, which is emphasized throughout its business strategies (often referred to as the "Copy Exactly" principle). Copy Exactly means that any time a specification or task is transferred between functions or suppliers, the other party is responsible for exactly reproducing the requirements. This requirement is spelled out in detail in the contract.

The process used by Intel to create and manage Copy Exactly facility maintenance contracts is as follows:

1. *Quantify shortfall in internal support capability.* Purchasing calculates total support requirements using Mean Time Between Failure date and preventive maintenance schedules, and compares these figures to their own internal resources (both existing and planned). The result is a gap analysis that assesses the gross requirements to be supplied externally in terms of technicians' experience with the tool set, training capability, and local labor market.

2. *Forecast requirements to suppliers.* Based on this gap analysis, the external capability requirements are filled using supplier service contracts. This is often a function of constrained labor markets and long training lead times, such that internal capabilities are unavailable. Some of the key metrics used to quantify this shortfall include future headcount by quarter across different factories for service coordinators.

3. *Supplier-specific scope of work (SOW) requirements are negotiated.* Using the basic "boilerplate" agreement, supplier-specific SOWs are negotiated and inserted in the contract. Some of the details include

- Headcount and timing
- Job descriptions
- Expertise requirements
- Maintenance and repair responsibilities
- Continuous improvement process involvement
- General requirements

4. *Service pricing and terms and conditions are negotiated, and purchase order issued.* Using a "should-cost" model, purchasing calculates fair supplier pricing based on skills, training, relocation, etc. A detailed total cost of ownership model is applied to estimate these costs, based on past cost behaviors.

5. *Monitor supplier hiring and training against plan.* The supplier's progress in hiring and training the required people needed to meet requirements is monitored using a detailed matrix. Each employee goes through a detailed employee profile and information audit, which includes
    - Number of months working in fabrication
    - Type of degree (internal level of training)
    - Related or industry experience at the beginning of the contract (years)
    - Specific tool experience at the beginning of the contract (months)
    - Compensation status
    - Position in company
    - Date hired by supplier
    - Certification level (see next section for description)
    - Date the contract is to start and end

6. *Audit supplier technician certification levels.* To further manage risk, supplier training skill levels are audited just before or as they arrive at the factory, similar to an equipment source inspection.

7. *Take appropriate remedial and commercial actions, based on audit results.* Supplier technicians who have significant gaps in certification criteria are required to take immediate corrective action. Some of these actions (depending on prior negotiations) include
    - Replacement of supplier technician
    - Addition of temporary "mentor" supplier technician
    - Price reduction until certification
    - Cancellation of headcount from contract

8. *Monitor supplier performance to scope of work, turnover, etc.* Supplier service performance is monitored to ensure that requirements are met in the areas of
    - Safety requirements
    - Performance of equipment and technicians
    - Problem escalation
    - Staffing turnover
    - Cost reduction

Intel inserts detailed specification clauses into its contracts. In most cases, they do not ask the supplier to come in and try to "fix" the equipment if it does not function properly. This costs too much, and the impact on other processes is unknown (e.g., it could cause other problems). A clean room costs $4,000 per square foot to operate—and extra equipment takes up extra space, making it even more expensive. Over many process generations, losses are rolled into the next generation, and the supplier's sustaining labor is redirected to new process tools as one process becomes obsolete (depending on the percentage of equipment reused in successive processes, installation of new tools, etc.). This approach has been instrumental in keeping Intel ahead of the competition in designing and bringing new chip technology to the market in a rapid manner. ■

CONCLUSION

This chapter has provided an overview of the types of contracts used by purchasers, administration procedures applied, and methods of resolving contractual disputes. Although it is impossible to cover all potential situations where a specific contract should be applied, the rules of thumb developed here should provide a reasonable set of guidelines. As a final point, it is interesting to note that many organizations are eliminating contracts altogether, and are choosing to do business with suppliers on an informal basis. This type of arrangement requires the development of excellent supplier relationships and trust between the parties. It is highly unlikely, however, that contracts will ever disappear between buyers and sellers.

DISCUSSION QUESTIONS

1. What are the risks to buyers associated with each of the different types of contracts (fixed-price, incentive, or cost contracts)?
2. What are the risks to suppliers associated with each of the different types of contracts (fixed-price, incentive, or cost contracts)?
3. Which types of firms are most suited to using turnkey systems contracts for their information system development?
4. Suppose you are a purchase manager who is the contract administrator for a supplier installing a purchasing transaction management information system. What are some of the key elements that you would wish to include in the contract with this supplier?
5. Why do consultants typically want to avoid including detailed outcomes in their contracts?
6. Under what conditions are short-term contracts preferable to long-term contracts?
7. Certain industries, such as the computer industry, are faced with constantly changing technologies, short product life cycles, many small-component suppliers, and demanding customers. Under these conditions, what type of contract would you recommend for a critical component supplier? What other measures would you include in this contract?
8. What are the implications for contract writing as a result of electronic signatures now being enforceable by law?

9.   What are the dangers associated with taking an old contract and merely changing the name of the supplier for use in a new three-year contract with a different supplier?
10. Why do many firms attempt to avoid litigation in settling contract disputes?
11. What are the different venues available for arbitration settlements?
12. What are the implications of e-commerce on enforcing contracts? Where do you think the venue for resolution should be if a conflict arises?
13. What are the advantages and disadvantages associated with a "Copy Exactly" contract agreement such as that used by Intel?

ADDITIONAL READINGS

Alston, Frank M., Margeret M. Worthington, and Louis P. Goldsman. *Contracting with the Federal Government.* New York: Wiley, 1992.

Behn, Robert D. "Strategies for Avoiding Pitfalls of Performance Contracting." *Public Productivity and Management Review* (June 1999): 470–90.

Buvik, Arnt. "The Effect of Manufacturing Technology on Purchase Contracts." *International Journal of Purchasing and Materials Management* (Fall 1998): 21–28.

Carbonneau, Thomas E. *Alternative Dispute Resolution: Melting the Lances and Dismounting the Steeds.* Urbana, IL: University of Illinois Press, 1989.

Coulson, Robert. *Business Arbitration: What You Need to Know*, 2nd ed. New York: American Arbitration Association, 1982.

Fisher, Richard X. "Checklist for a Good Contract for IT Purchases." *Health Management Technology* (March 2000): 14–17.

Gordon, Stephen B. "Performance Incentive Contracting: Using the Purchasing Process to Find Money Rather Than Spend It." *Government Finance Review* (August 1998): 33–37.

Hancock, William A., ed. *The Law of Purchasing*, 2nd ed. Chesterland, OH: Business Laws, 1987.

Murray, John E. "How Do You Make a Contract?" *Purchasing* (November 1994): 28–32.

———. "Electronic Commerce Alters the Way People Seal Deals." *Purchasing* (September 15, 1998): 27–31.

Reyniers, Diane J., and Charles S. Tapiero. "Contract Design and the Control of Quality in a Conflictual Environment." *European Journal of Operational Research* (April 1995): 26–38.

Rice, Mitchell F. "Federal Set-Asides Policy and Minority Business Contracting." *International Journal of Public Administration* 22, no. 7 (1999): 1001.

Rohleder, Stephen. "Contracting for the Best Results." *Government Executive* (September 1999): 72.

Shenson, Howard L. *The Contract and Fee-Setting Guide for Consultants and Professionals.* New York: Wiley, 1990.

Seide, Katharine, ed. *A Dictionary of Arbitration and Its Terms.* Dobbs Ferry, NY: Oceana Publishing, 1970.

MacCollum, David V. *Construction Safety Planning.* New York: Van Nostrand Reinhold, 1990.

Singer, Linda R. *Settling Disputes: Conflict Resolution in Business, Families, and the Legal System.* Boulder, CO: Westview Press, 1990.

Tepedino, Francis J. *Contract Claims and Litigation Avoidance.* San Diego: Condor Group, 1991.

Werner, Curt. "Contract Compliance a Double-Edged Sword for Most Suppliers." *Health Industry Today* (May 1998): 1–2.

Wright, Benjamin. "Contracts Without Paper." *Technology Review* (July 1992): 57–62.

ENDNOTES

1. Robert B. Handfield, "A Resource Dependence Perspective of Just-in-Time Purchasing," *Journal of Operations Management* 11 (1993): 289–311.
2. Robert B. Handfield, *Re-engineering for Time-based Competition* (Westport, CT: Greenwood Publishing, 1995), 103.
3. Robert Handfield and Ronald Pannesi, "Managing Component Life Cycles in Dynamic Technological Environments," *International Journal of Purchasing and Materials Management* (Spring 1994): 20–27.
4. Kelly Kevin and Kathleen Kerwin, "There's Another Side to the Lopez Saga," *Business Week,* August 23, 1993, 26.
5. James C. Wetherbe, "Executive Information Requirements: Getting It Right," *MIS Quarterly* 15, no. 1 (March 1991): 51–65.
6. White Paper, "'Do Good' Won't Do It on the Supply Front," *Purchasing* (February 16, 1995): 87–92.
7. White Paper, "Why Aren't Minority Supplier Programs More Successful?," *Purchasing* (February 16, 1995): 97–100; White Paper. "The Problems Coming From Supplier-Base Downsizing?," *Purchasing* (February 16, 1995): 101–103.
8. White Paper, "Do Good."
9. Howard L. Shenson, "The Contract and Fee-Setting Guide for Consultants and Professionals (New York: Wiley, 1990), 131–134.
10. David V. MacCollum, *Construction Safety Planning* (New York: Van Nostrand Reinhold, 1990).
11. Nancy M. Samelson and Raymond E. Levitt, "Owner's Guidelines for Selecting Safe Contractors," *ASCE National Spring Convention Proceedings* (April 26–30, 1982): 617–23.
12. John Barrett, "Why Major Account Selling Works," *Industrial Marketing Management* 15, no. 1 (1986): 63–73.

13. William A. Hancock, ed., *The Law of Purchasing*, 2nd ed. (Chesterland, OH: Business Laws, 1987), 68.02.
14. Linda R. Singer, *Settling Disputes: Conflict Resolution in Business, Families, and the Legal System* (Boulder, CO: Westview Press, 1990), 5.
15. Robert Coulson, *Business Arbitration: What You Need to Know*, 2nd ed. (New York: American Arbitration Association, 1982), 5.
16. Coulson, *Business Arbitration*.
17. Singer, *Settling Disputes*.

16 PURCHASING LAW AND ETHICS

Napster's Challenge to Copyright Laws on the Web

In January 1999, Shawn Fanning, a freshman at Northeastern University, dropped out of school to finish writing the software program for a product called Napster. Shawn had discovered a superior technology to existing search engines that allowed people to find and download MP3 music files. On June 1, Napster began its operations, letting people download free software that would enable them to swap music stored in their computer. In just a few days, Napster was downloaded by thousands of people. The company soon received seed money, first from Shawn's uncle, and then from a group of venture capitalists from Boston.

College students throughout the United States were discovering Napster and couldn't get enough of it. At Oregon State University, Napster was taking up 10% of the school's Internet bandwidth, and at Florida State, 20% to 30% of the school's pipes. At the University of Illinois, Napster was hogging up to 80% of the university's bandwidth. By October 1999, Napster had passed the 1 million-download mark. In October of that year, Napster and the major record companies were holding talks about cooperating to distribute music over the Net. The talks centered around selling a minority stake in Napster to record companies and allowing Napster to license music from one label. That deal could then be used as leverage to approach another record label. However, Napster's new CEO, Eileen Richardson, was unable to develop a business model palatable to the record industry. Finally, on December 7, 1999, the recording industry had had enough; the Recording Industry of America (RIAA) sued for copyright infringement, asking for damages of $100,000 each time a song was copied.

Napster saw these legal actions coming. From the start its founders studied the law—and concluded that they would be free to dispense music to the masses after a major legal battle. John Fanning, Napster's chief business strategist and Shawn Fanning's uncle, said he personally read the entire U.S. Court of Appeals for the Ninth Circuit's rulings on copyright law and determined that the highest courts in the land would side with the company. "We're an Internet service provider that is protected by the 1998 Digital Millennium Copyright Act," Fanning claimed. "We're like a VCR, which the Supreme Court has ruled has 'substantial noninfringing uses.'" However, the RIAA countered that Napster is more like an information-location tool and is therefore not eligible for protection. In fact, they claim, Napster was being used predominantly for the purpose of copyright infringement.

Rock musicians have been extremely upset about Napster. In April 2000, the rock band Metallica sued Napster and three schools (Yale University, University of Southern California, and Indiana University) for copyright infringement. Meanwhile, scores of universities banned Napster because heavy student use was overwhelming their computer systems. On June 13, 2000, the RIAA filed a motion for a preliminary injunction to block

→ → →

all major-label content from being traded through Napster. Napster in turn announced plans to work with digital rights technology company Liquid Audio to try to make its music downloads safe for copyright holders. Despite these efforts, on July 26, 2000, U.S. District Judge Marilyn Patel ruled in favor of the record industry and ordered Napster to stop allowing copyrighted materials to be swapped over its network by midnight two days later. Nine hours before Napster would have had to shut down, the Ninth U.S. Circuit Court of Appeals ruled that the company should be allowed to continue operating. In April 2001, Napster made a frank public admission that its music-swapping service continues to violate a judge's orders. However this situation is finally resolved in the future, this small company has set off an ongoing debate over whether the music and film industries must ultimately bend to the will of cutting-edge technologies like Napster.

Source: Adapted from Spencer Ante, "Inside Napster," *Business Week*, August 14, 2000, 113–120; Don Clark, "Steps on Piracy by Music Labels May Be Futile," *Wall Street Journal*, September 19, 2000, A3; Spencer Ante, "Can Microsoft's Nemesis Save Napster?" *Business Week*, July 3, 2000, 46; Bridis, Ted, "Online Music: Is It Time to Rewind or Fast Forward?" *Wall Street Journal*, April 4, 2001, B3.

Today's global business environment has made it more important then ever for purchasing managers to understand the changing nature of law at the international, federal, state, and regional level. Purchasing's daily activities are essentially concerned with the laws regarding *contracts* and the laws regarding *agency*. The majority of purchasing law is derived primarily from the laws regarding contracts.

Contract law essentially determines the nature of agreements that are enforceable and create legal rights between the parties. The characteristics of offer and acceptance, satisfaction, and nonperformance have all been clearly established by the law. Contracts between two or more parties allow the shifting of risk between the entities and constitute the foundation and fabric for every type of supply chain relationship. Agency law, on the other hand, deals with the role of managers as individual representatives acting on behalf of their organization. It is important that purchasing managers understand the role they play as an agent of their organization, so that they do not exceed the responsibilities bestowed upon them in this role. As agents of their organization, purchasing managers also wield a great deal of power in allocating the business of the company to their suppliers. They must also be aware of the potential for ethical abuses of this power that may be encountered.

Although we cannot provide a comprehensive treatment of these issues here, this chapter will introduce some of the basic legal concerns that purchasing managers must be aware of in their profession. Specifically, we begin with a discussion of the roles and responsibilities of purchasing managers as individuals representing their organization. Next, we present an overview of purchasing ethics and then discuss the major features of the Uniform Commercial Code. The major features of contract law are reviewed as well as the important area of patents and intellectual property. Finally, other laws that affect purchasing are discussed.

LEGAL AUTHORITY AND PERSONAL LIABILITY OF THE PURCHASING MANAGER

Laws of Agency

The laws regarding agency are concerned with governing the relationship of principals and agents. An *agent* is a person or entity who has been authorized to act on behalf of some other person or entity. A *principal*, on the other hand, is the corresponding person or entity for whom agents carry out their authority. The purchasing manager/buyer is typically considered to be a general agent for the buying firm (the principal). That means that a supplier dealing with this manager/buyer has a right to rely on the individual's statements, both in written form and verbally. Conversely, the sales representative can also be considered to be an agent of the selling firm (also a principal). The sales representative may have either a broad or narrow range of powers depending on whether he or she is a general or special sales agent.

Legal Authority

Purchasing managers generally have final authority over purchasing decisions within their firms. However, this final decision may be reached through the input provided by a cross-functional sourcing team. In the end, however, someone has to sign the contract, so the purchasing manager is most often considered as the general agent. (A general agent role merely implies that the guidelines provided by the employer for this individual are quite broad and general in nature.) Since purchasing managers are responsible for a significant amount of expenditures, the employer's instructions to their purchasing managers should be expressed clearly and succinctly. The purchasing agency relationship is created between the employer and employee when the company hires an individual to perform the purchasing job. Typically, a job description provides the basis for an agreement between the employing firm and purchasing agent/manager regarding actual scope of authority.

Purchasing managers have the right to require clear and unequivocal instructions from their employers regarding the scope of their day-to-day job performance expectations (as described in Chapter 4). From a legal perspective, if purchasing managers carry out their duties in a faithful, ethical, and conscientious manner, then their obligations to the employers are fulfilled. However, in agreeing to perform the purchasing duties for the employer, the purchasing manager does not imply that he or she will never make mistakes. The purchasing manager's responsibilities are essentially to keep the best interests of the employer in mind when accomplishing his or her day-to-day activities.

Personal Liability

Certain individuals in many organizations have interpreted the statement "acting in the best interests of the employer" in radically different ways. There are a number of ways in which purchasing managers can be held personally liable in the conduct of

EXHIBIT 16.1   *Laws of Agency*

	Actual Authority (what the agent is authorized to buy)	
	Within	Exceed
Apparent Authority (what the seller perceives) — **Within**	OK	Employer responsible for performance of contract
Apparent Authority (what the seller perceives) — **Exceed**	Not relevant	Purchasing manager liable (dire consequences)

their day-to-day activities, even if they were supposedly following these guidelines. Depending on the issue at hand, this personal liability can take the form of either a civil or criminal suit. The concept of apparent versus actual authority is the determining factor in such cases.

Actual authority stems from the instructions and granting of authority to the purchasing manager via the job description provided by the employer. These documents typically define the limits and parameters under which the purchasing manager is expected to operate. *Apparent authority*, on the other hand, is that level of authority perceived by the seller to be *available* to the purchasing manager. In most instances, this level of apparent authority can be defined as the scope of authority possessed by other purchasing managers of similar positions in other organizations within the same industry.

If a purchasing manager, in carrying out normal procurement responsibilities, exceeds his or her actual but not apparent authority, then the employer is still responsible for performance of the resulting contract but could seek legal action against the purchasing manager personally. Exceeding both actual and apparent authority can have dire consequences; an individual may be held directly liable by the supplier or other third party (see Exhibit 16.1).

It is in the purchasing manager's own self-interest to ensure that all suppliers or other third parties are aware that his or her actions are on behalf of the employing firm. All contracts should be signed in such a manner that demonstrate the agency relationship. The following language might be used in a contract:[1]

President Signs E-Signature Bill

On June 20, 2000 in Philadelphia, President Clinton signed into law a bill that makes electronic signatures as valid as their pen-and-ink counterparts. The Electronic Signatures in Global and National Commerce Act paves the way for a new era of electronic commerce in which organizations will be able to complete transactions online instead of in person. "Under this landmark legislation, online contracts will now have the same legal force as equivalent paper contracts," says the president. "Firms across America are moving their supply and sales channels online, improving customer service and reducing costs." By making electronic signatures equally valid, "companies will have the legal certainty they need to invest and expand in electronic commerce," he adds. The measure took effect on October 1, 2000, and as of March 1, 2001, organizations can begin the electronic retention of legal records such as mortgages and financial securities.

Source: Anonymous, *Purchasing Today* (August 2000): 4.

[your name] on behalf of [your company] or [your company name] by [your name]

Purchasing managers can be held personally liable for their damaging and illegal activities if they perform them without the authority of their firm. This personal liability may occur even if the purchasing manager believes (incorrectly) that he or she actually possesses the authority. Any damaging acts performed outside of the manager's scope of authority (whether actual or apparent) can lead to personal liability even though such acts were intended to benefit the employer. In essence, any act that causes damage to any other person could cause a legal liability to the purchasing manager who performs such an act.

Other areas of activity for the purchasing manager that could lead to personal liability include the following:[2]

- Deception for personal gain while behaving as an agent for the principal firm (includes taking bribes)
- Violating the lawful protection of items owned by others, such as patent infringement
- (Mis)use of proprietary information
- Violation of antitrust laws
- Unlawful transportation of hazardous materials and toxic waste

These activities are related to another important aspect of purchasing law: ethical behavior.

A good rule of thumb is to remember that purchasers must always act in the best interests of their employer. This includes maintaining loyalty, respecting confidential information, and avoiding compromising relationships that may lead to a conflict of interest. This in turn leads to the next topic, purchasing ethics.

Purchasing Ethics

Ethics have their basis in the field of philosophy, and identify common principles associated with appropriate versus inappropriate actions, moral duty, and obligation. Ethics are the set of moral principles or values guiding our behavior. In a business setting, ethical behavior is the use of recognized social principles involving justice and fairness throughout a business relationship. When interacting with suppliers, an ethical buyer treats them in a just, decent, fair, honest, and fitting manner. Being ethical means following a code viewed as fair by those within the profession as well as the community.[3]

Three rules are understood to be a part of ethical behavior. First, a buyer must commit his or her attention and energies for the organization's benefit rather than personal enrichment at the expense of the organization. Ethical buyers do not accept outside gifts or favors that violate their firm's ethics policy. Ethical buyers are also not tempted or influenced by the unethical practices of salespeople and do not have personal financial arrangements with suppliers. Second, a buyer must act ethically toward suppliers or potential suppliers. This means treating each supplier professionally and with respect. Finally, a buyer must uphold the ethical standards set forth by his or her profession. A code or statement of professional ethics usually formalizes the set of ethical standards.

Purchasing managers, more than any other group within a firm, experience enormous pressure to act in unethical ways. This occurs for several reasons. First, purchasing has direct control over large sums of money. A buyer responsible for a multimillion-dollar contract may find sellers using any means available to secure a favorable position. The very nature of purchasing means that a buyer must come in contact with outside, and occasionally, unethical sellers. A second reason is due to the pressure placed on many salespeople. A seller who must meet aggressive sales goals might resort to questionable sales practices.

Risks of Unethical Behavior

A buyer who performs an unethical act runs the risk that the act is also illegal. For example, a government buyer who accepts payment from a defense contractor clearly committed an unethical and illegal act. If this payment becomes known, the buyer risks legal penalty as defined by the law. The buyer's firm also risks a legal penalty. At a minimum, the buyer will probably lose his or her job.

Unethical behavior also presents a personal risk to a buyer's professional reputation. Sellers quickly become aware of buyers who are open to offers "on the side." Once a buyer earns a reputation within an industry, it is difficult to change it. A buyer also runs a risk that management will discover his or her lack of ethics and terminate employment. A professional reputation is something a buyer carries throughout an entire career. If a buyer is found guilty of accepting a bribe, companies will not only terminate the buyer, but may often pursue litigation as well. Personal financial bankruptcy or even jail sentences can result for buyers who are found guilty of accepting large bribes.

A final risk of unethical behavior is the risk to a firm's reputation. A buyer who makes purchase decisions based on factors other than legitimate business criteria risks the reputation of the entire firm. For example, quality may suffer if a buyer accepts substandard performance from a supplier who offered outside inducements. A buyer's unethical behavior can jeopardize the livelihood of others dependent on a firm's success. World-class suppliers do not have to practice unethical behavior to win contracts.

To summarize the legal perspective, accepting a supplier's outside gifts and favors in exchange for special treatment is a form of corruption. The U.S. business environment does not treat unethical behavior lightly. Buyers who practice unethical behavior subject themselves and their firms to increased risk and diminish the integrity of the purchasing profession. Firms dealing with global sourcing sometimes encounter unethical behavior, particularly in developing countries where bribery may be viewed as a routine source of extra income. However, global firms are increasingly adopting an unequivocal "zero tolerance" stance toward any form of bribery, even if it means sacrificing short-term profitability to maintain a global reputation of integrity and honesty in its dealings with suppliers.

A Framework of Ethical Behavior

The manner in which a buyer responds to an ethical situation is a function of four variables: (1) organizational environment, (2) personal experiences, (3) cultural environment, and (4) industry environment. Exhibit 16.2 presents these variables within a framework of ethical purchasing behavior. Each variable presented affects a buyer's perspective when confronted with an ethical decision or issue, and include the following:

- *Organizational environment:* Every organization has a history of accepted ethical behavior or norms. This history may be formally or informally accepted throughout the organization. Also, different managers within the same firm may have different ethical values, which can further influence a buyer's ethical perspective.
- *Personal experiences:* Each buyer's personal experiences affect his or her ethical perspective. These experiences affect a buyer's personal moral and ethical beliefs about what is right and wrong.
- *Cultural environment:* Society affects a buyer's ethical perspective by further defining the boundaries of right and wrong. Certain behaviors may be acceptable in one culture and totally unacceptable in another. Cultural environment exerts a strong influence on behavior through the passage of laws and regulations.
- *Industry environment:* Accepted or common practices within an industry can affect a buyer's perspective and behavior. These can also define acceptable boundaries of behavior.

Let's assume a buyer at Firm XYZ has the highest moral and ethical values—the buyer has strong beliefs about what is proper behavior within the purchasing profession. Conflict can occur if a manager asks the buyer to do something the buyer feels is unethical. Here, the organizational environment and personal experiences exert conflicting influences. For example, a manager may ask a buyer to award a contract

EXHIBIT 16.2   *A Framework of Ethical Behavior*

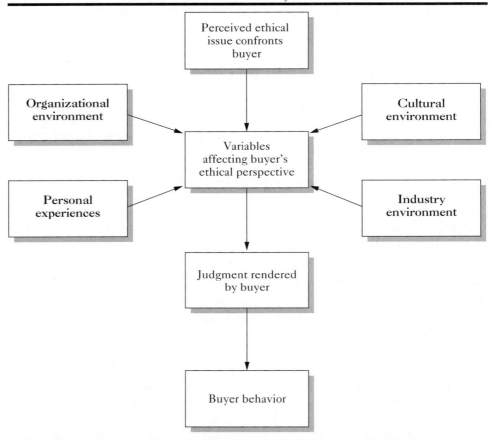

because of a personal friendship with a supplier. The buyer may feel this is unethical. Does the buyer simply award the contract in compliance with the manager's instruction, and ignore his or her own personal and moral values? Or does the buyer refuse to award the contract, thereby challenging the authority of a manager and jeopardizing his or her career? While a professional buyer should know the difference between right and wrong, organizational pressures can force a buyer to behave in ways that conflict with personal values, which creates a difficult situation for most buyers.

Types of Unethical Purchasing Behavior

The definition of ethical behavior can differ from buyer to buyer or from firm to firm. Despite these possible differences, most professionals recognize certain behavior or actions as unethical.

Reciprocity   This action involves giving preferential treatment to suppliers who are also customers of the buying organization.[4] In simple terms, it refers to a purchasing arrangement that dictates "I'll buy from you if you buy from me." The Federal Trade Commission (FTC) has taken an aggressive stance against reciprocal buying arrangements, ruiling that it is illegal "to abusively use large buying power to restrict competitive market opportunities." In the early 1970s, many larger firms entered into agreements with the FTC forbidding reciprocal purchasing. These firms also eliminated their internal trade departments established to coordinate these arrangements.[5] FTC rulings have convinced most firms to prohibit reciprocal purchasing. Most firms do recognize a customer's right for consideration as a potential supplier. A buyer, however, must rely only on legitimate performance criteria to evaluate supplier capability.

Personal Buying   This occurs when a purchasing department purchases material for the personal needs of its employees. Some states have outlawed such practices with statutes called *trade diversion laws*. These laws prohibit purchasing from engaging in personal buying for items not required during the normal course of business. Some exceptions to these laws do exist. For example, a firm can purchase safety shoes, hats, gloves, or even special tools required by the employee. A purchasing department can use its knowledge to purchase products conforming to specific quality standards. Personal buying is a gray area for some purchasing departments. Some firms view personal buying as a fringe benefit and service to the employee. Other firms flatly prohibit the practice. A buyer confronted with a request for personal buying should determine the legal status of the practice, and then discuss the subject with management. Personal buying can quickly get out of hand.

Accepting Supplier Favors   Accepting gifts and favors from a supplier is the most common ethical infraction involving buyers. These gifts and favors can affect a buyer's judgment to evaluate and select the most capable suppliers. The policy on supplier offerings is often a confusing issue. At what point does a supplier's gift or favor depart from a friendly showing of appreciation for a firm's business to an attempt to influence a buyer's purchase decisions? Accepting free items from potential suppliers is especially questionable. Here, a supplier does not even have a purchase contract. Firms can address this issue in their ethics policy by specifying exactly what a buyer may accept from a supplier.

Sharp Practices   A *sharp practice* is any misrepresentation by a buyer that falls just short of actual fraud.[6] Sharp practice occurs whenever a buyer "plays games" with a supplier and operates in an underhanded manner. The practice includes many different behaviors:

- *Willful use of misinformation, when a buyer knowingly deceives a supplier to realize some advantage.* For example, requesting quotes on inflated volumes and then placing smaller orders at the reduced price is a willful use of misinformation.
- *Exaggerating problems.* A buyer who exaggerates the size of a supplier-caused problem to extract a larger penalty or concession from a supplier is using a sharp practice.

- *Requesting bids from unqualified suppliers for the sole purpose of driving a qualified supplier's price lower.* A buyer should request bids from qualified suppliers only.
- *Gaining information unfairly through deception.*
- *Sharing information on competitive quotations.* The integrity of the competitive bid process requires confidentiality. Buyers who share supplier-quoted information violate the ethics of the bid process.
- *Not compensating a supplier for design or other work.* Buyers often request design and cost-saving assistance from suppliers. A supplier who helps a buyer should receive fair compensation for their efforts.
- *Taking unfair advantage of a supplier's financial situation.* A buyer who knowingly pressures a financially troubled supplier into providing a lower than normal price places the supplier in further financial jeopardy. Taking advantage of a financially susceptible supplier is an unethical business practice.
- *Lying or misleading.* Any instance of lying or misleading a seller is a sharp practice.

Financial Conflicts of Interest When a buyer awards business to a supplier because the buyer, the buyer's family, or relatives of the buyer have a direct financial interest in a supplier, this is considered a major unethical practice. This behavior is one reason many companies require employees to detail any investments in outside companies. Awarding a purchase contract to a company in which a buyer has a significant personal financial interest (versus owning a mutual fund that owns a small amount of stock in the company) is a serious breach of ethics. This action is similar to an executive buying or selling stock because of inside knowledge, which is an illegal act.

SMI Professional Code of Ethics

The Supply Management Institute (SMI) (formerly the National Association of Purchasing Managers (NAPM)) is the largest organization representing the purchasing profession. In 1959, the SMI officially adopted its initial Standards of Conduct. The document serves as a guide for the SMI membership by imposing rules of conduct, particularly when a buyer's own company lacks a policy or statement of ethics. In the words of the code, "It is necessary for all of us to exercise a strict rule of personal conduct to insure that relations of a compromising nature, or even the appearance of such relations, be scrupulously avoided." The document reflects the SMI's commitment to ethical behavior and fair business dealings.

The Standards of Conduct specifies three guiding principles of purchasing practice: (1) loyalty to company, (2) justice to those with whom a buyer deals, and (3) faith in the purchasing profession. From these principles SMI derived its standards of purchasing practice or Code of Ethics:

1. Consider, first, the interest of your company in all transactions and carry out and believe in its established policies.
2. Be receptive to competent counsel from your colleagues and be guided by such counsel without impairing the dignity and responsibility of your office.
3. Buy without prejudice, seeking to obtain the maximum value for each dollar of expenditure.

4. Strive consistently for knowledge of the materials and processes of manufacture and establish practical methods for the conduct of your office.
5. Subscribe to and work for honesty and truth in buying and selling, and denounce all forms and manifestations of commercial bribery.
6. Accord a prompt and courteous reception, so far as conditions will permit, to all who call on a legitimate business mission.
7. Respect your obligations and require that obligations to you and to your concern be respected, consistent with good business practice.
8. Avoid sharp practice.
9. Counsel and assist fellow purchasing managers in the performance of their duties, whenever the occasion permits.
10. Cooperate with all organizations and individuals engaged in activities designed to enhance the development and standing of purchasing.

These standards often help guide a firm's ethical code of conduct and policy. While suggestions for modifying certain sections of the Code of Ethics have been put forth, the basic 1959 code is still intact. The SMI standards specifically state that its members should maintain standards on an even higher plane than those accepted by society—what becomes the "true test of greatness." This is stated as follows in the code:

Nothing can undermine respect for the purchasing profession more than improper action on the part of its members with regard to gifts, gratuities, or favors. People engaged in purchasing should not accept from any supplier or prospective supplier any money, gift, or favor that might influence, or be suspected of influencing their buying decisions. We must decline to accept or must return any such gift or favor offered us or members of our immediate family. The declination of these gifts or favors must be done discreetly and courteously. Possible embarrassment resulting from refusals does not constitute a basis for exception.

The SMI Standards of Conduct is a powerful document. It holds the purchasing profession to the highest levels of ethical conduct. Companies of all sizes from many industries have used the Code of Ethics as a guide when developing their own ethical policies.

Supporting Ethical Behavior

A firm can take many actions to make sure its employees conduct business in an ethical manner. The following sections summarize the actions a firm can take to enhance the ethical behavior of its purchasing personnel.

Developing a Statement of Ethics   Most research on purchasing ethics concludes that adopting a formal ethics policy helps define and deter potentially unethical purchasing behavior. An earlier study found that firms without formal ethical policies disclosed supplier bid prices to other suppliers at a much higher rate than firms with a formal policy prohibiting this practice.[7] Also, firms without a formal ethics policy were more likely to make discounted purchases for their employees, a questionable practice in some states. A formal ethics policy helps define the boundaries of ethical behavior.

Top-Management Commitment Executive management sets the ethical code of behavior within a firm. While the highest executive may not actually write a firm's purchasing or marketing code of ethics, the ethical behavior of top executives sends a message about whether or not unethical behavior is tolerated. Lower-level managers quickly recognize top management's commitment to ethical behavior and imitate the commitment.

Closer Buyer-Seller Relationships Dealing with a smaller supply base or a single supplier for an item will probably do more for ethical purchasing behavior than any other recent trend or action. Firms are increasingly using buying teams to evaluate potential suppliers across different performance categories. Using a team approach to evaluate a supplier's capabilities limits the opportunity for unethical behavior. Unethical suppliers will find it tougher to influence a team of professionals. Buyers, or any other personnel within a buying firm, will also find it harder to practice unethical behavior when a team oversees the supplier selection process.

Ethical Training New buyers, usually at larger firms, often enter a training program before actually assuming their professional duties. One part of the training usually deals with purchasing ethics. Such a program is an opportunity to train a new buyer about a firm's ethics policy. Firms often use role playing to help buyers learn how to identify different types of unethical behavior and how to confront and deal with these situations. (See the Good Practice Example on Lockheed Martin at the end of this chapter.) Ethics training reinforces a firm's commitment to the highest ethical standards.

Developing Consistent Behavior Confusion about proper ethical behavior can arise when marketing and purchasing have separate ethical standards. A firm that prohibits its purchasing personnel from accepting gifts from suppliers but allows its marketing department to distribute gifts to its customers is not acting consistently. When different standards of behavior exist within the same firm, it becomes easier for one group to rationalize or justify unethical behavior. How can it be ethical for one group (marketing) to provide gifts and favors but unethical for another group (purchasing) within the same firm to accept any items?

Internal Reporting of Unethical Behavior Executive purchasing management should create an atmosphere that supports the reporting of unethical behavior. A buyer should be able to approach management about an ethical impropriety with confidence that management will correct the problem. A firm should also encourage suppliers to report instances of unethical behavior by anyone within the buying firm. This practice notifies suppliers that a buying firm is committed to ethical business practices. It also tells a firm's buyers that top management will not tolerate certain types of behavior. Another strategy involves preventive management to reduce the possibility of unethical purchasing behavior.

Preventive Measures One common strategy is to rotate buyers among different items or commodities, which prevents a buyer from becoming too comfortable with any particular group of suppliers. While a buyer should become familiar with purchased items and suppliers, it is often a good idea to rotate personnel between buying assignments. Rotation usually occurs every several years.

Another preventive measure is to limit a buyer's purchase authority without higher-level approval. For example, a firm's policy may limit a buyer's authority for awarding purchase contracts to amounts of $10,000 or less. Contracts greater than $10,000 then require a manager's signature. A buyer must justify the selection decision based on sound purchasing criteria before obtaining the final sign-off. This provides a system of checks and balances and reduces the possibility of unethical supplier selection.

Although a fine line exists between ethical and legal behavior, we believe that ethics should always come first. However, it is also important that a qualified purchasing manager develop a fine intuition for purchasing law, as this can have a significant impact on daily and long-term actions in the profession. In the remainder of the chapter, we will discuss some of the more important aspects of purchasing law, beginning with the most important: the Uniform Commercial Code.

THE UNIFORM COMMERCIAL CODE

Sources of U.S. Purchasing Law

Before we discuss the Uniform Commercial Code, it is worthwhile to briefly review what we mean by "purchasing law." U.S. federal purchasing law is composed of three distinct sources:

- Written law, which originates in the legislative branch of government
- Administrative law, which is derived by the executive branch through the issuance of rules and regulations
- Common law, which stems from judicial branch rulings and court decisions

Written law is composed of the various acts and laws passed by elected representatives of the relevant legislative bodies. In the case of the federal government, the U.S. Congress is the source of laws and acts. In the case of individual states, the respective state legislatures are responsible for writing laws and acts governing intrastate matters. A prime example of written law might be the Motor Carrier Act of 1980, which changed the ways motor carriers were able to set rates.

Administrative law is created through the issuance of rules and regulations by different governmental agencies acting within the scope of their legal authority. This source of law can originate from agencies at either the state or federal level of government. Examples of relevant U.S. agencies that have had a major impact on purchasing operations are the Internal Revenue Service within the Department of the Treasury and the Interstate Commerce Commission within the Department of Transportation.

Common law created by the judicial system plays a variety of roles because it can modify or overturn other sources of laws. In areas where written law is either indistinct or missing, the courts can actually create law through court decisions that establish a *precedence* for deciding similar cases in the future. In addition, the courts can rule that otherwise-applicable laws are unconstitutional and, subsequently, no longer applicable. Although this process may create some degree of confusion and uncertainty regarding conflicting interpretations of law between different court jurisdictions, the decisions of the judicial branch at either the state or federal level can have a significant long-term impact on buyer-seller relationships. At different times, and in different situations, there may be more than one source of law that affects different areas of purchasing practice. Although we will not go into these details, it is worthwhile noting that a great deal of confusion between conflicting sources of law has been eliminated through the passage of the Uniform Commercial Code.

Purchasing Law Before the UCC

In today's society, we take for granted that there is a certain level of fairness and predictability in the legal system. This was not always the case. Laws differed from nation to nation, state to state, and city to city. In the United States, every state had, and still does have, the power to enact is own laws concerning business transactions. Federal law is applicable only to interstate (trade between states) and foreign commercial transactions, while intrastate (within state) commerce is technically governed by state law.

Beginning in the 1950s, a national editorial board of legal scholars drafted the body of laws concerning business transactions, which was intended to make business transactions regular and predictable. The goal was to reduce the number of state-by-state variations. The resulting code was the federal Uniform Commercial Code (UCC). In 1952, all of the states (with the exception of Louisiana) adopted the UCC. A number of subsequent revisions to the UCC have kept its provisions more responsive to changing business conditions. The UCC that is in use today consists of the following ten articles:

1. General introductory provisions
2. Sales of goods and products
3. Transactions in commercial paper (bank checks, liability for endorsements)
4. Bank deposits and collections
5. Letters of credit (financial instruments issued by banks and other institutions)
6. Bank transfers
7. Warehouse receipts, bills of lading, and other documents of title to goods
8. Transfers in investment securities
9. Secured transactions
10. Technical matters

The primary portion of the Uniform Commercial Code that concerns purchasing is Article 2, which deals with sales contracts. The UCC provides benefits to the buying firm in four ways:[8]

1. If a seller makes an offer in writing, the seller has to live up to it for the period of time stated.
2. Verbal agreements, when confirmed in writing and if no objection is made, are valid.
3. The conflict between a buyer's purchase order terms and a seller's acknowledgment terms has been generally resolved in favor of the buyer.

4. As far as warranties are concerned, the purchasing manager can legally rely on the supplier to provide the item needed to do the job.

The real effect of Article 2 is to support the buying firm's position in its commercial dealings with its suppliers. The UCC, as opposed to other laws such as the Uniform Sales Act, establishes each party's rights and obligations based on the concepts of fairness and reasonableness, which are founded on accepted business practices. It should also be noted that the *sale of services is not outlined* but is covered under common law (system of jurisprudence). In cases where either the common law or the UCC may apply, the prevailing condition is the location where the bulk of funds is expended. One can also agree in a contract to override parts of the UCC—so it is important to read the "fine print" on contracts, being aware of the words "unless otherwise agreed." Because the UCC does *not* apply outside the boundaries of the United States—international law may have a wide range of agreements related to business transactions—the rule of thumb is "buyer beware."

The most basic elements of Article 2 within the UCC involve the following four issues:

- Warranties
- Transportation terms and risk of loss
- Seller's rights
- Buyer's rights

Warranties

Warranties ensure that a buyer can legally rely on a supplier to provide the item needed to do a job. In its most basic form, a warranty is defined as "a promise or representation made by the seller, which, if necessary, can be legally enforced."[9] In order for a warranty to be legally enforceable, it must be a formal part of the contract.

There are two major types of warranties: express and implied. An *express warranty* is one in which the manufacturer makes specific statements concerning promises, affirmations of fact, specifications, samples, and descriptions regarding the goods or services that are being sold. Express warranties may be either oral or written and it is not necessary that the words "warranty" or "guarantee" be specifically used in order to create such an express guarantee.

Buyers must be aware that the legal system in the United States has repeatedly ruled that suppliers' sales representatives (i.e., special agents) have a natural tendency to promote the capabilities and performance of their products and services for the sole purpose of making a sale. In other words, it is not illegal for sellers to *exaggerate* the merits of their product during their sales pitch. Because sales personnel are considered special (not "general") agents, it is *not illegal* for them to exaggerate the merits of their product. Such exaggerations are *not* considered warranties unless one of the following situations occurs:[10]

- The guarantee is confirmed by the employer or someone in his or her organization authorized to do so.
- The employer (supplier) has notified the purchaser that he or she will be bound by guarantees made by the sales representative.

- The employer (supplier) has in the past, without notification, accepted responsibility for such guarantees.
- The guarantee constitutes actual fraud, in which case the employer (supplier) is responsible for the action of his or her employee even though the employer did not authorize the salesperson to make the fraudulent statement or guarantee, either expressly or by implication.

For example, consider the following:

Mike's bakery needs flour, so Mike goes to Billy Bob's Flour Power Mill. Billy Bob says that he has a shipment of Grade A flour ready to sell. Billy Bob says that the shipment is all Grade A flour, and he gives a sample of the flour to Mike to inspect. The sample is fine Grade A flour. Mike buys the flour, pursuant to a contract of sale for "Grade A flour." However, when the shipment arrives at the bakery, it is not Grade A flour; it is spoiled and full of worms.

Mike can probably sue Billy Bob for violating an express warranty that the flour was Grade A flour: The contract said the shipment would be Grade A flour, and Billy Bob made an affirmation of fact when he told Mike that the shipment was Grade A flour. Further, the sample of flour was an express warranty that the rest of the flour would be as good as the sample.

The other form of warranty is the *implied warranty*, which deals with the concept of *fitness for use* and *merchantability*. The implied warranty of fitness for use (particular purpose) means when the seller at the time of contracting has reason to know of any particular purpose for which the goods are required, and the buyer is relying on the seller's skill or judgment to select or furnish suitable goods, there is unless excluded or modified an implied warranty that the goods shall be fit for such purpose. For example:

Mike goes to buy an industrial air-conditioning unit for his bakery. He goes to Joe's Air-Conditioning Supply Company. Mike describes the size of his bakery, the amount of heat produced by the machinery, how cool he wants to keep the facility, etc. Joe recommends the NotSoHot 1000, and Mike buys it. The machinery turns out to be inadequate: It can't keep the bakery cool, and it blows out after a few days.

In this case, Mike may be able to sue Joe for breach of the implied warranty of fitness for a particular purpose, since Joe had reason to know that Mike was buying an air conditioner for a particular purpose and that Mike relied on Joe's skill and judgment to select a suitable machine. A warranty of merchantability means that the good being exchanged meets the standards of the trade and its quality is appropriate for ordinary use. This means that people who are in the business of selling certain products imply to their customers that the products are of "fair average quality." For example:

Mike's bakery sells 10,000 glazed doughnuts to Dot. Dot runs a retail business called Dot's Donut Dollies that sells coffee, doughnuts, and other breakfast items. The doughnuts turn out to have been mistakenly glazed with salt instead of sugar and, as a result, have a nauseating flavor.

Dot may be able to sue Mike for breach of an implied warranty of merchantability, since Mike's bakery is a merchant with respect to doughnuts and the doughnuts were certainly not of fair average quality.

The purchasing manager in day-to-day activities may occasionally encounter two other types of warranties: warranty of title and warranty of infringement. *Warranty of title* essentially indicates that the supplier warrants that it has title to the goods and that they are not stolen or subject to any security interest or liens. In our example, Billy Bob warrants that the flour is his to sell to Mike, and that it is not stolen property. When there are doubts as to the legitimacy of the title to the goods, purchasing managers will need to take additional steps to ensure proper transfer of title, and ensure that the supplier has the right to sell the product.

The *warranty of infringement* refers to the supplier's guarantee that the goods being exchanged do not illegally infringe on another party's patent protection. The costs and penalties for patent infringement are so severe that most standard purchasing agreements contain an appropriate patent indemnification clause. If patent infringement is determined, then the damaged party can sue for an injunction to prevent further use of that item, potentially disrupting a firm's sales of products containing the item in dispute. A simple warranty of infringement in the purchaser's contracts is not enough protection. A more broad *patent indemnification clause* provides a greater level of safety for the buying organization. For example, if a firm provides design specifications that infringe on a third party's patent, the organization as well as the maker of that particular part may be subject to litigation. Patent infringement goes both ways and should be adequately protected against.

The following general suggestions can help purchasing managers to protect their organizations against warranty problems:[11]

- Write a good purchase order (and order acceptance form).
- Build a file.
- Write letters and save letters.
- Use good standard terms and conditions.
- Consider calling the seller's attention to the warranties.

Transportation Terms and Risk of Loss

Although very important, transportation documentation and delivery terms are frequently overlooked as a significant factor in many purchasing contracts. Transportation documents are used in domestic transportation to govern, direct, control, and provide information about a shipment.[12]

The *bill of lading*—perhaps the most common and singularly important shipping document—describes the origin of the shipment, provides specific directions for the carrier, delineates the transportation contract terms, and functions as a receipt for the shipment. In some circumstances, the bill of lading may also serve as a certificate of title for the shipment. The bill of lading contains the following information:

- Name and address of the consignor and consignee
- Routing instructions for the carrier
- Description of the goods being transported

- The number of items with corresponding commodity descriptions
- The freight class or rate for the commodity being shipped

The *freight bill* serves as the carrier's invoice for the freight charges involved in the movement of a particular shipment. As part of the freight bill, the Interstate Commerce Commission regulations require that credit terms be listed to avoid potential price discrimination between shippers. Freight bills may be classified as either prepaid or collect, to determine when the freight bill is to be tendered, regardless of whether the charges are paid in advance or not. On prepaid shipments, the freight bill is presented on the effective date of shipment. On collect shipments, the freight bill is presented on the effective date of delivery. Also, any adverse condition of the shipment should be noted here to facilitate any potential freight claims with the carrier.

Under the UCC, the risk of loss is with the *seller* until the title passes to the buyer. However, the following conditions can apply:

- The buyer and seller can agree in their contract as to when in the transaction the risk of loss becomes the buyer's rather than the seller's.
- If the seller is to ship goods by a third-party carrier, but the seller is *not* required to deliver the goods to a specific place (just to take the goods to the carrier), the risk of loss becomes the buyer's when the goods are delivered to the carrier.
- If the seller is required to ship goods to a specific place, the risk of loss becomes the buyer's when the goods are delivered to the specific place.
- If the goods are held by a third party who is responsible for their storage, such as a commercial warehouse, the risk of loss becomes the buyer's when the buyer receives certain documents of title or the third party acknowledges the buyer's right to take the goods.
- If the goods are defective, the risk of loss does not become the buyer's unless the defects are fixed or the buyer agrees to accept the defective goods.

Delivery terms essentially describe who is responsible for the selection of a carrier, payment of the freight bill, and the method in which the title of goods passes between the purchaser and the supplier. The term *F.O.B. (free on board)* delineates the point at which the supplier is responsible for freight charges and where the purchaser assumes title to the shipment. *F.O.B. shipping point* (or *F.O.B. origin*) indicates that the purchaser is responsible for payment of transportation costs and assumes title of the goods at the supplier's shipping dock. *F.O.B. destination* (or *F.O.B. delivered*) tells us that the supplier is responsible for transportation, and the purchaser assumes title of the goods at his or her own shipping dock. The F.O.B. term also defines which party is responsible for filing any freight damage claims. Essentially, the party who possesses title to the goods is responsible for filing the claim. The designation *C.I.F.*— similar to F.O.B. but referring to international shipments—stands for *cost, insurance, and freight*, so that essentially the contract price includes these costs in addition to the price of the goods. These costs may also include tariffs, customs duties, inspections, and so on, so buyers should be especially careful when agreeing to C.I.F. terms.

In most cases, a loss results in a freight claim being filed with the carrier to recover payment as a result of shipment loss, damage, or delay. Such documents can also be filed with the carrier to recover overcharge premiums. In order to be valid, freight claims must be filed within nine months of the date of actual or reasonable date of delivery. The carrier must respond with an acknowledgment of receipt of the claim within 30 days and then notify the claimant regarding whether or not the claim will be paid within 120 days. If the claim is not resolved within an additional 120 days, the carrier must notify the claimant of the reasons for not settling the claim each 60 days. If the carrier has refused to pay the claim, then the claimant has two years from the time the claim was disallowed to file for legal relief in the courts.

It is recommended that purchasing managers clearly specify delivery terms in the purchase contract to ensure that they receive the shipping and freight terms expected. It is important to signify these terms in as much detail as possible, even to the point of spelling out exact locations including street addresses and dock locations, if applicable. When in doubt, err on the side of increased detail. Unless otherwise specified in the purchase contract, the UCC recognizes F.O.B. origin as the default delivery term.

Seller's and Buyer's Rights

Seller's Rights   Article 2 of the UCC is very specific about sellers' and buyers' rights. Specifically, sellers have the right to do the following:

- Sue the buyer for the purchase price of the goods if the buyer basically refuses to pay for them.
- Recover reasonable costs and expenses incurred if goods have to be resold.
- Receive compensation for additional costs and expenses incurred by reason of the buyer's wrongful conduct.

The right to sue for the purchase price of goods is basically a breach of contract lawsuit. However, if there are still goods in the seller's possession, the buyer may be required to try to resell the goods for a fair price in order to offset what the buyer owes. This becomes especially important in end-of-life strategies. The buyer should let the seller know well in advance if a product is going to be discontinued to allow the seller to deplete existing inventories.

Buyer's Rights   According to the UCC, a buyer's rights include the right to do the following:

- Reject defective goods that the seller cannot repair within a reasonable time.
- Sue for breach of contract.
- Revoke acceptance of goods if the buyer discovers defects.
- Seek a court order forcing the seller to deliver the goods ("specific performance").
- Recover any extra expense incurred for having to purchase replacement goods from another seller.
- Retain the right to recover costs and expenses caused by a breach of warranty.

According to Article 2 of the UCC, a buyer cannot reject defective goods that cannot be remedied before the time required. However, the buyer has responsibilities with respect to seller goods in the buyer's possession. When a buyer accepts delivery of goods from a supplier (including a pickup from the supplier's plant), the buyer is responsible if it does not "catch" the defects. This is an excellent argument for certifying suppliers' processes and not relying on inspection as a means to ensure quality. In most cases, a supplier will want to remedy the problem to avoid conflict, but not always. If absolutely necessary, a buyer can get a court order to force the seller to deliver the goods. This might occur in a capacity problem, and is known as "specific performance." A buyer can also recover costs and expenses caused by a breach of warranty, including inspection costs, storage costs, return shipment costs.

Contract Law

Essential Elements of a Contract

Commercial law is defined as that "body of [the] law that refers to how business firms (parties) enter into contracts with each other, execute contracts, and remedy problems that arise in the process."[13] There are two major topical areas of commercial law that are of day-to-day interest to the purchasing professional: the laws regarding agency and the laws regarding contracts. We have already discussed agency law to some extent earlier in the chapter. Thus, we will turn our attention to the laws regarding contract.

In its most basic form, a *contract* can be defined as an agreement between two or more parties that can be legally enforced. Note that people make agreements every day, but not every agreement can be considered a contract. A contract is an agreement between two or more people to do specified things in exchange for other specified things. For example:

Shirley wants to go to the store to buy some potato chips but she doesn't have a car. She says to Rich, "I will pay you a dollar to take me to the store to buy some potato chips." Rich agrees and takes Shirley to the store.

The above statement can be characterized as a contract. Shirley agreed to do a specified thing *(pay Rich a dollar)* in exchange for another specified thing *(take Shirley to the store)*. In legal thinking a contract has three essential elements:

- Offer
- Acceptance
- Consideration

If any one of these elements is lacking, then an enforceable contract does not exist. Let's take a closer look at these three elements.

Offer   An *offer* is a proposal or expression by one person that he or she is willing to do something for certain terms. For example:

Betsy goes into Mimi's wholesale video store and says to Mimi, "I want to buy 1,000 videotapes of the movie Exterminator *from you. I will pay you $15 for each videotape."*

Betsy has made a specific offer—to purchase a specific movie—in specific volumes (1,000)—at a specific price ($15,000). This constitutes a valid offer. Somewhat different is a *conditional offer*, which includes additional criteria for completion of the agreement. For example:

Betsy goes into Mimi's wholesale video store and says to Mimi, "I want to buy 1,000 videotapes of the movie Exterminator *from you. I will pay you $15 for each videotape IF you deliver them to my place of business on February 1, 2001."*

In this case, a deadline has been added to the offer. The offer is valid if the conditions are met.

Acceptance   The second important part of the contract is the *acceptance*. Legally, a contract does not exist until the offer is *formally* accepted, either verbally or in written form. The offer and acceptance have to match. If they match, there is an agreement leading up to a contract. If they don't, it's more like a negotiation: an offer, to which someone responds with a counteroffer rather than an acceptance, which continues until both sides reach an agreement or a "meeting of the minds."

It is important to note that a contract exists only when there is an agreement resulting from both an offer and an acceptance. The agreement doesn't exist until the supplier accepts the offer, and a so-called "meeting of the minds" occurs. An acceptance, as recognized by the UCC, can be in "any manner and by any medium reasonable to the circumstances." In other words, the manner and medium of acceptance by the supplier can be met either through the promise of an acceptance or by the supplier's performance of the terms and conditions of the contract—that is, the actual delivery of the requested goods or services without prior verbal advance notice.

Many customer purchase orders typically contain a written copy that outlines the procedures for acknowledgment or acceptance by suppliers. However, suppliers frequently accept or acknowledge customer orders on their own forms, which may contain different language and terms than the customers' original purchase orders. When this occurs, the supplier's terms will automatically be incorporated into the final contract unless one of the following conditions is present:

1.   The supplier's terms substantially or materially alter the original intent of the offer (purchase order).
2.   The buyer objects to the supplier's acceptance terms in writing.
3.   The purchase order explicitly states that no alteration of terms is acceptable.

When the terms of the buyer's purchase order and the supplier's acceptance or acknowledgment conflict, and none of the conditions listed above are present, all of the terms of both the purchase order and the acceptance become part of the resulting contract *except the conflicting terms and conditions*. In effect, the conflicting terms and conditions are simply disregarded. The purchasing manager must therefore ensure that the terms and conditions of all supplier acceptance forms are carefully reviewed. If the buyer wants to avoid any dispute over the terms and conditions of the contract, the purchase order should include a statement to the effect that "Absolutely no deviation from the terms and conditions contained herein is permitted."

Consideration   The third element of a contract is difficult to define. *Consideration*, which has nothing to do with being considerate or nice to people, but rather is a form of "mutual obligation"—with each party bound to perform at certain levels and agreeing to carry out their responsibilities. The law has required consideration for centuries, but it has never been able to say exactly what it is or what it is not. Consideration is something of value in the formation of the contract that gives it legal validity. In the business world, mutual promises in a contract of sale, whether express or implied, are generally sufficient consideration. For example, in the previous example, Betsy made an offer that Mimi accepted. There has also been consideration. Betsy's consideration is express: she promised to pay $15 per tape. Mimi's consideration is implied: by saying "OK," she implied that she promised to sell Betsy 1,000 tapes for $15 apiece.

Two other elements are important to consider in contract law: competent parties/mutual assent and legal subject matter.

Competent Parties / Mutual Assent   The parties to a legally enforceable contract must have full contractual capacity through being either principals or qualified agents as described earlier. In addition, both the buyer and the seller must not have engaged in any fraudulent activities when formulating the agreement. The use of force or coercion to reach an agreement is not acceptable in signing a contract because both parties must enter into the agreement on their own free will. Both parties must indicate a willingness to enter into the agreement and be bound by its terms.

Legal Subject Matter   If an agreement has been made regarding a purpose that is illegal, then the resulting contract is null and void. The performance of a party in regard to the contract must not be an unlawful act if the agreement is to be enforceable. However, if the primary purpose of a contract is legal, but some terms contained within the agreement are not, then the contract may or may not itself be illegal depending on the seriousness of the illegal terms and the degree to which the legal and illegal terms can be separated.

The Purchase Order—Is It a Contract?

In most instances, the contracting parties participate in a series of negotiation deliberations through which the various terms and conditions of the contract are discussed, outlined, and agreed upon. As shown in Exhibit 16.3, a process takes place before the purchase order develops. This is initiated by the request for quotation, sent by the buyer to the supplier. The RFQ contains the following:

- Standard terms and conditions of the transaction
- Quantity/conditions of delivery
- End use of the item
- If customized, reviewed by legal counsel before the RFQ is submitted
- If a competitive bid, description of the manner and time period in which the bids will be evaluated
- Services

EXHIBIT 16.3   *The Contracting Process*

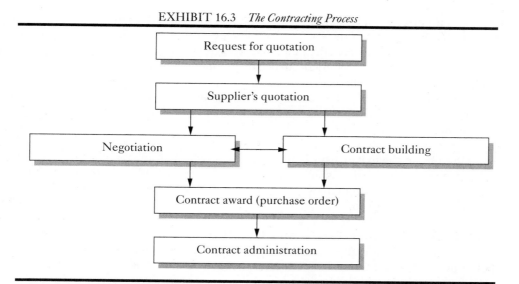

The RFQ is not an offer but a request for price and availability. The supplier will generally respond to the RFQ with a quote, which may then initiate further discussion and negotiation between the purchasing commodity team and the supplier's team. Eventually, this leads to a contract, which documents all of the different offers and counteroffers. Most commercial contracts are comprised of similar sets of general terms and conditions. With the exception of a description of the parties involved, a description of the basic subject of the contract and statement of work including dates, and a clearly definable or determinable quantity, the UCC can be relied upon to supply all other terms.

Once accepted, a purchase order becomes a contract. The major parts of a purchase order include

- Fixed prices and quantities (including taxes)
- Buyer's right of inspection and rejection
- Right to make specification/design changes
- Holding buyer harmless, patent infringement
- Supplier's right to assign contract to a third party
- Instructions regarding risk of loss
- Statement of credit and payment terms
- Identification
- Packing and preparation
- Statements of warranty
- Shipment quantities/dates
- Assignment of seller's rights
- Arbitration clause
- Right to cancel unshipped portion

It is worthwhile to go over several of these terms.

Price The price term is perhaps the single most important element of the entire contract. Section 2-305 of the UCC entitled "Open Price Term" indicates explicitly that the parties do not necessarily need to reach agreement on a price in order to have an enforceable contract. Although this clause promotes flexibility in setting prices, the possibility of being charged an unacceptable price increases. If the contract indicates that the price is to be determined at some point in the future or by some other mechanism, two basic requirements must be satisfied.[14] First, both parties must intend to make a binding contract even though the price remains open. Second, there must be some "reasonably certain basis for giving relief (or determining value)."

A purchasing manager who is in doubt as to whether an enforceable contract might have been reached without agreeing upon a price, should indicate in any correspondence with the supplier that no contract or agreement exists unless there is agreement on a specific price.

Boilerplate Contract Terms and Conditions In addition to the negotiated terms of price determination, description of the goods, delivery, and quantity, a number of other standard terms and conditions (often referred to as *boilerplate*) are typically included in most commercial contracts and purchase order agreements. Usually preprinted on the back of forms used by the purchaser (and the seller), these terms and conditions are intended to provide a measure of protection for the purchaser against undesirable actions by a supplier, and require the supplier to conform to certain business practices and procedures.

Since boilerplate language and the wording of other preprinted purchase order and sales documents may often conflict, it is important to communicate clearly with suppliers *exactly* which terms are in effect. (If in doubt, don't sign it and assume that things can be worked out later!) Many purchase orders are placed over the telephone, in person, and increasingly, through the Internet; purchasing managers must thus be aware of the potential pitfalls of oral contracts. It is important to remember that a contract is a relationship—not a physical entity—between the parties involved. When the contract is reduced to writing, the written document is not the actual contract but simply hard evidence of the existence of the underlying contractual relationship. Also, whenever a contract is reduced to writing, the written document supersedes all previous oral evidence. It is therefore important to ensure that all relevant negotiated data and warranty-related oral statements deemed to be part of the agreement are also reduced to writing in the contract. The UCC under section 2-201 specifies the following:[15]

- In order for a contract to exist, there must normally be some written (and signed) notation if the value of the order for the sale of goods is $500 or more.
- If the supplier provides a written confirmation memorandum that is not in accordance with the purchaser's understanding of an oral order, the purchaser must give a notice of objection to the supplier within ten days of receipt of the memorandum.

A good example of this situation might occur when you are purchasing a new or used vehicle. The salesperson may exaggerate the virtues of a particular car while

Alabama Bill Allows Longer-Term Contracts

Alabama public supply managers, who have been lobbying vigorously to extend the state's three-year contract limit for suppliers, have succeeded in their efforts. A recent bill (labeled SB 260) passed by the Alabama state legislature will amend the state law to allow contracts to be assigned for extended periods under certain conditions. According to SB 260, "any contract that generates funds or will reduce annual costs by awarding the contract for a longer term than a period of three years which is let by or on behalf of a state two-year or four-year college or university may be let for periods not greater than 10 years." The bill also allows contracts previously awarded for less than 10 years to be extended up to 10 years from the initial award, provided the contract terms are not altered or renegotiated during the extended period. The passing of the bill marks a victory for Alabama supply managers who wish to work more strategically with their suppliers to harness greater value and cost savings.

Source: Anonymous, *Purchasing Today* (August 2000): 4.

walking around the lot, yet when you sit down to review the contract, you may find that many of the "promises" are no longer in writing. In order to determine the true conditions of the sale, you may need to write down exactly what you have been told, and ask for the salesperson's written signature underneath your notes while still out on the lot.

CANCELLATION OF ORDERS AND BREACH OF CONTRACT

A good contract will protect the interests and rights of both buyer and seller. As a result, contractual obligations are equally binding upon both parties to the agreement. People cannot go around arbitrarily canceling or defaulting on their contracts. Actress Kim Bassinger found this out when she signed a contract for a major movie and decided she wasn't going to do it at the last minute. She was subsequently sued and lost in court, and was required to pay millions of dollars in losses to the studio. In some instances, however, one of the parties to a contractual arrangement may seek to cancel the agreement after it has been made. In other cases, the supplier simply fails to perform in the manner agreed to in the contract. Under these conditions, the buyer will always go back to the original contract to determine what the potential remedies are to these situations. If they are not spelled out in detail, the UCC once again provides some help.

Cancellation of Orders

Contract cancellations can generally be classified into three categories: (1) cancellation for default, (2) cancellation for convenience of the purchaser ("anticipatory breach"), or (3) cancellation by mutual consent.

Cancellation for default can be defined as failure of one of the parties to live up to the terms and conditions of the contract. Supplier actions that can result in this type of breach of contract include late deliveries, failing to meet product specifications, or otherwise failing to perform in accordance with contract provisions. The types of damages that might be awarded include production cost penalties, additional overtime, or expedited transportation costs. In actual practice, more effective settlements can be reached through negotiation with the supplier rather than through the litigation process.

Cancellation for the convenience of the purchaser, or *anticipatory breach,* makes the purchaser liable for any resulting injury to the supplier. A general rule here is that the supplier should not be called upon to incur any loss due to the purchaser's default. Generally speaking, purchasers should stay away from this term altogether in their purchase contracts. The term is highly interpretable in court and can result in any number of negative actions.

Cancellation by mutual consent indicates that cancellation of a previously agreed-upon contract does not automatically lead to legal action. If both parties mutually agree to terminate the agreement, then they have, in effect, created another contract with the intent of nullifying the first agreement. If there is no potential loss, the supplier will often accept a purchaser's cancellation in good faith as a normal risk of doing business. Even when suppliers have purchased special components or materials in the anticipation of fulfilling their responsibilities under the agreement, the parties can usually reach a mutually agreeable resolution through the process of negotiation rather than through litigation.

Breach of Contract

Under a commercial contract, the supplier is obligated to deliver the goods according to the contract's terms and conditions, and the purchaser is likewise obligated to accept and tender payment for the goods according to the terms of the agreement. A breach of contract occurs when either party fails to perform the obligations due under the contract (without a valid or legal justification). A breach may entitle the offended party to certain remedies or damages (discussed in greater detail in the next section). For example:

Mimi's wholesale video store and Betsy now have a valid contract. Betsy has promised to buy 1,000 videotapes for $15 apiece, and Mimi has promised to deliver them to Betsy's place of business on February 1. However, Mimi never shows up with the delivery.

Mimi may indeed be liable for breach of contract. However, one of the basic rules of the UCC is that each party to a contract must give the other party the total time agreed upon to complete his or her obligations under the contract.

Buyers should avoid the practice of routinely tolerating suppliers that breach purchase contracts. Doing so may result in the buyer forfeiting the right to legal action. If you, as the purchaser, have systematically accepted late deliveries from a supplier in the past and continue to accept late deliveries even though you must expedite late shipments, then you may have waived your right to pursue legal action for damages caused by the late shipments. For example:

A buyer and a supplier have been doing business for several years. During the past year, approximately one-third of the shipments from the supplier arrived a week or so late, but the buyer accepted them without serious complaints. In the eyes of the law, these acceptances by the buyer may well have set a precedent that waives the buyer's rights to timely delivery on future contracts.

To regain his or her legal rights, the buyer must give explicit written notice to the supplier and provide the supplier a reasonable period of time to gear up to meet the new delivery requirements. The new contract should also include the minimal lead time required for design changes, etc.

In major contracts, it is often apparent that a breach of contract may create major headaches for either the buyer or supplier; the level of damages in such cases is difficult to determine. To avoid this confusion, many organizations include an up-front termination or liquidated damages provision in the contract at the time of negotiation. This type of provision stipulates the mechanism to be used in determining any costs and damages to the injured party in the event of a breach of contract. Once again, spelling it out in the contract helps avoid confusion later on.

Damages

The concept of damages in the UCC is based on the remedy of a party being "made whole." In other words, a purchaser who is damaged by a breach of contract must receive damages that bring the purchaser back to the position where he or she would have been if the breach had not occurred. Damages include either actual damages (which include losses that are real, known, or can be reasonably estimated), as well as punitive damages (extra money over and above as "punishment" for the defendant's bad behavior). The UCC is quite clear on the point that punitive damages are not allowed, even if such a provision is contained in the contract. There are essentially three types of damages available to the purchaser:

- *Restitution:* Money the plaintiff actually paid to the defendant in connection with the contract.
- *Reliance:* Money the plaintiff lost because he or she was relying on the contract, depending on the defendant to live up to their obligations under the contract.
- *Expectancy:* Money the plaintiff was hoping to gain from the contract.

Back at Mimi's wholesale video store, Mimi and Betsy had a valid contract. Betsy promised to buy 1,000 videotapes for $15 apiece, and Mimi promised to deliver them to Betsy's place of business. Betsy gave Mimi $2,000 as a down payment on the delivery. Betsy also spent $5,000 building new shelves in her retail video store to hold the tapes. Finally, Betsy expected to make *a profit of $20,000 after expenses from selling and/or renting the tapes to her customers. However, Mimi never delivers the tapes, and Betsy sues for breach of contract. What damages is she entitled to?*

Betsy can sue for $2,000 in restitution damages for loss of the down payment, $5,000 in reliance damages for the shelves, and $20,000 in expectancy damages for the $20,000 in profits she expected to make (for a total of $27,000).

When calculating damages, there are various methods of doing so.[16] General damages are equal to the difference between the value of the purchased goods at the time of delivery against the goods' value at the time of specified delivery. Incidental damages include expenses reasonably incurred in inspection, receipt, transportation, and the care and custody of goods appropriately rejected by the purchaser. Consequential damages are those expenses incurred by the purchaser because the goods were not delivered when expected or as specified. Liquidation damages are those that result if the terms of the contract are not fulfilled and, as discussed above under remedies, are typically defined prior to the breach under the terms of the contract.

Acceptance and Rejection of Goods

The UCC allows the purchaser to accept part of the shipment and reject the remainder for cause, or to accept or reject the entire shipment. After the point of acceptance, the supplier's rights increase and the purchaser's rights decrease. Once the purchaser accepts the goods, there is only one recourse—to make a claim against the supplier. The UCC specifies that the purchaser does not have the legal right to withhold payment from the supplier once acceptance has been made. The purchaser also does not have the right at this point to send the goods back unless the supplier consents to this action.

The legal concept of acceptance is closely related to the concept of inspection. Purchasers have a legitimate right to inspect contracted goods before accepting or rejecting them. The law is quite explicit when it states that the purchaser accept the goods within a reasonable time whether or not the goods are physically inspected. Obvious defects must be discovered and rejected within this reasonable time frame, or the purchaser has no recourse against the seller. "Latent" defects are those that could not have been easily discovered during an inspection and do not fall under this rule. In certain limited situations, the purchaser is able to revoke an acceptance of delivered goods. A purchaser may revoke a prior acceptance if a problem is discovered that substantially impairs the value of the goods.

When the goods delivered by the supplier are actually rejected by the purchaser due to nonconformance, the purchaser must provide notice to the supplier within a reasonable period of time. The purchaser should be specific in notifying the supplier that he or she is in breach of contract. General statements about the problems at hand without stating that the supplier is considered in breach of contract are not adequate notification. The exact terms "breach of contract" must be used, or the purchaser stands to lose his or her right to recourse from the supplier.

Once goods are accepted there are two obligations that the purchaser must meet in order to recover his or her rights. First, the purchaser must carry the burden of proof that the goods did not conform to the terms and conditions of the contract. Second, the purchaser must, within a reasonable time after the breach is discovered, notify the supplier of that breach or lose the chance for remedy.

Acceptance of the contracted goods by the purchaser means that ownership of the goods has been transferred. There are no rituals or formalities required to make the transfer of ownership. Any words or acts by the purchaser that provide an indication of the purchaser's intention to transfer ownership are enough to effect the transfer. Even though the goods may have been formally rejected by the purchaser, actions typifying ownership may indicate that acceptance has instead been accomplished.

In order to prevent or mitigate problems arising from the acceptance or rejection of goods, a number of steps to manage the acceptance process can be implemented by the purchaser:[17]

- The receiving department should stamp all receipts of goods with a statement something to the effect of "Received subject to inspection, count, and testing."
- A thorough set of purchase order terms and conditions should indicate that all receipts from suppliers are subject to inspection, count, and testing.
- All delivered goods should be inspected as quickly as possible, and ideally, immediately upon delivery.
- If goods are not inspected until they are used, it is a good idea to maintain a stock rotation system to ensure that older quantities of goods are used first.
- In some cases, purchasers may want to consider putting language in their purchase order terms and conditions that defines the reasonable time for inspection and acceptance.
- An internal reporting system should be set up to ensure that defects encountered in the organization are reported to the purchasing department within a reasonable time so that remedies can be pursued.
- Contracts for such items as production equipment should contain a clause stating that acceptance will not be made until the equipment has been installed and run satisfactorily for a certain period of time.
- For hardware- and software-related contracts, the purchaser should carefully define the acceptance criteria and notify the supplier of the specific process that this equipment and software will be subjected to.

Honest Mistakes

Sometimes, in spite of the best efforts of the purchaser and the supplier, honest mistakes occur when parties draw up a purchase agreement. In such instances, careful consideration of all the circumstances are necessary to determine whether or not the resulting contract is valid or invalid. Generally, honest mistakes by a single party to the contract will *not* void the contract. If the other party was truly unaware of the mistake, then the contract is still intact. Note that mistakes made by *both* parties also do not necessarily affect the validity of the contract.

SOURCING SNAPSHOT

A Breach of Contract for Turkish Tapioca

International Agri Trade (a U.S. company) sold Bern Dis, a Turkish importer, some tapioca on the terms of the Grain and Feed Train Association (GAFTA) (an international law) form 100. The delivery was to be made to Bern Dis in Turkey, but after the contract was made, the Turkish government banned the import of tapioca, and an import license was refused. The seller did not unload the tapioca, and told the buyer that the vessel had sailed, that it held the buyer for all transportation costs involved, and that it would also not pay for the tapioca. GAFTA form 100 stated that "the party other than the defaulter shall . . . have the right . . . to sell or purchase . . . against the defaulter, and such sale or purchase shall establish the default price. Further, the damages payable shall be based on the difference between the contract price and the default price established upon the actual or estimated value of the goods on the date of default." The High Court of Turkey ruled that these damages were recoverable on normal contractual provisions, regardless of GAFTA form 100. This was based on Section 50 of the International Sale of Goods Act 1979 which provides that "the measure of damages is the estimated loss directly and naturally resulting, in the ordinary course of events, from the buyer's breach of contract." In other words, if there is an available market for the goods in question, damages are to be worked out by looking at the difference between the contract price and the market price. In the end, the High Court ruled that the basic principle set out in the Sale of Goods Act overruled Clause 28 from GAFTA, which was not clear enough. Specifically, the words "shall be based on" in Clause 28 are not the same as "shall be limited to." Also, the buyer's interpretation could produce anomalous results. For example, if the market value and the contract value of the goods on the day of default were the same, the seller would get nothing, even if it had to cancel the charter of a vessel.

Source: Anonymous, *Purchasing Today* (August 2000): 6.

Mistakes are not covered under the UCC. The parties must rely on traditional contract law to solve any dispute resulting from a mistake. "As a general rule, a party will not be given relief against a mistake induced by his own negligence. But the rule is not inflexible and in many cases relief may be granted although the mistake involved some element of negligence, particularly when the other party has been in no way prejudiced." [18] The rules for determining whether or not a contract exists after a mistake has been made are the basic fairness rules. The judicial system will more than likely allow a supplier to be absolved from the contract due to a mistake if the supplier gave the purchaser notification of the mistake before the purchaser relied on the bid. Buyers should therefore attempt to minimize the occurrence of contractual mistakes.

PATENTS AND INTELLECTUAL PROPERTY

As suppliers become increasingly integrated in new-product development, intellectual property agreements are becoming the norm. The U.S. Constitution provides the framework for the intellectual property legal system, including patent and copyright law, as we know it today through Article 1, Section 8, Clause 8, which says that "Congress shall have the Power . . . To promote the Progress of Science and useful Arts, by securing for limited Times to Authors and Inventors the exclusive Right to their respective Writings and Discoveries."[19] There are three kinds of intellectual property in the United States: (1) patents, (2) copyrights, and (3) trade secrets. Patent law has been established in several federal patent statutes including the Patent Act of 1790, 35 U.S.C. Section 1, and companion laws. Copyright law is founded in the federal statutes, particularly in the Copyright Act of 1976. Federal patent and copyright laws overrule any contradictory state statutes. By contrast, trade secret law is grounded in common law and is intended to protect unique ideas that would not otherwise have legal protection under patent and copyright law. Since common law varies by state, there is some variance in actual statutes. However, most states have created laws that are very similar.

In its most basic form, a *patent* is an agreement between the inventor and the federal government. The inventor receives the right to exclusive use of his or her invention for a period of *seventeen years* in exchange for a full public disclosure of that invention. Although the inventor has exclusive rights (i.e., a monopoly) to the invention during the patent period, others gain that right to the benefits of the invention following expiration of the protection period, thereby providing public benefit. A U.S. patent is applicable only to the inventor's exclusive use within the borders of the United States. Inventors wishing to expand their patent protection to other countries must file appropriate patent applications in each country in which protection is desired. Note that in some countries such as China and India, copyrights and patents may not be recognized at all.

A firm needs to protect itself from inadvertent patent infringement whenever it purchases a product from a supplier. This can best be done by including a patent indemnification clause in all purchasing documents. This clause should consist of three parts:

1. An indemnification, which seeks the supplier's assurances that the goods being contracted for do not infringe on any other party's patents
2. The right to require the supplier to defend any patent infringement suit itself
3. The right to have the purchaser's own attorneys involved in defense of any lawsuit concerning patent infringement

The UCC provides minimal protection for the purchasers in defending themselves against legal actions stemming from patent infringement. Therefore, indemnification agreements should be included in contracts with suppliers whenever possible.

A *copyright* is designed to afford protection for persons who create such original works as books, software, songs, and films. Copyright law does not require a formal application as does patent law. In addition, it is not necessary for the copyright originator to place any legend or indication on the protected material indicating that the material is copyrighted. Copyright is automatically assumed. However, most legal experts recommend that some sort of language in the form of a copyright notice be included on any works desired to be protected, along with the copyright symbol,©. This notice provides evidence that the creator of the article in question intends to maintain copyright privileges in the event of infringement.

A *trade secret* (also known as *confidential information*) is a very broad category of intellectual property. Virtually any information believed to be confidential and important to an organization can be deemed to be a trade secret or confidential information. Resources as diverse as formulas, supplier and customer lists, procedures, and training programs could all be regarded as trade secrets. In order to receive trade secret protection under the law, the organization must take steps to minimize or preclude the distribution of its sensitive information. The information must also be deemed to possess the following three characteristics:

- It is economically valuable.
- It is not generally known.
- It is kept as a secret.

Trade secret protection becomes essentially self-serving through the actions of the organization itself. For instance, if information that could otherwise be considered trade secrets is not protected through devices such as limited access or other security precautions, then the courts have ruled that this information is not confidential and, therefore, not entitled to protection. This test of confidential information can also be applied to any information that suppliers provide to the purchasing firm through the normal course of business dealings. As before, however, the supplier must make it known that the information is proprietary and is to be kept confidential. As a precaution, any information provided to a supplier should be accompanied by notification that the information is provided in confidence and should be treated as such by the supplier. This is typically known as a *nondisclosure agreement* (NDA). See Exhibit 16.4 for an example of a nondisclosure agreement.

OTHER LAWS AFFECTING PURCHASING

Laws Affecting Global Purchasing

Many laws—U.S., foreign, and international—affect global commerce. The following briefly summarizes some of the laws that can affect a purchaser's international business dealings.[20]

Foreign Corrupt Practices Act This law prohibits payments (such as bribes) that might benefit a foreign official personally. While usually pertaining to sellers, purchasers should understand this law's provisions so they can recognize situations addressed by the act.

EXHIBIT 16.4   *Nondisclosure Agreement*

Supplier's Name
Supplier's Address
City, State, Zip Code

Re: *Nondisclosure Agreement*

 In conjunction with recent discussions, our Company has disclosed and it is anticipated in the future that our Company will disclose to your company or your company will observe, or come in contact with certain confidential information that is the property of our Company. This information will include, without limitation, certain proprietary items related to our Company's know-how, processes, machinery, and manufacturing aspects of our Company's business.

 In consideration thereof, it is our understanding that except as hereafter specifically authorized in writing by our Company, your company shall not disclose to any party (a) the fact that it is assisting our Company in this matter; (b) any confidential information heretofore or hereafter disclosed by our Company to your company or that your company observes or comes in contact with, not in the possession of your company prior to the date of such disclosure, observance, or contact; or (c) any marketing, financial, or technical information developed or generated by your company for our Company at our request and direct or indirect expense. Your company shall neither use nor furnish to any party any equipment or material embodying or made by the use of such information, provided however, that:

1. Should any of the aforesaid information be published or otherwise made available to the public through sources that are entitled to disclose the same, and should your company demonstrate to our Company that it has obtained said information from a source available to the public, then in that event your company shall be free with respect to this understanding to disclose said information to any party;

2. Your company understands that nothing herein shall be construed to grant any right or license under any industrial property rights (patents, trademarks, and copyrights) of our Company.

Will you please indicate your company's concurrence in the foregoing understanding by signing and returning to us the enclosed duplicate of this letter.

Very truly yours,

_____

(Name and title)

XXX:xxx

Accepted By: _____

Name:_____

Title:_____

Date:_____

Anti–Boycott Legislation Various laws address doing business with countries that support the boycott of one nation against another. Examples include the boycott of Israel by Arab countries and the boycott of Taiwan by mainland China. These laws require reporting of any request to participate in a boycott, which purchasers often fail to do.

Export Administration Act Various laws and regulations govern, and sometimes even restrict, the export of goods, information, and services. Purchasers may not perceive that they are engaged in exporting. However, the law views certain types of drawings, specifications, and prototypes forwarded to a foreign entity as restricted exports of technology. Purchasers are urged to seek the advice of an expert when questions arise in this area.

Customs Laws This body of law addresses the importation of goods into the United States. Customs brokers who are familiar with customs laws can be quite valuable in understanding the rules and regulations governing importation.

Foreign Laws In addition to the U.S. laws that apply to foreign transactions, the laws and regulations of other countries involved in a business transaction may also apply. These laws will likely address contract law, export control, currency control, and criminal law. Some transactions could be illegal if structured in a certain manner.

International Laws Other laws may apply to a business transaction that are not part of any specific country's laws and regulations. Maritime laws are a good example of international laws that affect international commerce. Several international documents are also pertinent to international transactions. These include *The United Nations Convention on Contracts for International Sale of Goods* (CISG) and *International Contracting Terms* (INCOTERMS).

Laws Affecting Antitrust and Unfair Trade Practices

A number of federal laws deal with antitrust and competitive practices of interstate commerce. Each law seeks to promote the fair conduct of business. While most of these laws apply to the conduct of the seller, some provisions apply directly or indirectly to purchasers.

Sherman Antitrust Act (1898) This law prohibits actions that are "in constraint of trade" or actions that attempt to monopolize a market or create a monopoly. Legal actions under this law typically involve price fixing or other forms of collusion among sellers. However, the law also prohibits reciprocity or reciprocal purchase agreements, which was discussed in the ethics section.

Federal Trade Commission Act (1914) This act authorizes the Federal Trade Commission to interpret trade legislation, including the provisions of the Sherman Antitrust Act that deal with restraint of trade. The FTCA also addresses unfair competition and unfair or deceptive trade practices.

Clayton Antitrust Act (1914) This law makes price discrimination illegal and prohibits sellers from exclusive arrangements with purchasers and/or product distributors.

Robinson-Patman Act (1936) This law further addresses the issue of price discrimination. It prohibits sellers from offering a discriminatory price where the effect of discrimination may limit competition or create a monopoly. There is also a provision that prohibits purchasers from inducing a discriminatory price. While a seller may legally lower price as a concession during negotiations, the purchaser should not mislead or trick the seller, thus resulting in a price that is discriminatory to other buyers in the market.

The laws governing purchasing are complex and varied. Other laws address environmental and labor issues. This overview simply points out that today's purchaser must be aware of the laws and regulations governing domestic and international purchasing. A purchaser is urged to discuss with legal counsel any questions that arise during the performance of job responsibilities. Ignorance of the law is not a valid defense.

GOOD PRACTICE EXAMPLE
Tracking Ethics Electronically at Lockheed Martin

■ ■ ■

Lockheed Martin Corporation is turning business ethics into rocket science. While some companies worry about workers wasting time on the Web, the aerospace giant is aggressively steering them into cyberspace as part of a broad program—born of a bribery scandal—to audit, record, and perfect the measurement of employee morals. Using internal computer programs with names like Merlin and Qwizard, many of Lockheed Martin's 160,000 employees go online these days for step-by-step training on ethics and legal compliance. The system records each time an employee completes one of the sessions, which range from sexual harassment and insider trading to kickbacks and gratuities. It is also tracking the number of days to complete an internal investigation of ethics violations (30.4), people fired for ethics violations since 1995 (217), and percentage of ethics allegations involving conflicts of interest (4.8%).

One big reason for these complex ethics metrics is legal protection in the event the company faces charges. Lockheed Martin did not have such a sophisticated program in place in 1995, when, on the eve of its merger with Martin Marietta Corporation, it agreed to pay a $24.8 million fine and plead guilty to conspiring to violate U.S. antibribery laws. Lockheed admitted that it illegally paid $1 million to an Egyptian lawmaker in 1990 for helping sell its C-130 aircraft in that country. To keep from losing government contracts, Lockheed Martin submitted to an administrative agreement that amounted to a three-year probationary period. The company was required to turn over to the U.S. Air Force periodic ethics reports, including details of ethical complaints made to its employee hotline and other misconduct allegations. This is a critical element for the survival of the company—fully 70% of its $26.3 billion in sales comes solely from the U.S. government. As part of the training, the ethics department developed numerous "interactive" training sessions on security, software-licensing compliance, and labor charging. The courses, with actors playing out hypothetical cases, were produced for CD-ROMS. Clicking along at a workstation, an employee usually takes about 45 minutes to complete a session. A sample question from the kickback-and-gratuity clinic:

A kickback may be in the form of:

a.   Cash
b.   Gift to a family member
c.   Donation to a charity at your request
d.   All of the above [the correct answer]

These actions have made a good impression on the U.S. Air Force. Steve Shaw, the deputy general counsel who held a debarment ax over Lockheed Martin until the probationary period ended last year, says he is pleased the company is still keeping close statistical tabs on ethical conduct and compliance training. He adds: "To me, that says a lot about a company that large. You'll always have people who will make mistakes." ■

Source: Adapted from Michael McCarthy, "How One Firm Tracks Ethics Electronically," *Wall Street Journal*, October 21, 1999, B1.

CONCLUSION

The field of purchasing is dynamic and changing rapidly. When dealing with suppliers in contract negotiations, contract management, breach of contracts, potential damages, and patent or trade secret disputes, purchasing managers must be sure to stipulate the appropriate terms and conditions. Nevertheless, many legal disputes are being handled through discussions with suppliers instead of being referred to legal departments. Both purchasing managers and suppliers also generally prefer using negotiation as an alternative to court decisions. In either case, purchasing managers must be aware of the potential pitfalls implicit in standard legal terminology and must seek to prevent the occurrence of such disputes. An operational rule of thumb is when in doubt, err on the side of prudence.

DISCUSSION QUESTIONS

1.   Why is it important for purchasing managers to understand the law? Isn't this the business of lawyers?
2.   What is the relationship between contract law, the UCC, and commercial law?

3.   What does the term "agent" mean? Under what conditions can a purchasing agent be held personally responsible for "abusing" his or her position?

4.   Suppose you arrive at a verbal agreement with someone on the price of purchasing his or her vehicle. Under what conditions have you reached an enforceable contract?

5.   Suppose you sign a contract with a supplier for $5,000 worth of steel castings. You tell the supplier that you are only authorized to sign contracts for $4,000 without approval from the comptroller of your company, but the supplier agrees anyway. Later, you find out that you only need $2,500 worth of castings. How many dollars worth of castings are you legally bound to purchase from the supplier?

6.   Discuss the concept of ethics. Why is the purchasing profession particularly sensitive to this topic?

7.   What are the different risks associated with unethical behavior?

8.   Discuss the reasons why some issues that confront a buyer are not often clear from an ethical perspective.

9.   What should a buyer do if he or she suspects a seller of unethically trying to influence the buyer?

10.   What is the purpose of a professional code of purchasing ethics?

11.   When interacting with a supplier or potential supplier, why do many firms allow lunch meetings between a buyer and seller but prohibit dinners?

12.   Why is it important for a firm to have a written ethics policy? What is the importance of top management's commitment to the policy?

13.   Discuss some of the steps a firm can take to promote ethical behavior. Which of the steps do you believe are the most important?

14.   What are the most important federal laws related to purchasing? Which part of the purchasing manager's job is most affected by these laws?

15.   A seller verbally tells you that his cleaning product can remove any stain from the surface of a vehicle. You later find out that this is not the case. In fact, you find that the cleaning product does not work very well at all in removing paint stains. Do you have a legal claim against this seller? What types of damages are you entitled to?

16.   In the above case, the seller points to the fine print on the product, which states that the product can only be used in temperatures above 40 degrees Fahrenheit. You were using it in temperatures of 35 degrees. Do you have a claim?

17.   What are the important items that should be used any time you decide to enter into a long-term contract (e.g., more than one year) with a supplier?

18.   Briefly, what is the Uniform Commercial Code? Is it enforceable in other countries? Is it enforceable in all U.S. states?

19.   Suppose a supplier gives you a price on a contract and then later comes back and claims that he mistakenly wrote down the wrong price. Do you have the right to sue the supplier over breach of contract? What conditions are important here?

20.   How long do you have to correct overcharges in freight billing?

21.   Increasingly, companies are involving suppliers in new-product development efforts, and may be performing a great deal of design work (in addition to manufacturing of the product). What are some of the important legal terms that should be included in a contract with such a supplier?

ADDITIONAL READINGS

Bailey, Henry J., III and Richard B. Hagedorn. *Secured Transactions in a Nutshell*, 3rd ed. St. Paul, MN: West Publishing, 1988.

Barlow, C. Wayne, and Eisen, Glenn P. *Purchasing Negotiations*. Boston, MA : CBI Publishing, 1983.

Henry, Gabriel. *Practitioner's Guide to the Convention on Contracts for the International Sale of Goods (CISG) and the Uniform Commercial Code (UCC)*. New York: Oceana Publishing, 1994.

Meverowitz, Steve A. *An Ounce of Prevention: Marketing, Sales, & Advertising Law for Non-lawyers*. Detroit, MI: Gale Research, 1994.

Johnston, Donald F. *Copyright Handbook*. New York: R. R. Bowker, 1978.

Mayer, Jeffrey. "You Can't Always Get What You Want." *Purchasing Today* (August, 2000): 12.

Murray, John. "Contract Was Only a Joke." *Purchasing* (October 1994): 34–36.

"The Terrible Twos: How Articles 2, 2A and the Emerging 2B Are Addressing Common Issues." Presented by the Committee on Uniform Commercial Code and Young Lawyers Division, American Bar Association Section of Business Law, Chicago, 1997.

Woods, John A., ed. *The Purchasing and Supply Yearbook*. New York: McGraw-Hill, 2000.

ENDNOTES

1. William A. Hancock, ed., *The Law of Purchasing*, 2nd ed. (Chesterland, OH: Business Laws, 1989), 30.07.
2. Joseph L. Cavinato, *Purchasing and Materials Management: Integrative Strategies* (St. Paul, MN: West Publishing, 1984), 146.
3. P. J. Haynes and M. M. Helms, "An Ethical Framework for Purchasing Decisions," *Management Decision* (UK) 29, no. 1 (1991): 35; H. Page, "More on Ethics—Helping Your Buyers," *Purchasing World* 30, no. 12 (December 1986): 60.
4. Haynes and Helms, "An Ethical Framework," 36.
5. R. C. Parker, G. C. Fordyce, and K. P. Graham, "Ethics in Purchasing," in *Purchasing Handbook*, L. G. Farrell and L. A. Alijian, ed. (New York: McGraw-Hill, 1982), 7–16.
6. Haynes and Helms, "An Ethical Framework," 36.
7. L. B. Forker and R. L. Janson, "Ethical Practices in Purchasing," *International Journal of Purchasing and Materials Management* 26, no. 1 (Winter 1990): 19–26.
8. Stuart Heinritz, Paul V. Farrell, Larry C. Giunipero, and Michael G. Kolchin, *Purchasing: Principles and Applications*, 8th ed. (Englewood Cliffs, NJ: Prentice-Hall, 1991), 243.
9. Heinritz et al., *Purchasing*, 249–50
10. John Stockton and Frederick Miller, *Sales and Leases of Goods in a Nutshell*, 3rd ed. (St. Paul, MN: West Publishing, 1992) 84–87.
11. Hancock, *The Law of Purchasing*, 30.09.
12. John J. Coyle, Edward J. Bardi, and C. John Langley, Jr., *The Management of Business Logistics*, 4th ed. (St. Paul, MN: West Publishing, 1988), 360.

13. Eberhard E. Scheuing, *Purchasing Management* (Englewood Cliffs, NJ: Prentice-Hall, 1989), 55.
14. Hancock, *The Law of Purchasing*, 7.06
15. Stockton and Miller, *Sales and Leases*, 49–50
16. Cavinato, *Purchasing and Materials Management*, 134.
17. Hancock, *The Law of Purchasing*, 10.18–23
18. Hancock, *The Law of Purchasing*, 22.05–06.
19. Earl W. Kintner and Jack L. Lahr, *An Intellectual Property Law Primer* (New York: Macmillan, 1975), 6.
20. Martin J. Cabarra, J.D., and Ernest Gabbard, J.D., "What's on the Books: Other Laws Affecting Purchasing and Supply," *The Purchasing and Supply Yearbook*, ed. John A. Woods (New York: McGraw-Hill, 2000), 332–39.

17 MANAGING SUPPLY CHAIN INVENTORY

A Great Renewal at A&P

The Great Atlantic & Pacific Tea Company, Inc. (A&P) announced the next phase of its ongoing Project Great Renewal—an after-tax investment of approximately $250 million over four years to develop a state-of-the-art supply chain and business operations technology system. Christian Haub, president and chief executive officer, said the initiative will upgrade all processes and business systems related to the flow of information and products between A&P-operated offices, distribution points, and stores, and between A&P and its suppliers.

A&P selected IBM as its strategic partner for Project Great Renewal to implement business process changes, a new application portfolio and technical architecture, and assist in project and change management. A&P expects to improve margins, lower operating costs, reduce working capital through better management of inventory, and improve product availability. When this new phase of Project Great Renewal has been fully implemented, the Company anticipates improvement of ongoing annual pre-tax operating income of approximately $100 million. A&P also said it expects these initiatives will enhance its ability to increase sales by attracting more customers and increasing sales per transaction.

Initial work on Project Great Renewal will focus on reengineering the systems that support purchasing, inventory management and control, warehouse and transportation management, category management, pricing, promotion analysis, store space allocation, automatic replenishment, direct store delivery, and store operations. The resulting new technology and communication platform also will enable A&P to utilize Internet-based, business-to-business (B2B) e-commerce with its suppliers to improve supply chain and inventory efficiencies and develop more customer-focused and mutually profitable supplier relationships.

In support of this project, IBM and Retek Inc., a provider of B2B solutions for the global retail marketplace, are working together to create a merchandising solution to help food and drug retailers determine the right mix of products, pricing, and promotions across all channels, including store, telephone, Internet, and catalog sales. A&P will be the first retailer to use this new merchandising solution as part of its new business operations and technology system.

Merchandising solutions allow retailers to enhance customer service by improving all aspects of the supply chain, including purchasing, replenishment, space allocation, receiving, inventory management, and price/promotion management. The new offering will be developed using IBM's Application Framework for e-business, a technology roadmap with IBM's software that helps developers integrate Internet technologies with traditional information technology.

In October 1999, IBM began working with A&P senior management to build a comprehensive business case for the transformation of A&P's supply chain and business operations systems as the next phase of Project Great Renewal. This investment in A&P's future

→ → →

follows the people and store development improvements that were recently launched. It represents the third critical component of the Great Renewal strategy charted in 1998. A&P expects these combined efforts to drive top (sales) and bottom line (profitability) improvements by maximizing the impact and productivity of its market offering.

Source: Adapted from "A&P Launches Phase II of Project Great Renewal; Will Upgrade Supply Chain Business Process Systems," *Business Wire* (March 13, 2000).

If U.S. companies learned anything over the last ten years, it is that managing inventory efficiently and effectively is central to remaining competitive, as the opening vignette illustrates. Although maintaining high levels of inventory was an accepted practice for many years, it resulted in high carrying costs, reduced profit, and diminished market share. Furthermore, high inventory levels often hid other problems such as poor material quality, inaccurate demand-forecasting systems, and unreliable supplier delivery. To avoid having to deal with these problems, it was often easier to increase safety stock levels or increase the amount ordered from suppliers. Managers felt secure knowing there was more than enough inventory available to support production or customer requirements.

Today's highly competitive world does not allow wasteful inventory management practices. A firm's inventory investment requires close management in which every dollar of inventory investment is compared to its related inventory cost. The driving rule of thumb that underlies modern inventory policies stresses two points:

1. The costs associated with inventory investment should never exceed the benefits derived from the investment.
2. When inventory begins to hide operational problems, the inventory must be eliminated to identify the underlying problems.

The primary objective of this chapter is to provide an understanding of the importance of managing and controlling supply chain inventory investment. In the following sections, we discuss the principles and functions of inventory, the factors leading to inventory waste, the concept of the lean supply chain, and the major approaches for controlling inventory investment. The chapter concludes with a Good Practice Example involving inventory management.

UNDERSTANDING SUPPLY CHAIN INVENTORY

The best place to start our discussion of supply chain inventory is to understand the basic principles of inventory management. This section discusses the different types of inventory, the costs associated with holding inventory, and the changing view of inventory as a financial and operating liability rather than asset.

Types of Inventory

Inventory represents the largest single investment in assets for most manufacturers, wholesalers, and retailers. The five primary categories of inventory include (1) raw material and semifinished inventory; (2) work-in-process inventory; (3) finished-goods inventory; (4) maintenance, repair, and operating (MRO) supplies inventory; and (5) in-transit/pipeline inventory.

Raw Material and Semifinished Item Inventory This category includes the items purchased from suppliers or produced internally to directly support production requirements. Raw materials include those items purchased in a bulk or unfinished condition. Bulk quantities of chemicals, resins, or petroleum are examples of purchased raw materials. Semifinished inventory includes those items and components used as inputs during the final production process. Every producer relies on some level of raw material or semifinished inventory to support final production requirements. This type of inventory is managed primarily by purchasing, a material planning group, or supply chain managers.

Work-in-Process Inventory At any given point in time, work-in-process (WIP) is the sum total of inventory within all processing centers. Work-in-process is incomplete—it has not yet been transformed to a saleable finished good. This includes materials that are

- Waiting to be moved to another process
- Currently being worked on at a work center
- Queuing up at a processing center due to a capacity bottleneck or machine breakdown

If WIP increases over a certain level, this may indicate production bottlenecks or delays. One study found that in most facilities, 36% of WIP inventory is in queue waiting to be worked on, 27% is waiting to be moved to another work area or center, 4% is in the process of being moved, and only 24% is actually in process.[1] If WIP builds up at a workstation, a scheduler may have to reroute the flow of material to another work center.

Finished-Goods Inventory Finished-goods inventory includes completed items or products that are available for shipment or future customer orders. A firm that produces items in anticipation of customer orders should monitor its finished-goods inventory closely. A higher-than-anticipated level of finished goods may mean that a decrease in customer demand is occurring. A lower-than-anticipated finished-goods inventory level may indicate that customer demand is increasing. Either condition may also indicate that the forecasts of anticipated customer demand do not match current output levels.

When firms produce goods in anticipation of future customer orders, they are operating in a make-to-stock environment. They expect to hold finished inventory in anticipation of future demand. When firms produce in response to a customer order,

SOURCING SNAPSHOT

U.S. Technology Industry Leads in Inventory Management

The U.S. technology industry has led in inventory performance improvement over Japan and Europe for the past five years, according to a recent study by management consultants PRTM. Inventory turns for U.S. companies increased to an overall average of 5.4 per year in 1998, up from 4.8 turns in 1997. Inventory turns for Japanese companies decreased to 4.4 turns from 4.6, and European companies hit 3.9 turns, up from 3.8.

The inventory performance improvement trend in the United States has been driven by the need to support profit margins, as overall profit growth has dwindled from a high of nearly 15% per year to just over 6%. Emphasis on inventory improvement is no surprise, given the important role inventory plays in creating an efficient supply chain and the amount of attention given to supply chain management.

Traditional reasons for holding inventory are being challenged in today's business world. The movement of inventory upstream in the supply chain is being enabled through the use of advanced information-management tools and techniques, such as e-commerce, as well as redesigned business processes oriented toward an integrated supply chain. Companies no longer have to have physical possession of their inventory to achieve the optimum balance that will maximize profitability. Leading companies have significantly lowered their "four wall" inventory levels by partnering with suppliers, and have turned inventory levels from a cost to be controlled to an operating philosophy that is a competitive advantage.

Source: Adapted from *Business Wire*, February 29, 2000.

they are operating in a make-to-order environment. Just-in-time firms usually operate in a make-to-order environment.

Maintenance, Repair, and Operating Supplies Inventory MRO inventory includes the items used to support production and operations. These items are not physically part of a finished product but are critical for the continuous operation of plant, equipment, and offices. The Good Practice Example at the end of this chapter summarizes one company's success at managing this category of inventory. Examples of MRO inventory include office supplies, spare parts, tools, and computers.

Pipeline/In-Transit Inventory This inventory is in transit to a customer or is located throughout distribution channels. Most consumable goods inventory is either on trucks or on grocery store shelves. In fact, grocery stores only provide a shelf for the product but do not own any of the inventory. The supplying company or distributor owns the inventory, which receives payment when the consumer buys the product.

Inventory-Related Costs

One of the drawbacks of holding excessive inventory is the effect this has on a firm's working capital—the funds committed to operating a business, including the purchase and holding of inventory. If we hold excessive inventory, then funds are tied up unnecessarily. These funds could likely have been used more productively elsewhere. Ordering and carrying physical inventory results in a number of costs. It is critical to identify these costs so they can be better managed.

Unit Costs   The most basic and the easiest inventory-related cost to quantify and track is unit cost. We can view the calculation of unit costs in several ways. First, each item or good purchased from a supplier or another internal facility has a related unit cost, which is the price a firm pays. Second, a finished product has a unit cost. The calculation of this cost may be more complex. Besides the direct material used to manufacture the finished product, the product also has a labor cost and allocated overhead. Cost accountants are largely responsible for identifying and assigning these costs.

Ordering Costs   Ordering costs are a composite of the costs associated with the release of a material order. These costs may include the cost of generating and sending a material release, transportation costs, and any other cost connected with acquiring a good. If a firm produces an item or good itself, the ordering cost will also include machine setup costs.

Carrying Costs   Carrying costs consist of three separate components: (1) cost of capital; (2) cost of storage; and (3) the costs of obsolescence, deterioration, and loss. The dollar amount invested in physical inventory has an opportunity cost associated with it. Resources committed to inventory are not available for other economic uses. Therefore, committing financial resources to holding physical inventory creates an inventory-carrying cost.

The physical storing of inventory creates costs, including any costs related to storage space, insurance costs, or the cost to maintain the inventory (such as performing cycle counts). Carrying costs vary with the level of inventory, which makes these costs variable. Fixed costs are not included as part of inventory-carrying costs because inventory levels typically have no effect on a fixed cost, at least in the short run.

Holding inventory also increases the risk of theft, damage, spoilage, and obsolescence. For example, obsolescence is a major issue in the computer industry, where inventory loses about 1.5% of its functionality a week due to rapidly changing technology, making the extended holding of any inventory financially risky.

For most industries, inventory costs typically range from 15% to 25% of the value of the inventory, depending on the company's cost of capital. As shown in Exhibit 17.1, these costs are made up of a variety of different costs that may or may not be formally measured by a company. Carrying cost is calculated as follows:

Inventory carrying cost = Average inventory in units × Unit price × Carrying cost per year

EXHIBIT 17.1   *Inventory-Carrying Cost Components*

Element	Average	Ranges
Capital cost	15.00%	8–40%
Taxes	1.00%	0.5–2%
Insurance	0.05%	0–2%
Obsolescence	1.20%	0.5–2%
Storage	2.00%	0–4%
Total	19.25%	9–50%

Source: Donald J. Bowersox and David J. Closs, *Logistical Management*, McGraw-Hill: New York, 1996, 255.

If a company averages 1,000 units in inventory, for which the unit price is $1.00 per unit, and the annual carrying cost is 25%, the total inventory carrying cost per year for that level of inventory is (1,000 × $1 × .25) = $250.

Quality Costs Quality costs include any cost associated with nonconforming items or goods. The total cost of inventory ownership is more than simply the unit, ordering, and carrying costs. Quantifying the cost of poor quality can help identify the causes of problems. Examples of additional costs due to defective inventory include field failure costs, rework, losses due to poor product yields, inspection, lost production, and warranty costs.

Other Costs The holding of inventory may create other costs. Examples include duties, tooling costs, exchange rate differentials, packaging costs, transportation and logistics costs, and administrative costs.

It is often difficult to quantify the total costs associated with ordering and carrying physical inventory. Part of this results from the historical neglect of calculating total inventory costs along with a lack of systems capable of identifying inventory-related costs. Most cost accounting systems are not yet capable of identifying and assigning the true costs related to maintaining physical inventory. However, accounting systems based on activity-based costing (ABC) principles are increasingly able to quantify the distinct costs associated with holding inventory. The new types of enterprise resource planning (ERP) systems also aid managers to more accurately measure the actual level of inventory on hand, as opposed to "guesstimating."

Inventory Investment—Asset or Liability?

Financial managers have historically viewed inventory as a material asset with value. As Exhibit 17.2 shows, inventory appears under the Current Assets column on balance sheets. Using a financial perspective, an asset is something worth maximizing—it has value to a firm.[2] Unfortunately, this perspective neglects the total cost impact of not controlling inventory investment. From a balance sheet perspective, there is no obvious disadvantage of carrying too much inventory. However,

EXHIBIT 17.2 *Consolidated Balance Sheet*

	June 30	
	2000 (in thousands)	1999 (in thousands)
Current Assets		
Cash and cash equivalents	$ 647,595	$ 408,378
Marketable securities	242,952	421,111
Receivables	638,974	632,870
Inventories	917,495	771,233
Prepaid expenses	84,588	70,211
Total Current Assets	2,531,604	2,303,803
Investments and Other Assets		
Investments in and advances to affiliates	205,835	160,455
Long-term marketable securities	770,808	813,631
Other assets	56,735	40,314
	1,033,378	1,014,400
Property, Plant, and Equipment		
Agricultural processing	2,275,016	1,724,460
Transportation	420,609	407,347
	2,695,625	2,131,807
	$6,260,607	$5,450,010

inventory costs affect financial performance directly. Exhibit 17.3 compares two firms that are identical in every way but one—the amount of inventory they have on hand. This exhibit assumes that having less inventory results in reduced handling and carrying costs. Hence, Firm B has a better profit margin. This exhibit shows the effect of reduced inventory on some key financial performance measures. Firm B has a return on investment that is 23% higher than Firm A due to better inventory management.

Another reason for the historical neglect of inventory investment is related to traditional corporate performance measurement and evaluation systems. Profit and loss performance largely determined a manager's evaluation. Because inventory affects profit and loss indirectly (through material costs), most managers emphasized higher sales as the primary means to increase profit. Only recently have managers begun to pay more attention to inventory as measurement systems include performance ratios such as asset turns, inventory turns, and return on investment figures. The denominator of each of these ratios includes the value of inventories. As the denominator of these ratios increases, the worse the overall performance ratio appears. For companies such as Dell that purchase all of their materials from suppliers and only pay them once the materials have been paid for by their customers, they hold close to zero inventory on-hand. Dell's inventory turns are in the 300 to 400 range per year!

EXHIBIT 17.3   *Linking Supply Chain Management and Financial Performance*

	Firm A	Firm B
Sales	$200	$200
Profit Margin	6%	7%*
Assets		
Cash	$ 10	$ 10
Securities	$ 15	$ 15
Receivables	$ 8	$ 8
Inventories	$ 20	$ 10
Plant and equipment	$ 75	$ 75
Total Assets	**$128**	**$118**
Financial Formulas		
Inventory turns = Sales/ inventories	$200/$20 = 10 turns/year	$200/$10 = 20 turns/year
Asset turnover = Sales/total assets	$200/$128 = 1.56 turns/year	$200/$118 = 1.69 turns/year
Return on investment = Profit margin × Asset turnover	6% × 1.56 = 9.36%	7% × 1.69 = 11.55%

Note: All figures in millions of dollars.

*Assumes more efficient supply chain operations and less waste

The transition from viewing inventory as a material asset to seeing it as a supply chain cost driver has been gradual. When U.S. companies competed mainly against other U.S. companies, an increase in inventory turns (a ratio of sales to average inventory) from five to ten a year appeared impressive. However, the 1990s demonstrated that this level of performance was not enough to compete at world-class levels when many firms maintain minimum inventory. The efficient control of inventory investment is now a major metric that is calculated by all world-class competitors.

The Right Reasons for Carrying Inventory

Physical inventory plays an important role in all supply chains. Without inventory companies cannot build products, provide customer service, or run their operations. When deciding whether or not to maintain an investment in inventory, a single premise can be used to summarize the relative benefits of inventory: *Inventory should be held only when the benefit of holding inventory exceeds the cost of holding the inventory.* Inventory ceases to provide a benefit when it is used to disguise problems or other inefficiencies. The following section examines the proper reasons for carrying inventory, and also suggests a number of situations in which inventory is used inappropriately.

SOURCING SNAPSHOT

Eastman Chemical Manages the Entire Supply Chain

Eastman Chemical, nestled among the eastern Tennessee hills, has processes that use 1,500 different raw materials that arrive from 850 suppliers. To make sure that as little inventory as possible sits idle, Eastman devised what it calls "stream inventory management." "We try to see the entire supply chain operating like a pipeline," said the vice president of materials management. "When an order comes in from the customer, we take one pound of product out of the tail end. We've then got the raw material function working with the supplier to put another pound in on the other end. We want to achieve a continuous flow."

Stream inventory management processes reams of information crunched by the company's Global Business Integrated Information System (Globiis). This system provides visibility to customer demand and inventory levels across the entire supply chain. When customer orders consume inventory, the Globiis system calculates the type and amount of raw material required to replenish the supply chain. This maintains a balance between what exits the supply chain and what must enter. Furthermore, one executive manager has responsibility for tracking and managing inventory across the entire supply chain.

Is this total view of the supply chain working? Twenty years ago the company maintained, on average, 18 million pounds of paraxylene on hand, a material that winds up in plastic soda bottles. Today, Eastman maintains only 14 million pounds of paraxylene on hand, even though the production that requires this material has tripled in volume. The company has also reduced its wood pulp inventory from a three-month supply to a nine-day supply. It further hopes to reduce this to a four-day supply. Overall, Eastman's inventories have fallen from 11.5% of sales in 1989 to 8%.

Source: Adapted from Eryn Brown, "The Push to Streamline Supply Chains," *Fortune*, March 3, 1997, 108 [C]–108 [L].

Support Production Requirements

One of the primary reasons for inventory is to support physical production requirements. Even in an era of just-in-time production, almost all firms hold some level of preproduction inventory, which may include bulk supplies of raw materials, semifinished goods, or material to support the packaging and shipping of finished products.

Production inventory consumes a major portion of inventory investment. For this reason, firms emphasize the development of systems designed to control and reduce the amount of production-related inventory maintained at any given time. The reduction of production inventory (particularly work-in-process) results in lower inventory investment costs. While the need to support production requirements is still a primary reason to hold physical inventory, it is not a reason to hold excessive quantities.

Support Operational Requirements

Nearly every organization carries MRO inventory—maintenance, repair, and operating supplies—to support operations. The true cost of MRO inventory often goes unnoticed because firms fail to track these with the same intensity as production inventory. Over time, many organizations have little idea of their current total investment in MRO items. Multiple or obsolete items may be held in stock, and inventory pilferage can further lead to inventory-shrinking losses if proper tracking systems are not established.

Most firms are increasingly trying to control the costs associated with ordering and maintaining MRO items. Some of the techniques being applied include the use of a central MRO stores location, online requisitioning systems, and the use of full-service suppliers. Such suppliers are responsible for managing the entire supply and demand for MRO inventory items, and may charge an additional fee for their services. These suppliers may work on-site in the MRO inventory stockroom and can often save a significant amount in terms of inventory investment.

Support Customer Service Requirements

Many products such as computers, appliances, and automobiles require service or replacement parts. A lack of adequate spare parts inventory increases the risk of not meeting customer service requirements. To avoid this possibility, some companies maintain a significant inventory of service and replacement parts that represents a major investment.

Service and replacement parts are a major source of inventory waste or customer dissatisfaction if incorrect inventory levels are selected. Accurate part forecasts and material control systems are critical when maintaining inventory levels for service and replacement parts.

Hedge Against Marketplace Uncertainty

Supply chains are sensitive to changes in markets, including changes in the availability of material supply as well as price changes. When purchasers anticipate material shortages or price increases, they often increase purchase quantities as a hedge against these uncertainties. Material hedging is a common response, for example, when a strike by a key supplier appears likely. Another reason to hedge occurs when potential shortages in common commodities (e.g., lumber) appear imminent, with the knowledge that price increases are likely. In these situations, purchasers will carry out *forward buys* by ordering larger-than-normal quantities. On the other hand, if purchasers believe that prices are falling, they will pursue spot buying, which involves ordering only small quantities with the expectation that lower prices will be available shortly.

Increasing inventory levels in response to a legitimate threat of a shortage can be a good reason, at least in the short run, for holding additional material. One of the primary objectives of purchasing and supply chain management is to support the continued and uninterrupted operations. If this requires increased inventory to avoid a material shortage, then a purchaser should consider such an action, assuming that additional sources of supply are not readily available. The Sourcing Snapshot about palladium illustrates the challenges of managing a volatile item that is critical to production.

Managing Inventory in a Volatile Market

The auto industry has been fretting about the soaring price of an obscure, grayish metal called palladium. For anyone wanting to make a cleaner car or sports-utility vehicle, the little-known precious metal is a must. Unfortunately, the main exporter of palladium is Russia, which has created chaos on the market for the past few years by holding up deliveries at the start of each year, including releasing the metal from its huge stockpile. Recent concerns that political infighting in Moscow could choke supplies drove the price of palladium to nearly $1,000 an ounce, or about 10 times the levels seen in the early 1990s. Although there is less than an ounce of palladium in most vehicles—it is used inside the catalytic converter—that kind of price surge means palladium suddenly is becoming a big-ticket inventory item for auto companies.

Automakers brought much of this inventory management problem on themselves. In the mid-1990s, they agreed to accelerate their adoption of tighter national emission standards as part of a deal to head off separate state-by-state rules, which would have played havoc with manufacturing and distribution. Palladium looked like the best solution, since it began cleaning exhaust sooner after starting up the engine than platinum, then the dominant metal in catalytic converters. Plus, the price for little-used palladium hadn't gone above $200 an ounce in more than a decade, while platinum had jumped above $400. Engineers designed palladium into the emission control system. In the process, they created a tremendous amount of demand for a metal having volatile supply.

Purchasing has become central to the palladium problem. In 1998, GM, along with Ford and Japan's Mitsubishi Corporation, signed five-year supply deals with the only major palladium producer outside of Russia and South Africa, Stillwater Mining Company. Stillwater announced plans to more than double production to 1.2 million ounces a year by 2001 at its mine in the Beartooth Mountains of southern Montana. Economics dictates that other producers should boost output to bring the palladium market into balance in this kind of situation. But geology makes palladium special. In nature, it occurs mostly with other metals, nickel in Russia and platinum in South Africa, and in both places there is much less palladium per ton of ore than the other metals. Even if palladium prices take off, big producers won't add to output, since that would mean flooding the nickel and platinum markets. Supply chain inventory management sometimes means just getting the inventory.

Source: Adapted from Gregory L. White, "Unruly Element: Russian Maneuvers Are Making Palladium Ever More Precious," *Wall Street Journal*, March 6, 2000, A1.

Take Advantage of Order Quantity Discounts

Suppliers often offer quantity discounts to encourage larger orders from purchasers. A purchaser might consider releasing for a two-month supply versus a one-month supply, for example, in exchange for a per-unit discount. At one time most companies felt these discounts were worthwhile because they resulted in a lower average purchase price. However, a lower purchase price does not necessarily translate into a lower total inventory cost. Lower total inventory costs result only if the benefit from reduced ordering costs (larger purchase quantities means ordering less frequently) and a lower per-unit price outweigh the cost to hold additional inventory. It sometimes makes economic sense from a total cost perspective to take advantage of the quantity discounts offered by suppliers and to hold larger amounts of inventory.

Each of the reasons just discussed can result in holding some level of physical inventory. Regardless of the reason for holding inventory, supply chain managers must be aware of total inventory costs. The key is to minimize inventory investment wherever possible while still meeting competitive and customer requirements.

$\mathcal{T}$HE WRONG REASONS FOR CARRYING INVENTORY

Any inventory discussion must differentiate between good and bad reasons for carrying inventory. Almost all unnecessary inventory results from a single word—uncertainty. Uncertainty results in not being able to adequately plan inventory requirements because of supply chain variability. It is also a consequence of variability in forecasting accuracy and inconsistent logistics, which usually results in greater amounts of safety stock being held as protection. The following discussion considers the sources of variability or uncertainty that, if left uncorrected, encourage an increase in inventory. These are the wrong reasons for carrying inventory.

Poor Quality and Material Yield

Poor quality and material yield have been major sources of unnecessary inventory investment. Unfortunately, it is easier to increase a material release by 10% or carry safety stock to cover supplier quality problems than to correct a problem's root cause. It became a routine practice for many companies to order more than required to cover expected supplier quality variability and uncertainty. A certain level of material defects was an accepted part of the transaction.

Variable material yield also may also contribute to unnecessary levels of inventory. *Material yield* is a term typically associated with raw materials. A purchaser who specifies a raw material at a particular grade expects to receive a shipment conforming to that specification. Poor quality affects material yields when a portion of the shipment is a lower grade or quality than what was specified, therefore providing less output than expected. When this happens purchasers must often increase their purchased quantity to guarantee that their receipt yields the proper amount of usable material. This increases the inventory investment while providing nothing of value in return.

Unreliable Supplier Delivery

Suppliers who cannot meet delivery schedules create delivery uncertainty. To compensate for unreliable delivery, supply chain managers usually increase safety stock levels. Delivery uncertainty is often the result of poor supplier scheduling or production systems and can be a problem when buying from small suppliers who do not have the resources or experience to develop sophisticated scheduling and control systems. It can also be the result of discrepancies and logistics problems. Missed shipments, delays at international customs points, bad weather, and many other unexpected problems can result in late deliveries.

Purchasers must also accept part of the blame for delivery uncertainty. Suppliers value a stable production schedule with reasonable production lead times. A purchaser who provides suppliers with short notice or requests frequent changes to the release schedule increases the probability of delivery uncertainty. A major step toward eliminating delivery uncertainty is a commitment to stable release schedules with realistic (but not overly generous) supplier lead times.

Extended Buyer-Supplier Order-Cycle Times

A major business objective today is to reduce the total time between the recognition of a purchase requirement and the physical receipt of material from a supplier—that is, the order-cycle time between purchaser and seller. As order-cycle times lengthen, a common practice has been to carry a higher level of inventory to compensate for greater uncertainty. The ability to plan material requirements accurately decreases as order-cycle time lengthens. A six-month order-cycle lead time from a supplier introduces greater uncertainty than a two-week order-cycle period. It is more difficult to plan over extended periods of time. Much more can happen to disrupt plans over a six-month period than a two-week period.

Inaccurate or Uncertain Demand Forecasts

Inaccurate or uncertain demand forecasts are a common source of uncertainty affecting inventory levels, particularly for companies that produce products in anticipation of future orders. Increased safety stock levels are often used to compensate for demand uncertainty or inaccurate forecasts. Some firms simply have poor forecasting systems. When this is the case, inventory may be increased to protect against material stock outs. Companies should periodically evaluate the accuracy of their forecasting system by comparing forecasted demand to actual requirements. Forecasting systems should have a goal of minimizing the difference between a forecasted requirement and an actual requirement to avoid having to carry higher inventory levels as protection.

Specifying Custom Items for Standard Applications

Specifying custom items for standard applications is an area of great debate between purchasing and engineering. Purchasers would like to buy industry-standard parts wherever possible while still meeting engineering's quality and design requirements. Specifying customized parts when standardized parts are available adversely affects material inventory because customized parts are almost always more expensive than standardized parts. A supplier usually designs and creates specific tooling for each customized item. In addition, a supplier usually produces smaller batches of the item due to its custom specification. The smaller batches result in an increased piece-part cost. Customized parts, due to higher design and production costs, increase total unit and inventory-carrying costs.

Extended Material Pipelines

Long distances between supply chain members can result in higher inventory levels and costs. Distance increases delivery uncertainty, often for reasons outside the control of a supplier or buyer. Overseas shipments can experience a variety of delays at customs. Longer shipping distances also increase the potential for in-transit shipping damage, theft, or obsolescence. Furthermore, someone in the supply chain (the buyer, purchaser, or end customer) owns the inventory as it travels over great distances. Long material pipelines are a major consideration when comparing the cost of domestic versus international purchasing (see Chapter 11 on worldwide sourcing).

Inefficient Manufacturing Processes

A producer whose manufacturing system is not efficient must hold higher-than-necessary inventory levels to compensate for poor quality or process yield. One indication of an inefficient scheduling or production system is a large amount of work-in-process inventory located behind each machine. Inefficient scheduling and productions often create congested work areas as inventory accumulates in production centers. This increases total inventory-carrying costs because longer production times increase work-in-process inventory. Inefficient production processes also lead to higher costs through poorer yield or quality.

Most inventory waste results from underlying problems that management has failed to correct. When inventory is used to disguise operating inefficiencies, this accepts inefficiencies as part of conducting business. Failure to correct these underlying problems makes the inefficient producer vulnerable to challenges from cost-efficient producers. Whereas balance sheet accounting presents inventory as an asset, experienced supply chain managers recognize it is an asset worth controlling and, when necessary, even eliminating.

CREATING THE LEAN SUPPLY CHAIN

When inventory moves so fast that firms essentially hold zero inventory on hand, they are following a system known as the *lean supply chain*—a combination of JIT purchasing, JIT transportation, and JIT production. All three elements combine to create a

Can JIT Reduce Inventory Too Much?

When manufacturers were pummeled in the 1980s by foreign competition, many shifted to production methods embraced by their overseas rivals. Workforces were cut, just-in-time inventory methods were added, and extra controls were put in place to track production. Such methods helped U.S. companies beat back foreign competition. Now lean operations may have come back to haunt them. "We leaned things out so much, got rid of so many people that you just don't have the capacity anymore," says Bill Swanton, vice president for manufacturing strategies at AMR Research Inc. in Cambridge, Massachusetts. For example, with auto sales booming, Intermet Corporation (an auto-parts supplier) faces red-hot demand for the iron and aluminum castings it produces for sports-utility vehicles and light trucks. The crush of orders is so huge that Intermet is running 24 hours a day. Lines can't be shut down for needed maintenance. Stressed-out workers are quitting. Meanwhile, escalating production costs—for overtime, repairs, and premium freight charges—cut third-quarter profits by 20%, to $7.4 million, even as revenue jumped 16% to $225 million. Goodyear Tire and Rubber Company's third-quarter profits slipped a stunning 56% to $97.2 million, in part because executives didn't anticipate a big spike in demand for tires. Brett Hoselton, an auto-parts analyst with McDonald Investments Inc. in Cleveland notes that "Every supplier I talk to has to deal with extra costs just to keep up with demand." At Intermet, chairman and chief executive John Doddridge admits he badly underestimated demand. His company already produces only what is ordered each day, but it was still overwhelmed. Lean manufacturing systems "have done great things" he says, "but they allow little margin for error." When auto sales surged to 17 million—instead of the 15 million that Doddridge and others had anticipated—Intermet could not turn on a dime: Building more production capacity takes years. By then, of course, the economy may have cooled a bit.

Source: Adapted from Peter Galuszka, "Just-in-Time Manufacturing Is Working Overtime," *Business Week*, November 8, 1999, 36–37.

supply chain that minimizes inventory investment and eliminates waste. John Shook defines lean as "a philosophy that seeks to shorten the time between the customer order and the shipment to the customer by eliminating waste."[3] James Womack and Daniel Jones, in their book *Lean Thinking*, argue that all activities associated with lean attempt to achieve three objectives: flow, pull, and striving for excellence.[4] *Flow* means that inventory moves through the supply chain continuously with minimal queuing or non–value-added activity being performed. *Pull* means that customer orders start the work process. An upstream work center will not create output unless a

EXHIBIT 17.4   *Common Types of Supply Chain Waste*

Type of Supply Chain Waste	Effect on Inventory Investment	How to Eliminate This Waste
Overproduction	Creates excessive finished-goods inventory excessive component and raw material inventory at suppliers	Produce only to customer requirements
Waiting	Increases average levels of supply chain inventory as material remains in a non–value-added state longer	Coordinate flows between supply chain activities; balance the flow between work centers through coordinated production and ordering quantities
Excessive transportation and material handling	Increases possibility of damage; adds time and inventory to the material pipeline	Locate supply chain members and work centers geographically closer; use a dedicated transportation network
Unneeded production steps	Creates higher levels of work-in-process inventory as production cycles are lengthened	Process reengineer to reduce the number of steps required to produce
Excessive work-in-process inventories	Creates higher levels of supply chain inventory-carrying costs as inventory takes longer to become finished goods to the customer	Reduce setup times; better coordinate schedules between work centers; build only to customer order quantities
Unnecessary motion and effort	Creates higher levels of work-in-process inventory as production cycles lengthen	Perform industrial engineering studies to optimize movement
Defective products	Requires safety stock; rework, material, reordering, production, and transportation costs increase	Pursue zero defects throughout the supply chain, including the suppliers
Unnecessary staff	Unnecessary staff can make product lines uncompetitive, leading to reduced sales and obsolete inventory	Place decision-making authority closer to direct supply chain participants; replace staff with information
Incomplete or incorrect information	Requires safety stock or buffers across the supply chain; may result in excessive production; may result in wrong production	Develop integrated information systems; build trust among supply chain members

downstream work center directly requests (i.e., pulls) that output. The output is needed and consumed, leading to no inventory or waste. The third element, *striving for excellence*, means that supply chains must have perfect quality. Anything less than perfect quality leads to waste.

Exhibit 17.4 identifies the various types of supply chain waste. This exhibit explains how to eliminate the waste, and why the presence of that waste often leads to additional supply chain inventory. The elimination of supply chain waste, and the inventory that accompanies that waste, is perhaps the primary objective of a lean supply chain.

The following sections detail the three primary elements of a lean supply chain: (1) just-in-time purchasing, (2) just-in-time transportation, and (3) just-in-time production.

Just-in-Time Purchasing

Implementing a just-in-time (JIT) purchasing system is the first major element of a lean supply chain. A JIT purchasing system means receiving frequent receipts of material from suppliers to meet immediate requirements. The following features define a true JIT purchasing system:

- A commitment to zero defects by the buyer and seller
- Frequent shipment of small lot sizes according to strict quality and delivery performance standards
- Closer, even collaborative, buyer-seller relationships
- Stable production schedules sent to suppliers on a regular basis
- Extensive sharing of information between supply chain members
- Electronic data interchange capability with suppliers

Not simply a series of techniques, a JIT purchasing system is an operating philosophy that does not tolerate high inventory levels, less than perfect quality, or other inefficiency and waste between buyer and seller. JIT purchasing also requires permanent changes concerning how a firm conducts business. It is not a one-time effort or a project but rather a continuous supply chain improvement process. A true JIT purchasing system requires cultural and personnel mind-set changes at the purchaser and at suppliers. And perhaps most important, JIT purchasing does not mean pushing inventory back to the supplier. JIT purchasing requires cooperation, coordination, and information sharing to eliminate inventory throughout the supply chain.

Structural JIT Purchasing Barriers JIT purchasing between U.S. companies has been slowed or even prohibited by a variety of structural barriers that are part of the U.S. business system and culture, although industries are affected differently. Fortunately, some of these barriers are not as great as they were when JIT first became popular during the early and mid-1980s. Key factors include the following:

- *Dispersed supply base:* Most purchasers have a geographically dispersed supply base. Since JIT relies on frequent deliveries of smaller quantities from suppliers, it may be difficult to achieve a level of consistent delivery reliability from suppliers located 800 or even 8,000 miles away. The greater the distance between buyer and seller, the greater the variability around delivery times.
- *Historical buyer-seller relationships:* Buyers and sellers often lack the cooperative relationship required to pursue JIT purchasing. A true JIT system requires mutual trust and respect between parties. The historical relationship between U.S. buyers and sellers has been closer to adversarial rather than cooperative.
- *Number of suppliers:* Some supply chains still have too many suppliers to support an efficient JIT system. Like other progressive purchasing strategies, JIT requires a drastically reduced supply base to minimize the interaction and communication costs between parties. It is also impossible to develop closer relationships with thousands of suppliers.

EXHIBIT 17.5   *JIT Purchasing—Supplier Expectations*

- A longer-term business arrangement
- Fair financial return
- Adequate time for planning
- Accurate forecasts
- Correct and firm material and product specifications

- Parts designed to match the supplier's process capability
- Smoothly timed order releases
- Minimum number of change order

- *Supplier quality performance:* Some sellers simply have not achieved the levels of near-perfect quality required for JIT purchasing. A total commitment to product and delivery quality is a prerequisite for a successful JIT system.

These barriers are not as common with Japanese and other international competitors. The geographic size of Japan, for example, almost guarantees that buyers and suppliers are located near each other. Furthermore, Asian manufacturers historically have had closer relationships with their key suppliers—so close that buyers think of suppliers as virtual extensions of the buying company and treat them as such. This closeness allows the two firms to work together at a higher level. Nevertheless, not all has been easy for the Japanese. They face more congestion on the highways for their deliveries than encountered in the United States.

The structural barriers limiting the increased use of JIT purchasing in the United States are beginning to break down. A reduction in the number of suppliers is the most obvious change. JIT purchasing has clearly been a major factor behind the supply-base reduction effort of most U.S. companies. Another change includes buyers and sellers developing closer working relationships. The two parties are increasingly willing to share information such as production scheduling and future product development plans. Information sharing has contributed to the greater use of electronic systems linking between supply chain members.

Progressive suppliers have shown an increased willingness to locate facilities closer to key customers. For example, DuPont invested over $1 billion during the 1980s and early 1990s to establish facilities in southeast Michigan to support the technical and production requirements of U.S. automakers. Another trend has been the development of measurement systems to evaluate supplier quality performance, including the initial evaluation of supplier capability as well as continuous performance measurement. JIT purchasing will fail if a supplier cannot meet world-class quality levels.

Getting suppliers to cooperate in a JIT purchasing system is critical to success. One way to get that involvement and commitment is to understand the expectations that suppliers have within a JIT purchasing system. Exhibit 17.5 lists some of these expectations.

Just-in-Time Transportation

JIT transportation, another key element of a lean supply chain, refers to the efficient movement of goods between the buyer and seller. This involves frequent deliveries of smaller quantities directly to the point of use at the purchaser. A lean transportation

EXHIBIT 17.6   *JIT Transportation Delivery Systems*

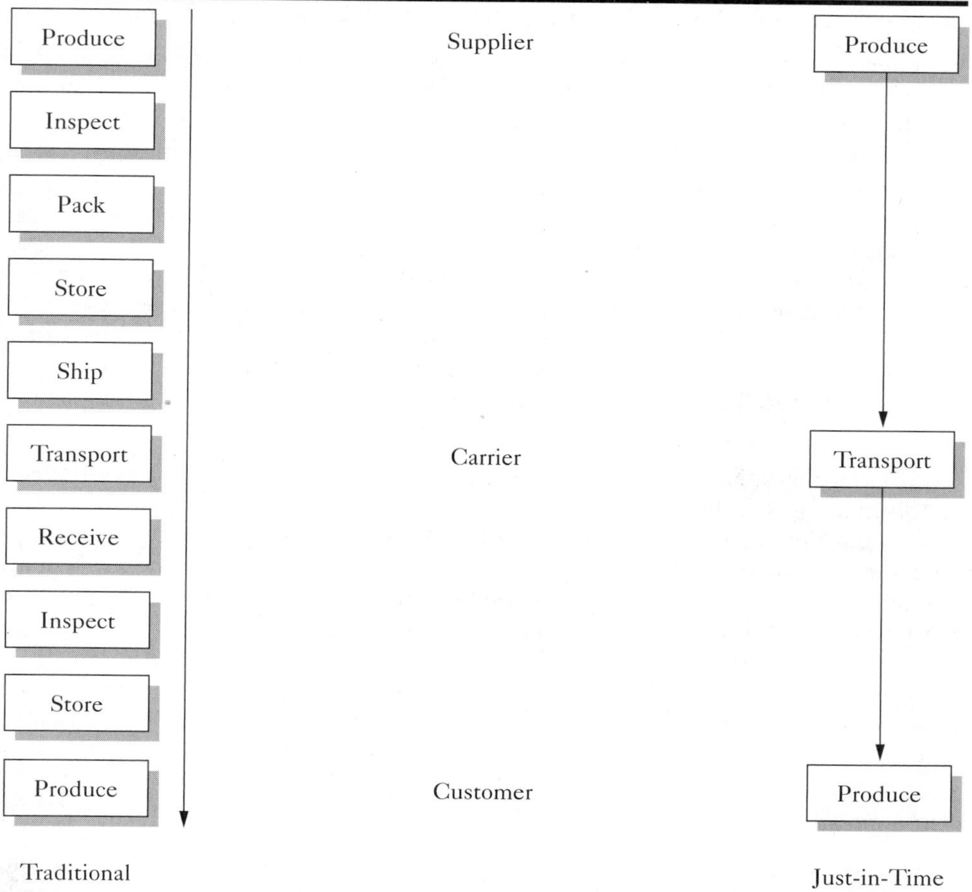

Produce	Supplier	Produce
Inspect		
Pack		
Store		
Ship		
Transport	Carrier	Transport
Receive		
Inspect		
Store		
Produce	Customer	Produce
Traditional		Just-in-Time

network relies on company-owned or contracted vehicles that pick up and deliver according to a regular and repeatable schedule in a *closed loop*—a system that moves goods from supplier to purchaser and then from purchaser back to supplier with return material, such as containers. Long-term dedicated contract carriage replaces commercial carriage as the primary mode of transportation in a closed-loop transportation system.

Exhibit 17.6 compares a traditional delivery system with a just-in-time delivery system. In a traditional system, the supplier and purchaser do not coordinate their material requirements or production schedules. As a result, suppliers produce material and then store that material awaiting an order from the purchaser. In a JIT system, suppliers coordinate production schedules with customer schedules. Production moves from the supplier's work center to the carrier directly to the purchaser. A JIT transportation network can eliminate up to 80% of the activities required in a traditional system. Designing a JIT transportation network involves certain steps:

- *Change the organizational structure:* Examples of organizational changes required to support JIT deliveries may include establishing cross-functional teams to manage the transition to JIT transportation.
- *Reduce the number of carriers:* Reduce the number of carriers, perhaps even to one per region.
- *Use longer-term contracts:* Negotiate longer-term agreements with carriers that formalize the dedicated transportation network.
- *Establish electric linkages:* Establish electronic linkages with suppliers and carriers to coordinate and control the movement of material through the network.
- *Implement a closed-loop system:* Pick up all freight from suppliers and deliver on a regular schedule. Use returnable containers to eliminate packaging waste.
- *Efficiently handle material:* Use state-of-the-art material-handling equipment and technology.

JIT transportation systems feature certain innovations that can further eliminate supply chain waste. The first includes specialized transportation vehicles that allow easy loading and unloading of smaller quantities. A common configuration resembles a beverage truck with side-loading doors. These trucks are smaller, more efficient, and more versatile. The second innovation includes the extensive use of returnable plastic or steel containers. As drivers pick up material from suppliers, they leave empty containers that were used in earlier deliveries. A third innovation involves point-of-use doors at production facilities. Since excessive material handling and travel within a facility is wasteful, delivery should be made to the door closest to where the material is needed.

Just-in-Time Production

This aspect of the lean supply chain involves taking raw and semifinished material and converting it to finished goods to satisfy customer orders. A narrow view of lean tends to focus on JIT production only while minimizing the importance of JIT purchasing and transportation. A truly lean supply chain requires all three pieces to be in place.

JIT production consists of the following elements, some of which are discussed further:

- Uniform facility loading and level scheduling
- Equipment setup reduction
- Inventory pull systems with visible signals
- Facility layout changes
- Total quality and continuous improvement
- Standardized material handling and containers
- Product and process simplification
- Total preventive maintenance
- Flexible workforce featuring teamwork
- Right performance measures

Ideally, a purchaser has suppliers that are also practicing lean supply chain production practices.

Equipment Setup Reductions Setup reduction involves reviewing how to minimize equipment downtime between part changeovers to facilitate small-volume production. An analogy that illustrates setup reduction is moving from a traditional tire change (longer downtime) to an Indy pit stop (downtime measured in seconds). With the Indy pit stop, the process is idle for the least amount of time possible.

Many companies start their lean production efforts by focusing on setup time reduction. There are five major approaches for improving setup times:

1. Reduce the time a piece of equipment is down for a changeover. This is achieved by planning and staging, which means knowing which part is coming next, knowing when the change will take place, and having the required tools and equipment ready before the change.
2. Study setup methods extensively. Time and motion studies will help identify wasted movement and methods.
3. Eliminate on-machine adjustments as much as possible.
4. Purchase new equipment that is easier and quicker to change.
5. Track progress toward stated time-reduction targets in order to focus the improvement efforts.

In short, setup time should become a nonevent that allows the production of small lot sizes or quantities.

Inventory Pull Systems with Visible Signals Customer orders serve as a "pull" signal in a lean supply chain. Cells, work centers, and even suppliers make a component, subassembly, or product only when requested by a downstream work center. Production and movement of goods are triggered by a visible signal, such as a production card, empty container, empty designated floor space, electronic signal, or other nonverbal communication. An empty container or floor space is the trigger to produce at a work station—empty meaning that a downstream work center used that material (which is why it is empty) and more will be required shortly for the next customer order. Because material is produced only when requested by a work center requiring that material, no excess or unbalanced production occurs.

Pull and push systems differ dramatically. In a push system material is produced upstream and then sent, or pushed, to the next work center in the supply chain. Usually the next center is unaware that material is on its way until it arrives, which often leads to bottlenecks. This is common when producing to a forecast of anticipated demand. Eventually the material reaches the end of production and is placed in warehouse storage.

Facility Layout Changes The objective of changing the layout of a facility is to overcome the limitations of traditional layouts, which include excessive material movement, workers with narrow job classifications or specialization, and complex material-tracking requirements. The most common layout change involves moving from

EXHIBIT 17.7   *Process Facility Layout Organized Around Production Processes*

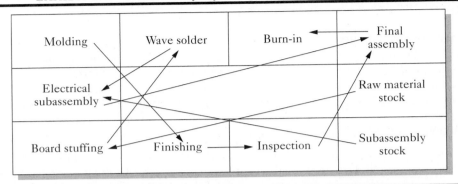

a process layout, where similar equipment is grouped into work centers, to a cellular layout, where dissimilar operations are grouped together to focus on a specific product line or customer. The goal is to minimize the movement of products. The cell also supports grouping employees into work teams with total accountability for a product and its quality. Exhibits 17.7 and 17.8 highlight the physical difference between a process facility and product or cellular layout.

Changing to a cellular approach is not as easy as it may sound. It can be difficult to overcome years of employee and departmental specialization, and some equipment does not lend itself to being grouped with other equipment. Also, the process of rearranging a facility is a major task that can easily disrupt production schedules and interfere with customer deliveries. Finally, equipment utilization often declines in a just-in-time system. Concern with factory utilization must shift to a concern with low inventory, balanced production, and quality assurance. This can be a problem if the performance measurement system stresses output and volume. Having equipment stand idle is better than using it to produce unneeded components, subassemblies, and finished products.

Uniform Loading and Level Scheduling Uniform plant loading is essential for a lean and integrated supply chain. The premise behind uniform loading is that all work centers, including work centers at the supplier, are not independent of one another. Batch sizes of component or subassembly production cannot be calculated separately from the finished-product requirements. The entire supply chain must be linked to finished-quantity requirements so there is a balanced flow of material through the supply chain with no queues or shortages.

Level scheduling means planning to build the same product mix and quantity every day during a given period. This works best for products that have a fairly consistent pattern of customer demand, such as making automobiles. Level scheduling removes the volatility that can disrupt the smooth flow of goods through the supply chain.

While entire books have been written on the topic of the lean supply chain, this discussion should at least make you aware of the basic elements and how being lean demands the identification and removal of supply chain waste.

EXHIBIT 17.8   *Product or Cellular Layout Organized Around Work Cells*

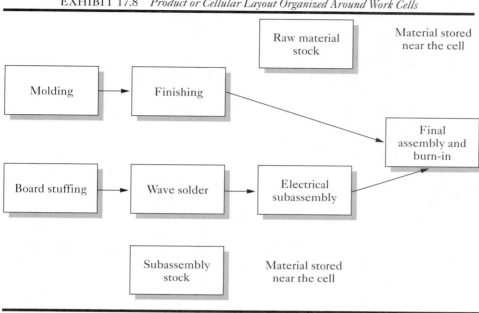

APPROACHES FOR CONTROLLING INVENTORY INVESTMENT

Besides the activities associated with a lean supply chain, companies rely on a variety of other techniques and methods to control inventory investment throughout the supply chain. The following summarizes some of the most common, along with a brief description of each approach.

Continuous Review of Excess and Obsolete Inventory

One way to control inventory investment involves evaluating inventory status on a regular basis. A reduction in problem inventory (such as obsolete inventory) creates benefits by lowering total inventory investment levels. Lower inventory levels lead to lower inventory carrying costs, increased cash flow, better utilization of storage space, and improved inventory turnover. Identification of the root causes of obsolete inventory should result in future savings by learning to better manage inventory investment. There are several basic steps to follow when reviewing inventory investment:

1. Define problem inventory.
2. Automate the inventory review system.
3. Review current inventory investment.

SOURCING SNAPSHOT

BFGoodrich and Grainger Team Up to Manage Inventory

The BFGoodrich Company and W. W. Grainger announced that they have signed a 10-year agreement that will better enable BFGoodrich to leverage purchasing activities, streamline procurement procedures, and significantly reduce materials management costs. With 1999 sales of $4.5 billion, Grainger is the leading North American provider of maintenance, repair, and operating (MRO) supplies, services, and related information to businesses and institutions. Under this agreement, Grainger will provide general industrial hardware products and MRO supplies estimated at $300 million while working with BFGoodrich to achieve an estimated $30 million in process and product cost savings over the 10-year period. "Managing our supply chain is a critical component of our overall productivity program, including lean manufacturing and other initiatives to reduce costs, cut lead times and reduce inventories for our advantage and the benefit of our customers," said Marshall Larsen, president and chief operating officer of BFGoodrich's aerospace segment.

The agreement provides consolidated sourcing opportunities for the entire BFGoodrich organization in the United States and Canada to obtain the best product or service solution at the lowest cost. Grainger services include customer-specific pricing, Internet expertise, logistics support, inventory management, on-site tool crib management, purchasing and procurement logistics, process improvement measurements, commodity management, and product sourcing. Grainger's nationwide presence and buying power in the marketplace were also key criteria in its selection.

"While many companies have asked Grainger to provide a single MRO solution, this is the first opportunity we've had to demonstrate our entire end-to-end value proposition," said Richard L. Keyser, chairman of the board and CEO of Grainger. "We are very pleased to be working with BFGoodrich in this collaborative effort."

Source: Adapted from "BFGoodrich and Grainger Enter Enterprise Purchasing Agreement," *PR Newswire*, March 8, 2000.

4. Determine courses of action.
5. Correct the underlying causes of excessive and obsolete inventory.

Inventory may eventually become classified as problem inventory for a number of reasons. A firm may have inadequate inventory control and record-keeping procedures that result in lost inventory. When the item is eventually located, it may not be required for production or service. Marketing may be too optimistic about future sales forecasts, which results in ordering too much inventory to support lower-than-expected production schedules. Economic shifts or technological changes may bring about a sudden shift in a product mix and create excess or obsolete inventory. One particular situation occurs when a part has a short life cycle. Discussions with suppliers and supply chain managers in high-tech industries reveal that a series of smaller life cycles exists within the total product life cycle, referred to as *component life cycles*. Whatever the reason, the continuous review of excess and obsolete inventory should be a regular part of the inventory management process.

Part Simplification and Redesign

Part simplification and redesign involves the detailed analysis of a physical product to identify potential design or material changes. Successful product simplification and redesign positively affects inventory investment in three ways. First, a simplified product design usually requires fewer parts, resulting in lower inventory management costs due to a reduced number of total part numbers. Second, the elimination of unnecessary components through simplification or redesign reduces a part's total cost. A lower part cost reduces the total cost of the inventory required to support part production. Third, product redesign can result in the greater use of standardized versus customized items and/or lower-cost material substitutes. The use of standardized parts almost always results in a lower total part cost, which also reduces inventory costs and improves profit. Most product designers are trying to apply the principles of redesign and simplification during initial product design by asking certain questions:

- Can any part of the product be eliminated without impairing the operation of the complete unit?
- Can the design of the part be changed to reduce its basic cost?
- Can the design of the part be changed to permit the use of simplified and less costly production methods?
- Can less expensive but equally satisfactory materials be used in the part?
- Are standardized items available that can replace customized components?

A thorough review of these questions during product design may lead to a less costly product, which positively affects inventory investment.

Review Safety Stock Levels and Forecasting Techniques

Inaccurate forecasting techniques cause several major problems for supply chain planners. Underforecasting actual customer demand causes production and service problems (not enough is available to satisfy customer requirements). When underforecasting occurs, the supply chain must expedite additional shipments of material at a premium charge. Lost sales may also result due to a lack of finished product or inability to satisfy customer service requirements. On the other hand, an overforecasted demand requirement results in too much inventory. While a supply chain with too much inventory can meet its production schedules, it now has unnecessarily high inventory-carrying costs.

Evaluating the accuracy of the forecasting system should be a continuous activity. The starting point is a comparison of actual demand requirements to forecasted requirements over an extended period of time. The following questions should be asked when evaluating the accuracy of forecasting techniques:

- Are forecasts consistently over or under actual demand, or are forecasting errors randomly distributed?

- Do we understand why actual demand varies from forecasted demand?
- When actual demand patterns change, is the system sensitive enough to realize the change or is there an unacceptable lag?
- Are better forecasting tools or refinements available?
- Are forecasts being manually overridden by planners? If so, why?
- Is the time interval between forecasts adequate?

On-Site Supplier-Managed Inventory

Throughout this book we refer to the importance of closer supplier-buyer relationships. These relationships are crucial for achieving performance improvements, including improvement in the control of inventory investment. One area that features closer supplier-buyer relationships is the use of on-site suppliers to manage inventory.

Almost all organizations use distributors to provide at least some portion of their MRO requirements. A distributor may stock and sell a full range of items from different manufacturers. If the purchaser has enough volume, then the distributor may be willing to locate an employee at the purchaser's facility to manage the inventory.

Purchasers are increasingly entering into partnerships or formal agreements with distributors featuring on-site support. Besides the on-site support, these agreements stipulate that a supplier/distributor will stock a wider range of items and provide agreed-upon service levels. The buyer, in exchange for purchasing solely from the distributor, no longer stocks inventory for items under contract. The on-site representative orders on an as-needed basis, often directly into the distributor's order-processing system. This reduces the amount of paperwork required to submit an order. A buying firm avoids stocking or managing this inventory while the distributor benefits from a higher share of a purchaser's total purchase requirements. Not stocking the items relieves the purchaser of carrying inventory.

The purchase of most MRO items is a nuisance because (1) they require a disproportionate amount of a buyer's time and (2) they are usually lower-value items. A formal agreement providing on-site supplier support can reduce the MRO ordering problem. These arrangements offer an opportunity to control a category of inventory that usually does not receive enough attention. By reducing the time and effort required to obtain route inventory, purchasers and supply chain managers can focus their attention on other value-adding activities.

Material Requirement Planning Systems

When we discuss systems that forecast future demand, we are referring to independent-demand systems. This means that demand for an item is not directly dependent upon the demand for any other item. A major task of the materials manager, however, is to control the inventory of items whose demand is dependent on the production of other items. A riding lawn mower is an example of an independent-demand item. Demand for the final part is independent—expected orders determine the final amount produced. The demand for the steering wheel or tires that go on the mower, for example, are dependent on the demand for the final part number (i.e., for the lawn mower). The production and scheduling system calculates the demand for the components or subassemblies with certainty. The component part or subassembly demand is simply a function of the production schedule for the final part number.

The availability of cost-efficient computer systems has allowed firms to make great progress controlling dependent-demand inventory. A widely used system that controls dependent-demand inventory is the material requirements planning (MRP) system. This system relies on production schedules developed for final part numbers in the master production schedule (MPS) to determine the timing and quantities of materials required for components or subassemblies. See Appendix H on the Web site.

Distribution Resource Planning Systems

Distribution resource planning (DRP) systems attempt to make the most effective use of finished-goods inventories. These systems, which are concerned with inventory that has left the work-in-process status, perform many functions:

- Forecasting finished-good inventory requirements
- Establishing correct inventory levels at each stocking location
- Identifying optimal stocking locations
- Determining the timing and replenishment of finished-goods inventories
- Allocating items in short supply
- Transportation planning and vehicle load scheduling

It is easy to see how a DRP system, combined with upstream supply chain planning systems such as MRP, can provide a total supply chain perspective.

Supply Chain Inventory Planning and Control

The establishment of a supply chain or logistical planner position responsible for coordinating and integrating material and information movement throughout the entire supply chain is gaining popularity as a way to manage inventory investment. A supply chain planner, a position often organized along product lines, manages the flow of inventory and information from suppliers through end customers. This position ties together the requirements of purchasing/materials management, production, inventory control, and product distribution.

The planner coordinates the movement and placement of inventory throughout the supply, production, and distribution channel. This person also serves as the liaison between various groups in the supply chain. Other assignments include developing production schedules, establishing production targets from marketing forecasts, determining inventory deployment at field warehouses, and continuously evaluating inventory safety stock levels. The supply chain planner also works closely with purchasing to coordinate material requirements to support production targets.

Automated Inventory-Tracking Systems

Automated inventory control systems involve computerized material and electronic data interchange (EDI) systems that track the flow of inventory throughout the entire supply chain. This approach electronically connects suppliers, production plants, field distribution centers, and even customers. A customer may be a retail outlet or an independent distributor.

An integrated systems approach relies on new forms of information technology, such as EDI and bar-code scanning, to link the entire supply chain electronically. Wal-Mart, for example, has benefited greatly from automated inventory-tracking systems, using bar-code technology to manage inventory at the point of sale to the consumer back up the supply chain to suppliers. Tracking sales allows Wal-Mart to identify what is selling and to replenish shelves quickly. Automated tracking systems present an opportunity for controlling inventory investment throughout the entire supply chain.

Supplier-Buyer Cycle-Time Reduction

Shortening the material pipeline in terms of time between suppliers and a buyer can reduce the average amount of inventory in a system at any given time. One area of emphasis will be to support reduced order-cycle times with suppliers. A reduced (and reliable) order-cycle time positively affects inventory investment by allowing more frequent orders received in smaller quantities. Planning horizons are also shorter, which reduces the need to carry safety stock.

There are several actions that support reduced order-cycle time with suppliers:

- *Expanded EDI capability:* The electronic exchange of information in a supply chain supports paperless procurement, faster data movement, and increased information accuracy. Electronic data interchange has the potential to reduce order-cycle times by 15% to 40% from current levels.
- *Supplier development support:* Supplier development means working directly with key supply chain members to improve performance. This support may include working directly at a supplier's facilities to speed order entry, production, and delivery through the removal of waste.
- *Measure order-cycle time:* Tracking order-cycle times helps identify areas of improvement. We expect to see greater emphasis on the development of performance measures that are time oriented.
- *Focus on second- and third-tier suppliers:* Total supply chain management requires working with first-, second-, and even third-tier suppliers. The ability of a purchaser to reduce order-cycle time and inventory with its immediate suppliers is partly a function of a supplier being able to work with its suppliers. A supplier's suppliers will become an increasingly important point of interest to supply chain managers.

These are not the only actions that supply chain managers can or will emphasize to manage inventory investment. This discussion points out, however, that creative approaches exist for achieving systemwide control and management of inventory investment.

GOOD PRACTICE EXAMPLE
Managing Low-Value Inventory for High-Value Savings at Lockheed

■ ■ ■

Lockheed Martin Energy Systems (LMES) has taken an aggressive step to control its MRO inventory. Confronted by a constant flow of small-dollar purchase requests, thousands of individual MRO suppliers, and difficulty tracking inventory and usage, LMES created its Accelerated Vendor Inventory Delivery (AVID) system. This system links LMES electronically with a preselected group of MRO distributors and allows users to order online using electronic catalogs. Exhibit 17.9 provides an overview of the AVID system.

Relying extensively on electronic data interchange between the user and suppliers, AVID allows users to control the purchase of low-dollar off-the-shelf items while significantly reducing the transaction costs of processing low-value purchases. Items typically acquired electronically through the system include electrical items, paper, lab supplies, building supplies, personal computers, electronics, and office supplies. The AVID system, which can trace its origin back to 1988, now allows more than 3,400 users to conduct transactions with 36 suppliers. Recently, the system accounted for 225,000 transactions involving $55 million in one year. The company has attained certain benefits from this system, most of which directly affect MRO inventory investment:

- Established a just-in-time delivery system for MRO purchasing.
- Increased purchasing power due to larger volumes with fewer suppliers.
- Eliminated the need for stocking MRO items at the company's facilities.
- Created a streamlined channel of electronic communication between LMES and suppliers.
- Reduced the total order-cycle time drastically.
- Improved overall quality of MRO items and reduced inventory aging.
- Reduced inventory-carrying costs drastically.
- Reduced paperwork and improved productivity through the use of bar-coded labels on all receipts.
- Improved accountability from both users and suppliers.

LMES offers selected suppliers the opportunity to become the company's sole supplier for a wide range of items. In return, the company requires a price reduction on MRO items, 24-hour turnaround on regular replenishment orders, two-hour emergency deliveries, and no paperwork. In addition, suppliers are asked to broaden their own inventory levels and depth to meet company requirements. LMES purchases a large volume from these suppliers, and holds a significant

EXHIBIT 17.9   *Lockheed Martin Energy Systems AVID System Overview*

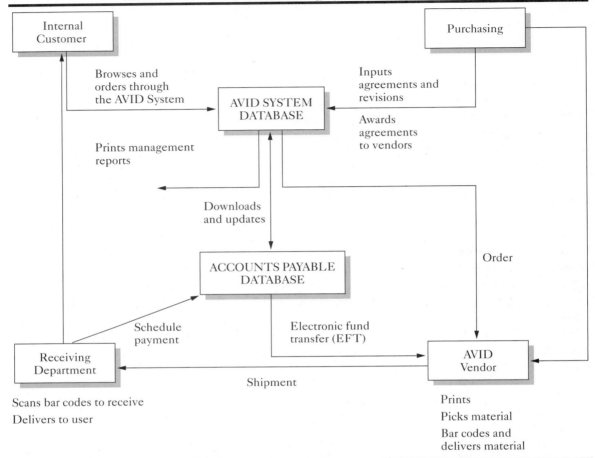

amount of leverage in order to set these terms. Not all companies may have this degree of leverage.

When the AVID system was developed, a steering committee was put in place that included representatives from executive management, accounts payable, accounts receivable, procurement, treasury, and business systems. In addition, an AVID project team and an AVID advisory team were established to monitor the operation of the system and to assume responsibility for the selection of AVID suppliers.

The selection criteria for AVID suppliers include technical and price considerations. The technical criteria include the supplier's warehouse and delivery capabilities, inventory management, financial strength, and the ability to work with the AVID system. Technical criteria during the selection process are weighted 60% while price is weighted 40%. Quality and time are critical considerations during selection. For example, can a chosen supplier deliver the correct product in 24 hours?

In the future, a Web-based version of AVID will include the current suppliers but will also allow LMES to increase the number of electronic catalogs that are part of the system. The AVID system has clearly demonstrated that a company can successfully manage low-value inventory to create high-dollar savings. ■

Source: Adapted from Robert J. Trent and Michael G. Kolchin, *Reducing the Transactions Costs of Purchasing Low Value Goods and Services* (Tempe, AZ: Center for Advanced Purchasing Studies, 1999): 113–118.

CONCLUSION

The dollars committed to inventory represent a major investment in most organizations. Like any investment, inventory must be managed to ensure that it provides an adequate return. Supply chain managers, including purchasing, play an important role in the management of inventory investment. The goal of this chapter was to create an awareness of the function of inventory, the operational problems that tempt firms to increase inventory levels, and some of the major approaches used to manage inventory investment. While inventory is technically an asset, it directly affects an organization's financial performance.

The following analogy is a useful way to envision the role of inventory investment. Inventory is the water in a river while operational problems are rocks piled along the river's bottom. One approach makes sure boats can safely pass (i.e., keep the business running) by raising the water level (inventory) until the rocks (operational problems) are comfortably covered by water. Since the rocks are covered, boats can pass without fear, even though the cost to pass may be far too high. A second approach requires lowering the water (for example, reducing inventory safety stock levels) until the rocks are exposed one by one. As a rock becomes exposed, an effort is made to permanently remove the rock (the operational problem). In the long run, which approach will be the most cost effective—the approach that covers problems with inventory or the one that permanently eliminates problems one by one? As purchasing and supply chain professionals, it may be your responsibility to manage the flow of physical inventory from suppliers. Throughout this flow you will encounter problems along the way, so it is important to remember the river analogy and the correct ways to manage and control inventory.

DISCUSSION QUESTIONS

1. What does it mean to say that high levels of inventory almost always disguise underlying problems? What types of problems would these be?
2. How is purchasing directly and indirectly involved in the control of a firm's inventory investment?

3.   What are some of the operational problems that excessive work-in-process inventory might indicate?

4.   Discuss several reasons why managers often neglect the true costs of holding physical inventory. What has happened to change our perspective about holding physical inventory?

5.   Why is the control of maintenance, repair, and operating (MRO) inventory typically a difficult task for most companies?

6.   What are the benefits of calculating the total cost of ownership associated with carrying physical inventory?

7.   Of the following functions of physical inventory, select the one that purchasing is most likely to be directly involved: (a) support of production requirements, (b) support of operational requirements, or (c) support of customer service requirements. Explain your choice.

8.   Describe the actions that purchasing can take to reduce uncertainty associated with (a) supplier quality, (b) supplier delivery, (c) long order-cycle times, (d) extended material pipelines, and (e) inaccurate demand forecasts.

9.   What problems are created by consistently overforecasting demand? What can a company do to resolve the problem of forecasting inaccuracy?

10.   What are the structural barriers U.S. firms face when implementing a true just-in-time (JIT) purchasing system? What can a company do to reduce the structural barriers to JIT purchasing?

11.   The chapter discussed various approaches for the control of inventory investment. Discuss three additional approaches not included that might involve supply chain managers.

12.   What are the main characteristics of a JIT purchasing system? Why does JIT purchasing require a cultural change at most firms?

13.   What is a lean supply chain? Explain the three primary elements of a lean system.

14.   What is a closed-loop transportation system? Why does such a system require dedicated or contracted transportation carriers?

15.   When a company shifts to a JIT purchasing system, what changes typically occur in the ordering and transportation system between buyer and seller?

16.   Discuss the advantages of taking a systemwide approach to the control of inventory investment. Are there any disadvantages? If yes, discuss the disadvantages.

ADDITIONAL READINGS

Bernard, Paul. *Integrated Inventory Management.* New York: Wiley, 1999.

Langenwalter, Gary. *Enterprise Resource Planning and Beyond: Integrating Your Entire Organization.*" Boca Raton, FL: St. Lucie Press, 2000.

Lewis, Colin. *Demand Forecasting and Inventory Control: A Computer Aided Learning Approach.* New York: Wiley, 1998.

Narasimhan, Seetharama L. *Production Planning and Inventory Control.* Englewood Cliffs, NJ: Prentice-Hall, 1995.

Orlicky, Joseph. *Materials Requirements Planning.* New York: McGraw-Hill, 1994.

Silver, Edward A. *Inventory Management and Production Planning and Scheduling.* New York: Wiley, 1998.

Wild, Tony. *Best Practice in Inventory Management.* New York: Wiley, 1998.

Zipkin, Paul Herbert. *Foundations of Inventory Management.* New York: McGraw-Hill, 2000.

ENDNOTES

1. Robert Handfield, "Distinguishing Attributes of JIT Systems in the Make-to-Order/Assemble-to-Order Environment," *Decision Sciences Journal* 24, no. 3 (1993): 581–602.
2. Some types of inventory, such as miscellaneous office supplies, may be treated as expense items. When this is the case, wasteful inventory practices affect profit and loss directly by increasing expenses.
3. John Shook, as quoted in Jeffrey K. Liker, ed., *Becoming Lean* (Portland, OR: Productivity Press, 1998).
4. James P. Womack and Daniel T. Jones, *Lean Thinking* (New York: Simon and Shuster, 1996).

18 PURCHASING TRANSPORTATION SERVICES

The Ford and UPS Connection: Finding a New Way to Track Vehicles

Ford Motor Company is tapping into the expertise of logistics provider United Parcel Service (UPS) to track millions of vehicles as they make their way from factories to dealerships. The automaker hopes to alleviate longtime distribution problems, cut in half the time it takes to ship vehicles from assembly plants to dealerships, and reduce distribution costs by 40%. Using bar codes and the Internet, UPS's logistics unit will track the more than 4 million cars and trucks Ford producs annually. This partnership continues the trend of making more of the car-buying process accessible through the Internet.

This combined information and transportation system allows Ford to log onto an Internet site to find out exactly where the vehicles they have ordered are in the distribution system, much the same way consumers can track UPS packages on the Internet using a tracking number. In the future, dealers and others familiar with the system said such a tracking program could be useful when consumers custom-order cars online through a dealer. "When the optimized network is fully complete," said a UPS executive, "Ford customers can expect the same on-time delivery reliability they get from UPS package delivery." A Ford dealer commented, "This system provides an unprecedented connection between Ford, its dealers, and its customers."

For Atlanta-based UPS, the agreement with Ford is a big boost for its six-year-old logistics division, which has seen its annual revenue surge over the last several years. Current UPS customers include Nike Inc., for which UPS handles online orders from a warehouse in Kentucky, and DaimlerChrysler, which recently brought in UPS to help overhaul a system used by dealers to order spare parts. The Ford contract is expected to boost the unit's revenue and its profile as a logistics expert, especially for Internet companies.

UPS has spent heavily in recent years to build a vast information technology platform, right down to handheld devices used by UPS drivers to transmit delivery-status information to company computers —and then onto the UPS Website. Tracking cars and trucks, however, has been a much less exact science over the years. Once vehicles leave the factory, the companies have been unable to tell dealers exactly when vehicles will arrive on their lots, making it impossible for dealers to tell consumers the arrival date of their vehicle. "Consumers are spoiled," said one Ford dealer. "They can track a package on FedEx, but I can't tell them when a vehicle will be in my dealership." The new system may not completely solve all transportation problems, but it's a step in the right direction. "Even with the logistical problems of delivery, whether by rail or truck, providing consumers information about where their car is in transit is an absolute home run," said one automotive analyst. Ford hopes that by streamlining internal operations, using the power of information technology, and partnering with a full-service logistics provider, the outbound distribution of cars will become a source of new competitive advantage.

Source: Adapted from Fara Warner and Rick Brooks, "Ford Is Hiring UPS to Track Vehicles as They Move from Factories to Dealers," *Wall Street Journal*, February 2, 2000, A6.

EXHIBIT 18.1   *Types of Logistics/Transportation Links*

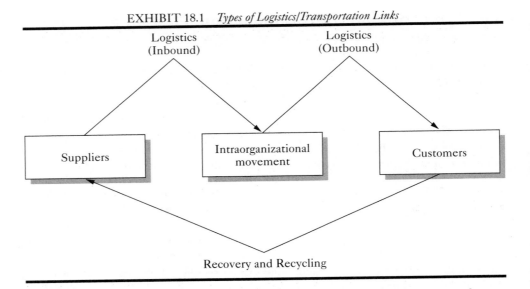

The timely and efficient movement and management of goods is critical to effective supply chain management. Many companies, like Ford, are aggressively using transportation and logistics providers to create advantages that customers benefit from directly.[1] Without effective transportation, getting the right product to the right place at the right time becomes nearly impossible. Selecting the right transportation and logistics provider is as critical as any other supplier evaluation and selection decision made within an organization.

Transportation service providers support the four major linkages throughout a typical supply chain shown in Exhibit 18.1: (1) inbound logistics, (2) intraorganizational movements, (3) outbound logistics, and (4) recovery and recycling. The first link includes all inbound shipments moving between a supplier and a buyer's facilities. In addition, a purchaser should theoretically also be concerned with the transportation linkages between its second-, third-, and fourth-tier suppliers. Any disruption in service or high costs at subtier supplies may eventually affect the buyer.

Companies with multiple production and warehouse facilities usually have a second major transportation link—intraorganizational movement. This includes movement of materials between production facilities within the same organization as well as movement to warehouse storage locations. A storage location may be in the same manufacturing complex as the production facility or at some other geographic location, which another company may control. Some companies directly control the movement of goods within this link through the use of company-owned transportation vehicles. Others are increasingly bypassing this link by producing only when they have a customer order, which allows shipment directly to the customer, and thus reduces the need for costly warehouse and distribution facilities.

The third link—outbound logistics—establishes the link between a company and its customers. The opening vignette relates to this link. Historically, the transportation department controlled the movement of outbound goods while suppliers arranged the movement of inbound freight. Since the deregulation of the transportation industry in the early 1980s, purchasing's involvement with the control of all three transportation links has increased greatly. The fourth link is one that companies are increasingly becoming concerned with—recovery and recycling of obsolete products and goods. This "reverse logistics" flow will require companies to find innovative methods of recovering and recycling products to minimize the impact on the environment.

This chapter focuses on the purchase of transportation services. Without the effective and efficient purchase and management of transportation services, world-class supply chain management can never be achieved. Topics discussed in this chapter include buying transportation services in an era of deregulation, purchasing's role in buying transportation services, a decision-making framework for developing transportation strategy, controlling and influencing transportation, and trends affecting the use of transportation services.

BUYING TRANSPORTATION SERVICES IN AN ERA OF DEREGULATION

Legislation passed in the United States during the late 1970s and early 1980s encouraged purchasing's involvement in the buying and management of transportation services. Congress passed the Air Cargo Deregulation Act in 1977; the Air Passenger Deregulation Act in 1978; and shortly after that the Motor Carrier Act of 1980 and the Staggers Act of 1980 (deregulating railroads) became law. Other major deregulation legislation includes the Transportation Industry Regulation Reform Act (TIRRA) of 1994, and the Ocean Shipping Reform Act (OSRA) of 1998.[2]

The primary objective of each of these deregulation laws was to make the U.S. transportation system more efficient by allowing increased competition to exist within the transportation industry. From a buyer's perspective, the new laws offered opportunities to negotiate transportation rates and service levels. From the carrier's perspective, the laws took away a comfortable blanket of government protection and significantly reduced profit margins on almost all national contracts. Transportation providers now had to compete against new entrants, existing providers, and even aggressive competition from other transportation modes. They also had to contend with requests for discounts from published tariff rates (although filing published tariff rates with the government in the motor carrier is no longer required). The legislative changes reshaped the domestic transportation industry. Purchasing and transportation managers began to discover they had the power to influence transportation cost and service levels. Increasingly, purchasers became involved in the buying of transportation services, something that did not occur as frequently when transportation was highly regulated.

The Air Cargo Deregulation Act of 1977 eliminated economic regulation and permitted air carriers to publish cargo rates without the approval of the Civil Aeronautics Board. The act also allowed new air carriers easier entry into the marketplace. These

changes encouraged competition by allowing purchasers of air carrier services to negotiate rates and by allowing new competitors to begin service. The Air Passenger
Deregulation Act of 1978 freed carriers from government regulation in the areas of
passenger fares and entry into the airline industry. One effect of air deregulation was
a dramatic increase in the number of new airlines formed during a five-year period
following the passage of the law. The increase indirectly affected buyers of air transportation because new passenger carriers also had the ability to move freight in the
cargo holds of their planes.

The Motor Carrier Act of 1980, while still requiring published tariff rates, allowed
carriers increased rate-making flexibility. Carriers could now offer discounts from
published rates to buyers of transportation services, which opened the door for rate
negotiations between buyers and carriers. Also, it became easier to obtain a "certificate of public convenience and necessity," a document providing a motor carrier with
a legal right to operate. The relaxation of the rules controlling the granting of operating certificates resulted in a dramatic increase in the number of motor carriers offering transportation services. The Motor Carrier Act also allowed carriers, both public
(i.e., common carriers) and private, to haul a wider range of goods. For example, creative shippers began to take advantage of a private carrier's need to fill trucks for return back-haul shipments. The Transportation Industry Regulation Reform Act
(TIRRA) of 1994 further deregulated the trucking industry. Specifically, this act
deregulated intrastate trucking; eliminated the need for carriers to file individually
set tariffs or rates; eliminated the need to provide notice of rate changes; provided
rate-making confidentiality between carriers and shippers; allowed off-bill discount-
ing; and removed some antitrust exemption for rate-making bureaus.

The Staggers Act, which applies to railroads, also provided carrier rate-making
flexibility. In addition to rate flexibility, railroads could now enter into long-term contracts with shippers. This was an important provision for firms that purchased large
volumes of raw materials and relied on railroads for transportation. The act also deregulated a form of intermodal transportation—trailer on flat car (i.e., piggyback). As a
result, piggyback intermodal transportation has enjoyed steady volume increases
since the passage of the deregulation law.

In the maritime industry, Congress passed the Ocean Shipping Reform Act
(OSRA) in 1998, a law that allows shippers and liner carriers to enter into confidential
service contracts. Although such contracts will continue to be filed with the Federal
Maritime Commission, rates, service commitments, and intermodal origin and destination points will no longer be public.[3] Industry statistics put the percentage of cargo
moving under contracts at less than 50%. This should rise to more than 75% within the
next five years, indicating the need for effective purchase negotiation with carriers.

This brief discussion of transportation deregulation is critical for understanding
purchasing's involvement with the buying of transportation services. If Congress had
not deregulated the transportation industry, purchasing probably would not have
taken as great an interest in the evaluation, selection, and control of transportation
providers. While each piece of legislation created some level of uncertainty for shippers and carriers, the legislation also created opportunities for innovate purchasers to
add value through the purchase of transportation services.

$\mathscr{P}$URCHASING'S ROLE IN BUYING TRANSPORTATION SERVICES

Effectively managing transportation services is important for several reasons. First, transportation is a major cost center at most manufacturing companies. Typically, transportation costs comprise 10% (on average) of a product's total cost structure. For many firms, logistics expenses now are second only to material costs in terms of their impact on cost of goods sold, and logistics expenditures represent one of the largest costs in international commerce. According to conservative estimates, in 1996 firms spent more than US$3.4 trillion to move goods and materials from one part of the globe to another. In North America, logistics accounted for a staggering 10.7% of total gross domestic product.[4] Robert A. Gallant, chief of supply management at Canadian National Railways (CNR), believes that firms can achieve 15% to 45% savings when coordinating and controlling the movement of material throughout the supply chain. He adds that once CNR adopted an integrated supply chain management perspective the railroad saved more than $60 million over the next two years.

Perhaps more important than cost savings is the direct impact transportation has on operations. Transportation affects production and scheduling systems, inventory levels, and customer order management. Companies that do not effectively manage transportation may experience increased waste and reduced competitiveness. While often taken for granted, transportation can have serious consequences if not managed properly. When managed properly, world-class transportation systems can satisfy end-customer needs faster and at a lower cost. For example, Mitsubishi Motor Manufacturing of America gives GATX Logistics a two-week view of its production schedule, which has helped keep its assembly line running without disruption. Also, GATX links directly to Mitsubishi's 360 suppliers via EDI and has three cross-docking facilities near Mitsubishi's suppliers in the Midwest. These services provide an additional $1 million per year in savings to the automaker. A senior vice president at Ryder Integrated Logistics says using transportation as part of supply chain management can drive inventory out of the process by keeping material in constant motion. (See Chapter 17, which discusses the lean supply chain.)

Deregulation has created major opportunities for purchasing to negotiate improved rates and service levels for transportation services. During the early 1980s, it became apparent that transportation offered significant cost savings if managed properly. Purchasing began to take an active role in the selection of and negotiation with transportation service providers. One observer offered this comment shortly after the passage of the major transportation laws in the 1980s:

From the purchasing point of view, it's more important than ever for a company to get hold of its transportation costs. A lot of purchasing people tend to buy goods on a free on board (F.O.B.) destination basis, which means the purchase price includes the transportation cost. Consequently, many companies don't even know their transportation costs—they get buried in the piece price. Result: the shipper, but not the buying firm, benefits from deregulation. A company must get hold of its transportation costs before it can truly benefit from the opportunities of deregulation.[5]

As purchasing professionals take a more active role in transportation management, what exactly are the duties they assume? What are the different activities of a purchasing and transportation professional when buying transportation services?

A study conducted in the early 1990s found that purchasing was predominantly involved with four major categories of transportation decisions.[6] The highest degree of involvement was the choice of transportation mode (88%), the choice of carrier (85%), price determination (67%), and rating of carrier performance (67%). Choice of mode refers to the selection of the type of transportation carrier—for example, rail versus motor carrier. Almost half the purchasing departments surveyed also indicated some involvement in outbound transportation. While purchasing rarely controls the outbound flow of material, it can involve itself with carrier selection and evaluation or other issues related to the purchase of transportation services. Many purchasing departments are now using detailed performance measurement systems, not only with their suppliers of goods, but with their transportation providers as well. Purchasing can support the purchase of inbound and outbound transportation services just as it supports the purchase of other products and services required throughout a firm.

When purchasing takes an active role in transportation decisions, managers often become involved with identifying and selecting inbound transportation providers, although involvement with outbound transportation providers is becoming more common. Purchasing may also negotiate freight agreements and evaluate carrier performance in a manner similar to the evaluation of suppliers of purchased items. The transportation department, if one still exists, usually involves itself with the day-to-day management of the transportation system or the development of transportation strategies that do not involve purchasing. This includes arranging pick-up and deliveries, processing damage claims, tracing and expediting shipments when required, coordinating intraplant and outbound movements, and auditing freight bills for accuracy. Both purchasing and transportation departments can combine their individual expertise when developing transportation strategies.

$\mathcal{A}$ DECISION-MAKING FRAMEWORK FOR DEVELOPING A TRANSPORTATION STRATEGY

The development of a transportation strategy involves a series of decisions. Exhibit 18.2 presents a general framework outlining some of the decisions and issues a purchaser faces when formulating a transportation strategy. How a transportation network is organized will vary depending on the type of commodity or material being moved. For example, bulk raw material usually requires rail transport, while small, expensive electronic components can use quicker but more expensive modes such as airfreight. No single approach or strategy covers the entire transportation needs of a company that purchases different items and raw materials.

EXHIBIT 18.2   *Transportation Strategy Development—A Decision-Making Process*

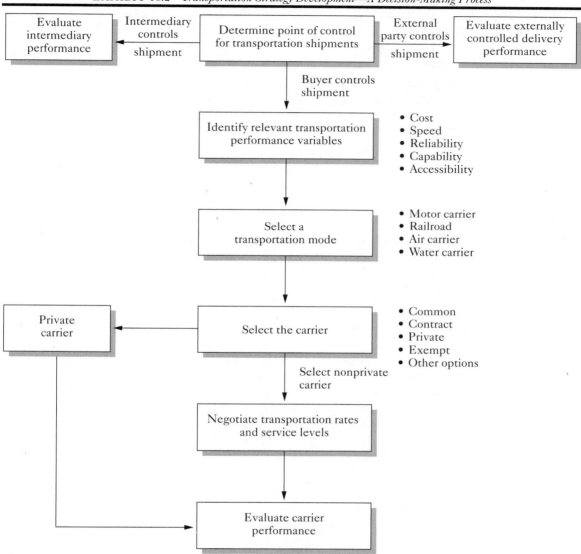

Determine When and Where to Control Transportation

An initial decision regarding an organization's transportation requirements involves determining when and where to control shipments. A significant amount of inbound material, for example, is still shipped *F.O.B. destination.* This designation means the seller retains title to the goods and controls the shipment until it is physically

EXHIBIT 18.3   *Defining Domestic Transportation Shipping Terms*

Shipper's Facility   Carrier   Buyer's Facility
F.O.B. Shipping Point   F.O.B. Destination

What does F.O.B. shipping point mean?   **What does F.O.B. destination mean?**

- Buyer controls or directs shipment
- Buyer assumes title to goods and risk of loss at seller's shipping point, unless agreed to otherwise (UCC Section 2-401)
- Seller has certain responsibilities (UCC Section 2-504):
  - To put the goods in the possession of the carrier
  - To make a proper contract for the transportation of the goods, taking into consideration the nature of the goods and other circumstances
  - To obtain and promptly deliver to the buyer any documents necessary for the buyer to take possession of the goods
  - To promptly notify the buyer of the shipment

- Seller is required at own risk and expense to transport goods to that place and there tender delivery (UCC Section 2-319)
- Seller assumes title to goods and risk of loss until satisfactory delivery to buyer's facility, unless agreed to otherwise (UCC Section 2-401)

received at a purchaser's facility. Unless otherwise negotiated, this also means the seller is responsible for the cost of the physical transportation, which the buying company inevitably pays for in the unit cost of the purchased item. Controlling inbound shipment usually requires a shipping designation of *F.O.B. shipping point*.

When a seller includes transportation charges as part of the unit cost of a good, the buyer often loses the ability to track transportation expenses. This also inflates the value of the purchaser's inventory, which has tax and other financial implications. Even when a supplier assumes responsibility for transportation costs, many purchasers require the supplier to identify transportation-related costs separately from material costs. Exhibit 18.3 compares the two primary F.O.B. shipping designations and the Uniform Commercial Code (UCC) sections that apply to domestic transportation designations.

The choice of whether to insource or outsource transportation is similar to a make-or-buy decision. A purchaser who chooses to have an external party, such as a supplier or logistics service, arrange and control material movement has no further decision to make concerning transportation. For some shipments, particularly small-volume shipments, a purchaser may determine it is not worthwhile to spend the time and energy to arrange transportation. When this is the case, a possible option is to provide suppliers with a list of acceptable transportation providers. The purchaser may even have negotiated a contract with the carrier for discounted freight rates. A purchaser who relinquishes control of inbound transportation to a supplier should still evaluate the delivery performance of supplier-arranged shipments.

EXHIBIT 18.4   *Criteria Used to Measure Transportation Performance*

Performance Measure	Description
Total cost	In addition to the fee charges, total cost includes the cost of extra inventory, warehousing, buffer stock, and in the case of international shipments, broker fees, customs, etc. Other cost factors such as extra managerial time may also have to be factored in.
Speed	Measured as time from when the shipment is released at the supplier's facility to the time of receipt at the buyer's receiving dock.
Reliability	Sometimes described as *fill rate*. Refers to the ability to deliver on time. Can be measured in different ways, but is typically a window of time when the delivery must be made. The measure is thus the percentage of deliveries made within the specified window.
Capability	Refers to the ability of the carrier to move the material, including special materials, hazardous materials, etc.
Accessibility	Refers to whether the carrier is capable of picking up the shipment and delivering it door-to-door.

Another option at this phase of the decision-making process involves the use of a transportation broker or intermediary. While this option also means giving up direct control of transportation shipments, a buyer may realize some benefits. A broker or intermediary should have the buyer's best interest in mind because the buyer is a customer of the intermediary. The broker or intermediary acts as a buyer's agent when arranging transportation. The intermediary can combine shipments with other customers' shipments to achieve a lower total transportation cost. Intermediaries can also perform valuable services such as expediting shipments through customs or negotiating favorable rates directly with carriers. This option is popular for firms lacking the resources or experience to manage their transportation system. It is also an option for small shipments.

Identify Key Transportation Performance Variables

Different performance variables must be assessed carefully when developing a thorough transportation strategy. The following set of variables is assessed when comparing transportation modes as well as specific carriers within the same mode.

The criteria used to measure transportation performance are shown in Exhibit 18.4.

Total Cost Total cost plays a major role in the transportation decision-making framework. If cost were not an issue, more shipments would arrive via air carrier instead of truck and rail. Cost, however, is only one of a number of important variables. Selecting a mode or carrier based solely on the lowest initial cost ignores the total cost of the decision. The lowest cost mode or carrier may not provide reliable delivery or other services that separate marginal from exceptional providers. The cost variable, while important, should not be the only variable used to arrive at a transportation decision. Furthermore, cost evaluation should always be in a total cost context. A transportation carrier that appears less costly may end up costing more than a seemingly higher-cost carrier.

Speed   This variable refers to the in-transit delivery time of a mode or carrier. For some items, such as bulk raw materials, speed may not be an important factor. For producers operating in a just-in-time environment, speed may be a critical factor for inbound shipments from suppliers or outbound shipments to customers. Companies that ship products directly to customers after receiving an order are likely to be focused on speed as a key performance variable.

Items that must arrive as soon as possible from a supplier or reach a customer quickly require a different mode of transportation than items of a less critical nature. Certain items, simply by their physical nature, will always arrive by the same type of transportation mode. When this is the case, a lack of transportation flexibility concerning the speed variable is something a purchaser must manage.

Reliability   A critical performance variable for any type of mode or carrier is reliability, which refers to the accuracy and on-time consistency of the transportation service. It also relates to a carrier's ability to deliver a shipment in an undamaged condition. For example, if a carrier says a shipment will arrive Monday morning, a recipient will expect that the shipment will actually arrive at the promised date and time. Reliability differs from speed—it is the measure of actual arrivals against planned arrivals. A reliable carrier requiring a longer in-transit time may be better than an unreliable carrier with a faster average in-transit time, particularly from an operational planning perspective.

Capability   This variable refers to a mode or carrier's ability to provide the equipment and services for the movement of material. This variable has several dimensions. First, does the transportation mode have the capability to transport an item? Can an air carrier move a hazardous material? Can a motor carrier transport a bulk chemical? Second, does a carrier have the equipment to perform the job? Does a specific motor carrier have the equipment and resources to transport a full shipment each day from a single shipping location? Capability is important because it affects a mode or carrier's ability to provide consistent transportation service (or even provide the service in the first place).

Accessibility   Transportation accessibility refers to a mode or carrier's ability to provide a service over a geographic area. A totally accessible mode or carrier is capable of picking up a shipment and delivering it directly to its final destination. Geographic constraints, however, restrict some modes. Inland water carriers, for example, are usually not accessible for most shippers. Use of this form of transportation often requires another mode to pick up or deliver material to the waterway. A carrier that cannot offer total accessibility for its customers is not necessarily bad. However, each time a shipment changes hands additional shipment time must be added and the risk of transportation damage increases.

A carrier may not have the regulatory authority or physical routes to transport goods between two points, or to operate in a specific geographic region. Carriers lacking legal authority to move goods directly between two points are not highly accessible. Motor carriers sometimes market their service on the basis of their authority to operate in 48 states. Instead of using different carriers for different shipments around the country, one carrier may be capable of meeting an organization's total transportation requirements.

Select a Transportation Mode

A match must exist between the key transportation performance variables identified in the previous section and the ability of the different modes or types of transportation to satisfy the requirements of these variables. For some items, it is not a difficult decision to make. For example, overseas shipments usually arrive by ocean vessel or, in a limited number of cases, by air carrier. Bulk or liquid commodities, such as raw materials or chemicals, usually arrive by rail. The most common modal decisions involve comparisons and trade-offs between rail and motor carrier; rail and inland water; and motor and air carrier. The most common modal decision for international shipments from outside of North America is between ocean vessel and air transportation.

There are five principal modes of transportation available to purchasers of transportation services: (1) motor, (2) rail, (3) air, (4) water, and (5) pipeline. A summary of the major advantages and disadvantages of each is shown in Exhibit 18.5.

Motor Carriers The greatest competition between transportation modes involves rail carriers and motor carriers. Before World War II, most freight between cities moved via rail carriers. The development of the U.S. highway system after World War II, combined with the flexibility of motor carriers, resulted in the growth of motor transportation at the expense of rail carriers.

It should come as no surprise why over-the-road carriers are a popular transportation option. They have a unique ability to provide door-to-door service, making it a flexible form of transportation. In addition, motor carriers are ideal for carrying smaller-volume (less-than-truckload) shipments. A well-established motor network exists for the movement of less-than-truckload quantities in the United States. It is difficult for a rail carrier to accommodate shipments smaller than a rail car. Motor carriers also have an advantage of speed and reliability over other modes, particularly for full truckload shipments.

Probably the major disadvantage of a motor carrier is its cost relative to other forms of transportation. Motor carrier transportation is six times more expensive than rail on a volume basis and 24 times more expensive than water. Also, motor carriers have limited ability to transport bulk commodities.

Motor carriers are characterized by higher variable costs due to labor costs, fuel, equipment maintenance, and other costs resulting from compliance with rules and regulations. A limit to the amount of weight a motor carrier can transport at one time also makes variable costs higher. Furthermore, each trailer, or tandem of trailers, requires a separate power unit. A motor carrier does not have the volume flexibility of a rail carrier.

EXHIBIT 18.5   *Advantages and Disadvantages of Transportation Modes*

Transportation Mode	Advantages	Disadvantages
Motor carrier	• High flexibility • Good speed • Good reliability • Good for JIT delivery • Can negotiate rates	• High cost • Limited to domestic or regional transportation • Cannot be used for large volumes
Rail carrier	• Lower cost • Can handle wide range of items • Piggyback service can increase flexibility • Direct between major cities • Greater intermodal service • Safe for hazardous materials	• Limited access to rail line or spur • Longer in-transit lead times • Less flexible—may not have rails to all locations
Air carrier	• Quick and reliable • Good for light/small, high-value shipments (e.g., electronics) • Good for expediting/emergency situations	• Very high cost • Location of large airports limits shipping points • Cannot be used for large, bulky, or hazardous shipments
Water carrier	• Good for bulk commodities (inland) and heavy, large items (international) • Can handle most types of freight • Low cost	• Limited flexibility • Seasonal availability • Very long lead times • Poor reliability (may encounter delays at ports, etc.)
Pipeline	• Good for high-volume liquids and gases • Low cost once installed	• High up-front installation costs • Limited to only certain items

Rail Carriers A primary advantage of a rail carrier is the wide range of items it is capable of hauling. While a large proportion of the freight on rail carriers today is of a commodity nature, a rail car can handle virtually any type of shipment. Another advantage of a rail carrier, and perhaps its major advantage, is the relatively low cost of rail transport. The ability to move large amounts of freight over long distances at a per-unit cost that is lower than other transportation modes is a primary reason rail carriers still command a large share of all intercity ton-mile shipments.

The costs associated with equipment, rail yards, and rail lines means rail carriers have high fixed costs. However, low variable costs allow rail carriers to move freight at a relatively low rate per mile. A single engine can move an additional rail car with only a minimal increase in total variable cost.

Firms that rely on rail shipments must have access to a rail line or spur. This constraint limits the use of rail carriers and highlights perhaps the major disadvantage of rail carriers—limited accessibility. Rails have attempted to overcome this limitation by shipping trucks directly on flat rail cars (referred to as *piggyback* service).

Another disadvantage of rail carriers, and one that motor carriers have successfully exploited, is long in-transit times. A two-day shipment by truck can take a week or more by rail. Few trains move as a single unit over long distances. Rail companies ship rail cars between cities by placing the cars with an outbound train moving in the direction of the customer's facility. A cross-country journey may require several switches of a customer's rail car at various rail yards. Each switch at a rail yard increases total shipping time. At the destination city, a local train makes the final delivery to the customer's facility.

In recent years, the rail industry has had to undergo major consolidation and mergers, a process that has eliminated thousands of miles of track from the rail system. The final impact on users and purchasers of rail transportation has yet to be determined.

Rail carriers will always be the mode of choice for certain items. Rail transport is particularly economical for the shipment of agricultural products, output from extractive industries (coal or chemicals, for example) or products associated with heavy manufacturing (steel or autos). It is doubtful that new methods of transportation will become available that shift these items away from the rail transportation mode.

Air Carriers   Air carriers are the least-used transportation mode for the movement of commercial freight, partly because of the high cost of air travel and partly because of the limited types of freight a plane can carry. A major reason for using an air carrier historically has been to satisfy emergency requirements. For example, a machine breakdown may require a replacement part as soon as possible. An air carrier may be the only option capable of meeting the performance variable of speed.

More firms are evaluating air transportation in relation to their just-in-time inventory systems. Shipping a highly priced component via an air carrier may actually be a cost-effective option, particularly if the material does not require much space. A significant amount of competition exists among air carriers today, which supports lower rates and increased service levels.

Higher cost is the primary disadvantage to the increased use of air transportation. Air shipments cost about 20 times more than rail carriers and three times more than motor carriers on a per-unit basis. Air has a high variable-cost-to-fixed-cost ratio due to the high costs of operating a flight. Because of the need to cover variable costs, air-freight rates are higher than other modes of transportation. Air carriers also suffer from limited capacity and flexibility. The dimensions of the plane limit the size and weight of a shipment. Furthermore, the location of larger airports limits the shipping points available to an air carrier. Once a shipment arrives at a destination city via air, a motor carrier almost always makes the final delivery to the customer.

Speed is the major advantage of air transportation. The speed/cost trade-off becomes clear when evaluating the cost of using this form of transportation. Also, as producers attempt to reduce warehousing, it might be an attractive option to use air to ship directly to a facility and bypass costly handling and storage. Over a two-year period, National Semiconductor closed six warehouses around the globe and began air-freighting its microchips to customers worldwide from a new 125,000-square-foot distribution center in Singapore.[7] This reduced standard delivery time 47%, reduced distribution costs 25%, and increased sales 34%.

Water Carrier   This transportation mode includes inland water and oceangoing vessels. Inland water carriers transport items such as bulk commodities and raw materials (chemicals, cement, agricultural products). For example, it is common to see freighters moving raw materials required for steel production from Minnesota to the point of production in southern Michigan. This material moves via the Great Lakes inland waterway system.

Inland water carriers rarely transport finished or semifinished products. The main advantage of water transportation is the large volume an inland barge or ship can move at one time, as well as the relatively low cost. The major disadvantages include limited flexibility of shipping points, seasonal shipment in some areas of the country, slow speed, and the potential for natural disasters such as oil spills, which have devastating effects on the natural environment.

Two-way international trade has increased the amount of freight moving on oceangoing vessels. If a buyer purchases from an international supplier, the modal decision is usually straightforward. Most shipments move across the ocean on deepwater vessels and, to a lesser extent, via air carrier. Ocean carriers are capable of handling virtually any type of freight or raw material. While selection of the form of transportation is usually not an issue for international shipments across the ocean, carrier selection is still important.

Pipeline   The use of a pipeline is usually not part of the decision trade-off between transportation modes. Pipelines primarily transport petroleum or natural gas. Even if a buyer purchases petroleum or coal, it is not likely the buyer will make the decision to use a pipeline for transportation. Another decision maker further up the supply chain sources from raw material suppliers who use a pipeline. Deciding on the use of a pipeline is rarely something a buyer who purchases directly from a supplier must consider. This discussion mentions pipeline only because it is a legitimate mode of transportation.

The cost structure of pipelines is similar to rail carriers. The equipment and physical pipeline (i.e., the right of way) has a high fixed cost and a low variable operating cost. The actual cost to ship via a pipeline is relatively low compared with other forms of transportation, as are labor costs.

Exhibit 18.6 presents the relative ranking of the different transportation modes against five performance criteria. It is easy to see why the motor carrier's popularity has increased with buyers of transportation services. Overall, motor carriers hold a real advantage over other modes when viewing the performance variables in total.

Select the Carrier

Once a purchaser makes a decision about what form of transportation is best suited to transport an item, the next step involves selecting the transportation provider to transport the material. A purchaser has several options available besides simply contacting a for-hire company and arranging shipment. Firms can select a public (common) carrier,

EXHIBIT 18.6   *Relative Ranking of Domestic Transportation Modes*

	Lowest per-unit cost	Speed	Reliability	Capability	Accessibility
Air	5	1	4	3	3
Rail	3	3	3	1	2
Pipeline	1	4	1	5	5
Motor	4	2	2	2	1
Inland water	2	5	5	4	4

1 = Highest rated compared to other modes
5 = Lowest rated compared to other modes

negotiate for services with a contract or exempt carrier, arrange shipments on company-owned vehicles (private carrier), or use a special type of carrier (such as FedEx or UPS). The most common decision is whether to use a common, contract, or exempt carrier (see Exhibit 18.7).

Common Carriers   By law, a *common carrier* serves the general public without discrimination. Part of its operating authority comes from its obligation to serve transportation users in a fair and nondiscriminatory manner. Besides its duty not to discriminate against transportation users, a common carrier must offer reasonable rates, although rates are not published as they were during regulation. A purchaser deciding to use a common carrier, particularly a motor carrier, often has a wide choice of carriers within a geographic region. Examples of common carriers include Roadway, Werner, and Schneider, noted for its bright orange trucks.

Contract Carriers   Companies that rely heavily on precise and frequent transportation might consider the use of a *contract carrier*. A contract carrier does not hold itself out to serve the general public as does a common carrier. The contract carrier serves a shipper (i.e., a buyer) under specific contract terms. A contract carrier, sometimes referred to as a *dedicated carrier*, serves the transportation requirements of the party with which it has a legal agreement. Contract carriers are popular with firms practicing just-in-time purchasing and delivery.

EXHIBIT 18.7   *Overview of Interstate Motor Carrier Industry*

```
                          ┌─────────────────┐
                          │  Motor carrier  │
                          │    industry     │
                          └─────────────────┘
                    ┌─────────────┴──────────────┐
              ┌───────────┐               ┌───────────┐
              │  For-Hire │               │  Private  │
              └───────────┘               └───────────┘
            ┌──────┴────────┐
      ┌──────────┐    ┌──────────┐
      │  Local   │    │ Intercity│
      └──────────┘    └──────────┘
       ┌────┴─────┐    ┌─────┴──────┐
  ┌──────────┐┌────────┐┌──────────┐┌──────────┐
  │Regulated ││ Exempt ││Regulated ││  Exempt  │
  └──────────┘└────────┘└──────────┘└──────────┘
                     ┌──────┴──────┐
               ┌──────────┐  ┌──────────┐
               │  Common  │  │ Contract │
               └──────────┘  └──────────┘
           ┌───────┴────────┐
     ┌──────────┐   ┌──────────────┐
     │Truckload │   │ Less-than-   │
     └──────────┘   │  truckload   │
                    └──────────────┘
             ┌───────────┴──────────┐
     ┌──────────────┐      ┌──────────────┐
     │   General    │      │   Special    │
     │ commodities  │      │ commodities  │
     └──────────────┘      └──────────────┘
```

Household goods
Heavy machinery
Petroleum products
Refrigerated liquids
Refrigerated solids
Dump trucking
Agricultural commodities
Motor vehicles
Amored truck service
Building materials
Films and associated commodities
Forest products

Contract carriers can offer many benefits to the transportation buyer. Besides negotiating a favorable rate, a buyer can usually receive a higher level of service than might otherwise be expected. After all, the carrier and buyer have a continuous contractual relationship.

Private Carriers   A private carrier includes the vehicles that a purchaser controls through direct ownership or management. Typically these vehicles move goods between company-owned facilities or from a company to its customers. At times these vehicles may be used for the inbound movement of material. Besides greater control, this offers the opportunity to increase the utilization of company-owned assets.

Probably the major drawback to using company-owned vehicles for inbound shipments is a lack of dedication to this task. It might be difficult to arrange shipments from a supplier's facility on a regular basis using company-owned vehicles. Practical experience with a number of firms indicates the use of private carriers for inbound shipments is the exception rather than the rule. When firms use a private carrier for receiving purchased items, it is usually the result of a geographically convenient arrangement between a purchaser and supplier.

Exempt Carriers   Exempt carriers are free of any regulation with respect to economic issues. They are able to gain this status because of the type of commodity they haul and the nature of their operation. These carriers usually transport agricultural products, newspapers, livestock, or fish. Exempt carriers are primarily local water carriers of bulk items.

Other Carriers   A buyer can also evaluate other shipping options, which is increasingly the case with electronic commerce (business to consumer) Internet companies. For example, FedEx and UPS fall into this category. The use of these carriers is increasingly becoming an option for smaller shipper and shipments. They are convenient, relatively inexpensive, and extremely reliable. They also offer linked information systems that provide a substantial advantage over their competitors. For this reason, many distributors and mail order companies use FedEx and UPS as their primary provider of transportation services.

Determining the type of carrier is only part of the decision process during this phase. Purchasing must also evaluate and compare different carriers against those variables that are critical to performance. Purchasers should even evaluate their own private carrier to make sure it can meet the same performance standards required of for-hire carriers. Selecting a carrier for transportation services should be no different or less rigorous than selecting a supplier for a purchased component.

Negotiate Transportation Rates and Service Levels

A purchaser with fairly substantial transportation requirements across its supply chain will likely negotiate directly with a carrier for dedicated or contracted services. This does not mean that buyers negotiate only with contract carriers. Negotiation can also occur with a common carrier, particularly over transportation rates and service requirements.

A major result of transportation deregulation has been the shift of the pricing function from published tariffs and rate bureaus to the negotiating table. A purchaser can use the negotiating session to detail required service levels while the carrier can indicate what freight volumes are necessary to support a particular service level or rate. The negotiating session(s) can cover a number of topics:[8]

- Service performance guarantees with penalties and rewards based on performance
- Commitment to ship a minimum amount of volume during the life of the contract
- Handling of freight claims
- Type of equipment to be used by the carrier
- Frequency of shipments
- Establishment of information-sharing systems
- Rate discounts
- Creative and innovative joint methods to reduce total transportation costs

A purchaser does not necessarily negotiate a contract with every carrier it uses. A smart buyer, however, will take advantage of the opportunities offered in today's transportation environment by combining transportation volumes with fewer carriers to achieve shipping economies of scale.

CONTROLLING AND INFLUENCING TRANSPORTATION

A purchaser can take a number of actions to affect transportation service and performance throughout the supply chain. Although we referred briefly to some of these actions, approaches, and techniques throughout the chapter, this section summarizes the more important steps that should be taken to influence and control an organization's transportation activities.

Gain Access to Critical and Timely Data

Accurate and timely information is power to a decision maker. It is difficult to manage material shipments without the ability to collect and analyze critical transportation data. Ideally, the following transportation-related information should be available:

- Number of carriers providing inbound, intraorganizational, and outbound transportation services
- Total transportation expenditures by specific carrier and form of transportation
- Number of suppliers shipping material (the number of shipping points) to a purchaser
- Volume and transportation costs associated with shipments from each supplier
- Breakdown of volumes by commodity type (type of purchased material)
- Performance ratings of individual carriers
- Percentage of shipments arranged by suppliers versus buyers

Exhibit 18.8 presents a simple analysis of one type of data breakdown, detailing the transportation costs associated with shipments from suppliers on different carriers over a one-month period. For example, the data reveal that each supplier, except for supplier E, had over $20,000 in transportation costs associated with shipments to the

EXHIBIT 18.8　*Comparison of Supplier Inbound Transportation Freight Costs by Carrier (Over a One-Month Period)*

		Supplier						
		A	B	C	D	E	F	Total
Carrier	1	$ 2,500	—	$ 3,000	—	—	—	$　5,500
	2	—	$ 5,000	$ 2,000	$ 1,500	—	—	$　8,500
	3	—	$ 2,500	$ 3,750	—	$ 1,000	—	$　7,250
	4	$ 3,500	$ 7,000	—	$ 16,000	—	$ 15,000	$　41,500
	5	$ 4,000	$ 1,500	—	$ 1,200	$　500	—	$　7,200
	6	$ 10,000	$ 5,000	$ 20,000	$ 11,000	—	$ 9,500	$　55,500
	7	$ 1,000	$ 1,500	—	—	—	—	$　2,500
	8	—	—	$ 9,500	—	$ 2,000	$ 7,000	$　18,500
	Total	$ 21,000	$ 22,500	$ 38,250	$ 29,700	$ 3,500	$ 31,500	$ 146,450

purchaser. However, carriers 4 and 6 clearly received a larger share of the transportation dollars, while carriers 1 and 7 had a relatively small share of the business. A buyer can examine these data and begin to make better decisions about where to allocate transportation purchases. This information may also be valuable if the purchaser decides to reduce the total number of carriers serving its facilities.

Develop System Visibility to Material Shipments

Up-to-the-minute data about the location of shipments can provide, at least partially, the visibility required for total material control. The need to achieve this control supports the development of electronic data systems between carrier and buyer.

Motor carriers are increasingly marketing themselves based on their ability to link electronically with transportation buyers through global positioning systems. These carriers offer detailed tracking systems to provide current updates of shipment location. Several levels of complexity exist in these systems. One-way information systems allow a buyer to gain information about the location of a shipment on a real-time basis. A buyer simply requests data directly from a carrier's information system.

Two-way informational systems allow carrier and buyer to send data transmissions between each party's system.

Develop Closer Relationships with Fewer Providers

A common theme throughout this book is that buyers and sellers can often benefit from closer relationships. This logic also applies to transportation buyers and providers. Transportation buyers are increasingly reducing the number of carriers they do business with on a companywide basis with the intention of working closer with the remaining carriers. This allows a transportation buyer to realize additional service and benefits that otherwise might not be available through a traditional business relationship. For example, a transportation buyer may receive a guarantee that equipment will always be available to service the buyer's needs. A sophisticated and detailed two-way electronic data interchange (EDI) system is not feasible or cost-effective with many transportation providers. Controlling and managing the movement of goods is easier and more efficient when a buyer selects only the best carriers available and then develops a closer working relationship with them.

Establish Companywide Transportation Contracts

All companies use transportation services. In larger, diversified firms, however, wasted cost-saving opportunities often occur between business units, divisions, or facilities. The selection of a transportation carrier is often a decision made by local personnel. Real cost and service benefits are possible when transportation volumes between locations, divisions, or business units are combined for increased purchasing leverage.

Examples of such consolidation policies abound. A diversified energy and automation company recognized the potential of combining its purchases of transportation services between its six divisions, 21 production facilities, and six distribution centers. The corporate purchasing manager formed a companywide traffic council that gave the company a single, strong presence in the transportation marketplace.[9] The traffic council includes representatives from each major corporate location. A steering committee is responsible for carrying out the directives of the council. Over a three-year period, a companywide approach to transportation purchasing reduced total transportation expenditures by 14% while sales increased 18% during the same period. The centrally coordinated team approach has reduced the number of carriers the company uses, combined freight volumes to realize lower freight rates, and developed longer-term agreements with remaining carriers. The traffic council and steering committee rely on direct input from transportation users throughout the company as they develop an integrated transportation strategy.

Evaluate Carriers as Suppliers

Purchasers should evaluate transportation providers with the same rigor they evaluate a supplier of a physical good. It is not difficult for supplier evaluation systems to include performance ratings of transportation providers. They should be evaluated on

SOURCING SNAPSHOT

UPS's New eVentures Unit Plans to Expand Logistics Business

United Parcel Service, trying to adapt its rigid culture to the freewheeling Internet economy has formed a subsidiary called eVentures. This unit will help manage the supply chain for small- and medium-sized companies, ranging from picking orders off a warehouse shelf to handling phone calls and returns from customers—all at a price lower than what UPS currently charges its big logistics clients. One instant advantage for UPS in this new venture is that no logistics rival can match UPS's recognizable (and huge) fleet of brown delivery trucks. "They've got a brand name, and they've done all this stuff before" for big logistics customers, said Chris Newton, a supply chain management analyst. The creation of eVentures is part of a major push inside the world's largest package-delivery company to capitalize fully on the emerging Internet economy. One reason eVentures was set up as a separate unit is so it can essentially break the sometimes rigid rules governing the traditional UPS culture. UPS officials acknowledge that some of the 93-year-old company's traditions, such as a strict dress code or not allowing employees to drink coffee at their desks, are out of step with the more relaxed cultures of many Internet-related companies. This new unit provides an attractive alternative for new companies that are trying to establish themselves through Internet-based marketing.

Source: Adapted from Rick Brooks, "UPS's New eVentures Unit Plans to Expand Logistics Business," *Wall Street Journal*, February 7, 2000, A4.

cost competitiveness, delivery reliability, service levels, responsiveness, equipment condition and availability, and quality. Continuous improvement requires the timely visibility of a carrier's performance.

Use Computer Decision-Support Tools and Computer Modeling

Complex transportation systems can benefit from the use of computer models simulating the movement of material. Computer models range from basic PC-based spreadsheets analyzing simple decisions to the complex modeling of entire systems with multiple variables. Modeling allows a buyer to explore many different transportation (and warehousing) options at a relatively low cost before reaching a final decision. Logistics and transportation models support decisions based on quantitative data instead of guesswork.

Other Actions

A broad range of actions can lead to the development of innovative approaches for greater control of transportation. For example, a transportation provider and purchaser may pursue a piggyback arrangement that combines low rail rates with a motor carrier's

SOURCING SNAPSHOT

FedEx Creates Web Unit for Freight Bidding

Memphis-based FedEx Corporation, through one of its operating units, has created an Internet-based company dedicated to online bidding for expedited freight shipping services. The newly created company is called UrgentFreight Inc., and it is located near Akron, Ohio, the home of FedEx Custom Critical (formerly Roberts Express), the expedited, time-critical shipment arm of FedEx. UrgentFreight, in development since December 1999, was officially incorporated as an independent operating subsidiary of FedEx Custom Critical in June 2000. The Website (http://www.urgentfreight.com) was launched August 21, 2000. UrgentFreight marks FedEx's low-key entry into the growing pool of providers of online freight bidding services. That means that UrgentFreight specializes in shipments of more than 150 pounds requiring delivery by noon the next business day. It gives shippers free access to an interactive electronic forum where they can post information about a shipment and receive bids from urgent and airfreight carriers within 15 minutes. Once the shipper selects a bid, freight pickup and delivery arrangements are usually made between the shipper and carrier. With little or no publicity and without FedEx's brand name prominently displayed on the site, about 73 shippers and eight carriers have registered so far. Rick Rennder, UrgentFreight's managing director, notes that "It's a carrier-neutral site. We didn't display FedEx's name because we didn't want to fly any [carrier's] flag over another." In this type of site, UrgentFreight could be considered a competitor to FedEx Custom Critical, although that is not its chief purpose. UrgentFreight wants to expand the market for expedited and urgent freight services, and targets mid- to large-size shippers that need to transport heavyweight cargo such as car parts or computer services in a hurry. "A lot of shippers in today's market really don't know who to use," Renner says.

Source: Richard Thompson, *The Commercial Appeal*, September 13, 2000, B1.

---

accessibility and flexibility. A purchaser may also pool shipments with other shippers to realize a lower total transportation rate and better service. Another option is to use a company's private transportation fleet to carry another company's freight to avoid empty return trips. A progressive, innovative buyer of transportation services has a large set of options available when seeking to improve the transportation network.

$\mathcal{T}$RENDS AFFECTING TRANSPORTATION

Based on changes over the last 20 years, it is possible to look ahead and discuss several trends affecting transportation. In one sense, each of the actions discussed in the previous section represents a trend—the trend toward increased use of decision-support tools, reduced carriers, companywide contracts, increased partnerships, among others. Several other important trends will affect purchasing's involvement with transportation.

Increased Use of Full-Service Transportation Providers

One clear trend is that many carriers will no longer market themselves simply as providers of physical transportation. For complex movements of freight (movements requiring multiple parties or multiple handling), many carriers will perform duties previously requiring the use of in-house personnel or third parties. A growing trend is reflected by the use of full-service transportation providers, particularly when material crosses international boundaries. Full-service providers, in addition to picking up and delivering goods, may consolidate shipments, provide simplified billing, ship just-in-time from local storage points, handle complex oversees shipments, coordinate shipments with other carriers or transportation modes, or configure final products for shipment directly to end customers. This allows a transportation buyer to focus on strategy development while the full-service carrier manages the routine and clerical details of the transportation network.

There are many examples of using transportation suppliers for more than just transportation. UPS handles all the worldwide after-market spare part business for Allison Engine. Burlington Air Express has reduced a computer company's order-cycle time by warehousing inventory, configuring PCs with correct software, and delivering directly to customers. Internet services provided by carriers are expanding as well. UPS and FedEx provide full tracking of packages via the Internet, and FedEx has created software that allows users to complete entire shipping transactions via the Internet.

Increased Combining of Intermodal Resources

We are also witnessing a trend toward increased collaboration between competitive transportation modes, which can benefit a purchaser if the resulting transportation service combines the best performance features both modes have to offer. For example, a major motor carrier combined resources with a major railroad to offer an intermodal arrangement between key east-west geographic destinations. The program offers its customers door-to-door service, a single communication contact, common billing procedures, a single total rate, and expedited terminal operations. The rail carrier cannot, by itself, offer door-to-door service. The motor carrier can offer door-to-door service but at a higher rate. By combining their best performance features, the two carriers can offer transportation users an attractive delivery package. Transportation providers will increasingly combine resources and work more closely together in the future.

Organizational Trends

We expect the purchasing and transportation functions to become more closely aligned within the organizational structure. In many cases, transportation support personnel will report to or at least be located with purchasing personnel, perhaps

SOURCING SNAPSHOT

Full-Service Logistics Firms Take Advantage of Outsourcing

Not only does FedEx move computers for quick delivery, but it takes consumers' phone orders for the computer maker. Ryder System, known mainly for trucks, hauls tractor repair kits for farmers and assembles the parts in each kit. Deere and Company, the farm equipment giant, uses Ryder to store and move parts for its big plant in Waterloo, Iowa, as well as label and package repair kits sent out to customers. Xerox lets workers for Ryder's logistics unit put some parts on copy machines. What's more, Ryder employees deliver the copiers, set them up, and explain to buyers how they work. What's going on here? For years, truckers, shipping lines, and package delivery companies have been expanding into full-service logistics, the enormous business of not only moving goods, but storing and packaging them as well. Now transportation companies are going even further—in some cases taking over the entire operations of a firm. Major manufacturers and retailers are sending more and more of their functions to logistics providers, helping to keep their expenses low by outsourcing. In fact, 75% of large manufacturers are relying on these mega-shippers today, twice the percentage of just four years ago. As one John Deere manager explained, "We don't think the farmer really cares who stores the parts, but he does want John Deere to build his tractor. You need to decide what you're really good at and focus on that."

Source: Adapted from Anna Wilde Mathews, "Logistics Firms Flourish Amid Trend in Outsourcing," *Wall Street Journal*, June 2, 1998, B4.

working on cross-functional logistics teams. This trend supports closer communication between the two groups. Overall, organizations are moving toward an integrated materials and logistics management function, which combines purchasing, transportation, warehousing, distribution, order entry and order management, internal manufacturing planning and control, and even first- and second-tier suppliers.

Focus on Inbound Transportation Pickup Versus Delivery

With the increased use of just-in-time purchasing and manufacturing, we can expect more firms to physically control the pick up of material at a supplier versus waiting for physical delivery from a transportation carrier. A JIT system cannot operate with missed delivery schedules, delays, or uncertainty. Firms are increasingly using private or contract carriers to transport JIT material on a regularly scheduled basis from suppliers.

   Purchasing will play a key role in a JIT inbound pick-up system. Whenever possible, buyers must evaluate and select suppliers who are located within a reasonable distance from the production facility. They must also work with suppliers to make

Compaq Uses Logistics to Create a Build to Order Model

Recently, Compaq Computer Corporation changed its entire manufacturing strategy from an inventory-based model to a "build to order" approach, running plants only to fill customers' orders. Internally, the PC-maker adapted its production processes and modified its generic ERP to make that shift happen. Externally, however, Compaq faced the daunting task of managing the inflows of more than 6,000 different parts from 200-plus suppliers—all at varying levels of technological sophistication.

Compaq contracted with CTI, a third-party logistics provider based in Jacksonville, Florida, to set up a 410,000-square-foot material center in Houston. This center acts as the information and material hub through which all materials from suppliers flow on their way to Compaq assembly lines. The cornerstone of the project is the development by CTI of a sophisticated electronic data interchange (EDI)/digital portal, which provides both suppliers and Compaq visibility into the flow of material through the supply chain. The communications manager becomes a portal to information flow. It allows suppliers, as well as Compaq, perpetual real-time visibility into inventory levels. Such information allows Compaq to make swift, strategic decisions essential to supply chain execution. The Houston Material Center, located just 20 minutes from Compaq's production plant, has reduced order-cycle times from four hours to less than two hours. Compaq and CTI intend to cut order-cycle time even further, thereby increasing inventory turns and decreasing capital assets.

Source: Adapted from Lisa Harrington, "Win Big with Strategic 3PL Relationships," *Transportation and Distribution* 40, no. 10 (October 1999): 118–36.

sure material is available when required. The trend toward the use of a JIT delivery system supports the increased integration of purchasing and transportation.

Time-Based Logistics

A powerful trend today involves increasing responsiveness by reducing transportation time throughout the supply chain. A key task in eliminating time within the supply chain involves visualizing each step as individual links in the order-to-delivery cycle, thereby allowing managers to focus on the processes that are the most time consuming and restructuring operations to eliminate the non–value-added elements. This involves identifying all the possible sources of variance and unnecessary steps that can delay the movement of goods and information. A study focusing on a large consumer packaged-goods company found that order-cycle times varied from 5 to 32 days, with an average of 12 days.[10] The study also noted that the administrative burden required to fully process and close an order was considerable, and contained many elements that were potential areas for lead-time reduction.

The primary measures of logistics performance involve tracking total costs and evaluating customer service. In time-based logistics, performance is usually measured with respect to the number of processes or steps completed per standard unit of time. Typical examples include pounds, pallets, cubic feet, dollar value, trailer loads, lines, cases, or units received or shipped per day; shipping and receiving employees used per pallet load moved daily; cube or payload utilization of inbound or outbound carriers; or total receiving and shipping cycle times. Each of these measures establishes a standard for time-related performance that is critical in becoming a time-based competitor.

Cross-Docking

A critical activity related to warehouse performance is *cross-docking*—a capability related to the increasing trend of customer demand pulling products into the market rather than companies pushing product into the marketplace (replenishment logistics). This logistics strategy strives to take inventory and other related costs out of the pipeline, shorten cycle time, and smooth product flow, while improving customer service. To derive these benefits, a flow-through distribution system must be created. One approach to creating a flow-through system is cross-docking, which can potentially save millions of dollars in storage and transportation costs for those willing to make the investment.

In theory, cross-docking is simple. It is a process that takes place at a distribution center and covers any method for processing shipments that avoids putting the product into storage before sending it to retail stores or other distribution outlets. Instead, the distributor simply moves stock from the receiving dock to the shipping dock, or holds it in a temporary staging area before moving it to the outbound dock.

Cross-docking provides a quick means for moving individual containers or pallet loads directly from the receiving area to the shipping area within a distribution center. This approach eliminates the intermediate put-away, transfer, and retrieval steps inherent in traditional warehousing. Some of the primary benefits include the reduction of time, labor, storage space requirements, inventory, and inventory-related costs involved in handling items. Companies can take advantage of savings derived from buying in large quantities while fulfilling customer needs for fast service through shorter order-cycle time.

DaimlerChrysler effectively uses information technology to quickly and efficiently cross-dock repair parts through a central distribution center in Center Line, Michigan, to regional centers around the United States. U.S. suppliers deliver after-market parts daily to a central facility. Upon receipt, an advanced IT system assesses the inventory condition of 14 regional stocking locations. If a regional site requires material, replenishment tickets for the regional centers are printed at the central facility. The material is then moved from receiving at the central facility to an outbound transportation truck destined for a regional facility, usually departing the same day. Material that is not required for a regional distribution center is stored in the central facility for future use.

GOOD PRACTICE EXAMPLE
Danka Uses Logistics Providers for More Than Transportation

■ ■ ■

Several years ago Danka Office Imaging Inc. faced a huge challenge. The third largest office equipment distributor in the United States needed to relocate a major repair parts depot from Rochester, New York, to a yet-to-be-determined location in 120 days. This required moving some 250,000 stockkeeping units to a new facility that could support same-day, next-day, and at most two-day customer delivery service. An interruption to shipping parts would have severe consequences on Danka's performance. Service, repair parts, and supplies provides 85% of Danka's operating margin. Ongoing service and parts support is a key differentiator between Danka and such giant retailers as Office Depot. Danka customizes service packages to each specific customer's needs. To support its U.S. customers, Danka operates a network of approximately 285 offices throughout the country, employs 3,500 full-time technicians, 1,100 selling representatives, and 4,500 administrative support personnel. The St. Petersburg, Florida, distributor also operates a fleet of 4,000 vehicles. Growth forced the company to consider a new parts depot location.

Under advisement from an external consultant, Danka opted to outsource both the relocation and ongoing management of the new parts depot. The external consultant also helped Danka determine its exact requirements and expectations for the project so Danka could clearly specify expectations to all third-party logistics (3PL) bidders. "We, along with several other 3PL firms, were invited to participate in the request for information [RFI] and subsequent request for quotation [RFQ] for the Danka project," recalls David Groveunder, chief operating officer of Burnham Inc. in Atlanta. "From the beginning, we established a cross functional team to meet with peers at Danka to discuss issues and complete the RFQ. They were very open with us and allowed very candid conversations." As part of Burnham's RFQ response, the 3PL mapped out its process for migrating Danka to the new facility. Burnham also preselected the site for the parts depot, submitting the idea of locating in Indianapolis after they saw the locations of all Danka's branches and field technicians. From Indianapolis, Danka could reach 80% of its destination points by road within two days. Indianapolis is also near a good airport and near the hubs of Danka's strategic air transportation partners (UPS, FedEx, and Airborne Express).

In addition, Burnham identified a building, contacted the building owner, and found material handling equipment vendors. In the latter case, the 3PL researched delivery lead times and had equipment orders ready to go as soon as the outsourcing contract was signed. Danka and Burnham's goal was to make sure the distributor's customers were never without the part they needed. To do this, an IT team—its members drawn from Danka, Burnham, and the external consultant—orchestrated and managed the systems integration on a daily basis.

The move to Indianapolis went smoothly and Danka accomplished its intended goal: to move its parts distribution center from Rochester to a state-of-the-art facility in Indianapolis with no interruption in customer service. In fact, the move to Indianapolis enabled Danka to extend its ordering time window to later in the day, and provide more reliable service to customers. From the start, all players adopted a trusting, collaborative attitude toward the project. Members of the project team at both Burnham and Danka were identified early on and those people saw the project through in its entirety.

Outsourcing stories like Danka's, where the 3PL provider and its customer enter into a complex, strategic partnership, are becoming more common. Danka was willing to entrust the most critical and profitable part of its business—the recurring revenue stream from parts and service support—to an outside party. For 3PLs, becoming strategically integrated in their clients' business does not typically happen overnight. While some progressive companies include 3PLs in their strategic planning activities from the start, most businesses still do not. Instead, they adopt a more cautious, incremental approach to their 3PL relationship, giving providers additional responsibilities as they prove their skill. As a result, 3PLs must be able to prove up front that they can do what they say they can. The performance bar for 3PLs has been rising steadily, and those that are not up to the challenge are exiting the industry. ■

Source: Adapted from Lisa H. Harrington, "Win Big with Strategic 3PL Relationships," *Transportation and Distribution* 40, no. 10 (October 1999): 118–126.

CONCLUSION

Logistics and transportation are exciting and dynamic parts of supply chain management. A study by Ernst and Young titled "Corporate Profitability and Logistics: Innovative Guidelines for Executives" concluded that firms should follow some basic principles for logistics and transportation success. Because purchasing plays a greater role in transportation management, the conclusions of this study directly affect purchasing professionals. This study maintains that a number of principles underlie world-class logistics and transportation performance:

- Link logistic and transportation activities directly to corporate strategy.
- Organize logistics and transportation activities under a single executive-level position.
- Expand and use the power of information and information-processing technology within logistics and transportation.

- Form partnerships and alliances with external parties throughout the supply chain.
- Focus on financial performance by treating some logistical and transportation activities as cost or profit centers.
- Combine transportation volumes on a companywide basis to realize increased purchase leverage and control.
- Measure logistics and transportation performance to sustain superior performance.

One topic that is critical to transportation and logistics management is the role of information technology. Systems such as electronic data interchange, electronic funds transfer, automatic identification, bar coding, global positioning systems, material tracking through the Internet, and automated materials handling are the technological enablers that support an integrated logistics system.

Managing a transportation system presents opportunities and challenges. An integrated logistics system can help firms gain or maintain industry leadership in terms of customer service and time-based competition. As global sourcing and global trade continues to increase, integrated logistics systems will become necessary in order to compete. Purchasing's involvement, although fairly recent by historical standards, will continue to grow. Excellent opportunities exist for the purchasing professional to make major contributions in this important but often overlooked area.

DISCUSSION QUESTIONS

1.   Discuss the business and legislative changes that resulted in an increased awareness by purchasing of transportation activities.

2.   What are the benefits associated with maintaining control of and visibility to transportation shipments?

3.   What were the major features of the Motor Carrier Act and the Staggers Act of 1980? How did the passage of these two laws benefit the buyer of transportation services?

4.   Why did deregulation create additional competition among motor carriers?

5.   Discuss the conditions under which a buyer might prefer that a supplier arrange and control the transportation of purchased items.

6.   Discuss the reasons an organization might consider the use of a transportation broker or other intermediary to arrange transportation services.

7.   Why is it often desirable to reduce the total number of transportation providers?

8.   Discuss each transportation performance variable. What could make some of the variables more important than others when making a transportation decision?

9.   What are the major advantages and disadvantages of air carriers? Motor carriers? Rail carriers?

10. What are the major differences between a common and a contract carrier? Can a buyer negotiate with a common carrier? Why or why not?

11. Why is access to transportation data essential to a buyer when developing a transportation strategy? What are some examples of data that might be valuable?

12. Assume you are a buyer responsible for developing a transportation strategy. List and discuss the major actions you would take to manage the movement of material throughout your supply chain. Do not limit yourself to the approaches discussed in this chapter.

13. What is a full-service transportation carrier? What are some of the value-added services provided by transportation and logistics companies?

14. Discuss the advantages and disadvantages of creating an executive position responsible for coordinating the movement of goods throughout an entire organization.

15. Why would an organization locate purchasing and transportation personnel near each other? Discuss the types of duties that a buyer might perform connected with transportation. Discuss the types of duties that transportation personnel might perform connected with purchasing.

16. Discuss the different strategies available to companies in developing a time-based logistics capability.

ADDITIONAL READINGS

Ballou, Ronald. *Business Logistics Management*, 4th ed. Englewood Cliffs, NJ: Prentice-Hall, 1998.

Bowersox, Donald J., and David J. Closs. *Logistical Management: The Integrated Supply Chain Process*. New York: McGraw-Hill, 1996.

Gibson, Brian J. *Supplier Certification: Utilization and Value in the Purchase of Industrial Transportation Services*. Knoxville: University of Tennessee, 1995.

Kasilingam, Raja G. *Logistics and Transportation: Design and Planning*. Boston: Kluwer Academic Publishers, 1998.

Perry, Charles L. *Purchasing Transportation*. West Palm Beach, FL: PT Publications, 1998.

Gentry, Julie J. *The Role of Carriers in Buyer/Supplier Strategic Alliances*. Tempe, AZ: Center for Advanced Purchasing Studies, 1995.

Tilanus, Bernard, ed. *Information Systems in Logistics and Transportation*. Tarrytown, NY: Pergamon, 1997.

Wood, Daniel F., Daniel L. Wardlow, Paul Regis Murphy, and James C. Johnson. *Contemporary Logistics*. Englewood Cliffs, NJ: Prentice-Hall, 1999.

ENDNOTES

1. The Council of Logistics Management defines *logistics* as "the process of planning, implementing, and controlling the efficient, effective flow and storage of goods, services, and related information from the point of origin to the point of consumption for the purpose of conforming to customer requirements." Transportation is a key element of logistics, and logistics, in turn, is a key element of supply chain management.

2. A complete discussion of transportation regulation is far beyond the scope of this book. For a complete discussion of the topic, see Donald J. Bowersox and David J.

Closs, *Logistical Management: The Integrated Supply Chain Process* (New York: McGraw-Hill, 1996).

3. Lisa H. Harrington, "A New Era Dawns: Shippers and Maritime Carriers Get Their Wished-for Deregulation," *Industry Week* (January 4, 1999): 48.

4. Donald J. Bowersox and Roger Calantone, "Executive Insights: Global Logistics," *Journal of International Marketing* 8, no. 4 (1998): 83–93.

5. William Hendrickson, "Viewpoint with Richard Haupt of Ford Motor Company: How to Take Advantage of the New Era of Deregulation," *Purchasing* (February 23, 1984): 39, as cited in Peter J. Walters, "The Purchasing Interface with Transportation," *International Journal of Purchasing and Materials Management* (Winter 1988): 22.

6. Julie Gentry, *Purchasing's Involvement in Transportation Decision Making* (Tempe, AZ: Center for Advanced Purchasing Studies, 1991).

7. Ronald Henkoff, "Delivering the Goods," *Fortune* (November 28, 1994): 66.

8. Anonymous, "Trends Facing Transportation Buyers/Carriers," *Purchasing World* (September 1998): 34.

9. Peter Bradley, "Roadwork Succeeds for This Transportation Team," *Purchasing* 5 (April 1990): 58–62.

10. W. C. Copacino, "Time to Review Order Management," *Traffic Management* (June 1993): 108–109.

19 SUPPLY CHAIN INFORMATION SYSTEMS AND ELECTRONIC COMMERCE

Reinventing Herman Miller

Managers at Herman Miller are justifiably proud of their furniture plant in Holland, Michigan. The place is so bright and airy that it's called the "Greenhouse." But best of all is the plant's performance. A sign near the front door boasts there has not been a late order in 70 days. Indeed, the factory has managed to solve a host of other problems plaguing office furniture makers. Herman Miller, the country's second-largest manufacturer of office furniture, built the plant five years ago to serve a new division: SQA, which stands for simple, quick, affordable. A key to the effort was linking all sales and purchasing operations via the Internet—something Herman Miller's competitors are only now starting to do. "No one is going to lead in this industry without leading in technology" says CEO Michael Volkema. When founded in 1995, the SQA division was intended to serve small- and medium-sized businesses of five to 150 employees. This market, which Herman Miller had largely ignored, values quick delivery of their furniture. SQA set a goal of delivering anything in its product line within two weeks, compared with six to eight weeks for the rest of the company. To do that, the unit had to scale back the number of choices it offers customers. Chair finishes, for example, come in only gray or black, compared with 11 color selections in the broader Herman Miller line.

To accommodate demand for fast turnaround and lower prices, the company turned to the Web to reduce inventory, cut costs, and slash delivery times. The SQA process works as follows. First, SQA sends a salesperson armed with three-dimensional design software to a customer's office. The software runs on the salesperson's laptop, allowing the customer to select furniture from limited ranges of options, colors, configurations, and styles. Variants are shown on the laptop screen in 3D with the cost of various options tallied by the program. Next, the customer settles on furniture and an office layout. The salesperson generates a final bill, logs onto the Net, and transmits the order to Herman Miller factories in Michigan or California. Within two hours, the customer receives e-mail confirmation of the delivery date. Scheduling software reserves the time and day for production, and space is reserved on a delivery truck. Another e-mail notifies the local dealer to schedule a crew to install the order. On the manufacturing day scheduled by the system, the order is broken down into components, and employees on various production lines start work at the same time. Factory workers gather parts for the order, staple fabrics on chairs and screens, and assemble the furniture. When the delivery truck arrives, components are brought together on the loading dock. Several times a day, suppliers of the components and materials head to the SQA Website to check order volumes to see if inventory is running low and needs restocking. Finally, the furniture is installed on the customer site between three days and two weeks after the date of sale.

The system provides nearly 99% on-time deliveries. Herman Miller is also setting up EZ-Connect, a dedicated Website for its best customers such as insurer Nationwide and

→ → →

stove-builder Viking Range. Clients around the world can order furniture from a limited menu at previously negotiated prices. And EZ-Connect zaps a bill to the customer's accounts payable department via the Net.

The company developed another program to give its network of more than 500 suppliers access to its ordering system on the Web. That means companies that produce chair coverings or laminated surfaces can check what the factory's needs will be weeks in advance. As soon as inventories are expected to drop below a certain level—usually a day's worth of production—the supplier sends more. And to give suppliers an incentive to make their deadlines, each is given a daily rating based on punctuality of deliveries and quality of their goods sold.

Source: Adapted from David Rocks, "Reinventing Herman Miller," *Business Week E.Biz*, April 3, 2000, 92–96.

Many organizations that survived through the difficult final two decades of the twentieth century were able to do so through a metamorphosis known as *business process reengineering*. During this period, almost every major Fortune 500 company went through some form of restructuring, as thousands of workers and managers were shed in an effort to increase productivity and reduce costs. In conjunction with this change, organizations adapted computers and information systems to perform tasks done previously by these workers. They installed systems such as material requirements planning (MRP), distribution requirements planning (DRP), and its broader application, enterprise resource planning (ERP). This was followed up by worries about the Year 2000 (Y2K) bug, requiring careful analysis of these "legacy" systems to determine if any computer programming bugs existed as companies entered the new millennium.

Today companies are restructuring their businesses to function in the new era of electronic commerce. Presented with a deluge of information on dot-coms, servers, business to business (B2B) requirements, and online customer and supplier linkages, organizations are now struggling to catch up with this new world of business.

This chapter is not a technical presentation of computerized information systems. Instead, it focuses on a host of issues that managers in the supply chain must be aware of to appreciate the role of information systems within purchasing. Many purchasers will at some point become involved in the development of different types of purchasing information systems, and knowledge of information systems applications is necessary in order for future managers to realize purchasing performance objectives. Topics presented in this chapter include drivers of new supply chain systems and applications, ERP systems, purchasing databases and data warehouses, electronic data interchange (EDI), business to business electronic commerce, and advanced supply chain systems and applications.

DRIVERS OF NEW SUPPLY CHAIN SYSTEMS AND APPLICATIONS

To be successful in the new virtual e-based economy, even companies in traditional "rust-belt" industries are sitting up and taking notice of the need for new information systems. This is because the next generation of systems will promote the free flow of perfect information instantaneously up and down the supply chain, effectively creating the foundation of a perfectly competitive market. The supply chains that support the new economy will be vehicles of equilibrium and advantage. Survival under these conditions requires fluid and swift supply chains whose primary competitive advantage is speed and excellence of execution. Several drivers are behind this new e-economy.

Internal and External Strategic Integration   As supply chain members increasingly work together, integration must occur between different functions that are *internal* to the organization (purchasing, engineering, manufacturing, marketing, logistics, accounting, etc.), as well as between parties that are *external* to the organization (end customers, third-party logistics, retailers, distributors, warehouses, transportation providers, suppliers, agents, financial institutions, etc.).

Both types of integration present their own set of challenges. Internal strategic integration requires that all members within a company use the same information system that spans across business sites and functions. This is most often accomplished through a companywide enterprise resource planning system (ERP) that links these internal groups together via a single integrated set of master records. We will discuss the challenges of ERP later in the chapter. External integration refers to the systems that link external suppliers and distributors to the focal company. This is needed to forecast demand and balance the levels of supply and demand at different points in the supply chain. Systems used to integrate supply chain members include Internet linkages, network communications, and electronic data interchange.

Globalization and Communication   While the notion of a global market is easy to envision, carrying out business in different cultures and geographies is an extremely challenging proposition. Companies require systems that enable them to manage suppliers and customers in all corners of the world, calculate total global logistics costs, increase leverage and component standardization worldwide, and improve communication of strategies across global business units and supply chain partners. Although English is becoming a universal language of the Internet, supply chain systems must be able to communicate in a variety of languages and alphabets.

Data Information Management   New forms of servers, telecommunication and wireless applications, and software are enabling companies to do things that were once never thought possible. These systems raise the accuracy, frequency, and speed of communication between suppliers and customers, as well as internal users. Information systems must be able to effectively filter, analyze, and "mine" an abundance of data to enable effective decision making. Users must be able to enter databases and "extract" the information they need to make better supply chain decisions. This is often achieved through systems known as *data warehouses* (described later in the chapter) and associated decision-support systems.

New Business Processes   Although many companies underwent reengineering efforts in the 1980s and 1990s, these reorganizations have not remained static. Business processes are constantly being changed in response to a rapidly shifting external environment. Such processes—which include customer order management, supplier evaluation and selection, and new-product development—are being mapped, studied, and changed in order to reduce redundancies, delays, and waste. In so doing, organizations can create a "rapid response" capability that allows them to quickly adopt to their customers' changing needs and control costs whenever possible. Information systems such as computer networks and ERP are enabling companies to link these processes in a more effective manner.

Replacement of Obsolete Systems   As companies adopted systems over time, people became familiar with the new procedures. In so doing, however, companies often adopted a "piecemeal" approach to system usage, such that each function (accounting, purchasing, engineering) used its own system, which was not linked to other functional systems. These obsolete systems (often called *legacy systems*) have now been integrated into a single enterprise-wide system used by everyone in the supply chain. Promising to solve hardware incompatibilities that existed before and to reduce excessive maintenance and programming costs, the systems are also being adopted to exploit the new hardware technologies emerging in the areas of computer networking, telecommunications, and Web-based applications.

Strategic Cost Management   Throughout the complete supply chain cycle, from order fulfillment back to purchasing and order payment, millions of transactions take place between different parties. In the past, these transactions were all done on paper. In order to determine specific cost drivers behind different business processes, companies often "estimated" costs based on outdated cost accounting systems (see Appendix F on the Website). New systems promise to automate data capture throughout supply chain systems, thereby automating the transactions that occur in the traditional procurement cycle. Not only will this reduce the costs of operating purchasing and logistics departments, but it will also enable the effective allocation of resources and enable immense reductions in inventory held in warehouses and stockrooms throughout the entire supply chain.

In the remainder of the chapter, we discuss the four primary forms of information systems used in managing supply chains: (1) enterprise resource planning, (2) data warehouses and purchasing databases, (3) Internet and network linkages, and (4) decision-support systems. Although we cannot hope to do justice to the breadth of these areas in one chapter, this is meant as an introduction to the area with the understanding that continuous learning and evolution of user needs in these systems is required.

Buildscape and E-Bricks Sell Construction Materials Online

As part of Harvard Business School's annual business plan competition for MBA students, Tawfik Hammond came up with the idea for e-Bricks. Simultaneously at another location, Steven Wilson, the chairman of Wickes Corporation, a $1.1 billion lumberyard, came up with the vision for another similar Website called Buildscape. Both parties imagined a site where any builder could order any construction material from an electronic catalog. Both Web operations have yet to prove themselves, but each has learned that the key to online success will be leveraging the old ways of doing business, not wrecking them. To illustrate this point, both parties felt they could sell plywood and other materials to contractors over the Web at a price discount of as much as 20%. However, the team almost immediately realized that they needed to hire insiders from the industry, from buyers and sellers, to be their conduit to the market. They also realized that the scope of their original vision was too broad. Managing a market for big bulky products such as roofing material and two-by-fours would be almost impossible with a network of existing distribution centers around the country. It also turned out that there was a rationale behind many of the construction industry practices that at first looked so inefficient. Indeed, contractors' basic buying habits work against the original e-Bricks model, which would have pitted all suppliers against one another in a brutal electronic price competition. Contractors actually don't want to shop endlessly for the lowest prices. They follow an Old Economy maxim that when buying truly critical supplies, buy from a trusted source—one that consistently shows up on time and with the right stuff. "As time went on, we realized how those relationships actually work," says Mr. Parini, one of the founders of e-Bricks. Soon, e-Bricks realized it had to win over "trading clusters"—well-established groups of buyers and sellers with longstanding relationships—without threatening the suppliers' prices. The focus of e-Bricks became to streamline a cluster's transactions, cut processing costs, shorten the time required for orders, and eventually increase sales between the parties. The team also focused on engineers and architects who order huge quantities of those materials for big commercial projects. As these initiatives move forward, the only certainty is that it is not enough to put up a Website and expect it to drive revenues without understanding the marketplace.

Source: Adapted from Douglas Blackmon, "In the New Economy, Who Are the Hunters and Who the Hunted?" *Wall Street Journal,* April 12, 2000, 1.

ENTERPRISE RESOURCE PLANNING SYSTEMS

An *enterprise resource planning (ERP) system* is an integrated transaction processing and reporting system. The different software applications and forms of ERP support the reengineering of business processes. Expressed in simpler terms, ERP systems provide the means for tracking organizational resources, including people, processes, and technology. The system serves as the "backbone" to the organization in terms of providing the information and support required for making decisions.

ERP systems add a "process logic" to an organizational information system and create a fundamental discipline in business processes. Whereas in the past managers and staff were free to make decisions independent of other functional areas, ERP systems effectively "force" people to interact together in a single system, even if they would prefer not to! As shown in Exhibit 19.1, ERP systems also create a process logic between the closely related areas of customer order management, manufacturing planning and execution, purchasing processes, and financial management and accounting. In effect, ERP systems enable people in these very different parts of the business to communicate with one another.

In an ideal case of moving information across the supply chain, sales representatives enter customer orders directly into a company's ERP via a laptop and modem. The sales reps access the sales order planning and master production schedule. Once the orders are input in the system, the sales reps can provide an "available-to-promise" report and can inform customers when they can expect order delivery. The master production schedule drives the material requirements system, which automatically generates purchase orders to ensure that suppliers deliver parts, components, and services in time to produce the customer's order.

The material requirements planning module converts material requirements into purchase requisitions that purchasing places with selected suppliers. When the supplier delivers the components, this information is passed through to the scheduling system that ensures that the components are linked to the specific production order on the shop floor. Once production begins, the sales person in the field also knows that the order will soon be delivered to the customer. Once delivered, customer billing and payment are also automatically generated by the ERP system.

The idea of having a single information system that links sales, production, transportation, warehousing, and purchasing appears to be an inherently obvious way to manage these different business processes. Historically, individual systems were able to fulfill the informational requirements of sales, purchasing, production, etc., but were not linked to one another in any way. Most importantly, different legacy systems did not communicate with accounting or financial reporting systems. This made it difficult, if not impossible, to be able to extract cost data to allocate overhead costs to different parts of the business.

A typical ERP system is designed around four primary business processes (see Exhibit 19.1):

1. *Selling a product or service:* Customer order management process
2. *Making a product:* Production planning and execution process

EXHIBIT 19.1   *Business Process Integration in ERP*

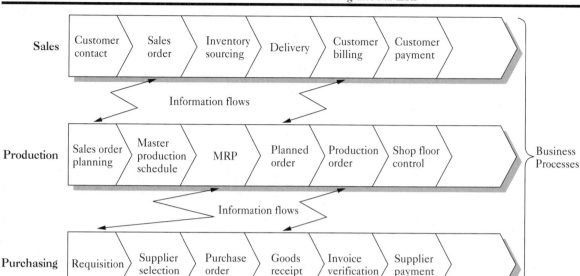

3. *Buying a product:* Procurement process
4. *Costing, paying the bills, collecting:* Financial/management accounting and reporting process (integrated across the prior three processes).

ERP systems facilitate the integration of these processes by adopting a single customer, product, and supplier database. One master record is used for the enterprise with multiple views. All processes use a common database, and information is captured only once, essentially eliminating the possibility of inaccurate data entering the database. Information is rolled down to the affected business process in real time, eliminating delays of information sharing. Visibility of specific transactions taking place in each business process is accessible to everyone in the organization; theoretically, anyone wanting to find out information such as where an order is in the process or whether a supplier has been paid, can obtain the latest updates by going through the system (instead of making phone calls, etc.). In addition, all business processes are linked with the work flow through the use of templates for entering information about transactions at every step.

The actual process of implementing a new ERP system in an environment where people have grown accustomed to using their single familiar legacy system has proved to be a monumental task in many organizations. Many implementation efforts have turned into multimillion-dollar projects involving consultants residing on-site for months and even years. Why is the task of ERP implementation proving to be so difficult and expensive?

Implementing ERP Systems

When businesses implement an ERP system, they must by definition adhere to a more rigorous set of business processes. In Chapter 12 we discussed process mapping as a tool to identify what exactly happens within any given business process. Before organizations actually implement ERP, they must first create a process map for every process shown in Exhibit 19.1. When companies actually map what they "believe" a process looks like, they discover that the actual process is quite different than what they thought it should look like. In some cases, no formal process exists, since everyone in the functional organization has done it their own "unique" way. When it comes time to create an information system around the business processes, many companies discover that they must also "reengineer" or change their business processes before they can build an information system around it. In some cases, changing these business processes requires a major organizational and cultural change. Although ERP consultants can effectively create a system around a well-defined business process, they cannot create a system around a business process that has not been well defined or explained to them by employees.

In order to effectively implement an ERP system, a company must go through four steps to ensure that the business processes are effectively reengineered and improved:

1. *Define the current process "as is."* An ERP implementation team of subject-matter experts document what the current process looks like.
2. *Define what the "best-in-class" business processes should be.* At this point, the team must have a clear understanding of what the final objective of the process is. Further, they must understand what the ERP system will replace, and how the benefits are likely to occur.
3. *Develop the system.* This is an iterative process in which consultants work in conjunction with those managers who are most familiar with the business processes in question.
4. *Work through all final "bugs" and then "flip the switch."* A danger that often exists when flipping the switch—switching over from the old system to the new system—is that the company may not be ready for the change, nor is the system completely configured to handle the specific activities that keep the business running.

ERP Meltdowns

Although ERP systems hold out the promise of improved integration, some companies are finding the implementation process to be expensive, and in come cases, ineffective. Consider, for instance, the case of Hershey Foods. Just a few days before the biggest candy binge of the year, Halloween 1999, one of their largest warehouses in Michigan displayed empty shelves where there should have been Hershey's chocolate bars, Reese's Peanut Butter Cups, and Rolos. Unfortunately, an order for 20,000 pounds of candy that the regional distributor had placed hadn't arrived. In fact, the distributor had not received any orders for five weeks. The $4.4 billion candymaker had flipped the switch on a $112 million system that was supposed to automate and modernize everything from candy orders to putting pallets on trucks. The project called for 5,000 personal computers as well as network hubs and servers and several different vendors.

What happened? Despite the complexity of the system, Hershey decided to go online with a huge part of the implementation all at once—a so-called "big bang" that computer experts says is rare and dangerous. Initially, the confectioner planned to start up in April, a slow period. When bug development and testing weren't complete, the start-up date was pushed to July, when Halloween orders were beginning to arrive. The result of this huge mistake: net income dropped 19% in the third quarter of 1999, and market share was lost to competitors. Unfortunately, Hershey also lost out on a good portion of the Christmas 1999 sales as well.[1]

An important lesson learned from the Hershey disaster was that ERP systems may be very good for integrating *internal* business processes but oftentimes do not have the capabilities for linking suppliers and distributors both up and down the chain. In many respects, ERP systems should be installed *before* linked information systems are put in place with outside parties. There is no point in sending out inaccurate information to outside suppliers and distributors—rushing to do so before one's own "house" is in order. In the next section, we discuss purchasing databases and data warehouses.

$\mathcal{P}$URCHASING DATABASES AND DATA WAREHOUSES

A prerequisite needed before introducing any type of ERP system that manipulates data is the development of a reliable *database*—an integrated collection of computer files capable of storing operational data essential for managing a department. Databases are highly efficient in the storage and retrieval of data because minimal overlapping of information between the files occurs. Reduced redundancy of information between files allows different systems to cross-reference and use efficiently the data contained in all files.[2] In the past, different user groups could share data from the files as needed but gain access only to the data necessary to support their system needs. The new forms of ERP systems are allowing more users from functional groups other than purchasing access to these files.

Although definitions vary, a data warehouse is generally thought of as a decision-support tool for collecting information from multiple sources and making that information available to end users in a consolidated, consistent manner. Rather than trying to develop one unified system or linking all systems in terms of processing, a data warehouse provides the means to combine the data in one place and make it available to all of the systems.

In most cases, a data warehouse is a consolidated database maintained separately from an organization's production system databases. Many organizations have multiple databases, often containing duplicate data. A data warehouse, in theory, is organized around informational subjects rather than specific business processes. The data warehouse stores data fed to it from multiple production databases in a format that is readily accessible by end users. Data held in data warehouses are time-dependent, historical data and may also be aggregated. For example, separate production systems may track sales and coupon mailings. Combining data from these different systems may yield insights into the effectiveness of coupon sales promotions that would not be immediately evident from the output data of either system alone. Integrated within a data warehouse, however, such information could easily extracted.

Purchasing processes require a variety of information maintained on different databases that make data warehouses very useful. The purchasing system must be able to pull data from and store data into the host data file. If a proposed purchasing system requires nonexistent data, then a new database must collect and store the information. A basic purchasing and materials information system requires, at a minimum, access to a number of databases or files. A *file* may be a collection of specific data, sorted in alphanumeric order, or by criteria chosen by the user. Examples of some of these files include the following:

- *Part files:* Records the part numbers that all manufacturing firms rely on to identify the thousands of unique purchased entities within a system. The actual content of the part file is a function of a firm's specific informational requirements. The time required to capture information on part numbers and enter them into a database can be significant.
- *Supplier name and address file:* Contains the names and addresses (including e-mail addresses) of each supplier with which a firm does business.
- *Historical usage file:* Stores historical usage by part number and using location. This information supports inventory analysis and updating of material forecasts with actual historical data.
- *Open-order and past-due file:* Maintains the status of open material releases and stores an order as pending until a firm physically receives the scheduled release. Any orders not received by their due date become past due. This file provides data that a buyer or material planner requires to maintain visibility and control of the material pipeline.
- *Bill of material file:* Details the component requirements of a part number. It is an integral part of the material requirements planning (MRP) system. If the material system generates a release for an end-item or subassembly part number, then the system must also generate releases for all components as well. This file also provides visibility about sourcing requirements for new parts with components.
- *Engineering requirements file:* Provides visibility to the specific engineering requirements and specifications for a part number.
- *Forecasted demand file:* Calculates anticipated demand requirements for each part number in the part file. It relies on the historical usage file to update and calculate projected future requirements.

These databases support the development of both basic and sophisticated purchasing and material information systems. While purchasing is not responsible for directly maintaining all of the data on these files, it must have access to the data to support its operating requirements.

ERP Modules and Access to Purchasing Databases

ERP systems are typically organized around specific "modules." A module generally contains the software required to enter data about a set of transactions that are specific to certain business processes. For example, the financial module allows users to enter information and obtain data about current amounts receivable, current inventory dollars, etc. Although the financial module is typically the first module developed for companies, the next to be implemented is generally the purchasing and materials management module.

This section describes the *module*—a basic feature of an ERP system that is unique to the purchasing processes. The purchasing and materials management module is typically integrated into a single system used by all functions in the organization. In addition to the data just presented, the purchasing module must contain the purchasing function information and data from a variety of processes including the following:

- Inventory management and control
- Material requirements planning (MRP)
- Material releases
- Request for quotation processing
- Supplier selection assistance
- Purchase order issuance
- Supplier performance measurement and control
- Receiving and inspection
- Management and reporting capabilities

The role of these different processes within the ERP purchasing module is described next.

Inventory Management and Control   The module must provide control and visibility to the status of individual items maintained in inventory. The main functions are to maintain inventory record accuracy and to generate material requirements for all purchased items. The system should also have the capability to analyze inventory performance of purchased items (inventory turns, for example).

Material Requirements Planning (MRP)   This module must allow planning of material requirements generated in the inventory management and control module. This part of the system also allows the manual input of requirements to handle one-time purchase requirements when no established need or requirement exists within the system. The module generates automatic purchase requisitions and passes that information to the material release system.

Material Releases   This module must allow for the physical generation and forwarding of material releases to suppliers (either electronically or by mail/fax). A material requirement does not reach this stage unless it has an assigned purchase order. In a nonelectronic environment, the material release is a paper-generated document sent directly through the mail or faxed to suppliers. In an electronic environment, the supplier receives the release electronically from the purchaser, either through an electronic data interchange (EDI) system or via the Internet. Both types of systems rely upon this module to generate the actual material requirement.

Request for Quotation Processing The first three business processes described here may or may not be the purchasing department's responsibility. Within most large companies, the routine reordering of items with established purchase orders is the responsibility of a materials group not directly connected to purchasing. The request for quotation module is the direct responsibility of purchasing. When a user generates a material request with no current supplier, it is often the responsibility of purchasing to identify potential suppliers. One method to accomplish this is to generate requests for quotes (RFQs). An RFQ is a request to submit a proposal based on a set of specifications provided by a buyer. The module assists in identifying qualified suppliers to receive RFQ requests. The module automatically generates, issues, and tracks the progress of the RFQs throughout the system. Again, this may be done either electronically or manually, depending on the company's level of maturity in introducing the process.

Supplier Selection Assistance The module should be organized around a critical task assigned to the purchasing department: supplier selection. Firms are placing an increasing emphasis on supplier selection because of the contribution the supply base makes to strategic performance objectives. The supplier selection assistance module uses a basic set of mathematical algorithms to assist a buyer when evaluating different supply and cost scenarios. This is discussed later in a section on decision-support system applications.

Purchase Order Issuance The module supports the generation of purchase orders, which involves the automatic assignment of purchase order numbers for selected items along with the transfer of purchase order information to the proper database(s). The module provides purchasing with visibility to current purchase orders on file.

Supplier Performance Measurement and Control The module provides visibility to open-item status and measures and analyzes supplier performance. The key features include automatic inquiry of item status, monitoring of order-due dates, and supplier performance analysis. The module should have the capability to monitor planned receipts against due dates, provide immediate visibility to past-due items, and flag those items likely to become past due. The system should generate summary reports of supplier performance compared against predetermined performance criteria, which may include due-date compliance, quality ratings, price variances, quantity discrepancies, and total transportation charges.

Receiving and Inspection This module updates system records upon receipt of an item. Most systems hold a received item in a protected state (unavailable for use) until all inbound processing is complete. Sophisticated systems are able to do this via a bar-code reader that automatically transmits all necessary information into the data-

NTT Seeks to Redefine Japanese Markets

Nippon Telephone and Telegraph (NTT), the $72 billion communications giant, is creating a consortium of top Japanese electronics suppliers that will pool their suppliers and buyers in a Web trading network. The company is in negotiations with potential consortium partners, including $10.5 billion Ricoh Company. The network, launched in the second quarter of 2000, will trade more than $2 billion worth of goods and services within five years and eliminate 10% of NTT's procurement costs. In addition, NTT will levy transaction fees on the business it generates from the site. The savings from such group buys may be simple math, but the structure of these new buying networks is as complex as a Japanese *keiretsu*. The NTT consortium, for example, will accommodate a variety of buyer-seller relationships allowing "any buyer to purchase from any supplier," says Noriyoshi Osumi, a vice president of NTT America who serves as an architect of the parent company's consortium. In some cases, the members of the electronics consortium may decide to buy parts or components from one another. Or they may all decide they want better deals on, say, paper, and so invite a new member to supply that item. According to Osumi, NTT will facilitate—and profit from—any combination.

Source: Adapted from "Purchasing in Packs," *Business Week E.Biz*, November 1, 1999, EB33–38.

base. This processing includes tasks such as inspection (if required), material transfer, and stockkeeping.

Management and Reporting Capabilities   A well-designed ERP purchasing module has the ability to generate timely management reports providing visibility to the entire materials process. In a modern systems environment, many firms no longer generate a paper copy of each report. Instead, users view the reports via networked computers placed throughout the organization, although a user can usually generate a printed copy of the report if needed. In creating these reports, more and more companies are turning to *data warehouses* (described earlier).

Most systems have the capability to generate new reports assuming data are available or can be generated by using other data. Another capability of a well-designed system is that the frequency of data reporting and system updating matches a user's operational needs. A system that operates in a real-time environment provides the most current data. *Real-time updating* is a process in which all data files that include a specific address are automatically updated within the system. In contrast to real-time updating is the *data bucket*—a process of storing each transaction in a temporary file and updating the system at scheduled times throughout the day or on a weekly basis. *Batch updating* refers to the process of downloading all data buckets into the main system on a regularly scheduled basis.

Electronic Data Interchange: The Predecessor to E-Commerce

Traditional information flows between buyers and suppliers often necessitate a lengthy sequential process composed of multiple steps required to support the servicing as well as the fulfillment of the order. Examples of these information flows include transmission of the product specifications from buyer to supplier, submission of a bid, acceptance of the contract, inspection and receiving documents associated with the shipment, accounting audits, and submission of payment. Some of the problems that occur within these traditional information flows include increased transaction time, low accuracy due to data-handling errors, high utilization of staff time and resources, and increased uncertainty in the form of both mailing and processing delays.[3]

An early approach to facilitating transactions electronically was *electronic data interchange* (EDI)—a communications standard that supports interorganizational electronic exchange of common business documents and information. First implemented in the 1980s and 1990s, EDI represented a cooperative effort between buyer and seller to become more competitive by streamlining the communication process through the elimination of many of the steps involved in traditional information flows. The basic components of an EDI system include the following:

1. *A standard form (EDI standards):* Include the basic rules of formatting and syntax agreed upon by the users in the network. The American National Standards Institute (ANSI) ACS X12 series of EDI standards was one of the first adopted by many companies.
2. *A translation capability (EDI software):* Translates the company-specific database information into EDI standard format for transmission.
3. *A mail service (EDI network):* Responsible for the transmission of the document, usually in the form of a direct network or through a third-party provider. Such a value-added network (VAN) serves as an intermediary "post office" for the systems.

The process that occurs when buyer and supplier go through an EDI transaction ideally progresses in the following manner.

1. The computer in the buying company monitors the real-time inventory status of the item purchased using technologies such as bar-code scanners.
2. When it is determined, according to a predefined reorder criterion, that there is a need to order more of the item, the application program notifies the translation software.
3. An EDI purchase order is created and released against a prenegotiated blanket amount, and the purchase order is sent to the supplier.
4. The supplier's computer receives the order and the EDI software translates the order into the supplier's format.
5. A functional acknowledgment, which indicates receipt of the order, is automatically generated and transmitted back to the buyer.

6. When the original EDI purchase order is created, a number of additional electronic transactions may occur. Bridging software transmits the relevant data to the buyer's accounts payable application, to the buyer's receiving file, to the supplier's warehouse or factory file, and to the supplier's invoicing file.

7. Once the order is filled from the supplier's warehouse or factory, a shipping notice is created and transmitted to the buyer. This shipping notice may require some manual data entry by the shipper. However, this is the first time that any manual keystrokes are required in the entire process.

8. Upon receipt of the goods, a shipping notice is electronically entered into the receiving file. Although additional keying may be required, technology often eliminates this step as well.

9. The receipt notice is transmitted through bridging software to the accounts payable application and to the supplier's invoicing application, whereupon an invoice is electronically generated and transmitted to the buyer.

10. Once the invoice is received by the buyer's computer, it is translated into the buyer's format and the invoice, receiving notice, and purchase order are electronically reconciled (eliminating the need for an accounting audit).

11. A payment authorization is electronically created and transmitted to accounts payable, the receivables application is updated to indicate an open receivable, and payment is transmitted electronically from the buyer's bank to the supplier's bank.

12. An electronic remittance advice is transmitted to the supplier, and upon receipt, this information is translated into accounts receivable and the buyer is given credit for payment.

Within this process, there are only three instances of manual data entry. In traditional information flows, each step would require that paperwork be completed and filed by clerical staff. Thus EDI saves a great deal of time and paperwork—as well as allowing fewer opportunities for errors, no mailing or physical transmission delays, and lower clerical costs.

EDI and the Internet

Despite the promise of greater diffusion of EDI via value-added networks, EDI remained a technology that required significant investment by companies to implement. EDI technology required investment in application-specific hardware that could not be used for different purposes. Because there are service fees associated with VANs, they may be more expensive to use than direct networks. Smaller suppliers in particular found it difficult to justify the investment in EDI technology, and struggled with the demands placed on them from different companies to adopt differing EDI systems. Finally, EDI was never considered an "interactive" mode of communication. Each time a transmission was sent, it implied that a "decision" had been made: an order for a fixed amount placed, a forecast of future demand fixed, a lead time for delivery specified, etc. There was never any means for the buying and supplying parties to actually interact, collaborate, and reach a decision through joint,

EXHIBIT 19.2   *Internet EDI with Virtual Private Networks*

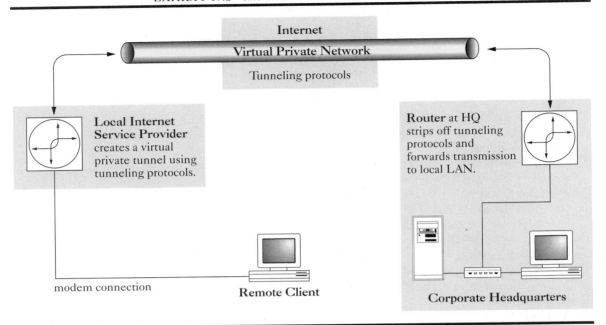

bilateral communication. In the last five years, however, Internet technology emerged that has changed business to business information systems.

As shown in Exhibit 19.2, the Internet facilitates collaboration between parties in the supply chain through a *virtual private network (VPN)*. A virtual private network is similar to a VAN, but is hosted on a third party's Website and server, and does not require any significant investment on the part of either buyer or supplier. Instead of having to invest in a significant amount of "hard" technology, a supplier can be connected to a large customer through EDI simply by having a computer, a modem, and software. In other cases, a T1 line may be used to transmit higher volumes of data. A T1 line is a high-speed optical network line that enables quicker response time when a user goes online. Ford, for example, has offered to connect their suppliers to the Internet for as little as $8 a month, which they recover in improved communication with their supply base.

Let's look at an example to see the way this system works. Suppose a supplier wishes to notify a customer that they are shipping an order. First, a local Internet service provider (ISP) creates a virtual private tunnel using tunneling protocols—tunneling protocols are essentially the "alphabet" and "rules of grammar" that allow different systems to work together—including PPTP, L@F, L2TP, and others, which may be clustered around different industry groups. For example, many high-tech companies have adopted rosettanet (http://www.rosettanet.org), while U.S. automotive

Inside IBM: Internet Business Machines

In his annual meeting with Wall Street, CEO Lou Gerstner observed that "I am not suggesting that you view us as an Internet company, but I think that it is worth noting that IBM is already generating more [e-business] revenue and certainly more profit than all of the top Internet companies combined." Indeed, IBM estimates that 25% of its revenue—some $20 billion—is driven by e-business demand. That's nearly 50% more than Internet darling Sun, whose servers are used for most Web businesses. IBM does not just promote the Internet to its customers—it also uses it for its own business, believing that the best way to learn is by doing. By moving purchasing onto the Web, the company expects to save $240 million on the $11 billion in goods and services it will buy this year. So far, IBM has plugged more than 6,700 suppliers into its online procurement system. Now, IBM can cut out rogue buying—employees who buy from suppliers that are not preapproved. IBM is also helping other companies to turn over entire business processes to IBM that are conducted over the Web. IBM also uses the Web for internal training and expects 30% of its internal training materials to be delivered online with anticipated savings of more than $120 million. Finally, the company also uses the Net for service calls handled through ibm.com. This year, IBM expects to handle 35 million online service requests, saving an estimated $750 million in customer support costs.

Source: Adapted from Peter Burrows, David Rocks, and Diane Brady, "Inside IBM: Internet Business Machines," *Business Week E.Biz*, December 13, 1999, EB20-40.

companies are adopting protocols established by the Automotive Industry Action Group (http://www.aiag.org). Using this protocol, data are transferred from the supplier to the customer's router at their headquarters over the Internet. The router at headquarters strips off the tunneling protocols and forwards transmission to a local area network (LAN) and then to the right individuals. When the customer wishes to place an order with the supplier, the reverse process takes place.

Internet EDI is certainly an important application providing numerous benefits. This approach is typically much less expensive than a traditional "hard-wired" EDI system and presents fewer standards issues, but it also typically requires a common platform on either end (e.g., common ERP systems). The tunneling protocol used helps to addresses security concerns that users may have when relying on the Internet to transmit data. However, the true benefits of the Internet go far beyond this. In fact, the Internet enables buyers and suppliers to achieve a level of collaboration that extends far beyond EDI technology as it was originally conceived. To truly understand how this collaboration takes place, we need to delve into the details of how the Internet evolved and understand the properties of "Net-centrism."

$\mathcal{B}$USINESS TO BUSINESS ELECTRONIC COMMERCE: A NEW FORM OF PURCHASING

Attributes of the Internet

The growth of the Internet has been explosive. One group of researchers at the Center for Research in Electronic Commerce at the University of Texas found that the Internet spans 200 million users, with 100,000 new users every day. Internet traffic growth has been doubling every 90 days. Although the U.S. gross domestic product grew by 3.6% from 1995 to 1999, the Internet economy grew from $5 billion to $507 billion during this period, a rate of growth surpassing 212%.[4] Although a large number of the dot-coms have since failed due to a lack of poor business models, a number of "old economy" firms are nevertheless filling this void with their own industry and private trade exchanges. A trade exchange brings together buyers and sellers on a Website to enable users to virtually buy and sell materials and services, logistics services, disposal, maintenance repair and operating supplies, and provide value-added market information to all participants. Through all of this growth, two important lessons have emerged about the Internet:

1. Those who move first and fast will win the market. (Consider that companies such as Yahoo, Amazon, and eBay were the first to exploit their ideas, and quickly became the recognized market leader.)
2. The marginal cost of bytes approaches zero. This means there is no limit as to the amount of information that can be stored and transmitted via the Web. In effect, the upper boundaries for other forms of data, such as voice, digital, and audiovisual, are limitless.

Before we begin a detailed description of the specific applications of the Internet to purchasing, let's consider some of the attributes of the Internet that make it different from previous forms of interorganizational information systems.

Several attributes of the Internet make it markedly different from previous forms of business to business transactions such as EDI. (For more information on e-commerce, visit the learning Website http://ecommerce.ncsu.edu.)

Internet "B's" and "C's"   Certain Websites are structured around different types of transactions occurring between groups of Internet users. As shown in Exhibit 19.3, there are four major types of Internet transactions that can occur between individual consumers and businesses in four possible combinations (2×2):[5]

1. Business to consumer (B2C), which embraces normal retail activity on the Web, such as bookselling by Amazon.com or online stockbroking by Charles Schwab.
2. Consumer to business (C2B), which takes advantage of the Internet's power to drive transactions the other way around—for example, would-be passengers bidding for airline tickets on Priceline.com, leaving the airlines to decide whether to accept these offers.
3. Consumer to consumer (C2C), which covers the new fashion for consumer auctions, epitomized by the auction site eBay.com.

EXHIBIT 19.3   *Internet Transactions*

	Consumer	Business
Business	B2C Retail Sales Amazon.com Charles Schwab	B2B Sales GE Cisco Oracle
Consumer	C2C Auctions eBay.com	C2B Bidding Priceline.com

4.   Business to business (B2B), which represents the biggest volume of trade. This typically involves the sites for suppliers to communicate with large companies such as General Electric. Several technology companies, including Cisco and Oracle, have transferred almost all their purchasing (and indeed most of their sales) to the Web. Even such long-established businesses as America's two biggest automakers, Ford and GM, say they are transferring all their purchasing to the Web within the next few years.

Core Technology Architecture   One of the reasons the Internet grew so quickly was because of its core technology designs. Although in the early years the hardware was composed exclusively on centralized mainframe computers located at large universities and research institutions, it quickly evolved to a system of open distributed communication between smaller minicomputers or "servers." These servers were linked through a set of packet-switched communication protocols, which essentially constituted the "rules of the road" for exchanging information in a format that could be readily interpreted by all. The development of HyperText Markup Language (HTML) was a foundation for this protocol. One way of thinking about the Internet is as a large brain consisting of a network of electrical circuits that allows completely free flows along each network.

Software Standards   Many of the applications developed in today's Web rely on software such as HTML, Java, C++, Visual Basic, and others. However, many of the software applications used for years by companies rely on more mature software that does not always communicate well with these other forms and must thus be upgraded to support the needs of a modern Web-based network. World Wide Web browsers enable users to search the entire network for information linked to keywords and search criteria. The first such browser was Netscape, but others include Microsoft Internet Explorer, Lycos, and Yahoo. Netscape (purchased by AOL) is still the most common browser, although Yahoo is the site visited most by people seeking information on the Web. The Yahoo site gets an average of 30 million "hits" a day.

Lack of Central Control Despite the growth of the Internet, no central "Webmaster" exists to control what information is passed along the Web. Although the widespread acceptance of protocol exists, the fact that no control exists means that growth is unabated. Because everyone owns their data, it is difficult to ensure reliability and control. The downside of this phenomenon is that there is the potential for misinformation to appear on the Web. Another downside is the danger of security being breached by "hackers" who create destructive viruses that systematically attack Websites and computer files via e-mail.

Who Pays for the Internet? Although in the early years the Internet was essentially sponsored by government and universities operating the mainframe computers that formed the network, the development of HTML and the "point and click" technology quickly attracted the interest of businesses willing to invest in the new communication form. Today, users can get onto most Websites and access a wealth of information virtually for free. However, is the Internet really free? Upon closer examination, it is not entirely free—someone has to pay for the servers and the cost of maintaining Websites. Some Websites provide free information but charge for advertising; others charge for information or provide a product or service—from personal computers (sales at Dell, the largest, average $3 million a day on their site), travel, books and music, to flowers, food, and beverages.

Intranets and Extranets One of the largest areas of growth in the Internet is the evolution of business to business transactions, as noted earlier. Most of this is occurring through the application of Internet technology (i.e., Web-based information, hypertext linkages, and browsers) to organizational applications known as intranets and extranets. *Intranets* use Internet technologies for internal use. For example, Motorola University has a site that provides updates on classes, information, and texts available to internal users who wish to learn more about a specific topic or upgrade their job skills. *Extranets*, on the other hand, use Internet technologies for external use. For instance, FedEx has a purchasing Website that all suppliers can access to view their recent supplier scorecard rating. Extranets are especially well suited to supply chain management applications.

Advantages and Disadvantages of the Internet

The Internet clearly provides a number of advantages over traditional buying channels. First, it is more convenient. Buyers can quickly access the Web and search various sites to determine the lowest price and best service available. In addition, a company selling on the Web does not have to worry about shelf space at its various retail outlets; stock can be kept at a central location and distributed to customers when required. Customers also have faster access to new products and information, and they can research products before purchasing them.

A single Website, once established, can be used to cover the globe and to branch from selling one product to another. The Web also allows things like customer aggregation and auctions to be done in ways that are impossible in the real world. Data can be exploited far more readily on the Internet and everything can be recorded—not just every transaction but which Web pages customers visit, how long they spend there, and what banner ads they click on. In summary, the Internet allows reach (size of the audience), richness (service customization), and affiliation (response to customers' needs).

Some of the challenges or barriers to buying and selling on the Internet are also beginning to emerge. To begin with, Websites have not been successful in replicating the social function of shopping or negotiating a contract, or in generating the purchases that come from visits to a shopping area or mall or trade shows. E-commerce cannot offer the instant gratification that today's purchasers have come to expect. Order fulfillment also comes into the equation. Goods that are heavy or bulky will be harder and more expensive to sell online compared with light, easily transportable ones. Many Websites that set up shop for the Christmas 1999 shopping period were unequipped logistically to deal with the rush of orders, and only two-thirds of orders placed on the Web a month before Christmas 1999 on many sites actually reached their destination by Christmas day. Obtaining sufficient bandwidth to handle customers and running and servicing a Website to ensure that it is 99.999% reliable (the ideal "five nines" goal) is not cheap. Logistics and distribution are so critical to an e-commerce venture's success that it often has to spend heavily on them, as well as heavy marketing expenses to generate customer "hits" for a newly emerging Website.

The Different Forms of B2B E-Commerce

One of the real benefits of the Internet was that it eliminated many of the difficulties associated with traditional business to business transactions. Early applications of the Internet to B2B e-commerce included the development of virtual private networks, as described earlier. Today, Internet computing is largely for viewing and entering data. However, the applications that lie in the future go far beyond this initial approach. The pivotal change that is underway is moving the industry to a more interactive Internet that enables users to not only view but also make active use of data. Such transitions will enable business systems to evolve from supplier-centric to customer-centric systems. We can identify four stages of progression toward increased integration of buyers and suppliers via B2B electronic commerce: (1) Web presence, (2) e-commerce, (3) data delivery, and (4) automation. Stages 1 and 2 are supplier-centric, while Stages 3 and 4 are customer-centric.[6]

Stage 1: Web Presence   Today's Internet is largely a supplier-centric computing environment that allows suppliers to create a Web presence for providing product and service information directly to their customers. This process, known as *disintermediation*, adds value by enabling businesses to communicate directly with customers, in addition to established channels of communication, such as sales and marketing or customer service (see Exhibit 19.4). For example, a customer can go directly to a

EXHIBIT 19.4   *Stage 1: Web Presence (Supplier-Centric)*

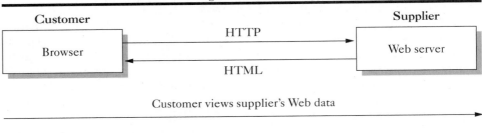

Customer views supplier's Web data

HTTP: Hyper Text Tunneling Protocol
HTML: Hyper Text Markup Language

computer hardware vendor to download information on the latest driver or to check "Frequently Asked Questions" with no human intervention. The Web server is a stand-alone server owned and operated by a third party, usually outside the company's security firewall, that is not linked with any existing business systems. Many businesses establish this type of Web presence through an Internet service provider.

Stage 2: E-Commerce   This stage entails a higher level of integration that allows suppliers to go beyond displaying electronic "brochures" describing their products, services, and company information. The e-commerce services offered allow customers to place orders directly by linking to an internal line of business systems (Exhibit 19.5). An example is Barnes and Noble, which uses a Web presence for e-commerce that ties into the fulfillment systems the company already had in place to support their catalog sales. We have also seen the rise of a new set of intermediaries who consolidate information made available from a number of external Web sources to provide a single site for their customers to get information from many suppliers. The intermediaries allow different legacy systems at different locations to effectively communicate with one another. If Stage 1 was the stage of disintermediation, this is the stage of *reintermediation* (a new intermediary is involved in the supply chain). An example of reintermediation is Travelocity and Expedia, travel sites that incorporate information from other Web sources to provide their travel customers services such as airline tickets and hotel room and rental car reservations. They interface effectively with all of the legacy systems owned by these different organizations.

EXHIBIT 19.5   *Stage 2: E-commerce (Supplier-Centric)*

Customer views supplier's data and buys X

EXHIBIT 19.6   *Stage 3: Data Delivery (Customer-Centric)*

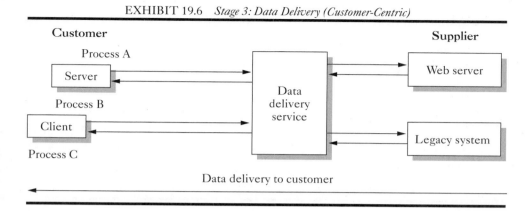

Data delivery to customer

Stages 1 and 2 are supplier-centric models. In supplier-centric computing, customers go to suppliers to get one-size-fits-all data. All customers receive the same data (no personalization). There are still many suppliers without a Web presence today. We will continue to see explosive growth in Stages 1 and 2, since these models provide new ways for suppliers to advertise, market, and sell their products and services.

Stage 3: Data Delivery   For tomorrow's Internet, we will see a significant transition to customer-centric computing—a process reflecting the shift from customers using their browser to obtain data from their suppliers, to suppliers delivering personalized data directly to their customers (tailored to what they care about) (see Exhibit 19.6). Suppliers begin to deliver electronic data that can be integrated into their customers' and suppliers' spreadsheets and business systems. For example, the supplier might supply a component that automatically updates the customer's spreadsheet whenever an order status changes. Having this data delivered allows the customer to proactively take steps to deal with issues like inventory shortages or missed delivery windows.

The major difference between supplier-centric and customer-centric computing is that the supplier-centric approach requires the user to search for information one page at a time (i.e., what is displayed on the area of a computer monitor). In customer-centric computing, binary data is shipped to the user to make the job easier, and is transported directly from multiple sources into the user's business applications. The advantage of data delivery is that it helps to improve a customer's decision-support capability. For example, when customers check inventory to determine whether they will be able to fill a sales order on time. The available inventory is a combination of internal stock, stock in transit, and stock that could arrive (from one or more suppliers) in time to fill the sales order. Stage 3 combines information from both internal and external business systems. It also initiates a radically different relationship between suppliers and customers—one in which suppliers compete on the basis of how effectively they can integrate their information with those of their customers and suppliers to create a positive service experience.

EXHIBIT 19.7   *Stage 4: Automated Interbusiness Processes*

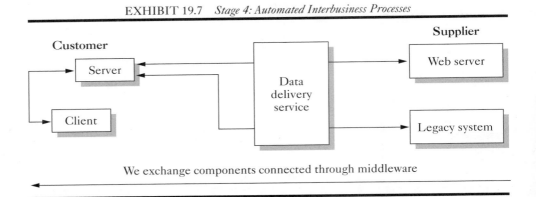

We exchange components connected through middleware

Stage 4: Automated Interbusiness Processes
Process integration between the decision-making systems of businesses and their suppliers and customers becomes bidirectional and tightly integrated during this stage (see Exhibit 19.7). Suppliers can interact dynamically and can initiate business processes within each other's information systems by predefining business rules that trigger events across systems (known as "middleware"). This means that physical supply chains can become at least partially automated. For example, when an order comes to a supplier, orders to the supplier's suppliers to replace committed stock are automatically generated, as is a ripple effect through the supply chain. Less human intervention is required at each step as interbusiness processes become more automated and rules based.

As this stage evolves, customers' and suppliers' business systems are able to make more intelligent business decisions. For example, if one supplier's price drops below that of other suppliers, the customer's application might automatically move that supplier up in the "supplier of choice" list on the business rules engine. The customer consulting this list before ordering would see the supplier at the top and place an order with that supplier. Other applications of automation of decision-making processes between businesses would also occur. In effect, the key value of Stage 4 involves automated integrated databases, which convey more than information between businesses. The rapid, two-way flow of information accelerates the business cycle, enables just-in-time delivery, reduces the cost per transaction, and streamlines the way resources flow through the supply chain.

To summarize, the e-business transition from a supplier-centric to a customer-centric environment is one in which suppliers must follow two strategies:

- Use the universal communications medium of the Internet to tightly link their business information systems.
- Win customer loyalty and increase the value of their supply chain by using their own information technology systems to increase their customers' and suppliers' decision-making effectiveness.

Customer-centric e-business suppliers will compete not only on the price and quality of their products and services but also on the quality of their information

The Big Three's TradeXchange Site

Forming an unprecedented alliance, General Motors, Ford, and Daimler-Chrysler announced a joint venture to build a network to streamline business with their vast array of suppliers. If successful, the new company would handle much of the $240 billion in purchasing of raw materials, parts, and even office supplies made each year by the three automakers, creating what could be the largest Internet company in terms of revenues. The venture underscores just how powerful the promise of the Internet has become to traditional businesses. The automakers believe the new business to business company will slash costs, save time, and make operations more efficient for them and tens of thousands of suppliers around the world. The base for the new company will be the two similar exchanges GM and Ford launched last fall—GM's TradeXchange and Ford's AutoXChange. All three automakers will have an equal stake in the company, which will be run independently. Oracle Cor-poration and Commerce One, the software companies that partnered with Ford and GM for their exchanges, will have a smaller ownership stake. Officials said that other automakers will be offered stakes in the company. "Nobody will be better," said Harold Kutner, vice president for GM worldwide purchasing. "Nobody will be faster. Nobody will offer more to everyone involved."

Source: Adapted from Associated Press, "Internet Beckons Industry," February 27, 2000.

services and e-business links. Suppliers who operate within intelligent supply chains will be able to reduce inventory, be more responsive, and improve customer service.

Advanced Supply Chain Systems and Applications

This section addresses other forms of information technology that supply chain professionals will encounter in the next few years and which will dramatically effect supply chain management strategies.

B2B Hubs and Marketplaces[7]

The appeal of doing business on the Web is clear. By bringing together huge numbers of buyers and sellers and by automating transactions, Web markets expand the choices available to buyers, give sellers access to new customers, and reduce transaction costs for all players. By extracting fees for the transactions occurring within the

EXHIBIT 19.8   *The B2B Matrix*

	Operating inputs	Manufacturing inputs
How businesses buy / **Systematic sourcing**	MRO Hubs Ariba W.W. Grainger MRO.com BizBuyer.com CommerceOne	Catalog Hubs Chemdex Sciquest.com PlasticsNet.com
Spot sourcing	Yield Managers Employease Adauction.com CapacityWeb.com Youtilities eLance iMark	Exchanges e-Steel PaperExchange.com Altra Enegry IMX Exchange

What businesses buy

Source: Kaplan and Sawhney, May 2000.

B2B marketplaces, market makers can earn vast revenues. And because the marketplaces are made from software—not bricks and mortar—they can scale with minimal business investment, promising even more attractive margins as the markets grow. However, there is a need to classify the different types of B2B marketplaces in order to make some sense of this burgeoning sector of the economy. Kaplan and Sawhney introduced the 2 × 2 matrix shown in Exhibit 19.8 as a means to classify the B2B marketplaces.

As shown in this exhibit, the authors first classify all purchases as either manufacturing inputs or operating inputs. Manufacturing inputs are the raw materials and components that go directly into a product or process. These are usually purchased from industry-specific, or vertical suppliers and distributors. They also tend to require specialized logistics and fulfillment mechanisms—UPS and FedEx do not deliver hydrochloric acid or high-density polyethelene. Operating inputs, by contrast, are not parts of finished products. Often called maintenance, repair, and operating (MRO) items, they include the office supplies, spare parts, airline tickets, and services most every business needs. As a result, they are frequently purchased from horizontal suppliers, such as Staples and American Express, that serve all industries. These items are much more likely to be shipped through generalists such as UPS.

The second classification in the matrix is how products and services are bought. Companies can engage either in *systematic sourcing* or in *spot sourcing*. Systematic sourcing involves negotiated contracts with qualified suppliers. Because the contracts tend to be long term, the buyers and sellers often develop close relationships. In spot sourcing, the buyer's goal is to fulfill an immediate need at the lowest possible cost. Commodity trading for things like oil, steel, and energy exemplifies this approach. Spot transactions rarely involve a long-term relationship with the supplier—in fact, the buyer often does not know who they're buying from. Using these categories, we can now explore each of the quadrants shown in Exhibit 19.8.

MRO Hubs These e-commerce providers are horizontal markets that enable systematic sourcing of operating inputs. In MRO hubs, the operating inputs tend to be low-value goods with relatively high transaction costs. These e-hubs provide value largely by improving efficiencies in the purchasing process. Many of the best known players in this arena, including W.W.Grainger, MRO.com, BizBuyer.com, Ariba, and Commerce One, started out by licensing expensive software for e-procurement to large companies, which used the software on their own intranets. Now, instead of licensing their software to individual companies, the e-hubs are hosting it on their own servers to provide an open market. These markets give buyers access to consolidated MRO catalogs from a wide array of suppliers. Newer entrants in this area include PurchasingCenter.com, and ProcureNet. Because MRO hubs can use third-party logistics suppliers to deliver goods, they can disintermediate, or bypass, existing intermediaries without having to replicate their fulfillment capabilities and assets.

Yield Managers These hubs create spot markets for common operating resources like manufacturing capacity, labor, and advertising, which allow companies to expand or contract their operations on short notice. This type of e-hub adds the most value in situations with a high degree of price and demand volatility, such as the electricity and utilities markets, or with huge fixed-cost assets that cannot be liquidated or acquired quickly, such as manpower and manufacturing capacity. Examples of yield managers include Youtilities (for utilities), Employease and eLance (for human resources), iMark.com (for capital equipment), CapacityWeb.com (for manufacturing capacity), and Adauction.com (for advertising).

Exchanges Close cousins of traditional commodity exchanges, online exchanges allow purchasing managers to smooth out the peaks and valleys in demand and supply by rapidly exchanging the commodities or near-commodities needed for production. The exchange maintains relationships with buyers and sellers, making it easy for them to conduct business without negotiating contracts or otherwise hashing out the terms of relationships. In fact, in many exchanges, the buyers and sellers never even know each other's identity. Examples of exchanges include e-Steel (for the steel industry), Paper Exchange.com (for the paper industry), Altra Energy (for the energy industry), and IMX Exchange (for the home mortgage industry).

Catalog Hubs Catalog hubs automate the sourcing of noncommodity manufacturing inputs, creating value by reducing transaction costs. Like MRO hubs, catalog hubs bring together many suppliers at one easy-to-use Website. The only difference is that catalog hubs are industry-specific. They can also be buyer focused or seller focused— that is, some catalog hubs essentially work as virtual distributors for suppliers; others work to represent buyers in their negotiations with sellers. Examples of catalog hubs include Chemdex (initially in the specialty chemicals industry), SciQuest.com (in the life-science industry), and PlasticsNet.com (in the plastics industry). Because the products they offer tend to be specialized, catalog hubs often work closely with distributors to ensure safe and reliable deliveries.

Decision-Support System Applications in a Purchasing Environment

Decision-support systems (DSS) represent an extension of computer technology that moves past the basic emphasis on structured tasks and the information processing characteristic of electronic data processing and management information systems. Decision-support systems attempt to overcome the shortcomings of earlier system applications by using both data and structured mathematical models to support the decision-making process.[8] All definitions of DSS stress that it is an interactive system designed to support managers in making effective decisions about nonstandard problems. Decision-support tools have many applications in a purchasing environment.

Budget Development and Planning Computer spreadsheets combined with budget-planning algorithms can support the development of annual purchasing budgets. Purchasing can incorporate quantity discount information, forecasted annual volumes, exchange rates, cost structure data, price data, and other critical information into a decision-support tool to determine the annual purchasing budget. Management can also determine the budget impact for changes to any of these variables.

Make-or-Buy Analysis Decision-support tools are excellent for make-or-buy analysis because of the structured nature of the make-or-buy decision. The manipulation of variables allows purchasing to determine the impact of variable changes on the make-or-buy decision over a wide range of values. A user can perform make-or-buy analysis on spreadsheet software once all decision criteria appear in equation form on the spreadsheet.

Supplier Performance Evaluation While routine performance reporting can occur within the purchasing transaction system, decision-support tools allow estimates of future supplier performance relating to any key variable. For example, by extrapolating current rates of performance change a buyer can forecast a supplier's cost structure, performance, or price expected at a future time period.

Price Forecasting Price forecasting requires the construction of a model to identify the variables affecting an item's price, including the length of an item's product life cycle, the life cycle stage the item is in, and the item's price history. Life cycle cost curves can forecast expected price performance through time. Purchasing can use these projections to develop budget projections.

Total Cost Models Different types of templates supported by databases can aid purchasers to estimate the total cost of ownership for products and services. These models incorporate shipping, freight, duty, imports and tariffs, inventory costs, and quality costs.

Project Management   Project management tools allow the purchasing professional to manage simultaneously many activities related to the same project. This approach lets the manager update a project's status through time and have immediate visibility to estimated project completion dates. Project managers can use project management tools to provide the most current estimates of project completion, identify possible project delays, or identify activities with excess resources or time.

Training   Decision-support tools offer a number of attractive features as they relate to supply chain training:

- The use of decision-support tools for training extends a firm's capabilities to develop programs adaptable to a user's level of experience. Some applications allow users to enter their current skill sets, and provide "career path" requirements for the individual. In some cases, this may require external online training classes in supply chain management, such as those provided by North Carolina State University (http://scrc.ncsu.edu) and Arizona State University (http://www.asu.edu).
- A firm can easily schedule the training exercise since the sessions can be accessed online whenever the user has time available.
- The use of decision-support tools provides prompt feedback to participants on what they need to do to advance within the organization.

Integration of ERP Systems and B2B E-Commerce

Although we discussed ERP systems and B2B e-commerce separately in this chapter, it would be a mistake for students to think that these systems are already integrated. ERP systems often work independently of decisions made by managers using the Web to order materials and transmit forecasts. In the future, we will see a change and increased integration between standalone ERP systems and the systems that communicate information between buyers and suppliers. We are more likely to witness a convergence of customer-focused applications that link suppliers with internal production schedules and production schedules between different plants in a single enterprise. Not only will the requirements between plants be consolidated and communicated to suppliers via a supply chain planning module, but these schedules will also be linked forward to customers. Sales representatives in the field will be able to promise exact delivery dates to customers using an available to promise (ATP) module, a system that allows sales people to access plant schedules and determine if enough capacity is available to produce the product for the customer by a certain date, and also whether suppliers will be able to deliver the materials in time to produce it.

In addition, other modules will facilitate transactions between buyers and suppliers. A distribution planning module will help identify the transportation requirements and distribution center inventory levels in time to meet customers' delivery requirements. A demand planning module will help identify whether long-term capacity requirements will be sufficient to meet the demand for new products coming on-stream. Finally, a supplier collaboration module will help ensure that future supplier capacity requirements will be in place to meet future demand requirements for new products and services. In effect, these linked systems would enable a single view of the entire supply chain. Managers could analyze the factory and the supply chain simultaneously, and synchronize demand and supply. Distribution centers would act as a shock absorber for customer demand variability and would help to facilitate stable production schedules at the plants, thereby "collapsing the cycles." These types of systems are only now beginning to emerge.

As we speak, many of the technologies discussed in this chapter are changing and being replaced with alternative technologies. Many of the strategies being pursued within supply chain organizations will rely on e-commerce solutions, as organizations seek to integrate suppliers and distributors, share information, link ERP systems to sales personnel in the field, outsource manufacturing and logistics systems, and develop supplier on-site engineering and maintenance activities. These strategies will require new e-commerce channels, Web-based applications to enable information sharing, and most importantly, an effective order fulfillment process with rapid delivery. While many solutions providers promise these capabilities, in fact, they are extremely difficult to deploy. Moreover, many companies lack the fundamental supply chain infrastructure required to be able to apply these technologies across multiple tiers of customers and suppliers. To learn to crawl before learning to walk and then run—organizations must address the current flawed designs of their existing supply chains and only then build these B2B applications around their reengineered networks. A Web-based application cannot fix the problems associated with a large and poorly performing supply base, a fragmented logistics and distribution network, an adversarial set of relationships, and an unwillingness to share information due to a lack of trust. In order to succeed in the B2B world, organizations must be willing to share risks and rewards, and build the underlying infrastructure to apply B2B technology.

GOOD PRACTICE EXAMPLE
SMTC Collaborates with Dell via eSupply Chain Hub

■ ■ ■

SMTC Manufacturing Corporation is a Canadian-based producer of PC boards that supports a wide variety of customers, including Dell, IBM, and Compaq. Along with other suppliers in the electronics industry, SMTC is facing an increasing number of supply chain challenges, including short product life cycles, constant new-product introduction, continuous engineering changes, demand volatility, demands for greater product variety, increased demands for customer service, and volatility in component prices and availability.

One of SMTC's largest customers, Dell Computer, developed a business model to sell computers on the Web. When orders are taken via Dell's Website, customers can configure their computers to include different types of monitors, modems, CD-ROMs or DVDs, memory, and microprocessors. Once customers place an order and pay for the computer, Dell orders the specific components from its suppliers, then performs the final assembly and test of the product (in a few hours) once supplier shipments arrive. In essence, Dell carries no inventory and does not order it until they have the customer's payment (enabling them to enjoy an enormous return on assets). Many other large computer manufacturers such as IBM and even automotive manufacturers are seeking to mimic the Dell model.

SMTC produces PC boards and is responsible for improving supply chain performance, managing supply problems associated with components, developing collaborative forecasts for their suppliers, and dealing with the impact of changes in orders on short notice. Meanwhile, customers such as Dell are seeking to reduce inventory, expediting, and the order-to-delivery cycle with improved customer service. This means that each of SMTC's eight manufacturing sites must also seek to meet these same objectives, and also require their suppliers to do the same. In fact, Dell requires SMTC to carry 150% of their inventory requirements at all times to ensure availability. (Dell requires this of all their suppliers.)

With a complex supply chain consisting of over 50 customer and 700 suppliers, SMTC decided to create an eSupply Chain Hub that would enable greater visibility to their supply chain planning system and improved communication with its suppliers. At the time, SMTC was one of the few suppliers to Dell that developed such a site. One of these major suppliers connected to the hub was Philips Electronics, a supplier of microchips to SMTC.

Early in 1999, SMTC was told by Philips managers that a chip shortage was imminent. Due to market conditions, Phillips advised SMTC that they should increase their inventory of chips to avoid possible shortages. SMTC in turn informed Dell of this situation, and let them know that they should increase inventory and plan for possible shortages of certain types of PC boards. Managers at Dell were skeptical of this information. Dell managers checked with other suppliers and was told that there would be "no problem" in obtaining microchips. Five days later, the sudden shortage occurred, as predicted by SMTC and Philips. Although SMTC was able to meet Dell's requirements during this period due to their foresight in increasing inventory of microchips, several other Dell suppliers were caught by surprise and unable to meet their order commitments.

As a result of this event, Dell decided to reward SMTC with more business for doing something innovative that the other players in the industry were not doing. Following this event, SMTC was able to increase its customer satisfaction ratings with Dell, increase its business with Dell by five times, and increase revenues from $200 million to $1.2 billion. Today, SMTC is considered by Dell as one of its best suppliers, along with Philips Electronics. By moving quickly to establish a B2B Web-based presence and collaborating with its partners in the supply chain, SMTC has become a major player in the electronics supply chain. ∎

Source: Adapted from Dan Russell, "Strategic Technologies." Paper presented at North Carolina State University, Raleigh, NC, March 2000.

CONCLUSION

Purchasing must expand its use of information technology to increase both individual and functional performance. The use of Web-based applications, ERP, and decision-support systems can help professional buyers shift attention from routine to strategic tasks. For example, systems that support the making of better supplier selection decisions—one of a firm's most strategic tasks—can reduce or eliminate future supply-base problems. Also, a system that monitors supplier performance can provide timely visibility concerning potential supply problems.

Ordering and implementing new ERP systems requires planning and work. The final decision about a system usually represents a long-term commitment to the selected features and equipment. Purchasing professionals must identify systems that meet current operating requirements with the capability to meet future needs. Progressive purchasing functions should always be looking five years ahead to identify system trends, operating requirements, and systems applications. For purchasing to contribute to a firm's performance objectives, it must have the resources and ability to develop world-class information systems supported by leading-edge technology.

DISCUSSION QUESTIONS

1. Why do you believe there has been such an emphasis on information systems in purchasing transactions in the last 20 years?
2. Discuss why some firms, particularly smaller firms, are reluctant to adopt new information systems.
3. Why are ERP systems not typically considered a means to improve external integration?
4. What are some of the major barriers encountered by firms seeking to implement ERP systems?
5. One executive noted that "ERP systems take too long to implement and are not worth the cost." Do you agree or disagree with this statement? Explain why.
6. Another executive made this comment: "Many of our suppliers are too small to implement ERP systems." Do you think that this situation may change in the future?
7. Why do you believe that more companies did not adopt EDI over the past 20 years?
8. Most of the Internet applications we see today are of the B2C or C2C nature, yet B2B is probably the largest future sector. Why do you think the Internet evolved in this manner?
9. What are some Websites not listed in this chapter that fall into the B2B, B2C, C2C, and B2C categories?
10. Why should purchasing professionals have an understanding of the role of the Internet?
11. Of the modules that comprise a basic purchasing and materials management system, which are most likely to be the direct responsibility of purchasing to maintain? Which modules are the responsibility of an inventory control group?

12. Imagine walking into the purchasing office of the future. How might you go about completing your tasks for the day using future information technologies?

13. What are the possible benefits and risks that may occur in using decision-support systems and linked databases in purchasing applications?

ADDITIONAL READINGS

Achieving Supply Chain Excellence Through Technology, "eCommerce Requires Intelligent Supply Chains." Anderson Consulting, 1999, pp. 188–190, Chicago, IL.

Balsmeier, Phillip W., and Wendell J. Voisin. "Supply Chain Management: A Time-Based Strategy." *Industrial Management* (September/October 1996): 28–36.

Broadbent, Marianne, and Peter Weill. "Management by Maxim: How Business and IT Managers Can Create Infrastructures." *Sloan Management Review* (Spring 1997): 24–30.

Cross, J., M. Earl, and J. Sampler. "Transformation of the IT Function at British Petroleum." *MIS Quarterly* 21 (1997): 401–23.

Davenport, T. *Process Innovation: Reengineering Work Through Information Technology.* Boston, MA: Harvard Business School Press, 1993.

Emmelhainz, M. *EDI: A Total Management Guide.* Agawam, MA: Penfield Productions, 1990.

Huizing, A., E. Koster, and W. Bouman. "Balance in Business Reengineering: An Empirical Study of Fit and Performance." *Journal of Management Information Systems* 14, no. 1 (1997): 93–118.

Kaplan, Steven, and Mohanbir Sawhney. "E-Hubs: The New B2B Marketplaces." *Harvard Business Review* (May-June 2000): 97–103.

Turban, Efraim, Ephraim McLean, and James Wetherbe. *Information Technology for Management: Improving Quality and Productivity*, New York: Wiley, 1996.

Venkatraman, V. "Beyond Outsourcing: Managing IT Resources as a Value Center." *Sloan Management Review* (Spring 1997): 51–64.

Wetherbe, James C., and Nicholas P. Vitalari. *Systems Analysis and Design: Best Practices*, 4th ed. St. Paul, MN: West Publishing, 1994.

ENDNOTES

1. Emily Nelson and Evan Ramstad, "Hershey's Biggest Dud Has Turned Out to Be New Computer System," *Wall Street Journal*, October 29, 1999, A1; Shelly Branch, "Hershey Net Sinks by 19%; Snafus Linger," *Wall Street Journal*, October 26, 1999, A3.

2. James Bradley, *Introduction to Data Base Management* (New York: Holt, Rinehart and Winston, 1987), 7.
3. R. Handfield, *Reengineering for Time-based Competition* (Westport, CT: Quorum Press, 1995).
4. Working paper, *Center for Research in Electronic Commerce,* University of Texas, 1999.
5. "Define and Sell," *The Economist,* February 26, 2000. p. 78–81.
6. George Moakley, "eCommerce Requires Intelligent Supply Chains," in *Achieving Supply Chain Excellence Through Technology,* Anderson Consulting, 1999, 188–90, Chicago, IL.
7. This section is based on an article by Steven Kaplan and Mohanbir Sawhney, "E-Hubs: The New B2B Marketplaces," *Harvard Business Review* (May-June 2000): 97–103.
8. Hossein Bidgoli, "DSS Products Evaluation: An Integrated Framework," *Journal of Systems Management* (November 1989): 27.

PERFORMANCE MEASUREMENT AND EVALUATION 20

Measuring Perfect Supply Chain Performance at Kellogg's

Kellogg Company was founded around the turn of the twentieth century when a doctor by the name of William Keith Kellogg arrived from Chicago and established a sanitarium in the small town of Battle Creek, Michigan. Kellogg actively advocated a healthy lifestyle, consisting of no meat, a high-fiber diet, and plenty of exercise. The sanitarium was designed to help people achieve this goal and became very popular. A student of Kellogg's, Dr. C. W. Post, soon joined him and built another sanitarium in Battle Creek.

The cereal industry has come a long way since the early days of Kellogg's sanitarium. Today the competition in the cereal industry is fierce and is steadily increasing. Most recently, cereal manufacturers have been challenged to dramatically reduce their costs. This is forcing Kellogg's to more closely monitor and measure its supply chain costs and performance to key customers. The company has 14 teams that work directly with customers that represent 50% of total sales, including Wal-Mart, Kroger, Publix, and Safeway. Each of these teams reports to the sales group at corporate headquarters. Customers place their orders via electronic data interchange systems directly to a customer service group.

Customer service has recently been located within the marketing function. Its main function is to receive orders and determine if they meet a set of reasonable criteria. For instance, customer service will check to ensure that the order is of a reasonable volume (e.g., at least a truckload), how quickly the customer wants it, and whether Kellogg's can meet the requested delivery date.

Once a customer commitment is made, the order is released internally. At this point, customer service decides if the order can be filled by a Kellogg's plant or by a regional distribution center. If the order comprises a full truckload quantity that can be filled by one of the plants, it is shipped directly from a plant. If the order has a high mix of different products from different plants and/or the customer wants a rapid turnaround, it is filled from one of the distribution centers.

If an order is released to the plant, an order fulfillment team takes over—responsible for picking, packing, and loading the order. Because of the complexities associated with the movement of cereal in the United States, Canada, Europe, and now Asia, Kellogg's must constantly monitor and improve its distribution network to ensure that only the freshest product arrives in the store for consumers.

Kellogg's has determined that the ultimate measure when filling customer requests is the Perfect Order. Such an order meets the customer's deadline, is delivered on time, has perfect invoice accuracy, and is damage-free. Kellogg's current service record is excellent – over 95%. This has been achieved in spite of a 30% reduction in North American manufacturing capacity. During this same period, service levels improved while inventory was continually reduced. In the future, the perfect order concept will be one of the most important measures for consumer product companies that supply large retailers.

Source: Global Procurement and Supply Chain Benchmarking Initiative, Michigan State University, 1998.

All businesses and business functions require measurement systems that influence behavior and track performance progress. The purchasing function, however, has traditionally lagged behind other functions, including supply chain activities such as the ones highlighted in the opening vignette, in the development of sophisticated performance measurement and evaluation systems. As a result, purchasing performance measures have tended to be internal, with minimal linkages to corporate goals and objectives. Furthermore, few standardized measures of efficiency or effectiveness have emerged over time.

This chapter begins with a basic overview of performance measurement and evaluation, including the reasons to measure performance and the problems associated with measurement and evaluation. Next, there is a discussion of the most common purchasing and supply chain measurement categories with specific examples of performance measures presented. The third section discusses the development of a performance measurement and evaluation system. The last section discusses performance benchmarking, which is a process involving comparisons against leading firms to establish performance plans and objectives. The chapter concludes with observations about performance measurement and evaluation.

$\mathcal{P}$URCHASING AND SUPPLY CHAIN PERFORMANCE MEASUREMENT AND EVALUATION

A purchasing and supply chain performance evaluation system represents a formal, systematic approach to monitor and evaluate purchasing performance. While this sounds easy, it is often difficult to develop measures that direct behavior or activity exactly as intended. Some firms still rely on measures that harm rather than support long-term performance objectives. For example, the ability to win price concessions from a supplier is still a major objective for certain price/cost performance measures. However, if a purchaser continuously squeezes short-term price reductions from a supplier, will that supplier have the financial resources or the commitment to invest in longer-term performance improvements?

Modern purchasing and supply chain performance measurement and evaluation systems contain a variety of measures. Most of these measures fall into two broad categories: effectiveness and efficiency measures. *Effectiveness* refers to the extent to which, by choosing a certain course of action, management can meet a previously established goal or standard. Efficiency refers to the relationship between planned and actual sacrifices made to realize a previously agreed-upon goal.[1] Efficiency measures usually relate some input to a performance output.

Almost all measures include a standard or target against which to evaluate performance results or outcomes. It is incomplete to say, for example, that a measure will track improvement in supplier quality. We still need to compare actual improvement against a preestablished target or objective. Meeting this target, which is presumably based on world-class performance levels, will bring value to an organization. Each performance measure should include actual performance levels and a targeted performance level.

Why Measure Performance?

A number of reasons exist for measuring and evaluating purchasing and supply chain activity and performance.

Support Better Decision Making   Measurement can lead to better decisions by making performance and results visible. It is difficult to develop performance improvement plans without understanding the areas in which performance falls short. Measurement provides a track record of purchasing performance over time and directly supports decision-making activity by management.

Support Better Communication   Performance measurement can result in better communication across the supply chain, including within purchasing, between departments, with suppliers, and with executive management. For example, a purchaser must communicate clearly performance expectations to suppliers. The measures that quantify supplier performance reflect a purchaser's expectations.

Provide Performance Feedback   Measurement provides the opportunity for performance feedback, which supports the prevention or correction of problems identified during the performance measurement process. Feedback also provides insight into how well a buyer, department, team, or supplier is meeting its performance objectives over time.

Motivate and Direct Behavior   Measurement motivates and directs behavior toward desired end results. A measurement system can accomplish this in several ways. First, the selection of performance categories and objectives indicates to purchasing personnel those activities that an organization considers critical. Second, management can motivate and influence behavior by linking the attainment of performance objectives to organizational rewards, such as pay increases.

Problems with Purchasing and Supply Chain Measurement and Evaluation

Measuring and evaluating performance, including purchasing and supply chain performance, historically has had certain problems and limitations. Mark Brown, an expert on performance measurement, argues that most managers and professionals today are like a pilot trying to fly a plane with only half the instruments needed and many additional instruments that measure irrelevant data.[2] He states that practically every organization has some type of problem with its measurement system.

Too Much Data and Wrong Data   Having too much data is the most common problem an organization has with its measurement system. A second and more serious problem is that the data that managers pay attention to are often the wrong data. The metrics are selected because of history or a feeling that the measure is related to success, which may not be the case at all. In fact, measures that managers follow may sometimes be in conflict with measures used in other units or functional areas. As a general rule, no employee should monitor more than a dozen measures, with a half of those being the most critical.

Measures That Are Short-Term Focused   Many small- and medium-sized organizations have a problem of relying on measures and data that are short-term focused. Typically the only data they collect are financial and operating data. In purchasing, this would mean a short-term focus on workload and supply chain activities, while ignoring the longer-range or strategic measures.

Lack of Detail   At times the data that are reported are summarized so much as to make the information meaningless. A measure that reports on a single measure of monthly supplier quality probably lacks detail. A supply manager will want to know what are the specific types of defects the supplier is experiencing, what the defects cost the buyer's company, and the supplier's quality performance over time.

An operations manager at a major automotive regional parts distribution facility receives a monthly measure of the facility's quality as measured by claims made by customers. However, he also receives reports that detail the following:

- The type of errors that are occurring (wrong part picked, damage, shortages, missed shipments, etc.)
- Which customers are making the quality claims
- Which employees are responsible for the quality errors
- The total cost of the quality claims against the facility
- The part numbers that have quality claims against them

With this information the manager can take action that will attack the root causes of the quality problems at his facility.

Drive the Wrong Performance   Unfortunately, many measures drive behavior that is not what was intended or needed. If buyers are measured on the number of purchase orders written, then they will make sure to split orders between suppliers to generate as many purchase orders as possible. Part of this is due to the fact that measuring intellectual work is difficult. However, organizations still want to look for factors that can be measured and reported. These factors may not, however, always be the right factors.

Measures of Behavior Versus Accomplishments   The problem with measuring behavior is there is no guarantee the behavior will lead to desired results. A behavioral measure that tracks the amount of purchase volume covered by corporate-wide contracts, for example, is becoming increasingly common. A better measure, however, is one that tracks the total savings due to the use of corporate-wide contracts. Another example of a behavioral measure is one that measures the number of meetings held by a commodity team each quarter. A better set of measures will track the performance results that occurred because of the team's actions. Although some set of behavioral measures will always be present, measures that capture accomplishments will be the ones that really matter.

Purchasing and Supply Chain Performance Measurement Categories

Hundreds of purchasing and supply chain measures are in existence. Perhaps the best way to summarize the vast number of separate measures is by developing performance measurement categories. Within each category, many separate measures appear that relate to each general category. Most purchasing and supply chain measures fall into one of the following categories:

1. Price performance
2. Cost effectiveness
3. Purchasing workload
4. Administration and control
5. General efficiency measures
6. Material status and control
7. Supplier performance
8. Supply chain performance
9. Strategic performance
10. Regulatory, societal, and environmental
11. Purchasing planning and research

The following sections discuss each of these categories.

Price Performance Measures

Purchasing uses various indicators to evaluate *price performance measures*—in other words, how effectively it spends purchase dollars. The most common price performance measures include actual purchase price versus planned purchase price comparisons, actual purchase price(s) compared to a market index, comparisons of actual-to-actual purchase prices for individual and aggregated items between operating plants or divisions within an organization, and target prices achieved. Two price performance measures that are gaining importance are target prices achieved and price to market index comparisons.

Actual Price Compared to a Plan A common price performance measure is the difference between actual and planned purchase prices. Measurement of planned purchase price variance can occur at different organizational levels. One level includes actual-to-planned purchases for the total material budget; this is an aggregated price performance measure. Other levels show comparisons that provide greater detail. For example, purchasing may calculate actual-to-planned price variances for each individual purchased item. Exhibit 20.1 presents various methods to calculate purchase price variance from a plan.

Actual Prices-to-Market Index Purchase price to market index measures provide information about the relationship between actual prices and published market

The Tight Squeeze at Chrysler

Sales representatives from Detroit-area auto suppliers have been complaining about the cost-cutting pressure coming from the U.S. unit of DaimlerChrysler, which is hurting the cooperative relationships that existed between suppliers and the automotive manufacturer. During the 1990s, Chrysler extensively measured the savings generated from supplier-provided ideas. Now, facing lower sales, high rebate costs, and the cost of launching new vehicles, DaimerChrysler recently announced that it would report a $600 million quarterly loss at its Chrysler unit. The red ink will likely increase the pressure at Chrysler to cut more than $2 billion as part of a $5.7 billion corporate belt-tightening. A supplier doing $300 million in business with Chrysler will now have to find an extra $3 million, and many suppliers are already struggling with razor-thin margins. Pre-merger Chrysler was renowned for working closely with its suppliers, and received an enthusiastic response as new products were jointly developed that helped reduce Chrysler's manufacturing costs. By 1998, this strategy had helped Chrysler measure up as one of the lowest-cost producers in the world, with the highest profits per vehicle. One supplier, complaining about the shift in performance metrics, suggests that his company may market its best technology at other automakers if the trend continues. And that is a cost that Chrysler can ill afford.

Source: Jeff Green, "The Tight Squeeze at Chrysler," *Business Week*, October 9, 2000, 33–34.

---

prices. These measures are most appropriate for market-based products where pricing is primarily a function of supply and demand. This also applies to standard and readily available products. Index measures take into account the difference between a published index number over a designated period (such as a quarter) and the change in the actual price paid. The following illustrates this concept:

1a. Market-based index for Item X		March 31, 2001	=	125
1b. Market-based index for Item X		June 30, 2001	=	128
1c. Market index change	=	$(128 - 125)/125$	=	2.4% increase
2a. Actual price paid for Item X		March 31, 2001	=	$150
2b. Actual price paid for Item X		June 30, 2001	=	$152
2c. Price paid change rate	=	$(\$152 - \$150)/\$150$	=	1.3% increase
3. Comparison to market		$2.4\% - 1.3\% = 1.1\%$		**Better by 1.1%**

Price Comparisons Between Operations Actual price comparisons between plants, divisions, or business units for similar items also occur. These comparisons provide an opportunity to identify purchase price differences within a firm. This provides visibility as to which unit is negotiating or securing the best purchase price. The comparison activity can also help identify commonly purchased items between units for purchase consolidation.

EXHIBIT 20.1   *Purchase Price Variance from Plan*

Various Formats for Measuring Purchase Price Variance
1. Purchase price variance = Actual price − Planned price
2. Purchase price variance percentage = Actual price/Planned price
3. Total purchase price variance = (Actual price − Planned price) × Purchase quantity or estimated annual volume
4. Current year dollar impact of purchase price variance = (Actual price − Planned price) × (Estimated annual volume × Percentage of requirements remaining)

Units of Measure
　Dollars or percentages

Performance Reported by
　Purchase item
　Commodity or family group
　End product
　Project
　Buying location or department
　Buyer
　Management group
　Supplier

Although firms are increasingly focusing on cost versus price, price performance measures are still popular, especially with firms that lack detailed cost data. Price performance measures are also commonly used when purchasing raw materials, other commodity or standard-type items, components, systems, and contract services.

Target Prices Achieved   Target pricing is the process of determining what the external customer is willing to pay for a product or service and then assigning specific cost targets to the components, assemblies, and systems that make up the product or service. Target costing uses the following formula to determine allowable costs:

$$\text{Target price} - \text{Profit target} = \text{Allowable cost}$$

Allowable cost is then allocated to various elements that make up the final product or service.

Cost-Effectiveness Measures

The measures in this category focus attention on efforts to reduce purchase costs. Cost measures fall into two general categories: cost changes and cost avoidance.

　The use of cost measures requires a word of caution. The method used to achieve cost reductions is critical. A cost reduction based on mutual cooperation is the same, on paper, as a cost reduction resulting from heavy-handed pressure on a supplier. While the end result (i.e., a cost reduction) appears to be the same, the process used to achieve that result can have longer-term implications. Cooperation may reduce costs through joint improvement while heavy-handed cost pressure may force a supplier to cut corners, resulting in poor quality.

Cost Changes   A cost-change measure compares the actual cost of an item or family of items over a period of time. A cost change is the increase or decrease in cost resulting from a change in purchasing strategy or practice brought about by an individual or a group.

Cost Avoidance   Cost avoidance represents the difference between a price paid and a *potentially* higher price (which might have occurred if purchasing had not obtained the lower price through a specific effort or action). For example, assume that purchasing paid $5 per unit for an item in the past, but the supplier now quoted a price of $5.50 per unit. If the buyer negotiates a price of $5.25 per unit, then he or she achieved a cost avoidance of $.25 per unit, even though the price was still $.25 higher than the prior price. Unfortunately, finance often argues that cost-avoidance savings rarely show up on a firm's profit line.

Cost-change and cost-avoidance measures differ slightly. Cost-change represents an actual change from a prior period price while cost avoidance refers to the amount that would have been paid minus the amount actually paid. Purchasing departments that require tangible cost improvement should focus more on the cost-change approach. This represents actual changes that can impact a firm's overall profitability. Cost-avoidance figures almost always require manual calculation and are sometimes subject to exaggeration. As a result, some observers have described cost-avoidance measures and figures as "soft," "funny money," and "easy to manipulate."

Purchasing Workload Measures

Workload measures are efficiency indicators of total work. This type of measure quantifies the status of purchasing's workload. The primary objective of purchasing workload measures is to help determine workload levels and to provide information for staff scheduling, work assignments, or justification for staff increases or reduction. These measures are more common for purchasing groups that are operational or reactive. They do not capture the strategic value of higher-level purchasing activities. The three most common workload measures include workload-in, workload-in-process, and workload-completed.

Workload-in   Measures of workload-in are typically simple counts of work received in a certain period but not yet in-process or scheduled. These measures identify new work requests received over a given time period. Different measures of inbound work include purchase requests/requisitions received, purchase or engineering change notices received, and pricing requests received for items.

Workload-in-Process   Measures included in the workload-in-process category identify the amount of work currently being worked on within purchasing. All noncompleted work represents work-in-process. The most common measurement indicators in this category include open purchase requests/requisitions on hand, line items awaiting purchase, and open purchase orders.

If purchasing can assign a time to each assignment, it can convert in-process workload into a number of days of work. The following formula converts the number of line items waiting to be purchased into a total workload figure (in days):

$$\text{Work-in-process (in days)} = \frac{\text{Line items to be purchased}}{\left[\dfrac{\text{Cumulative line items purchased}}{\text{(Cumulative worker hours/8)}}\right] \times \text{Number of available persons}}$$

This information helps management approximate its current workload level.

Workload-Completed   These measures report the volume of work completed by the purchasing department over a selected period of time. Examples of different measured activities can include purchase orders placed, line items purchased, dollar value of purchases placed, contracts written, and pricing proposals written. Workload-completed measures help provide comparisons of purchasing activity across points in time.

Workload-related measures reflect a past interest in making purchasing a productive, efficient operation. These measures assume that most purchasing tasks are routine and predictable. For most firms, this type of performance measure by itself provides marginal value except for the most clerical and routine tasks. The strongest characteristic of workload measures is the opportunity to gain a rough idea about current work volumes for various purchasing tasks. The weakest characteristic of workload measures, and one that has to be considered strongly, is the emphasis on purchasing efficiency over purchasing effectiveness.

Workload measures provide some insight into the magnitude of work in a purchasing department. However, they are not useful for comparing across companies due to differences in work assignments, processes, and technology used.

Administration and Control Measures

Management uses administration and control measures to plan purchasing's annual administrative budget and to help control administrative expenses during a budget period. Budgeted expense items commonly include salaries, travel and living expenses, training expenses, office supplies, and other miscellaneous expenses. Salaries traditionally take the largest share of the purchasing administrative budget. The two most common methods to establish the purchasing administrative budget are the current budget plus adjustment and the use of control ratios.

Current Budget Plus Adjustment   The most common method of establishing a budget uses the current administrative budget as a starting point. Management then adjusts the budget for the next period (usually the next fiscal year) upward or downward depending on expected business conditions or other departmental requirements. Budget adjustments reflect management's view about projected purchasing workload and a firm's profitability. Decreasing workload or profits can result in a budget reduction. Conversely, increasing workload or profits may justify a budget increase.

Control Ratios With the control ratio approach, the purchasing administrative budget is a percentage of another measure that reflects purchasing's workload. Planned dollar expenditure for direct material is often the selected workload measure.

   The historical control ratio as well as negotiation between purchasing and higher management often determines the control ratio percentage used during calculation of the administrative budget. A projection of direct material purchase requirements for the next period then affects the administrative budget. Purchasing workload is assumed to be proportional to planned dollar expenditures for direct material. The purchasing administrative budget becomes

   Purchasing budget = Estimated expenditures for direct material × Control ratio

   Purchasing managers use the total budget figure to allocate resources among different departmental uses. Management must determine how many buyers are required, the size of the clerical support staff, and other budget-related issues.

Other Approaches Current budget plus adjustment and control ratios are not the only methods used to arrive at a purchasing administrative budget. Some firms, and particularly certain U.S. government agencies, use detailed and complex time-standard models to identify headcount and budget requirements. Unfortunately, a time-standards approach treats purchasing as a production function that performs only buying. Again, we must warn about emphasizing purchasing efficiency over purchasing effectiveness as a strict indicator of performance.

General Efficiency Measures

Different measures exist that relate a purchasing input to a purchasing output. Efficiency measures can help determine the level of resources consumed or identify the resources required to accomplish a set of purchasing tasks.

Two-Factor Measures This type of efficiency measure includes basic measures that relate some purchasing department output against a resource input. These measures are ratios or averages of an input to an output. Examples of two-factor measures include worker hours per line item, worker hours per purchase order, administrative dollars per contract, total company purchases per purchasing employee, active suppliers per purchasing employee, or purchasing operating expense per purchasing employee. Two-factor measures must relate some output against some input.

   Excessive reliance on two-factor efficiency measures can have unforeseen consequences in other performance areas—quantity can become more important than quality. Purchasing must strive for the right mix of quantity and quality to meet its functional objectives.

Purchasing Administrative Lead Time   Most public and private purchasing organizations track purchasing administrative lead times—the elapsed time from the arrival of a purchase requisition until placement of a purchase order with a supplier. It is purchasing's responsibility to provide a level of service that satisfies its internal customers. Tracking lead-time efficiency is one way to measure purchasing's level of customer service. Increasingly, the ordering of routine items is performed by users rather than by purchasing.

Material Status and Control Measures

Most organizations maintain a series of reports or measures that evaluate the flow of material from the seller to the purchaser. Material status and control measures usually fall into four categories: (1) identification of open purchase orders and their due dates, (2) identification of past-due open purchase orders, (3) identification of immediate manufacturing material requirements, and (4) measurement of how well suppliers are meeting delivery schedules.

The most common uses of these measures and reports are to expedite past-due material and to maintain the orderly flow of material throughout the production system. The reports are also valuable when evaluating supplier delivery performance. This includes not only a supplier's performance against expected due dates but also performance against the ordered quantity. These measures provide valuable ordering lead-time information and support tracking lead-time performance improvement.

Supplier Performance Measures

Supplier performance measurement is an area in which many firms have made great progress. Purchasers generally track supplier quality, cost, and delivery along with other performance areas. Furthermore, firms are beginning to quantify the cost associated with each act of supplier nonperformance. The resulting cost figure represents the total cost of doing business with a supplier. Supplier total-cost measures allow direct comparisons between suppliers.

The supplier performance evaluation model developed by Hewlett-Packard represents one way to evaluate supplier performance. This model evaluates supplier performance (and the teams that manage those suppliers) in the areas of T (technology contribution), Q (quality), R (supplier responsiveness), D (delivery performance), C (cost), and E (environmental performance). The FedEx supplier scorecard featured in Chapter 8 provides additional detail about supplier performance measurement systems.

Supply Chain Performance Measures

Many measures relate to how well various aspects of the supply chain are operating.

Inventory   It is common to have multiple measures that track different aspects of a firm's inventory investment. These measures are common with physical distribution centers. Examples include dollar value of total inventory, percentage of active to inactive

The Perfect Order at Procter and Gamble

The perfect order represents the ability of the supply chain to provide 100% availability in a timely, error-free manner. Procter and Gamble (P&G), a manufacturer and distributor of consumer products, defines the perfect order metric as on time to the buyer's requested delivery date, shipped complete, invoiced correctly, and not damaged in transit. In 1992, P&G began to measure their "perfect orders." Initially, managers were shocked to discover that the number of perfect orders was only around 75%. Since that time, substantial improvements have been made. In 1995, 82% of orders were perfect; and by 1998, 88% were perfect. This has been achieved through continuous replenishment, having customer service representatives work closely with major customers, and improved information systems. Procter and Gamble estimates that every imperfect order costs approximately $200 due to redelivery, lost revenue, damage, warehouse and shipping costs, deductions, and backorders. P&G knows that continuous supply chain improvement requires measuring what is really important to the customer. And to the customer, the perfect order is important.

Source: Presentation by Ralph Drayer, the Eli Broad Graduate School of Management, Michigan State University, East Lansing, MI, December 1998.

---

part numbers, total number of part numbers, working capital savings, total inventory investment, days supply of inventory, and inventory investment by type of purchased item (for example, production items, maintenance items, packaging materials).

It is also common to have measures that track the speed or velocity of inventory as it moves through the supply chain. This includes raw material, work-in-process, and finished-goods inventory turns. The amount of inventory maintained as safety stock is also a common measure. The accuracy of computer records that are part of the inventory location system is also closely tracked.

Transportation Transportation measures include tracking actual transportation costs against some preestablished objective, demurrage and detention costs, transportation carrier quality and delivery performance levels, and transportation lead-time indicators.

Customer Orders These measures evaluate how well an organization is satisfying its commitment to downstream customers. Various measures include the percentage of on-time delivery, total time from customer order to customer delivery, returned orders, and warranty claims. While we have focused primarily on purchasing and upstream supply chain activities, purchasing and material planners are increasingly responsible for managing inventory from a total supply chain perspective. This may also include downstream activities.

EXHIBIT 20.2   *Examples of Strategic Purchasing Measurement Indicators*

- Percentage of purchasing's operating budget committed to on-site supplier visits
- Proportion of quality-certified suppliers to total suppliers
- Percentage of receipts free of inspection and material defects
- Total number of suppliers
- Proportion of suppliers participating in early product design or other joint value-added activities
- Revenue increase as a result of supplier-provided technology that differentiates end products to customers
- Percentage of operating budget allocated to supplier development and training
- Total cost supplier selection and evaluation measures
- Supplier lead-time indicators
- Purchasing's contribution to return on assets, return on investment, and economic value-added corporate measures
- Purchasing success with achieving cost reductions with tier 2 and tier 3 suppliers
- Percentage of purchase dollars committed to longer-term contracts
- Savings achieved from the use of companywide agreements
- Purchasing's contribution to product development cycle time reduction
- Percentage/dollar value of items purchased from single sources
- Percentage of purchase dollars committed to highest-performing suppliers
- Percentage of purchase transactions through electronic data interchange (EDI) or Web-based systems
- Percentage of total receipts on a just-in-time basis
- Supplier quality levels, cost performance, and delivery performance compared with world-class performance targets
- Supplier development costs and benefits
- Continuous supplier performance improvement measures
- Reductions in working capital due to purchasing and supply chain efforts
- Contribution to return on investment and assets realized from strategic outsourcing efforts
- Savings achieved from part number reduction efforts
- Savings achieved from part standardization efforts

Strategic Performance Measures

Purchasing requires measures that reflect its ability to support overall corporate and functional goals, which means a reduced emphasis on pure efficiency measures (e.g., the cost to issue a purchase order or current workload status) and greater emphasis on effectiveness measures (those that reflect purchasing's strategic contribution). Examples of the latter include tracking early supplier involvement in product design, performance gains resulting from direct supplier development efforts, or supplier-provided improvement suggestions. Within most industries, purchasing must shift from measuring itself as an administrative support function to one that provides strategic value.

Exhibit 20.2 provides examples of key strategic purchasing measures. Notice that these measures are a combination of activity and results-oriented measures. Emphasis shifts from strict indicators of personnel performance or efficiency to how well the purchasing function supports strategic supply-base management goals and objectives.

To shift from an operational to a strategic perspective, the purchasing measurement and evaluation system must also shift.

The performance indicators in Exhibit 20.2 are more strategically and externally focused than traditional performance indicators. They are also specified in terms of broader purchasing goals rather than specific activity. For example, a buyer may be responsible for a performance objective stating that 75% of the buyer's suppliers will be quality certified by the third quarter of 2002. This differs from a measure that states a buyer must process ten requests for quotation per day on average.

Additional Purchasing Measures

Organizations use additional purchasing measures in varying degrees.

Regulatory/Societal/Environmental These measures provide information about purchasing's achievement of regulated public policy objectives and/or societal and environmental objectives that management considers important. Examples in this category include purchase dollars placed with small businesses or minority suppliers, dollars spent on supplier development of small or disadvantaged suppliers, or percentage of materials purchased from recycled materials.

Purchasing Planning and Research These measures indicate the level and accuracy of purchasing planning and research activities. Examples include: the number of strategic procurement plans established per year, material availability and price forecasting accuracy, the number of make/buy studies completed, and delivery lead-time forecasting accuracy.

Depending on the objectives of the purchasing manager, different types of measures can be used to achieve different purposes. Moreover, no single set of measures can be used universally for any purchasing performance system. These categories of measures point out that purchasing managers must properly link measures with purchasing strategy objectives, and they also ensure that the right measures are used in tracking the success of each strategy.

DEVELOPING A PERFORMANCE MEASUREMENT AND EVALUATION SYSTEM

The development of a measurement and evaluation system requires the leadership, support, and commitment of executive management, who must commit the financial resources necessary for system development. Management must also require all purchasing locations to use the same system structure, which can reduce duplication of effort and save development and training costs. This does not mean that each location must use the same performance objectives or performance criteria. It means only that the system's basic design is similar. Executive management support also sends a message about the seriousness of tracking and improving performance.

EXHIBIT 20.3   *Developing a Purchasing and Supply Chain Performance Measurement and Evaluation System*

Develop specific performance measures

Determine which performance categories to measure

Price effectiveness
Cost effectiveness
Workload
Administration
General efficiency
Material status
Supplier performance
Strategic performance
Other

Features:
Objective
Clear
Nonmanipulable
Dynamic
Promotes creativity
Uses available data
Relates to purchasing objectives

Establish performance objectives through

Historical data
Internally derived
  comparisons
Competitive analysis
  (i.e., benchmarking)

Performance Measurement and Evaluation System Development

Finalize system details

Implement and review system performance and measures

Pilot test
Update over time

Reporting frequency
Education and training
How to use system output

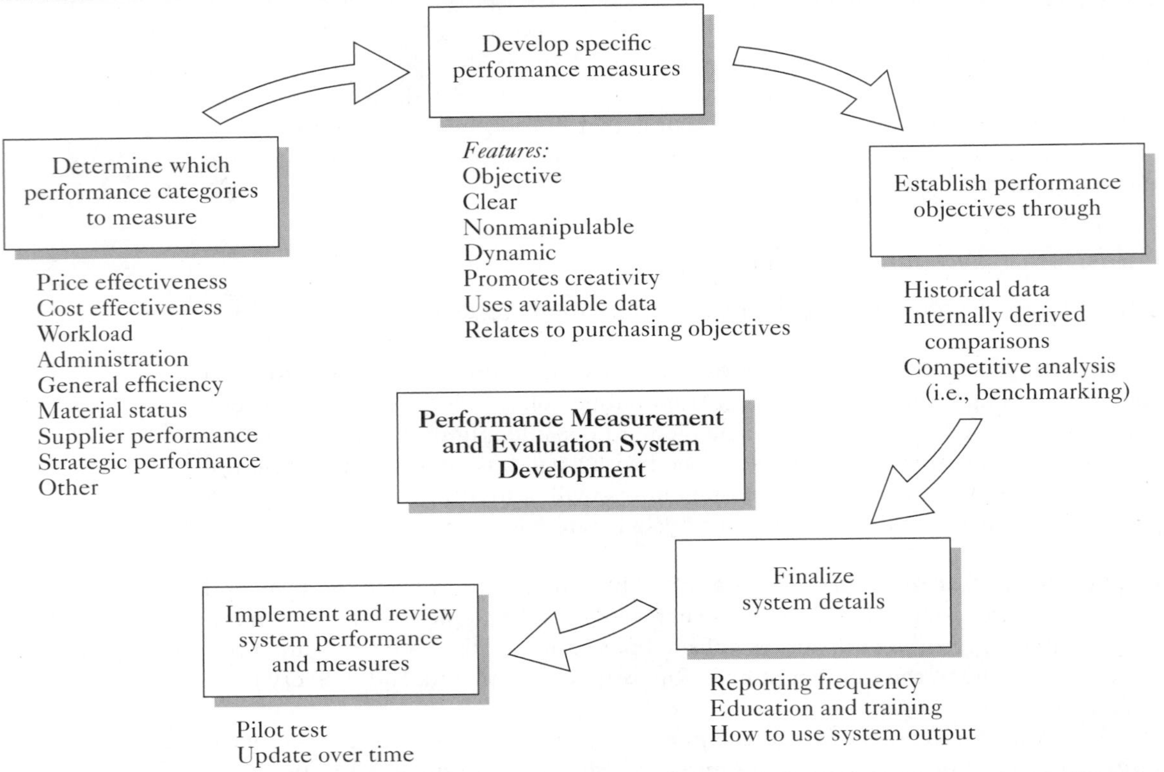

Development of an effective measurement and evaluation system follows a general sequence of activities. These include determining which performance categories to measure, developing specific performance measures, establishing performance standards for each measure, finalizing system details, and implementing and reviewing the system and each performance measure. Exhibit 20.3 presents an overview of the development of a purchasing and supply chain performance measurement system.

Determine Which Performance Categories to Measure

A previous section discussed various performance measurement categories. The first step of the development process requires identifying which measurement categories to emphasize. Also, a firm can weigh its performance measures and categories differently. Management does not concern itself with specific performance measures during this phase of system development. The selected performance categories must relate broadly to organizational and to purchasing and supply chain goals and objectives. Selecting the performance measure categories is a critical step prior to developing specific performance measures.

Develop Specific Performance Measures

Developing specific performance measures begins once management identifies the measurement categories it will emphasize. Certain features characterize successful purchasing and supply chain performance measures.

Objectivity   Each measure should be as objective as possible. The measurement system should rely on quantitative data instead of qualitative feelings and assessments. Subjective evaluation can create disagreement between the rater and the individual or group responsible for the performance objective.

Clarity   Personnel must understand a performance measure's requirements in order to direct performance toward the desired outcome and minimize misunderstandings. All parties must be clear about what each performance measure means, agree on the performance objectives associated with the measure, and understand what it takes to accomplish the measure. Well-understood measures are straightforward and unambiguous.

Use of Accurate and Available Data   Well-defined measures use data that are available and accurate. If a measure requires data that are difficult to generate or unreliable, the probability of using the measure on a consistent basis declines. The cost of generating and collecting the required data should not outweigh the potential benefit of using the performance measure.

Creativity   A common misconception is that a performance evaluation system should measure every possible activity. When this occurs, the measures can stifle individual creativity. The measures control behavior so tightly that the system eliminates room for personal initiative. A successful system measures only what is important while still promoting individual initiative and creativity, which may mean focusing on five or six important, clearly defined measures instead of 25 vague measures.

Directly Related to Organizational Objectives   Exhibit 20.4 illustrates how corporate goals and objectives influence purchasing goals and objectives. Other functional objectives also can influence purchasing. For example, manufacturing's goals can have a direct impact on purchasing since purchasing supports the manufacturing process. To meet its goals and objectives, purchasing executives develop strategies and action plans. Finally, management develops measures that evaluate the output or performance from the activities required to accomplish purchasing's strategies and plans. The measures serve as indicators of purchasing's progress.

EXHIBIT 20.4   *Linking Purchasing Measures and Corporate Objectives*

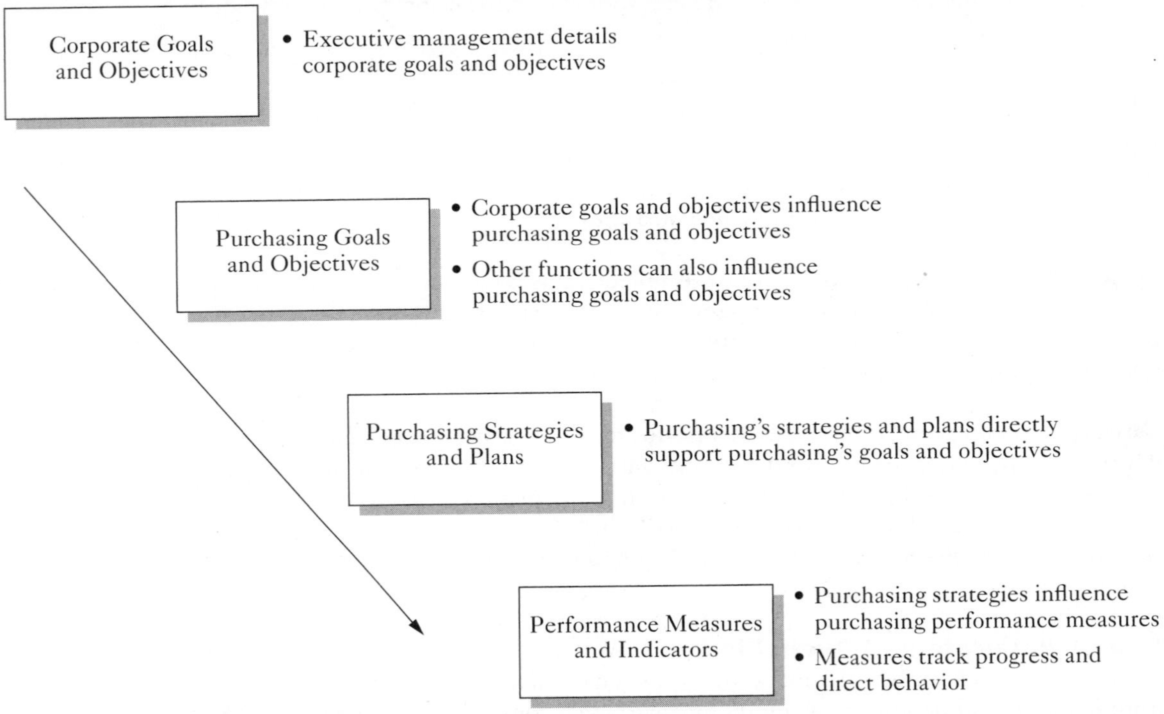

Corporate Goals and Objectives
- Executive management details corporate goals and objectives

Purchasing Goals and Objectives
- Corporate goals and objectives influence purchasing goals and objectives
- Other functions can also influence purchasing goals and objectives

Purchasing Strategies and Plans
- Purchasing's strategies and plans directly support purchasing's goals and objectives

Performance Measures and Indicators
- Purchasing strategies influence purchasing performance measures
- Measures track progress and direct behavior

Joint Participation Joint participation means that the personnel responsible for each measure participate in developing the measure or establishing the measure's performance objective. Joint participation can go a long way toward getting the support of the personnel responsible for achieving the measure.

Dynamic Over Time A dynamic system is one that management reviews periodically, to determine whether existing measures still support purchasing's goals and objectives, the possible need for new measures, or if performance standards or objectives require updating.

Nonmanipulable A nonmanipulable measure means that personnel cannot inappropriately influence performance results (i.e., the measure is cheat-proof). Ideally, the individual(s) responsible for the measure should not be responsible for supplying the data to the reporting system. This becomes an issue of accountability and integrity. The measure's output should be a true reflection of actual activity or performance results. Systems receiving their input from automated or computerized systems are generally less susceptible to data manipulation.

Establish Performance Objectives for Each Measure

Establishing an objective for each performance measure is critical. Objectives quantify the desired performance target or goal. Management must not specify objectives that are too easy. The too-easy objective can become an accepted performance standard within a department.

Performance standards or objectives must be realistic, which means the measure is challenging yet achievable through a solid effort. An objective should not be so easy that it requires minimal effort. It should not be so difficult that it discourages personnel from even attempting to achieve the objective. The objective must also reflect the realities of a firm's competitive environment. An objective that is challenging internally yet does not reflect the competitive environment is not part of a well-defined measure.

Firms commonly use three methods when establishing performance measure objectives: (1) historical data, (2) internal comparisons, and (3) external analysis.

Historical Data This method uses past data about an activity as the basis for establishing a formal performance objective. Historical performance is often modified with a performance improvement factor to arrive at a current objective. Purchasing and supply chain managers often use the historical approach with efficiency-related measures.

Relying on historical data can create some problems. The possibility exists that past performance was less-than-optimal. By establishing an objective based on suboptimal performance, even with an improvement factor, a firm risks continuing suboptimal performance. Also, historical data provide no insight about the performance capabilities of competitors or other leading firms.

Internally Derived Goals or Objectives A firm can perform internal comparisons between departments or business units. The best internal performance level can become the basis for a companywide performance objective. Firms with multiple business units often compare and rank performance internally across different performance categories.

This approach, which offers some advantages over the historical approach, also has disadvantages. A firm that stresses comparisons between internal units can lose sight of its external competition. Unhealthy rivalry can also develop between internal business units or departments. Furthermore, no guarantee exists that the best performing internal unit matches the best performing unit of a direct competitor.

External Analysis This approach requires examination of the practices and performance objectives of competitors or other leading firms. The advantage of this approach is that it requires an external assessment at very specific levels of detail. A later section discusses benchmarking as a competitive-analysis approach for establishing performance objectives.

Finalize System Details

The next phase of implementation requires management to consider issues such as the frequency of performance reporting, the education and training of system users, and the final determination about how to use system output.

Performance-Reporting Frequency A sound measurement and evaluation system provides regular reporting of performance results. The actual reporting frequency can differ from measure to measure. Management must determine what frequency supports the most effective use of each measure. A measure that tracks the status of inbound transportation shipments, for example, must be available on a frequent (daily or real-time) basis. A summary measure evaluating overall supplier performance may require only weekly or monthly reporting.

Education and Training A firm must train its personnel and suppliers to use the performance measurement and evaluation system. Each participant must understand his or her accountability and responsibility under the system and how to use the system's output to improve performance. The measurement and evaluation system is a tool, and like all tools, it requires proper education and training in its use.

Using System Output Managers use the output of a performance measurement and evaluation system in a number of ways. Some managers rely on the output to evaluate directly the performance of purchasing personnel or suppliers. Managers may use the system to track the effectiveness of individual buyers. System output may also identify better-performing suppliers that deserve future purchase contracts. Managers must give careful thought concerning how best to use system output.

Implement and Review System Performance and Measures

All systems have an implementation phase, which may include pilot or trial runs to make sure the system performs as planned. The measurement and evaluation system, along with each performance measure, must be subject to periodic review. A system that contains obsolete or inappropriate measures can be more damaging than having no formal system at all.

PERFORMANCE BENCHMARKING: COMPARING AGAINST THE BEST

An increasingly popular approach for establishing performance standards, processes, measurements, and objectives is *benchmarking*, a process that is not exclusively a purchasing or supply chain practice or approach per se. Rather, it is an approach used by corporate- and functional-level executives and managers. Benchmarking has definite applications, however, when establishing purchasing and supply chain management performance objectives and action plans. Before discussing specific benchmarking applications, we must first gain an understanding of the benchmarking process.

Benchmarking Overview

Benchmarking is the continuous measuring of products, services, processes, activities, and practices against a firm's best competitors or those companies recognized as industry or functional leaders.[3] Formally, the benchmarking process or activity requires measuring performance against that of best-in-class companies, determining how the best-in-class achieve their performance levels, and using that information as the basis for establishing a company's performance targets, strategies, and action plans.[4]

Benchmarking does not always involve comparisons against competitors. Firms often rely on comparisons with noncompetitors as a source of information, especially when benchmarking a process or functional activity common to firms across different industries (for example, supply chain management). It is usually easier to obtain benchmarking data and information from a cooperative noncompetitor.

Benchmarking is necessary for firms that are not industry leaders. Unfortunately, many U.S. firms recognized the need for performance benchmarking after foreign competitors captured worldwide market share. Industry leaders should also practice performance benchmarking on a regular basis. A firm may not retain market leadership if it is unaware of the actions and capabilities of its competitors.

Types of Benchmarking There are three basic types of performance benchmarking.[5] The first type is *strategic benchmarking*, which involves a comparison of one firm's market strategies against those of another. Strategic benchmarking usually involves comparisons against leading competitors and allows a firm to gain an in-depth understanding of the market strategies of its leading competitors.[6] With this knowledge, a firm can develop strategies and plans to counter or preempt the competition.

The second type of benchmarking is *operational benchmarking*, a process that the purchasing function follows when it performs benchmarking comparisons. Operational benchmarking focuses on different aspects of functional activity and identifies methods to achieve best-in-class performance. Selecting the function and the activities within that function to benchmark are critical to the success of operational benchmarking. Firms should benchmark functional activities that provide the greatest return over time.

The third type of benchmarking is *support-activity benchmarking*. During this process, support functions within an organization demonstrate their cost effectiveness against external providers of the same support service or activity. Firms are increasingly using support-activity benchmarking as a way of controlling internal overhead and rising costs.

Benchmarking Benefits A company that actively pursues performance benchmarking hopes to benefit from the process in a number of ways.[7] The benchmarking process helps identify the best business or functional practices to include in a firm's business plans, which can lead directly to performance improvement. Benchmarking can also break down a reluctance to change. Managers begin to see what it takes to maintain corporate or functional leadership by viewing the outside world. Benchmarking can also serve as a source of market intelligence. For example, competitive benchmarking may uncover a previously unrecognized technological breakthrough. Finally, valuable professional contacts between firms can result from the benchmarking process.

Benchmarking Critical Success Factors Certain factors are critical to benchmarking success. Performance benchmarking must become an accepted process within a firm or function and not simply another fashionable program or fad. Personnel must view performance benchmarking as a permanent part of a system that establishes goals, objectives, and competitive strategies. Executive management support for the process is critical.

A firm must also be willing to commit the necessary legwork toward data gathering. A firm must identify which company is the best-in-class for an activity, identify why that company is best, and quantify the benchmarked performance measure. The success of the benchmarking process relies on detailed and accurate benchmarked data and information that becomes part of a firm's action plans and performance objectives.

Managers must view benchmarking as a way to learn from outside companies and improve internal operations on a continuous basis.[8] Some individuals resist the benchmarking process because of a reluctance to recognize the value of a competitor's way of doing business—the "not invented here" syndrome. One way around this syndrome is to benchmark a noncompetitor's activities and performance wherever possible. Obviously, strategic benchmarking requires comparisons against direct competitors. For functional activities, however, a firm can study the performance and methods of noncompetitors.

Information and Data Sources A solid source of benchmarking data includes trade journals, other business library resources, and the World Wide Web. Trade journals and other industry publications often feature firms that have distinguished themselves in some way. If this is not adequate, a firm can contact a benchmark target directly to request further information.

Industrywide conferences and professional seminars are also good sources of information, particularly at a functional level. These meetings often serve as a forum for the exchange of ideas about different topics. Leading firms often make presentations at industry trade meetings. These meetings can provide clues about which firms are the most highly regarded in a particular business area or practice.

Suppliers are another source of information. Purchasers can ask suppliers to identify the firms they believe are the best for each benchmark performance area. A firm can also rely on a professional consultant or other industry experts to identify benchmarking candidates.

A major purchasing benchmarking initiative is currently being conducted through CAPS Research, a joint effort between the Center for Advanced Purchasing Studies (CAPS), Arizona State University, and the National Association of Purchasing

Management (NAPM). This effort includes specific industry-by-industry benchmarks and the results of Project 10X, a study providing information and data about future purchasing and supply chain strategies and practices. In addition, data are provided to participating companies through an online assessment, which is a comparative benchmarking tool, and the Sourcing and Supply Excellence Model. Data are collected via focus group visioning sessions, field research, and Internet-based systems. Information about CAPS Research and Project 10X can be found at http://www.capsresearch.org.

The Benchmarking Process

Robert Camp notes that distinct steps or phases exist before a firm fully receives the benefits of the performance benchmarking process.[9] Exhibit 20.5 graphically presents these five phases.

Planning   During this initial phase of the benchmarking process, a firm addresses issues such as which products or functions to benchmark, which companies to select as benchmarking targets (competitors, noncompetitors, or both?), and how to identify data and information sources. Benchmarking plans should focus on process and methods rather than simply on quantitative performance results. The process and methods cause the quantitative end results.

Analysis   Data and information collection and analysis occur during the second phase. A firm must determine how and why the benchmarked firm is better. A variety of questions should be asked:

* In what product or functional areas is the benchmarked company better?
* Why is the benchmarked company better?
* How large is the gap between the benchmarked company and our company?
* Can we include the benchmarked company's best practices directly into our operating plans?
* Can we project future performance levels and rates of change?

This phase is critical because it requires management to interpret and understand the benchmarked company's processes, methods, and activities.

Integration   Integration is the process of communicating and gaining acceptance of the benchmarking findings throughout an organization. During this phase, management begins to establish operational targets and functional goals based on the benchmarking findings.

Action   The action phase requires translating the benchmark findings into detailed action plans. Critical items during this phase include having personnel directly responsible for carrying out the plans involved with formulation of the plans, developing a schedule for updating plans and objectives over time, and developing a reporting system to communicate progress toward benchmarking goals.

EXHIBIT 20.5   *Benchmarking Implementation Phases*

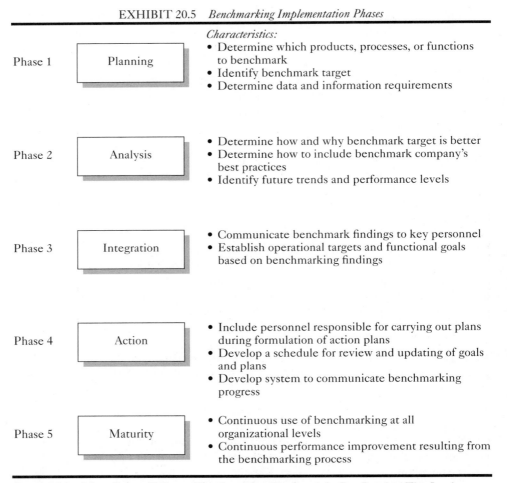

Phase 1	Planning	*Characteristics:* • Determine which products, processes, or functions to benchmark • Identify benchmark target • Determine data and information requirements
Phase 2	Analysis	• Determine how and why benchmark target is better • Determine how to include benchmark company's best practices • Identify future trends and performance levels
Phase 3	Integration	• Communicate benchmark findings to key personnel • Establish operational targets and functional goals based on benchmarking findings
Phase 4	Action	• Include personnel responsible for carrying out plans during formulation of action plans • Develop a schedule for review and updating of goals and plans • Develop system to communicate benchmarking progress
Phase 5	Maturity	• Continuous use of benchmarking at all organizational levels • Continuous performance improvement resulting from the benchmarking process

Source: Adapted from Robert C. Camp, "Benchmarking: The Search for Best Practices That Lead to Superior Performance," *Quality Progress* (February 1989): 15.

Maturity A firm reaches maturity when benchmarking becomes an accepted process for establishing performance plans and objectives. Another indicator of benchmarking maturity occurs when a firm realizes continuous performance improvement as a direct result of performance benchmarking.

A formal process, such as benchmarking, is essential for establishing performance targets and action plans that are externally focused. Without external comparisons, most organizations run the risk of losing sight of what defines best practices or what the competition is doing. Purchasing and supply chain managers must endorse this practice when attempting to establish plans, measures, and objectives that represent best-in-class performance.

$\mathcal{A}$ Summary of Purchasing Measurement and Evaluation Characteristics

A review of purchasing and supply chain performance and measurement systems supports a number of conclusions. These fall into two categories: system characteristics and human resource characteristics.

System Characteristics

1. Measurement is not free. An evaluation system must compare the costs associated with measurement against the benefits. Furthermore, increased measurement does not necessarily mean improved performance. The amount and type of measurement should be enough to achieve the intended result but not cause negative or dysfunctional behavior.
2. Not all aspects of performance lend themselves to quantitative measurement. Negotiating skill and obtaining supplier cooperation are two examples of performance categories that are difficult to quantify.
3. Purchasing and supply chain managers are better served by a few precisely defined and thoroughly understood measures than by many poorly defined measures.
4. An effective measurement system requires a database that provides consistent and reliable data. All personnel must have access to the same data when calculating and reporting purchasing performance indicators.
5. Periodic review of the purchasing and supply chain measurement system should occur to eliminate unimportant or unnecessary performance measures, add new measures as required, and reevaluate performance measure objectives or targets.
6. No best way exists to measure performance. Performance measures differ from firm to firm and industry to industry. No established industry purchasing performance standards have yet emerged. However, the movement toward performance benchmarking does support the development of performance indicators common to more than one firm.
7. Measurement-reporting requirements and content vary by position and level within the organization. Careful planning helps guarantee effective use of the system at each organizational level.
8. A single, overall productivity measure representing purchasing and supply chain performance is not feasible.
9. Many industries need to shift from operational measures focusing on activity to strategic measures assessing a desired end result (for example, increased participation by suppliers during new-product development).
10. The strategies and plans used to produce a performance measure's result are probably more important than the end performance result itself.

Human Resource Characteristics

1. A measurement and evaluation system is not a substitute for solid management. The system is a tool that can be used to assist in the efficient and effective operation of the purchasing and supply chain function.

2. An effective system requires communication. Responsible personnel must clearly understand the performance measure, its performance expectation, and the role of the measure during the performance evaluation process.
3. Measures must reinforce positive behavior and not serve as punitive tools. If management uses the measures solely as a means to identify nonperforming individuals, negative, dysfunctional, or "beat-the-system" behavior may result.

GOOD PRACTICE EXAMPLE
Using Measurement to Drive Continuous Supply Chain Improvement at Accent Industries

■ ■ ■

Accent Industries, a U.S.-based consumer goods company, produces products for direct shipment to retailers worldwide. This company's strategy is to excel across various operational aspects of service by being the industry leader in price, service, and convenience. Accent has developed a set of organizational objectives that it believes are critical to worldwide success. These objectives include being a low-cost producer, providing the highest quality to customers, and offering the best customer service, delivery, and responsiveness in the industry. The company has also developed a set of purchasing and supply chain performance measures that it believes supports directly its organizational directives.

When implementing its purchasing and supply chain measurement system, Accent followed a series of defined steps:

•   Step 1: Conduct cross-functional discussions and benchmarking to establish measures, measurement objectives, and performance targets.
•   Step 2: Formalize measurement objectives into written policy and procedures.
•   Step 3: Formally communicate measures and objectives to the supply base.
•   Step 4: Receive feedback from suppliers.
•   Step 5: Modify, if necessary, performance measures and their objectives.
•   Step 6: Implement final distribution of the measurement objective and process.
•   Step 7: Collect and maintain performance data.

Accent relies on a wide range of purchasing and supply chain measures that relate directly to the company's corporate objectives. A sample of the more critical measures include the following:

Quality
•   Supplier defects in parts per million
•   Internal manufacturing defects in parts per million
•   Internal process capability (Cpk)
•   Damage
•   Number and cost of warranty claims

Price/Cost
- Actual price to market price comparisons
- Price/cost reductions
- Tooling cost management
- Transportation cost management

Cycle Times
- New-product development cycle time

Delivery and Service
- Supplier on-time delivery

Inventory/Forecasting
- Total inventory dollar value over time
- Raw material, work-in-process, and finished-goods inventory turns
- Forecast accuracy

Supplier quality performance is determined during on-site supplier visits and statistical inferences from product receipts. The frequency of calculation varies with each supplier's current quality levels. Suppliers with known quality problems or higher levels of defects are targeted for more frequent measurement.

Accent uses its performance measurement system to establish and convey performance objectives, track progress, and promote continuous improvement. Each supplier is provided clear, comprehensive goals and timely feedback. Factors that are critical to effective measurement include a process for establishing aggressive but attainable goals, supplier consensus that the goals are achievable, senior management support, and accurate measurement with regular feedback.

In the future the company plans to expand its use of total cost of ownership models for supplier evaluation and selection. In addition, Accent wants to pursue the open measurement and sharing of cost elements with its suppliers. ▪

Source: Based on interviews with company managers. Company name has been changed at the request of the company.

CONCLUSION

A purchasing and supply chain performance measurement and evaluation system should directly support corporate goals and objectives. A measurement system that directs behavior and activity away from those goals and objectives is counterproductive and can cause greater harm than good.

A need exists to create measurement systems that are responsive to change. Firms will also increasingly require measures that focus on end results rather than on specific activities. Emphasis will increasingly shift from efficiency measures to effectiveness measures. In addition, executive management must have the ability to distinguish between good and poor purchasing practices and results. A well-developed performance measurement and evaluation system can help provide this distinction.

DISCUSSION QUESTIONS

1. What is a purchasing performance measurement and evaluation system? Why would a firm want to measure purchasing performance?

2. Why would a firm want to measure supplier performance? Describe the kinds of measures that can be used to measure supplier performance.

3. What is performance benchmarking? Why is it increasingly being used when establishing purchasing performance goals and objectives?

4. What are the three types of performance benchmarking? Which type is most commonly used by the purchasing function?

5. What is the difference between effectiveness and efficiency measures? When should a firm focus on purchasing effectiveness measures? When should a firm focus on purchasing efficiency measures?

6. Discuss the reasons why measuring and evaluating purchasing performance has historically had certain problems or limitations. Do you think the purchasing function should increase or decrease its effort to measure performance? Why or why not?

7. Consider the following statement: *Some firms still rely on measures that harm rather than support purchasing's long-term performance objectives.* What does this mean? Provide examples of performance measures that might actually result in a negative longer-term effect on purchasing performance.

8. What is the benefit of developing performance measures that focus on cost versus purchase price?

9. Discuss the major difference between cost-reduction and cost-avoidance measures. Why have some described the reported savings in cost-avoidance measures as "soft," "funny money," and "easy to manipulate"? When can purchasing take credit for a legitimate cost reduction or cost avoidance?

10. Assume you are responsible for developing a benchmarking program. Describe how you would go about establishing the benchmarking process. Be sure to discuss the critical issues you must address.

11. Discuss what is meant by each of the following statements:
    a. Purchasing measurement is not free.
    b. No best way to measure purchasing performance exists.
    c. Many industries need to shift from operational measures focusing on buyer activity to strategic measures focusing on a desired end result.
    d. A purchasing measurement and evaluation system is not a substitute for solid management.

12. Why is it sometimes advantageous to benchmark performance against a noncompetitor?

13. Effective performance measurement systems have certain characteristics. Select three characteristics and discuss why a measure should possess that characteristic.

14. Discuss the different uses a manager has for purchasing and supply chain performance data.

ADDITIONAL READINGS

Brown, Mark Graham. *Keeping Score: Using the Right Metrics to Drive World-Class Performance.* New York: American Management Association, 1996, 15–26.

Chao, C., E. E. Scheuing, and W. A. Ruch. "Purchasing Performance Evaluation: An Investigation of Different Perspectives." *International Journal of Purchasing and Materials Management* (Summer 1993): 33–39.

Cooper, Robin, and Robert Kaplan. "Measure Costs Right: Make the Right Decisions." *Harvard Business Review* (September-October 1988): 23–28.

Dumond, E. "Moving Toward Value-Based Purchasing." *Purchasing Today* (April 1994): 3–8.

Eccles, Robert G. "The Performance Measurement Manifesto." *Harvard Business Review* (January-February, 1991): 131–37.

"Inside Purchasing: Four Pillars of Supply Strategy." *Purchasing* 118, no. 10 (June 15, 1995): 13. (Anonymous)

Kaplan, Robert S., and David P. Norton. "The Balanced Scorecard—Measures That Drive Performance." *Harvard Business Review* (January-February 1992): 71–79

Sharman, Paul. "How to Implement Performance Measurement in Your Organization." *CMA Magazine* (May 1995): 33–38.

Timme, Stephen, and Christine Williams-Timme. "The Financial-SCM Connection." *Supply Chain Management Review* (May-June 2000): 33–40.

Vitale, R. and Sarah C. Mavrinac. "How Effective Is Your Performance Measurement System?" *Management Accounting* (August 1995): 43–47.

ENDNOTES

1. Arjan J. van Wheele, "Purchasing Performance Measurement and Evaluation," *International Journal of Purchasing and Materials Management* (Fall 1984): 18–19.
2. Mark Graham Brown, *Keeping Score: Using the Right Metrics to Drive World-Class Performance* (New York: American Management Association, 1996), 15–26.
3. Robert C. Camp, "Benchmarking: The Search for Best Practices That Lead to Superior Performance: Part I," *Quality Progress* (January 1989): 66.
4. Lawrence S. Pryor, "Benchmarking: A Self-Improvement Strategy," *Journal of Business Strategy* (November/December 1989): 28.
5. Pryor, "Benchmarking," 29–30.
6. Pryor, "Benchmarking," 29.
7. Robert C. Camp, "Benchmarking: The Search for Industry Best Practices That Lead to Superior Performance: Part III," *Quality Progress* (March 1989): 77–80.
8. Timothy R. Furey, "Benchmarking: The Key to Developing Competitive Advantage," *Planning Review* (September-October 1987): 32.
9. Robert C. Camp, "Benchmarking: The Search for Best Practices That Lead to Superior Performance: Part II," *Quality Progress* (February 1989): 71.

21 PURCHASING AND SUPPLY CHAIN CHANGES AND TRENDS

FedEx Retools for the Future

While we often think that modern industrial success stories involve software and electronic companies, a company in Memphis, Tennessee, has changed the way the world views time, logistics, and supply chain management. Operating with only a small fleet of jets, almost 30 years ago, Fred Smith created the overnight package delivery business and became an American industrial legend. Unfortunately, the package delivery business has become mature and intensely competitive. What was once a comfortable niche is now a major industry with global players. Future success means controlling costs, inventing new products and features that customers value, and having employees who are capable of responding to and creating change. For some parts of FedEx, this has meant a retooling of the workforce so it is equipped to meet future challenges.

One area where FedEx is actively retooling its personnel is within the company's Strategic Sourcing and Supply (SS&S) group, a diverse organization with over 300 people in the United States. Edith Kelly-Green, the energetic vice president of strategic sourcing and supply, saw the need for purchasing and supply chain personnel to shift from a reactive, short-term, and operational perspective to one that creates value at the highest levels of the company. As a result of her vision, FedEx has created a series of ten purchasing and supply chain courses that all SS&S employees in the United States have attended with plans to develop an international version.

The curriculum developed by FedEx, with the help of external educators, examines the many topics, skills, and knowledge areas that today's purchasing and supply chain specialists must be familiar with to be effective. Each employee attends ten separate course modules, with each module lasting two days. The leading-edge training areas address a variety of topics:

- Cycle time management
- Process mapping and control
- Cross-functional teaming
- Supplier integration
- Supplier development
- Sourcing strategy development
- Alliances and partnerships
- Longer-term contracting
- Supply chain changes and trends
- Cost management

Throughout their training, FedEx personnel work in groups to propose and present projects that relate to class material. Some of these projects become opportunities for FedEx to improve its supply chain. Employees even have to take a final exam, which involves a major case that encompasses major course topics.

→ → →

FedEx knows that the changes, trends, and pressures affecting its industry are powerful and unrelenting. Executive management also knows that future competitive advantage requires personnel who are at the forefront of mastering new knowledge and skills. For Strategic Sourcing and Supply at FedEx, the future is now.

Source: Based on company interviews with FedEx managers and corporate trainers.

A common theme throughout this book is that the functional area called purchasing, along with the activities that support supply chain management, are experiencing dramatic change. Once regarded as a reactive activity capable only of neutral or negative contribution, purchasing and supply chain managers must today be at the forefront of responding to and creating change. As AT&T's executive vice president for telephone products once remarked, "Purchasing is by far the largest single function at AT&T. Nothing we do is more important."[1]

This chapter outlines the real and projected changes and trends that have affected and will continue to affect purchasing and supply chain professionals. These changes and trends appear within seven areas: (1) performance improvement requirements; (2) purchasing and supplier importance; (3) organization and human resources; (4) information systems development; (5) performance measurement; (6) supply-base management; and (7) purchasing responsibilities and activities. Each area is supported by data collected annually from purchasing and supply chain managers.

Performance Improvement Requirements

Over the last ten years purchasing managers have overwhelmingly recognized the need for continuous improvement, including the need to realize time-based reduction targets. Performance improvement requirements have been a driving force behind the execution of innovative purchasing and supply chain practices. This section examines the improvement targets that respondents expect to achieve in the years ahead.

- **There will be continuous improvement in internal and external cycle time, cost, quality, and delivery performance.**

Stringent customer requirements and increasingly competitive markets require improvement across all major performance categories. This has forced managers to make continuous improvement an integral part of their planning processes. Over the next several years, firms expect to achieve the following improvement targets as part of their continuous improvement efforts:

> More than 70% of companies expect no change or a decrease in *purchased material costs* (after adjusting for inflation/deflation.) Firms expecting to or achieve material cost decreases (55% of firms) anticipate annual decreases averaging 2-3%.

More than 92% of firms expect average annual *product quality* improvements of 10-13%. This improvement relates to whatever method respondents use to measure quality.

Almost 91% of firms expect average annual *delivery performance* improvements of 7-10%.

Continuous improvement expectations make purchasing's contribution crucial to longer-term success. Purchasing and supply chain managers must develop practices and approaches that link to and support business improvement targets. A later section identifies the activities that respondents expect will help them realize these performance gains.

- **The reduction of time, particularly during product and process development, will become increasingly important.**

While high quality and low cost will always be important, time-related capabilities are rapidly becoming the next generation of order winners in the eyes of the customer. In particular, product support and best customer service with short lead times and the ability to bring new products from concept-to-customer in the shortest time will begin to rival cost and quality as critical market attributes.

Most managers agree that reduced cycle times are essential for market success. Competition is no longer between big and small but rather fast and slow firms. Purchasing plays an important role in time-based competition because of its ability to affect time-related processes and activities. For example, reducing material ordering cycle times with suppliers can also help reduce internal manufacturing cycle times. Faster supplier responsiveness supports faster responsiveness to end customer requirements, particularly as planning horizons become shorter and less certain. While beyond the scope of this discussion, material ordering cycle time has four components that supply chain practices affect directly: (1) transmission of requirements to suppliers; (2) the suppliers' ordering and manufacturing cycle time; (3) delivery from suppliers; and (4) incoming receiving and inspection.

Perhaps the most obvious area where firms are concentrating their time-reduction efforts is during product and process development. Major changes have occurred in the methods and time required for developing products and processes over the last eight years, such as the use of product development teams, rapid prototyping technologies, and shared computer aided design systems with suppliers. As a result, average product development cycle time has declined from 3.2 years in 1990 to less than 2.5 years currently. In 1990, executive management reported that the importance of reduced product development cycle time for achieving competitive goals was 4.7 on average versus almost 5.4 currently (where 1 = limited importance and 7 = significant importance).

Companies will continue to reduce cycle times in areas sensitive to time-based competition and performance, particularly product development. Most business units expect a 40% to 45% reduction from existing levels in product development cycle time over the next several years. This has and will continue to require purchasing to pursue actions directed at shortened cycle times. For example, early supplier design involvement increased from 29% of firms stressing this activity in 1990 to almost 70%

today. Computer-aided design interface with suppliers grew from 21% of firms stressing this activity in 1990 to almost 40% currently. Both activities support shortened cycle time by involving suppliers during product development.

$\mathcal{P}$URCHASING AND SUPPLIER IMPORTANCE

In the mid- 1960s, a respected purchasing professional, Bruce D. Henderson, remarked about the state of affairs facing purchasing.[2] He stated that purchasing was a neglected function in most organizations because executive managers sensed it was not important to mainstream problems. He further explained that some executives found it hard to visualize a company becoming more competitive because of superior procurement. In his view, this was incorrect since firms often derived a competitive edge from other functions such as research, marketing, finance, or manufacturing. In his words, "Procurement is regarded by executive management as a negative function—it can hinder the company if not done well, but can make little positive contribution." During the 1990s, we have observed an almost total reversal of this belief, where today's suppliers and purchasing/sourcing have the attention and respect of executive managers.

• **Executive perception of supplier and purchasing importance will continue to increase.**

The average perception that *executive managers have of supplier importance* has increased from 3.1 in 1990 to 3.84 in 2001 to 4.53 expected in 2003 (where 1 = not important and 5 = extremely important). In addition, 98% of companies now say supplier importance is *quite* or *extremely important*. The shift in supplier importance is a result of at least five factors affecting most industries. These include (1) the need to control unit costs, (2) the need to reduce the total cost of acquisition, (3) the increasing influence that suppliers have on the purchaser's ability to respond to end customers, particularly as it affects time-related requirements, (4) an increased reliance on fewer suppliers, and (5) a willingness of purchasers to rely on suppliers to design and build entire subassemblies and subsystems.

Executive purchasing management's awareness of supplier importance in supporting product development has also increased steadily, growing from 4.5 in 1990 to 5.9 today (where 1 = limited importance and 7 = significant importance). Executive managers recognize the contribution that qualified suppliers should make during product development, such as providing design and technical expertise for components and subassemblies. Progressive firms include suppliers early during their product development process.

A major sign of purchasing and supply chain importance involves the number of firms where purchasing and supply chain personnel make strategy presentations to the highest executive levels. In 1990, only 18% of firms said they made strategy presentations to the Board of Directors versus almost 50% today. Just over 50% said they made strategy presentations to the executive committee in 1990 versus 86% today.

This growth reflects a maturing of purchasing to the point where it can assume a position on par with other functional groups. An earlier study by Bales and Fearon revealed that two-thirds of CEO's and presidents from various sized companies viewed the purchasing function as very important to the overall success of their firm.[3] Furthermore, almost 90% of the CEO's and presidents in their study showed an interest in reviewing purchasing performance measures.

- **A growing reliance on external suppliers for product and process technology will continue.**

A dependence on suppliers as a source of product and process technology provides additional evidence of growing supplier importance. Since 1990, reliance on external sources for *product* technology has increased from 37% to 44% of total requirements, with reliance on suppliers for *process* technology remaining steady at around 40%. Concentrating on core competencies and technologies with a greater emphasis on the outsourcing of non-core requirements almost guarantees continued growth in external reliance. Also, pressure to differentiate products by including the latest technology in product designs makes supplier contribution increasingly vital.

ORGANIZATION AND HUMAN RESOURCES

The right organizational structure and human resource skills are essential for effective purchasing and supply chain management. Today, the right structure often means using higher-level teams to evaluate, select, manage, and develop suppliers. Furthermore, the need to support accelerated product development and other cross-organizational tasks requires purchasing to take an end-item rather than strict commodity focus. Leading firms are beginning to include suppliers as a part of their organizational structure. This may involve providing space for a supplier's engineers to work during new product development. Furthermore, suppliers are increasingly assuming roles as formal members on cross-functional teams.

- **Expect a continued change in purchasing and supply chain organizational structures.**

While most companies still organize purchasing around commodities, a real change continues in the number of purchasing groups organized by finished product, process, or other hybrid structures. The shift toward end-item and other types of structures reflects a growing need for purchasing to become more integrated with other parts of the organization. Purchasing participation on product development teams, for example, forces the purchasing member to assume a product rather than commodity perspective. Some organizations have developed both a product and commodity focus to their purchasing structure, with commodity teams or specialists supporting product development teams with commodity information as required. Other organizations are moving from a vertical structure to a horizontal structure organized around key supply chain processes, which Exhibit 21.1 illustrates.

EXHIBIT 21.1   *Process Organizational Structure*

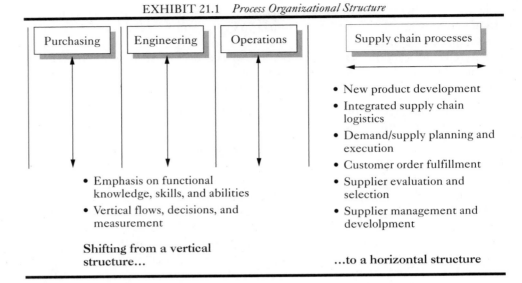

| Purchasing | Engineering | Operations | | Supply chain processes |

- Emphasis on functional knowledge, skills, and abilities
- Vertical flows, decisions, and measurement

- New product development
- Integrated supply chain logistics
- Demand/supply planning and execution
- Customer order fulfillment
- Supplier evaluation and selection
- Supplier management and develolpment

Shifting from a vertical structure...

...to a horizontal structure

- **Organizations will continue to rely on cross-functional sourcing teams.**

A major change during the last ten years has involved the use of cross-functional teams to support sourcing decision making. In 1990, less than 50% of firms said they emphasized the use of cross-functional teams to support sourcing decisions. This has increased to more than 80% of firms using these teams today. Cross-functional sourcing teams are assuming greater responsibility for evaluating, selecting, and managing suppliers. These teams include members from various disciplines, with perhaps only one member with formal purchasing or supply management experience.

Perhaps the greatest challenge confronting cross-functional sourcing teams has been getting nonpurchasing or supply chain members and functions to support team tasks. Because sourcing team assignments are usually part-time, members work within a dual reporting structure. Members report not only to the team but also to their functional managers, some of whom perceive the team's tasks to be part of traditional purchasing responsibilities. Continued use of cross-functional sourcing teams requires a careful examination of the difficulties surrounding their use.

Purchasing as a functional group may even disappear at some organizations. The process of evaluating, selecting, and managing suppliers will increasingly belong to cross-functional teams. Once a team selects a supplier, then users throughout the organization order routinely from that supplier.

- **There will be increased separation of strategic and tactical job responsibilities.**

Most organizations are taking action to reduce the burden of ordering and expediting small, routine orders. Certain trends are occurring that will result in purchasing

Measuring Future Purchasing Skill Requirements

As the purchaser's job has evolved, so have the skills needed to handle both day-to-day and strategic tasks. What's lacking, however, is a corporate understanding of how to evaluate those skills and define expectations for higher-level procurement positions, according to Larry Giunipero, who authored the study "A Skills Based Analysis of a World Class Purchaser" for the Center for Advanced Purchasing Studies.

According to Giunipero's report, companies that will show the way in this area must continually assess the skills and knowledge of their purchasers; measure those skills against an ideal; make training convenient and readily available to their purchasers; understand the importance of having suppliers involved in the training process; and establish quantifiable metrics that can be converted into measurable training goals.

To get to the next level, companies should consider devising a weighted skill matrix, a technique that defines the skills required by individuals for a particular position and uses a rating scale where each number represents proficiency in a particular skill set. Before setting up the matrix, however, companies must define what skills are needed for the position today and in the future. From there, companies can evaluate the level of skills currently demonstrated and identify the gaps between an ideal skills set and what an employee possesses. Once those gaps are defined, top management and the purchasing department can establish a plan to foster the future growth of skills.

Source: Adapted from Larry Giunipero, "A Skills-Based Analysis of the World Class Purchaser," Center for Advanced Purchasing Studies, Tempe, AZ, 2000.

professionals performing less day-to-day buying. For example, most organizations now issue credit cards to selected users. These cards allow holders to obtain what they require directly from approved sources. The credit card provider issues reports, performs billing, and assumes many responsibilities performed previously by purchasing. Operational activities become the responsibility of internal users, allowing purchasing and supply chain specialists to concentrate on more important activities.

The expanded use of information technology will further reduce the operational burden placed on purchasing and supply chain professionals. By relying on information systems, users can order what they require through their system or the Internet directly from an approved supplier's system. Also, ordering for production items can occur automatically once a firm generates its production schedules. The production control system will forward component requirements immediately to suppliers, greatly reducing the need for human involvement.

Another development that will reduce the clerical work assumed by purchasing is the use of third-party suppliers to manage inventory. Suppliers are increasingly

EXHIBIT 21.2   *Separating Strategic and Tactical Responsibilities*

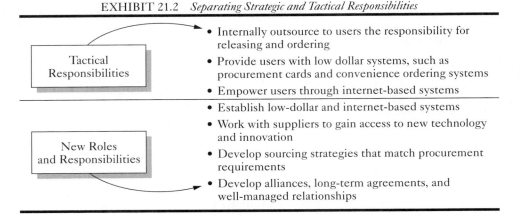

locating personnel at a purchaser's site to manage tool cribs, storerooms, maintenance supplies, and so on in a classic example of outsourcing. Since the purchaser no longer has primary responsibility for these items, purchasing professionals are free to pursue other activities. Exhibit 21.2 identifies one way to separate tactical and strategic job responsibilities.

These changes concern some purchasers. If an individual's main responsibility has been to routinely place purchase orders, what happens when job requirements change? A changing profession calls for continuing education and skill development. Many buyers are ill equipped to respond to the changes that are taking place.

- **New purchasing and supply chain skills will be required to compete effectively.**

Managing the future purchasing and supply chain organization requires a new, emerging set of skill requirements. The skills, abilities, and knowledge required today are much more extensive than just a few years ago. Firms require individuals who understand strategic sourcing and supply chain management, which means being proficient in many different areas (see Exhibit 21.3). Personnel who lack the necessary skills and abilities must further their education and training. The vignette opening this chapter highlighted the efforts FedEx has taken to retool its purchasing and supply chain personnel.

INFORMATION SYSTEMS DEVELOPMENT

Given the growing need to coordinate supply chain activities across many locations, assume an organizational rather than functional perspective, and take on complex and strategic responsibilities with existing staff, it is understandable why most companies expect to emphasize purchasing and supply chain systems development over the next several years. Furthermore, the increased complexity and importance of information

Teamwork and Cooperation Comes Slowly Between Functions

Companies are taking steps to get different departments to work together effectively, but they're still falling short of the goal. And while most purchasing professionals agree that teamwork and cooperation are the best mechanisms for getting different corporate functions to work together, they also point out that neither attribute exists naturally in a corporate setting.

The results of a recent survey indicate that while there are good signs of cooperation between corporate departments, many companies are not doing enough to foster cooperation between purchasing and other functions. Even worse, many such efforts are actually counterproductive. "There's too much competition among departments," says Ronald Blizzard, material administrator for Massachusetts-based Guilford Rail System. His response was typical of many purchasers who say that long-standing rivalries between groups do not die easily or quickly.

Most of the survey participants say their companies are not taking the most effective approach to the problem of trying to promote teamwork and cooperation. Some survey respondents say that employees themselves are the root of the problem, that staff members simply refuse to play along or work well with others. But the majority of survey respondents lay the responsibility at the feet of management. They say whatever process is adopted, it must receive the blessing and support of upper management. Too often, the departments of production, planning, design, quality, and purchasing have different leaders to answer to. Those who have watched this process work well report that their purchasing departments were successfully linked with operations management, logistics and planning, materials, and warehouse receiving/shipping departments. Management must continually reinforce the common goal of teamwork, reminding employees that they are part of a company, not only a department.

Source: Adapted from Brian Milligan, "Despite Attempts to Break Them, Functional Silos Live On," *Purchasing* (November 4, 1999): 24–26.

---

systems help explain why development is becoming less the responsibility of purchasing and more the responsibility of information technology specialists.

- **Internet-based systems will become the platform for sourcing and integrated supply chain management.**

Internet-based systems that integrate processes within and between firms will become increasingly common and critical. Integrative systems include electronic data interchange (EDI), Internet home pages, intranets, computer-aided-design capability with suppliers, shared production control and scheduling systems, and any other

EXHIBIT 21.3   *Emerging Skill Requirements*

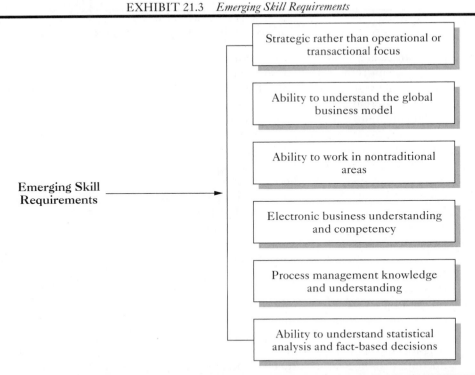

systems that transfer information and data between parties. These Internet-based systems should facilitate and manage the flow of information between parties effectively and efficiently. Exhibit 21.4 highlights some of the applications that should increasingly occur through the Internet.

•   **The use of supply chain planning and execution software will increase dramatically.**

The concept of the integrated supply chain implies the increased use of supply chain planning and execution software. Companies such as i2 Technologies, Man-ugistics, and LOG-NET have made great strides in the development and installation of planning and execution modules that help coordinate the two-way flow of material, information, and funds across the supply chain. Supply chain planning software is designed to improve forecast accuracy, optimize production scheduling, reduce inventory costs, decrease order cycle times, reduce transportation costs, and improve customer service. The goal of such software is to procure and manage the flow of products from suppliers all the way through distribution to help ensure delivery to the right location and customer using the best delivery methods. Exhibit 21.5 highlights the various modules and activities contained in supply chain execution software.

EXHIBIT 21.4   *Sourcing and Supply Chain Management Through the Internet*

The Internet ⟶

- Web-based intelligent agents will allow buyers to globally search for best price, delivery, and availability.
- Internet-based tools will provide the structure, the ability to measure progress and performance, the means to share information, and the rules to administer integrated supply chain management.
- The buying and selling of commodity and standard industrial goods through Internet auctioning will increase, creating risks and opportunities.
- Internet-exchanges will lead to huge consortia with members leveraging information and volumes across the entire supply chain.
- Emergent market sourcing will increase as expanded connectivity through the Internet provides visibility to worldwide sources.

PERFORMANCE MEASUREMENT

Performance measurement is essential for gauging overall effectiveness. It enables purchasing and supply chain managers to identify (1) supplier performance and improvement opportunities, (2) performance trends, (3) the best suppliers, both for routine purchase requirements and for critical items that would benefit from longer-term purchase agreements, (4) the best places to commit limited supplier development resources, and (5) the overall effectiveness of supply chain improvement efforts. A formal supplier measurement system also provides an efficient way to express performance requirements across a supply chain. Several trends involve purchasing performance measurement.

- **There will be continued increase in the measurement of purchasing and supply chain contribution and performance.**

As purchasing shifts its focus from operational to more strategic activities, certain performance measurement areas will gain importance. These areas include (1) purchasing's support of concept-to-customer cycle time reduction for new products, (2) purchasing's ability to introduce new technology from suppliers, (3) purchasing process cycle time measurement, (4) the ability to reduce the total cost of ownership, and (5) the ability of purchasing and supply chain managers to affect key corporate indicators like return on investment (ROI) and economic value add (EVA). Exhibit 21.6 shows how purchasing and supply chain management supports financial performance. New measurement areas will emphasize purchasing effectiveness and contribution to revenue growth rather than just efficiency.

EXHIBIT 21.5   *Modules and Activities Contained in Supply Chain Execution Software*

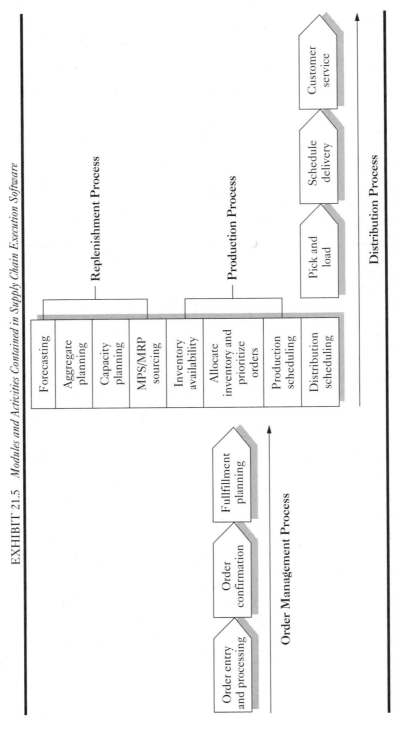

Source: Adapted from Raui Kalakota and Marcia Robinson, *e-Business: Roadmap for Success*, 1999. Addison-Wesley Publishing Company.

EXHIBIT 21.6   *Purchasing and Supply Chain Contribution to Financial Performance*

Responsibility for
Revenue Growth

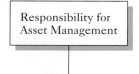

Responsibility for
Asset Management

Responsibility for
Cost Management

- Growing need to
  indentify suppliers that
  provide early access to
  new technology, which
  supports product
  differentiation and
  market growth
- Greater coordination
  with marketing and new
  product development

- Greater involvement with
  insourcing/outsourcing
  and capital acquisition
  decisions
- Emphasis on effective
  management of inventory
  investment

- Use of web-based
  approaches for managing
  purchase cost, including
  auctions and industry-
  based Internet
  procurement exchanges
- Creation of new systems
  to remove transactions
  costs
- Use of leading-edge
  practices to manage
  price/cost

- **There will be an increase in the development of formalized systems for measuring supplier performance.**

An often-ignored area involves the continuous measurement of supplier performance. Many organizations, large and small, have failed to recognize the importance of supplier-related measurement. This has resulted in shifting systems development resources to more "critical" areas. As a result, wide differences exist in the quality and capability of supplier measurement systems. Some firms perform monthly qualitative assessments of supplier performance while others measure performance against stringent daily targets. A small percentage calculates the total cost of supplier-caused nonconformance while others fail to evaluate supplier performance at all.

In 1990, only 47% of companies had a formal system to measure continuous supplier performance, and only 36% maintained specific minimum levels of acceptable supplier performance. By 2000, 75% of firms said they had a formalized system, with 60% maintaining defined minimum levels of acceptable performance. For smaller firms, these figures decline rapidly. Firms are expected to enhance their supplier-related measurement capabilities, often as part of their systems development effort.

SUPPLY-BASE MANAGEMENT

Not long ago, most U.S. companies believed that how they managed suppliers made little difference in their overall performance. Buyers played suppliers off against each other, switched suppliers frequently, and offered only short-term contracts. This adversarial model, while not ideal, worked when all industry members practiced the same

SOURCING SNAPSHOT

TRW Looks to the Future

TRW—a global technology, manufacturing and service company—has a new president: David Cote, a 25-year veteran with General Electric. Although Cote is still learning his way around the automotive industry, one conclusion he has already reached is that his new company must undergo some major changes in purchasing and supply chain management to ensure future growth and prosperity. Cote said he's concentrating on three areas: (1) reducing material purchasing costs from TRW's current level of 50% of sales; (2) reducing inventories to boost working capital, and (3) eliminating products that do not add value for TRW customers. "Quite honestly, we just make too much stuff," he said.

As for the auto industry as a whole, TRW's president said he doesn't expect the supplier consolidation trend of recent years to erase what he called the "often difficult" relationships among suppliers and between suppliers and OEMs, even if it means fewer, larger players. "This is just a difficult industry where you've got to be trying to bring better cost, quality, delivery, and technology every day," Cote said. "I don't see that changing."

Source: Adapted from Susan Carney, "TRW's Future: Cut, Cut, Cut," *Automotive News* (March 13, 2000): 46F.

---

form of supply management. The model changed, however, when global competitors showed that collaborating with suppliers could lead to competitive market advantages. Now, changes are occurring in how firms approach and manage their supply base.

- **There will be a continued reduction in the size of a purchasers' supply bases.**

An unquestionable trend involves the willingness of most firms to reduce the number of suppliers they maintain. Almost 75% of firms decreased the number of suppliers they maintained over the last five years. More than 80% of firms expect a continued reduction in the size of their supply base over the next several years, although the reductions will not be as aggressive as they were in the late 1980s and early 1990s. Respondents anticipating a reduction from 1999 levels estimate a 20% to 30% decrease in the size of their supply base.

Interestingly, supplier reduction sometimes involves only a reduction in the number of *first-tier* suppliers. A trend within the automotive industry, for example, has been to rely on larger, full-service suppliers to design and build entire subsystems. Instead of many smaller suppliers providing components for the subsystem, the purchaser uses one major subsystem supplier, who then depends on smaller suppliers to provide components. Former first-tier suppliers have become second-tier suppliers. While the purchaser maintains fewer first-tier suppliers, integrated supply chain management requires that buyers maintain a keen interest in first, second, and even third tier suppliers.

Optimization is only a first step toward world-class supply base performance. Advanced sourcing strategies requiring closer interaction between the purchaser and the seller simply are not viable with a large supply base.

- **Longer-term contracting will continue to grow.**

A steady increase in longer-term contracting has taken place over the last decade. The percentage of longer-term contracts to total contracts has increased from 24% of total contracts in 1990 to 37% today, representing an increase of 50%. Additionally, the dollar value of purchases represented by longer-terms contracts has increased from 34% to 54% of total purchase dollars. Within the next several years, expect half of all contracts to be longer-term, representing two-thirds of the value of total purchases.

Most firms no longer pursue short-term contracts characterized by frequent competitive bidding. Instead, purchasers are choosing to direct their efforts toward value-adding activities. Perhaps most importantly, longer-term purchase agreements are prerequisites to activities requiring closer cooperation between a purchaser and supplier. As purchasers expand their use of activities requiring closer relationships, such as early supplier design involvement, the use of longer-term agreements will continue to increase. Furthermore, many longer-term agreements can be expected to evolve to partnerships or alliances between buyers and sellers. The Good Practice Example featured at the end of this chapter highlights a long-term agreement that is highly collaborative.

- **There will be increased purchase volume accumulation or consolidation, especially across worldwide locations.**

Severe competition has forced firms to search for innovative ways to reduce total costs. Because of the lower emphasis placed on purchase consolidation during the 1980s, this approach has created significant cost savings throughout the 1990s. Firms consolidate (i.e., combine) their purchase volumes of common items or families of items across buying locations to receive lower prices and better service. Although consolidation efforts have increased over the last ten years, respondents say their efforts have resulted in only a moderate level of consolidation, even when opportunities for consolidation exist. Purchase consolidation remains an evolving opportunity at most organizations.

Firms will increasingly concentrate their consolidation efforts across worldwide buying units. This usually involves selecting suppliers who have global design, production, and technical support capabilities. Worldwide consolidation requires the development of global databases and commodity coding schemes to coordinate the consolidation effort. Unfortunately, 60 percent of companies do not have access to a global purchasing database, although this number has improved over the last five years.

- **There will be increased efforts to develop supplier performance capabilities.**

Historically, U.S. firms committed few resources toward developing supplier performance capabilities. Traditional buyer/seller relationships, characterized by limited trust, did not support collaborative efforts. Today, a smaller supply base requires a commitment and investment in relationships rather than switching suppliers at the first sign of a problem. Progressive companies have increasingly practiced supplier development activities that are direct and aggressive. Examples of supplier development include many activities:

Conducting education or training programs
Providing technology
Providing personnel
Providing equipment
Agreeing to contingent liabilities
Providing progress payments
Providing capital

Supplier development is an activity that begins to separate those firms that are truly committed to leading-edge supply chain management practices from those that maintain more traditional sourcing relationships. Expect purchasers to be increasingly willing to help develop their key suppliers within a smaller supply base.

PURCHASING RESPONSIBILITIES AND ACTIVITIES

If an increase in purchasing importance is taking place, then we would expect to see shifting responsibilities over time that reflect this importance. Since 1990, we have witnessed dramatic changes in purchasing and supply chain activities stressed by companies.

- **There will be a continued increase in externally focused and higher-level purchasing activities.**

Many activities have experienced major changes in their emphasis since 1990. The percentages shown in the list below reflect the growth compared with 1990 levels in the number of firms saying they emphasize an activity. This shows how aggressive purchasing and supply chain management activities have become at most firms.

- Benchmarking against leading firms (+146%)
- Use of full-service suppliers (+125%)
- Joint ventures and supplier partnerships (+117%)
- Supplier technology demonstration days (+96%)
- Value analysis/value engineering (+96%)
- Global sourcing (+74%)
- Total cost of ownership supplier selection and management (+72%)
- CAD interface with suppliers (+71%)
- System or subsystem sourcing (+67%)
- Cross-functional sourcing teams (+62%)
- Single sourcing (+44%)
- Supplier recognition through awards (+43%)

EXHIBIT 21.7   *Sourcing Challenges Faced in Emergent Markets*

- Physical infrastructure inadequacies
- Ethics, laws, and regulatory differences
- Absence of reliable data
- Difficulty in obtaining duty drawbacks
- Countertrade demands
- Country by country differences as material crosses borders
- Tariffs and duties
- Government corruption
- Less developed business processes
- Longer pipelines, inconsistent delivery reliability, and quality variability

- **Purchasing and supply chain management will increasingly become a global activity.**

Several trends and changes reveal that purchasers have increasingly assumed a global perspective over the last ten years. As mentioned, the focus of purchase volume consolidation today is across worldwide buying units. We have observed a major increase since 1990 in the number of firms saying that purchasing is involved with international supply chain management. Respondents also expect the development of global databases to be a primary area of systems growth. Finally, an unquestionable increase in worldwide sourcing is occurring.

Purchases from foreign sources have increased from 9% of total purchases in 1990 to 30% of total purchases today. This increase is due primarily to cost reduction pressures and the need to gain exposure to worldwide process and product technology. These pressures ensure that a gradual increase in total purchases from foreign sources will continue.

The trend toward increased global purchasing and emergent markets is clear. However, the need to manage currency risk, extended material pipelines, global databases, and cultural and language differences (to name a few) creates greater complexity. The question becomes whether organizations have the resources and capabilities required for coordinating worldwide purchasing activities. Exhibit 21.7 identifies some of the issues when purchasing in emerging markets.

- **Outsourcing of non-core competencies and capabilities will occur.**

Vertical integration, where a firm controls most of its supply chain, is no longer considered desirable within industries that demand flexibility and responsiveness. A focus on core competencies and capabilities has influenced the strategic planning process at most firms. Debate will always exist about which activities or production should be performed internally and which should be outsourced. Because purchasing deals extensively with external sources, it becomes involved with the insourcing/outsourcing process. The trend toward outsourcing should continue, although firms have to be careful about being too aggressive with their outsourcing or relying on outsourcing

SOURCING SNAPSHOT

IBM Expects Purchasing to Add Value

Ten years ago when IBM was vertically integrated, purchasing was basically an administrative function that was not very important to the company. Purchasers executed the buying transaction after being told what to buy. But in the early 1990s, there was a change in IBM's business philosophy when Lou Gertsner became chief executive officer. His view was to leverage the size of IBM—a process that involved outsourcing and a reliance on outside suppliers. According to Nicholas Donofrio, senior vice president of technology and manufacturing, IBM's procurement organization was driven by a change in business philosophy. "We wanted to focus on the things that make a big difference and do them ourselves. Where there are competitive alternatives, we want to buy them."

Under the direction of chief procurement officer Gene Richter, commodity teams were formed to manage the purchase of components and services globally. IBM combined the requirements of all its divisions and locations to gain buying clout. Purchasers began evaluating the performance of suppliers, reducing the number of suppliers, and identifying potential new ones.

Donofrio says procurement has become more strategic to IBM and will become even more so in the future once the company's purchasing process moves to the Internet. "The vast majority of our expenditures are going to be done via the Internet," says Donofrio. "There will be an exception process when something can't be purchased over the Internet. We process 5 million pieces of paper per year. Within the next few years that will go to zero. We intend to wipe out paper as part of our transaction process," he says. IBM's Internet procurement initiative will reduce cost and procurement cycle time and will free up buyers to work on more important issues.

Source: Adapted from "An Executive View of Procurement," *Purchasing*, (September 16, 1999): 45.

---

partners that do not fulfill their performance promises. There are a number of reasons why an emphasis on outsourcing will continue:

- As mentioned earlier, the pressure to reduce costs is severe and will only increase. Cost-reduction pressures are forcing organizations to use their productive resources more efficiently. As a result, executive management will increasingly rely on insourcing/outsourcing decisions to provide a way to effectively manage costs.
- Firms are continuing to become more highly specialized in product and process technology. Increased specialization implies focused investment in a process or technology, which contributes to greater cost differentials between firms.
- Firms will increasingly focus more on what they excel at while outsourcing areas of nonexpertise. Some organizations are formally defining their core competencies to help guide the insourcing/outsourcing effort. This has affected decisions concerning what businesses a firm should engage.

- The need for responsiveness in the marketplace is increasingly affecting insourcing/outsourcing decisions. Shorter cycle times, for example, encourage greater outsourcing with less vertical integration. The time to develop a production capability or capacity may exceed the window available to enter a new market.
- Wall Street recognizes and rewards firms that achieve higher return on investment. Since insourcing usually requires an assumption of fixed assets (and increased human capital), financial pressures are causing managers to closely examine sourcing decisions. Avoidance of increased fixed costs is motivating many firms to rely on external rather than internal assets.
- Improved computer simulation tools and forecasting software enable firms to perform insourcing/outsourcing comparisons with greater precision. These tools allow the user to perform sensitivity (what-if) analysis that permits comparisons of different sourcing possibilities.

GOOD PRACTICE EXAMPLE
General Motors Works to Secure Its Future

■ ■ ■

General Motors understands that future success will belong to those firms that are maximizing the value received from a world-class supply chain. The automaker has taken aggressive action by signing a 10-year long-term agreement to buy a substantial portion (around 25%) of its worldwide aluminum requirements from Alcan Aluminum Ltd. This agreement is unusual in two regards. First, its length is much longer than is typical for longer-term agreements. Second, the agreement attempts to provide stable pricing, which is not a characteristic of the aluminum market. Prices will be linked to production costs rather than the nuances of the aluminum market.

A primary driver behind this innovative agreement is the need to sharply reduce the weight of future autos to improve gas mileage and reduce emissions. Montreal-based Alcan calculates that every one-ton reduction in vehicle weight results in a 20-ton reduction in carbon dioxide emissions over the vehicle's life. Carbon dioxide is the principal greenhouse gas linked to global warming. GM's chairman, John F. Smith, Jr., considered this agreement so important that he signed it himself.

GM said it expects aluminum's use to increase by at least 7% annually. While GM will not disclose its pricing mechanisms, GM's vice president in charge of purchasing says that the mechanism for keeping prices stable involves a formula that guarantees Alcan a return on its investment, as well as involving third-party financing. Aluminum's price volatility, sometimes 30% to 40% in a year, reflects trading and speculation on commodity markets and has been a handicap in expanding the use of the material in autos and trucks.

This agreement, which represents a trend toward greater collaboration between key supply chain members, also calls for GM and Alcan to set up a joint research program at GM's technical center in Warren, Michigan. The center employs several dozen engineers from the two companies. The engineers are working to invent new ways to use aluminum in autos and to make aluminum parts as recyclable as soda cans. An executive for Alcan said his company has spent $200 million over the last ten years on research to increase and improve the use of aluminum in vehicles. Alcan's goal is to "establish ourselves as the leading supplier to the auto industry."

This agreement shows that traditional ways of doing business must give way to innovative approaches that capture the value that supply chain collaboration potentially offers. GM sees creative sourcing and supply chain practices as a way to meet the environmental and cost challenges of the future. ■

Source: Adapted from: Robert L. Simison, "GM Commits to Aluminum in Alcan Pact," *Wall Street Journal,* November 9, 1998, Page A3.

CONCLUSION

This chapter—as well as this book—presents purchasing and supply chain management as a dynamic field of study. Surviving in an era of rapid change and intense competition requires a commitment to (1) develop the skills of purchasing professionals, (2) actively use information technology across the supply chain, (3) pursue activities and practices that capture the full benefit of a world-class supply base, and (4) create responsive new organizational structures. Competing today requires purchasing and supply chain managers to play an active role in helping achieve an organization's cost, quality, time, and technology goals—or risk losing market share to competitors who are benefiting from world-class supply chain management.

DISCUSSION QUESTIONS

1. Given the trends described in this chapter, what do you think the future purchasing organization will look like?
2. What are some of the primary skills that purchasing and supply chain managers will need to be successful in the future?
3. What will the role of the Internet be in supporting purchasing and supply chain management activities?
4. Why will there be an increase in using suppliers for product and process technology?
5. Why will the development of global databases increase? What kind of information should a global database provide?
6. Why will global sourcing increase?
7. Do you believe the total number of suppliers within a typical firm's supply bases will increase or decrease? Why?
8. The need to reduce cycle time is important. How can purchasing help in this process?

ADDITIONAL READINGS

"Across the Border Supply Chain Management Trends," *Transportation & Distribution*, 39 no. 7 (1998): 75.

Anderson, R. "Logistics and Supply-Chain Recruitment Trends," *Logistics Focus: The Journal of the Institute of Logistics*, no. 1 (1999): 28.

Carter, Phillip, "The Future of Purchasing and Supply: A Ten-Year Forecast," *Journal of Supply Chain Management*, 36, no. 1 (2000): 14.

Katzorke, Michael, "Cessna Charts a Supply Chain Flight Strategy," *Purchasing* 129, no. 4 (2000): 42.

"One on One: An Interview with Gene Richter—A Leading Purchasing and Supply Management Professional Shares his Views on Technology and Trends," *Journal of Supply Chain Management* 36 no. 1 (2000): 2.

"One on One: An Interview with Edith Kelly-Green—A Leading Purchasing and Supply Management Professional Shares Her Views on Technology and Trends," *Journal of Supply Chain Management* 36 no. 2 (2000): 2.

"One on One: An Interview with David L. Sorenson—A Leading Purchasing and Supply Management Professional Shares His Views on Technology and Trends," *Journal of Supply Chain Management* 36 no. 3 (2000): 2.

Pooley, John and Steven C. Dunn, "A Longitudinal Study of Purchasing Positions: 1960–1989," *Journal of Business Logistics* 15 no. 1 (1994): 193.

Sochocki, Larry Jr. and Paul Kaminski, "When Supply Chain Strategy Changes, What Doesn't Change?" *Hospital Materiel Management Quarterly*, 20, no. 3 (1999): 46.

Trent, Robert J. and Robert M. Monczka, "Purchasing and Supply Management: Trends and Changes Throughout the 1990s," *International Journal of Purchasing and Materials Management* 34 no. 4 (1998): 2.

ENDNOTES

1. Shawn Tully, "Purchasing's New Muscle," Fortune, February 20, 1995, p. 75.
2. Bruce T. Henderson, "The Coming Revolution in Purchasing," Journal of Purchasing, vol. 11. no. 2 (Summer 1975), p. 44. (Note: From a reprint of an article first appearing in 1964).
3. Harold E. Fearon and William A. Bales, "CEOs' Presidents/Perceptions and Expectations of the Purchasing Function," Center for Advanced Purchasing Studies, 1993.

Appendixes

*This appendix can be found on the Product Website at http://monczka.swcollege.com.

$\mathcal{A}$ppendix A   Glossary of Key Terms

Capacity planning Decisions a company makes regarding how many products it will make or how many customers it will serve over a period of time.

Commodity analysis Researching the requirements for a commodity purchase. Some of the elements of a thorough commodity analysis include the buyer's/supplier's needs and objectives, importance of the item, cost/quality/delivery/packaging requirements, manufacturing process, cost structure and pricing trends, substitutions, major suppliers and customers, and other relevant information that can facilitate a sound sourcing decision.

Continuous improvement A management philosophy embraced by companies who constantly improve the quality and productivity of their operations in order to survive. A wide range of approaches to continuous improvement exist, including total quality management (TQM), and statistical process control (SPC).

Contract An agreement between two or more parties that can be legally enforced. A contractual relationship between two or more commercial entities allows the shifting of risk between the entities in order to obtain the stated purpose of the contract.

Customer service The function within an organization responsible for taking orders from customers and ensuring that the finished goods or services are delivered at the right time and in the right condition and quantity, and are billed correctly. This function may be located in the marketing, logistics, or operations part of an organization.

Disposition Activities that involve the management of excess or waste packaging and materials. In the past, organizations frequently used landfills for disposition. Today, more organizations are increasingly exploring alternative environmentally friendly forms of disposition, including recycling, reuse, remanufacturing, and other similar options. This approach is sometimes referred to as *reverse logistics*.

Electronic commerce Information systems that allow transactions between parties in a supply chain to be automatically completed via electronic data interchange (EDI), electronic funds transfer (EFT), bar codes, and a variety of other electronic mediums. The "paper" transactions of the past are becoming increasingly obsolete. At the same time, the proliferation of new telecommunications and computer technology has also made instantaneous communications a reality. Such information systems—like Wal-Mart's satellite network—can link together suppliers, manufacturers, distributors, retail outlets, and ultimately, customers, regardless of location.

Electronic data interchange (EDI) A communications standard that supports the interorganization electronic exchange of common business documents and information between buyers and sellers.

Extended enterprise An organizing principle that views multiple tiers of suppliers and multiple tiers of customers as part of the integrated supply chain.

Forecasting An important activity that provides operations and supply chain managers with the numbers needed to make both long-term capacity decisions and short-term planning decisions. For example: What will the total demand for a new product be over the next 5 years? How many customers will we serve next week?

Inventory Materials used in producing a final product. **Raw materials inventory** includes items purchased from suppliers to directly support production requirements. **Work in process inventory** is the total inventory that exists within and and among all processing centers located throughout the operations system. **Finished goods inventory** includes completed items or products that are available for shipment or future customer orders. **Maintenance, repair, and operating (MRO) inventory** includes all the items used to support operations but which are not directly in the finished product. **Pipeline or in-transit inventory** includes items on their way to customers or located throughout a firm's distribution channels.

Inventory management Activities involved in ensuring that the right materials and goods are in the right place at the right time at the lowest cost possible. Inventory management (also called *materials management* in some organizations) may involve automated and/or manual systems for tracking inventory, as well the physical facilities for storing the materials.

Just-in-time system A system in which a firm receives frequent receipts of material to meet its immediate production requirements. This system affects purchasing, manufacturing, and inbound and outbound logistics.

Logistics Also called *physical distribution*, logistics focuses on the physical movement and storage of goods and materials. Managers in this area must evaluate various transportation options, develop and manage networks of warehouses when needed, and manage the physical flow of materials into and out of the organization, what are often called **in-bound** and **out-bound logistics**. In some cases, logistics managers help decide on the appropriate type of packaging for the product. Logistics must also work closely with marketing to determine the appropriate channels (e.g., wholesalers, retailers, mail order) by which to market the firm's products and services.

Materials management An approach to management that seeks to organize and coordinate the activities responsible for managing the inbound flow of materials and information from suppliers through to the point of finished goods. The various functions that often fall under the materials umbrella include *material planning and control, materials and procurement research, purchasing, incoming traffic, receiving, incoming quality control, stores, materials movement,* and *scrap and surplus disposal*.

Material requirements planning (MRP) An information system that generates automatic purchase requisitions and shop floor requirements, based on existing part inventories in a production system.

Negotiation A process of formal communication, either face to face or electronic, where two or more people come together to seek mutual agreement about an issue or issues.

Operations The collection of people, technology, and systems within a company that has primary responsibility for providing the organization's products or services.

Operations management The design, implementation, and improvement of a firm's operations. All organizations have an operations function. But not all organizations *manage* their operations. A firm must constantly ask itself, "How can we use our operations to create the greatest value for our customers and to meet our business strategy?"

Physical distribution management An approach to management that seeks to organize and coordinate the activities responsible for managing the outbound flow of materials and information from finished goods operations through to end customers. The various functions that often fall under the physical distribution umbrella include *distribution planning and control, forecasting, outbound transportation, material handling, inventory planning and control,* and *warehousing.*

Price/cost analysis The ongoing evaluation of price and cost trends. **Price analysis** is the process of comparing supplier prices against external price benchmarks, without direct knowledge of the supplier's actual costs. **Cost analysis** is the process of analyzing each individual cost element that together add up to the final price.

Production scheduling The systems and activities involved with coordinating materials, manpower, and machines to produce a given amount of finished product or service and meet customer requirements.

Purchasing (or **procurement**) A functional activity carried out in just about every organization, most often referring to the day-to-day tactical management of material flows and information. It begins with the determination of needs and specifications for internal customers, matching market and commodity information to customer needs, developing a **purchase order** (a paper or electronic form that specifies that type and quantity of material or service required), tracking and follow-up on the order, and issuing a payment to the supplier.

Strategic activities Refers to activities that support the "long-term" objectives of an organization. Examples include strategic planning, strategic sourcing, etc.

Strategic sourcing A cross-functional process that involves members of the firm other than those who work in the purchasing department. A strategic sourcing team may include members from engineering, quality, design, manufacturing, marketing, accounting, strategic planning and other departments. The focus of strategic sourcing management involves integrating supplier capabilities into organizational processes to achieve a competitive advantage through cost reduction, technology development, quality improvement, cycle time, and delivery capabilities to meet customer requirements.

Supply chain The activities associated with the flow and transformation of goods from the raw materials stage (extraction), through to the end user, as well as the associated information flows. Material and information flows both up and down the supply chain. The supply chain includes systems management, manufacturing and assembly, sourcing and procurement, production scheduling, order processing, inventory management, warehousing, and customer service.

Supply chain management The integration of the activities in the supply chain through improved supply chain relationships, information systems, and other means to achieve a sustainable competitive advantage. The supply chain includes the management of information systems, sourcing and procurement, production scheduling, order processing, inventory management, warehousing, customer service, and after-market disposition of packaging and materials.

Supplier development The process providing on-site help, training, or other improvement measures to suppliers.

Supplier evaluation and selection The process of determining if a given supplier is capable of meeting a purchasing organization's needs. This is typically carried out by an on-site visit to the supplier's facility.

Supplier identification The process of searching multiple sources (Internet, catalogs, interviews, trade shows, etc.) to find potential suppliers to meet a need.

Supplier integration The process of involving suppliers in new product development and ongoing production processes.

Supplier network A group of organizations that provide inputs, either directly or indirectly, to the focal firm.

Supplier management The ongoing coordination of all suppliers being used. This is a broad term that often includes supplier identification, evaluation, performance measurement, and development.

Supplier performance measurement The ongoing process of tracking cost, quality, delivery, and service performance of suppliers, as well as updating a database of all supplier's performance over time.

Tactical activities The short-term activities associated with the day-to-day management. Over time, tactical activities serve to eventually support the organization's long-term strategic goals.

Warehousing The management of distribution of products to a market by storing a product in a facility. Warehouses often include the following activities: **consolidation** (combining a large number of small shipments into a smaller number of large shipments, in order to gain transportation economies, by getting truckload rates); **mixing** (providing a mix of different items in a single shipment, using a "cross-dock" operation); **service** (making items available when needed, and reducing lead time for delivery); **contingencies uncertainties** (holding inventory in a warehouse as safety stock, in order to accommodate unpredictably high demand for a product); and **smoothing** (decoupling one entity from another in the supply chain—e.g., decoupling the manufacturer from his supplier, or decoupling the manufacturer from his market).

$\mathcal{A}$ppendix B   Using Purchasing and Supply Chain Analysis Software

Sourcing Decision Support Inc. has created software designed to meet the analytic needs of purchasing and supply chain professionals. Many companies, including Honeywell and Johnson & Johnson, have trained their sourcing professionals on SDS NoteBooks, a software package containing four separate notebooks. This software easily allows users to evaluate quantity discounts, learning curves, supplier financial condition, break-even points, and other quantitative applications. The purpose of this software is to allow the purchasing and supply chain professional to replace subjective analysis with objective analysis, particularly during negotiations with suppliers. This software relates to many of the topics presented in Chapters 8 (supplier financial ratios), 12, and 13.

The following table summarizes the many applications that are part of this software.

SDS NoteBooks Software Applications

NoteBook	*Specific Software Application*
NoteBook 1 **Quotation Analysis Notebook** Evaluates supplier price	• *Quantity Discount Analysis* for specific quantities and ranges of quantities validates volume discounts • *Fixed and Variable Cost Analysis* determines volumes and identifies variable costs • *Experience Curve Analysis* forecasts total supplier productivity • *Economic Order Quantity Analysis* balances acquisition and inventory carrying costs
NoteBook 2 **Cost Analysis Notebook** Evaluates costs and identifies waste	• *Fixed and Variable Cost Analysis* determines volumes and identifies variable costs • *Price Productivity Analysis* targets cost take-out opportunities • *Typical Learning Curve* shows the theory of learning curves • *Learning Curve Analysis* evaluates purchase price due to changes in direct labor at suppliers • *Stanford-B Analysis* captures and evaluates prior learning • *Break-Even Analysis* determines the point where total costs = total revenue
NoteBook 3 **Performance Analysis Notebook** Targets areas for improvement	• *Supplier Performance Analysis* identifies waste caused by suppliers • *Throughput Analysis* finds costs in the "hidden factory" • *Value Indices* determine the rate at which suppliers are contributing value

	• *Total Supplier Productivity* measures total supplier value contributions • *Assessments of Relationships, Organizations, and Teams* helps prepare for negotiations
NoteBook 4 **Financial Analysis Notebook** Determines supplier financial analysis	• *Solvency Ratios* determines the liquidity of suppliers • *Leverage Ratios* identifies the sources of operating capital for suppliers • *Profitability Ratios* identifies if suppliers are making enough to operate or making so much to be able to give a price break • *Z-Score Analysis* forecasts possible supplier financial distress

Note: More information is available at www.sdsnotebooks.com.

*A*ppendix C   Guidelines for Writing a Contract

The basic components of a contract include title, recitals, body, signatures, acknowledgments, and exhibits. As much as anything else, writing a good purchase contract or agreement involves organization and practice. When possible, the contract administrator should begin by reviewing existing or previously used contracts that have been employed for prior purchases within the same commodity or service family. To minimize confusion and potential misinterpretation later on, special attention should be paid to the use of grammar, spelling, punctuation, page and paragraph numbering, paragraph indentation, page breaks, signature lines, and consistent application of defined terms (especially those that are open to interpretation). When in doubt, be specific and spell out in detail exactly what the party to a contract means. It is particularly easy for technical terms and jargon to be misconstrued by nontechnical personnel when taken out of context.

When drafting contractual terms and conditions, it is important for the purchaser to keep in mind the legal doctrine of *good faith*, which means "honesty in fact and the observance of reasonable commercial standards of fair dealing in the trade."[1] The good-faith doctrine may limit the enforceability of some of the purchaser's terms and conditions if there is leeway for interpretation that is attributable to the discretion of the purchaser's actions. The discretion of the purchaser (and the seller) must be exercised in good faith. The good-faith standard must be determined by the parties' actions, not specifically by the literal words of the written agreement. Examples of clauses in purchase agreements that have potential good-faith implications include:

- Termination for convenience clause
- Inspection clause
- Make changes clause
- Setoff clause
- Termination for cause clause
- Delivery clause
- Waiver of rights clause
- Warranty clauses

Other guidelines regarding "contract language" include the following:

1. *Agrees to:* Do not use "agrees to" in the body of the contract. By law every obligation has already been agreed to when the contract is signed. Instead, use "shall."
2. *By whom:* Whenever an obligation is stated in the contract, specifically state whose obligation it is—"The equipment will be installed on or before February 28, 2002—and add "by Seller."
3. *Checklists:* Should identify necessary changes included for each contract; reviewed and modified in each case ("see enclosed").
4. *Data and software:* A big area of concern; specify what data and software to be delivered, when, and with what rights?

5. *Dates for delivery:* Be specific; not "sixteen months after award" but "on February 28, 2002."

6. *Documents:* Specify the date for each document referenced. A statement of work referenced, but not dated, can cause litigation, especially if revised.

7. *Definitions clause:* Use for complex items; gives a common language that helps prevent misunderstandings at a later date.

8. *Effective date:* Clearly state the effective date; not necessarily the date performance commences, it should be the date that starts the clock running for other obligations.

9. *Format:* Present all provisions in alphabetical order; put all general and special provisions in exhibits; when changes occur, only the specific exhibit will need revision rather than whole contract; use headings to orient the reader; doublespace all contracts; if a clause is too long, break it into subsections using subheadings.

10. *Generic terms:* Use whenever possible; eliminates retyping entire contract when used for different clients; use a glossary with terms such as Buyer, Seller, Owner, Contractor, etc.

11. *Incorporate documents by reference:* Put major documents at the end of the contract, and refer to them in the body of the contract. Including a Statement of Work within a clause makes reading it difficult, and if it must be revised, the whole contract has to be redone. Other documents to include by reference include general provisions, special provisions, detailed payment provisions, delivery schedules with multiple deliveries, milestone schedules, codes, and standards.

12. *Negotiable clauses:* If a clause is subject to negotiation, include it in the first part of the contract, not the body.

13. *Notices:* Include a provision indicating where notices and correspondence are to be sent; be specific—name a person.

14. *Order of precedence:* Include a clause specifying the order in which conditions take precedence, determined on a case-by-case basis.

15. *Purchase order:* If article is "off the shelf" or slightly modified, use a purchase order. If nonstandard, write up using this checklist.

16. *Scope of work:* Include a scope of work clause in every contract to highlight in summary fashion what is to be performed with reference to a specific statement of work.

17. *Signatures:* Type names and titles of persons signing, attesting, or witnessing a contract under the signature line.

18. *Small value contract:* Use when purchasing a service or having minor construction work performed, if the dollar value is not large.

19. *Statement of work:* The heart of the contract. Define here what the seller is going to deliver to the buyer. It should be an exhibit incorporated by reference in the contract. Many contracts do not incorporate by reference but include it into a long, difficult to read clause. The statement of work should include inspection and acceptance, quality assurance requirements, packing and marking, data requirements (manuals and drawings), and training.

20. *Warranty:* Set forth a one-year warranty period, which may be varied. Should be more specific for complex items.

A good rule of thumb regarding good faith is to try and evaluate your actions or potential actions from the viewpoint of the other party. Do your actions conform with the terms and conditions as written, or do they conflict? Other general considerations for writing, negotiating, and administering a purchase agreement refer to the protection of one party against actions or opportunism by the other. The contract, particularly if it is a long-term or ongoing agreement, should address contingencies such as pricing mechanisms or delivery changes. Spelling out the process of mediation, arbitration, or one of the other dispute resolution methods is also recommended because it is nearly impossible to avoid misinterpretation of all contractual terms and conditions. Be sure to specify the legal venue and applicable court system where legal disputes are to be heard in the event that alternative dispute resolution is ineffective (see Chapter 16 on legal considerations). Payment schedules should also be spelled out in detail to ensure that both parties understand the flow of funds. In the event of litigation between the parties, or in the case of a third-party lawsuit for such things as product liability or patent infringement, responsibility for the payment of attorneys' fees should be stipulated.

[1] Hancock, 1987.

3M Corporation	http://www.mmm.com/us
AARP	http://www.aarp.org/
Automotive Industry Action Group	http://www.aiag.org
Black & Decker, Inc	http://www.blackanddecker.com
Cast	http://www.cast.org/bobby/
The Defense Systems Management College	http://www.dsmc.dsm.mil
Dow Chemical Company	http://dow.com/environment/ehs.html
Ecommerce Learning Center of North Carolina State University	http://ecommerce.ncsu.edu.
Edgar Online, Inc	http://www.FreeEDGAR.com
Federal Express	http://www.fedex.com/ investorrelations/1999annualreport
Fed Ex Center for Cycle Time Research	http://www.people.memphis.edu/ %7Ecctr/cycle.htm
The Forest Stewardship Council (FSC)	http://www.fscus.org.html/about_fsc/ index.html
Hamilton Strategic Management Group, Inc	http://www.hsmg.com/index.htm
Home Depot, Inc	http://www.homedepot.com/
Lycos, Inc	http://www.hotbot.com
Market Watch. Com, Inc	http://cbs.marketwatch.com
National Association of Purchasing Management	http://www.napm.org/
NMSDC of Florida	http://www.nmsdcfl.com/business.htm
Nortel Networks, Ltd.	http://www.nortelnetworks.com/ prd/suppliers/index.html
North Carolina State University	http://www4.ncsu.edu
Product Design and Development	http://www.pddnet.com/
Rosettanet	http://www.rosettanet.org
Stock Selector. Com, Inc	http://www.411stocks.com
The Street. Com, Inc	http://www.thestreet.com
Thinking Cap Solutions, Inc	http://www.ice-alert.com
Urgent Freight, Inc	http://www.urgentfreight.com
US Department of Commerce	http://www.census.gov/prod/ www/abs/industry.html
US Government	http://www.whitehouse.gov
World Bank Group	http://www.worldbank.org/prospects
Yahoo	http://www.yahoo.com
Yahoo	http://biz.yahoo.com

$\mathscr{C}$ASES

$\mathcal{M}$ANAGING SUPPLIER QUALITY: INTEGRATED DEVICES I

This case examines many issues relating to supplier quality management. A key point of this case is that simple, relatively inexpensive items can cause nonconformance costs disproportionate to the value of the item. Here, a molding bracket with a unit price of $1.55 is causing the failure of the finished product and disrupting production schedules. Both conditions affect the producer's ability to service end-customers in a timely and defect-free manner. To compete today, firms cannot afford a "hands-off" attitude as it relates to supplier quality.

Case Objectives

This case has several learning objectives. The case requires participants to:

* Develop a process for proactively managing supplier quality
* Understand how objective quality tools support supplier quality management
* Appreciate the consequences of poor supplier quality on a producer's ability to satisfy end-customer requirements

Case Details

Bill Edwards is a quality engineer assigned to the Injected Molding Commodity Team at Integrated Devices. The commodity team is responsible for evaluating, selecting, and negotiating agreements with plastic-injected molding suppliers to be used throughout Integrated Devices. The team is also responsible for improving material and service quality that Integrated Devices receives from its suppliers. Bill's role after supplier selection involves working directly with suppliers who require training or technical assistance concerning quality control and quality improvement. The company spends about 70 percent of each sales dollar on purchased goods and services, so suppliers have a major impact on product quality.

Bill just received a call concerning a reoccurring manufacturing problem at Integrated System's Plant No. 3. The plant buyer said the plant is experiencing some quality variability problems with a key plastic-injected molding component supplied by Trexler Plastics. The component is sometimes too short or too long to fit properly with other components within the finished product. On occasion, the bracket snaps, causing end-product failure. While the unit cost of the plastic-injected molding component is only $1.55, these quality problems (length variability and snapping) are creating problems that far exceed the component's purchase price.

The local buyer announced he was having difficulty resolving the problem and asked for support from the corporate commodity team. The buyer said, "You corporate guys selected this supplier that we all have to use. The least you can do is to help us out of the jam *your* supplier choice is causing." The buyer's comment surprised Bill, although Bill would soon come to understand that plant personnel resented not being able to select their own suppliers.

After investigating the problem during a tension-filled meeting with Plant No. 3 personnel, Bill determined he would have to visit the supplier directly. He would work with Trexler's process engineers to address the manufacturing variability caused by the nonconforming component. Bill went back and reviewed his team's actions when selecting a single supplier to provide *an entire family* of plastic-injected moldings. Trexler quoted the lowest price of all competing suppliers and had provided samples that passed Integrated System's engineering tests.

Upon his arrival at the supplier, Bill learned that Trexler did not have a dedicated process engineer. One engineer, Steve Smith, was responsible for plant layout, process, quality, and industrial engineering. This individual, who was hired only two months previously, was still becoming familiar with Trexler's procedures. When Bill asked to review the supplier's quality control procedures, Steve had to ask several people before he could locate Trexler's procedures' manual.

Bill decided that his first step should be to understand the capability of the process responsible for producing the defective component. At an afternoon meeting, Bill asked Steve for actual output data from Trexler's process. Steve explained they did not collect data, either for process proving studies or for statistical control charting of continuous production. However, he did say that sometimes, "things don't seem to be operating well" with the equipment that produces the component. Trexler uses an inspector to examine each finished item to determine if it should be shipped to the customer.

After explaining the basics of process proving to Steve, Bill asked him to collect data from the process that produced the bracket component. Bill requested that Steve take exact measurements periodically from the process so they could draw statistical conclusions. Bill said he would return in three days to examine the data.

Upon his return three days later, Steve shared with Bill the details of the data collection effort (Exhibit 1):

Component:	#03217666
Description:	Bracket
Design specification:	4 +/- .06 inches

EXHIBIT 1   *Process Output Data Part #03217666*

4.01	4.02	4.00	3.99	3.98	4.00	4.00	4.03
4.04	4.02	4.07	3.95	3.98	4.01	4.03	4.00
4.00	3.96	3.94	3.98	3.99	4.02	4.01	4.00
4.05	3.98	3.97	4.03	4.07	4.04	4.02	4.01
3.99	3.96	4.00	4.00	4.01	4.02	4.02	4.01
3.98	3.99	3.94	3.93	4.00	4.02	4.00	3.97
3.99	4.02	4.04	4.00	3.96	3.97	4.00	4.01

Once Bill calculated a preliminary process capability from this data and examined the training and quality control procedures at Trexler, he realized he had some serious work ahead of him.

Case Requirements

1. Calculate the Cp and Cpk of the process that produces the component purchased by Integrated Devices. Remember—Process width = 6× the standard deviation of the sample. Can the process at Trexler satisfy design requirements? What should be a target Cpk level?

2. Why is it important to prove that a process is proven capable before developing statistical control limits (i.e., SPC charts)?

3. Is Integrated Devices being reactive or proactive when in comes to managing supplier quality? Why?

4. Discuss the possible advantages of negotiating quality requirements directly into supplier contracts.

5. What is the risk of relying on product samples when selecting suppliers? What is the risk of relying too heavily on unit cost when making the selection decision?

6. Why was it so important for Bill to work with Plant No. 3 personnel before visiting Trexler?

7. The local buyer at Integrated Devices did not seem pleased that a corporate team selected the supplier that the local plants must use. Why do firms use corporate commodity teams to select suppliers? How can firms get support from plant personnel for company-wide suppliers?

8. Is quality a major emphasis at this supplier? Why?

9. What are the possible effects if Trexler's inspector approves components for shipment that should be rejected due to nonconformance (Type II error)? What are the possible effects if Trexler's inspector rejects components for shipment that are in conformance with specifications (Type I error)? How can we control error of measurement?

Potential Consequences of Type I Errors	Potential Consequences of Type II Errors

10. When evaluating supplier quality, why is it important to focus on the *process* that produces the material or service rather than on the material or service itself? What did Integrated Devices rely on?

11. Discuss the likelihood that Bill will resolve the problem(s) with this component.

12. If Integrated Devices decides to continue using Trexler as a supplier, what must both companies do to begin improving Trexler's component quality?

13. Design a supplier quality management process for Integrated Devices that focuses on the *prevention* of supplier defects. (Hint: activities performed during supplier evaluation and selection should be part of this process. Process proving may also be part of your supplier quality management process.)

Sourcing and Commodity/Purchase Family Strategy Development

Emily Smith sat in her office thinking, looking out the window. As director of corporate procurement for United Express, a company specializing in overnight package delivery, she was responsible for all supply management strategies and issues that affected the company. Emily had just left a staff meeting with Bernie Nickels, the vice president of supply chain management.

Bernie opened the meeting by comparing the supply management group to the marketing group, a comparison that did not evoke a pleasant response among the supply managers present. He said that he had just spent an entire day with the vice president of marketing in a strategy alignment meeting. During this meeting, it became evident how seriously and creatively marketing took its responsibility for developing customer-focused marketing strategies. Bernie said it was "embarrassing" when it was his turn to outline current and future sourcing strategies, which he said paled in comparison to the marketing department's strategies. The staff assembled at this meeting soon realized that Bernie was not about to suffer this embarrassment alone. In the words of one staff member, "Bernie really read us the riot act."

Bernie argued that the sourcing strategies developed at United Express were inconsistent and sometimes conflicting. For example, he said that while one group wants a partnership with a supplier, another group is out "beating suppliers over the head for a lower price." Meanwhile another group wants a single source contract at the same time a second group insists on maintaining more than one supplier for every purchased item. An animated discussion of long versus short-term contracting finally sent Bernie looking for aspirin. Bernie concluded the meeting by saying:

"The bottom line is that we need to get our act together. Each supply group is off doing its own thing while reinventing the wheel every time we have a purchase requirement. We are not consistent. We are not developing strategies that align with what this company must do to be successful. We operate in our own little world, and from where I sit, that world doesn't command much respect around this corporation. Emily, I want you and your people to address these issues right away."

Emily was troubled by Bernie's comments, particularly his concern that United Express pursued widely divergent sourcing strategies. While admitting to herself that sourcing groups sometimes developed strategies that appeared inconsistent, wasn't it possible that some of these groups were responding rationally to the demands placed on them by each sourcing decision? As she thought about this question, however, it became evident that United Express would benefit from a purchasing/commodity strategy development process or framework that would guide the strategy development groups. This process must be robust enough so that all sourcing groups could use it. It was also evident to Emily that United Express required a tool or approach for segmenting purchase requirements. She felt that segmenting purchase requirements would require each group to develop a strategy that was a reasonable response to that purchase requirement. Should United Express really be buying low-dollar office supplies the same way it buys high-dollar aircraft parts?

Assignment

1. Develop a multi-step strategy development process or framework that provides consistency and structure to the development of United Express's purchasing/sourcing strategies.
2. Develop and discuss a portfolio matrix approach that requires users to segment purchase requirements according to variables that you determine are important. Be sure to identify where this segmentation tool fits within the strategy development framework.

GUAVA PUREE AT ACREAGE FOODS

Betty Johnson is a senior buyer of fruit products for Acreage Foods, a major U.S. multinational food processing company. This California company uses a wide variety of fruit concentrates, purees, flavors, and extracts in many of its popular food products. One of Betty's responsibilities is to negotiate annual purchase contracts for these ingredients. One such ingredient, guava puree, is grown and harvested on a seasonal basis in various countries around the world.

Betty is currently examining the costs associated with using one of her existing suppliers, a Philippine grower/processor. Acreage Foods has used this supplier's high-quality product for a number of years. The product is grown in a remote area of the Philippines and transported to the processing plant where it is pureed and packaged for transoceanic shipment. This particular variety of guava is highly prized for its flavor, which is maintained by the aseptic method of processing used by the supplier.

The guava puree (currently priced at $0.29/pound, FOB vessel) is aseptically packaged in foil bags, each containing 50 pounds of product, then inserted into corrugated boxes. The boxes are stacked on wooden pallets, 40 to a pallet, for loading into overseas containers. Each container holds 20 pallets and is shipped via ocean freighter. The ocean freight charge is $2,300 per container. Once the containers reach the U.S. port, they are shipped for $250 per container to a local warehouse for storage. Import duties are calculated by U.S. customs to be 15% of the shipment's original purchase price excluding freight charges. Acreage Foods' requirement is one container-load per month.

Each container is warehoused locally until needed for processing. The monthly storage charge is $5.50 per pallet. In addition, the warehouse charges a one-time in/out fee of $6.00 per pallet to cover administrative costs. Acreage Foods' cost of capital is 18%. Production demand of the guava puree is assumed to be constant over the year.

When a container of guava puree is required at the plant, the container is moved from the warehouse via a local freight company, which charges $150 per container. Incoming quality-control procedures are estimated to cost $2 per pallet. Because of the nature of the product and the distance involved in purchasing and storing the guava puree, the company estimates it incurs a loss of 2% of the total puree purchased. The budgeted factory yield of the guava puree when blending into company products is calculated at 97%; that is, 3% of the product by volume is wasted and nonrecoverable.

Occasionally, undetected usage of spoiled guava puree will require an FDA-mandated product recall from grocer's shelves. Out-of-pocket costs incurred typically total $20,000 for each product recall incident; these costs are not recoverable from the supplier. The company's records indicate that such an incident occurs about once every eight months. In addition, corporate accounting policy requires that a 15% assessment on purchased product total cost be applied to cover general and administrative overhead costs.

Assignment

1. Identify all the cost categories besides purchase price that apply to the purchase, transporting, and use of the guava puree.
2. Identify the cost per pound of the guava puree from the Philippines to the U.S. port.
3. Identify the dock-to-warehouse cost per pound.
4. Identify the warehouse-through-production cost per pound.
5. Determine the total cost per pound to Acreage Foods of purchasing the guava puree. Be sure to include all the additional costs presented in the case.
6. Why is it important to identify all the costs associated with purchasing and using a product?
7. If Acreage Foods establishes a goal of reducing the total cost of its purchased materials, discuss some specific alternatives that the company might employ across the guava puree supply chain to reduce its costs (based on your analysis).

$\mathcal{W}$IRING HARNESS PURCHASE

Bill Major, a buyer at a Detroit-based producer of subassemblies for the automotive market, has sent out Requests for Quotations (RFQs) for a wiring harness to four prospective suppliers. Only two of the four suppliers indicated an interest in quoting the business: PDF Systems in Atlanta and Nippon Automotive Assemblies (NAA) of Tokyo, Japan. The estimated demand for the harnesses is 5,000 units a month. The supplier will incur some cost to retool for this particular harness. The harnesses will be prepackaged in 24" × 12" × 6" cartons. Each packaged unit weighs 10 pounds.

Quote 1

The first quote received is from PDF Systems located in Atlanta, Georgia. The quote includes unit price, tooling, and packaging. The quoted unit price does not include shipping costs. PDF Systems requires no special warehousing of inventory.

PDF Systems Quote:
Unit price = $31.00
Packing costs (containerization) = $0.75 unit
Tooling = $4,500 one-time fixed charge
Freight cost = $7.30 per hundred pounds

Quote 2

The second quote received is from Nippon Automotive Assemblies (NAA) of Tokyo, Japan. The supplier must pack the harnesses in a container and ship via inland transportation to the port in Japan, have the shipment transferred to a container ship, ship material to Seattle, and then have material transported inland to Detroit. The quoted unit price does not include international shipping costs, which the buyer will assume.

NAA Quote:
Unit price = $21.50
Shipping lead time = 6 weeks
Tooling = $3,000

In addition to the supplier's quote, Bill must consider additional costs and information before preparing a comparison of the supplier quotations:

- Each monthly shipment requires three 40-foot containers
- Packing costs for containerization = $1.00 per unit
- Cost of inland transportation to port of export = $200 per container
- Freight forwarder's fee = $100 per shipment (letter of credit, documentation, etc.)

- Cost of ocean transport = $2,067 per container
- Marine insurance = $.50 per $100 of shipment
- U.S. port handling charges = $640 per container
- Customs duty = 5% of unit cost
- Customs broker fees = $150
- Transportation from Seattle to Detroit = $18.6 per hundred pounds
- Need to warehouse two weeks of inventory in Detroit at a warehousing cost of $1.00 per cubic foot per month, to compensate for leadtime uncertainty. Bill must also figure the costs associated with committing corporate capital for holding inventory. Bill has spoken to some accountants, who typically use a corporate cost of capital rate of 15%.
- Cost of hedging currency—broker fees = $400 per shipment
- Additional administrative time due to international shipping = 4 hours per shipment × $25 hour (estimated)
- Additional paperwork = $100 per year (estimated)

The additional costs associated with international purchasing are estimated but are nevertheless present. If Bill does not assume these costs directly, then both suppliers have agreed to either pay them and invoice Bill later, or build the costs into a revised unit price. Bill feels that the U.S. supplier is probably less expensive, but he is unsure about how to calculate the total costs for each option.

Assignment

1. Calculate the total cost per unit of purchasing from PDF Systems.
2. Calculate the total cost per unit of purchasing from NAA.
3. Based on the total cost per unit, which supplier should Bill recommend?
4. Are there any other issues besides cost that Bill should evaluate?
5. Based on this case, do you think international purchasing is more or less complex than domestic purchasing? Why? Is it worth the additional effort?

PLASTIC SHIELD PRICE ANALYSIS

A buyer is looking for pricing irrationalities within a family of plastic shields. Any unusual pricing might require further analysis and negotiation with suppliers. The buyer is performing this analysis by reviewing the pricing history of various shields purchased over the previous four years. Volumes for each of the part numbers have been similar, so any price differences are not the result of material volume discounts. Design changes occurred for parts 4 and 5 in 1998. The number below the per-unit price in 1997 and 1998 (for parts 4 and 5) is the total amount of plastic required for each part.

| | Price History by Part Number per Unit Part Number | | | | |
	1	2	3	4	5
2000	$2.43	$2.70	$2.25	$3.15	$3.25
1999	$2.36	$2.62	$2.25	$3.00	$3.19
1998	$2.25	$2.47	$2.23	$2.99	$3.19
				1.60 lb.	1.63 lb.
1997	$2.25	$2.47	$2.23	$2.89	$3.09
	1.95 lb.	1.85 lb.	1.90 lb.	1.85 lb.	1.95 lb.

The buyer has also collected other data to help with the analysis:

Laminated Plastic Price Index Cost Elements by Percentage		(at year ending)	
Direct materials	45%	2000	203.2
Direct labor	15%	1999	201.6
Manufacturing burden	25%	1998	191.7
General and administrative	8%	1997	188.2
Profit	7%	1996	188.3
Selling price	100%	Base year 1980 = 100	

Labor Monthly Statistics Hourly Earnings Index	
2000	184.4
1999	178.8
1998	174.5
1997	172.2
1996	168.6
Base year 1980 = 100	

Assignment

1. Identify what you consider to be pricing irrationalities that require further analysis and perhaps negotiation with the supplier.
2. Assume that different suppliers provided the five part numbers. Does the buyer have all the information required to perform a *precise* comparative analysis? What information might be helpful when comparing parts supplied by different suppliers?

NORTHWEST PRODUCTS— PLASTICS COMMODITY STRATEGY

Ron Mitchell is a commodity team leader at Northwest Products, a large manufacturer of computer components. Northwest has traditionally sourced plastic directly from its three plants located in Arizona, Michigan, and North Carolina. However, Northwest has recently reorganized their supply management organization to consolidate purchasing activity through cross-functional commodity teams, responsible for developing and implementing sourcing strategies. Working out of the North Carolina plant for several years, Ron was responsible for sourcing all of the resins and plastics for the facility and thus brings with him a good degree of knowledge. Along with Ron, the other members of the team include Linda Angell, a manufacturing engineer, Sanjay Ahire, a quality specialist, and Cecil Hahn, a line supervisor on the plastic injection molding line. Resins and plastic products purchased have standard industry quality, and all of the suppliers have a good delivery record to the local plants. The group is reviewing some recent pricing data from a group of five suppliers that Northwest has used in the past. Some data are missing because certain suppliers have only begun to sell to Northwest in the last five years when the Michigan and North Carolina plants were expanded.

	Prices Paid ($ per pound) by suppliers								
Supplier	1992	1993	1994	1995	1996	1997	1998	1999	2000
Advantix (California)	0.79	0.82	0.83	0.80	0.90	0.91	0.92	0.90	1.10
Bearcar (California)	NA	NA	0.85	0.84	0.86	0.87	0.87	0.89	0.90
Crane (Michigan)	NA	NA	NA	0.87	0.88	0.87	0.95	0.96	0.97
Dogwood (N. Carolina)	NA	NA	NA	NA	0.77	0.90	0.92	0.96	0.98
Exeter (N. Carolina)	NA	NA	NA	NA	0.86	0.89	0.89	0.90	0.91

In addition to the above data, Ron has recently downloaded Producer Price Index (PPI) data for plastics and resins from the Bureau of Labor Statistics homepage (http://www.bls.gov). He recently attended a seminar on strategic sourcing, where the instructor demonstrated the use of PPI data to track prices of standard commodities and determine pricing irregularities. He printed out the page (shown here) and brought it with him to the commodity meeting. The team has also determined that all of the suppliers have enough capacity to supply all three divisions with their requirements if necessary.

Producer Price Index Revision—Current Series

Series Id: PCU2821#
Industry: Plastic materials and resins
Product: Plastic materials and resins
Base Date: 8012

Year	Jan	Feb	Mar	Apr	May	Jun	Jul	Aug	Sep	Oct	Nov	Dec	Ann.Avg
1991	150.0	149.5	144.7	141.1	138.5	135.9	132.8	132.8	132.5	132.3	131.8	133.5	137.9
1992	132.0	132.0	130.2	130.1	131.3	129.9	132.8	132.5	133.2	133.2	132.4	132.6	131.8
1993	132.8	132.9	132.5	132.2	131.5	132.0	132.2	132.8	132.7	132.3	131.9	131.9	132.3
1994	130.8	130.4	130.3	132.1	133.2	134.6	135.3	136.9	141.1	146.3	148.8	152.6	137.7
1995	156.9	160.6	161.5	164.5	164.7	164.5	162.7	160.8	158.2	154.6	151.1	147.8	159.0
1996	146.1	144.7	145.0	144.4	147.2	148.7	149.8	151.9	154.4	154.5	154.6	154.2	149.6
1997	154.1	154.8	155.6	155.6	155.5	156.0	155.7	154.0	152.4	152.3	151.1	150.3	153.9
1998	150.4	147.6	145.1	144.4	142.6	140.1	138.3	137.0	133.2	131.8	130.4	129.2	139.2
1999	130.1	129.7	130.8	132.3	136.2	137.5	142.6	144.3	147.9	161.3	161.3	159.1	142.8
2000	158.3	159.5	163.2	164.3	167.5	167.0	167.3	167.8	163.7	166.0	165.7(P)	163.2(P)	164.6(P)
2001	169.1(P)	170.3(P)											

P: Preliminary. All indexes are subject to revision four months after original publication.

Source: Data extracted on April 11, 2001.

The commodity team has been asked to make a decision on the sourcing strategy and to implement the decision immediately.

Assignment

1. Compare the difference in prices paid by the different Northwest divisions paid to the different suppliers to the increases and decreases shown by the PPI index. Do you think the PPI is a good predictor of pricing strategies by suppliers?
2. What do you think accounts for the differences in pricing strategies for each supplier? Try to determine what the underlying pricing strategy is in each case (low-balling, demand skimming, etc.)
3. Based on the available information, what do you recommend as the sourcing strategy for this commodity team? How should the team implement the decision (i.e., detail the specific activities that should take place)?

LEARNING CURVE A

Craig Phillips is a buyer at Socon, a manufacturer of large industrial pumps. He has a requirement for a customized subassembly that his preferred supplier, Oriel, is building for the first time. He is preparing for negotiation with Oriel, where a key issue will be the price of the subassembly. Given the unique nature of this subassembly, Craig expects to incorporate into the contract price reduction targets based on learning curve estimates.

While Craig does not have specific data for Oriel, he has accumulated data for a subassembly that was similar in design and manufacturing complexity.

Units	Total Labor Hours	Average Labor per Unit	Learning Rate
1	6	————	******
2	10.8	————	————
4	19.2	————	————
8	35.2	————	————
16	64	————	————
32	115.2	————	————
64	211.2	————	————
128	384	————	————
Overall average improvement rate:			————
Applicable learning curve:			————

Assignment

1. Given the above data, calculate the average labor per unit given the cumulative total labor hours provided.
2. Calculate the appropriate learning rate and the overall average improvement rate for this data set.
3. Plot the data on an *X-Y* chart. Label the *X* axis "Units Produced" and the *Y* axis "Average Labor Per Unit."
4. Are gains from learning realized early in production or at a later point?
5. A learning curve applies to improvements in the direct labor portion of a process. How does the learning curve differ from the experience curve?

$\mathcal{L}$EARNING CURVE B

A buyer has placed an order with a supplier for 100 pieces at a per-unit price of $281 and has collected the following cost data:

Material	$100
Direct labor	50 (5 hours at $10 per hour)
Overhead	75 (150% of direct labor)
Total costs	225
Profit (25%)	56
Total per unit	281

The buyer now wants to place an order for an additional 700 pieces.

Assignment

1. What do you estimate the buyer should pay per unit for the next 700 pieces assuming the supplier demonstrates a 75% learning curve?
2. Why can we use rough estimates when applying learning curves?
3. Why do manual processes experience greater learning curves than automated processes?
4. Are there factors besides learning that can help reduce costs as volume increases?

QUANTITY DISCOUNT ANALYSIS

Aleda Marucheck has received the following quote from a supplier of replacement ink cartridges used in laser jet printers:

Quantity	Unit Price
1	$23
2	19
5	17
10	13
13	12

Assignment

1. Using the format illustrated in Chapter 12, calculate a quantity discount analysis for a quote using specific quantities.
2. What quantity should Aleda order if she wants to receive the lowest incremental costs between quantities?
3. Is there anything unusual about this quote?
4. What must a buyer consider when determining what quantity to purchase?

That same day Aleda receives a quote for a separate item. The supplier has quoted a discount schedule using ranges instead of specific quantities.

Quantity Range	Unit Price
1–5	$9.00
6–10	8.85
11–20	8.75
21–30	8.00
31–40	7.60
41–50	7.30
51–99	7.00

Assignment

1. Using the format illustrated in Chapter 12, calculate a quantity discount analysis for a quote specifying quantity ranges.
2. What do you conclude about this quotation? Does it appear reasonable based on your analysis? Why or why not?

THE NOTSOHOT COMPANY

During the past two years, the Notsohot Company has been showing a weakening of financial results that are causes for potential concern. The 1999 downturn of the widget sector has been a major factor in this year's results, as has an ongoing labor conflict at their South American plant. Notsohot obviously needs to make some intelligent management decisions in order to make the right steps to return toward profitability. The following summary reviews their latest financial results.

The projection of 1999 net sales is $425 million—a 30% decrease from 1998 net sales of $710 million and a 25% decrease from 1997 net sales of $690 million. The company's 1998 annual report indicates the decrease is primarily due to the labor strike in South America. The 1999 third-quarter 10-Q filed attributes the continued sales decline to the U.S. widget market and the extended shutdown of its major OEM (original equipment manufacturer) customers in that market. During this same period, the projected net loss for 1999 is $(7.3 million). Notsohot pointed to the same factors depressing sales as those primarily influencing its income.

The table below depicts key balance asset accounts used to evaluate Notsohot's current financial position.

(in millions)	Est. YE 99	YE 98	YE 97	99 vs. 97
Accounts receivable	$100	$100	$110	(9.09%)
Inventories	$140	$145.5	$150	(6.67%)

The table below shows key asset and liability accounts used to evaluate Notsohot's current financial position.

(in millions)	Est. YE 99	YE 98	YE 97	99 vs. 97
Cash and equivalents	$5	$10	$25	(80%)
Long-term debt	$300	$300	$250	20%
Cash to LT debt ratio	0.050	0.060	0.120	(56.41%)

Based on comparable industry information, the 1998 industry average of cash to long-term debt ratio was 0.432, which is obviously a stronger, more desirable financial position.

Additionally, the following ratio shows the coverage of current maturities by cash flow from operations. Since cash flow is the primary source of debt retirement, this ratio measures the ability to service principal repayment.

	Est. YE 99	YE 98	YE 97	99 vs. 97
(NI + depreciation) / current portion LT debt ratio	0.90	6	7	(87.4%)

The following table of key liquidity ratios is used to evaluate Notsohot's current financial position.

	Est. YE 99	YE 98	YE 97	99 vs. 97	Industry Average
Days' sales	85.9	51.4	57.4	30%	40
Days' inventory	127.8	96.6	91.3	25%	39
Current ratio	1.72	1.71	2.8	(33%)	above 2
Quick ratio	0.72	0.63	1.08	(45%)	above 0.8

Based on comparable industry information, the industry average of the days' sales ratio is 44.5 days, or just under 40% lower than Notsohot. Comparatively, the industry average for inventory is 41.5 days, or roughly 70% lower than Notsohot.

The following table of liquidity ratios for the Even Better Company can be used for comparison purposes.

	Est. YE 99	YE 98	YE 97	99 vs. 97
Days' sales	75	53	45	66%
Days' inventory	75	73	70	7%

Assignment

1. Based on the above financial information, discuss some of the critical trends in financial data that may be of concern if considering the Notsohot Company as a supplier.
2. What would be your next steps if you were currently using this supplier as a major source for widgets in your company?

TOTAL COST OF OWNERSHIP—PERSONAL COMPUTERS

Supply manager Megan Mittlestadt was considering the purchase of 1,000 personal computers for her organization. The life cycle was three years and the organization's cost of capital was 12%. She calculated the total cost of ownership for one of the purchase options as follows.

Cost Elements	Cost Measures
Purchase Price	
Equipment	Supplier quote: $1,200 per PC
Software License A	Supplier quote: $300 per PC
Software License B	Supplier quote: $100 per PC
Software License C	Supplier quote: $50 per PC
Acquisition Cost	
Sourcing	2 full-time equivalent @ $85K and $170K for 2 months
Administration	1 purchase order @ $150, 12 invoices @ $40 each
Usage Costs:	
Installation	$700 per PC (PC move, install, network)
Equipment support	$120 per month per PC - supplier quote
Network support	$100 per month - supplier quote
Warranty	$120 per PC for a 3-year warranty
Opportunity cost—lost productivity	Downtime 15 hours per PC per year @ $30 per hour
End of Life	
Salvage value	$36 per PC

Source: Adapted from Sanjit Menezes, "Total Cost of Ownership" in *Purchasing Today*, March 2001: 20–21.

Assignment

1. Determine the total cost of this contract over three years.
2. How would you approach this supplier about reducing the total cost of ownership for computers over the life of this contract?

SUPPLY CHAIN MANAGEMENT AT BOSE CORPORATION

Bose Corporation, headquartered in Framingham, Massachusetts, offers an excellent example of integrated supply chain management. Bose, a producer of audio premium speakers used in automobiles, high-fidelity systems, and consumer and commercial broadcasting systems, was founded in 1964 by Dr. Bose of MIT. Bose currently maintains plants in Massachusetts and Michigan as well as Canada, Mexico, and Ireland. Its purchasing organization, while decentralized, has some overlap that requires coordination between sites. It manages this coordination by using conference calls between managers, electronic communication, and joint problem solving. The company is moving toward single sourcing many of its 800 to 1,000 parts, which include corrugated paper, particle board and wood, plastic injected molded parts, fasteners, glues, woofers, and fabric.

Some product components, such as woofers, are sourced overseas. For example, at the Hillsdale, Michigan, plant, foreign sourcing accounts for 20% of purchases, with the remainder of suppliers located immediately within the state of Michigan. About 35% of the parts purchased at this site are single sourced, with approximately half of the components arriving with no incoming inspection performed. In turn, Bose ships finished products directly to Delco, Honda, and Nissan and has a record of no missed deliveries. Normal lead time to customers is 60 working days, but Bose can expedite shipments in one week and air freight them if necessary.

The company has developed a detailed supplier performance system that measures on-time delivery, quality performance, technical improvements, and supplier suggestions. A report is generated twice a month from this system and sent to the supplier providing feedback about supplier performance. If there is a three-week trend of poor performance, Bose will usually establish a specific goal for improvement that the supplier must attain. Examples include 10% delivery improvement every month until 100% conformance is achieved, or 5% quality improvement until a 1% defect level is reached over a four-month period. In one case, a supplier sent a rejected shipment back to Bose without explanation and with no corrective action taken. When no significant improvement occurred, another supplier replaced the delinquent supplier.

Bose has few written contracts with suppliers. After six months of deliveries without rejects, Bose encourages suppliers to apply for a certificate of achievement form, signifying that they are qualified suppliers. One of the primary criteria for gaining certification involves how well the supplier responds to corrective action requests. One of the biggest problems observed is that suppliers often correct problems on individual parts covered by a corrective action form without extending these corrective actions to other part families and applicable parts.

Bose has adopted a unique system of marrying just-in-time (JIT) purchasing with global sourcing. Approximately half of the dollar value of Bose's total purchases are made overseas, with the majority of the sourcing done in Asia. Because foreign sourcing does not support just-in-time deliveries, Bose "had to find a way to blend low inventory with buying from distant sources," says Lance Dixon, director of purchasing and logistics for Bose.

Visualizing itself as a customer-driven organization, Bose now uses a sophisticated transportation system—what Bose's manager of logistics calls "the best EDI system in the country." Working closely with a national less-than-truckload carrier for the bulk of its domestic freight movements, including shipments arriving at a U.S. port from oversees, Bose implemented an electronic data interchange (EDI) system that does much more than simple tracking. The system operates close to real time and allows two-way communication between every one of the freight handler's 230 terminals and Bose. Information is updated several times daily and is downloaded automatically, enabling Bose to perform shipping analysis and distribution channel modeling to achieve reliable lowest total cost scenarios. The company can also request removal from a terminal of any shipment that it must expedite with an air shipment.

This state-of-the-art system provides a snapshot of what is happening on a daily basis and keeps Bose's managers on top of everyday occurrences and decisions. Management proactively manages logistics time elements in pursuit of better customer service. The next step, Dixon feels, is to implement this system with all major suppliers rather than just with transportation suppliers. In the future, Bose plans to automate its entire materials system.

Perhaps one of the most unique features of Bose's procurement and logistics system is the development of JIT II. This system was pioneered by Lance Dixon at corporate headquarters and has been reported on extensively in trade journals. The basic premise of JIT II is simple: The person who can do the best job of ordering and managing inventory of a particular item is the supplier himself. Bose negotiated with each supplier to provide a full-time employee at the Bose plant who was responsible for ordering, shipping, and receiving materials from that plant, as well as managing on-site inventories of the items. This was done through an EDI connection between Bose's plant and the supplier's facility. Colocating suppliers and buyers was so successful that Bose is now implementing it at all plant locations. In fact, many other companies have also begun to implement colocation of suppliers.

Assignment

The following assignment questions relate to ideas and concepts presented throughout this book. Answer some or all of the questions as directed by your instructor.

1. Discuss how the strategy development process might work at a company like Bose.
2. What should be the relationship between Bose's supply management strategy and the development of its performance measurement system?
3. Why is purchased quality so important to Bose?

4. Can a just-in-time purchase system operate without total quality from suppliers?

5. Why can some components arrive at the Hillsdale, Michigan, plant with no incoming inspection required?

6. Discuss the reasons why Bose has a certificate of achievement program for identifying qualified suppliers.

7. Bose is moving toward single sourcing many of its purchased part requirements. Discuss why the company might want to do this. Are there any risks to that approach?

8. Discuss some of the difficulties a company like Bose might experience when trying to implement just-in-time purchasing with international suppliers.

9. Why does a company like Bose have to source so much of its purchase requirements from offshore suppliers?

10. What makes the JIT II system at Bose unique? Why would a company pursue this type of system?

11. Why is it necessary to enter into a longer-term contractual arrangement when pursuing arrangements like the one Bose has with its domestic transportation carrier?

12. Why is it important to manage logistics time elements proactively when pursuing higher levels of customer service?

13. What role does information technology play at Bose?

14. What advantages do these systems provide to Bose that might not be available to a company that does not have these systems?

15. Why has Bose developed its supplier performance measurement system?

16. Do you think the performance measurement systems at Bose are computerized or manual? Why?

$\mathcal{M}$ITOLA 600

You are the purchasing manager for an electronics firm responsible for a make-or-buy decision analysis for a key component used in one of your firm's most popular products, the Mitola 600—a voice synthesizer used widely in a variety of personal computers. The component in question, the MT-1A, is an electronic assembly that is critical to the Mitola 600's performance. Quality is an important issue to consider in the analysis.

Your firm has been manufacturing the MT-1A since the component's introduction three years ago. Management has determined there is a possibility of converting the manufacturing area and equipment used on the MT-1A to manufacture a new component, the AMP-2, which will be used on a new line of products scheduled for introduction in two years.

In the course of analysis, you have gathered a variety of cost information. You have negotiated a tentative purchase price under a three-year contract with a long-term supplier that would result in a purchase price of $5.675 per unit FOB supplier. Due to the location of the supplier, freight costs are estimated to be $0.328 per unit. In your conversations with the quality assurance and logistics departments, you have determined jointly that receiving and incoming inspection costs would be $0.132 per unit. Your marketing group projects MT-1A volumes to be 400,000 units next year with a 10% annual growth rate.

Accounting and finance departments have reviewed costing of the WZO-1A to provide the most current cost information available. The following per-unit costs apply given the expected annual volume of 400,000 units:

Purchased materials	$2.724
Inbound freight	0.157
Direct labor	0.908
Engineering and design costs	0.093
Depreciation	0.222
Corporate office administration	0.099
Transfer price (includes 8% profit)	$7.000

Transfer price is a term used to describe an internal sale from one part of a business to another. In addition, variable burden is 100% of direct labor per unit and fixed burden is 150% of direct labor. Also, approximately $200,000 in discontinuation or switching costs would be incurred if a make-or-buy decision occurs.

Assignment

1. Develop the make-or-buy analysis for the MT-1A and report your recommendation in the form of a written report to management.

2. When and why do make-or-buy decisions originate?

3. When outsourcing a component, assembly, or finished product, what are some of the qualitative (i.e., nonquantitative) issues that management must consider?

4. One of the major challenges when conducting a make-or-buy analysis involves collecting accurate data. Discuss the various groups that purchasing must involve when conducting a make-or-buy analysis. What types of information can these other groups contribute?

5. Make-or-buy decisions are becoming increasingly important within most firms today. Discuss the reasons why you think make-or-buy decisions can have an important impact on a firm's business.

ELECTRIC MOTOR OUTSOURCING DECISION

You are a member of a make-or-buy review team for electrical components, and work for a division of a large U.S. industrial power equipment manufacturer located in the Midwest. You have been assigned the responsibility of analyzing whether or not your company should outsource or internally manufacture a motor assembly that controls a key function on a new line of power equipment. As an initial step, the team is responsible for gathering the required information to guide its decision process.

Your marketing group estimates the following volumes for the motor assembly: year 1–1,500 units; year 2–2,700 units; and year 3–4,000 units. A long-time supplier of electric motors has quoted a price of $150 per unit, FOB supplier, with 10% price decreases per year for years 2 and 3. You assume these price decreases are due to lower material costs from higher volumes, the positive effects of learning at the supplier, and greater operating efficiencies. If the new line of industrial power equipment is successful, it is estimated that the life cycle will be seven years, reaching a total of 20,000 units. Shipping and handling costs, using a just-in-time delivery system, are expected to be $4.50 per unit for years 1 through 3.

The cost engineering department has provided the following *per-unit* cost estimates for internally manufacturing and assembling the motors during year 1 of a three-year planning cycle:

Direct labor	$18.750	Cost of receiving components	$ 1.250
Direct materials	36.250	Indirect labor	5.500
Factory supplies	3.135	Transfer price profit	18.750

In addition, initial tooling and line modification costs would total approximately $14,000. Fringe benefits for direct labor are 50% of direct labor rates, variable burden is assigned at 100% of direct labor rates, and fixed overhead is 250% of direct labor rates. Fringe benefits on indirect labor are assigned at 50% of indirect labor rates.

Depreciation expense and engineering/design costs over the next three years are $20,000 and $80,000, respectively, to be spread evenly across the three-year total volume.

In years 2 and 3, management expects a 4% annual decrease in material costs and a 3% rise in direct and indirect labor rates. Assume that this will increase the per-unit direct and indirect labor costs by 3%.

Assignment

1. Prepare a three-year make-or-buy per-unit cost analysis. Be sure to include all costs.

2. Prepare a three-year make-or-buy analysis that looks at the total cost of each sourcing alternative.
3. What is your recommendation to management?
4. What other non-cost variables would be helpful in this analysis?

$\mathscr{N}$EGOTIATION—AUTOMOTIVE SUPPLIER

This simulation involves negotiating the purchase of a sheet metal product. The information presented here is common to all groups participating in the negotiation.

There are four potential manufacturers of sheet metal parts:

- Athena Corporation: Annual sales of approximately $8 million dollars, located in Bowling Green, Kentucky
- Cybaris Corporation: Annual sales of approximately $10 million dollars, located in Charlotte, North Carolina
- Medusa Corporation: Annual sales of approximately $4 million dollars, located in Columbus, Ohio
- Orion Corporation: Annual sales of approximately $7 million dollars, located in Grand Rapids, Michigan

There are four potential purchasers of sheet metal parts. These companies are first-tier automotive suppliers who supply the major automotive companies located in Michigan and Ohio and in the Southeast.

- King Corporation, located in Greenville, South Carolina, has requirements for 3,000 units of the sheet metal product for 2001. The products will be required in 2002 and 2003 according to current plans, and volumes are expected to increase.
- Queen Corporation, located in Knoxville, Tennessee, requires 5,000 units of the sheet metal product for 2001, but volumes for 2002 and 2003 are uncertain.
- Duke Corporation, located in Cleveland, Ohio, requires 2,000 units of the product, and production volumes required are expected to increase by 50% or more in 2002 and 2003.
- Duchess Corporation, located in Lansing, Michigan, requires 4,000 units of the product, and volumes are expected to decrease somewhat in 2002 and 2003.

These companies have all purchased in small quantities from all of the suppliers.

- Prices for similar sheet metal parts are in the $120 to $155 price range per unit.
- All identified suppliers are able to produce to specifications provided by the purchasing company. However, quality performance related to the product can vary greatly.
- Individual cost structures of the firms providing the sheet metal parts can vary significantly.
- Suppliers provide widely different levels of service and technical support.
- All suppliers have to satisfy the same quality and delivery terms, payment terms, and transportation (F.O.B. seller's plant).
- Industry capacity utilization is about 75 percent.

- All purchasing companies have purchased relatively small amounts from all of the suppliers previously, never totaling more than $25,000 per purchase.

Assignment

Students will work in small groups and participate in one face-to-face negotiation session. Each team will receive buyer/seller specific information on the price and cost characteristics of the products being discussed. Group size will not exceed three to four people for either the buying or selling negotiating team.

Prior to the negotiation, each group will develop a brief written negotiating strategy that is to be handed in to the instructor and then conduct an actual negotiation session with an assigned buyer/supplier group from the class. (*Note:* An agreement may not always occur with an assigned group.) Eventually, each pair of groups will develop jointly a written contract that documents the outcome of the negotiation process. The instructor has an information packet for the buyer and the seller that provides additional information required to prepare for and conduct the negotiation. Buyers and sellers can share as little or as much of the information with each other as they desire during the actual negotiation.

Groups must prepare properly before conducting the negotiation. In particular, teams should study the price/cost characteristics of the product in question, and prepare a cost analysis for use in the negotiation. Each group's negotiation strategy should be developed *prior to* the negotiating session. All group members are to participate in the research planning as well as the actual negotiation. Remember, price is not the only variable subject to negotiation. Be creative when crafting your agreement.

$\mathcal{N}$EGOTIATION—PORTO

Due to competitive pressures, firms in the computer industry are constantly looking to reduce costs. Computer manufacturers compete fiercely for contracts based on meeting the technology, quality, and price requirements of customers. Profit margins and return-on-investment targets are almost always under pressure. Dell Computer recently saw its operating margins slip to a slim 7%.

Most computer manufacturers have programs designed to improve quality and reduce the costs associated with their products. One strategy that many producers use is to contract only with high-quality suppliers and develop longer-term buyer-seller relationships. One major computer company, Porto, also initiated a program requesting suppliers to continually improve productivity, which should lead to cost reductions. The objective of the program was to reduce purchase costs over the foreseeable future. Porto also expects its suppliers to contribute cost-saving ideas whenever possible.

The high-technology industry features high fixed costs due to large investment in plant and equipment. These companies also commit large expenditures to research and development.

Porto currently has a requirement for an electronic component termed the New Prod, which is part of a recently designed product. The estimated volume requirement of New Prod is 200,000 units with additional follow-on orders likely. For the New Prod component, Porto felt there were five to eight highly competitive suppliers capable of producing the item. These suppliers are located primarily along the east and west coasts of the United States. After a request for quote and preliminary analysis, the buyer for Porto decided to pursue further discussions with Technotronics.

Negotiation Session Requirements

Each negotiator must plan and prepare before conducting the negotiation. The group leader has information packets for the buyer and the seller that provides additional information and assignments required for conducting the negotiation. Buyers and sellers can share as little or as much of the information with each other as they desire during the actual negotiation.

Your negotiation strategy should be developed *prior to* the negotiating session. If working in groups, all group members should participate in the research planning as well as the actual negotiation. Remember, price is not the only variable subject to negotiation. In highly volatile industries like the computer industry, for example, capacity guarantees from suppliers are often critical. Be creative when crafting your purchase agreement.

Negotiation—Hubcaps

This negotiation involves a discussion between two individuals:

- **Individual 1:** You are vice-president of marketing for HubbaBubba Inc., a producer of hubcaps for the auto industry. HubbaBubba has been supplying the auto industry for ten years, primarily providing hubcaps to BMW as they began manufacturing operations in North America. In recent years you have maintained some of the BMW business (40% of your revenues), but you have developed other customers including HQBA, a manufacturer of luxury automobiles. They comprise 40% of your revenues as well.

  You are about to meet with the director of aesthetic sourcing for HQBA. The meeting is to allow you to negotiate product characteristics and prices for hubcaps to be used on next year's models. From previous discussions, and meetings with other manufacturers, you have learned that HQBA is introducing a new model, the HQBA-T, which is a higher-quality vehicle than their original model, the HQBA-A. Both models are available in a sedan or station wagon design.

- **Individual 2:** You are director of external aesthetic sourcing for HQBA Inc., a relatively new auto company that currently has two models, a high-quality sedan/ station wagon known as the HQBA-A, and a higher quality sedan/station wagon known as the HQBA-T. Over the past five years that you have been in business, market growth has been greater than any of your marketing staff had expected, and pressure has been placed on the company to expand the product line to meet the demand of consumers that are interested in the top-of-the-line autos. That is why the company recently introduced the HQBA-T. The intent of the HQBA-T is to take the basic design of the HQBA-A, and upgrade the quality of materials and parts used in the vehicle. In other words, the HQBA-T is the same vehicle design as the HQBA-A, but with better quality inputs.

Assignment

All participants will receive confidential information from the instructor before meeting to negotiate an agreement. After reaching an agreement with the other party, you are to use the contract shown here to identify the financial terms of the agreement. The goal is to maximize all benefits.

Contract

Original product price $ _____

Original product volume _____

Type of material used in the original product _____

Type of production process used in the original product _____

New product price $ _____

New product volume _____

Type of material used in the new product _____

Type of production process used in the new product _____

_____	_____
Buyer's signature	Seller's signature

Calculation Sheet

Original Product

Buyer calculation (price × volume) (A)   Seller calculation (price × volume) (A)

Buyer calculation (if material is Grade B)   Seller calculation (product cost × volume) (B)
  (volume × .04) (B)   Seller calculation (representative benefit)

Buyer calculation (if production process is)   ([A − B] × .10) (C)
  (machine stamping)
  (volume × .06) (C)

Buyer calculation ({[B + C] × price} X 2) (D)

Buyer calculation ({[B + C] × .10} X $2,000) (E)

Buyer calculation (A − D − E) (F)

New Product

Buyer calculation (price × volume) (A)   Seller calculation (price × volume) (A)

Buyer calculation (if material is Grade B)   Seller calculation (product cost × volume) (B)
  (volume 3 .04) (B)   Seller calculation (representative benefit)

Buyer calculation (If production Process is)   ([A − B] 3 .15) (C)
  (machine stamping)
  (volume × .06) (C)

Buyer calculation ({[B + C] × Price} × 2)
  (D)

Buyer calculation ({[B + C] × .10} × $2,000)
  (E)

Buyer calculation (volume × $200) (F)

Buyer calculation (A − D − E + F) (G)

Total

Buyer total (original F + new G)   Seller calculation (original C + new C)

$\mathcal{E}$XPRESS DELIVERY SERVICE

Your manager, the director of supply management at Express Delivery Service, has come to you regarding your company's sourcing strategy for a high volume critical electronic component that is used in a majority of your company's vehicles. Many different suppliers have the capability to produce the component. In the past, your firm has used competitive bidding, but has typically relied on three different suppliers. The suppliers' ratings are as follows:

	Cheapo	*Best*	*Excel*
Price/unit	$2.30	$2.50	$2.60
Quality	99%	98.5%	1,000 PPM
Delivery on-time	95% on-time	99% on-time	98% on-time
Order Cycle time	2 weeks	3 weeks	24 hours

Assignment

1. Respond to your manager's request by discussing the critical factors that you should consider when deciding whether to single source or multiple source this critical item.
2. Provide your recommendation for awarding this contract using a formal weighted point supplier evaluation tool that you have developed.
3. What other factors might a buyer or buying team consider when evaluating the worthiness of potential suppliers?

CUSTOMER AND SUPPLIER INTEGRATION INTO KEY SUPPLY CHAIN PROCESSES

William Janis, the popular CEO of United Express, a global package delivery company, stood in front of thousands of employees to discuss the company's future. He said that the days of charging a premium price for the services the company provided were over. Today's customers, he argued, have never had a wider choice of options and providers. To remain successful, United Express must be at the forefront of innovation, be the low cost, high quality provider, and integrate with suppliers and customers to create new supply chain opportunities and value. United Express must be responsive to market changes, understand customers and their requirements, act entrepreneurial, and be willing to take risks.

It was not long after this talk that managers across the company began proposing projects and improvements that aligned directly with Mr. Janis's vision. One project that was receiving a great deal of attention involved the introduction of a new process sorting technology. Package sorting is an area that has differentiated this company from its competitors, although the performance gap with competitors has narrowed significantly during the last five years. What separated this project from previous or proposed development projects was its scope and urgency. The project team would be responsible for extensively refining and adapting a supplier-provided technology for installation at each United Express sorting center. Executive management mandated that project completion be within one year, which was well below the team's initial estimate. The project team also received a budget that was 20% less than its initial estimates.

The head of the project team was Jill Stevens, a bright and energetic engineer with an ability to manage project tasks while maintaining excellent interpersonal skills. The more Jill thought about this project, the more she became convinced that this project could benefit from early supplier involvement. She had been reading extensively about the potential benefits of involving suppliers early on during product and process development. As Jill considered the pros and cons of early supplier involvement with such an important project, she had to admit that she was apprehensive. Jill knew that her organization lacked experience in this type of activity, which was true of most North American firms. She also had to admit that project delay or even failure could result if the early integration efforts were unsuccessful.

Assignment

1. What is the logic behind pursuing early supplier design involvement with key suppliers?
2. Develop and discuss a multi-step supplier integration process that will guide this organization as it seeks to involve suppliers in projects such as the one highlighted in this case. (This question assumes that the project team has decided to involve suppliers. This question does not ask for the presentation of a new product/process/service development process that may or may not include supplier involvement.)
3. What are some of the barriers that might inhibit the success of early supplier involvement during process development? How can this organization overcome these barriers?
4. Discuss what is meant by white box, gray box, and black box supplier integration.

$\mathcal{I}$NDEX